The History of the Crusades
Vol. II

by

J. Fr. Michaud

The History of the Crusades
Vol. II
by J. Fr. Michaud

ISBN: 978-93-62762-12-2

Published by

DOUBLE 9 BOOKS

2/13-B, Ansari Road
Daryaganj, New Delhi – 110002
info@double9books.com
www.double9books.com
Tel. 011-40042856

ABOUT THE AUTHOR

J. Fr. Michaud was a French historian and publicist. Michaud was born in either La Biolle or Albens in the Duchy of Savoy. He was schooled in Bourg-en-Bresse and then worked as a writer in Lyon, where the French Revolution instilled in him a deep distaste for revolutionary beliefs that would last his entire life. In 1791, he traveled to Paris and worked as an editor for various royalist periodicals, putting his life in danger. One of these was the Gazette Universelle, which he formed alongside Pascal Boyer and Antoine Marie Cerisier. His Bourbon sympathies landed him in prison briefly in 1800, and when he was released, he temporarily abandoned journalism in favor of writing and editing books. In 1806, he wrote the first work of its sort, Biographie moderne ou dictionnaire des hommes qui se sont fait un nom en Europe since 1789, with his brother Louis Gabriel Michaud and two collaborators. In 1811, he published the first volume of his Histoire des Croisades (History of the Crusades) and the first volume of his Biographie Universelle. In 1813, he was elected Academician, filling the vacancy caused by the death of Jean-François Cailhava de L'Estandoux. In 1814, he resumed editing La Quotidienne.

CONTENTS

BOOK IX
A.D. 1195-1198

FOURTH CRUSADE

When we cast a retrospective glance over the periods we have described, we congratulate ourselves upon not having lived in those times of war and trouble; but when we look around us, and reflect upon the age of which we form a part, we fear we have little reason to boast over the epochs commonly termed barbarous. During twenty-five years a revolution, born of opinions unknown to past ages, has pervaded cities, agitated nations, and shaken thrones. This revolution has for auxiliaries war and victory; it strengthens itself with all the obstacles that are opposed to it; it is for ever born again from itself, and when we believe we can perceive the end of its ravages, it re-appears more terrible and menacing than ever. At the moment in which I resume the account of the Crusades, [1] the spirit of sedition and revolt, the fanaticism of modern doctrines, which seemed to slumber, all at once awake, and again threaten the world with universal disorder; nations which tremble for their liberty and their laws, are aroused, and spring up in arms; a coalition of all kings and of all nations, a general crusade is formed not to defend the tomb of Christ, but to preserve that which Europe possesses of its ancient civilization. It is amidst the rumours of a new revolution, of a formidable war, that I am about to describe the revolutions and wars that disturbed the East and the West in the middle ages. May I, whilst deploring the calamities of my country, profit by the events of which I am a witness, and by the frightful spectacle which is before my eyes, to paint with greater truth the passions and the troubles of a remote age, and revive in the hearts of my contemporaries a love of concord and peace.

The death of Saladin was followed by that which almost always is to be observed in the dynasties of the East,—a reign of agitation and trouble succeeding a reign of strength and absolute power. In these dynasties, which have no other support but victory, and the all-powerful will of a single man, as long as the sovereign, surrounded by his soldiers, commands, he is tremblingly obeyed; but as soon as he has closed his eyes, his people precipitate themselves towards license with the same ardour that they had yielded to servitude; and passions, long restrained by the presence of the despot, only blaze forth with the greater violence when there remains nothing of him but a vain remembrance.

Saladin gave no directions respecting the order of succession, and by this want of foresight prepared the ruin of his empire. One of his sons, Alaziz, [2] who commanded in Egypt, caused himself to be proclaimed sultan of Cairo; another [3] took possession of the sovereignty of Aleppo, and a third of the principality of Amath. [4] Malek-Adel, the brother of Saladin, assumed the throne of Mesopotamia, and the countries in the neighbourhood of the Euphrates. The principal emirs, and all the princes of the race of the Ayoubites, made themselves masters of the cities and provinces of which they held the command. [5]

Afdhal, [6] eldest son of Saladin, was proclaimed sultan of Damascus. Master of Syria, and of the capital of a vast empire, sovereign of Jerusalem and Palestine, [7] he appeared to have preserved something of the power of his father; but all fell into disorder and confusion. The emirs, the old companions of the victories of Saladin, endured with reluctance the authority of the young sultan. Several refused to take the oath of obedience, [8] drawn up by the cadis of Damascus; others consented to take it, but on condition that their fiefs should be secured to them, or that new ones should be bestowed upon them. Far from labouring to reduce the power of this haughty soldiery, Afdhal neglected the duties of his throne for the pleasures of debauchery, to which he gave himself up entirely, abandoning the welfare of his empire to a vizier, [9] who rendered him odious to the Mussulmans. The army demanded the dismissal of the vizier, whom they accused of having usurped the authority of the prince: the vizier, on his part, advised his master to banish the seditious emirs. The weak sultan, who only saw with the eyes of his minister, annoyed by the presence and complaints of a discontented army, dismissed from his service a great number of soldiers and emirs, who went among all the neighbouring princes, complaining of his ingratitude, and accusing him of forgetting, in the bosom of idleness and effeminacy, the holy laws of the prophet and the glory of Saladin.

The greater number of them, who went into Egypt, exhorted Alaziz to take arms against his brother. The sultan of Cairo gave ear to their advice, and under the pretence of avenging the glory of his father, conceived the project of possessing himself of Damascus. He assembled his forces, and marched into Syria at the head of an army. At the approach of danger, Afdhal invoked assistance from the princes that reigned over the countries of Amath and Aleppo. Soon a formidable war blazed forth, into which was dragged the whole of the family of the Ayoubites. Alaziz laid siege to

Damascus. The hopes of an easy conquest animated his emirs, and made them believe that they were fighting in a just cause; but as they at first had but little success, and as victory seemed every day to fly further from their banners, the war began to appear to them unjust. At first they murmured; then they revolted from Alaziz, and at length rejoined the troops of Syria. The sultan of Cairo, upon being thus abandoned, was obliged to raise the siege disgracefully, and return into Egypt. The sultans of Damascus and Aleppo pursued him across the desert, with the design of attacking him in his capital. Afdhal, at the head of a victorious army, soon carried terror to the banks of the Nile. Alaziz was about to be dethroned, and Egypt to be conquered by the Syrians, if the brother of Saladin, guided by a policy, whose motive might be easily divined, had not opposed the authority of his counsels to the arms of the conqueror, and re-established peace in the family of the Ayoubites.

The princes and emirs respected the experience of Malek-Adel, and allowed him to be the arbitrator of their differences. The warriors of Syria and Egypt, accustomed to see him in camps, looked upon him as their leader, and followed him with joy to battle; whilst nations, that he had often astonished by his exploits, invoked his name in their reverses and dangers. The Mussulmans now perceived with surprise that he had been in a manner exiled in Mesopotamia, and that an empire, founded by his valour, was abandoned to young princes who bore no name among warriors: he himself grew secretly indignant at not having received due recompense for his labours, and was aware of all that the old soldiers, he had so often led to victory, might one day do to further his ambitious views. It was important to his designs that too much of the empire should not be in the same hands, and that the provinces should remain for some time longer shared by two rival powers. The peace which he had brought about could not be of long duration and the discord ever on the point of breaking out among his nephews, must soon offer him an opportunity of reaping the rich harvest of the vast heritage of Saladin.

Afdhal, warned by the dangers he had run, resolved to change his conduct. Hitherto he had scandalized all faithful Mussulmans by his intemperance in the use of wine. Aboulfeda, who was descended from the family of Saladin, [10] says, in his history, that the sultan of Damascus, during the early years of his reign, passed his life amidst banquets and indulgence, taking delight in nothing but listening to songs and composing verses. On his return from Egypt, Afdhal exhibited an entire alteration in his manners; but he only fell from one excess into another; he was now constantly at prayers, or employed in the most minute practices of the Mussulman religion; but, in his excessive devotion, as in his dissipated life, he was perfectly inattentive to the duties of a monarch, and submitted himself, without reserve, to the counsels of the same vizier who had already nearly cost him his dominions. "Then," says Aboulfeda, "complaints against him were heard from all quarters, and tongues that had been loud in his praise became silent."

Alaziz thought this opportunity favourable for again taking up arms against his brother; and Malek-Adel, persuaded that war was most likely to minister to his ambition, no longer advocated peace, but placed himself at the head of the army of Egypt. Having intimidated by his threats, or won by his presents, the principal emirs of Afdhal, he at once took possession of Damascus in the name of Alaziz, and soon governed as sovereign the richest provinces of Syria.

Every day fresh quarrels broke out among the emirs and princes; all those who had fought with Saladin, thought the moment was come at which to put forth and establish their pretensions; and the princes who still remained of the family of Noureddin began to entertain hopes of regaining the provinces wrested from the unfortunate Attabeks by the son of Ayoub. All the East was in a state of fermentation. Bloody divisions desolated Persia, a prey to the various claims of the feeble remains of the race of the Seljoucides. The empire of the Carismians, which conquest was every day extending, threatened at the same time the capital of Corosan and the city of Bagdad, in which the pontiff of the Mussulman religion lived in perpetual fear. For a long time the caliphs had been unable to take any active part in the events that changed the face of Syria; and the only authority they possessed was exercised in consecrating the victories of the triumphant party, whoever that might be. Afdhal, driven from Damascus, called in vain upon the caliph of Bagdad for protection; all that shadow of power could afford him was a recommendation to exercise patience, and an assurance "*that his enemies would have to render an account to God of what they had done.*"

Among the rivalries that convulsed the Mussulman states, Malek-Adel met with no obstruction to his projects; the troubles and disorders which his usurpation gave birth to, even the wars undertaken against him, all contributed to the consolidation and extension of his unjustly-obtained power. It became evident that he must soon unite under his sway the greater part of the provinces conquered by Saladin. Thus was verified, for the second time within a few years, the observation of an Arabian historian, who expressed himself in the following words when speaking of the succession of Noureddin: "*The greater part of the founders of empires have not been able to leave them to their posterity.*" This instability of power is not a thing to be wondered at in countries where success renders everything legitimate, where the caprices of fortune are frequently laws, and where the most formidable enemies of an empire founded by arms, are the very men whose bravery has assisted in raising it. The historian we have quoted, deplores the revolutions of military despotism, without duly searching for the natural causes of them; and can explain so many changes only by referring to the justice of God, always ready to punish, at least in their children, all who have employed violence or shed the blood of man to attain empire.

Such were the revolutions which, during many years, agitated the Mussulman states of Syria and Egypt. The fourth crusade, which we are about to describe, and in which the Christians might have greatly profited by the troubles of the East, only served to reunite the scattered members of the empire of Saladin. Malek-Adel owed the progress of his power not only to the divisions of the Mussulmans, but to the spirit of discord that reigned among the Christians.

After the departure of the king of England, as was always the case at the termination of every crusade, the Christian colonies, surrounded by perils, advanced more rapidly to their fall. Henry of Champagne, charged with the government of Palestine, disdained the title of king, as he was impatient to return to Europe, and looked upon his kingdom as a place of exile. The three military orders, detained in Asia by their vows, constituted the principal strength of a state which but lately had had all the warriors of Europe for its defenders. Guy of Lusignan retired to Cyprus, took no more interest in the fate of Jerusalem, and had full occupation in keeping himself on his new throne, shaken by the continual revolts of the Greeks and threatened by the emperors of Constantinople.

Bohemond III., grandson of Raymond of Poictiers, and descended, in the female line, from the celebrated Bohemond, one of the heroes of the first crusade, governed the principality of Antioch and the county of Tripoli. Amidst the misfortunes that afflicted the Christian colonies, the sole aim of this prince was the extension of his dominions, and every means appeared to him good and just that could forward his designs. Bohemond pretended to have claims to the principality of Armenia; and employed by turns force and stratagem to get possession of it. After several useless attempts, he succeeded in decoying into his capital Rupin of the Mountain, one of the princes of Armenia, and detained him prisoner. Livon, the brother of Rupin, determined to take signal vengeance for such an outrage; and, under the pretence of treating for peace, invited Bohemond to repair to the frontiers of Armenia. The two princes engaged by oath to come without escort or train to the place of conference; but each formed a secret design of laying a snare for his adversary. The Armenian prince, better seconded by either his genius or fortune, remained conqueror in this disgraceful contest. Bohemond was surprised, loaded with chains, and carried away to a fortress of Lesser Armenia. The war was instantly renewed with fury; the people of both Armenia and Antioch rushed to arms, and the countries and cities of the two principalities were speedily by turns invaded and ravaged. At length peace became desirable, and after some disputes upon the conditions, the prince of Antioch was sent back to his states, and Rupin of the Mountain was restored to the nations of Armenia. By an agreement entered into by the two princes, Alice, the daughter of Rupin, married the eldest son of Bohemond. This union promised to be the pledge of a durable peace; but the germ of so many divisions still subsisted; the two parties retained a strong feeling of the outrage they had received; and every treaty of peace becoming a fresh subject of discussion, war was always ready to be rekindled.

In another direction, ambition and jealousy set at variance the orders of the Temple and St. John. At the period of the third crusade, the Hospitallers and the Templars were as powerful as sovereign princes; they possessed in Asia and Europe villages, cities, and even provinces. [11] The two orders, rivalling each other in power and glory, attended far less to the defence of the holy places than to the augmentation of their own renown and riches. Every one of their immense possessions, every one of their prerogatives, the renown of the knights, the credit of the leaders, all, even to the trophies of their valour, were for them subjects of rivalry, and, at length, this spirit of discord and jealousy produced an open, war. A French gentleman, established in Palestine, possessed, as a vassal of the Hospitallers, the castle of Margat, situated towards the frontiers of Arabia. The Templars pretended that this castle belonged to them, and took possession of it by main force. Robert,—that was the name of the gentleman,—carried his complaints to the Hospitallers, who immediately flew to arms and drove the Templars from the castle. From that time the knights of the two orders never met without provoking each other to the combat most of the Franks and Christians always taking a part in the quarrel, some for the order of St. John, others for that of the Temple. The king of Jerusalem and the most prudent of the barons made many useless attempts to restore peace; and several Christian princes endeavoured in vain to reconcile the two rival orders. The pope himself had much difficulty in getting his sacred mediation to be accepted; and it was only after long debates that the Holy See, sometimes armed with evangelical thunders, sometimes employing the paternal language of the head of the Church, terminated, by its wisdom and supreme ascendancy, a contest which the knights themselves would have preferred deciding with sword and lance.

During these fatal divisions none thought of defending themselves against the general enemy, the Saracens. One of the most melancholy consequences of the spirit of faction is, that it always leads to a lamentable indifference for the common cause. The more violently the parties attacked each other, the less perception they seemed to have of the dangers that threatened the Christian colonies; neither the knights of the Temple or of St. John, nor the Christians of Antioch or Ptolemaïs, ever thought of asking for succour against the infidels; and history does not say that one person was sent from the East to make Europe aware of the griefs of Sion.

The situation of the Christians in Palestine was besides so uncertain and perilous, that the wisest could form no idea of coming events, or dare to adopt a resolution. If they appealed afresh to the warriors of the West, they broke the truce made with Saladin, and exposed themselves to all the resentment of the infidels; if they respected treaties, the truce might be broken by the Mussulmans, ever ready to profit by the calamities which fell upon the Christians. In this state of things, it appeared difficult to foresee a new crusade, which was neither called for by the wishes of the Christians of Asia, nor promoted by the interests of Europe. In fact, when we cast our eyes over the Christian colonies of the East, as they are described to us in these unhappy times, and see the spirit of ambition and discord displacing in all hearts the holy spirit of the Gospel, we cannot wonder that Christendom took so little interest in their fate. Again, when contemporary history represents to us these colonies a prey to license and division, and destitute of everything that could render them flourishing, we can scarcely believe that the West was again likely to lavish its wealth and its blood to support and defend them. But the great name of Jerusalem still produced a powerful effect upon the minds of all; the remembrance of the first crusade still aroused the enthusiasm of Christians; and the veneration for the holy places, which appeared to grow weaker in the kingdom of Christ itself, was yet cherished beyond the seas and in the principal countries of the West.

Celestine III. had, by his exhortations, encouraged the warriors of the third crusade; and, at the age of ninety, pursued with zeal all the projects of his predecessors; ardently wishing that the last days of his pontificate should be illustrated by the conquest of Jerusalem. After the return of Richard, the news of the death of Saladin had spread joy throughout the West, and revived the hopes of the Christians. Celestine wrote to all the faithful to inform them that the most formidable enemy of Christendom had ceased to live; and, without regarding the truce made by Richard Cœur de Lion, he ordered his bishops and archbishops to preach a new crusade in their dioceses. [12] The sovereign pontiff promised all who would take the cross the same privileges and the same advantages as in the preceding crusades. The profanation of the holy places; the oppression under which the faithful of the East groaned; the ever-increasing insolence and audacity of the Saracens—such were the motives by which he supported his holy exhortations. He addressed himself particularly to the bishops of England, and commanded them to use every persuasion to induce Richard again to take up arms against the infidels.

Richard, although returned, had never laid aside the cross, the symbol of pilgrimage; and it might be supposed he still intended to repair again to the Holy Land; but, scarcely escaped from an unjust captivity, taught by his own experience how great were the difficulties and perils of a distant enterprise, his thoughts and time were engrossed by his endeavours to remedy his losses, to defend or aggrandize his states, and to be on his guard against the insidious attempts of Philip Augustus. His knights and barons, whom he himself exhorted to resume the cross, professed, as he did, a warm devotion for the cause of Jerusalem; but they could not make up their minds to return to a country which had been to them a place of suffering and exile.

Although the appearance of the preachers of the crusade everywhere inspired respect, they had no better success in France, where, only a few years before, a hundred thousand warriors had been roused by the summons to defend the holy places. If the fear of the enterprises of Philip was sufficient to detain Richard in the West, the dread of the vindictive and jealous disposition of Richard exercised the same influence over Philip. The greater number of his knights and nobles followed his example, and contented themselves with shedding tears over the fate of Jerusalem. The enthusiasm for the crusade was communicated to only a small number of warriors, amongst whom history names the count de Montfort, who afterwards conducted the cruel war against the Albigeois.

From the commencement of the crusades, Germany had never ceased to send its warriors to the defence of the Holy Land. It deplored the recent loss of its armies, destroyed or dispersed in Asia Minor, and the death of the Emperor Frederick, who had gained nothing but a grave in the plains of the East; but the remembrance of so great a disaster did not extinguish in all hearts the zeal for the cause of Jerusalem. Henry VI., who occupied the imperial throne, had not partaken, as the kings of France and England had, the perils and reverses of the last expedition. Unpleasant remembrances or fears of his enemies in Europe could have no effect in preventing him from joining in a new enterprise, or deter him from a holy pilgrimage which so many illustrious examples seemed to point out as a sacred duty.

Although this prince had been excommunicated by the Holy See, only the preceding year, the Pope sent an embassy to him, charged with the duty of recalling to his mind the example of his father Frederick, and urging him to assume the cross. Henry, who sought every occasion to conciliate the head of the Church, and who likewise entertained vast projects in which a new crusade might be very serviceable, received the envoy of Celestine with great honours.

Of all the princes of the middle ages, no one evinced more ambition than Henry VI.; his imagination, say historians was filled with the glory of the Cæsars, and he wished to be able to say with Alexander, *all that my desires can embrace belongs to me*. Tancred, a natural son of William II., king of Sicily, chosen by the Sicilian nobility to succeed his father, was recently deceased; and the emperor, who had espoused Constance, the heiress of a throne founded by Norman Crusaders, and desirous of establishing his claims, judged that the time was come to carry out his designs and achieve his conquests. The expedition of which the Holy See desired him to be the leader, was exceedingly favourable to his ambitious projects; when, promising to defend Jerusalem, he only thought of the conquest of Sicily; and the conquest of Sicily had no value in his estimation but as opening the road to Greece and Constantinople. [13] At the same time that he professed entire submission to the will of the head of the Church, he endeavoured to form an alliance with the republics of Genoa and Venice, promising them the spoils of the conquered; but in his mind he nourished the hope that he should one day overthrow the Italian republics and lower the authority of the Holy See, and upon their remains revive, for himself and his family, the empire of Augustus and Constantine.

Such was the prince to whom Celestine sent an embassy, and whom he wished to persuade into a holy war. After having announced his intention of taking the cross, Henry convoked a general diet at Worms, in which he himself exhorted the faithful to take up arms for the defence of the holy places. Since Louis VII., king of France, who harangued his subjects to induce them to join in the crusade, Henry was the only monarch that had mingled his voice with that of the preachers of the holy war, to make his subjects acquainted with the sufferings and complaints of the Church of Jerusalem. His eloquence, celebrated by the historians of his time, but above all, the spectacle presented of a great emperor himself preaching a holy war against the infidels, made a profound impression upon the multitude of his auditors. [14] After this solemn address, the most illustrious of the prelates assembled at Worms ascended the evangelical pulpit to keep up the rapidly increasing enthusiasm of the faithful; during eight hours nothing was heard but the groans of Sion and the city of God. Henry, surrounded by his court, assumed the symbol of the Crusaders; a great number of German nobles followed his example, some to please God, *and others to please the emperor*. Among those who took the oath to combat the Saracens, history names Henry duke of Saxony; Otho marquis of Brandenburgh; Henry count palatine of the Rhine; Herman landgrave of Thuringia; Henry duke of Brabant; Albert count of Apsburg; Adolphus count of Schwemburg; Henry count of Pappenhein, marshal of the empire; the duke of Bavaria; Frederick, son of Leopold, duke of Austria; Conrad marquis of Moravia; Valeran de Limbourg; and the bishops of Wurtzburg, Bremen, Verdun, Habbastadt, Passau, and Ratisbon. [15]

The crusade was preached in all the provinces of Germany, and the letters of the emperor and the pope kindled the zeal of the Christian warriors everywhere; never had an enterprise against the infidels been undertaken under more favourable auspices. As Germany undertook the crusade almost singly, the glory of the German nations seemed as much interested in this war as religion itself. Henry was to command the holy expedition; and the Crusaders, full of confidence and hope, were preparing to follow him to the East. But Henry entertained other views; several nobles of his court, some who penetrated his secret designs, and others who believed they offered him prudent advice, conjured him to remain in the West, and direct the crusade from the bosom of his dominions; and Henry, after a slight resistance, yielded to their prayers, and gave his whole attention to the hastening of the departure of the Crusaders.

The emperor of Germany placed himself at the head of forty thousand men and took the route for Italy, where everything was prepared for the conquest of Sicily; the remainder of the Crusaders were divided into two armies, which, proceeding by different roads, were to meet in Syria. The first, commanded by the duke of Saxony and the duke of Brabant, embarked at ports of the German Ocean and the Baltic; the second crossed the Danube, and directed its march towards Constantinople, whence the fleet of the Greek emperor Isaac was to transport it to Ptolemaïs. To this army, commanded by the archbishop of Mayence and Valeran de Limbourg, were joined the Hungarians, who accompanied their queen Margaret, sister to Philip Augustus. The queen of Hungary, after having lost Bela her husband, had made a vow to live only for Christ, and to end her days in the Holy Land.

The Crusaders under the command of the archbishop of Mayence and Valeran de Limbourg, were the first to arrive in Palestine. Scarcely were they landed when they expressed their desire and resolution to begin the war against the infidels. The Christians, who were then at peace with the Saracens, hesitated to break the truce signed by Richard, and were, further, unwilling to give the signal for hostilities before they could open the campaign with some hopes of success. Henry of Champagne and the barons of Palestine represented to the German Crusaders the danger to which an imprudent rupture would expose the Christians of the East, and conjured them to wait for the army of the dukes of Saxony and Brabant. But the Germans, full of confidence in their own strength, were indignant at having obstacles thrown in the way of their valour by vain scruples and chimerical alarms; they were astonished that the Christians of Palestine should thus refuse the assistance sent to them by Providence itself, and added, in a tone of anger and contempt, that warriors of the West were not accustomed to defer the hour of battle, and that the pope had not induced them to take up arms and the cross to remain in a state of shameful inactivity. The barons and knights of the Holy Land could not listen to such injurious speeches without indignation, and replied to the German Crusaders that they had neither solicited nor wished for their arrival; that they were better acquainted than the northern warriors of Europe with what was advantageous to the kingdom of Jerusalem; that they had without any foreign succour braved the greatest perils, and that when the proper moment should arrive they knew how to prove their valour otherwise than by words. Amidst such warm debates the minds of both parties became daily more exasperated, and the most cruel discord thus prevailed among the Christians before war was declared against the infidels.

All at once the German Crusaders marched out in arms from Ptolemaïs, and commenced hostilities by ravaging the lands of the Saracens. At the first signal of war the Mussulmans gathered together their forces; and the danger that threatened them putting an end to their discord, from the banks of the Nile and from the remotest parts of Syria crowded hosts of warriors but lately armed against each other, but who now, assembled under the same banners, acknowledged no other enemies but the Christians.

Malek-Adel, towards whom all Mussulmans turned their eyes when the defence of Islamism was the question, marched from Damascus at the head of an army and repaired to Jerusalem, where all the emirs of the adjoining provinces came to take his orders. The Mussulman army, after dispersing the Christians who had advanced towards the mountains of Naplouse, laid siege to Jaffa.

In the third crusade much importance had been attached to the conservation of this city. Richard Cœur de Lion had fortified it at great expense, and when that prince returned to Europe he left a numerous garrison in it. Of all the maritime places, Jaffa was nearest to the city which was the object of the wishes of the faithful; if it remained in the hands of the Christians, a road was always open for them to Jerusalem, and the means of laying siege to that place were rendered more easy; but if it fell into the power of the Mussulmans, it gave them proportionate advantages for the defence of the holy city.

When it was known at Ptolemaïs that the city of Jaffa was threatened, Henry of Champagne, with his barons and knights, immediately took arms to defend it, and joined the German Crusaders, giving all their energies to the prosecution of a war which they found could now no longer be deferred or avoided. The three military orders, with the troops of the kingdom, were about to set forward on their march, when a tragical accident once more plunged the Christians in grief, and retarded the effects of the happy harmony which had been re-established at the approach of peril. Henry of Champagne, leaning against a window of his palace, at which he had placed himself to see his army defile from the city, the window all at once gave way, and in its fall precipitated him with it. [16] The unfortunate prince expired in sight of his soldiers, who, instead of following him to battle, accompanied him to his grave, and lost several days in celebrating his funeral obsequies. The Christians of Ptolemaïs were still weeping the death of their king, when the misfortune they dreaded increased their grief and consternation; the garrison of Jaffa having attempted a sortie, had fallen into an ambuscade, and all the warriors that composed it were either killed or taken prisoners. The Mussulmans entered the city almost without resistance, and twenty thousand Christians were put to the sword.

These disasters had been foreseen by all who had dreaded the breaking of the truce; but the barons and knights of Palestine lost no time in vain regrets, or in the utterance of useless complaints, and looked with eager impatience for the arrival of the Crusaders who had set out from the ports of the Ocean and the Baltic. These troops had stopped on the coast of Portugal, where they had defeated the Moors, and taken from them the city of Silves. Proud of their triumph over the infidels, they landed at Ptolemaïs at the moment the people were lamenting the loss of Jaffa and crowding to the churches to implore the mercy of Heaven.

The arrival of the new Crusaders restored hope and joy to the Christians, and they resolved to lose no time, but to march at once against the infidels. The army left Ptolemaïs and advanced towards the coast of Syria, whilst a numerous fleet kept along shore, loaded with provisions and warlike stores. The Crusaders, without seeking the army of Malek-Adel, laid siege to Berytus.

The city of Berytus, at an equal distance between Jerusalem and Tripoli, by the commodiousness of its port, its large population, and its commerce, had become the rival of Ptolemaïs and Tyre. The Mussulman provinces of Syria acknowledged it as their capital, and it was in Berytus that the emirs, who contended for the lordship of the neighbouring cities, came to display the pomp of their coronations. After the taking of Jerusalem, Saladin was here saluted sovereign of the city of God, and crowned sultan of Damascus and Cairo. The pirates, who infested the seas, brought to this city all the spoils of the Christians; the Mussulman warriors there deposited the riches acquired by conquest or brigandage; and the Frank captives, made in late wars, were crowded together in the prisons of Berytus; so that the Christians had powerful motives for endeavouring to get possession of this place, and the Mussulmans had no less urgent ones for defending it.

Malek-Adel, after having destroyed the fortifications of Jaffa, advanced with his army as far as the mountains of Anti-Libanus, on the route to Damascus; but on hearing of the march and determination of the Crusaders, he crossed the mountains on his left, and drew near to the coast: the two armies met on the plain watered by the river Eleuthera, between Tyre and Sidon. The trumpets soon sounded to battle; the army of the Saracens, which covered an immense space, endeavoured at first to surround the Franks, and then to get between them and the coast; their cavalry precipitated itself by turns on the flanks, the van, and the rear of the Christians. The Christians closed their battalions and on all sides presented impenetrable ranks. Whilst their enemies showered arrows and darts upon them, their lances and swords were bathed in the blood of the Saracens. They fought with different arms, but with the same bravery and fury. The victory remained for a long time uncertain; the Christians were several times on the point of losing the battle; but their obstinate valour at length triumphed over all the resistance of the Mussulmans, and the sea-coast, the banks of the river Eleuthera, and the declivities of the mountains were covered with dead. The Saracens lost a great many of their emirs. Malek-Adel, who displayed, during the whole of this day, the skill of a great captain, was wounded on the field of battle, and only owed his safety to flight. All his army was dispersed; some fled towards Jerusalem, whilst others hurried along the road to Damascus, whither the news of this bloody defeat carried consternation and despair. [17]

In consequence of this victory, all the cities on the coast of Syria, which still belonged to the Mussulmans, fell into the power of the Christians; the Saracens abandoned Sidon, Laodicea, and Giblet. When the Christian fleet and army appeared before Berytus, the garrison was surprised, and did not venture to offer any resistance. This city contained, say historians, more provisions than would have sufficed for the inhabitants during three years; two large vessels, add the same chronicles, could not have contained the bows, arrows, and machines of war that were found in the city of Berytus. In this conquest immense riches fell into the hands of the victors, but the most precious reward of their triumph doubtless was the deliverance of nine thousand captives, impatient to resume their arms, and avenge the outrages of their long captivity. The prince of Antioch, who had joined the Christian army, sent a dove [18] to his capital to announce to all the inhabitants of the principality the miraculous victory gained by the soldiers of the cross. In all the Christian cities thanks were offered up to the God of armies. The historians, who have transmitted to us the account of these glorious events, in order to paint the transports of the Christian people, content themselves with repeating these words of holy writ: *"Then Sion leaped with joy, and the children of Judah were filled with delight."*

Whilst the Crusaders were thus pursuing their triumphs in Syria, the emperor Henry VI. took advantage of all the means and all the powers that the crusade had placed in his hands, to achieve the conquest of the kingdoms of Naples and Sicily. Although, in the course of his victories, he unceasingly invoked religion, humanity, and justice, he only listened to the dictates of his ambition; and, tormented by the sentiment of an implacable revenge, he was neither touched by the misery of the conquered, nor the submission of his enemies. All who had shown any respect or any fidelity for the family of Tancred, were cast by his orders into dungeons, or perished in horrible tortures, which he himself had invented. The army he led but too well seconded his gloomy and savage policy; the peace which the conquerors boasted of having restored to the people of Sicily, caused them more evils, and made more victims than war itself. Falcandus, who died some years before this expedition, had deplored beforehand, in his history, the misfortunes that were about to desolate his country. He already saw the most flourishing cities and the rich country of Sicily laid waste by the irruption of the barbarians. "Oh! unfortunate Sicilians," cried he, "it would be less frightful for you still to endure the tyrants of old Syracuse, than to live under the empire of this savage nation, which advances to invade your territory, and plunge you into all the horrors of misery and slavery." [19]

Nevertheless, these pitiless soldiers wore the crosses of pilgrims; and their emperor, although not yet relieved from his excommunication, arrogated to himself glory as the first of the soldiers of Christ. Henry VI. was considered as the head of the crusade, and supreme arbiter of the affairs of the East. The king of Cyprus offered to become his vassal; Livon, prince of Armenia, begged the title of king of him. The emperor of Germany having no more enemies to dread in the West, gave his whole attention to the war against the Saracens, and in a letter addressed to all the nobles, magistrates, and bishops of his empire, exhorted them to hasten the departure of the Crusaders. The emperor undertook to keep up an army of fifty thousand men for one year, and promised to pay thirty ounces of gold to every one that should remain under his banners till the end of the holy war. A great number of warriors, seduced by this promise, entered into an engagement to cross the sea, and fight against the infidels. Henry had no further need of them for his own conquests, and therefore pressed their departure for the East. Conrad, bishop of Hildesheim, chancellor of the empire, whose counsels in the wars of Sicily had but too well aided the ambition and barbarous policy of his master, was charged with the task of leading the third army of the Crusaders into Syria.

The arrival of so powerful a reinforcement in Palestine rekindled the zeal and enthusiasm of the Christians, and it might be expected that they would signalize their arms by some great enterprise. The victory they had recently gained in the plains of Tyre, the taking of Berytus, Sidon, and Giblet, had struck the Mussulmans with terror. Some of the leaders of the Christian army proposed to march against Jerusalem. "That city," said they, "cannot resist our victorious arms; her governor is a nephew of Saladin, who endures with impatience the authority of the sultan of Damascus, and has often appeared disposed to listen to the propositions [20] of the Christians." Most of the barons did not, however, partake in this hope, and placed no confidence in the words of the Mussulmans. It was well known, that the infidels, after the departure of Richard Cœur de Lion, had very considerably augmented the fortifications of Jerusalem; [21] that a triple wall, and ditches of great depth, must render this conquest more perilous, and particularly more difficult, than in the time of Godfrey of Bouillon. Winter was approaching; the Christian army might be overtaken by the rainy season, and forced to raise the siege in face of the army of the Saracens. These considerations determined the Crusaders to put off the attack of the holy city to the following year.

It is not impertinent to remark here, that in the Christian armies they were constantly talking about Jerusalem, but that the leaders as constantly directed their efforts and their arms to the acquisition of other conquests. The holy city, situated far from the sea, contained within its walls no other treasures but religious relics and monuments. The maritime cities of Asia could boast of more worldly wealth, and held out far greater advantages to the conquerors; they afforded, likewise, more easy communication with Europe; and if the conquest of Jerusalem sometimes tempted the piety and devotion of the pilgrims, that of cities bordering upon the sea, constantly kept awake the ambition of the maritime and warlike nations of the West.

All the sea-coast from Antioch to Ascalon belonged to the Christians; the Mussulmans having only been able to keep possession of Thoron. The garrison of this fortress frequently made incursions into the neighbouring countries, and by continual hostilities, intercepted the communication between the Christian cities. The Crusaders resolved that before they set out for Jerusalem, they would lay siege to the castle of Thoron. This fortress, built by Hugh de Saint-Omer, in the reign of Baldwin II., was situated at some leagues from Tyre, on the summit of a mountain, between the chain of Libanus and the sea. It was only accessible across steep rocks, and by a narrow way bordered by precipices. The Christian army had no machines sufficiently lofty to reach the heights of the walls, and arrows or stones hurled from the foot of the mountain, could not injure the besieged; whilst beams and fragments of rock precipitated from the ramparts, made dreadful havoc among the besiegers. In the early attacks, the Saracens ridiculed the vain efforts of their enemies, and witnessed, almost without danger to themselves, prodigies of valour, and the most murderous inventions of the art of sieges, exercised ineffectually against their walls. But the almost insurmountable difficulties that might have been supposed likely to arrest the progress of the Christians, only redoubled their ardour and courage. [22] They every day made fresh attacks, each day seeming to increase their efforts, and their obstinate bravery was seconded by newly-invented machines of war. With incredible labour, they dug out the earth, and made themselves a way across the rocks; whilst some Saxons, who had worked in the mines of Rammesberg, were employed in opening the flank of the mountain. The Crusaders at length reached the bottom of the ramparts of the fortress; the walls, the foundations of which they demolished, began to shake in various parts, without being struck by the ram, and their fall, which seemed delayed by a miracle, filled the besieged with dread.

The Mussulmans now losing all hope of defending themselves, proposed to capitulate; but such was the disorder of the Christian army, with its multitude of leaders, that not one of them durst take upon himself to listen to the proposals of the infidels. Henry, palatine of the Rhine, and the dukes of Saxony and Brabant, who enjoyed great consideration among the Germans, could enforce obedience from none but their own soldiers. Conrad, chancellor of the empire, who represented the emperor of Germany, might have been able to exercise beneficial power; but, weakened by disease, without experience in war, always shut up in his tent, he awaited the issue of the contest, and did not even deign to be present at the councils of the princes and barons. When the besieged had come to the determination to capitulate, they remained several days without knowing to which prince it would be most proper to address themselves, and when their deputies came to the Christian camp, their propositions were heard in a general assembly, in which the spirit of rivalry, short-sighted zeal, and blind enthusiasm held much greater empire than reason and prudence.

The Saracens, in their speech, confined themselves to imploring the clemency of their conquerors; they promised to abandon the fort with all their wealth, and only asked life and liberty as the price of their submission. The suppliant attitude of the Saracens must have touched the pride of the Christian warriors; religion and policy united to procure a favourable answer to the proposals that were made to them, and the greater part of the leaders were disposed to sign the capitulation. But some of the most ardent could not see without indignation that it was wished to obtain by treaty that which they must soon gain by force of arms. "It is necessary," said they, "that all our enemies should be struck with terror; and if the garrison of this place perish by the sword, the affrighted Saracens will not dare to wait for us either in Jerusalem or the other cities still in their possession."

As their advice was not adopted, these ardent and inconsiderate soldiers resolved to employ every means to interrupt the negotiation, and whilst re-conducting the deputies to the fortress, said to them: "*Defend yourselves, for if you surrender to the Christians, you will all perish in tortures.*" In addition to this, they addressed the Christian soldiers, and informed them, with accents of anger and grief, that a disgraceful peace was about to be concluded with the enemies of Christ. At the same time, such of the leaders as inclined towards peace, spread themselves through the camp, and represented to the army that it was useless, and perhaps dangerous, to purchase by new contests that which fortune, or rather Providence itself, offered to the Crusaders. Among the Christian warriors, some yielded to the counsels of moderation, others were unwilling to trust to anything but the sword; such as preferred victory to peace, ran to arms, and they who accepted the capitulation, retired to their tents. The camp, in which some remained in inaction and repose, whilst others prepared for battle, presented, at the same time, an image of peace and war: but in this diversity of opinions, amidst so strange a spectacle as the army then presented, it was easy to foresee that they would very soon be unable either to treat with enemies or fight them.

The capitulation was, notwithstanding, ratified by the principal chiefs and by the chancellor of the empire. The hostages the Saracens were to send were looked for in the camp, and the Crusaders fancied they could see the gates of the castle of Thoron thrown open to them; but despair had all at once changed the resolutions of the Saracens. When the deputies to the Christian camp reported to their companions in arms what they had seen and what they had heard; when they told them of the menaces that had been made to them, and of the divisions that existed among the enemies, the besieged forgot that their walls were in ruins, that they wanted both arms and provisions; that they had to defend themselves against a victorious army; and they swore rather to die than treat with the Crusaders. Instead of sending hostages, they appeared in arms upon the ramparts, and provoked the besiegers to renew the contest. The Christians resumed the labours of the siege, and recommenced their attacks; but their courage grew weaker every day, whilst, in the same proportion, despair seemed to increase the bravery of the Mussulmans. The besieged laboured without intermission in repairing their machines and rebuilding their walls; sometimes the Christians were attacked in the subterranean passages they had dug, and perished, buried under masses of loosened earth; whilst arrows and stones were constantly showered upon them from the ramparts. Frequently the Saracens succeeded in surprising some of their enemies, whom they carried alive into the place, and then slaughtered without mercy; the heads of these unfortunate prisoners were exposed upon the walls, and afterwards hurled by the machines into the camp of the Christians. The Crusaders appeared to have sunk into a sort of dejection or apathy; some still fought and remembered their oaths; but others remained indifferent spectators of the dangers and death of their brethren. Many added the scandal of the most depraved morals to their indifference for the cause of God. There might be seen, says an historian, men who had quitted their wives to follow Christ, forgetting all at once the most sacred duties, and attaching themselves to vile prostitutes; in fact, the vices and disorders of the Crusaders were so disgraceful, that the authors of the old chronicles blush whilst they retrace the picture of them. Arnold of Lubec, after having described the corruption that reigned in the camp of the Christians, appears to ask pardon of his reader; and, that he may not be accused of writing a satire, he takes care to add that he does not recall such odious remembrances to confound the pride of men, but to warn sinners, and touch, if possible, the hearts of his brothers in Christ. [23]

Fame soon brought to the ears of the Christians that the kingdoms of Aleppo and Damascus were in arms, that Egypt had assembled an army, and that Malek-Adel, followed by a numberless multitude of warriors, was advancing by forced marches, impatient to avenge his late defeat. [24]

At this news, the leaders of the crusade resolved to raise the siege of Thoron; and to conceal their retreat from the enemy, they did not blush to deceive their own soldiers. On the day of the Purification of the Virgin, whilst the Christians were engaged in the offices of devotion, the camp was informed, by sound of trumpet, that it was intended to make a general assault on the morrow. The whole army passed the night in preparations for the fight; but, at break of day, they learnt that Conrad and most of the leaders had quitted the army and taken the road to Tyre. The men assembled in groups round their tents to ascertain the truth, and made inquiries of each other with the greatest inquietude. The blackest forebodings took possession of the minds of the Crusaders; as if they had been conquered in a great battle, their only thought was flight. Nothing had been prepared for the retreat, no order had been given; no man saw anything but his own danger, or listened to any advice but that suggested by his fear; some loaded themselves with everything valuable they possessed, whilst others abandoned even their arms. The sick and wounded dragged themselves along with pain in the steps of their companions; such as could not walk were abandoned in the camp. The confusion was general; the soldiers marched *pêle-mêle* with the baggage; they knew not what route to take, and many lost themselves in the mountains; nothing was heard but cries and groans, and, as if Heaven wished to denote its anger at this disorder, a frightful tempest came on; fierce lightning rent the clouds, the thunder rolled in awful peals, and torrents of rain inundated the country. [25] In their tumultuous flight, not one of the Crusaders ventured to turn his eyes to that fortress which, but a few days before, had offered to surrender to their arms: their terror was not abated till they beheld the walls of Tyre.

The army being at last re-assembled, it became a general inquiry, "What was the cause of the disorder they had experienced?" Then a new delirium took possession of the Christians; mistrust and mutual hatred succeeded to the panic terror of which they had been the victims; the most grave suspicions were attached to actions the most simple, and gave an odious meaning to words perfectly innocent. The Crusaders reproached each other, as with wrongs and proofs of treachery, with all the evils they had suffered or feared to suffer. The measures that an improvident zeal had counselled, as well as those that had been dictated by necessity and prudence, were the work of perfidy without example. The holy places, which so lately the Crusaders had contemplated with apparent indifference, now occupied their every thought; and the most fervent reproached the leaders with introducing none but profane views into a holy war; with having sacrificed the cause of God to their own ambition, and with having abandoned the soldiers of Christ to the fury of the Saracens. The same Crusaders proclaimed loudly, that God had been unfavourable to the Christians, because those whom he had appointed to lead the defenders of the cross, disdained the conquest of Jerusalem. Our readers may remember that after the siege of Damascus, in the second crusade, some Templars and Germans were accused of avarice, and of having sacrificed the zeal and bravery of the Christian warriors. Accusations quite as serious were renewed on this occasion, and with equal bitterness. If we are to believe the old chronicles, Malek-Adel had promised several leaders of the Christian army a great number of pieces of gold to engage them to raise the siege of Thoron; and the same chronicles add, that when the Mussulman prince paid them the sum agreed, he gave them nothing but false gold,—a worthy price of their cupidity and treachery. [26] The Arabian historians give no sanction to these odious accusations; but such was the spirit of animosity which then reigned among the Christian warriors, that they were judged with more severity by their brethren and companions in arms than by their enemies.

At length the rage of discord was carried so far that the Germans and the Syrian Christians would not remain under the same colours; the former retired to the city of Jaffa, the ramparts of which they restored, and the latter returned to Ptolemaïs. Malek-Adel, willing to profit by these divisions, marched towards Jaffa, and offered the Germans battle. A severe conflict took place at a short distance from the city. The duke of Saxony and the duke of Brabant both perished in the *mêlée*. [27] The Crusaders lost a great number of their bravest warriors; but the victory was in their favour. After a triumph which was due to their arms alone, the pride of the Germans knew no bounds; and they treated the Christians of Palestine with the greatest contempt. "We have," said they, "crossed the seas to defend their country; and, far from taking any part in our labours, these warriors, without either gratitude or courage, abandoned us in the hour of peril." The Christians of Palestine, on their side, reproached the Germans with having come into the East, not to fight but to command; not to assist their brethren, but to impose a yoke upon them more insupportable than that of the Saracens. "The Crusaders," added they, "only quitted the West to make a pleasurable military progress into Syria; they there found peace, but they left war behind them; like those birds of passage that announce the season of storms and tempests."

In these fatal divisions nobody had sufficient credit and power to restrain angry spirits, or reconcile discordant opinions. The sceptre of Jerusalem was in the hands of a woman; the throne of Godfrey, so often shaken, was destitute of support; the empire of religion and law was every day fading away, and violence alone possessed the privilege of making itself respected. Necessity and force were the only powers that commanded obedience; whilst the license and corruption that prevailed among the people, still called *the people of God*, made such frightful progress, that we are tempted to accuse contemporary authors and ocular witnesses of employing great exaggeration in their recitals.

In this state of decline, amidst such shameful disorders, the most wise and prudent of the prelates and barons thought the best step they could adopt would be to give an able and worthy leader to the Christian colonies, and they entreated Isabella, the widow of Henry of Champagne, to take a new husband, who might consent to be their sovereign. Isabella, by three marriages, had already given Palestine three kings. They proposed to her Amaury, who had recently succeeded Guy de Lusignan in the kingdom of Cyprus. An Arabian historian says that Amaury was *a wise and prudent man, who loved God and respected humanity*. He did not fear to reign, amidst war, troubles, and factions, over the poor remains of the unfortunate kingdom of Jerusalem, and came to share with Isabella the vain honours of royalty. Their marriage was celebrated at Ptolemaïs, with more pomp, say historians, than the posture of affairs warranted. Although this marriage might not remedy all the evils under which the Christians laboured, it at least afforded them the consolatory hope that their discords would be appeased, and that the colonies of the Franks, when better governed, might gather some fruit from so many victories gained over the infidels. But news which arrived from the West, soon spread fresh grief through the kingdom, and put an end to the barren exploits of the holy war. Amidst the festivities which followed the marriage and coronation of Amaury, the death of the emperor Henry VI. was announced. [28] The election of a new head of the empire would most probably produce a violent contest in Germany; and every one of the German princes or nobles then in Palestine, naturally turned his attention to that which he had to hope or fear in the events preparing in Europe: they determined to return immediately into the West.

The count de Montfort and several other French knights had but recently arrived in the Holy Land, and earnestly entreated the German princes to defer their return. The pope likewise, on receiving intelligence of the death of Henry VI., wrote to the leaders of the Crusaders, to implore them to finish their good work, and not to abandon the cause of Christ; but neither the prayers of the count de Montfort nor the exhortations of the pope could detain the Germans, impatient to return to their country. Of so many princes who had left the West to secure a triumph to the cause of God, the queen of Hungary alone was faithful to her vows, and remained with her knights in Palestine. [29] On quitting Syria, the Germans contented themselves with leaving a garrison in Jaffa. A short time after their departure, whilst celebrating the feast of St. Martin with every excess of drunkenness and debauchery, this garrison was surprised and massacred by the Saracens. [30] Winter was approaching; neither party could keep the field; discord reigned equally among Christians and Mussulmans; and both sides were desirous of peace, because they were incapable of carrying on the war. The count de Montfort concluded with the Saracens a truce for three years. Thus terminated this crusade, which only lasted a few months, and was really nothing but a pilgrimage for the warriors of the West. The victories of the Crusaders rendered the Christians masters of all the coasts of Syria; but their precipitate departure destroyed the fruits of their conquests. The cities they had obtained were left without defenders, and almost without inhabitants.

This fourth crusade, in which all the powers of the West miscarried in an attempt upon a little fortress of Syria, and which presents us with the strange spectacle of a holy war directed by an excommunicated monarch, furnishes the historian with fewer great events and a smaller number of great misfortunes than the preceding expeditions. The Christian armies, which made but a transient visit to the East, experienced neither the famine nor the diseases that had proved so fatal to the former enterprises. The foresight and attention of the emperor of Germany, who had become master of Sicily, provided for all the wants of the Crusaders, whose exploits were intended to assist his ambitious projects, and whom he considered as his own soldiers.

The German warriors that composed the Christian armies had not the requisite qualities to secure the advantages of victory. [31] Always ready to throw themselves blindly into danger; quite ignorant that it is possible to ally prudence with courage; listening to nothing but the violence of their own passions, and recognising no law but their own will; obedient to leaders of their own nation, and despising all others; full of an indomitable pride, which made them disdain the help of their allies and the lessons of experience, such men could neither make peace nor war.

When we compare these new Crusaders with the companions of Richard or Godfrey, we find in them the same ardour for fight, the same indifference for danger; but we find them very deficient in that enthusiasm which animated the first soldiers of the cross at the sight of the holy places. Jerusalem, which had never ceased to be open to the devotion of the faithful, no longer beheld within its walls that crowd of pilgrims which, at the commencement of the holy wars, repaired thither from all parts of the West. The pope and the leaders of the Christian army forbade Crusaders to enter the holy city without having conquered it; and they, who did not always prove so docile, obeyed the prohibition without pain. More than a hundred thousand warriors that had left Europe for the purpose of delivering Jerusalem, returned to their homes without having entertained perhaps one thought of visiting the tomb of Christ, for which they had taken up arms. The thirty ounces of gold promised by the emperor to all who should cross the sea to fight the infidels, very much increased the number of the Crusaders; this was not the case in former expeditions, in which the crowd of soldiers of the cross was influenced principally by religious motives. More religion than politics had entered into the other holy wars; in this crusade, although it had been directly promoted by the head of the Church, and was to a considerable extent directed by bishops, we may safely say there was more of politics than religion. Pride, ambition, jealousy, the most disgraceful passions of the human heart, did not make an effort, as in the preceding expeditions, to cover themselves with a religious veil. The archbishop of Mayence, the bishop of Hildesheim, with most of the other ecclesiastics who took the cross, attracted no admiration for either their wisdom or piety, or distinguished themselves by any personal quality. Conrad, the chancellor of the empire, on his return to Europe, was followed by the suspicions which had been attached to his conduct during the holy war; and when, a long time after, he was slain by several gentlemen of Wurtzburg, who conspired against him, the people considered his tragical death as a punishment from Heaven.

Henry VI., who had preached the crusade, only viewed this distant expedition as a means and an opportunity for increasing his power and extending his empire; whilst the West put up prayers for the success of a holy war, of which he was the life and soul, he prosecuted an impious war, desolated a Christian people for the purpose of subjecting them to his laws, and threatened the empire of Greece. [32] The son of Tancred was deprived of his sight, and cast into prison, and the daughters of the king of Sicily were carried away into captivity. Henry's barbarities were so excessive, that he irritated his neighbours, and created enemies in his own family. When he died, a report prevailed in Europe that he had been poisoned; the nations that he had rendered miserable could not believe that so many cruelties could remain unpunished, and they asserted that Providence had employed the wife of the emperor to be his executioner, and to avenge all the calamities he had inflicted upon the kingdoms of Naples and Sicily. At the approach of death, Henry remembered that he had persecuted Richard; that he had detained a prince of the Crusaders in chains, in spite of the solicitations of the father of the faithful; and he hastened to send ambassadors to the king of England, charged with the task of making him a solemn reparation for so great an outrage. After his death, as he had been excommunicated, it was thought necessary to address the sovereign pontiff to obtain permission to bury him in the Holy Land; and the pope coolly replied, that they were at liberty to bury him among Christians, but before they did so, they must offer up many prayers to mitigate the anger of God.

In taking possession of the beautiful and rich territories of Italy by perfidy and violence, Henry prepared for that unfortunate country a series of revolutions, to be renewed from age to age. The odious war he had made against the family of Tancred, naturally gave birth to other wars injurious to his own family. [33] In removing so far from Germany with his armies, Henry afforded opportunity for the formation of powerful parties, which, at his death, disputed the imperial sceptre with some success, and at length gave rise to a war in which the principal states of Europe were involved. Thus, whilst the other holy wars had contributed to maintain or establish public peace in Europe, this fourth crusade produced divisions among the states of Christendom, without at all diminishing the power of the Saracens, and only served to introduce trouble and confusion into many kingdoms of the West.

BOOK X
A.D. 1198-1204

FIFTH CRUSADE

"*Christian troops,*" says J. J. Rousseau, in his "Contrat Social," "*are, as they say, excellent; I deny it; show me such; for my part, I know no Christian troops.*" The events we have just related, and those we are about to make known, will, there is no doubt, suffice to refute this strange paradox of J. J. Rousseau. The author of the "Social Contract" does not dissemble, it is true, the objections that may be made to him from the history of the crusades; but, ever faithful to his system, and taking no account of historical truths, he answers, that "*the Crusaders, far from being Christians, were citizens of the Church; that they fought for their spiritual country, which the Church had rendered temporal nobody knows how.*" Strange abuse of reasoning, which confounds the sense of words, and refuses the title of Christians to those who fought in the name of Christ! In representing the Crusaders as citizens of the Church, Rousseau doubtless, meant to say that the popes were the origin of the crusades, and that the soldiers of the cross defended the temporal power of the popes. We at once reply that the crusades owed their birth and growth to the religious and warlike enthusiasm that animated the nations of the West in the twelfth century, and that without this enthusiasm, which was not the work of the heads of the Church, the preachings of the Holy See would not have been able to collect a single army under the banners of the cross. We may further add that, during the holy wars, the sovereign pontiffs were frequently driven from Rome and despoiled of their states, and that they did not summon the Crusaders to the defence of the power or *temporal country* of the Church. Not only were the Crusaders not always the blind instruments of the Holy See, but they sometimes resisted the will of the popes, and yet in their camps were no less models of valour united with Christian piety. No doubt, the leaders were often seduced by ambition, the love of glory, and a passion for war; but religion, well or ill understood, acted upon the greater number; the Christian religion which they defended, or believed they defended, by inspiring them with a desire for the blessings of heaven and a contempt for life, elevated them above all perils, and enabled them to brave death on every occasion. Here is the whole truth; but this truth is too simple for such as disdain common routes, and cannot form a judgment upon human affairs without displaying all the parade of a proud and austere philosophy. For ourselves, who are persuaded that true philosophy consists in studying the human heart and the spirit of societies, not in vain theories, but in the faithful history of past ages; we will not refute brilliant sophisms by long arguments; but to show in all its splendour the valour of *Christian soldiers*, we will content ourselves with pursuing our recital, and making known with impartiality the labours, the reverses, and the victories of the soldiers of the cross. [34]

The departure of the German Crusaders plunged the eastern Christians into grief and consternation; the colonies, when left to their own resources, were only protected by the truce concluded between the count de Montfort and Malek-Adel. The infidels had too great a superiority over their enemies to respect, for any length of time, a treaty which they considered as an obstacle to the progress of their power. The Christians, threatened by new perils, again turned their eyes to the West. The bishop of Ptolemaïs, accompanied by several knights, embarked for Europe, in order to solicit the aid of the faithful. The vessel in which he embarked had scarcely quitted the port, when it was swallowed up by the waves, and the bishop and every person of his suite perished. Other ships, that set sail a short time afterwards, were surprised by the tempest, and forced to return to the port of Tripoli; so that the prayers and complaints of the Christians of Palestine could not reach the ears of their brethren of the West. Nevertheless, the afflicting news of the situation of the feeble kingdom of Jerusalem soon became generally known; some pilgrims, escaping from the perils of the sea, described, on their return, the triumphs and threats of the Saracens; but in the state of Europe at that moment, nothing could be more difficult than to induce nations to undertake a new crusade. The death of the Emperor Henry VI. divided the princes and prelates of Germany, and Philip Augustus was still at war with Richard of England. One of the sons of Bela, king of Hungary, who pretended to take the cross, only assembled an army to agitate the kingdom, and get possession of the crown. Amidst the fierce contentions that disturbed Europe, the Christian people seemed to have forgotten the tomb of Christ: a single man was touched with the misfortunes of the faithful of the East, and was not without hope of alleviating them.

Innocent III., at the age of thirty-three, had recently gained the suffrages of the conclave. [35] At a period of life in which the passions are generally masters, devoted to the most austere retirement, constantly occupied with the study of holy books, and ready at all times to confound new heresies by the force of reason, the successor of St. Peter shed tears on being informed of his elevation; but when seated on the pontifical throne, Innocent all at once exhibited a new character: the same man, who had appeared to dread the splendour of a lofty position, became most eager, by any means, to increase his power, and displayed all the ambition and inflexible obstinacy of Gregory VII. His youth, which promised him a long reign; his ardour in the defence of justice and truth; his eloquence, his knowledge, his virtues, which drew upon him the respect of the faithful, all united to give birth to the hope that he would assure the triumph of religion; and that he would one day accomplish the projects of his predecessors.

As the power of the pope was founded upon the progress of the faith and the holy enthusiasm of the Christians, Innocent gave his first attention to the suppression of the dangerous innovations and imprudent doctrines that began to corrupt his age and menace the sanctuary; he particularly endeavoured to reanimate the ardour for the crusades: and, to master the minds of kings and nations, to rally all Christians, and make them concur in the triumph of the Church, he spoke to them of the captivity of Jerusalem; he pointed to the tomb of Christ, and the holy places profaned by the presence and the domination of infidels.

In a letter [36] addressed to the bishops, the clergy, the nobles, and people of France, England, Hungary, and Sicily, the sovereign pontiff made known the will, the menaces, and the promises of God. "Since the lamentable loss of Jerusalem," said he, "the Holy See has never ceased to cry towards Heaven, and to exhort the faithful to avenge the injury done to Christ, thus banished from his heritage. Formerly Uriah would not enter into his house, or see his wife, whilst the ark of the Lord was in the camp; but now our princes, in this public calamity, abandon themselves to illegitimate amours; immerse themselves in voluptuousness; abuse the blessings that God has given them; and pursue each other with implacable hatred; only thinking of revenging their own personal injuries, they never consider that our enemies insult us, saying: *'Where is your God, who cannot deliver himself out of our hands? We have profaned your sanctuary, and the places in which you pretend your superstition had its birth; we have crushed the arms of the French, the English, the Germans, and subdued a second time the proud Spaniards: what remains then for us to do? to drive out those you have left in Syria, and to penetrate into the West to efface for ever both your name and your memory.'"* Assuming then a more paternal tone: "Prove," cried Innocent, "that you have not lost your courage; be prodigal, in the cause of God, of all you have received from him; if, on an occasion so pressing, you refuse to serve Christ, what excuse will you be able to offer at his terrible tribunal? If God died for man, shall man fear to die for his God? Will he refuse to give up his transitory life and the perishable goods of this world for him who lays before us the treasures of eternity?"

Prelates were at the same time sent through all the countries of Europe, to preach peace among princes, and exhort them to unite against the common enemies of God. These prelates, clothed in the full confidence of the Holy See, were to engage cities and nobles to equip, at their own expense, for the Holy Land, a certain number of warriors, to serve there during two years at least. They promised remission of sins, [37] and the special protection of the Church [38] to all that would take up the cross and arms, or would contribute to the equipment and support of the soldiers of Christ. To receive the pious tribute of the faithful, boxes were placed in all the churches. At the tribunal of penitence, the priests were ordered to command all sinners to concur in the holy enterprise; no error could find grace before God, without the sincere will of participating in the crusade; zeal for the deliverance of the holy places appeared to be at that time the only virtue the pope required of Christians, and even charity itself lost some of its value, if not exercised in promoting the crusades. As the Church of Rome was reproached with imposing upon the people *burdens to which she only applied the tip of her own finger*, the pope exhorted the heads of the clergy, and the clergy themselves, to set an example of devotedness and sacrifices. Innocent ordered his gold and silver plate to be melted to defray the expenses of the holy war, and would allow none but vessels of wood and clay to be seen on his table whilst the crusade lasted.

The sovereign pontiff was so satisfied of the zeal and piety of the Christians, that he wrote to the patriarch and king of Jerusalem, to announce to them the coming succours from the West. He neglected nothing that could augment the numbers of the soldiers of Christ; he addressed himself to the emperor of Constantinople, and reproached him with indifference for the deliverance of the holy places. The emperor Alexius endeavoured, in his answer, to show his zeal for the cause of religion; but he added that the time of deliverance was not yet arrived, and that he feared to oppose himself to the will of God, irritated by the sins of the Christians. The Greek prince adroitly reminded him of the ravages committed in the territories of the empire by the soldiers of Frederick, and conjured the pope to direct his reproofs against those who, feigning to labour for Jesus Christ, acted against the will of Heaven. In his correspondence with Alexius, Innocent III. did not at all conceal his pretensions to universal empire, and spoke in the character of sovereign arbiter of the kings of the East and West. He applied to himself these words addressed to Jeremiah: "I have placed thee over the nations and over the kingdoms, to pull up and scatter, to edify and to plant." When speaking of the power of the popes and that of princes, he compared the one to the sun, which lights the universe during the day, and the other to the moon, which lights the earth during the night.

The pretensions that Innocent put forth, and the haughtiness with which he sought to establish them, were, no doubt, injurious to the effect of his exhortations, and must have weakened the zeal of the Christian princes whom he wished to persuade to undertake the crusade. The princes and bishops of Germany were divided between Otho of Saxony and Philip of Swabia; the sovereign pontiff pronounced strongly for Otho, and threatened with the thunders of the Church all who assisted the opposite party. In the dissensions occasioned by this momentous affair, some availed themselves of the opportunity to gain the favour of the pope, and others to secure themselves from the effects of his anger; but all Germany being engaged in the quarrel, nobody took the cross.

One of the pope's legates, Peter of Capua, succeeded in re-establishing peace between Richard Cœur de Lion and Philip Augustus. Richard, who was desirous of conciliating the good-will of the Holy See, constantly promised to equip a fleet and collect an army to go and make war against the infidels. He proclaimed a tournament in his capital, in the midst of which he called upon the barons and knights to follow him into the East; but all these demonstrations, the sincerity of which was very suspicious, remained unproductive. It was not long before war again broke out between France and England, and Richard, who on all occasions repeated his vow of combating the infidels, was killed in a petty quarrel with Christians.

Philip Augustus repudiated Ingeburge, daughter of the king of Denmark, to marry Agnes de Meranie. The sovereign pontiff, in a letter addressed to the faithful, strongly censured princes who gave themselves up to illegitimate amours; he ordered Philip Augustus to take back Ingeburge, and as Philip refused to obey, the kingdom of France was placed under an interdict. During several months all religious ceremonies were suspended; the pulpits of the Gospel ceased to give forth the holy word; church bells and the voice of prayer were silenced; Christian burial was refused to the dead; the sanctuary was closed against the faithful; a long mourning veil seemed to hang over cities and plains, from which the Christian religion was banished, and which might almost be fancied to be invaded by the Saracens. Although such as took the cross were exempt from the interdict, the spectacle which France presented discouraged and saddened its inhabitants. Philip Augustus, irritated against the pope, showed very little disposition to revive their zeal; and the clergy, whose influence might have had a powerful effect, had less reason to deplore the captivity of Jerusalem than the unhappy state of the kingdom.

At length a curé of Neuilly-sur-Maine began to fill France with the fame of his eloquence and his miracles. Foulques had at first led a very dissipated life, but, touched with sincere repentance, he was not satisfied with expiating his irregularities by penitence, but became desirous of bringing back all sinners to the paths of salvation, and travelled through the provinces endeavouring to awaken in the people a contempt for the things of this life. God, to try him, permitted that, in his early sermons, Foulques should be exposed to the ridicule of his auditors; but the truths he uttered soon obtained a marvellous ascendancy over all that came to hear him. Bishops invited him to preach in their dioceses; he received everywhere extraordinary honours, and both people and clergy flocked out to meet him, as if he had been an envoy of God. Foulques, says the chronicle of St. Victor, had nothing remarkable in his vestments or manner of living; *he travelled on horseback, and ate that which was given to him.* He preached sometimes in churches, at others in public places, and not unfrequently amidst the excitement of tournaments. His eloquence was simple and natural; safe, by his ignorance, from the bad taste of his age, he neither astonished his auditors by the vain subtleties of the schools, nor by an absurd mixture of passages from the Scriptures and profane quotations from antiquity. His words, from being unadorned by the erudition then so much admired, were the more persuasive, and found their way more directly to the heart. [39] The most learned preachers ranked themselves among his disciples, and declared that the Holy Ghost spoke by his mouth. Animated by that faith which performs prodigies, he enchained at his pleasure the passions of the multitude, and caused to resound, even in the palaces of princes, the *thunders of evangelical denunciations*. [40] At his voice, all that had enriched themselves by fraud, brigandage, or usury, hastened to restore that which they had unjustly acquired; libertines confessed their sins, and devoted themselves to the austerities of penitence; [41] prostitutes, following the example of Madeline, deplored the scandal of their lives, cut off their hair, exchanged their gaudy apparel for haircloth and mean garments, and made vows to sleep upon ashes and die in retirement. In short, the eloquence of Foulques of Neuilly effected such miracles, that contemporaries speak of him as of another St. Paul, sent for the conversion of his age. One of them even goes so far as to say that he dares not relate all he knows of him, fearing the incredulity of men. [42]

Innocent III. cast his eyes upon Foulques of Neuilly, and confided to him the mission that, fifty years before, had been given to St. Bernard. The new preacher of the crusade himself assumed the cross at a general chapter of the order of Citeaux. At the sound of his voice, the zeal for the holy war, which had appeared extinct, blazed out again in all parts. In every city he passed through, the people crowded to listen to him; and all who were in a condition to bear arms, took the oath to combat the infidels.

Several holy orators were associated with Foulques of Neuilly; Martin Litz, of the order of Citeaux, in the diocese of Bâle, and on the banks of the Rhine; Herloin, a monk of St. Denis, took his cause through the still wild countries of Bretagne and the lower Poitou; and Eustace, abbot of Flay, crossed the sea twice, to awaken the enthusiasm and holy ardour of the provinces of England.

These pious orators were not all endowed with the same eloquence; but all were animated by the most ardent zeal. The profanation of the holy places, the evils suffered by the Eastern Christians, and the remembrance of Jerusalem, imparted the most lively interest to their discourses, and touched all hearts. [43] Such was the spirit spread through Europe, that simply to mention the name of Christ, or to speak of the city of God, held in captivity by the infidels, melted auditors to tears, and gave birth to transports of enthusiasm. The people everywhere evinced the same piety and the same feelings; but the cause of Christ still wanted the example and courage of princes and nobles. As a celebrated tournament had been proclaimed in Champagne, at which the boldest warriors of France, Germany, and Flanders were expected to be present, Foulques repaired to the castle of Ecry-sur-Aisne, [44] which was the rendezvous of the knights. His eloquence procured attention to the complaints of Sion, even amidst the profane and violent amusements of chivalry; when Foulques spoke of Jerusalem, knights and barons neglected their jousts, the shivering of lances, or high feats of arms; they became insensible of the presence of *dames* and *demoiselles*, who accorded the prizes to valour; and turned a deaf ear to the gay minstrels who celebrated *la prouesse achetée et vendue au fer et à l'acier*. All took the oath to fight against the infidels; and it must have been surprising to see numerous defenders of the cross come forth from these warlike festivals that were so severely reprehended by the Church.

Among the princes and lords who enrolled themselves in the crusade, the most conspicuous were Thibault IV., count of Champagne, and Louis, count of Chartres and Blois, both relations of the kings of France and England. The father of Thibault had followed Louis VII. to the second crusade, and his elder brother had been king of Jerusalem. Two thousand five hundred knights owed him homage and military service, and the nobility of Champagne excelled in all the noble exercises of arms. [45] The marriage of Thibault with the heiress of Navarre brought to his standard a great number of warriors from the countries bordering on the Pyrenees. Louis, count of Chartres and Blois, reckoned among his ancestors one of the most illustrious chiefs of the first crusade, and was master of a province abounding in warriors of name. After the example of these two princes, the following distinguished leaders took the cross:—The count of St. Paul, the counts Gauthier and Jean de Brienne, Manassès de l'Isle, Renard de Dampièrre, Mathieu de Montmorency, Hugh and Robert de Boves, d'Amiens, Renaud de Boulogne, Geoffrey de Perche, Renaud de Montmirail, Simon de Montfort, who had just signed a treaty with the Saracens, but was no less ready on that account to take an oath to fight against them; and Geoffrey de Villehardouin, [46] marshal of Champagne, who has left us an account of this crusade in the unadorned language of his time.

Among the ecclesiastics, history names Nivelon de Chérisi, bishop of Soissons; Garnier, bishop of Langres; the abbot of Looz, and the abbot of Veaux-de-Cernai. The bishop of Langres, who had been the object of the censures of the pope, expected to find in the pilgrimage to the Holy Land, an opportunity of reconciling himself with the Holy See. The abbot of Looz and the abbot of Veaux-de-Cernai were both remarkable for their piety and learning; the former full of wisdom and moderation, the latter animated by a holy enthusiasm and an ardent zeal, which afterwards he but too strongly displayed against the Albigeois and the partisans of the count of Thoulouse.

When the knights and barons returned to their homes, bearing a red cross upon their baldrics and their coats of mail, [47] they aroused by their presence the enthusiasm of their vassals and brothers in arms. The nobility of Flanders, after the example of those of Champagne, were anxious to prove their zeal for the recovery of the holy places. Baldwin, who had taken the part of Richard against Philip Augustus, sought beneath the standard of the cross an asylum against the anger of the king of France, and swore, in the church of St. Donatien of Bruges, to go into Asia to combat the Saracens. Mary, countess of Flanders, sister of Thibault, count of Champagne, would not live separated from her husband; and although she was still in the flower of her youth, and was several months advanced in her pregnancy, took an oath to follow the Crusaders beyond the seas, and to quit a home she was doomed never to see again. The example of Baldwin was followed by his two brothers, [48] Eustace and Henry, count of Sarbuck; by Canon de Bethune, whose piety and eloquence were held in high estimation, and by Jacques d'Avesnes, son of him who, under the same name, had made himself so famous in the third crusade. Most of the knights and barons of Flanders and Hainault also took the oath to share the labours and perils of the holy war.

The principal leaders first met at Soissons, and afterwards at Compiègne. In their assembly, they gave the command of the expedition to Thibault, count of Champagne. It was decided also that the Crusaders should repair to the East by sea; and, in consequence of this determination, six deputies were sent to Venice, [49] in order to obtain from the republic the vessels required to transport the men and horses.

The Venetians were at that period in the highest state of their greatness and prosperity. Amidst the convulsions that had preceded and followed the fall of the Roman power, these industrious people had taken refuge in the islands that border the extremity of the Adriatic Gulf; and, placed upon the waves, had directed all their views to the empire of the sea, [50] of which the barbarians took no heed. Venice was at first under the dominion of the emperors of Constantinople; but, in proportion with the decline of the Greek empire, the republic acquired territory, strength, and splendour, which necessarily produced independence. From the tenth century, palaces of marble had replaced the humble huts of fishermen, scattered over the island of the Rialto. The cities of Istria and Dalmatia obeyed the sovereigns of the Adriatic Sea. The republic, become formidable to the most powerful monarch, was able, at the least signal, to arm a fleet of a hundred galleys, which it employed successively against the Greeks, the Saracens, and the Normans. The power of Venice was respected by all the nations of the West; and the republics of Genoa and Pisa in vain contended with her for the domination of the seas. The Venetians remembered with pride these words of Pope Alexander III., when the republic had protested against the emperor of Germany, who presented a ring to the doge, saying, *"Espouse the sea with this ring, that posterity may know that the Venetians have acquired the empire of the waves, and that the sea has been subjected to them as a woman is to her husband."*

The fleets of the Venetians constantly visited the ports of Greece and Asia; they transported pilgrims to Palestine, and returned laden with the rich merchandise of the East. The Venetians entered into the crusades with less eagerness and enthusiasm than other Christian nations, but knew well how to profit by them for their own interests; whilst the warriors of Christendom were fighting for glory, for kingdoms, or for the tomb of Christ, the merchants of Venice fought for counting-houses, stores, and commercial privileges; and avarice often made them undertake that which other nations could not have been able to effect but by an excess of religious zeal. The republic, which owed all its prosperity to its commercial relations, sought without scruple the friendship and protection of the Mussulman powers of Syria and Egypt; and often, even when all Europe was arming against the infidels, the Venetians were accused of supplying the enemies of the Christian nations with both arms and provisions.

When the deputies of the Crusaders arrived at Venice, the republic had for doge Dandolo, so celebrated in its annals. Dandolo had for a length of time served his country in important missions, and in the command of its fleets and armies; now, placed at the head of its government, he watched over its liberties and the operations of its laws. His labours in war and peace, his useful regulations of the money currency, with his administration of justice and public security, deservedly procured him the esteem and gratitude of his fellow-citizens. He had acquired the power of mastering, by words, the passions of the multitude, even in the stormy disputes of a republic.

Nobody was more skilful in seizing a favourable opportunity, or in taking advantage of the least circumstance for the furtherance of his designs. At the age of ninety, the doge of Venice exhibited no symptoms of senility but virtue and experience. [51] Everything that could save his country aroused his activity and inflamed his courage; with the spirit of calculation and economy which distinguished his compatriots, Dandolo mingled passions the most generous, and threw an air of grandeur over all the enterprises of a trading people. His patriotism, always sustained by the love of glory, appeared to possess something of that sentiment of honour, and that chivalric greatness of soul which formed the predominant characteristic of his age.

Dandolo [52] praised with warmth an enterprise that appeared glorious to him, and in which the interests of his country were not opposed to those of religion. The deputies required vessels to transport four thousand five hundred knights and twenty thousand foot, with provisions for the Christian army for nine months. Dandolo promised, in the name of the republic, to furnish the necessary provisions and vessels, on condition that the Crusaders should engage to pay the Venetians the sum of eighty-five thousand silver marks. [53] As he was not willing that the people of Venice should be unconnected with the expedition of the French Crusaders, Dandolo proposed to the deputies to arm, at the expense of the republic, fifty galleys, and demanded for his country half of the conquests that might be made in the East.

The deputies accepted without hesitation the more interested than generous proposals of the doge. The conditions of the treaty were first examined in the doge's council, [54] composed of six patricians; it was afterwards ratified in two other councils, [55] and at last presented for the sanction of the people, who then exercised supreme power. [56]

A general assembly was convoked in the church of St. Mark, and when the mass of the Holy Ghost had been celebrated, the marshal of Champagne, accompanied by the other deputies, arose, and addressing the people of Venice, pronounced a discourse, the simple and unaffected expressions of which paint, better than we possibly can, the spirit and feelings of the heroic periods of our history. [57] "The lords and barons of France, the most high and the most powerful, have sent us to you to pray you, in the name of

God, to take pity on Jerusalem, which the Turks hold in bondage; they cry to you for mercy, and supplicate you to accompany them to avenge the disgrace of Jesus Christ. They have made choice of you, because they know that no people that be upon the sea have so great power as your nation. They have commanded us to throw ourselves at your feet, and not to rise until you shall have granted our request, until you shall have had pity on the Holy Land beyond the seas." At these words the deputies were moved to tears, [58] and feeling it no degradation to humble themselves in the cause of Christ, [59] they fell upon their knees and held up their hands in a supplicating manner towards the assembly of the people. The strong emotion of the barons and knights communicated itself to the Venetians, and ten thousand voices replied as one, "*We grant your request.*" The doge, ascending the tribunal, praised highly the earnestness and loyalty of the French barons, and spoke with enthusiasm of the honour God conferred upon the people of Venice in choosing them from amongst all other nations, [60] to partake in the glory of the most noble of enterprises, and associate them with the most valiant of warriors. He then read the treaty entered into with the Crusaders, and conjured his assembled fellow-citizens to give their consent to it in the forms ordained by the laws of the republic. Then the people arose, and cried with an unanimous shout, "*We consent to it.*" All the inhabitants of Venice were present at this meeting; an immense multitude covered the place of St. Mark and filled the neighbouring streets. Religious enthusiasm, love of country, surprise and joy were manifested by acclamations so loud and general, that it might be said, according to the expression of the marshal of Champagne, "*that the world was about to engage in one common conflict.*"

On the morrow of this memorable day, the deputies of the barons repaired to the palace of St. Mark, and swore on their swords and the Gospel, to fulfil all the engagements they had made. The preamble of the treaty recalled the faults and the misfortunes of the princes who had to that time undertaken the deliverance of the Holy Land, and praised the wisdom and prudence of the French lords and knights, who neglected nothing to assure the success of an enterprise full of difficulties and perils. The deputies were charged to endeavour to cause the conditions they had sworn to to be adopted by their brothers in arms the barons and knights, by *the whole of their nation*, and *if possible, by their sovereign lord the king of France*. The treaty was written on parchment and sent immediately to Rome, to receive the approbation of the pope; and, full of confidence in the future, as well as in the alliance they had contracted, the French knights and the patricians of Venice exchanged the most touching protestations of friendship. [61] The doge lent the barons the sum of ten thousand silver marks, and the latter swore never to forget the services the republic had rendered to Jesus Christ. "There were then shed," says Villehardouin, "many tears of tenderness and joy."

The government of Venice was a new spectacle for the French nobles; deliberations of the people were perfectly unknown to them, and must have struck them with astonishment. On the other side, the embassy of the knights and barons could not fail to flatter the pride of the Venetians; the latter felicitated themselves upon being thus acknowledged as the greatest maritime nation, and, never separating their glory from their commercial interests, rejoiced at having made so advantageous a bargain. The knights, on the contrary, only thought of honour and the cause of Christ; and although the treaty was ruinous to the Crusaders, they bore back the news to their companions in arms with the greatest joy and satisfaction. [62]

The preference given to the Venetians by the Crusaders naturally excited the jealousy of the other maritime powers of Italy; thus the French deputies, upon going to Pisa and Genoa to solicit the aid of the two republics in the name of Jesus Christ, met with a cold reception and a perfect indifference for the deliverance of the holy places.

The account of what had taken place at Venice, and the presence of the barons, did not fail, however, to arouse the enthusiasm of the inhabitants of Lombardy and Piedmont; a great number of them took the cross and arms, and promised to follow Boniface, marquis of Montferrat, to the Holy Land.

The marshal of Champagne, whilst crossing Mount Cenis, met Gauthier de Brienne, who had taken the cross at the castle of Ecry, and was on his way to Apulia. He had married one of the daughters of Tancred, last king of Sicily. Followed by sixty knights of Champagne, he was going to endeavour to make good the claims of his wife, and conquer the kingdom founded by the Norman knights. The marshal Villehardouin and Gauthier de Brienne congratulated each other upon the brilliant prospects of their expeditions, and promised to meet again in the plains of Egypt and Syria. Thus the future presented nothing to the knights of the cross but victories and trophies; and the hope of conquering distant kingdoms redoubled their ardour.

When the deputies arrived in Champagne, they found Thibault dangerously ill. The prince was so delighted at learning the success of their embassy, that, heedless of the disease that had confined him to his bed, he insisted upon putting on his armour and mounting on horseback; but "this was great pity and misfortune," says Villehardouin; "for the malady increased, and gathered such strength, that he declared his will, took leave of his friends, and got no more on horseback." Thibault, the model and hope of the Christian knights, died in the flower of his age, deeply regretted by his vassals and companions in arms. He deplored before the barons the rigorous destiny that condemned him thus to die without glory, at the moment that he was about to gather the palms of victory or of martyrdom in the plains of the East; he exhorted them to perform the vow he had made to God to deliver Jerusalem, and left them all his treasures to be employed in this holy enterprise. An epitaph in Latin verse, which still exists, celebrates the virtues and pious zeal of Count Thibault, recalls the preparations for his pilgrimage, [63] and terminates by saying, that this young prince *found the heavenly Jerusalem, when about to seek the earthly Jerusalem.*

After the death of the count of Champagne, the barons and knights who had taken the cross, assembled to choose another leader, and their election fell upon the count de Bar and the duke of Burgundy. The count de Bar refused to take the command of the Christian army. Eudes III., duke of Burgundy, still mourned the death of his father, who had died in Palestine after the third crusade, and could not be induced to quit his duchy to undertake the pilgrimage to the East. The refusal of these two princes was a subject of scandal for the soldiers of the cross; and contemporary history informs us that they afterwards repented of the indifference they had evinced for the cause of Christ. [64] The duke of Burgundy, who died within a few years, was desirous of taking the cross on his bed of death, and, to expiate his fault, sent several of his warriors into Palestine.

The knights and barons then offered the command to Boniface, marquis of Montferrat. [65] Boniface belonged to a family of Christian heroes; his brother Conrad had rendered himself famous by the defence of Tyre, and he himself had already fought many times against the infidels: he did not hesitate in complying with the wishes of the Crusaders. He came to Soissons, where he received the cross from the hands of the curé of Neuilly, and was proclaimed leader of the crusade in the church of Notre Dame, in the presence of the clergy and the people.

Two years had passed away since the sovereign pontiff had ordered the bishops to preach the crusade in their dioceses. The situation of the Christians of the East became every day more deplorable; the kings of Jerusalem and Armenia, the patriarchs of Antioch and the holy city, and the grand masters of the military orders, addressed day after day their complaints and lamentations to the Holy See. Touched by their prayers, Innocent again exhorted the faithful, and conjured the Crusaders to hasten their departure; warmly censuring the indifference of those who, after having taken the cross, appeared to be forgetful of their vow. The Christian father, above all, reproached the ecclesiastics with their tardiness in paying the fortieth part of their revenues, destined to the expenses of the holy war: "and you and we," said he, "and all persons supported by the goods of the Church, ought we not all to fear that the inhabitants of Nineveh should appear against us at the day of judgment, and pronounce our condemnation? for they were made penitent by the preaching of Jonas; and you, not only you have not rent your hearts, you have not even opened your hands to succour Christ in his poverty, and repulse the opprobrium with which the infidels load him." The epoch of a holy war being for Christians a season of penitence, the sovereign pontiff proscribed, in his letters, sumptuousness in living, splendour in dress, and public amusements; and although the new crusade had been first preached at the tournament of Ecry, tournaments were in the number of diversions and spectacles forbidden to all Christians by the holy father during the space of five years.

To reanimate the courage and confidence of those who had taken the cross, Innocent told them of the new divisions that had sprung up among the Mussulman princes, and of the scourges with which God had recently afflicted Egypt. "God," cried the pontiff, "has struck the country of Babylon with the rod of his power; the Nile, [66] that river of Paradise, which fertilizes the land of the Egyptians, has not had its accustomed course. This chastisement has given them up to death, and prepared the triumph of their enemies." The letters of the pope had the desired effect. The marquis of Montferrat went into France, towards the autumn of the year 1201, and the whole winter was devoted to preparations for the holy war. These preparations were unaccompanied by disorder, and the princes and barons refused to receive under their banners any but disciplined soldiers and men accustomed to the use of the lance and the sword. Some voices were raised against the Jews, whom they desired to force to contribute to the expenses of the holy war; [67] but the pope took them under his protection, and threatened all who made attempts upon their lives or liberty with excommunication.

Before they left their homes, the Crusaders had to deplore the loss of the holy orator who had awakened their zeal and animated their courage. Foulques fell sick, and died in his parish of Neuilly. Some time before, loud murmurs had been heard respecting his conduct, and his words had ceased to exercise their accustomed power over the minds of his auditors. Foulques had received considerable sums of money destined for the expenses of the holy war, and as he was accused of appropriating these to his own use, the more money he amassed, says James of Vitri, [68] the more consideration and credit he lost. The suspicions attached to his conduct were not, however, generally credited. The marshal of Champagne informs us, in his history, that the knights and barons were deeply affected by the death of the curé of Neuilly. Foulques was buried in the church of his parish with great pomp; his tomb, a monument of the piety of his contemporaries, attracted, even in the last century the respect and veneration of the faithful. [69]

With the earliest days of spring the Crusaders prepared to quit their homes, "and knew," says Villehardouin, "that many tears were shed at their parting, and at taking leave of their relations and friends." The count of Flanders, the counts of Blois and St. Paul, followed by a great number of Flemish warriors and their vassals; the marshal of Champagne, accompanied by several Champenois knights, advanced across Burgundy, and passed the Alps to repair to Venice. The Marquis Boniface soon joined them, bringing with him the Crusaders of Lombardy, Piedmont, Savoy, and the countries situated between the Alps and the Rhone. Venice also received within its walls the warriors from the banks of the Rhine, some under the command of the bishop of Halberstadt, and others under that of Martin-Litz, who had persuaded them to take arms, and still continued to animate them by the example of his virtues and piety.

When the Crusaders reached Venice, [70] the fleet that was to transport them into Asia, was ready to set sail: they were at first received with every demonstration of joy; but amidst the festivities that followed their arrival, [71] the Venetians called upon the barons to redeem their word, and pay the sum agreed upon for transporting the Christian army; and then it was that, with deep grief, the barons became aware of the absence of a great number of their companions in arms. Jean de Nesle, châtelain of Bruges, and Thierri, son of Philip, count of Flanders, had promised Baldwin to bring to him, at Venice, Marguerite, his wife, and a chosen band of Flemish warriors: they did not keep their appointment, for having embarked upon the ocean, they had directed their course to Palestine. Renaud de Dampierre, to whom Thibault, count of Champagne, had left all his treasures to be employed in the voyage to the Holy Land, had embarked with a great number of Champenois knights at the port of Bari. The bishop of Autun, Gilles, count of Ferez, and several other leaders, after having sworn upon the Gospel to join the other Crusaders, had set out from Marseilles, and others from Genoa. Thus half the Crusaders did not come to Venice, which had been agreed upon as the general rendezvous of the Christian army: "by which," says Villehardouin, "they received great shame, and many misadventures afterwards befell them in consequence of it."

This breach of faith might prove very injurious to the enterprise; but what most grieved the princes and barons assembled at Venice, was the impossibility of fulfilling their engagements with the republic without the concurrence of their unfaithful companions. They sent messengers into all parts to warn the Crusaders that had set out, and to implore them to join the main army; but whether most of the pilgrims were dissatisfied with the agreement entered into with the Venetians, or whether it appeared to them more convenient and safe to embark at ports in their own vicinity, a very small number of them could be prevailed upon to repair to Venice. Those who were already in that city, were neither sufficiently numerous nor sufficiently rich to pay the promised amount, or fulfil the engagements made in their names. Although the Venetians were more interested in the crusade than the French knights, as they possessed a part of the cities of Tyre and Ptolemaïs, which they were going to defend, they were unwilling to make any sacrifice, and the barons, on their side, were too proud to ask any favour, or to solicit the Venetians to change or moderate the conditions of the treaty. Each of the Crusaders was required to pay the price of his passage. The rich paid for the poor; soldiers as well as knights being eager to give all the money they possessed, persuaded, they said, that God was powerful enough to return it to them a hundred-fold, when it should please him. The count of Flanders, the counts of Blois and St. Paul, the marquis of Montferrat, and several other leaders despoiled themselves of their plate, their jewels, and everything they had that was most valuable, [72] and only retained their horses and arms. Notwithstanding this noble sacrifice, the Crusaders still were indebted to the republic a sum of fifty thousand silver marks. The doge then assembled the people, and represented to them that it was not honourable to employ too much rigour, and proposed to demand of the Crusaders the assistance of their army for the republic, until they could discharge their debt.

The city of Zara had been for a length of time under the dominion of the Venetians; but thinking the government of a king less insupportable than that of a republic, it had given itself up to the king of Hungary, and, under the protection of a new master, braved the authority and menaces of Venice. After having obtained the approbation of the people, Dandolo proposed to the Crusaders to assist the republic in subduing a revolted city, and promised to put off the entire execution of the treaty until God, by their common conquests, should have given them the means of fulfilling their promises. This proposition was received with much joy by the greater part of the Crusaders, who could not support the idea of being unable to keep their word; the barons and knights deemed it prudent to conciliate the Venetians, who were so serviceable to them in carrying out their enterprise, and thought they did but little to pay their debts by an affair in which they should expend nothing but their blood.

Some murmurs, however, arose in the Christian army; many of the Crusaders recollected the oath they had taken to fight the infidels, and could not make up their minds to turn their arms against a Christian people. The pope had sent the Cardinal Peter of Capua to Venice, to deter the pilgrims from an enterprise which he termed sacrilegious. "The king of Hungary had taken the cross, and by doing so had placed himself under the especial protection of the Church; and to attack a city belonging to him was to declare themselves enemies of the Church itself." Henry Dandolo braved menaces and reproaches that he deemed to be unjust. "The privileges of the Crusaders," said he, "could not screen the guilty from the severity of laws divine and human. Crusades were not undertaken to promote the ambition of kings or protect rebellious nations. [73] The pope had not the power to enchain the authority of sovereigns, or turn the Crusaders aside from a legitimate enterprise; from a war made against revolted subjects, against pirates whose brigandage perilled the freedom of the seas, and jeopardized the safety of pilgrims on their way to the Holy Land."

To complete his conquest over all scruples, and dissipate all fears, the doge resolved to associate himself with the perils and labours of the crusade, and to engage his fellow-citizens to declare themselves the companions in arms of the Crusaders. The people being solemnly convoked, Dandolo ascended the pulpit of St. Mark, and demanded of the assembled Venetians permission to take the cross. "Seigneurs," said he to them, "you have made an engagement to concur in the most glorious of enterprises; the warriors with whom you have contracted a holy alliance, surpass all other men in piety and valour. For myself, you see that I am laden with years, and have need of repose; but the glory that is promised to us restores me courage and strength to brave all the perils, to support all the labours of war. I feel by the ardour that leads me on, by the zeal which animates me, that nobody will merit your confidence, nobody will conduct you so well as the man you have chosen as head of your republic. If you will permit me to fight for Jesus Christ, and allow my son to perform the duties you have confided to me, I will go and live or die with you and the pilgrims."

At this discourse, his whole auditory was much affected, and the people loudly applauded the resolution of the doge. Dandolo descended from the tribunal, and was led in triumph to the foot of the altar, where the cross was attached to his ducal cap. A great number of Venetians followed his example, and swore to die for the deliverance of the holy places. By this skilful policy, the doge completely won the Crusaders, and placed himself, in a manner, at the head of the crusade. He soon found himself sufficiently powerful to deny the authority of the cardinal of Capua, who spoke in the name of the pope, and pretended to have a right to direct the holy war, in his character of legate of the Holy See. Dandolo told the envoy of Innocent, that the Christian army stood in no need of leaders to conduct it, and that the legates of the sovereign pontiff ought to content themselves with edifying the Crusaders by their examples and discourses.

This bold, free language very much astonished the French barons, accustomed to respect the will of the Holy See; but the doge, by taking the cross, had inspired them with a confidence nothing could shake. The cross of the pilgrims was, for the Venetians and French, a pledge of alliance, a sacred tie, which united all their interests, and made of them, in a manner, but one same nation. From that time no one listened to those who spoke in the name of the Holy See, [74] or persisted in raising scruples in the minds of the Crusaders. The barons and knights showed the same zeal and ardour for the expedition against Zara as the Venetians themselves. The army of the Crusaders was ready to embark, when there happened, says Villehardouin, "a great wonder, an unhoped-for circumstance, the strangest that ever was heard of." [75]

Isaac, emperor of Constantinople, had been dethroned by his brother Alexius. Abandoned by all his friends, deprived of sight, and loaded with irons, this unhappy prince languished in a dungeon. The son of Isaac, named also Alexius, who shared the captivity of his father, having deceived the vigilance of his guards and broken his chains, had fled into the West, in the hope that the princes and kings would one day undertake his defence, and declare war against the usurper of the imperial throne. Philip of Swabia, who had married Irene, the daughter of Isaac, [76] received the young prince kindly; but he was not then in a position to undertake anything in his favour, being fully engaged in defending himself against the arms of Otho and the menaces of the Holy See. Young Alexius next in vain threw himself at the feet of the pope, to implore his assistance. Whether the pontiff saw in the son of Isaac only the brother-in-law of Philip of Swabia, then considered an enemy to the court of Rome, or whether all his attention was directed towards the East, he gave no ear to the complaints of Alexius, and seemed to dread countenancing a war against Greece. The fugitive prince had in vain solicited most of the Christian monarchs, when he was advised to address himself to the Crusaders, the noblest warriors of the West. The arrival of his ambassadors created a lively sensation at Venice; the knights and barons were impressed with generous pity by the account of his misfortunes; they had never defended a more glorious cause. To avenge injured innocence, to remedy a great calamity, stirred the spirit of Dandolo; and the proud republicans, whose head he was, feelingly deplored the fate of a fugitive emperor. They had not forgotten that the usurper preferred to an alliance with them one with the Genoese and Pisans; it appeared to them that the cause of Alexius was their own, and that their vessels ought to bear him back to the ports of Greece and Byzantium.

Nevertheless, as everything was prepared for the conquest of Zara, the decision of this business was deferred to a more favourable opportunity; and the fleet, with the Crusaders on board, set sail amidst the sounds of martial music and the acclamation of the whole population of Venice. Never had a fleet so numerous or so magnificently equipped been seen in the Adriatic Gulf. The sea was covered with four hundred and eighty ships; the number of the combatants, horse and foot, amounted to forty thousand men. After having subdued Trieste and some other maritime cities of Istria that had shaken off the yoke of Venice, the Crusaders arrived before Zara on the 10th day of November, 1202, the eve of St. Martin. Zara, [77] situated on the eastern side of the Adriatic Gulf, sixty leagues from Venice, and five leagues north of Jadera, an ancient Roman colony, was a rich and populous city, fortified by high walls, and surrounded by a sea studded with rocks. The king of Hungary had sent troops to defend it, and the inhabitants had sworn to bury themselves beneath the ruins of the place rather than surrender to the Venetians. At the sight of the ramparts of the city, the Crusaders perceived all the difficulty of the enterprise, and the party opposed to this war again ventured to murmur. The leaders, however, gave the signal for the assault. As soon as the chains of the port were broken, and the machines began to make the walls shake, the inhabitants forgot the resolution they had formed of dying in defence of their ramparts, and, filled with dread, sent deputies to the doge, who promised to pardon them on account of their repentance. But the deputies charged with the petition for peace, met with several Crusaders among the besiegers, who said to them, "Why did you surrender? you have nothing to fear from the French?" These imprudent words rekindled the war; the deputies, on their return, announced to the inhabitants that all the Crusaders were not their enemies, and that Zara would preserve its liberty if the people and soldiers were willing to defend it. The party of the malcontents, whose object was to divide the army, seized this opportunity for reviving their complaints; the most ardent amongst them, insinuating themselves into the tents of the soldiers, and endeavouring to disgust them with a war which they termed impious.

Guy, abbot of Vaux de Cernai, of the order of Citeaux, made himself conspicuous by his endeavours to secure the failure of the enterprise against Zara; everything that could divert the march of the Crusaders from the route to the holy places, [78] was, in his eyes, an attack upon religion. The most brilliant exploits, if not performed in the cause of Christ, could command neither his esteem nor his approbation. The abbot of Cernai was deficient in neither subtlety nor eloquence, and knew how to employ both prayers and menaces effectively; he had that influence over the pilgrims that an inflexible mind and an ardent, obstinate character always obtains over the multitude. In a council, he arose, and forbade the Crusaders to draw their swords against Christians, and was about to read a letter from the pope, when he was interrupted by threats and cries.

Amidst the tumult which followed in the council and the army, the abbot of Cernai would have been in danger of his life, if the count de Montfort, who partook his sentiments, had not drawn his sword in his defence. The barons and knights could not, however, forget the promise they had made to fight for the republic of Venice; nor could they think of laying down their arms in presence of an enemy that had promised to surrender, and who now defied their attacks. The greater the efforts of the count de Montfort and the abbot of Cernai to interrupt the war, the more they conceived their honour and glory to be engaged to continue the siege they had begun. Whilst the malcontents were giving vent to their scruples and complaints, the bravest of the army proceeded to the assault. The besieged, whose hopes were built upon the divisions among their enemies, placed crosses upon the walls, persuaded that this revered sign would protect them more effectually than their machines of war; but they were not long in finding that there was no safety for them except in submission. On the 5th day of the siege, without having offered their enemies any serious resistance, they opened their gates, and only obtained from the conqueror liberty and life. The city was given up to pillage, and the booty divided between the Venetians and the French.

One of the results of this conquest was a fresh quarrel in the victorious army, in which more blood flowed than had been shed during the siege. The season being too far advanced to allow the fleet to put to sea, the doge proposed to the Crusaders to winter at Zara. The two nations occupied different quarters of the city; but as the Venetians had chosen the handsomest and most commodious houses, the French loudly proclaimed their dissatisfaction. After a few complaints and many threats, they had recourse to arms, and every street became the theatre of a conflict; the inhabitants of Zara beheld with delight the sanguinary disputes of their conquerors. The partisans of the abbot of Cernai applauded in secret the deplorable consequences of a war they had condemned; whilst the doge of Venice and the barons employed every effort to separate the combatants. Their prayers and threats at first had no effect in appeasing this horrible tumult, which was prolonged to the middle of the night. On the morrow, all the passions that divided the army were near breaking out with increased fury. Whilst interring their dead, the French and Venetians renewed their disputes and menaces. The leaders were, for more than a week, in despair of being able to calm the irritated spirits of their followers, and reunite the soldiers of the two nations. Scarcely was order re-established when a letter was received from the pope, who disapproved of the capture of Zara, ordered the Crusaders to renounce the booty they had made in a Christian city, and to engage themselves, by a solemn vow, to repair the injuries they had inflicted. Innocent reproached the Venetians bitterly with having seduced the soldiers of Christ into this impious and sacrilegious war. This letter from the pope was received with respect by the French, with disdain by the Crusaders of Venice. The latter openly refused to bow to the decisions of the Holy See; and to secure the fruits of their victory, began to demolish the ramparts of Zara. The French barons could not endure the idea of having incurred the anger of the pope, and sent deputies to Rome to endeavour to mitigate the displeasure of his holiness, and solicit their pardon, alleging that they had only obeyed the law of necessity. The greater part of them, though fully determined to retain all they had obtained, promised the pope to restore their spoils: they undertook, by a solemn act, addressed to all Christians, to repair the wrongs they had done, and to merit by their conduct pardon for past errors. [79] Their submission, far more than their promises, disarmed the anger of the pope, who replied to them with mildness, and commanded the leaders to salute the knights and pilgrims, giving them absolution and his benediction, as to his children. He exhorted them, in his letter, to set out for Syria, *without turning to the right or the left*; and permitting them to cross the sea with the Venetians, whom he had just excommunicated, [80] *but only from necessity, and with bitterness of heart*. If the Venetians persisted in their disobedience, the sovereign pontiff advised the barons, when they arrived in Palestine, to separate themselves from a people reproved of God, for fear of bringing a malediction upon the Christian army, as formerly Achan had brought down the divine wrath upon the Israelites. Innocent promised the Crusaders to protect them in their expedition, and to watch over their wants during the perils of the holy war. "In order that you may not want provisions," said he to them, "we will write to the emperor of Constantinople to furnish you with them, as he has promised; if that be refused to you which is refused to none, it will not be unjust, if, after the example of many holy persons, you take provisions wherever you may find them; for it will be known that you are devoted to the cause of Christ, to whom all the world belongs." [81] These counsels and these promises, which so completely reveal to us the spirit of the thirteenth century and the policy of the Holy See, were received by the knights and barons as evidence of the paternal goodness of the sovereign pontiff: but the face of things was about again to change; and fortune, which sported with the decisions of the pope as well as those of the pilgrims, was not long in giving an entirely new direction to the events of the crusade.

Ambassadors from Philip of Swabia, brother-in-law of young Alexius, arrived at Zara, and addressed the council of the lords and barons, assembled in the palace of the doge of Venice. "Seigneurs," said they, "the puissant king of the Romans sends us to recommend to you the young prince Alexius, and to place him in your hands, under the safeguard of God. We do not come for the purpose of turning you aside from your holy enterprise, but to offer you an easy and a certain means of accomplishing your noble designs. We know that you have only taken up arms for the love of Christ and of justice; we come, therefore, to propose to you to assist those who are oppressed by unjust tyranny, and to secure at once the triumph of the laws of religion and humanity: we propose to you to turn your victorious arms towards the capital of Greece, which groans under the rod of an usurper, and to assure yourselves for ever of the conquest of Jerusalem by that of Constantinople. You know, as well as we do, how many evils, our fathers, the companions of Godfrey, Conrad, and Louis the Young, suffered from having left behind them a powerful empire, the conquest and submission of which would have become a source of victories to their arms. What have you not now to dread from this Alexius, more cruel and more perfidious than his predecessors, who has gained a throne by parricide, who has, at once, betrayed the laws of religion and nature, and whose only means of escaping from the punishment due to his crime is by allying himself with the Saracens? We will not tell you how easy a matter it would be to wrest the empire from the hands of a tyrant hated by his subjects, for your valour loves obstacles and delights in dangers; nor will we spread before your eyes the riches of Byzantium and Greece, for your generous souls aim at nothing in this conquest, but the glory of your arms and the cause of Jesus Christ."

"If you overturn the power of the usurper in order that the legitimate sovereign may reign, the son of Isaac promises, under the faith of oaths the most inviolable, to maintain, during a year, both your fleet and your army, and to pay you two hundred thousand silver marks towards the expenses of the war. He will accompany you in person in the conquest of Syria or Egypt; and if you think proper, will furnish ten thousand men, as his portion of the armament; and, moreover, will maintain, during the whole of his life, five hundred knights in the Holy Land. But that which must weigh above all other considerations, with warriors and Christian heroes, is that Alexius is willing to swear, on the holy Gospel, to put an end to the heresy which now defiles the empire of the East, and to subject the Greek Church to the Church of Rome. So many advantages being attached to the enterprise proposed to you, we feel confident you will listen to our prayers. We see in Holy Writ that God sometimes employed men the most simple and the most obscure to make known his will to his chosen people; on this occasion, it is a young prince he has appointed the instrument of his designs; it is Alexius that Providence has commissioned to lead you in the way of the Lord, and to point out to you the road you must follow to render certain the triumph of the armies of Jesus Christ."

This discourse made a strong impression upon a great number of the knights and barons, but it did not command the suffrages of the whole assembly. The doge and the lords dismissed the ambassadors, telling them they would deliberate upon the proposals of Alexius. Warm debates then ensued in the council; those that had been averse to the siege of Zara, among whom the abbot of Vaux de Cernai was still conspicuous, opposed the expedition to Constantinople with great vehemence; they were indignant that the interests of God should be placed in the balance against those of Alexius; they added that this Isaac, whose cause they were called upon to defend, was himself an usurper, elevated by a revolution to the throne of the Comnenas; that he had been, during the third crusade, the most cruel enemy of the Christians, the most faithful ally of the Turks; as for the rest, the nations of Greece, accustomed to the change of masters, supported the usurpation of Alexius without murmuring, and the Latins had not quitted their homes to avenge the injuries of a people that really did not call upon them for aid.

The same orators further said, that Philip of Swabia exhorted the Crusaders to assist Alexius, but was content himself with making speeches and sending ambassadors; they warned the Christians not to trust to the promises of a young prince, who engaged to furnish armies, and had not a single soldier; who offered treasures, and possessed nothing; who, besides, had been brought up amongst the Greeks, and would, most likely, some day turn his arms against his benefactors. "If you are so sensible to misfortune," added they, "and impatient to defend the cause of justice and humanity, listen to the groans of our brethren in Palestine, who are menaced by the Saracens, and who have no earthly hope but in your courage." They moreover told the Crusaders, that if they wished for easy victories and brilliant conquests, they had but to turn their eyes towards Egypt, the population of which was at that moment devoured by a horrible famine, and which the seven plagues of Scripture yielded up to the arms of the Christians almost without defence.

The Venetians, who had cause of complaint against the emperor of Constantinople, were not at all affected by these arguments, and appeared much more inclined to make war upon the Greeks than the infidels; they were anxious to destroy the warehouses of their rivals the Pisans, now established in Greece, and to see their ships crossing the straits of the Bosphorus in triumph. Their doge nourished a keen resentment on account of some personal offence; and to inflame the minds of his compatriots, he magnified all the wrongs inflicted by the Greeks on his own country and the Christians of the West.

If ancient chronicles may be believed, Dandolo was impelled by another motive, which he did not avow before the Crusaders. The sultan of

Damascus, made aware of a Christian army being assembled at Venice, and terrified at the crusade that was preparing, had sent a considerable treasure to the republic, to engage it to divert the Crusaders from an expedition into the East. Whether we yield faith to this account, or whether we consider it as a fable invented by hatred and party spirit, such assertions, collected by contemporaries, at least prove that violent suspicions were then entertained against the Venetians by the dissatisfied Crusaders, and particularly by the Christians of Syria, justly irritated at not being assisted by the soldiers of the cross. [82] Nevertheless, we feel bound to add that the majority of the French Crusaders stood in no need of being stimulated by the example or speeches of the doge, to undertake a war against the Greek empire. Even those who opposed the new expedition the most strongly, as well as all the other Crusaders, entertained an inveterate hatred and a sovereign contempt for the Greeks; and the discussions had only the more inflamed the general mind against a nation considered inimical to the Christians.

Several ecclesiastics, having at their head the abbot of Looz, a personage remarkable for his piety and the purity of his manners, did not accord in opinion with the abbot of Vaux de Cernai, and maintained that there was much danger in leading an army into a country devastated by famine; that Greece presented much greater advantages to the Crusaders than Egypt, and that there could be no doubt that the conquest of Constantinople was the most certain means of securing to the Christians the possession of Jerusalem. These ecclesiastics were particularly fascinated by the hope of one day seeing the Greek Church united to that of Rome, and they constantly announced in their discourses the approaching period of concord and peace among all Christian people.

Many knights contemplated with satisfaction the prospect of the union of the two churches, likely to be brought about by their arms; but they yielded further to motives not less powerful over their minds; they had sworn to defend innocence and the rights of the oppressed, and they believed they performed their duty in embracing the cause of Alexius. Some of them, without doubt, who had heard of the vast wealth of Byzantium, might believe that they should not return from such a brilliant undertaking empty handed; but such was the spirit of the lords and knights, that by far the greater number were attracted by the mere prospect of the perils, and still more by the wonders of the enterprise. After a long deliberation, it was decided in the council of the Crusaders that the proposals of Alexius should be accepted, and that the Christian army should embark for Constantinople at the commencement of spring.

Before the siege of Zara, the report of the armament of the Crusaders, and of an expedition against Greece had reached the court of Byzantium.

The usurper of the throne of Isaac immediately sought for means to avert the storm about to fall upon his states, and hastened to send ambassadors to the pope, whom he considered the arbiter of peace and war in the West. These ambassadors were ordered to declare to the sovereign pontiff that the prince who reigned at Constantinople was the only legitimate emperor; that the son of Isaac had no right to the empire; that an expedition against Greece would be an unjust enterprise, dangerous, and adverse to the great designs of the crusade. The pope, in his reply, did not at all seek to calm the fears of the usurper, but told his envoys that young Alexius had numerous partisans among the Crusaders, because he had made a promise to succour the Holy Land in person, and to put an end to the rebellion of the Greek Church. The pope did not approve of the expedition against Constantinople; but, by speaking in the way he did, he thought that the sovereign who then reigned over Greece might be induced to make the same promises as the fugitive prince, and would be more able to fulfil them; he conceived a hope that they might treat advantageously, without having recourse to the sword, and that the debates concerning the empire of the East would be referred to his supreme tribunal. But the elder Alexius, whether he was persuaded that he had sufficiently interested the pope in his cause, or whether he deemed it most prudent not to appear alarmed, or, in short, whether the prospect of a distant danger could not remove his habitual indolence, sent no more ambassadors, and made not the least exertion to prepare against the invasion of the warriors of the West.

In another direction, the king of Jerusalem and the Christians of Palestine never ceased to give vent to their complaints, and to implore the assistance that the head of the Church had promised them. The pope, much affected by their prayers, and always zealous for the crusade he had preached, renewed his efforts to direct the arms of the Crusaders against the Saracens. He sent the cardinals, Peter of Capua, and Siffred, into Palestine, as legates of the Holy See, to revive the courage of the Christians, and announce to them the approaching departure of the army of Crusaders; but when he learnt that the leaders had determined upon attacking the empire of Constantinople, he poured upon them the most bitter reprimands, and reproached them with *looking behind them,* as Lot's wife had done. "Let none among you," said he, "flatter himself that he may be allowed to invade or plunder the lands of the Greeks, under the pretence that the empire is not sufficiently submissive, or that the emperor has usurped the throne of his brother; whatever crime he may have committed, it is not for you to constitute yourself the judge of it: you did not assume the cross to avenge the injuries of princes, but that of God."

Innocent finished his letter without bestowing his benediction upon the Crusaders; and, to frighten them from their new enterprise, threatened them with the maledictions of Heaven. The barons and knights received the remonstrances of the sovereign pontiff with respect; but did not at all waver in the resolution they had formed.

Then the opponents of the expedition to Constantinople renewed their complaints, and employed no sort of moderation in their discourses. The abbot of Vaux de Cernai, the abbot Martin Litz, one of the preachers of the crusade, the count de Montfort, and a great number of knights employed every effort to shake the determination of the army; and when they found they could not succeed, resolved to leave them, some to return to their homes, and others to take the route to Palestine. Those who abandoned their colours, and those who remained in the camp, mutually accused each other with betraying the cause of Christ. [83] Five hundred soldiers having thrown themselves on board a vessel, were shipwrecked and all swallowed up by the waves; many others, in crossing Illyria, were massacred by the savage inhabitants of that country. These perished cursing the ambition and errors which had turned the Christian army aside from the true object of the crusade; whilst those who remained faithful to their standards, deplored the tragical death of their companions, saying among themselves: *"The mercy of the Lord has remained with us; evil be to them who stray from the way of the Lord."*

The knights and barons regretted in secret that they had not been able to obtain the approbation of the pope, but were persuaded that, by means of victories, they should justify their conduct in the eyes of the Holy See; and that the father of the faithful would recognise in their conquests the expression of the will of Heaven.

The Crusaders were upon the point of embarking, when young Alexius himself arrived at Zara. His presence created a fresh enthusiasm for his cause; he was received amidst the sounds of trumpets and clarions, and presented to the army by the marquis of Montferrat, [84] whose elder brothers had been connected by marriage and the dignity of Cæsar, with the imperial family of Constantinople. The barons hailed young Alexius as emperor, with the greater joy, that they hoped his future grandeur would be the work of their hands. Alexius took arms to break the chains of his father, and they admired in him a most touching model of Christian piety: he was about to combat usurpation, to punish injustice, and stifle heresy, and they looked upon him as an envoy of Providence. The misfortunes of princes destined to reign affect us more sensibly than those of other men; in the camp of the Crusaders, the soldiers talked over the story of Alexius among themselves, and they pitied his youth, and deplored his exile and the captivity of Isaac. Alexius, accompanied by the princes and barons, went constantly among the soldiery, and replied by demonstrations of the warmest gratitude to the generous interest the Crusaders evinced in his favour.

Animated by sentiments which misfortune inspires, and which not unfrequently terminate with it, the young prince was lavish of vows and protestations, and promised even more than he had done by his envoys, without thinking that he placed himself under the necessity of failing in his word, and drawing upon himself, one day, the reproaches of his liberators.

The Crusaders, however, renewed every day their vow to place young Alexius on the throne of Constantinople; and Italy and the whole West rung with the fame of their preparations. The emperor of Byzantium appeared to be the only person ignorant of the war declared against his usurped power, and slept upon a throne ready to crumble from under him.

The emperor Alexius, like the greater part of his predecessors, was a prince without virtues or character; when he deposed his brother, he allowed the crime to be committed by his courtiers, and when he was upon the throne he abandoned to them the charge of his authority. He was lavish of the treasures of the state, to secure pardon and oblivion for his usurpation; and, to repair his finances, he sold justice, ruined his subjects, and plundered the merchant ships that traded between Ramisa and Constantinople. The usurper scattered dignities and honours with such profusion, that no one thought himself honoured by them, and there remained in his hands no true reward for merit. Alexius had associated his wife Euphrosyne with himself in the sovereign authority, and she filled the empire with her intrigues, and scandalized the court by the laxity of her morals. Under his reign the empire had been several times menaced by the Bulgarians and the Turks; Alexius occasionally visited the army, but he never faced the enemy. Whilst the Bulgarians were ravaging his frontiers, he employed himself in levelling hills, and tracing gardens on the shores of the Propontis. Abandoned to a shameful effeminacy, he disbanded a part of his army; and fearing to be disturbed in his pleasures by the din of arms, he sold the sacred vases, and plundered the tombs of the Greek emperors, to purchase peace of the emperor of Germany, who had become master of Sicily. The empire had no navy left; the ministers had sold the rigging and equipments of the vessels, and the woods that might have furnished timber for new ships, were reserved for the pleasures of the prince, and guarded as strictly, says Nicetas, as those formerly consecrated to the gods. [85]

Such numbers of conspiracies never were heard of; under n, prince who was rarely visible, the government appeared to be in a state of interregnum; the imperial throne was as an empty seat, which every ambitious man aspired to occupy. Devotedness, probity, bravery, were no longer held in esteem by courtiers or citizens. Nothing was deemed worthy of public approbation or reward but the invention of a new pleasure or the fabrication of a fresh impost. Amidst this general depravity, the provinces knew nothing of the emperor but by the exaction of taxes; [86] and the army, without discipline and without pay, had no leaders capable of commanding it. Everything announced an approaching revolution in the empire; and the peril was the greater from no one having the courage to foresee it. The subjects of Alexius never dreamt of obtruding truth upon the imperial ear; birds, taught to repeat satires, alone interrupted the silence of the people, and published from the roofs of houses, and in the high streets, the scandals of the court and the disgrace of the empire.

The Greeks, at the same time superstitious and corrupt, still preserved some remembrances of ancient Greece and old Rome; but these remembrances, instead of creating a noble, emulative pride, only nourished in their hearts a puerile vanity, and their history, of which they were so vain, only served to render more striking their own degradation and their empire's too evident decay. The voice of patriotism was never heard, and no influence was obeyed but that of the monks placed at the head of affairs of all kinds, who attracted and preserved the confidence of both people and prince by frivolous predictions and senseless visions. The Greeks wasted their time in vain disputes, which enervated their character, increased their ignorance, and stifled their patriotism. At the moment the fleet of the Crusaders was about to set sail, Constantinople was in a state of ferment with discussing the question whether the body of Jesus Christ, in the Eucharist, is corruptible or incorruptible; each opinion had its partisans, whose defeats or triumphs were, by turns, loudly proclaimed—and the threatened empire remained without defenders.

The Venetians and French left Zara, and the isle of Corfu was appointed as the place of meeting for the whole fleet. [87] When they landed on the shores of Macedon, the inhabitants of Duras brought young Alexius the keys of the city, and acknowledged him as their master. The people of Corfu were not tardy in following this example, and received the Crusaders as liberators: the acclamations of the Greek people, in the passage of the Latins, was a happy augury for the success of their expedition.

The island of Corfu, the country of the Phœnicians, so celebrated by the shipwreck of Ulysses and by the gardens of Alcinoüs, afforded the Crusaders pasturage and abundance of provisions. The fertility of the island induced the leaders to remain there several weeks; but so long a repose did not fail to produce evil consequences in an army supported by enthusiasm, to which no time for reflection should have been allowed, and, amidst indulgence and idleness, the complaints and murmurs of the siege of Zara broke out again.

They learnt that Gauthier de Brienne had conquered Apulia and the kingdom of Naples. This conquest, effected in a few months, by sixty knights, inflamed the imagination of the Crusaders, and furnished the malcontents with a fresh opportunity for blaming the expedition to Constantinople, the preparations for which were immense, the perils evident, and the success uncertain. "Whilst we are going," said they, "to exhaust the resources of the West in a useless enterprise, in a distant war, Gauthier de Brienne has made himself master of a rich kingdom, and is preparing to fulfil the promises he has entered into with us to deliver the Holy Land; why should we not demand vessels of him? why should we not set out for Palestine with him?" These speeches prevailed over a great number of the knights, who were ready to separate themselves from the army.

The chief malcontents had already assembled in a secluded valley to deliberate upon the means of executing their project, when the leaders of the army were warned of their plot, and immediately united all their efforts to prevent the fatal consequences of it. The doge of Venice, the count of Flanders, the counts of Blois and St. Paul, the marquis of Montferrat, and several bishops clothed in mourning habits, with crosses borne before them, repaired to the valley in which the malcontents were met. As soon as they, from a distance, perceived their unfaithful companions, who were deliberating on horseback, they alighted, and advanced towards the place of assembly in a suppliant manner. The instigators of the desertion, seeing the leaders and prelates of the army coming thus towards them, suspended their deliberations, and themselves dismounted from their horses. The parties approached each other; the princes, counts, and bishops threw themselves at the feet of the malcontents, and, bursting into tears, swore to remain thus prostrated till the warriors who wished to abandon them, had renewed the oath to follow the army of the Christians, and to remain faithful to the standard of the holy war. "When the others saw," says Villehardouin, an ocular witness, "when they saw their liege lords, their dearest relations and friends thus cast themselves at their feet, and, so to say, cry to them for mercy, they were moved with great pity, and their hearts were so softened, they could not refrain from weeping, and they told them that they would consider of it together (Qi'ils s'en aviseraient par ensemble)." After having retired for a moment to deliberate, they came back to their leaders, and promised to remain with the army until the beginning of autumn, on condition that the barons and lords would swear upon the Gospel to furnish them at that period with vessels to convey them to Syria. The two parties engaged themselves by oath to perform the conditions of the treaty, and returned together to the camp, where nothing now was spoken of but the expedition to Constantinople.

The fleet of the Crusaders quitted the island of Corfu under the most happy auspices; the historians who have described its progress through that archipelago, so full of remembrances of antiquity, have not been able to refrain from employing the language of poetry. The wind was favourable, and the sky pure and serene; a profound calm reigned over the waves; three hundred vessels of all sizes, with their colours floating from their sterns, covered an immense space; the helmets and cuirasses of thirty thousand warriors reflected the rays of the sun; now were heard sounding over the waters the hymns of the priests, invoking the blessings of Heaven; and then the voices of the soldiers, soothing the leisure of the voyage with warlike songs; and the braying of trumpets and neighing of horses, mingled with the dashing of oars, resounded from the coasts of the Peloponnesus, which presented themselves to the eyes of the pilgrims. The Crusaders doubled Cape Matapan, known formerly as Tenara, and passed before the heights of Malea, without dread of the rocks so much feared by ancient navigators. Near Cape Malea they met two vessels returning from Palestine, in which were many Flemish pilgrims. At sight of the Venetian fleet, a soldier on board one of the two ships, slipped down a rope, and bade adieu to his companions, saying: *"I leave you all I have on board, for I am going with people who intend to conquer kingdoms."* [88]

The Crusaders landed at several islands they fell in with on their passage; the inhabitants of Andros and Negropont came out to meet Alexius, and acknowledged him as their emperor. It was the period of harvest, and the land presented, everywhere, a spectacle of the richest abundance. The enjoyment of a beautiful climate, the satisfaction at the submission of the Greeks, so many riches, so many wonders, so many unknown regions, all daily increased the enthusiasm of the Crusaders. At length the fleet arrived at the entrance of the Bosphorus, and cast anchor in the port of St. Stephen, three leagues from the capital of the Greek empire.

Then the city of Constantinople, of which they were about to effect the conquest, broke full upon the view of the Crusaders; [89] bathed on the south by the waves of the Propontis, on the east by the Bosphorus, and on the north by the gulf that serves as its port, it presented a spectacle at once magnificent and formidable. A double enclosure of walls surrounded it in a circumference of more than seven leagues; a vast number of splendid buildings, whose roofs towered above the ramparts, appeared to proclaim the queen of cities. The shores of the Bosphorus to the Euxine and to the Hellespont, resembled an immense faubourg, or one continued line of gardens. The cities of Chalcedon and Scutari, built on the Asiatic shore, and Galata, placed at the extremity of the gulf, appeared in the distance, and crowned the immense and magnificent picture which lay before the warlike hosts of the Crusaders.

Constantinople, situated between Europe and Asia, between the Archipelago and the Black Sea, joins together the two seas and the two continents. In the times of its splendour, it held at its pleasure the gates of commerce open or shut; its port, which received the vessels of all the nations of the world, deserved to be termed by the Greeks, *the golden horn*, or *the horn of abundance*. Like ancient Rome, Constantinople extended over seven ascents, and, like the city of Romulus, it sometimes bore the name of the city of the seven hills; in the times of the crusades, its walls and its towers were compared to those of Babylon; its deep ditches were converted at will into a large and rapid lake, and the city could, at the least signal, be surrounded by waters, and separated from the continent.

The monarch who founded it reigned over all the known nations of the world, and in the execution of his designs he had the advantage of making the arts and sciences of Greece concur with the genius and power of the Romans. Not content with employing the beautiful marbles of the isles of the Archipelago, he caused materials to be transported from the extremities of Europe and Asia; all the cities of the Roman empire, Athens, and Rome itself, were spoiled of their ornaments to embellish the new city of the Cæsars. Several of the successors of Constantine had repaired the edifices that were crumbling into ruins, and had erected fresh monuments in Constantinople, which in its temples, upon its public places, and around the walls, everywhere recalled the memory of twenty glorious reigns. The city was divided into fourteen quarters; it had thirty-two gates; it contained within its bosom circuses of immense extent, five hundred churches, among which St. Sophia claimed attention as one of the wonders of the world; and five palaces, which themselves looked like cities in the midst of the great city. More fortunate than its rival Rome, the city of Constantine had never beheld the barbarians within its walls; it preserved with its language the depository of the masterpieces of antiquity, and the accumulated riches of the East and the West.

It would be difficult to paint the enthusiasm, the fear, the surprise that took possession of the minds of the Crusaders at the aspect of Constantinople. [90] The leaders landed, and passed one night in the abbey of St. Stephen. This night was employed in anxious deliberation upon what they had to do; at one time they resolved to land upon the isles; then they determined to make a descent upon the continent. In the very same instant they drew back in terror and gave themselves up to a wild joy; they could not come to any fixed determination, but changed their plans and their projects a thousand times. At daybreak Dandolo, Boniface, Baldwin, and the count de Blois ordered all the standards of the army to be unfurled; the escutcheons and coats of arms of the counts and knights were ranged along the vessels, [91] to display the military pomp of the West and recall to the warriors the valour of their ancestors. The signal was given to the fleet, which entered into the canal, and, driven on by a favourable wind, passed close to the walls of Constantinople. An immense population, [92] who only the day before were ignorant of the arrival of the Latins, crowded the ramparts and covered the shore. The warriors of the West, clad in complete armour, [93] stood erect upon the decks of their vessels; [94] some stones and arrows were launched from the towers and fell upon the ships: "there was no heart," says Villehardouin, "so bold as not to be moved; for never was so great an affair undertaken." Every warrior turned his eye towards his sword, thinking the time was come in which to make use of it. The Crusaders fancied that in the crowd of spectators they beheld the defenders of Constantinople; but the capital of the empire was only defended by the memory of its past glory, and by the respect of the nations ignorant of its weakness. Of true soldiers the imperial army only mustered two thousand Pisans, who despised the Greeks, and the troop of Varangians, mercenary soldiers from the northern parts of Europe, with whose origin and country the Greeks themselves were scarcely acquainted. [95]

The Crusaders made a descent upon the Asiatic shore of the Bosphorus, pillaged the city of Chalcedon, and established themselves in the palace and gardens in which the emperor Alexius had so long forgotten his own dangers and those of his empire. At the approach of the Venetian fleet, this prince had retreated to Constantinople, where, like the last king of Babylon, he continued to live amidst pleasures and festivities, without reflecting that he had been judged, and that his hour was nearly come. His courtiers, in the intoxication of the banquet, celebrated his power and proclaimed him invincible; amidst the pomp that surrounded him, and which appeared to him a rampart against the attacks of his enemies, he, in his speeches, insulted the simplicity of the Latins, and believed he had conquered them because he had called them barbarians.

When he saw the Crusaders masters of his palace and gardens, he began to entertain some degree of fear, and sent an Italian named Rossi, with orders to salute the lords and barons. "The emperor my master," said the envoy of Alexius, "knows that you are the most puissant and most noble princes among those who do not wear crowns; but he is astonished that you should have come to bring war into a Christian empire. Rumour proclaims that your design is to deliver the Holy Land from the yoke of the Saracens;

the emperor applauds your zeal, and solicits the honour of being associated with your enterprise; he is ready to assist you with all his power. But if you do not quit his states, he shall feel obliged to direct against you the forces he would willingly have employed in your cause and in that of Christ. Accept, then, the generous offers that he makes to you by me; but do not believe that this pacific language is dictated by fear. The emperor Alexius reigns over Greece by the love of his people as well as by the will of God; with one single word he could gather around him innumerable armies, disperse your fleet and your battalions, and close against you for ever the routes to the East."

The envoy of the emperor thus terminated his speech without naming either Isaac or young Alexius. Conon de Béthune, [96] who answered for the leaders of the army, was astonished that the brother of Isaac should dare to speak as master of the empire, and that he had not thought fit to attempt to justify a parricide which had roused the indignation of all Christian nations. "Go and tell your master," said the orator of the Crusaders, addressing the emperor's envoy, "go and tell him, that the earth we tread upon does not belong to him, but that it is the heritage of the prince you see seated amongst us. If he be desirous of knowing the motive that brings us hither, let him ask his own conscience, and remember the crimes he has committed. A usurper is the enemy of all princes; a tyrant is the enemy of the whole human race. He who sent you has but one means of escaping the justice of Heaven and of men, that is, to restore to his brother and his nephew the throne he has wrested from them, and implore the pity of those same princes towards whom he has been so merciless. In that case we promise to add our prayers to his supplications, and to procure for him, with his pardon, the means of passing his life in a repose far preferable to the splendour of an usurped sovereignty; but if he is not willing to act justly, if he is inaccessible to repentance, tell him we disdain his threats as we do his promises, and that we have no time to waste in listening to ambassadors." This vehement reply was an actual declaration of war, and left the emperor no hope of either seducing or intimidating the Crusaders. The lords and barons were, however, astonished that the Greeks took no notice of young Alexius, and that the cause they came to promote found no partisans in the city of Constantinople. They resolved to ascertain the inclinations of the people. A galley, on board of which was the son of Isaac, was brought close to the walls of the capital; [97] Boniface and Dandolo held up the young prince, whilst a herald-at-arms repeated in a loud voice these words:— "Behold the heir of the throne; acknowledge your sovereign; have pity on him and on yourselves." The Greeks assembled in the ramparts remained motionless; some answered by insulting language, others maintained a sullen silence.

Whilst the Crusaders were thus making a last attempt to preserve peace, the most horrible tumult reigned in the interior of the city. The presence of the Latins irritated the multitude; they assembled in the public places; they excited each other to vengeance; the people ran to the quarter of the Franks, demolished several houses, and gave the rest up to pillage. A great number of Latins, threatened with loss of life, immediately sought an asylum in the camp of the Crusaders. Their presence, their accounts, their complaints, fired the easily kindled indignation of the knights and barons. From that moment the leaders saw no hopes but in the chance of war and in the protection of the Heaven that had confided to their hands the cause of innocence and misfortune.

Eighty knights succeeded in putting to flight a numerous body of troops that the emperor had sent across the Bosphorus. "The Greek commanders," says Nicetas, "were more timid than deer, and did not dare to resist men whom they called *exterminating angels, statues of bronze,* which spread around terror and death." The Crusaders, however, had great cause to fear that the Greeks, recovered from their first panic, might become aware of the small number of their enemies, and succeed in overwhelming them by their multitudes; they resolved, therefore, to take advantage of the fear they had inspired, and gave their whole attention to forward the preparations for attacking enemies that had provided nothing for their defence.

The Christian army assembled at Chrisopolis (Scutari [98]), and beheld full in front of them the capital of the Greek empire. After having put to flight some troops sent out to follow their march or skirmish with them, the leaders mounted on horseback and deliberated in full assembly, on the plan of action best to be pursued. They decided that the army should cross the canal of the Bosphorus, and encamp under the walls of Constantinople. "Then," says Villehardouin, "the bishops and the clergy addressed their remonstrances to all those of the camp, exhorting them to confess themselves, and make their testaments, for they did not know the hour at which it might please God to call them, and do his will by them; which they did very willingly, and with great zeal and devotion." When all was ready, and the Crusaders had invoked the protection of Heaven by their prayers, the signal for departure was given; the war-horses, saddled and covered with their long caparisons, were embarked in the flat-bottomed boats; the knights stood erect near their horses, helm on head and lance in hand; the remainder of the troops went on board the large ships, each of which was towed by a galley. The army of the Greeks, commanded by the emperor in person, was drawn up in battle array on the opposite shore, and appeared disposed to dispute the passage of the Crusaders. All at once the vessels heaved their anchors to the sounds of trumpets and clarions. Every soldier, with his eyes fixed on Constantinople, swore to conquer or die. On approaching the shore, the barons and knights cast themselves into the sea, fully armed, and contended for the honour of first gaining the strand occupied by the Greeks. The archers and foot-soldiers followed the example of the knights; in less than an hour the whole army was on the other side of the Bosphorus, and looked about in vain for an enemy over a plain they had so recently seen covered with arms and warriors. The army of Alexius took to flight; and, if we may believe a letter of the count de St. Pol, the swiftest arrows of the Latins could scarcely overtake a few of the fugitives. The Crusaders, following up their advantage, found the camp of the Greeks abandoned, and plundered the tents of the emperor, without meeting with one of his soldiers.

Night surprised them in the midst of their bloodless victory; and on the morrow they resolved to attack the fortress of Galata, which, erected upon a hill, commanded the port of Constantinople. From break of day the Greeks rushed in crowds to anticipate and surprise the Latins. At the first shock, Jacques d'Avesnes was wounded grievously, and placed *hors de combat*; the sight of his wound highly incensed the Flemish warriors, who precipitated themselves with fury into the *mêlée*. The Greeks were not able to withstand the impetuous attack of their enemies, and took to flight in great disorder; some, hoping to find an asylum in the ships in the port, perished in the waves, whilst others fled bewildered to the citadel, into which the conquerors entered with the conquered. Whilst the French thus got possession of Galata, the Venetian fleet, which was drawn up in line of battle before Scutari, turned its prows towards the port of Constantinople. The entrance of the gulf was defended by an enormous chain of iron, and by twenty galleys, which constituted the whole navy of the empire. The resistance of the Greeks was obstinate; but a vessel of extraordinary size, assisted by a favourable wind, struck the extended chain violently in its passage, and divided it with enormous shears of steel, which opened and shut by the operation of a machine. [99] The galleys of the Greeks were soon taken, or dispersed in fragments on the face of the waters, and the whole of the Venetian fleet rode in triumph into the port: it was then the Greeks were able to perceive what they had to dread from the invincible courage of these barbarians, who had till that period been the object of their contempt.

The French, masters of Galata, divided their army into six great battles or divisions. Baldwin, who had under his orders a great number of archers and crossbow-men, led the van. The rear was composed of Lombards, Germans, and Franks, from countries near the Alps, commanded by the marquis of Montferrat. The other four divisions, in which were ranged the crusaders from Champagne, Burgundy, and the banks of the Seine and the

Loire, had at their head Henry, brother of Baldwin, the counts of St. Pol and Blois, and Matthew de Montmorenci.

This army advanced [100] towards the west of the city, without meeting with a single foe in its passage, and encamped between the gate of Blachernæ and the tower of Bohemond.

The Greeks, in a single battle, had lost the empire of the sea, and had no longer the power to defend the approach to their capital. The Venetian fleet cast anchor near the mouth of the river Barbysses. [101] The Venetians, masters of the port, were secure from all surprise, and had no cause to fear being overpowered by numbers. If the whole army had been united on board the fleet, there is very little doubt it would have more easily triumphed over the efforts and multitudes of the Greeks, and it was the advice of the doge that such should be the plan; but the knights and barons could not be prevailed upon to fight on an element with which they were unacquainted; and they answered (we quote Villehardouin), that they could not act so well upon the sea as they could upon the land, where they could have their horses and their arms. Their army, which did not muster twenty thousand men under its banners, attacked without fear a city, which, according to the account of some historians, contained a million of inhabitants, and more than two hundred thousand men able to bear arms.

Before they began the assault, the Crusaders deemed it proper once more to invite the Greeks to make peace, by receiving the son of Isaac as emperor; and several barons drew near to the walls, crying with a loud voice that there was still time to listen to justice. Young Alexius was surrounded by the Latin leaders, and his presence among them explained sufficiently clearly the meaning of the words addressed to the inhabitants of Constantinople. Their only reply was hurling stones and javelins at the Crusaders; the people of Byzantium had been persuaded that young Alexius came for the purpose of changing the manners, religion, and laws of Greece.

History ought to add here, that since the intrigues of ambition and the caprices of fortune had enjoyed the privilege of bestowing masters upon them, the Greeks beheld with indifference the successions of power or the changes of their princes; the Greek nations had not forgotten that it was a revolution that lifted the family of Isaac to the imperial throne. With the impressions this family had left in their minds, the misfortunes and prayers of Alexius did not move them sufficiently to declare in his favour, or take arms to support his cause; since they were obliged to choose between two new princes, he who was reigning amongst them appeared preferable to him who implored their aid.

From that time the attention and efforts of the Crusaders were solely directed to the prosecution of their perilous enterprise. Their camp, placed between the gate of Blachernæ, and the castle of Bohemond, occupied but a very small space before walls many leagues in extent. Every day the Greeks made sorties; the country round was covered with the soldiers of the enemy; the army of the besiegers appeared to be themselves besieged by troops that were unceasingly renewed. Day and night the Crusaders were under arms, and had neither time to take their food nor refresh themselves by sleep. They had only provisions for three weeks, and could look for safety to nothing but a speedy victory; nevertheless, they continued to fill up the ditches, and make their approaches to the ramparts. Balistas, catapultas, rams, everything that could carry destruction and death into the city, were employed to second the bravery and indefatigable ardour of the besiegers; without cessation, enormous masses fell with fearful crash from the tops of the walls; and such was the surprising power of the machines of war then in use, that the houses and palaces of Constantinople were often shaken to their foundations by stones launched from the camp of the Latins. [102]

After ten days of labour and fighting, the Crusaders determined to storm the city. On the morning of the 17th of July, 1203, the trumpets and clarions sounded the signal; the count of Flanders, who commanded the attack, passed through the ranks, and directed the attention of his knights to the ramparts of Constantinople, *as the road which would conduct them to an eternal glory.* The army was immediately in motion, and every machine was directed against the walls. One tower, which had fallen in with a great crash, appeared to offer a passage to the troops of Baldwin. Ladders were planted, and the most intrepid contended for the honour of entering first into the city; but, this time, numbers prevailed over valour. A host of Greeks, encouraged by the presence of the Varangians and Pisans, hastened to the rampart, and overturned the ladders. Fifteen Frank warriors, braving stones, beams, and torrents of Greek fire, alone were able to maintain themselves on the walls, and yielded only after fighting with desperate valour. Two of these intrepid warriors were led to the emperor, who watched the fight from the windows of the palace of Blachernæ. Alexius had ceased to despise the Latins; and, in his fright, he had such an idea of their courage, that the sight of the two prisoners appeared to him a victory.

At the same time the Venetians attacked the city by sea. Dandolo ranged his fleet in two lines; the galleys were in the first rank, manned by archers, and laden with machines of war; behind the galleys advanced the large vessels, upon which were constructed towers exceeding the loftiest of the walls of Constantinople in height. At daybreak the contest began between the city and the fleet; the Greeks, armed with the Greek fire, the

Venetians, covered with their armour, the ramparts and the vessels charged with a thousand destructive instruments, cast from one to the other, by turns, terror, fire, and death. The incessant dashing of the oars, the shocks of the vessels against each other, the cries of the sailors and combatants, the hissing of the stones, javelins, and arrows, the Greek fire darting along the sea, seizing on the ships and boiling upon the waves, presented altogether a spectacle a thousand times more fearful than that of a tempest. Amidst this horrible tumult, Henry Dandolo was heard: standing erect in his galley, he excited his troops, and, with a terrible voice, threatened to hang every man that did not land. The orders of the intrepid doge were soon executed. The men of his galley took him in their arms and bore him swiftly to the shore, the standard of St. Mark floating over him. At sight of this, the efforts of the crews of the other galleys were redoubled, all struck the shore, and the soldiers rushed forward to follow their venerable leader. The vessels, which had hitherto remained motionless, now advanced and placed themselves between the galleys, so that the whole fleet was extended in a single line before the walls of Constantinople, and presented to the terrified Greeks a formidable rampart raised upon the waters. The floating towers lowered their drawbridges upon the ramparts of the city, and whilst, at the foot of the walls, ten thousand arms planted ladders and battered with rams, on the summit a fearful conflict was maintained with sword and lance.

All at once the standard of St. Mark appeared upon one of the towers, planted by an invisible hand; upon seeing this the Venetians uttered a loud shout of joy, persuaded that their patron saint fought at their head; their courage proportionately increased with the terror and despair of their enemies; the most intrepid cast themselves on to the walls, and soon twenty-five towers were in their possession. They pursued the Greeks into the city; but fearing to fall into some ambush or be overwhelmed by the people, crowds of whom filled the streets and covered the public places, they set fire to the houses as they came to them on their passage. The conflagration extended rapidly, [103] and drove before it the terrified and trembling multitude. Whilst the flames, preceding the conquerors, spread devastation on their path, and the greatest disorder prevailed in Constantinople, Alexius, pressed by the cries of the people, mounted on horseback, and ordered a sortie of the troops, by three different gates, to attack the French, who were less fortunate in this day's fight than the Venetians.

The army conducted by the emperor was composed of sixty battalions; clothed in all the marks of imperial dignity, Alexius rode along the ranks, animated his soldiers, and promised them victory. At his approach, the Crusaders abandoned the ramparts, and drew up in line of battle before their camp. [104] Villehardouin admits that the bravest knights were, for a moment, seized with fear. Dandolo, who saw the danger in which the French were placed, abandoned his victory, and flew to their aid. But all the Crusaders united, could not have resisted the imperial army, if the Greeks, but more particularly their leaders, had shown a spark of courage. The troops of Alexius would not advance nearer than within bow-shot, and contented themselves with showering a multitude of arrows from a safe distance. The son-in-law of the emperor, Lascaris, of whose courage the Greeks and even the Latins boast, demanded with loud cries that the Crusaders should be attacked in their intrenchments; but he could not prevail upon Alexius, surrounded by base courtiers who endeavoured to communicate their own alarms to him, and assured him that he had done enough for his glory in showing himself to his enemies. The emperor, without having fought, ordered a retreat to be sounded, and his numerous troops, who still bore the name of Romans, and before whom the eagles of Rome were carried, returned with him into Constantinople.

Every quarter of the capital resounded with lamentations and groans; the Greeks were more terrified at the cowardice of their defenders, than by the bravery of their enemies; the people accused the army, and the army accused Alexius. The emperor mistrusting the Greeks and dreading the Latins, now only thought of saving his own life: he abandoned his family, his friends, his capital; he embarked secretly in the darkness of night, and fled to seek a retreat in some obscure corner of his empire.

When daylight informed the Greeks that they had no longer an emperor, the disorder and excitement of the city became excessive; the people assembled in the streets, and freely discussed the errors and deficiencies of their leaders, the infamy of the favourites, and their own misfortunes. Now Alexius had abandoned his power, they remembered the crime of his usurpation, and a thousand voices were raised to invoke the anger of Heaven upon his head. Amidst the confusion and tumult, the wisest were at a loss what part to take, when the courtiers rushed to the prison in which Isaac languished, broke his chains, and led him in triumph to the palace of Blachernæ. Although blind, he was placed upon the throne, and, whilst he believed himself to be still in the hands of his executioners, his ears were saluted with the unexpected accents of flattery; on seeing him again clothed in the imperial purple, the courtiers for the first time became affected by misfortunes he no longer endured. All denied having been partisans of Alexius, and related what vows they had put up for his cause. They next sought out the wife of Isaac, whom they had forgotten, and who had lived in a retreat to which no one knew or had inquired the road during the preceding reign.

Euphrosyne, the wife of the fugitive emperor, was accused of having endeavoured to take advantage of the troubles of Constantinople, to clothe one of her favourites with the purple. She was cast into a dungeon, and reproached with all the evils that had fallen on her country, but most particularly with the lengthened miseries of Isaac. Such as had been loaded with favours by this princess, were conspicuous among her accusers, and pretended to make a merit of their ingratitude.

In political troubles, every change is, in the eyes of the people, a means of safety; they felicitated themselves upon this new revolution in Constantinople; hope revived in all hearts, and Isaac was saluted by the multitude with cries of joy and congratulation. Rumour soon carried to the camp all that had taken place in the city. At this news the council of the barons and knights was assembled in the tent of the marquis of Montferrat, and they returned thanks to Providence, which in delivering Constantinople, had, at the same time, delivered them from the greatest dangers. But when they recollected having seen only on the preceding day the emperor Alexius surrounded by an innumerable army, they could scarcely give faith to the miracle of his flight.

The camp was, however, soon crowded with a multitude of Greeks, who came to relate the wonders of which they had been witnesses. Many of the courtiers who had not been able to attract the attention of Isaac, flocked to young Alexius, in the hope of securing his first favours; they returned warm thanks to Heaven for having listened to the ardent vows they had put up for his return, and conjured him, in the name of his country and the empire, to come and share the honours and the power of his father. But all these testimonies could not persuade the Latins, so accustomed were they to mistrust the Greeks. The barons kept their army in the strictest order, and always prepared for battle, and then sent Matthew of Montmorenci, Geoffrey de Villehardouin, and two Venetian nobles to Constantinople to ascertain the truth.

The deputies were directed to congratulate Isaac, if he had recovered his throne, and to require of him the ratification of the treaty made with his son. On arriving in Constantinople, they were conducted to the palace of Blachernæ between two ranks of soldiers, who, the day before, had formed the body-guard of Alexius, and who had just taken the oath to defend Isaac. The emperor received the deputies on a throne sparkling with gold and precious stones, and surrounded by all the splendour of Eastern courts. "This is the manner," said Villehardouin, addressing Isaac, "in which the Crusaders have fulfilled their promises; it now remains with you to perform those that have been made in your name. Your son, who is with the lords and barons, implores you to ratify the treaty he has concluded, and commands us to say that he will not return to your palace until you have sworn to perform all he has promised us." Alexius had engaged to pay the Crusaders two hundred thousand silver marks, to furnish their army with provisions for a year, to take an active part in the perils and labours of the holy war, and to reduce the Greek Church to submission to that of Rome. When Isaac heard the conditions of the treaty, he could not forbear from expressing his surprise, and pointing out to the deputies how difficult it must be to perform such promises; but he could deny nothing to his liberators, and thanked the Crusaders for not requiring more: [105] *"You have served us so well,"* added he, *"that if we were even to give you the whole empire, you would have merited it."* The deputies praised the frankness and good faith of Isaac, and carried back to the camp the imperial patents, to which was affixed the seal of gold that confirmed the treaty made with Alexius.

The lords and barons immediately mounted on horseback, and conducted young Alexius into Constantinople. The son of Isaac rode between the count of Flanders and the doge of Venice, followed by all the knights, clad in complete armour. The people, who so lately had preserved a sullen silence on beholding him, now crowded around him on his passage, and saluted him with loud acclamations; the Latin clergy accompanied the son of Isaac, and those of the Greek Church sent out their magnificent *cortège* to meet him. The entrance of the young prince into the capital was a day of festivity for both the Greeks and the Latins; in all the churches thanks were offered up to Heaven; hymns of public rejoicing resounded everywhere, but it was particularly in the palace of Blachernæ, so long the abode of mourning and fear, that the greatest transports of joy were manifested. A father, blind, and immured during eight years in a dungeon, clasping in his arms a son to whom he owed the restoration of his liberty and crown, presented a new spectacle that must have penetrated every heart with lively emotions. The crowd of spectators recalled to their minds the long calamities of these two princes; and the remembrance of so many evils past, appeared to them a pledge for the blessings that Heaven had in store for the empire.

The emperor, reunited to his son, again thanked the Crusaders for the services they had rendered him, and conjured the leaders to establish themselves with their army on the other side of the Gulf of Chrysoceras. He feared that their abode in the city might give birth to some quarrel between the Greeks and the Latins, too long divided. The barons yielded to the prayer of Isaac and Alexius, and the army of the Crusaders took up their quarters in the faubourg of Galata; where, in abundance and repose, they forgot the labours, perils, and fatigues of the war. The Pisans, who had defended Constantinople against the Crusaders, made peace with the Venetians; all discords were appeased, and no spirit of jealousy or rivalry divided the

Franks. The Greeks came constantly to the camp of the Latins, bringing provisions and merchandise of all kinds. The warriors of the West often visited the capital, and were never tired of contemplating the palaces of the emperors, the numerous edifices, the masterpieces of art, the monuments consecrated to religion, and, above all, the relics of saints, which, according to the marshal of Champagne, were in greater abundance in Constantinople than in any other place in the world.

A few days after his entrance into Constantinople, Alexius was crowned in the church of St. Sophia, and admitted to a partition of the sovereign power with his father. The barons assisted at his coronation, and offered up sincere wishes for the happiness of his reign. Alexius hastened to discharge a part of the sum promised to the Crusaders. The greatest harmony prevailed between the people of Byzantium and the warriors of the West; the Greeks appeared to have forgotten their defeats, the Latins their victories. The subjects of Isaac and Alexius mingled with the Latins without mistrust, and the simplicity of the Franks was no longer the subject of their raillery. The Crusaders, on their side, confided in the good faith of the Greeks. Peace reigned in the capital, and seemed to be the work of their hands. They respected the two princes they had placed upon the throne, and the emperors retained an affectionate gratitude for their liberators.

The Crusaders, having become the allies of the Greeks, and the protectors of a great empire, had now no other enemies to contend with but the Saracens; and they turned their minds to the fulfilment of the oath they had made on taking the cross; but, ever faithful to the laws of chivalry, the barons and knights deemed it right to declare war before beginning it. Heralds-at-arms were sent to the sultan of Cairo and Damascus, to announce to him, in the name of Jesus Christ, in the name of the emperor of Constantinople, and in the names of the princes and nobles of the West, that he would soon experience the valour of the Christian nations, if he persisted in holding under his laws the Holy Land and the places consecrated by the presence of the Saviour.

The leaders of the crusade announced the wonderful success of their enterprise to all the princes and nations of Christendom. Whilst addressing the emperor of Germany, [106] they conjured him to take part in the crusade, and come and place himself at the head of the Christian knights. The account of their exploits excited the enthusiasm of the faithful; the news, when carried into Syria, spread terror among the Saracens, and revived the hopes of the king of Jerusalem and the defenders of the Holy Land: so much glorious success ought to have satisfied the pride and valour of the Crusaders; but, whilst the world resounded with their glory, and trembled at the fame of their arms, the knights and barons believed they had achieved nothing for their own renown, or for the cause of God, until they had obtained the approbation of the Holy See. The marquis of Montferrat, the count of Flanders, the count of St. Pol, and the principal leaders of the army, when writing to the pope, represented to him that the success of their enterprise was not the work of men, but the work of God. These warriors, filled with haughty pride, who had just conquered an empire; who, according to Nicetas, boasted of *fearing nothing but the falling of the heavens*, thus bent their victorious brows before the tribunal of the sovereign pontiff, and protested at the feet of Innocent, that no mundane view had directed their arms, and that he must only contemplate in them the instruments Providence had employed in accomplishing its designs.

Young Alexius, in concert with the leaders of the crusades, wrote at the same time to the pope, to justify his conduct and that of his liberators. "We avow," said he, "that the principal cause that induced the pilgrims to assist us, was that we had promised, with an oath, to recognise the Roman pontiff as our ecclesiastical head, and the successor of St. Peter." Innocent III. in replying to the new emperor of Constantinople, praised his intentions and his zeal, and pressed him to accomplish his promises; but the excuses of the Crusaders were not able to appease the resentment which the pope retained on account of their disobedience to the counsels and commands of the Holy See. In his answer, he did not salute them with his usual benediction, fearing that they were again fallen under excommunication, by attacking the Greek emperor in spite of his prohibition. If the emperor of Constantinople, said he to them, does not make haste to do that which he has promised, it will appear that neither his intentions nor yours have been sincere, and *that you have added this second sin to that you have already committed*. The pope gave the Crusaders fresh advice; but neither his counsels nor his threats produced any better effect than they had done at the siege of Zara: Providence was preparing in secret, events that exceeded the foresight of the Crusaders, or even that of the Holy See, and which would once again change the aim and object of the holy war.

BOOK XI
A.D. 1198-1204

When war and revolutions have shaken an empire to its foundation, evils arise against which no human wisdom can provide. It is then that princes, called to the throne, are more to be pitied than their subjects, and that their power is more likely to excite commiseration than to awaken the ambition or hatred of other men. The people, in the extreme of misery, know not what bounds to put to their hopes, and always demand of the future more than the future can possibly bring. When they continue to suffer irreparable misfortunes, they blame their leaders, by whose influence they expected all sorts of prosperity; the murmurs of unjust hatred soon succeed to the acclamations of an irreflective enthusiasm, and, not unfrequently, virtue itself is accused of having caused evils which are the effects of revolt, war, or bad fortune.

Nations themselves, when they have succumbed, and have for ever lost their political existence, are not judged with less severity or injustice than princes or monarchs: after the fall of an empire, the terrible axiom *væ victis*, receives its application even in the judgment of posterity. Generations, quite equally with contemporaries, allow themselves to be dazzled by victory, and entertain nothing but contempt for conquered nations. We shall endeavour, whilst speaking of the Greeks and their princes, to guard against the prejudices that history has transmitted to us, and when we shall pronounce a severe judgment upon the character and people of Greece, our opinion will be always founded upon authentic traditions and the testimony of the historians of Byzantium.

Whilst young Alexius had nothing to do but make promises and give hopes, he was gratified by the flattering benedictions of both Greeks and Crusaders; but when the time arrived for him to perform all he had promised, he met with nothing but enemies and obstacles. In the position in which his return had placed him, it was extremely difficult for him to preserve at the same time the confidence of his liberators and the love of his subjects. If, in order to fulfil his engagements, the young emperor undertook to unite the Greek Church with the Church of Rome; if, to pay that which he owed to the Crusaders, he oppressed his people with taxes, he must expect to hear violent murmurs arise throughout his empire. If, on the contrary, he respected the religion of Greece, if he lightened the excessive weight of the imposts, the treaties would remain unexecuted, and the throne he had so recently ascended, might be overturned by the arms of the Latins.

Dreading every day to see the fires of either revolt or war kindled, obliged to choose between two perils, after having long and earnestly deliberated, he did not dare to confide his destiny to the equivocal valour of the Greeks, and conjured the barons to become a second time his liberators. He repaired to the tent of the count of Flanders, and spoke as follows to the assembled leaders of the crusade. [107] "You have restored to me life, honour, and empire, and I have only one thing to desire: that is, to be able to perform all the promises I have made you. But if you abandon me now, in order to go into Syria, it will be impossible for me to find the money, the troops, or the vessels I have undertaken to furnish. The people of Constantinople have received me with joy; but the frequency of revolutions has caused them to lose the habits of submission and obedience. The laws of their country, the majesty of the throne, no longer inspire them with respect; a spirit of faction reigns in the capital, and throughout the too-long agitated provinces. I conjure you then, in the name of your own glory, in the name of your own interests, to finish your work, and render firm the power you have reëstablished. Winter is approaching, the navigation is perilous, and the rains will not permit you to commence the war in Syria; wait then till the spring, when the sea will present fewer dangers, and war greater success and glory; you will then have all Greece as auxiliaries in your enterprises; I shall myself be able to keep the oaths that chain me to your cause, and accompany you with an army worthy of an emperor." At the conclusion of his speech, Alexius promised to furnish all that the army would require, and to make such suitable arrangements with the doge, that the Venetian fleet might remain at the disposal of the Crusaders during their abode at Constantinople, and to the end of their expedition.

A council was called to deliberate upon the proposals of the young emperor: those who had been desirous of separating themselves from the army at Zara and Corfu, represented to the assembly that they had, until that time, fought for the glory and profane interests of princes of the earth, but that the time was now come for them to fight for religion and for Jesus Christ. They were indignant at new obstacles being raised to retard the holy enterprise. This opinion was warmly combated by the doge of Venice and the barons who had embarked their glory in the expedition against Constantinople, and could not make up their minds to lose the fruit of all their labours. "Shall we," said they, "allow a young prince, whose cause we have brought to a triumphant issue, to be delivered over to his enemies, who are as ours, and an enterprise so gloriously begun, become for us a source of shame and repentance? Shall we allow the heresy that our arms have stifled in humbled Greece, to reconstruct its impure altars, and be again a subject of scandal for the Christian church? Shall we leave the Greeks the dangerous faculty of declaring against us, and allying themselves with the Saracens, to war with the soldiers of Christ?" To these weighty motives the princes and lords did not disdain to add supplication and prayers; at length their opinion triumphed over an obstinate opposition, and the council decided that the departure of the army should be deferred until the festival of the Easter of the following year.

Alexius, in concert with Isaac, thanked the Crusaders for their favourable determination, and neglected nothing that could prove his gratitude to them. For the purpose of paying the sums he had promised, he exhausted his treasury, increased the imposts, and even melted the images of the saints and the sacred vases. Upon seeing the churches despoiled of the sacred images, the people of Constantinople were struck with surprise and terror, and yet had not the courage to utter their complaints aloud. Nicetas reproaches his compatriots bitterly with having remained quiet spectators of such sacrilege, and accuses them of having, by their cowardly indifference, drawn upon the empire the anger of Heaven. The most fervent of the Greeks deplored, as Nicetas did, the violation of their holy places; but scenes much more grievous were soon to be brought before their eyes.

The leaders of the army, influenced by the counsels of the Latin clergy and by the fear of the pontiff of Rome, required that the patriarch, the priests, and the monks of Constantinople should abjure the errors that separated them from the Romish church; and neither the clergy, nor the people, nor the emperor, attempted to resist this demand, although it alarmed every conscience and alienated all hearts. The patriarch, from the pulpit of St. Sophia, declared, in his own name, and in the name of the emperor and the Christian people of the East, that he acknowledged *Innocent, third of that name, as the successor of St. Peter, first vicar of Jesus Christ upon earth, pastor of the faithful flock*. The Greeks who were present at this ceremony believed they beheld the abomination of desolation in the holy place, and if they afterwards pardoned the patriarch the commission of such a scandal, it was from the strange persuasion in which they were, that the head of their church was deceiving the Latins, and that the imposture of his words redeemed in some sort the crime of blasphemy and the shame of perjury.

The Greeks persisted in believing that the Holy Ghost does not proceed from the Son, and quoted in support of their belief, the Creed of Nice; the discipline of their church differed in some points from that of the Church of Rome; in the early days of the schism it might have been easy to effect a reunion, but now the disputes of theologians had too much exasperated men's minds. [108] The hatred of the Greeks and the Latins appeared but too likely to separate the two creeds for ever. The law that was imposed upon the Greeks only served to promote the growth of their invincible resistance. Such among them as scarcely knew what the subject was of the long debates that had sprung up between Byzantium and Rome, showed no less fanaticism and opposition than all the others; whilst such as had no religion at all adopted with warmth the opinions of the theologians, and appeared all at once disposed to die for a cause which till that time had inspired them with nothing but indifference. The Greek people, in a word, who believed themselves to be superior to all other nations of the earth, repulsed with contempt all knowledge that came from the West, and could not consent to recognise the superiority of the Latins. The Crusaders, who had changed the emperors and conquered the empire, were astonished at not being able to change men's hearts likewise; but, persuaded that everything must in the end yield to their arms, they employed, in subduing minds and opinions, a rigour which only augmented the hatred of the vanquished, and prepared the fall of the emperors whom victory had replaced upon the throne.

In the mean time, the usurper Alexius, on flying from Constantinople, had found a retreat in the province of Thrace; several cities opened their gates to him, and a few partisans assembled under his banner. The son of Isaac resolved to seek the rebels and give them battle. Henry of Hainault, the count of St. Pol, and many knights, accompanied him in this expedition. At their approach, the usurper, shut up in Adrianople, quickly abandoned the city and fled away towards Mount Hemus. All the rebels who had the courage to await them, were either conquered or dispersed. But young Alexius and the Crusaders had a much more formidable enemy to contend with: this was the nation of the Bulgarians. These wild and ferocious people obedient to the laws of Constantinople at the time of the first crusade, had taken advantage of the troubles of the empire to shake off the yoke of its rulers. [109] The leader of the Bulgarians, Joannices, an implacable enemy of the Greeks, had embraced the faith of the Church of Rome, and declared himself a vassal of the sovereign pontiff, to obtain from him the title of king. He concealed under the veil of a new religion the most vindictive hatred and aspiring ambition, and employed the support and credit of the court of Rome to make war against the masters of Byzantium. Joannices made frequent incursions into the countries adjoining his own territories, and threatened the richest provinces of the empire with invasion. If young Alexius had been guided by prudent counsels, he would have taken advantage of the presence of the Crusaders to intimidate the Bulgarians, and compel them to remain on the other side of Mount Hemus: this expedition might have deservedly obtained him the confidence and esteem of the Greeks, and assured the repose of several provinces; but whether he was not seconded by the Crusaders, or that he did not perceive the advantages of such an enterprise, he contented himself with threatening Joannices; and, without having made either peace or war, after receiving the oaths of the cities of Thrace, his sole wish was to return to Constantinople.

The capital of the empire, which had already undergone so many evils, had just experienced a fresh calamity. Some Flemish soldiers, encouraged by the Latins established in Constantinople, had provoked and insulted the Jews in their synagogue, and the people had taken up the defence of the latter against the aggressors. Both sides had recourse to arms, and in the tumult of fight, chance, or malevolence, set fire to some neighbouring houses. The conflagration extended on all sides, during the night and the following day, with a rapidity and violence that nothing could stop or confine; the flames meeting from several points, rolled on with the swiftness of a torrent, consuming, as if of straw, galleries, columns, temples, and palaces. From the bosom of this frightful mass of fire issued fragments of burning matter, which, falling upon distant houses, reduced them to ashes. The flames, at first impelled by a north wind, were afterwards driven back, by a strong change, from the south, and poured upon places that had appeared secure from danger. The conflagration began at the synagogue, near the sea, on the eastern side of the city, and extended its ravages as far as the church of St. Sophia, on the western side, traversing a space of two leagues, and in its course including the port, where many ships were consumed upon the waters. [110]

During eight days the fearful element continued the destruction; the crash of houses and towers falling on all sides, and the roaring of the winds and flames mingling with the cries of a ruined and distracted multitude. The crowds of inhabitants rushed over and against each other in the streets, flying before the closely-pursuing fire, some bearing their goods and most valuable effects, others dragging along the sick and the aged. Such as perished in the conflagration were the least unfortunate, for multitudes of others, weeping the death of their relations and friends, and the loss of their whole worldly property, many of them wounded, some half-burnt, wandered about bewildered among the ruins, or were huddled together in the public places, without any means of subsistence, or the hope of finding an asylum.

The Crusaders viewed the progress of this horrible disaster from the heights of Galata, and deplored the calamities of Constantinople. A great number of knights lent their most earnest endeavour to subdue the raging element, and lamented that they had to contend with an enemy against which valour was powerless. The princes and barons sent a deputation to the emperor Isaac, to assure him how sincerely they participated in his sorrow, and to declare that they would punish the authors of the conflagration with the utmost severity, if they should prove to be among their soldiers. The protestations and assistance which they promptly and earnestly offered to the victims, could neither console nor appease the Greeks, who, whilst contemplating the ruins and misfortunes of their capital, accused the two emperors, and threw out horrible imprecations against the Latins.

The families of the Franks established at Constantinople, who, in spite of persecutions, had remained in the city, became again subject to the ill-treatment of the people; and, forced to seek an asylum without the walls, they took refuge in the faubourg of Galata. Their groans and complaints revived all the animosity of the Crusaders against the Greeks. Thus everything contributed to inflame the hatred of two nations, whom such great misfortunes ought to have more closely united, and to rekindle discords that were doomed to bring in their train new and incurable calamities.

When Alexius re-entered Constantinople in triumph, the people received him with moody silence; the Crusaders alone applauded victories he had gained over Greeks; and his triumph, which contrasted so keenly with the public calamities, and his laurels, gathered in a civil war, only served to render him more odious to the inhabitants of his capital. He was obliged, more than ever, to throw himself into the arms of the Latins; he passed his days and nights in their camp; he took part in their warlike games, and associated himself with their gross orgies. Amidst the intoxication of banquets, the Frank warriors treated Alexius with insolent familiarity, and more than once they pulled off his jewelled diadem to place on his head the woollen cap worn by Venetian sailors. The Greeks, who took great pride in the magnificence of their sovereigns, only conceived the stronger contempt for a prince, who, after abjuring his religion, degraded the imperial dignity, and did not blush to adopt the manners of nations that were only known at Constantinople under the name of barbarians.

Nicetas, whose opinions are not wanting in moderation, never speaks of this prince but with a sort of anger and violence. According to the historian of Byzantium, "Alexius had a countenance resembling that of the exterminating angel; he was a true incendiary; and far from being afflicted by the burning of his capital, he would have wished to see the whole city reduced to ashes." Isaac himself accused his son of having pernicious inclinations, and of corrupting himself daily by an intercourse with the wicked; he was indignant that the name of Alexius should be proclaimed at court and in public ceremonies, whilst that of Isaac was rarely mentioned. In his blind anger, he loaded the young emperor with imprecations; but, governed by a vain jealousy, much more than by any proper sentiment of dignity, whilst he applauded the hatred of the people for Alexius, he evaded the duties of a sovereign, and did nothing to merit the esteem of men of worth. Isaac lived retired in his palace, surrounded by monks and astrologers, who, whilst kissing his hands still scarred with the irons of his captivity, celebrated his power, made him believe that he would deliver Jerusalem, that he would plant his throne upon Mount Libanus, and would reign over the whole universe. Full of confidence in an image of the Virgin which he always carried with him, and boasting of being acquainted, by means of astrology, with all the secrets of policy, he could yet imagine, to prevent sedition, nothing more effective than to have transported from the hippodrome to his palace, the statue of the wild boar of Calydon, which was considered the symbol of revolt and the image of an infuriated people.

The people of Constantinople, no less superstitious than Isaac, whilst deploring the evils of their country, laid the blame upon both marble and brass. A statue of Minerva which decorated the Square of Constantine, had its eyes and arms turned towards the West; it was believed that she had called in the barbarians, and the statue was torn down and dashed to pieces by an exasperated mob: [111] "cruel blindness of the Greeks," cries an historical *bel esprit*, [112] "who took arms against themselves, and could not endure in their city the image of a goddess who presides over prudence and valour!"

Whilst the capital of the empire was thus agitated by popular commotions, the ministers of Alexius and Isaac were busied in levying taxes for the payment of the sums promised to the Latins. Extravagance, abuses of power, and numerous instances of injustice, added still further to the public calamities; loud complaints were proclaimed by every class of the citizens. It was at first intended to lay the principal burden of the imposts upon the people; but the people, says Nicetas, arose like a sea agitated by the winds. Extraordinary taxes were then, by necessity, laid upon the richer citizens, and the churches continued to be plundered of their gold and silver ornaments. All the treasures they could collect were not sufficient to satisfy the insatiable desires of the Latins, who began to ravage the country, and pillage the houses and monasteries of the Propontis.

The hostilities and violence of the Crusaders excited the indignation of the people to a greater degree than they moved that of the patricians and the great. In the course of so many revolutions, it is astonishing to find that the spirit of patriotism so frequently revives amongst the multitude, when it is extinct in the more elevated classes. In a corrupt nation, so long as revolutions have not broken forth, and the day of peril and destruction is not arrived, the riches of the citizens is a sure pledge of their devotedness and patriotism; but this pledge is no longer the same at the height of danger, when society finds itself in antagonism with all the enemies of its existence and its repose; a fortune, the loss of which is dreaded, is often the cause of shameful transactions with the party of the conquerors; it enervates more than it fortifies moral courage. Amidst the greatest perils, the multitude, who have nothing to lose, sometimes preserve generous passions that skilful policy may direct with advantage. Unfortunately, the same multitude scarcely ever obey anything but a blind instinct; and in moments of crisis, become a dangerous instrument in the hands of the ambitious, who abuse the names of liberty and patriotism. It is then that a nation has no less to complain of those who are not willing to save her, than of those who do not dare defend her; and that she perishes, the victim at once of culpable indifference and senseless ardour.

The people of Constantinople, irritated against the enemies of the empire, and urged on by a spirit of faction, complained at first of their leaders; and, soon passing from complaint to revolt, they rushed in a crowd to the palace of the emperors, reproached them with having abandoned the cause of God and the cause of their country, and demanded, with loud cries, avengers and arms.

Among those who encouraged the multitude, a young prince of the illustrious family of Ducas was conspicuous. He bore the name of Alexius, a name which must always be associated with the history of the misfortunes of the empire: in addition, he had obtained the surname of *Mourzoufle*, a Greek word, signifying that his two eyebrows met together. Mourzoufle [113] concealed a subtle spirit beneath that severe and stern air that the vulgar never fail to take for an indication of frankness. The words patriotism and liberty, which always seduce the people; the words glory and religion, which recall noble sentiments, were for ever in his mouth, and only served to veil the machinations of his ambition. Amidst a timid and pusillanimous court, surrounded by princes, who, according to the expression of Nicetas, *had greater fear of making war against the Crusaders, than stags would have in attacking a lion*, Mourzoufle was not deficient in bravery, and his reputation for courage was quite sufficient to draw upon him the eyes of the whole capital. As he possessed a strong voice, a haughty look, and an imperious tone, he was pronounced fit to command. The more vehemently he declaimed against tyranny, the more ardent were the wishes of the multitude that he should be clothed with great power. The hatred that he affected to entertain for foreigners, gave birth to the hope that he would one day defend the empire, and caused him to be considered the future liberator of Constantinople.

Skilful in seizing every available chance, and in following all parties, after having rendered criminal services to the usurper, Mourzoufle gathered the reward of them under the reign that followed the usurpation; and he who was everywhere accused of having been the gaoler and executioner of Isaac, [114] became the favourite of young Alexius. He neglected no means of pleasing the multitude, in order to render himself necessary to the prince; and knew how to brave, on fit occasions, the hatred of the courtiers, to augment his credit among the people. He was not tardy in taking advantage of this double influence to sow the seeds of new troubles, and bring about the triumph of his ambition.

His counsels persuaded young Alexius, that it was necessary for him to break with the Latins, and prove himself ungrateful to his liberators, to obtain the confidence of the Greeks; he inflamed the minds of the people, and to make a rupture certain, he himself took up arms. His friends and some men of the people followed his example, and, led by Mourzoufle, a numerous troop rushed from the city, in the hope of surprising the Latins; but the multitude, always ready to declaim against the warriors of the West, did not dare to face them. Mourzoufle, abandoned on the field of battle, had nearly fallen into the hands of the Crusaders. This imprudent action, that might have been expected to ruin him, only tended to increase his power and influence; he might be accused of having risked the safety of the empire by provoking a war without the means of sustaining it; but the people boasted of the heroism of a young prince, who had dared to brave the warlike hosts of the Franks; and even they who had deserted him in the fight, celebrated his valour, and swore, as he did, to exterminate the enemies of their country.

The frenzy of the Greeks was at its height; and, on their side, the Latins loudly expressed their dissatisfaction. In the faubourg of Galata, inhabited by the French and Venetians, as well as within the walls of Constantinople, nothing was heard but cries for war, and nobody durst speak of peace. At this period a deputation from the Christians of Palestine arrived in the camp of the Crusaders. The deputies, the principal of whom was Martin Litz, were clothed in mourning vestments, which, with the sadness of their aspect, made it sufficiently plain that they came to announce fresh misfortunes. Their accounts drew tears from all the pilgrims.

In the year that preceded the expedition to Constantinople the Flemish and Champenois Crusaders, who had embarked at the ports of Bruges and Marseilles, landed at Ptolemaïs. At the same time came many English warriors, commanded by the earls of Northumberland, Norwich, and Salisbury; and a great number of pilgrims from Lower Brittany, who had chosen for leader the monk Hélain, one of the preachers of the crusade. These Crusaders, when united with those who had quitted the Christian army after the siege of Zara, became impatient to attack the Saracens, and as the king of Jerusalem was averse to breaking the truce made with the infidels, the greater part of them left Palestine, to fight under the banners of the prince of Antioch, who was at war with the prince of Armenia. Having refused to take guides, they were surprised and dispersed by a body of Saracens, sent against them by the sultan of Aleppo; [115] the few that escaped from the carnage, among whom history names two seigneurs de Neuilly, Bernard de Montmirail, and Renard de Dampierre, remained in the chains of the infidels. Hélain, the monk, had the grief to see the bravest of the Breton Crusaders perish on the field of battle, and returned almost alone to Ptolemaïs, to announce the bloody defeat of the soldiers of the cross. A horrible famine had, during two years, desolated Egypt, and extended its ravages into Syria. Contagious diseases followed the famine; the plague swept away the inhabitants of the Holy Land; more than two thousand Christians had received the rights of sepulture in the city of Ptolemaïs, in one single day!

The deputies from the Holy Land, after rendering their melancholy account, invoked by tears and groans the prompt assistance of the army of the Crusaders; but the barons and knights could not abandon the enterprise they had begun; they promised the envoys from Palestine that they would turn their arms towards Syria, as soon as they had subdued the Greeks; and, pointing towards the walls of Constantinople, said: "*This is the road to salvation; this is the way to Jerusalem.*"

Alexius was bound to pay the Latins the sums he had promised; if he was faithful to his word, he had to apprehend a revolt of the Greeks; if he did not fulfil his engagements, he dreaded the arms of the Crusaders. Terrified by the general agitation that prevailed, and restrained by a double fear, the two emperors remained inactive in their palace, without daring to seek for peace, or prepare for war.

The Crusaders, dissatisfied with the conduct of Alexius, [116] deputed several barons and knights to demand of him peremptorily whether he would be their friend or their enemy. The deputies, on entering Constantinople, heard nothing throughout their passage but the insults and threats of an irritated populace. Received in the palace of Blachernæ, amidst the pomp of the throne and the court, [117] they addressed the emperor Alexius, and expressed the complaints of their companions in arms in these terms: "We are sent by the French barons and the doge of Venice to recall to your mind the treaty that you and your father have sworn to upon the Gospel, and to require you to fulfil your promises as we have fulfilled ours. If you do us justice, we shall only have to forget the past, and give due praise to your good faith; if you are not true to your oaths, the Crusaders will no longer remember they have been your friends and allies, they will have recourse to no more prayers, but to their own good swords. They have felt it their duty to lay their complaints before you, and to warn you of their intentions, for the warriors of the West hold treachery in horror, and never make war without having declared it; we offer you our friendship, which has placed you upon the throne, or our hatred, which is able to remove you from it; we bring you war with all its calamities, or peace with all its blessings: it is for you to choose, and to deliberate upon the part you have to take."

These complaints of the Crusaders were expressed with so little respect, that they must have been highly offensive to the ears of the emperors. In this palace, which constantly resounded with the acclamations of a servile court, the sovereigns of Byzantium had never listened to language so insolent and haughty. The emperor Alexius, to whom this menacing tone appeared to reveal his own helplessness and the unhappy state of his empire, could not restrain his indignation; the courtiers fully partook of the anger of their masters, and were desirous of punishing the insolent orator of the Latins on the spot; [118] but the deputies left the palace of Blachernæ, and hastened to regain the camp of the Crusaders.

The council of Isaac and Alexius breathed nothing but vengeance; and, on the return of the deputies, war was decided on in the council of the barons. The Latins determined to attack Constantinople; nothing could equal the hatred and fury of the Greeks; but fury and hatred cannot supply the place of courage: not daring to meet their enemy in the open field, they resolved to burn the fleet of the Venetians. The Greeks, on this occasion, had again recourse to that Greek fire, which had, more than once, served them instead of courage, and saved their capital. This terrible fire, skilfully hurled or directed, devoured vessels, soldiers, and their arms; like the bolt of Heaven, nothing could prevent its explosion, or arrest its ravages; the waves of the sea, so far from extinguishing it, redoubled its activity. Seventeen ships, charged with the Greek fire and combustible matter, were carried by a favourable wind towards the port in which the Venetian vessels lay at anchor. To assure the success of this attempt, the Greeks took advantage of the darkness of night; and the port, the gulf, and the faubourg of Galata were, all at once, illumined by a threatening and sinister light. At the aspect of the danger, the trumpets sounded the alarm in the camp of the Latins; the French flew to arms and prepared for the fight, whilst the Venetians cast themselves into their barks, and went out to meet vessels bearing within their sides destruction and fire.

The crowd of Greeks assembled on the shore, applauded the spectacle, and enjoyed the terror of the Crusaders. Many of them embarked in small boats, and rowed out upon the sea, darting arrows and endeavouring to carry disorder among the Venetians. The Crusaders encouraged each other; they rushed in crowds to encounter the danger, some raising plaintive and piercing cries towards Heaven, and others uttering horrible imprecations against the Greeks: on the walls of Constantinople, clapping of hands and cries of joy resounded, and were redoubled as the vessels covered with flames drew nearer. Villehardouin, an ocular witness, says that amidst this frightful tumult, nature appeared to be in confusion, and the sea about to swallow up the earth. Nevertheless, the Venetians, by the means of strong arms and numberless oars, succeeded in turning the course of the fire-ships wide of the port, and they were carried by the current beyond the canal. The Crusaders, in battle array, standing on their vessels or dispersed among the barks, rendered thanks to God for having preserved them from so great a disaster; whilst the Greeks beheld with terror their fire-ships consuming away upon the waters of the Propontis, without having effected the least injury.

The irritated Latins could not pardon the perfidy and ingratitude of the emperor Alexius: "It was not enough for him to have failed in his engagements and broken his oaths, he endeavoured to burn the fleet that had borne him triumphantly to the heart of his empire: the time was now come to repress the enterprises of traitors by the sword, and to punish base enemies, who were acquainted with no other arms but treachery and deceit; and, like the vilest brigands, only ventured to deal their blows in the darkness and silence of night." Alexius, terrified at these threats, could think of no other resource than that of imploring the clemency of the Crusaders. He offered them fresh oaths and fresh promises, and threw the blame of the hostilities upon the fury of the people, which he had not the power to restrain. He conjured his friends, his allies, his liberators, to come and defend a throne ready to fall to pieces beneath him, and proposed to give up his own palace to them.

Mourzoufle was directed to convey to the Latins the supplications and offers of the emperor, and, seizing the opportunity to augment the alarms and discontent of the multitude, he caused the report to be spread that he was going to deliver Constantinople up to the barbarians of the West. On learning this, the people assembled tumultuously in the streets and public places; the report became general that the enemies were already in the city, and all joined in the cry that to prevent the greatest calamities, not a moment was to be lost; the empire required a master who was able to defend and protect it.

Whilst the young prince, seized with terror, shut himself up in his palace, the crowd of insurgents flocked to the church of St. Sophia to choose a new emperor.

Since the imperial dynasties had become the playthings of the caprice of the multitude, and of the ambition of conspirators, the Greeks made the changing of their sovereigns quite a sport, without reflecting that one revolution produces other revolutions; and, to avoid present calamities, rushed headlong into new ones. The most prudent of the clergy and the patricians presented themselves at the church of St. Sophia, and earnestly endeavoured to prevent the evils with which the country was threatened. But it was in vain they explained to their excited auditory that by changing their master they were sure to overthrow both the throne and the empire. "When they asked my opinion," says the historian Nicetas, "I was careful not to consent to the deposition of Isaac and Alexius, because I felt assured that the man they would elect in their place would not be the most able. But the people," adds the same historian, "whose only motive of action is passion,—the people, who twenty years before had killed Andronicus and crowned Isaac, could not endure their own work and live under princes whom they themselves had chosen." The multitude reproached their sovereign with their misery, which was the bitter fruit of the war; and with the weakness of their government, which was but the result of general corruption. The victories of the Latins, the inefficiency of the laws, the caprices of fortune, the very will of Heaven, all were gathered into one great accusation to be brought against those who governed the empire. The distracted crowd looked to a revolution for everything; a change of emperors appeared to them the only remedy for the ills under which they groaned. They pressed, they solicited the patricians and senators,—they scarcely knew the names of the men they wished to choose as masters; but any other than Isaac, any other than Alexius, must merit the esteem and love of the Greeks. To be the wearer of a purple robe, was quite enough to entitle a man to ascend the throne of Constantine. Some excused themselves on account of age, others from alleged incapacity. The people, sword in hand, required them to accept the sovereign authority. At length, after three days of stormy debate, an imprudent young man, named Canabus, allowed himself to be prevailed upon by the prayers and threats of the people. A phantom of an emperor was crowned in the church of St. Sophia, and proclaimed in Constantinople. Mourzoufle was no stranger to this popular revolution. Several historians have thought that he promoted the election of an obscure man, to test the peril in some sort, and to become acquainted with the power and will of the people, in order, one day, to profit by it himself.

Alexius, made aware of this revolution, trembled in the recesses of his deserted palace; he had no hope but in the Latins; he solicited, by messages, the support of the barons; he implored the pity of the marquis of Montferrat; who, touched by his prayers, entered Constantinople by night, and came, at the head of a chosen troop, to defend the throne and the lives of the emperors. Mourzoufle, who dreaded the presence of the Latins, flew to Alexius, to convince him that they were the most dangerous enemies he had, and told him that all would inevitably be lost if the Franks once appeared in arms in the palace.

When Boniface presented himself before the palace of Blachernæ, he found all the doors closed; Alexius caused him to be informed that he was no longer at liberty to receive him, and conjured him to leave Constantinople with his soldiers. The sight of the warriors of the West had spread terror throughout the city; their retreat revived both the courage and fury of the people. A thousand different rumours prevailed at once; the public places resounded with complaints and imprecations; from moment to moment the crowd became more numerous and the tumult increased. Amidst all this confusion and disorder, Mourzoufle never lost sight of the prosecution of his designs; by promises and caresses he won over the imperial guard, whilst his friends pervaded the capital, exciting the fury and rage of the multitude by their speeches and insinuations. An immense crowd soon assembled before the palace of Blachernæ, uttering seditious cries. Mourzoufle then presented himself before Alexius: he employed every means to aggravate the alarm of the young prince, and, under the pretext of providing for his safety, drew him into a secluded apartment, where his creatures, under his direction, loaded him with irons and cast him into a dungeon. Coming forth, he boldly informed the people what he had done for the salvation of the empire; and the throne, from which he had dragged his master, benefactor, and friend, appeared but a just recompense for the devotedness of his services: he was carried in triumph to the church of St. Sophia, and crowned emperor amidst the acclamations of the people. Scarcely was Mourzoufle clothed with the imperial purple, than he resolved to possess the fruit of his crime in security; dreading the caprice of both fortune and the people, he repaired to the prison of Alexius, forced him to swallow an empoisoned draught, and because death did not keep pace with his impatience, strangled him with his own hands.

Thus perished, after a reign of six months and a few days, the emperor Alexius, whom one revolution had placed upon a throne, and who disappeared amidst the storms of another, without having tasted any of the sweets of supreme rank, and without an opportunity of proving whether he was worthy of it. This young prince, placed in a most difficult situation, had not the power, and perhaps not the will, to rouse the Greeks to oppose the Crusaders. On the other side, he had not the tact to employ the support of the Latins so as to keep the Greeks within the bounds of obedience; directed by perfidious counsels, ever vacillating between patriotism and gratitude, fearing by turns to alienate his unhappy subjects, or to irritate his formidable allies, he perished, the victim of his own weakness and irresolution. Isaac Angelus, on learning the tragical end of his son, died of terror and despair; thus sparing Mourzoufle another parricide, of which he was not the less suspected to be guilty. History makes no more mention of Canabus; the confusion was so great that the Greeks were ignorant of the fate of a man whom but a few days before they had elevated to the rank of their sovereign; four emperors had been dragged violently from the throne since the arrival of the Latins, and fortune reserved the same fate for Mourzoufle.

In order to profit by the crime that had ministered to his ambitious views, the murderer of Alexius formed the project of committing another, and to bring about by treachery the death of all the principal leaders of the army of the Crusaders. An officer, sent to the camp of the Latins, was directed to say that he came on the part of the emperor Alexius, of whose death they were ignorant, to engage the doge of Venice and the French nobles to come to the palace of Blachernæ, where all the sums promised by the treaties, should be placed in their hands. The barons at first agreed to accept the invitation of the emperor, and prepared to set out with great joy; but Dandolo, who, according to Nicetas, deservedly obtained the name of the *Prudent of the Prudent*, awakened their mistrust, and pointed out strong reasons for fearing a fresh perfidy of the Greeks. It was not long before they were fully informed of the death of Isaac, the murder of Alexius, and all the crimes of Mourzoufle. At this news the indignation of the Crusaders was strong and general; knights had difficulty in crediting such baseness; every fresh account made them tremble with horror; they forgot the wrongs of Alexius towards themselves, deplored his unfortunate end, and swore to avenge him. In the council, the leaders loudly exclaimed that an implacable war must be made against Mourzoufle, and that the nation that had crowned treachery and parricide should be punished. The prelates and ecclesiastics, more animated than all the others, invoked at once the thunders of religion and earthly war against the usurper of the imperial throne, and against the Greeks, untrue to their sovereign, untrue to God himself. Above all, they could not pardon the subjects of Mourzoufle, for willingly remaining plunged in the darkness of heresy, and escaping, by an impious revolt, from the domination of the Holy See. They promised all the indulgences of the sovereign pontiff and all the riches of Greece to the warriors called upon to avenge the cause of God and men.

Whilst the Crusaders thus breathed nothing but war against the emperor and people of Constantinople, Mourzoufle was preparing to repel their attacks; he earnestly endeavoured to attach the inhabitants of the capital to his cause; he reproached the great with their indifference and effeminacy, and laid before them the example of the multitude; to increase his popularity and fill his treasury, he persecuted the courtiers of Alexius and Isaac, and confiscated the property of all those who had enriched themselves in public offices. [119] The usurper at the same time set about reëstablishing discipline among the troops, and augmenting the fortifications of the city; he no longer indulged in pleasures or allowed himself repose; as he was accused of the greatest crimes, he had not only to contend for empire, but for impunity; remorse doubled his activity, excited his bravery, and proved to him that he could have no safety but in victory. He was constantly seen parading the streets, with his sword by his side, and an iron club in his hand, animating the courage of the people and the soldiers.

The Greeks, however, contented themselves with declaiming against the Crusaders. After having made another attempt to burn the fleet of the Venetians, they shut themselves up within their walls, and supported with patience the insults and menaces of the Latins. [120] The Crusaders appeared to have nothing to fear but famine; as they began to feel the want of provisions, Henry of Hainault, brother of the count of Flanders, undertook, in order to obtain supplies for the army, an expedition to the shores of the Euxine Sea; and, followed by several knights, laid siege to Philea. The city of Philea was the ancient Philopolis, celebrated in the heroic ages of antiquity for the palace in which were received Jason and the Argonauts, who, like the French knights, had left their country, to seek distant adventures and perils. Henry of Hainault, after a short resistance from the inhabitants, made himself master of the city, in which he met with a considerable booty, and found provisions in abundance; the latter he transported by sea to the army.

Mourzoufle, being informed of this excursion, marched out, by night, with a numerous body of troops, and placed himself in ambush on the route which Henry of Hainault would take on his return to the camp. The Greeks attacked the Crusaders unexpectedly, in the full persuasion that their victory would be an easy one; but the Frank warriors, without displaying the least alarm, closed in their ranks, and made so firm and good a resistance, that the ambuscaders themselves were very quickly obliged to fly. Mourzoufle was upon the point of falling into the hands of his enemies, and only owed his safety to the swiftness of his horse; he left behind on the field of battle, his buckler, his arms, and the standard of the Virgin, which the emperors were accustomed to have borne before them in all great perils. The loss of this ancient and revered banner was a source of great regret to the Greeks. The Latins, on their part, when they saw the standard and image of the patroness of Byzantium floating amongst their victorious ranks, were persuaded that the mother of God had abandoned the Greeks, and declared herself favourable to their cause.

After this defeat, the Greeks became convinced that there existed no other means of safety for them but the fortification of their capital; it was much more easy for them to find workmen than soldiers, and a hundred thousand men laboured day and night at the reparation of the walls. The subjects of Mourzoufle appeared satisfied that their ramparts would defend them, and handled the implements of masonry without repugnance, in the hope that they would prevent the necessity for their wielding the sword or lance.

Mourzoufle had learnt to dread the courage of his enemies, and as strongly doubted the valour of his subjects; therefore, before risking any fresh warlike attempts, he determined to sue for peace, and demanded an interview with the leaders of the Crusaders. The lords and barons refused with horror to have an interview with the usurper of the throne, the murderer, the executioner of Alexius; but the love of peace, and the cause of humanity, induced the doge of Venice to consent to listen to the proposals of Mourzoufle. Henry Dandolo repaired in his galley to the point of the gulf, and the usurper, mounted on horseback, approached him as near as possible. The conference was long and animated. The doge required Mourzoufle to pay immediately five thousand pounds' weight of gold, to aid the Crusaders in their expedition to Syria, and again to swear obedience to the Romish church. After a long altercation, Mourzoufle promised to give the Latins the money and assistance they demanded; but he could not consent to submit to the yoke of the Church of Rome. [121] The doge, astonished that, after having outraged all the laws of Heaven and nature, he should attach so much importance to religious opinions, casting a glance of contempt at Mourzoufle, asked him, if the Greek religion excused treachery and parricide? [122] The usurper, although much irritated, dissembled his anger, and was endeavouring to justify his conduct, when the conference was interrupted by some Latin horsemen.

Mourzoufle, on his return to Constantinople, convinced that he must prepare for war, set earnestly about his task, and determined to die with arms in his hand. By his orders, the walls and towers that defended the city on the side of the port, were elevated many feet. He constructed upon the walls galleries of several stages, from which the soldiers might launch arrows and javelins, and employ balistas and other machines of war; at the top of each tower was placed a drawbridge, which, when lowered upon the vessels, might afford the besieged a means of pursuing their enemies, even to their own fleet.

The Crusaders, although supported by their natural bravery, could not view all these preparations with indifference. [123] The most intrepid could not help feeling some inquietude on comparing the small number of the

Franks with the imperial army and the population of Constantinople; all the resources they had till that time found in their alliance with the emperors were about to fail them, without their having any hope of supplying their place but by some miraculous victory: for they had no succour to look for from the West. Every day war became more dangerous, and peace more difficult; the time was gone by for retreat. In this situation, such were the spirit and character of the heroes of this crusade, that they drew fresh strength from the very circumstances that would appear likely to have depressed them, and filled them with dread; the greater the danger, the more courage and firmness they displayed; menaced on all sides, expecting to meet with no asylum on either sea or land, there remained no other part to take but that of besieging a city from which they could not retire with safety: thus nothing could overcome their invincible bravery. [124]

On viewing the towers that the Greeks considered as a certain means of safety, the leaders assembled in their camp, and shared amongst them the spoils of the empire and the capital, of which they entertained no doubt of achieving the conquest. It was decided in the council of the princes, barons, and knights, that a new emperor should be nominated instead of Mourzoufle, and that this emperor should be chosen from the victorious army of the Latins. The chief of the new empire should possess by right a fourth of the conquest, with the two palaces of Blachernæ and Bucoleon. The cities and lands of the empire, as well as the booty they should obtain in the capital, were to be distributed among the Franks and Venetians, with the condition of rendering homage to the emperor. In the same council regulations were made to assign the proportions of the Latin clergy, and of the lords and barons. They regulated, according to the feudal laws, the rights and duties of the emperors and subjects, of the great and small vassals. [125] Thus Constantinople, under the dominion of the Greeks, beheld before its walls a small band of warriors, who, helm on head, and sword in hand, abolished in her walls the legislation of Greece, and imposed upon her beforehand the laws of the West. By this act of legislation, which they derived from Europe, the knights and barons appeared to take possession of the empire; and, whilst making war against the inhabitants of Constantinople, might imagine that they were already fighting for the safety and glory of their own country.

In the first siege of Byzantium, the French had been desirous of attacking the city by land, but experience had taught them to appreciate properly the wiser counsels of the Venetians. They determined, with an unanimous voice, to direct all their efforts to an attack by sea. They conveyed into the vessels the arms, provisions, and appointments of all kinds; and the whole army embarked on Thursday, the 8th day of April, 1204. On the morrow, with the first rays of the sun, the fleet which bore the knights and their horses, the pilgrims and all they possessed, the tents, the machines of the Crusaders, *and the destinies of a great empire,* heaved anchor, and crossed the breadth of the gulf. The ships and galleys, arranged in line, covered the sea for the space of half a league. The sight of the towers and ramparts, bristling with arms and soldiers, and covered with murderous machines and long tubes of brass, from which poured the Greek fire, did not in the least intimidate the warriors of the West. The Greeks had trembled with fright at seeing the fleet of the Crusaders in motion; but as they could look for no safety but in resistance, they appeared disposed to brave all perils in defence of their property and their families.

Mourzoufle had pitched his tents in the part of the city ravaged by the fire; his army was encamped amidst ruins, and his soldiers had nothing beneath their eyes but melancholy pictures, the sight of which he thought must necessarily excite them to vengeance. From the summit of one of the seven hills, the emperor was able to view the contest, to send succours where he saw they were wanted, and to reanimate at every moment the courage of those who defended the walls and towers.

At the first signal, the Greeks put all their machines in full operation, and endeavoured to defend the approach to the ramparts; but several ships soon gained the shore; the ladders are planted, and the walls shake beneath the continuous blows of the rams. The attack and defence proceed with equal fury. The Greeks fight with advantage from the tops of their elevated towers; the Crusaders, everywhere overpowered by numbers, cannot open themselves a passage, and find death at the foot of the ramparts they burn to surmount. The ardour for fight, itself, produced disorder among the assailants, and confusion in their fleet. The Latins faced all perils, and sustained the impetuous shock of the Greeks till the third hour of the evening: "It was then," says the marshal of Champagne, "that fortune and our sins decreed that we should be repulsed." The leaders, dreading the destruction of their fleet and army, ordered the retreat to be sounded. When the Greeks saw the Crusaders drawing off, they believed that their capital was saved; the people of Byzantium flocked to the churches to return thanks to Heaven for so great a victory, and, by the excess of their transports, proved how great the fear had been with which the Latins had inspired them.

On the evening of the same day, the doge and barons assembled in a church near the sea, to deliberate upon their future proceedings; they spoke with deep grief of the check they had sustained, and expatiated strongly upon the necessity of promptly retrieving their defeat. [126] "The Crusaders were still the same men that had already surmounted the ramparts of Byzantium; the Greeks were still the same frivolous, pusillanimous nation, that could oppose no other arms but those of cunning to those of valour. The soldiers of Mourzoufle had been able to resist for one day; but they would soon remember that the Latins had conquered them many times; the recollections of the past were sufficient to revive the confidence of the one party, and to fill the others with terror. Besides, it was well known that the Greeks only contended for the triumph of usurpation and parricide; whilst the Crusaders fought for the triumph of humanity and justice. God would recognise his true servants, and would protect his own cause."

These discourses could not reassure all the Crusaders, and many proposed to change the point of attack, and make a new assault on the side of the Propontis. The Venetians did not agree with this opinion, and dreaded lest the fleet should be drawn away by the currents of the sea. Some of the leaders despaired of the success of the enterprise; and, in their despair, would have been very willing, says an eyewitness, "that the winds and the waves should carry them away beyond the Archipelago." [127] The advice of the Venetians was, however, adopted; and the council decided that the attack upon Constantinople should be renewed on the same side, and at the same point at which the army had been repulsed. Two days were employed in repairing the vessels and machines; and on the third day, the 12th of April, the trumpets once more sounded the signal for battle. The fleet got into motion, and advanced in good order towards the ramparts of Constantinople. The Greeks, who were still rejoicing over their first advantage, could scarcely believe the approach of the Latins to be reality, and their surprise was by no means free from terror. On the other side, the Crusaders, who had met with a resistance they had not at all expected, advanced with precaution towards the ramparts, at the foot of which they had fought in vain. To inflame the ardour and emulation of the soldiers, the leaders of the Latins had proclaimed, by a herald-at-arms, that he that should plant the first banner of the cross upon a tower of the city, should receive a hundred and fifty silver marks.

The combat soon commenced, and was as quickly general; the defence was no less vigorous than the attack: beams, stones, javelins were hurled from one side to the other, crossed or met in mid-air, and fell with a loud noise on the ramparts and the ships; the whole shore resounded with the cries of the combatants and the clashing of swords and lances. In the fleet, the vessels were joined together, and proceeded two by two, in order that upon each point of attack, the number of the assailants might correspond with that of the besieged. The drawbridges are soon let down, and are covered with intrepid warriors, who threaten the invasion of the most lofty towers. The soldiers mount in file, and gain the battlements; the opponents seek, attack, and repulse each other in a thousand different places. Some, on the point of seizing victory, are overthrown by a mass of stone: others are consumed by the Greek fire; but they who are repulsed, again return to the charge, and the leaders everywhere set an example by mounting to the assault like common soldiers.

The sun had run half his course, and prodigies of valour had not been able to triumph over the resistance of the besieged, when a strong breeze from the north arose, and brought two ships that fought together close under the walls. The bishop of Troie and the bishop of Soissons were on board of these two vessels, called the *Pilgrim* and the *Paradise*. Scarcely were the drawbridges lowered, than two Frank warriors were seen upon one of the towers of the city. These two warriors, one of whom was a Frenchman, named D'Urboise, and the other a Venetian, Pietro Alberti, drew after them a crowd of their companions, and the Greeks were massacred or took to flight. In the confusion of the *mêlée*, the brave Alberti was slain by a Frenchman, who mistook him for a Greek, and who, on discovering his mistake, attempted to kill himself in despair. The Crusaders, excited by the fight, scarcely perceived this sad and tragical scene, but pursued the flying, disordered enemy.

The banners of the bishops of Troie and Soissons were planted on the top of the towers, and attracted the eager eyes of the whole army. This sight inflames those who are still on board the vessels; on all sides they press, they rush forward, they fly to the escalade. The Franks obtain possession of four towers: terror prevails among the Greeks, and the few who resist are slaughtered at every point they endeavour to defend; three of the gates of the city fall to pieces beneath the strokes of the rams; the horsemen issue from the ships with their horses, and the whole army of the Crusaders precipitates itself at once into the city. [128] A horseman (Pierre Bacheux), who preceded his fellows, advanced almost alone to the hill upon which Mourzoufle was encamped, and the Greeks, in their fright, took him for a giant. Nicetas himself says that his helmet appeared as large as a tower; the soldiers of the emperor could not stand against the appearance of a single Frank horseman. Mourzoufle, abandoned by his troops, fled: the Crusaders took possession of the imperial tents, continued their victorious course into the city, and put to the sword every Greek they met with. "*It was a horrible spectacle,*" says Villehardouin, "*to see women and young children running distractedly here and there, trembling and half dead with fright, lamenting piteously, and begging for mercy.*"

The Crusaders set fire to the quarter they had invaded, [129] and the flames, driven by the wind, announced to the other extremities of the city the presence of an irritated conqueror. Terror and despair prevailed in every street of Constantinople. Some Greek soldiers retired to the palace, whilst others, to escape recognition, threw away both their clothes and their arms. The people and the clergy took refuge in the churches, and the more wealthy inhabitants, in all parts, endeavoured to conceal their most valuable property by burying it in the earth. Many rushed out of the city, without at all knowing whither to direct their steps. [130]

Whilst all were flying before them, the Crusaders were in a state of astonishment at their own victory. At the approach of night, they dreaded an ambuscade, and did not venture to pursue the conquered enemy further; the Venetians encamped within sight of their vessels; the count of Flanders, by a happy augury, occupied the imperial tents, and the marquis of Montferrat advanced towards the palace of Blachernæ. The Latins entertained no idea that the conflict was ended, and kept careful watch under the ramparts they had invaded and won.

Mourzoufle went through many quarters of the city, endeavouring to rally the soldiers: he spoke to them of glory, he invoked the name of their country, he promised rich rewards for valour: but the voice of patriotism was no longer listened to, and neither the love of glory nor the hopes of reward could affect men whose whole thoughts were engaged in the means of saving their lives. Mourzoufle no longer inspired either respect or confidence, and the people, in reply to his exhortations, reproached him with his parricide, and attributed to him all the calamities of the war. When he found himself without hope, it became necessary to endeavour to escape both the pursuit of the conquerors and the resentment of the conquered, and he embarked secretly on the Propontis, with the purpose of seeking an army, or rather an asylum, in the mountains of Thrace. When his flight became known in Constantinople, his name was loaded with maledictions, and, as if it was necessary that an emperor should be present at the fall of the empire, a distracted crowd flocked to the church of St. Sophia, to choose a new master.

Theodore Ducas and Theodore Lascaris solicited the suffrages of the assembly, and contended for a throne that no longer existed. Lascaris was chosen emperor, but he did not dare to assume the imperial crown. This prince possessed both firmness and spirit; the Greeks even boasted of his skill in war, and he undertook to reanimate their courage and arouse their patriotism. "The Latins," said he, "are few, and advance with trembling caution into a city that has still numberless defenders; the Crusaders are afraid to leave their ships at any distance, as they know they are their only refuge in case of defeat: pressed by the approach of danger, they have called in the assistance of fire as their faithful auxiliary, and conceal their fears behind a rampart of flames and a heap of ruins. The warriors of the West neither fight for religion, nor their country, nor their property, nor the honour of their families. The Greeks, on the contrary, defend all they hold most dear, and must carry to the contest every sentiment that can increase the courage and inflame the zeal of citizens. If you are still Romans," added Lascaris, "the victory is easy; twenty thousand barbarians have shut themselves up within your walls; fortune has given them up to our arms." The new emperor then addressed the soldiers and the imperial guards; he represented to them that their safety was inseparably connected with that of Constantinople, that the enemy would never pardon being driven back by them several times from the ramparts of the capital; that in victory they would find all the advantages of fortune, all the pleasures of life: whilst in flight, neither land nor sea could afford them an asylum, and that shame, misery, and death itself would follow their footsteps everywhere. Lascaris did not neglect to flatter the pride, and endeavour to kindle the zeal of the patricians. He reminded them of the heroes of ancient Rome, and presented to their valour the great examples of history. "It was to their arms Providence had confided the safety of the imperial city; if, contrary to all hopes, the country should be subdued, they could have but few regrets in abandoning life, and would find perhaps some glory in dying on the same day on which the old empire of the Cæsars should be doomed to fall."

The soldiers only replied to his speech by demanding their pay; the people listened to Lascaris with more surprise than confidence, and the patricians preserved a gloomy silence, sensible to no other feeling but a profound despair. The trumpets of the Crusaders were soon heard, and at this signal, terror seized even the bravest; there was no longer any idea of disputing the victory with the Latins. Lascaris, left alone, was himself obliged to abandon a city which he could find no one to assist him in defending. Thus Constantinople, that had beheld two emperors in one night, was once again without a master, and presented the image of a vessel without a rudder, dashed about by the winds, and ready to perish amidst the howling of the tempest. The conflagration begun by the Latins, extended to several other quarters, and consumed, by the admission of the barons, more houses than three of the greatest cities of either France or Germany contained. The fire continued its ravages during the whole night, and before day the Crusaders prepared, by the light of its flames, to follow up their victory. Ranged in order of battle, they were advancing with precaution and mistrust, when their ears were saluted with supplicating voices that filled the air with lamentations and prayers. Women, children, and old men, preceded by the clergy, bearing crosses and images of saints, came in procession, to throw themselves at the feet of the conquerors. The leaders allowed their hearts to be touched by the cries and entreaties of this weeping crowd, and a herald-at-arms was ordered to pass through the ranks, and proclaim the laws of clemency; the soldiers were commanded to spare the lives of the inhabitants, and to respect the honour of women and maidens. The Latin clergy joined their exhortations with those of the leaders of the army, and threatened with the vengeance of the Church all who should abuse victory by outraging humanity.

In the mean time the Crusaders advanced amidst the braying of trumpets and the noise of clarions, and their banners were soon planted in the principal quarters of the city. When Boniface entered the palace of Bucoleon, which was supposed to be occupied by the imperial guard, he was surprised to find a great number of women, of the first families of the empire, whose only defence was their groans and tears. Marguerite, daughter of the king of Hungary, and wife of Isaac, and Agnes, daughter of a king of France, [131] the wife of two emperors, threw themselves at the feet of the barons, and implored their mercy. The marquis of Montferrat respected their misfortunes, and placed them under the protection of a guard. Whilst Boniface occupied the palace of Bucoleon, Henry of Hainault took possession of that of Blachernæ; these two palaces, filled with immense riches, were preserved from pillage, and were exempted from the lamentable scenes which, during several days, desolated the city of Constantinople. [132]

The Crusaders, impatient to gather the treasures they had shared beforehand, spread themselves through all the quarters of the capital, and carried off, without pity or consideration, everything that offered itself to their avidity. The houses of the poorest citizens were no more respected than the mansions of the rich. The Greeks, plundered of their property, ill-treated by the conquerors, and turned out of their homes, implored the humanity of the counts and barons, and pressed around the marquis of Montferrat, crying, *"Holy king marquis, have pity upon us!"* Boniface was touched by their prayers, and endeavoured to recall the Crusaders to some sentiments of moderation; but the license of the soldiers increased with the sight of booty; the most dissolute and most undisciplined gave the signal, and marched at their head, and their example led on all the rest: the intoxication of victory had no longer any restraint, — it was sensible to neither fear nor pity. [133]

When the Crusaders discontinued the slaughter, they had recourse to every kind of outrage and violence to plunder the conquered; no spot in Constantinople was free from brutal search. In spite of the frequently-repeated prohibitions of their leaders and priests, they respected neither the modesty of women nor the sanctity of churches. Some soldiers and followers of the army plundered the tombs and coffins of the emperors; the body of Justinian, which ages had spared, and which presented itself to their eyes in a fresh and undecayed state, could not repel their sacrilegious hands, or make them respect the peace of the grave; in every temple where a rag of silk shone, or a particle of gold glittered, their greedy fingers were stretched out to clutch them. The altar of the Virgin, which decorated the church of St. Sophia, and which was admired as a masterpiece of art, was beaten to pieces, and the veil of the sanctuary was torn to rags. The conquerors played at dice upon the marble tables which represented the apostles, and got drunk out of the cups reserved for divine service. Horses and mules led into the sanctuary, bent beneath the weight of the spoils, and, pierced by sword-points, stained with their blood and their ordure the vestibule of St. Sophia. A prostitute girl, whom Nicetas calls the follower of demons, the priestess of furies, mounted the patriarchal pulpit, sang an immodest song, and danced in the church, amidst a crowd of soldiers, as if to insult the ceremonies of religion.

The Greeks could not behold these impious scenes without trembling with horror. Nicetas, whilst deploring the misfortunes of the empire and the Greek Church, declaims with vehemence against the barbarous race of the Franks. "Here," says he, "is what was promised by that golden gorget, that haughty bearing, those elevated eyebrows, that closely shaven beard, that hand so ready to shed blood, those nostrils breathing anger, that proud eye, that cruel disposition, that prompt and hurried utterance." [134] The historian of Byzantium reproaches the Crusaders with having surpassed the Saracens in barbarity, and reminds them of the example of the soldiers of Saladin, who, when masters of Jerusalem, neither violated the modesty of matrons and virgins, nor filled the sepulchre of the Saviour with bloody carcasses, nor subjected Christians to fire, sword, hunger, or nakedness.

The country on the shores of the Bosphorus offered a no less deplorable spectacle than the capital. Villages, churches, country-houses were all devastated and given over to pillage. A distracted crowd covered the roads, and wandered about at hazard, pursued by fear, bending under fatigue, and uttering cries of despair. Senators, patricians, the offspring of a family of emperors, strayed homeless about, covered with rags, seeking for any miserable asylum. When the church of St. Sophia was pillaged, the patriarch fled away, imploring the charity of passengers; all the rich fell into indigence, and inspired nothing but contempt; the most illustrious nobility, the highest dignities, the splendour of talents or virtues, possessed nothing to create respect or attract admiration. Misery, like inevitable death, effaced all distinctions, and confounded all ranks; the dregs of the people completed the spoliation of the fugitives, at the same time insulting their misfortunes. A senseless multitude rejoiced at the public evils, applauded the degradation of the noble and the rich, and called these disastrous days, days of justice and equality.

Nicetas describes his misfortune and his own deplorable adventures; the house he had inhabited under the reign of the emperors was consumed by the flames of the second conflagration: having retired with his family to another house, built near the church of St. Sophia, he soon found himself in danger in this last asylum, and only owed his safety to devoted friendship and gratitude. A Venetian merchant, whom he had saved from the fury of the Greeks before the flight of Alexius, was desirous, in his turn, of saving his benefactor; he armed himself with a sword and a lance, assumed the dress of a soldier of the cross, and as he spoke the languages of the West, he defended the entrance of the house of Nicetas, saying it was his, the price of his blood, shed in fight. This vigilant sentinel at first repulsed all aggressors, and braved a thousand perils; a model of fidelity and virtue, amidst the horrid disorders that desolated Constantinople.

The turbulent crowd of soldiers that filled the streets and penetrated everywhere, became indignant that a single house should be thus exempt from their brutal searches. The despairing Venetian at length came to Nicetas, and told him that it was totally out of his power to defend him any longer. "If you remain here," said he, "to-morrow, perhaps, you will be loaded with chains, and your family become a prey to all the violences of the conquerors. Follow me, and I will conduct you out of the gates of Constantinople." Nicetas, with his wife and children, followed the faithful Venetian: their liberator, in armour, marched at their head, and led them as if they were prisoners.

This unfortunate family proceeded, filled with fear, meeting at every step soldiers greedy of pillage, who ill-treated the Greeks they plundered, and threatened every woman with insult. Nicetas, and some of his friends who had come to join him, carried their children in their arms, the only wealth that Heaven had left them; and defended alone by the pity which their despair and misery inspired. They walked together, placing their wives and daughters in the centre, after having advised the youngest to blacken their faces with earth. In spite of this precaution, the beauty of one young girl attracted the attention of a soldier, and she was borne away from the arms of her father, weighed down by age and infirmities. Nicetas, touched by the tears of the old man, flew after the ravisher, and addressing himself to all the warriors he met, he implored their pity, and conjured them, in the name of Heaven, the protector of virtue, in the name of their own families, to snatch a daughter from dishonour, to save a father from despair. The Frank warriors were affected by his prayer, and the unfortunate father soon saw his daughter restored to him, the only hope of his exile, the last consolation of his grey hairs. Nicetas and his companions in trouble encountered still further dangers, but at length got safely out of Constantinople by the Golden

Gate, happy at being able to quit a country so lately the object of all their affections. The generous Venetian received their blessings, and in return prayed Heaven to protect them in their exile.

Nicetas, with tears, embraced his liberator, whom he never had the good fortune to see again; then casting a look upon Constantinople, upon his unhappy country, he addressed to it these touching complaints, which express the griefs of his exile, and which he himself has transmitted to us: [135] — "O Queen of Cities, what power has been able to separate us from thee! What consolation shall we find on issuing from thy walls, as naked as we issued from the bosom of our mothers! Become the sport of strangers, the companions of wild animals that inhabit the forests, we shall never again visit thy august domes, and can only fly with terror around thee, like sparrows round the spot where their nest has been destroyed."

Nicetas arrived with his family at Cylindria, and afterwards retired to Nice, where he employed himself in retracing the history of the misfortunes of his country.

Constantinople did not cease to be the theatre of the frightful deeds of violence that war brings in its train. Amidst the sanguinary sports of victory, the Latins, to insult the effeminate manners of the Greeks, clothed themselves in long flowing robes, painted of various colours; they fastened to the heads of their horses linen hoods with their silken cords, in which the Orientals dress themselves; whilst others paraded the streets carrying in their hands, instead of a sword, some paper and an ink-horn; thus ridiculing the conquered, whom they termed scribes and copyers.

The Greeks had on all occasions insulted the ignorance of the Latins; the knights, without seeking to retort upon the quiet occupations of peace. With these dispositions it was not likely they should spare the monuments that decorated the public places, the palaces, or the edifices of Byzantium. Constantinople, which to this period had stood erect amidst the ruins of several empires, had collected within its walls the scattered relics of the arts, and was proud to exhibit the masterpieces that had been saved from the destruction of barbarous ages. The bronze, in which breathed the genius of antiquity, was cast into the furnace, and converted into money, to satisfy the greedy soldiers. The heroes and gods of the Nile, those of ancient Greece and of ancient Rome, the masterpieces of Praxiteles, Phidias, and the most celebrated artists, fell beneath the strokes of the conquerors.

Nicetas, who deplores the loss of these monuments, has left us a description, from which the history of art may derive some advantage. [136] The historian of Byzantium informs us that in the Place of Constantine stood, before the siege, the statue of Juno, and that of Paris offering to Venus the prize of beauty, or the apple of discord. The statue of Juno, which had formerly adorned the temple of the goddess at Samos, was of so colossal a size, that when it was destroyed by the Crusaders, eight harnessed oxen were required to drag the gigantic head to the palace of Bucoleon. In the same place was erected an obelisk of a square form, which astonished the spectator by the multitude and variety of the objects it presented to his view. On the sides of this obelisk the artist had represented, in basso-relievo, all sorts of birds saluting the return of the sun, villagers employed in their rustic labours, shepherds playing on their pipes, sheep bleating, lambs bounding on the grass; further on, a tranquil sea and fishes of a thousand sorts, some taken alive, others breaking the nets and regaining their deep retreats; at the back of the landscape, naked cupids playing and throwing apples at each other; at the top of the obelisk, which terminated in a pyramidal form, was the figure of a woman that turned with the least breath of air, which was called *the attendant of the winds.*

An equestrian statue [137] ornamented the place of Mount Taurus; the horse appeared to throw up the dust with his feet, and outspeed the winds in his course. As the horseman had his arm extended towards the sun, some supposed it to represent Joshua, commanding the star of day to stand still, on the plains of Gabaon; others believed the artist meant to describe Bellerophon mounted on Pegasus. [138]

A colossal statue of Hercules, [139] attributed to Lysippus, was one of the ornaments of the Hippodrome; the demigod had neither his bow nor his club; he was seated on a bed of osier; [140] his left knee bent, sustained his elbow; his head reclining on his left hand; his pensive looks and air expressing the vexation and sorrow caused by the jealousy of Eurystheus. The shoulders and chest of Hercules were broad, his hair was curled, and his limbs were large and muscular; his leg alone exceeded in height the stature of an ordinary man. The skin of the Nemean lion, exhibited over the shoulders of the son of Alcmena, the erected mane and the head of the animal, which might be fancied still to roar and terrify the passers by, who stopped to contemplate the statue.

Not far from the terrible Hercules, was a group of an ass and its driver, which Augustus placed in his colony of Nicopolis, to perpetuate the remembrance of a singular circumstance that had foretold the victory of Actium to him. Near this were the hyena or she-wolf that suckled Romulus and Remus, a monument from the old nations of the West; [141] the sphinx, with the face of a woman, dragging frightful animals behind her; the crocodile, an inhabitant of the Nile, with his tail covered with horrible scales; a man fighting with a lion; an elephant with his supple trunk; and the antique Scylla, showing before, the features of a woman, with large breasts and a deformed figure; and behind, such monsters as those that pursued Ulysses and his companions. In the same place was an eagle clutching a serpent in his talons, and bearing it away towards the azure vault; the bronze beautifully exhibited the pain of the reptile, and the haughty fierceness of the bird of Jupiter. When the sun shone on the horizon, the extended wings of the king of the air denoted, by lines skilfully traced, the twelve hours of the day.

All who, in that gross age, preserved any taste for the arts, admired the figure of a young woman, her hair plaited on her brow, and gathered into a knot behind, placed upon a column of the Circus; this young woman, as if by enchantment, bore in her right hand a horseman, whose horse she held by one foot; the horseman covered with his cuirass, and the spirited, neighing steed, seemed listening to the warlike trumpet, and to breathe nothing but eagerness for the fight. Near the eastern boundary of the Circus were represented in bronze, the charioteers who had gained prizes, and whose triumphs, in times gone by, had often divided the empire into two factions; they appeared standing in their chariots, running in the lists, pulling and loosening by turns the reins of their coursers, and encouraging them by gesture and voice. Not far from this, upon a basis of stone, were several Egyptian animals, the aspic, the basilisk, and the crocodile, all engaged in mortal combat,—an image of the war made by the wicked on each other; the hideous forms of these animals, the rage and pain expressed throughout their bodies, the livid poison which seemed to exhale with their bites, altogether inspired a feeling of disgust and terror. Another masterpiece, made to charm the sight, ought, at least, to have touched and disarmed the conquerors. Among the statues described by Nicetas, none is more conspicuous than a Helen with her charming smile and her voluptuous attitude; a Helen, with perfect regularity of features, her hair floating at the pleasure of the winds, her eyes full of languor, her lips, which even in the bronze were rosy; her arms, of which even the same bronze showed the whiteness; Helen, in short, with all her beauty, and such as she appeared before the old men of Ilium, who were ravished at her presence.

Constantinople contained many other splendid objects of art, which preceding ages had admired; almost all such as were of bronze were condemned to perish, the Crusaders seeing in these monuments nothing but the metal of which they were composed. "That which antiquity had judged," says Nicetas, "of inestimable value, became, all at once, a common matter; and that which had cost immense sums, was changed by the Latins into pieces of coin of very little value!" The statues of marble held out less temptation for the cupidity of the conquerors, and received no other injuries than such as were inseparable from the tumult and disorders of war.

The Greeks, who appeared so proud of their knowledge, themselves neglected the fine arts. The sciences of Greece, the profane wisdom of the Academy and the Lyceum, had given place among them to the debates of scholastic theology, they passed by the Hippodrome with indifference, and held nothing in reverence but relics and images of saints. These religious treasures, preserved with care in the churches and palaces of Byzantium, had, during several ages, attracted the attention of the Christian world; in the days that followed the conquest, they tempted the pious cupidity of the Crusaders. Whilst the greater part of the warriors bore away the gold, the jewels, the carpets, and the rich stuffs of the East, the more devout of the pilgrims, particularly the ecclesiastics, collected a booty much more innocent and appropriate to the soldiers of Christ. Many braved the prohibitions of their leaders and their superiors, and did not disdain to employ by turns supplications and menaces, stratagem or violence, to procure relics that were the objects of their respect and veneration. Contemporary history relates several examples of this, which serve to make us acquainted with the spirit of the pilgrim conquerors of Byzantium. Martin Litz, abbot of Paris, in the diocese of Bâle, entered into a church that had been given up to pillage, and penetrated, without being observed, into a retired place, where numerous relics were deposited, under the guardianship of a Greek monk. [142] This Greek monk was then at prayers, with his hands raised supplicatingly towards heaven. His old age, his white hairs, his fervent piety, and the grief impressed upon his brow, were calculated to inspire both respect and pity; but Martin, approaching the venerable guardian of the treasures with an angry manner, exclaimed in a threatening tone, "Miserable old man, if thou dost not instantly conduct me to the place where thy relics are hidden, prepare to die on the spot!" The monk, terrified by this menace, immediately and tremblingly arose, and pointed to a large iron coffer, into which the pious abbot eagerly plunged both his hands, and seized everything precious that he could grasp. Delighted with this conquest, he ran to conceal his treasures on board a vessel, and contrived, by a holy fraud, to keep them for several days from the knowledge of the leaders and prelates of the army, who had strictly ordered the pilgrims to bring to an appointed place all the relics that fell into their hands.

Martin Litz, at first, returned to the Christians of Palestine, who had sent him to Constantinople; and, a short time after, came back to Europe, loaded with spoils obtained from the clergy of Byzantium. Among the relics he exhibited on his return, were, a piece of the true cross, the bones of St. John the Baptist, and an arm of St. James. The miraculous translation of this treasure is celebrated with much pomp by the monk Gunther, in whom it created more surprise and joy than the conquest of a great empire.

If we may credit the account of the German monk, angels descended from heaven to watch over the relics of Martin Litz. On the route of the holy abbot, the tempests of the ocean were silent, pirates were struck motionless, and robbers, those pests of travellers, stopped short, seized with respect and fear. At length Martin Litz was received in triumph at Bâle, and the treasures he had preserved through so many perils, were distributed among the principal churches of the diocese.

Another priest, named Galon de Dampierre, of the diocese of Langres, less adroit or less fortunate than Martin Litz, had not been able to obtain any share of the spoils of the churches; he went and threw himself at the feet of the pope's legate, and implored him, with tears in his eyes, to permit him to carry back to his country the head of St. Mames. A third ecclesiastic of Picardy, having found the head of St. George, and the head of St. John the Baptist, concealed among the ruins, hastened to quit Constantinople, and, laden with such a rich prize, presented to the cathedral of Amiens, his country, the inestimable relics of which Providence had made him the possessor.

The princes and barons did not despise these holy spoils. Dandolo, receiving as his share [143] a piece of the true cross, which the emperor Constantine was accustomed to have borne before him to battle, made a present of it to the republic of Venice. Baldwin kept for himself the crown of thorns of Christ, and several other relics found in the palace of Bucoleon. He sent Philip Augustus, king of France, a portion of the true cross, a foot in length; some of the hair of Jesus Christ, when an infant; and the linen in which the Man-God was enveloped in the stable in which he was born.

The Greek priests and monks, thus plundered by the conquerors, parted with tears from the remains of the saints that had been confided to their keeping, and which every day cured the sick, made the lame to walk, restored sight to the blind, and strength to the paralytic. These holy spoils, that the devotion of the faithful had gathered together from all the countries of the East, went to illustrate the churches of France and Italy, and were received by the Christians of the West as the most glorious trophies of the victories God had enabled the Crusaders to obtain.

Constantinople fell into the power of the Latins on the 10th of April, towards the end of Lent. The marshal of Champagne, after relating some of the scenes we have described, says with great simplicity, "Thus passed the splendid festivities of Easter." The clergy called the Crusaders to penitence; the voice of religion made itself heard in hearts hardened by victory; the soldiers crowded to the churches they had devastated, and celebrated the sufferings and death of Christ upon the wrecks of his own altars.

This solemn epoch without doubt inspired some generous sentiments; all the Latins were not deaf to the language of the charity of the Gospel. We feel bound here to admit that the greater part of the knights and ecclesiastics protected the liberty and lives of the citizens, and the honour of matrons and virgins; but such was the spirit that then possessed the warriors, that all the Crusaders allowed themselves to be overcome by the thirst for booty; and the leaders, equally with the soldiers, exercised, without hesitation or scruple, the right which their victory had given them of plundering the conquered. It was agreed that all the spoils should be deposited in three churches, selected for the purpose; and the leaders commanded the Crusaders to bring, in common, the whole of the booty, and threatened with death and excommunication all who should abstract anything from the prize of the valour, and the recompense due to the labours of the whole army. Many soldiers, and even some knights, allowed themselves to be led away by avarice, and retained valuable objects that fell into their hands. "Which," says the marshal of Champagne, "made the Lord to begin to love them less." The justice of the counts and barons was inflexible towards the guilty; the count of St. Pol ordered one of his knights, who had withheld something from the common stock of booty, to be hung, with his escutcheon suspended from his neck. [144] Thus the Greeks, plundered by violence, might be present at the punishment of some of the ravishers of their property, and might contemplate with surprise the regulations of stern equity mingled with the disorders of victory and pillage. After the festival of Easter, the Crusaders shared the captured riches; the fourth part of the spoil was set aside for him who should be chosen emperor, and the rest was divided among the French and the Venetians. The French Crusaders, who had conquered Zara, to the sole advantage of the Venetians, were not the less called upon to pay the fifty thousand silver marks they owed to the republic; the amount was deducted beforehand from the portion of the booty that belonged to them. In the division that was made among the warriors of Lombardy, Germany, and France, each knight had a part equal to that of two horsemen, and every horseman one equal to that of two foot-soldiers. All the plunder of the Greeks only yielded [145] four hundred thousand silver marks; but although this sum far exceeded the revenues of all the kingdoms of the West, it did not by any means represent the value of the riches accumulated in Byzantium. If the princes and barons, upon making themselves masters of the city, had been satisfied with imposing a tribute upon the inhabitants, they might have received a much larger sum; but this pacific manner of obtaining wealth agreed neither with their character nor the humour they were in. History asserts that the Venetians, in this circumstance, offered them some very prudent advice, and made propositions that were rejected with scorn. The Frank warriors could not condescend to submit the advantages of victory to commercial calculations; the produce of pillage was always, in their eyes, the most worthy fruit of conquest, and the most noble reward of valour.

When they had thus shared the rich plunder of the Eastern empire, the Crusaders gave way to the most extravagant joy, without perceiving that they had committed a great fault in exhausting a country which was about to become their own; they did not reflect that the ruin of the conquered might one day bring on that of the conquerors, and that they might become as poor as the Greeks they had just despoiled. Without regrets, as without foresight, hoping everything from their own good swords, they set about electing a leader who should reign over a people in mourning and a desolated city. The imperial purple had still the same splendour in their eyes, and the throne, though shaken by their arms, was still the object of their ambition. Six electors were chosen from among the Venetian nobles, and six others from among the French ecclesiastics, to give a master to Constantinople; the twelve electors assembled in the palace of Bucoleon, and swore, upon the Gospel, to crown only merit and virtue.

Three of the principal leaders of the crusade had equal claims to the suffrages of the electors. If the purple was to be the reward of experience, of ability in council, and of services rendered to the cause of the Latins, Henry Dandolo, who had been the moving spirit, the very soul of the enterprise, certainly had the first claim to it. The marquis of Montferrat, likewise, had titles worthy of great consideration; the Latins had chosen him for their leader, and the Greeks already acknowledged him as their master. His bravery, proved in a thousand fights, promised a firm and generous support to a throne that must rise from amidst ruins. His prudence and moderation might give the Latins and the people of Greece reason to hope that, when once raised to empire, he would repair the evils of war. The claims of Baldwin to the imperial crown were not less cogent than those of his concurrents. The count of Flanders was related to the most powerful monarchs of the West, and was descended, in the female line, from Charlemagne. He was much beloved by his soldiers, whose dangers he was always ready to share; he had deservedly obtained the esteem of the Greeks, who, even amidst the disorders of conquest, celebrated him as the champion of chastity and honour. Baldwin was the protector of the weak, the friend of the poor; he loved justice, and had no dread of truth. His youth, which he had already illustrated by brilliant exploits and solid virtues, gave the subjects of the new empire hopes of a long and happy reign; the rank he held among the warriors, his piety, his intelligence, his love of study and learned men, rendered him worthy of ascending the throne of Augustus and Constantine.

The electors at first turned their attention towards the venerable Dandolo; but the republicans of Venice trembled at the idea of seeing an emperor among their fellow-citizens: "What shall we not have to dread," said they, "from a Venetian, become master of Greece, and of part of the East? Shall we be subject to his laws, or will he remain subject to the laws of our country? Under his reign, and under that of his successors, who will assure us that Venice, the Queen of the Seas, will not become one of the cities of this empire?" The Venetians, whilst speaking thus, bestowed just eulogiums upon the virtue and character of Dandolo: they added, that their doge, who was approaching the end of a life filled with great actions, had nothing left him but to finish his days with glory, and that he himself would find it more glorious to be the head of a victorious republic, than the sovereign of a conquered nation. "What Roman," cried they, "would have been willing to lay down the title of citizen of Rome, to become king of Carthage?"

On terminating their speeches, the Venetians conjured the assembly to elect an emperor from among the other leaders of the army. After this, the choice of the electors could only be directed towards the count of Flanders and the marquis of Montferrat; the most wise dreading that the one of the two concurrents who should not obtain the empire, would be sure to give vent to his dissatisfaction, and would desire the fall of the throne occupied by his rival. They still remembered the violent debates which, in the first crusade, had followed the election of Godfrey of Bouillon; and the troubles excited in the young kingdom of Jerusalem, by the jealous ambition of Raymond de St. Gilles. To prevent the effects of such a fatal discord, it was judged best to decree, at once, that the prince that should gain the suffrages for the imperial throne, should yield to the other, under the condition of fealty and homage, the property of the island of Candia, and all the lands of the empire situated on the other side of the Bosphorus. After this decision, the assembly turned their whole attention to the election of an emperor. Their choice was for a long time uncertain. The marquis of Montferrat at first appeared to have the majority of the suffrages; but the Venetians were fearful of seeing upon the throne of Constantinople a prince who had any possessions in the neighbourhood of their territories, and represented to the assembly that the election of Baldwin would be much more advantageous to the Crusaders, particularly as it would interest the warlike nations of the Flemings and French in the glory and support of the new empire. The interests and jealousies of policy, and, without doubt, also wisdom and equity, at length united all voices in favour of the count of Flanders.

The Crusaders, assembled before the palace of Bucoleon, awaited with impatience the decision of the electors. At the hour of midnight, the bishop of Soissons came forward under the vestibule, and pronounced, in a loud voice, these words: "This hour of the night, which witnessed the birth of a Saviour of the world, gives birth to a new empire, under the protection of the Omnipotent. You have for emperor, Baldwin, count of Flanders and Hainault." Loud cries of joy arose from among the Venetians and the French. The people of Constantinople, who had so often changed masters, received, without repugnance, the new one just given to them, and mingled their acclamations with those of the Latins. Baldwin was elevated upon a buckler, and borne in triumph to the church of St. Sophia. The marquis of Montferrat followed in the train of his rival; the generous submission, of which he presented an example, was much admired by his companions in arms, and his presence drew scarcely less attention than the warlike pomp that surrounded the new emperor.

The ceremony of the coronation was postponed till the fourth Sunday after Easter. In the mean time the marriage of the marquis of Montferrat with Margaret of Hungary, the widow of Isaac, was celebrated with much splendour. Constantinople beheld within its walls the festivities and spectacles of the West, and, for the first time, the Greeks heard in their churches the prayers and hymns of the Latins. On the day appointed for the coronation of the emperor, Baldwin repaired to St. Sophia, accompanied by the barons and the clergy. Whilst divine service was being performed, the emperor ascended a throne of gold, and received the purple from the hands of the pope's legate, who performed the functions of patriarch. Two knights carried before him the *laticlavici tunica* of the Roman consuls, and the imperial sword, once again in the hands of warriors and heroes. The head of the clergy, standing before the altar, pronounced, in the Greek language, these words: *"He is worthy of reigning;"* and all persons present repeated in chorus, *"he is worthy! he is worthy!"* The Crusaders shouting their boisterous acclamations, the knights clad in armour, the crowd of miserable Greeks, the sanctuary despoiled of its ancient ornaments, and decked with foreign pomp, presented altogether a spectacle solemn and melancholy—all the evils of war amidst the trophies of victory. Surrounded by the ruins of an empire, reflective spectators could not fail to remark among the ceremonies of this day, that in which, according to the custom of the Greeks, were presented to Baldwin a little vase filled with dust and bones, and a lock of lighted flax, [146] as symbols of the shortness of life and the nothingness of human grandeur.

Before the ceremony of his coronation, the new emperor distributed the principal dignities of the empire among his companions in arms. Villehardouin, marshal of Champagne, obtained the title of marshal of Romania; the count de St. Pol, the dignity of constable; the charges of master of the wardrobe, great cupbearer and butler, were given to Canon de Bethune, Macaire de St. Ménéhoult, and Miles de Brabant. The doge of Venice, created despot or prince of Romania, had the right of wearing purple buskins, a privilege, among the Greeks, reserved for members of the imperial family. Henry Dandolo represented the republic of Venice at Constantinople; half the city was under his dominion and recognised his laws; he raised himself, by the dignity of his character as well as by his exploits, above all the princes and all the nobles of the court of Baldwin; he alone was exempt from paying fealty and homage to the emperor for the lands he was to possess.

The barons began to be impatient to share the cities and provinces of the empire. In a council composed of twelve of the patricians of Venice and twelve French knights, all the conquered lands were divided between the two nations. Bithynia, Romania or Thrace, Thessalonica, all Greece from Thermopylæ to Cape Sunium, with the larger isles of the Archipelago, fell to the share and under the dominion of the French. The Venetians obtained the Cyclades and the Sporades, in the Archipelago; the isles and the oriental coast of the Adriatic Gulf; the coasts of the Propontis and the Euxine Sea; the banks of the Hebrus and the Vardas; the cities of Cypsedes, Didymatica, and Adrianople; the maritime countries of Thessalonica, &c. &c. Such was at first the distribution of the territories of the empire. But circumstances that could not be foreseen, the diversity of interests, the rivalries of ambition, all the chances of fortune and of war, soon produced great changes in this division of dominions. History would in vain endeavour to follow the conquerors into the provinces allotted to them; it would be more easy to mark the banks of an overflowing torrent, or to trace the path of the storm, than to fix the state of the uncertain and transitory possessions of the conquerors of Byzantium.

The lands situated beyond the Bosphorus were erected into a kingdom, and, with the island of Candia, given to the marquis of Montferrat. Boniface exchanged them for the province of Thessalonica, and sold the island of Candia to the republic of Venice for thirty pounds weight of gold. The provinces of Asia were abandoned to the count of Blois, who assumed the title of duke of Nice and Bithynia. In the distribution of the cities and lands of the empire, every one of the lords and barons had obtained domains proportionate with the rank and services of the new possessor. When they heard speak of so many countries of which they scarcely knew the names, the warriors of the West were astonished at their conquests, and believed that the greater part of the universe was promised to their ambition. In the intoxication of their joy, they declared themselves masters of all the provinces that had formed the empire of Constantine. They cast lots for the countries of the Medes and Parthians, and the kingdoms that were under the domination of the Turks and Saracens; [147] several barons expressed a great desire to reign at Alexandria; others disputed for the palace of the sultans of Iconium; some knights exchanged that which had been assigned to them for new possessions, whilst others complained of their share, and demanded an augmentation of territory. With the money which arose from the plunder of the capital, the conquerors purchased the provinces of the empire; they sold, they played at dice, for whole cities and their inhabitants. Constantinople was during several days a market, in which seas and their islands, nations and their wealth, were trafficked for; in which the Roman world was put up to sale, and found purchasers among the obscure crowd of the Crusaders.

Whilst the barons were thus distributing cities and kingdoms, the ambition of the Latin clergy was by no means idle, but was busy in invading the property of the Greek Church. All the churches of Constantinople were divided between the French and the Venetians; they named priests of the two nations, to minister in the temples torn from the conquered; and no other religious ceremonies were celebrated within the walls of the city but those of the West. The leaders of the crusade had agreed among themselves, that if the emperor of Constantinople should be chosen from the French, the patriarch should be a Venetian. According to this convention, which had preceded the conquest, Thomas Morosini [148] was elevated to the chair of St. Sophia; priests and Latin bishops were, at the same time, sent into the other conquered cities, and took possession of the wealth and the privileges of the Greek clergy. Thus the Romish worship associated itself with the victories of the Crusaders, and made its empire acknowledged wherever the banners of the conquerors floated.

Nothing now opposed the arms of the Crusaders; all trembled before them; fame wafted everywhere the accounts of their exploits and their power; but, on casting a glance into the future the leaders had great reason to fear that the retreat or death of their warriors would leave the empire they had founded destitute of defenders. The population, weakened and dispersed, were not sufficient for either the cultivation of the lands or the work of the cities. In this conjuncture, the counts and barons, who always expected with fear the judgments of the head of the Church, redoubled their submission to the sovereign pontiff, and sought his support, in the hope that the Holy See would bring the West to pronounce in their favour, and that at the voice of the father of the faithful, a great number of French, Italians, and Germans would come to people and defend the new empire.

After his coronation, Baldwin wrote to the pope, to announce to him the extraordinary victories by which it had pleased God to crown the zeal of the soldiers of the cross. The new emperor, who assumed the title of knight of the Holy See, recalled to the mind of the sovereign pontiff the perfidies and the long revolt of the Greeks. "We have brought under your laws," said he, "that city, which, in hatred for the Holy See, would scarcely hear the name of the prince of the apostles, and did not afford a single church to him who received from the Lord the supremacy over all churches." Baldwin, in his letter, invited the vicar of Jesus Christ to imitate the example of his predecessors, John, Agapetus, and Leo, who visited in person the Church of Byzantium. To complete the justification of the pilgrims who had made themselves masters of the Greek empire, the emperor invoked the testimony of all the Christians of the East. "When we entered into this capital," added he, "many inhabitants of the Holy Land, who were there, expressed greater joy than any others, and asserted aloud that we had rendered God a more agreeable service than if we had retaken Jerusalem."

The marquis of Montferrat at the same time addressed a letter to the sovereign pontiff, in which he protested his humble obedience to all the decisions of the Holy See. "As for me," said the king of Thessalonica, "who only took up the cross for the expiation of my sins, and not to obtain an opportunity of sinning with more license under the pretext of religion, I submit myself blindly to your will. If you judge that my presence in Romania may be useful, I will die there, contending against your enemies and those of Christ: if you think, on the contrary, I ought to abandon these rich countries, pay no regard to the wealth or dignities I possess there, I am ready to return to the West; for I am not willing to do anything that will draw upon me the anger of the sovereign judge."

The doge of Venice, who till that time had braved with so much haughtiness the threats and thunders of the Church, acknowledged the sovereign authority of the pope, and joined his protestations with those of Baldwin and Boniface. To disarm the anger of Innocent, they represented to him that the conquest of Constantinople had prepared the deliverance of Jerusalem, and boasted of the wealth of a country which the Crusaders had at length brought under the laws of the Holy See. In all their letters to the pope or the faithful of the West, the conquerors of Byzantium spoke of the Greek empire as of a new land of promise, which awaited the servants of God and the soldiers of Christ.

Innocent had been for a long time irritated by the disobedience of the Crusaders; in his reply, he reproached with bitterness the victorious army of the Latins for having preferred the riches of the earth to those of heaven; [149] he reprimanded the leaders for having exposed to the outrages of the soldiers and followers of the army, the honour of matrons and maidens, and virgins consecrated to the Lord; for having ruined Constantinople, plundered *both great and small,* violated the sanctuary, and put forth a sacrilegious hand upon the treasures of the churches. Nevertheless, the father of the faithful would not take upon him to fathom the judgments of God; he was satisfied to believe that the Greeks had been justly punished for their faults, and that the Crusaders were recompensed as the instruments of Providence, as the avengers of divine justice. "Dread," said he, "the anger of the Lord; hope with fear that he will pardon the past, if you govern the nations with equity; if you are faithful to the Holy See, and, above everything, if you entertain a firm resolution to accomplish your vow for the deliverance of the Holy Land."

Notwithstanding this outward show of anger, the sovereign pontiff was gratified to the depths of his heart by the prayers and submission of the heroes and princes whose exploits made the Eastern world tremble. Cardinal Peter of Capua had given absolution to the Venetians excommunicated after the siege of Zara. Innocent at first blamed the indulgence of his legate, but finished by confirming the pardon granted to Dandolo and his compatriots. The pope approved the election of Baldwin, who took the title of knight of the Holy See, and consented to recognise an empire to which he was to give laws. The more submissive the Crusaders showed themselves to his authority, the more plainly it appeared to him that their conquests must concern the glory of God and that of the vicar of Christ upon earth. He wrote to the bishops of France, that God had been willing to console the Church by the conversion of heretics; that Providence had humbled the Greeks, an impious, proud, and rebellious people; and again placed the empire in the hands of the Latins, a pious, humble, and submissive nation. The sovereign pontiff invited, in the name of the emperor Baldwin, the French of both sexes and all conditions, to repair to Greece to receive lands and riches proportioned to their merit and their quality. He promised the indulgences of the crusade to all the faithful, who, sharing the glory of the Crusaders, should go to defend and promote the prosperity of the new empire of the East.

The pope did not, however, lose sight of the Syrian expedition, and appeared persuaded that succours sent to Constantinople must contribute to the deliverance of the holy places. The king of Jerusalem implored more earnestly than ever, both by letters and ambassadors, the effective protection of the Holy See, as well as that of the princes of the East.

The new emperor of Byzantium did not renounce the hope of assisting the Christian colonies of Syria; and to raise the courage of his brethren of the Holy Land, he sent to Ptolemaïs the chain of the port and the gates of Constantinople. When these trophies reached Palestine, scarcity, famine, and all the evils of an unfortunate war ravaged both cities and plains. At the news of approaching aid, the people of Ptolemaïs passed at once from excessive grief and despondency to all the transports of joy. Fame, whilst publishing the miraculous conquests of the companions of Baldwin and Boniface, carried the hope of safety into all the Christian cities of Syria, and spread terror among the Mussulmans. The sultan of Damascus had recently concluded a truce with the Christians, and trembled lest it should be broken, when, all at once, he owed his safety to the very event that had caused his alarms.

The greater part of the defenders of the Holy Land, who had experienced nothing but the evils of war, became desirous of partaking of the glory and the good fortune of the French and Venetians. They even who had quitted the victorious army at Zara, who had so severely blamed the expedition to Constantinople, believed that the will of God called them to the shores of the Bosphorus, and they abandoned the Holy Land. The legate of the pope, Peter of Capua, was drawn away by the example of the other Crusaders, and went to animate with his presence the zeal of the Latin clergy, who were labouring for the conversion of the Greeks; the knights of St. John and the Temple also directed their course towards Greece, where glory and rich domains were the reward of valour; and the king of Jerusalem was left almost alone at Ptolemaïs, without means of making the truce he had entered into with the infidels respected.

Baldwin warmly welcomed the defenders of the Holy Land; but the joy he experienced at their arrival was much troubled by the intelligence of the death of his wife, Marguerite of Flanders. This princess had embarked in the fleet of John de Nesle, in the belief that she should meet her husband in Palestine; sinking under the fatigue of a long voyage, and perhaps the pains of disappointment, she fell sick at Ptolemaïs, and died at the moment she learnt that Baldwin had been crowned emperor of Constantinople. The vessel destined to convey the new empress to the shores of the Bosphorus only brought back her mortal remains. Baldwin, amidst his knights, wept for the loss of a princess he had loved tenderly, and who, by her virtues and the graces of her youth, he had hoped would be the ornament and example of the court of Byzantium. He caused her to be buried with great pomp in the same church in which, but a few days before, he had received the imperial crown. Thus the people of Constantinople witnessed, almost at the same time, the coronation of an emperor and the funeral of an empress;— days of joy and triumph mingled with days of mourning. This contrast of the pageantry of death and the pomps of victory and of a throne, appeared to offer a faithful image of the glory of conquerors, and the future destiny of the empire.

The emperor and his barons, with all the succours they had received from the East, had scarcely twenty thousand men to defend their conquests and restrain the people of the capital and the provinces. The sultan of Iconium and the king of the Bulgarians had long threatened to invade the lands contiguous to their states, and they thought that the dissensions and subsequent fall of the Greek empire presented a favourable opportunity for the outbreak of their jealousy and ambition. The nations of Greece were conquered without being subdued. As in the disorder which accompanied the conquest of Byzantium, no other right had been acknowledged but that of force and the sword, all the Greeks, who had still arms in their hands, were desirous of forming a principality or a kingdom. On all sides new states and empires sprang up from the bosom of the ruins, and already threatened that which the Crusaders had so recently established.

A grandson of Andronicus founded in a Greek province of Asia Minor the principality of Trebizonde; Leo Sgurre, master of the little city of Napoli, had extended his dominions by injustice and violence, and, to employ a comparison offered by Nicetas, he had grown greater, like the torrent that swells in the storm and is enlarged by the waters of the tempest. A barbarous conqueror, a fierce and cruel tyrant, he reigned, or rather he spread terror, over Argos and the isthmus of Corinth. Michael-Angelus Comnenus, employing the arms of treachery, gained the kingdom of Epirus, and subdued to his laws a wild and warlike people. Theodore Lascaris, who, like Æneas, had fled from his burning country, collected some troops in Bithynia, and caused himself to be proclaimed emperor at Nice, whence his family was destined at a future day to return in triumph to Constantinople.

If despair had imparted any degree of courage to the two fugitive emperors, they might have obtained a share of their own spoils, and preserved a remnant of power; but they had not profited by the lessons of misfortune. Mourzoufle, who had completed all the crimes begun by Alexius, did not hesitate to place himself in the power of his unfortunate rival, whose daughter he had married: the wicked sometimes take upon themselves the duty of punishing one another. Alexius, after having loaded Mourzoufle with caresses, inveigled him into his house, and caused his eyes to be put out. In this condition, Mourzoufle, abandoned by his followers, for whom he was now nothing but an object of disgust, went to conceal his existence and his misery in Asia; but on his road fell into the hands of the Latins. Being led to Constantinople, and condemned to expiate his crimes by an ignominious death, he was precipitated from the top of a column raised by the emperor Theodosius in the Place of Taurus. The multitude of Greeks that had offered the purple to Mourzoufle were present at his tragical end, and appeared terrified at a punishment that was much more new to them than the crimes for which it was inflicted. After the execution, the crowd contemplated with surprise a basso-relievo on the column of Theodosius, [150] which represented a king falling from a very elevated place, and a city stormed by sea. In these times of troubles and calamities, presages were discovered everywhere. Everything, even to marble and stone, appeared to have told of the misfortunes of Constantinople. Nicetas was astonished that such great misfortunes had not been announced by a shower of blood, or some sinister prodigies; the most enlightened Greeks explained the fall of the empire of Constantine by the verses of poets and sibyls, or by the prophecies of the Scriptures; the common people read the death of tyrants and their own miseries in the looks of statues, and upon the columns that remained standing in the capital.

The perfidy and cruelty of Alexius did not remain long unpunished; the usurper was obliged to wander from city to city, and, not unfrequently, to conceal the imperial purple under the garb of a mendicant. For a considerable time he only owed his safety to the contempt in which he was held by the conquerors. After having long strayed about in a state of destitution, he was given up to the marquis of Montferrat, who sent him a prisoner into Italy; escaping thence, he again passed into Asia, and found an asylum with the sultan of Iconium. Alexius could not be satisfied to live in peace in his retreat, but joined the Turks in an attack upon his son-in-law Lascaris, whom he could not pardon for having saved a wreck of the empire, and reigning over Bithynia. As the Turks were beaten, the fugitive prince fell at length into the hands of the emperor of Nice, who compelled him to retire to a monastery, where he died, forgotten by both Greeks and Latins.

Thus four emperors were immolated to ambition and vengeance:—a deplorable spectacle, and most worthy of pity! Amidst the convulsions and fall of an empire, we behold princes of the same family quarrelling for a phantom of authority, snatch from each other by turns both the sceptre and life, surpass the populace in fury, and leave them no crime, no parricide, to commit.

If we could believe Nicetas, Alexius was a model of mildness and moderation: he never made a woman put on mourning for her husband, he never caused a citizen to weep for the loss of his fortune. This eulogy of Nicetas throws a far greater light upon the nature of the government than upon the qualities of the monarch. If it be true that we ought to be thankful to despotism for every ill that it has not committed, we must not forget that Alexius only obtained the throne by infamous means; that he did not redeem his parricide by any public virtue; and that the crime of his usurpation gave birth to a thousand other crimes, brought about a horrible revolution, and caused the ruin of a nation. Nicetas treats Mourzoufle with much more severity; but some modern historians, dazzled by a few actions of bravery, have undertaken to justify a prince who sacrificed everything to his ambition. They have not hesitated to point out to us in a cruel, unscrupulous tyrant, a model and a martyr of the patriotic virtues, as if love of country was the same thing as a boundless love of power, and could possibly ally itself with treachery and parricide.

Whilst the Greek princes were thus making war against each other, and quarrelling for the wrecks of the empire, the French counts and barons quitted the capital to go and take possession of the cities and provinces that had fallen to their share. Many of them were obliged to conquer, sword in hand, the lands that had been assigned to them. The marquis of Montferrat set out on his march to visit the kingdom of Thessalonica, and receive the homage of his new subjects. The emperor Baldwin, followed by his brother Henry of Hainault, and a great number of knights, made a progress through Thrace and Romania, and everywhere on his passage, was saluted by the noisy acclamations of a people always more skilful in nattering their conquerors than in combating their enemies. When he arrived at Adrianople, where he was received in triumph, the new emperor announced his intention of pursuing his march as far as Thessalonica. This unexpected resolution surprised the marquis of Montferrat, who entertained the desire of going alone to his own kingdom. Boniface promised to be faithful to the emperor, to be always ready to employ his forces against the enemies of the empire; but he feared the presence of Baldwin's army in his cities, already exhausted by war. A serious quarrel broke out between the two princes. The marquis of Montferrat accused the emperor of wishing to get possession of his states; Baldwin fancied he could perceive in the resistance of Boniface the secret design of denying the sovereignty of the head of the empire. Both loved justice, and were not wanting in moderation; but now one had become king of Thessalonica, and the other emperor of Constantinople, they had courtiers, who endeavoured to exasperate their quarrel and inflame their animosity. Some told Boniface that Baldwin was entirely in the wrong, and that he abused a power that ought to have been the reward of virtues very different from his. Others reproached the emperor with being too generous to his enemies, and, in the excess of their flattery, said he was guilty of only one fault, and that was of having too long spared an unfaithful vassal. In spite of all the representations of the marquis of Montferrat, Baldwin led his army into the kingdom of Thessalonica. Boniface considered this obstinacy of the emperor as a flagrant outrage, and swore to take vengeance with his sword. Impelled by passion, he departed suddenly with several knights who had declared in his favour, and got possession of Didymatica, a city belonging to the emperor.

The marquis of Montferrat took with him his wife, Mary of Hungary, the widow of Isaac; and the presence of this princess, with the hopes of keeping up the division among the Latins, drew many Greeks to the banner of Boniface. He declared to them that he fought for their cause, and clothed in the imperial purple a young prince, the son of Isaac and Mary of Hungary. Dragging in his train this phantom of an emperor, around whom the principal inhabitants from all parts of Romania rallied, he resumed the road to Adrianople, and made preparations for besieging that city. Boniface, daily becoming more irritated, would listen to neither the counsels nor the prayers of his companions in arms; and discord was about to cause the blood of the Latins to flow, if the doge of Venice, the count of Blois, and the barons that remained at Constantinople, had not earnestly employed their authority and credit to prevent the misfortunes with which the new empire was threatened. Deeply afflicted by what they learnt, they sent deputies to the emperor and the marquis of Montferrat. The marshal of Champagne, the envoy to Boniface, reproached him, in plain terms, with having forgotten the glory and honour of the Crusaders, of whom he had been the leader; with compromising, to gratify a vain pride, the cause of Christ and the safety of the empire, and preparing days of triumph and joy for the Greeks, the Bulgarians, and the Saracens. The marquis of Montferrat was touched by the reproaches of Villehardouin, who was his friend, and who spoke in the name of all the Crusaders. He promised to put an end to the war, and to submit his quarrel with Baldwin to the judgment of the counts and barons.

In the meanwhile Baldwin had taken possession of Thessalonica. As soon as he heard of the hostilities of the marquis of Montferrat, he hastily marched back to Adrianople. He was brooding over projects of vengeance, and threatening to repel force by force, and oppose war to war, when he met the deputies, who came in the name of the leaders of the crusade, to speak to him of peace, and recall to his heart the sentiments of justice and humanity. A knight of the train of the count of Blois addressed a speech to the emperor, that Villehardouin has preserved, in which our readers will be pleased, without doubt, to meet with a picture of the noble frankness of the conquerors of Byzantium. "Sire," said he, "the doge of Venice, the Count Louis of Blois, my very honoured lord, and all the barons who are at Constantinople, salute you as their sovereign, and make complaint to God and you against those who, by their evil counsels, have created fatal discords. You did, certes, very wrong to lend an ear to these perfidious counsellors, for they are our enemies and yours. You know that the Marquis Boniface has submitted his quarrel to the judgment of the barons; the lords and princes hope that you will do as he has done, and that you will not hold out against justice. They have sworn, and we are charged to declare so in their name, not to suffer any longer the scandal of a war kindled between Crusaders."

Baldwin did not at first answer this speech, and appeared surprised at such language; but they spoke to him thus in the name of the doge of Venice, whose old age he respected, and whom he loved tenderly; in the name of the counts and barons, without whose help he could not hope to preserve his empire, and, at length, he listened to the united voices of reason and friendship. He promised to lay down his arms, and repair to Constantinople, to adjust the quarrel between him and the marquis of Montferrat. On his arrival, the counts and barons spared neither complaints nor prayers, and they found him docile to all their counsels. The marquis of Montferrat, who very shortly followed him, entered the capital with a degree of mistrust; he was accompanied by a hundred knights, with their men-at-arms; but the welcome he received from Baldwin and the other leaders completely appeased all his resentments, and dissipated all his misgivings. From that time the re-establishment of harmony and peace became the sincere object of the Crusaders. The doge of Venice, the counts and barons, with the most respected of the knights, who reminded the masters of the new empire of the redoubtable institution of the PEERS of the West, gave judgment in the quarrel that was submitted to them, and pronounced, without appeal, between the king of Thessalonica and the emperor of Constantinople. The two princes swore never to listen again to perfidious counsels, and embraced in presence of the army, who rejoiced at the return of concord, as they would have done at a great victory obtained over the enemies of the empire. "Great evil might they have done," says Villehardouin, "who excited this discord; for if God had not taken pity on the Crusaders, they were in danger of losing their conquests, and Christianity might have perished."

As soon as peace was re-established, the knights and barons again quitted the capital to pass through the provinces, and subdue such as were refractory. The count of Blois, who had obtained Bithynia, sent his knights across the Bosphorus; the troops of the Crusaders gained several advantages over those of Lascaris. Penamenia, Lopada, Nicomedia, and some other cities, opened their gates to the conquerors, after a feeble resistance. The Latins brought under their dominion all the coasts of the Propontis and the Bosphorus, as far as the ancient Eolis. Henry of Hainault was not idle in this new war; whilst the warriors of the count of Blois were pushing their conquests towards Nice, he led his men-at-arms into Phrygia, unfurled his triumphant banners in the plains where Troy once stood, fought at the same time both Greeks and Turks, in the fields which had been trod by the armies of Xerxes and Alexander, and took possession of all the country that extends from the Hellespont to Mount Ida.

At the same time the marquis of Montferrat, now the peaceable master of Thessalonica, undertook the conquest of Greece. [151] He advanced into

Thessaly, passed the chain of mountains of Olympus and Ossa, and took possession of Larissa. Boniface and his knights, without fear and without danger, passed through the narrow straits of Thermopylæ, and penetrated into Bœotia and Attica. They put to flight Leo Sgurre, who was the scourge of a vast province; and their exploits might have reminded the Greeks of those heroes of the early ages who travelled about the world fighting monsters and subduing tyrants. As all the Greeks, for so long a time oppressed, sighed for a change, the heroes of the crusades were everywhere received as liberators. Whilst Boniface was becoming possessed of the beautiful countries of Greece, Geoffrey de Villehardouin, nephew of the marshal of Champagne, established the authority of the Latins in the Peloponnesus. After having driven the troops of Michael Comnenus to the mountains of Epirus, he occupied, without fighting, Coronea and Patras, and met with no resistance except in the canton of Lacedæmonia. The conquered lands and cities were given to the barons, who rendered fealty and homage to the king of Thessalonica and the emperor of Constantinople. [152] Greece then beheld lords of Argos and Corinth, grand sieurs of Thebes, dukes of Athens, and princes of Achaia. French knights dictated laws in the city of Agamemnon, in the city of Minerva, [153] in the country of Lycurgus, and in that of Epaminondas. Strange destiny of the warriors of this crusade, who had quitted the West to conquer the city and lands of Jesus Christ, and whom fortune had conducted into places filled with the remembrances of the gods of Homer and the glory of profane antiquity!

The Crusaders were not allowed to felicitate themselves long upon their conquests. Possessors of an empire much more difficult to be preserved than invaded, they had not the ability to master fortune, who soon took from them all that victory had bestowed. They exercised their power with violence, and conciliated neither their subjects nor their neighbours. Joannice, king of the Bulgarians, had sent an ambassador to Baldwin, with offers of friendship; Baldwin replied with much haughtiness, and threatened to compel Joannice to descend from his usurped throne. When despoiling the Greeks of their property, the Crusaders shut out from themselves every source of prosperity, and reduced men to whom they left nothing but life, to despair. To fill up the measure of their imprudence, they received into their armies the Greeks, whom they loaded with contempt, and who became their implacable enemies. Not content with reigning over cities, they were desirous of subjugating hearts to their will, and awakened fanaticism. Unjust persecutions exasperated the minds of the Greek priests, who declaimed with vehemence against tyranny, and who, reduced to misery, were listened to as oracles and revered as martyrs.

The new empire of the Latins, into which the feudal laws had been introduced, was divided into a thousand principalities or lordships, and was nothing but a species of republic, governed with great difficulty. The Venetians had their particular jurisdiction, and the greater part of the cities were regulated by turns by the legislation of Venice and the code of feudalism. The lords and barons had among themselves opposite interests and rivalries, which, every day, were likely to bring on discord and civil war. The Latin ecclesiastics, who had shared the spoils of the Greek Church, did not at all conciliate peace by their example, but carried the scandals of their dissensions even into the sanctuary. It was their constant wish and endeavour to exalt the laws and authority of the court of Rome over those of the emperors. Many of them had usurped the fiefs of the barons, and as the fiefs they possessed were exempted from military service, the empire thus became weakened in its natural defences.

The delicious climate and the riches of Greece, with the long sojourn at Constantinople, enervated the courage of the conquerors, and fostered corruption among the soldiers of the cross. The nations in the end ceased to respect the power and the laws of those whose morals and manners they despised. As the Latins had separated, some to go into Greece, and others into Asia Minor, the Greeks, who no longer beheld great armies, and who had sometimes resisted their enemies with advantage, began to fancy that the warriors of the West were not invincible.

In their despair, the conquered people resolved to have recourse to arms; and, looking around them to find enemies for the Crusaders, they implored the alliance and protection of the king of the Bulgarians. There was formed a widely-extended conspiracy, into which all entered to whom slavery was no longer tolerable. All at once the storm burst forth by the massacre of the Latins; a war-cry arose from Mount Hemus to the Hellespont; the Crusaders, dispersed in the various cities and countries, were surprised by a furious and pitiless enemy. The Venetians and French, who guarded Adrianople and Didymatica, were not able to resist the multitude of the Greeks; some were slaughtered in the streets; others retired in disorder, and, in their flight, beheld with grief their banners torn down from the towers, and replaced by the standards of the Bulgarians. The roads were covered with fugitive warriors, who found no asylum in a country which lately trembled at the fame of their arms.

Every city besieged by the Greeks was ignorant of the fate of the other cities confided to the defence of the Latins; communications were interrupted; sinister rumours prevailed in the provinces, which represented the capital in flames, all the cities given up to pillage, and all the armies of the Franks dispersed or annihilated. The old chronicles, whilst speaking of the barbarity of the Greeks, also describe the terror that took possession of some of the barons and knights. The sense of danger appears to have stifled in their hearts every other feeling. In the hour of peril, crusaders abandoned their companions in arms, brothers abandoned brothers. An old knight, Robert de Trils, who, in spite of his grey hairs, had insisted upon following his son to the crusade, was besieged by the Greeks in Philippolis; the city was surrounded by enemies, and Robert had but slender hopes of safety. Even in such circumstances, his prayers and tears could not prevail upon either his son or his son-in-law to remain with him. Villehardouin informs us that these recreant warriors were slain in their flight; for God would not save those who had refused to succour their own father.

When the report of these disasters reached Constantinople, Baldwin assembled the counts and barons; it was determined to apply the promptest remedy to so many evils, and to put into action all the energies of the empire to stop the progress of the revolt. The Crusaders who were engaged in warlike expeditions on the other side of the Bosphorus, received orders to abandon their conquests, and to return immediately to the standards of the main army. Baldwin waited for them several days, but as he was impatient to begin the war, and wished to astonish the enemy by the promptitude of his proceedings, he set out at the head of the knights that remained in the capital, and, five days after his departure, appeared before the walls of Adrianople.

The leaders of the crusade, accustomed to brave all obstacles, were never checked or restrained by the small number of their own soldiers, or the multitude of their enemies. The capital of Thrace, surrounded by impregnable ramparts, was defended by a hundred thousand Greeks, in whom thirst of vengeance supplied the want of courage. Baldwin mustered scarcely eight thousand men around his banners. The doge of Venice soon arrived with eight thousand Venetians. The Latin fugitives came from all parts to join this small army. The Crusaders pitched their tents, and prepared to lay siege to the city. Their preparations proceeded but slowly, and provisions were beginning to fail them, when the report reached them of the march of the king of the Bulgarians. Joannice, the leader of a barbarous people, himself more barbarous than his subjects, was advancing with a formidable army. He concealed his ambitious projects and his desire for vengeance under an appearance of religious zeal, and caused a standard of St. Peter, which he had received from the pope, to be borne before him. This new ally of the Greeks boasted of being a leader of a holy enterprise, and threatened to exterminate the Franks, whom he accused of having assumed the cross for the purpose of ravaging the provinces and pillaging the cities of Christians.

The king of the Bulgarians was preceded in his march by a numerous troop of Tartars and Comans, whom the hopes of pillage had drawn from the mountains and forests near the banks of the Danube and the Borysthenes. The Comans, more ferocious than the nations of Mount Hemus, drank, it was said, the blood of their captives, and sacrificed Christians on the altars of their idols. Like the warriors of Scythia, accustomed to fight whilst flying, the Tartar horsemen received orders from Joannice to provoke the enemy, even in their camp, and to endeavour to draw the heavy cavalry of the Franks into an ambuscade. The barons were aware of this danger, and forbade the Crusaders to quit their tents, or go beyond their intrenchments. But such was the character of the French warriors, that prudence, in their eyes, deprived valour of all its lustre, and it appeared disgraceful to shun the fight in the presence and amidst the scoffs of an enemy.

Scarcely had the Tartars appeared near the camp, when the sight of them made even the leaders themselves forget the orders they had issued only the night before. The emperor and the count of Blois flew to meet the enemy, put them to flight, and pursued them with ardour for the space of two leagues. But all at once the Tartars rallied, and in their turn charged the Christians. The latter, who believed they had gained a victory, were obliged to defend themselves in a country with which they were unacquainted. Their squadrons, exhausted by fatigue, were surprised and surrounded by the army of Joannice; pressed on all sides, they made useless efforts to recover their line of battle, but had no power either to fly, or resist the barbarians.

The count of Blois endeavoured to retrieve his fatal imprudence by prodigies of valour; when seriously wounded he was thrown from his horse amidst the enemy's ranks, one of his knights raised him up, and wished to draw him out of the *mêlée*: "No," cried this brave prince, "leave me to fight and die. God forbid I should ever be reproached with having fled from battle." As he finished these words, the count of Blois fell, covered with wounds, and his faithful squire died by his side.

The emperor Baldwin still disputed the victory; the bravest of his knights and barons followed him into the *mêlée*, and a horrible carnage marked their progress through the ranks of the barbarians. Peter bishop of Bethlehem, Stephen count of Perche, Renaud de Montmirail, Mathieu de Valencourt, Robert de Rançai, and a crowd of lords and valiant warriors lost their lives in defending their sovereign. Baldwin remained almost alone on the field of battle, and still continued fighting bravely; but at length, overpowered by numbers, he fell into the hands of the Bulgarians, who loaded him with chains. The wreck of the army retired in the greatest disorder, and only owed their safety to the prudent bravery of the doge of Venice and the marshal of Champagne, who had been left to guard the camp.

In the night that followed the battle, the Crusaders raised the siege of Adrianople, and retook the route to the capital, amidst a thousand dangers. The Bulgarians and the Comans, proud of their victory, pursued without intermission the army they had conquered; this army, which had lost half of its numbers, was in great want of provisions, and had great difficulty in dragging along the wounded and the baggage. The Crusaders were plunged in a melancholy silence, their despair was evident in their actions and on their countenances. At Rodosto they met Henry of Hainault, and several other knights, who were on their way from the provinces of Asia, to join the army of Adrianople. The retreating leaders related with tears their defeat and the captivity of Baldwin. All these warriors, who knew not what it was to be conquered, expressed at once their astonishment and their grief; they mingled their lamentations and tears, and raised their hands and eyes towards heaven, to implore the divine mercy. The Crusaders who returned from the shores of the Bosphorus, addressed the marshal of Romania, and weeping, said to him: "Order us where the greatest danger exists, for we no longer wish to live: are we not sufficiently unfortunate in not having come in time to succour our emperor?" Thus the knights of the cross, though pursued by a victorious enemy, were still strangers to fear; the grief caused by the remembrance of their defeat scarcely allowed them to be sensible of the perils by which they were threatened.

All the Crusaders, however, did not exhibit this noble degree of courage; many knights [154] whom Villehardouin is not willing to name, that he may not dishonour their memory, abandoned the banners of the army and fled to Constantinople; they related the disasters of the Crusaders, and, to excuse their desertion, drew a lamentable picture of the misfortunes that threatened the empire. All the Franks were seized with grief and terror, on learning they had no longer an emperor. The Greeks that inhabited the capital, applauded in secret the triumph of the Bulgarians, and their ill-concealed joy still further increased the alarms of the Latins. A great number of knights, overcome by so many reverses, saw no safety but in flight, and embarked hastily on board some Venetian vessels. In vain the legate of the pope and several leaders of the army endeavoured to detain them, threatening them with the anger of God and the contempt of men: they renounced their own glory; they abandoned an empire founded by their arms, and went to announce the captivity of Baldwin in the cities of the West, where the rejoicings for the first victories of the Crusaders were still being celebrated.

In the mean time, Joannice continued his pursuit of the conquered army. The Greeks, united with the Bulgarians, took possession of all the provinces, and left the Latins no repose. Among the disasters of which contemporary history has left us a deplorable account, we must not forget the massacre of twenty thousand Armenians. This numerous colony had left the banks of the Euphrates, and established themselves in the province of Natolia. After the conquest of Constantinople, they declared for the Latins, and when the latter experienced their reverses, finding themselves menaced and pursued by the Greeks, they crossed the Bosphorus, and followed Henry of Hainault, who was marching towards Adrianople. The Armenians took with them their flocks and their families: they drew, in carriages, all that they possessed that was most valuable, and had great difficulty, on their march across the mountains of Thrace, in keeping up with the army of the Crusaders. These unfortunate people were surprised by the Tartars, and, to a man, perished beneath the swords of a pitiless conqueror. The Franks wept at the defeat and destruction of the Armenians, without being able to avenge them: they had nothing but enemies throughout the vast provinces of the empire. Beyond the Bosphorus, they only preserved the castle of Peges: on the European side, only Rodosto and Selembria. Their conquests in ancient Greece were not yet threatened by the Bulgarians; but these distant possessions only served to divide their forces. Henry of Hainault, who took the title of regent, performed prodigies of valour in endeavouring to retake some of the cities of Thrace; and lost, in various combats, a great number of the warriors that remained under his banners.

The bishop of Soissons and some other Crusaders, invested with the confidence of their unfortunate companions in arms, were sent into Italy, France, and the county of Flanders, to solicit the assistance of the knights and barons but the succour they hoped for could only arrive slowly, and the enemy continued to make rapid progress. The army of the Bulgarians, like a violent tempest, advanced on all sides; it desolated the shores of the Hellespont, extended its ravages into the kingdom of Thessalonica, repassed Mount Hemus, and returned, more numerous and more formidable than ever, to the banks of the Hebrus. The Latin empire had no other defenders but a few warriors divided among the various cities and fortresses, and every day war and desertion diminished the numbers and strength of the unfortunate conquerors of Byzantium. Five hundred knights, picked warriors of the army of the Crusaders, were attacked before the walls of Rusium, and cut to pieces by a countless multitude of Bulgarians and Comans. This defeat was not less fatal than the battle of Adrianople; the hordes of Mount Hemus and the Borysthenes carried terror everywhere. On their passage, the country was in flames, and the cities afforded neither refuge nor means of defence. The land was covered with soldiers, who slaughtered all who came in their way; the sea was covered with pirates, who threatened every coast with their brigandage. Constantinople expected every day to see the standards of the victorious Joannice beneath its walls, and only owed its safety to the excess of evils that desolated all the provinces of the empire.

The king of the Bulgarians did not spare his allies any more than his enemies; he burnt and demolished all the cities that fell into his hands. He ruined the inhabitants, dragged them in his train like captives, and made them undergo, in addition to the calamities of war, all the outrages of a jealous and barbarous tyranny. The Greeks, who had solicited his assistance, were at last reduced to implore the aid of the Latins against the implacable fury of their allies. The Crusaders accepted with joy the alliance with the Greeks, whom they never ought to have repulsed, and re-entered into Adrianople. Didymatica, and most of the cities of Romania, shook off the intolerable yoke of the Bulgarians, and submitted to the Latins. The Greeks, whom Joannice had urged on to despair, showed some bravery, and became useful auxiliaries to the Latins; and the new empire might have hoped for a return of days of prosperity and glory, if so many calamities could possibly have been repaired by a few transient successes. But all the provinces were strewed with ruins, and the cities and countries were without inhabitants. The hordes of Mount Hemus, whether victorious or conquered, still continued their predatory habits. They easily recovered from their losses; the losses of the Franks became every day more irreparable. The leader of the Bulgarians sought out everywhere the foes of the new empire; and, being abandoned by the Greeks of Romania, he formed an alliance with Lascaris, the implacable enemy of the Latins.

The pope in vain exhorted the nations of France and Italy to take up arms for the assistance of the conquerors of Byzantium; he could not awaken their enthusiasm for a cause that presented to its defenders nothing but certain evils, and dangers without glory.

Amidst the perils that continued to multiply, the Crusaders remained perfectly ignorant of the fate of Baldwin; sometimes it was said that he had broken his bonds, and had been seen wandering in the forests of Servia; [155] sometimes that he had died of grief in prison; sometimes that he had been massacred in the midst of a banquet by the king of the Bulgarians; that his mutilated members had been cast out upon the rocks, and that his skull, enchased in gold, served as a cup for his barbarous conqueror. Several messengers, sent by Henry of Hainault, travelled through the cities of Bulgaria to learn the fate of Baldwin; but returned to Constantinople, without having been able to ascertain anything. A year after the battle of Adrianople, the pope, at the solicitation of the Crusaders, conjured Joannice to restore to the Latins of Byzantium the head of their new empire. The king of the Bulgarians contented himself with replying, that Baldwin had paid the tribute of nature, and that his deliverance was no longer in the power of mortals. This answer destroyed all hopes of again seeing the imprisoned monarch, and the Latins no longer entertained a doubt of the death of their emperor. Henry of Hainault received the deplorable heritage of his brother with tears and deep regret, and succeeded to the empire amidst general mourning and sorrow. To complete their misfortunes, the Latins had to weep for the loss of Dandolo, who finished his glorious career at Constantinople, and whose last looks must have perceived the rapid decline of an empire he had founded. [156] The greater part of the Crusaders had either perished in battle, or returned to the West. Boniface, in an expedition against the Bulgarians of Rhodope, received a mortal wound, and his head was carried in triumph to the fierce Joannice, who had already immolated a monarch to his ambition and vengeance. The succession of Boniface gave birth to serious disputes among the Crusaders; and the kingdom of Thessalonica, which had exhibited some splendour during its short existence, disappeared amidst the confusion and the storms of a civil and a foreign war. In the brother and successor of Baldwin were united the civil and military virtues; but he could scarcely hope to restore a power so shaken on all sides.

I have not the courage to pursue this history, and describe the Latins in the extremes of their abasement and misery. On commencing my narration, I said: "*Evil to the conquered;*" on terminating it, I cannot refrain from saying: "*Evil to the conquerors.*"

An old empire which moulders away, a new empire ready to sink into ruins, such are the pictures that this crusade presents to us; never did any epoch offer greater exploits for admiration, or greater troubles for commiseration. Amidst these glorious and tragical scenes, the imagination is excited in the most lively manner, and passes, without ceasing, from surprise to surprise. We are at first astonished at seeing an army of thirty thousand men embark to conquer a country which might reckon upon many millions of defenders; a tempest, an epidemic disease, want of provisions, disunion among the leaders, an indecisive battle, all, or any of these, might have ruined the army of the Crusaders, and brought about the failure of their enterprise. By an unheard-of good fortune, nothing that they had to dread happened to them. They triumphed over all dangers, and surmounted all obstacles: without having any party among the Greeks, they obtained possession of their capital and the provinces; and, at the moment when they saw their standards triumphant all around them, it was that their fortune deserted them and their ruin began. A great lesson is this, given to nations by Providence, which sometimes employs conquerors to chastise both people and princes, and then, at its pleasure, destroys the instrument of its justice! There is no doubt that that Providence, which protects empires, will not permit great states to be subverted with impunity; and to deter those who wish to conquer everything by force of arms, it has decreed that victory shall sometimes bear none but very bitter fruits.

The Greeks, a degenerate nation, honoured their misfortunes by no virtue; they had neither sufficient courage to prevent the reverses of war, nor sufficient resignation to support them. When reduced to despair, they showed some little valour; but that valour was imprudent and blind; it precipitated them into new calamities, and procured them masters much more barbarous than those whose yoke they were so eager to shake off. They had no leader able to govern or guide them; no sentiment of patriotism strong enough to rally them: deplorable example of a nation left to itself, which has lost its morals, and has no confidence in its laws or its government!

The Franks had just the same advantages over their enemies that the barbarians of the north had over the Romans of the Lower Empire. In this terrible conflict, simplicity of manners, the energy of a new people for civilization, the ardour for pillage, and the pride of victory, were sure to prevail over the love of luxury, habits formed amidst corruption, and vanity which attaches importance to the most frivolous things, and only preserves a gaudy resemblance of true grandeur.

The events we have recorded are, doubtless, sufficient to make us acquainted with the manners and intellectual faculties of the Greeks and Latins. Two historians, however, who have served us as guides, may add by their style even, and the character of their works, to the idea that we form of the genius of the two races.

The Greek Nicetas makes long lamentations over the misfortunes of the vanquished; he deplores with bitterness the loss of the monuments, the statues, the riches which ministered to the luxury of his compatriots. His accounts, full of exaggeration and hyperboles, sprinkled all over with passages from the Scriptures and profane authors, depart almost always from the noble simplicity of history, and only exhibit a vain affectation of learning. Nicetas, in the excess of his vanity, [157] hesitates to pronounce the names even of the Franks, and fancies he inflicts a punishment upon them by preserving silence as to their exploits; when he describes the misfortunes of the empire, he can only weep and lament; but whilst lamenting, he is still anxious to please, and appears much more interested about his book than his country.

The marquis of Champagne does not pique himself upon his erudition, but even seems proud of his ignorance. It has been said that he could not write, and he himself confesses that he dictated his history. His narration, void of all spirit of research, but lively and animated, constantly recalls the language and the noble frankness of a *preux chevalier*. Villehardouin particularly excels in the speeches of his heroes, and delights in praising the bravery of his companions: if he never names the Grecian warriors, it is because he did not know them, and did not wish to know them. The marshal of Champagne is not affected by the evils of war, and only elevates his style to paint traits of heroism; the enthusiasm of victory alone can draw tears from him. When the Latins experienced great reverses, he cannot weep, he is silent; and it may be plainly seen he has laid down his book to go and fight. [158]

There is another contemporary historian, whose character may likewise assist us in forming a judgment upon the age in which he lived and the events he has related. Gunther, a monk of the order of Citeaux, who wrote under the dictation of Martin Litz, expatiates upon the preachings of the crusade, and on the virtues of his abbot, who placed himself at the head of the Crusaders of the diocese of Bâle. When the Christian army directs its course towards the capital of the Greek empire, Gunther remembers the orders of the pope, and becomes silent; if he affords us a few words upon the second siege of Constantinople, he cannot conceal the terror which this rash enterprise creates in him. In his recital, the valour of the Crusaders scarcely obtains a modest eulogy; the imagination of the historian is only struck by the difficulties and perils of the expedition; filled with the most sinister presentiments, he constantly repeats that there is no hope of success for the Latins. When they are triumphant, his fear is changed all at once into admiration. The monk Gunther celebrates with enthusiasm the unhoped-for success of the conquerors of Byzantium, among whom he never loses sight of his abbot, Martin Litz, loaded with the pious spoils of Greece.

When reading the three histories contemporary with the expedition to Constantinople, we plainly perceive that the first belongs to a Greek brought up at the court of Byzantium, the second to a French knight, and the third to a monk. If the two first historians, by their manner of writing and the sentiments they express, give us a just idea of the Greek nation and the heroes of the West, the last may also explain to us the opinions and the character of the greater part of those Crusaders, who were constantly threatening to quit the army after it had left Venice, and who, perhaps, were only so mindful of the oath they had made to go to the Holy Land, because the name alone of Constantinople filled them with terror. There were, as may be plainly seen, but very few of these timid Crusaders in the Christian army, and even these were governed by the general spirit that animated the knights and barons. Other crusades had been preached in councils, this crusade was proclaimed at tournaments; thus the greater parts of the Crusaders proved more faithful to the virtues and laws of chivalry than to the will of the Holy See. These warriors, so proud and so brave, were full of respect for the authority and judgment of the pope; but, governed by honour, placed between their first vows and their word given to the Venetians, they often swore to deliver Jerusalem, and were led, without thinking of it, to the walls of Constantinople. Armed to avenge the cause of Christ, they became subservient to the ambition of Venice, to which republic they esteemed themselves bound by gratitude, and overturned the throne of Constantinople to pay a debt of fifty thousand silver marks.

The chivalric spirit, one of the peculiar characteristics of this war, and of the age in which it was undertaken, kept up in the hearts of the Crusaders ambition and the love of glory. In the early days of chivalry, knights declared themselves the champions of beauty and innocence; at first they were appealed to for justice against injuries and robberies; but soon princes and princesses, deprived of their rights by force, came to demand of them the restitution of provinces and kingdoms. The champions of misfortune and beauty then became illustrious liberators and true conquerors.

At the same time that a young prince came to implore the Crusaders to assist him in replacing his father upon the throne of Constantinople, a young princess, the daughter of Isaac, king of Cyprus, despoiled by Richard Cœur de Lion, repaired to Marseilles, to solicit the support of the Crusaders, who were embarking for Palestine. She married a Flemish knight, and charged him with the task of recovering her father's kingdom. This Flemish knight, whose name history does not mention, but who belonged to the family of Count Baldwin, when he arrived in the East, addressed himself to the king of Jerusalem, and demanded the kingdom of Cyprus of him; he was supported in his demand by the châtelain of Bruges, and the greater part of his companions who had taken the cross. Amaury, who had received from the pope and the emperor of Germany, the title of king of Cyprus, far from yielding to such pretensions, ordered the Flemish knight, John of Nesle, and their companions, to quit his dominions. The knights who had embraced the cause of the daughter of Isaac, abandoned the idea of retaking the kingdom of Cyprus, and without stopping in the Holy Land, turned their steps towards the banks of the Euphrates and the Orontes, to seek for other countries to conquer.

Before there was a question of attacking Constantinople, we have seen a daughter of Tancred, the last king of Sicily, espouse a French knight, and transfer to him the charge of avenging her family and establishing her claims to the kingdom founded by the Norman knights. Gauthier de Brienne, after his marriage, set out for Italy, furnished with a thousand *livres tournois*, and accompanied by sixty knights. Having received at Rome the benediction of the pope, he declared war against the Germans, then masters of Apulia and Sicily; got possession of the principal fortresses, [159] and appeared likely to enjoy the fruits of his victories in peace, when he was surprised in his tent, and fell, covered with wounds, into the hands of his enemies. He was offered his liberty upon the condition of renouncing his claim to the crown of Sicily; but he preferred the title of king to freedom, and allowed himself to die with hunger rather than abandon his rights to a kingdom which victory had bestowed upon him.

This spirit of conquest, which appeared so general among the knights, might favour the expedition to Constantinople; but it was injurious to the holy war, by turning the Crusaders aside from the essential object of the crusade. The heroes of this war did nothing for the deliverance of Jerusalem, of which they constantly spoke in their letters to the pope. The conquest of Byzantium, very far from being, as the knights believed, the road to the land of Christ, was but a new obstacle to the taking of the holy city; their imprudent exploits placed the Christian colonies in greater peril, and only ended in completely subverting, without replacing it, a power which might have served as a barrier against the Saracens.

The Venetians skilfully took advantage of this disposition of the French knights; Venice succeeded in stifling the voice of the sovereign pontiff, who often gave the Crusaders counsels dictated by the spirit of the gospel. The republic had the greatest influence over the events of this war, and over the minds of the barons and knights, who allowed themselves to be governed by turns by the sentiments of honour and by a desire to win rich dominions, and thus exhibited throughout their conduct an inconsistent mixture of generosity and avarice.

The inclination to enrich themselves by victory had, particularly, no longer any bounds when the Crusaders had once beheld Constantinople; ambition took the place in their hearts of every generous sentiment, and left nothing of that enthusiasm which had been the moving principle of other crusades. No prodigy, no miraculous apparition came to second or stimulate the valour of knights to whom it was quite sufficient to point out the wealth of Greece. In preceding crusades, the bishops and ecclesiastics promised the combatants indulgences of the Church and eternal life; but in this war, as the Crusaders had incurred the displeasure of the head of the faithful, they could not be supported in their perils by the hope of martyrdom; and the leaders who were acquainted with the spirit that animated their followers, contented themselves with offering a sum of money to the soldier that should first mount the ramparts of Constantinople. When they had pillaged the city, knights, barons, and soldiers exclaimed, in the intoxication of their joy,—*Never was so rich a booty seen since the creation of the world!*

We have remarked that, in the conquest of the provinces, every knight wished to obtain a principality; every count, every lord, wished for a kingdom; the clergy themselves were not exempt from this ambition, and often complained to the pope of not having been favoured in the division of the spoils of the Greek empire.

To recapitulate, in a few words, our opinion of the events and consequences of this crusade, we must say that the spirit of chivalry and the spirit of conquest at first gave birth to wonders; but that they did not suffice to maintain the Crusaders in their possessions. This conquering spirit, carried to the most blind excess, did not allow them to reflect that among the greatest triumphs, there is a point at which victory and force themselves are powerless, if prudence and wisdom do not come to the assistance of valour.

The Franks, their ancestors, who set out from the North to invade the richest provinces of the Roman empire, were better seconded by fortune, but more particularly by their own genius. Respecting the usages of the countries that submitted to their arms, they only beheld in the conquered, fellow-citizens and supporters of their own power; they did not create a foreign nation in the midst of the nations they had desolated by their victories. The Crusaders, on the contrary, evinced a profound contempt for the Greeks, whose alliance and support they ought to have been anxious to seek; they wished to reform manners and alter opinions, —a much more difficult task than the conquest of an empire,—and only met with enemies in a country that might have furnished them with useful allies.

We may add that the policy of the Holy See, which at first undertook to divert the Latin warriors from the expedition to Constantinople, became, in the end, one of the greatest obstacles to the preservation of their conquests. The counts and barons, who reproached themselves with having failed in obedience to the sovereign pontiff, at length followed scrupulously his instructions to procure by their arms the submission of the Greek Church, the only condition on which the holy father would pardon a war commenced in opposition to his commands. To obtain his forgiveness and approbation, they employed violence against schism and heresy, and lost their conquest by endeavouring to justify it in the eyes of the sovereign pontiff. The pope himself did not obtain that which he so ardently desired. The union of the Greek and Roman churches could not possibly be effected amidst the terrors of victory and the evils of war; the arms of the conquerors had less power than the anathemas of the Church, to bring back the Greeks to the worship of the Latins. Violence only served to irritate men's minds, and consummated the rupture, instead of putting an end to it. The remembrance of persecutions and outrages, a reciprocal contempt, an implacable hatred arose and became implanted between the two creeds, and separated them for ever.

History cannot affirm that this crusade made great progress in the civilization of Europe. The Greeks had preserved the jurisprudence of Justinian; the empire possessed wise regulations upon the levying of imposts and the administration of the public revenues; but the Latins disdained these monuments of human wisdom and of the experience of many ages; they coveted nothing the Greeks possessed but their territories and their wealth. Most of the knights took a pride in their ignorance, and amongst the spoils of Constantinople, attached no value to the ingenious productions of Greece. Amidst the conflagrations that consumed the mansions and palaces of the capital, they beheld with indifference large and valuable libraries given up to the flames. It must be confessed, however, that, in these great disasters the Muses had not to weep for the loss of any of the masterpieces they had inspired. If the conquerors knew not how to appreciate the treasures of genius, this rich deposit was not to be lost for their descendants. All the books of antiquity that were known in the time of Eustathius [A. D. 750, Trans.], and of which that learned philosopher made the nomenclature some centuries before the fifth crusade, enriched France and Italy at the revival of letters.

We may add that the necessity for both conquerors and conquered of intercommunication must have contributed to the spreading of the Latin language among the Greeks, and that of the Greeks among the Latins. [160] The people of Greece were obliged to learn the idiom of the clergy of Rome in order to make their petitions and complaints known; the ecclesiastics charged by the pope to convert the Greeks could not dispense with the study of the language of Plato and Demosthenes, to teach the disciples of Photius the truths of the Roman Catholic religion.

We have spoken of the destruction of the masterpieces of sculpture; we must admit, nevertheless, that some of them escaped the barbarism of the conquerors. The Venetians, more enlightened than the other Crusaders, and born in a city constructed and embellished by the arts, caused several of the monuments of Byzantium to be transported into Italy. Four horses of bronze, [161] which, amidst the revolutions of empires, had passed from Greece to Rome, from Rome to Constantinople, were sent to decorate the place of St. Mark: many ages after this crusade, they were doomed to be carried away from Venice, in its turn invaded by victorious armies, and again to return to the shores of the Adriatic, as eternal trophies of war, and faithful companions of victory.

The Crusaders likewise profited by several useful inventions, and transmitted them to their compatriots; and the fields and gardens of Italy and France were enriched by some plants till that time unknown in the West. Boniface sent into his marquisate some seeds of maize, which had never before been cultivated in Italy: a public document, which still exists, attests the gratitude of the people of Montferrat. The magistrates received the innocent fruits of victory with great solemnity, and, upon their altars, called down a blessing upon a production of Greece, that would one day constitute the wealth of the plains of Italy. [162]

Flanders, Champagne, and most of the provinces of France, which had sent their bravest warriors to the crusade, fruitlessly lavished their population and their treasures upon the conquest of Byzantium. We may say that our intrepid ancestors gained nothing by this wonderful war, but the glory of having given, for a moment, masters to Constantinople, and lords to Greece. And yet these distant conquests, and this new empire, which drew from France its turbulent and ambitious princes, must have been favourable to the French monarchy. Philip Augustus must have been pleased by the absence of the great vassals of the crown, and had reason to learn with joy that the count of Flanders, a troublesome neighbour, and a not very submissive vassal, had obtained an empire in the East. The French monarchy thus derived some advantage from this crusade; but the republic of Venice profited much more by it.

This republic, which scarcely possessed a population of two hundred thousand souls, and had not the power to make its authority respected on the continent, in the first place, made use of the arms of the Crusaders, to subdue cities, of which, without their assistance, she could never have made herself mistress. By the conquest of Constantinople, she enlarged her credit and her commerce in the East, and brought under her laws some of the richest possessions of the Greek emperors. She increased the reputation of her navy, and raised herself above all the maritime nations of Europe. The Venetians, though fighting under the banners of the cross, never neglected the interests or glory of their own country, whilst the French knights scarcely ever fought for any object but personal glory and their own ambition. The republic of Venice, accustomed to calculate the advantages and expenses of war, immediately renounced all conquests the preservation of which might become burdensome and of her new possessions in the East, only retained such as she judged necessary to the prosperity of her commerce, or the maintenance of her marine. Three years after the taking of Constantinople, the senate of Venice published an edict, by which it permitted any of the citizens to conquer the islands of the Archipelago; yielding to them the proprietorship of all the countries they might subdue. After this there soon appeared princes of Naxos, dukes of Paros, and lords of Mycone, as there had been dukes of Athens, lords of Thebes, and princes of Achaia; but these dukes and princes were only vassals of the republic. Thus Venice, more fortunate than France, made the valour and ambition of her citizens subservient to her interests.

BOOK XII
A.D. 1200-1215

SIXTH CRUSADE

In the preceding books, the imposing spectacle has passed before our eyes of the fall of an old empire, and of the rise and rapid decline of a new one. The imagination of man loves to dwell upon ruins, and the most sanguinary catastrophes even offer him highly attractive pictures. We have reason to fear that our narration will create less interest, awaken less curiosity, when, after the great revolutions we have described, it will be our duty to turn our attention to the petty states the Christians founded in Syria, for the safety of which the nations of the West were constantly called upon to furnish warlike assistance.

At the present day, we have great difficulty in comprehending that enthusiasm which animated all classes for the deliverance of the holy places, or that powerful interest that directed the thoughts of all to countries almost forgotten by modern Europe. [163] During the height of the fervour for the crusades, the taking of a city or town of Judea caused more joy than the taking of Byzantium; and Jerusalem was more dear to the Christians of the West than their own country. This enthusiasm, of which our indifference can scarcely form an idea, renders the task of the historian difficult, and makes him often hesitate in the choice of the events that history has to record: when opinions have changed, everything has changed with them: glory itself has lost its splendour, and that which appeared great in the eyes of men, seems only fantastical or vulgar; the historical epochs of our annals have become the objects of our most sovereign contempt; and when, without due reference to the ages of the holy wars, we wish to submit these extraordinary enterprises to the calculations of reason, we resemble those modern travellers who have only found a dribbling rivulet in the place of that famous Scamander, of which the imagination of the ancients, and still more, the muse of Homer, had made a majestic river.

But if we have no longer the task of describing the revolutions and falls of empires, the epoch of which we are about to trace the picture, will still present to us but too many of those great calamities with which human life supplies history: whilst Greece was a prey to all the ravages of war, the most cruel scourges desolated both Egypt and Syria.

The Nile suspended its accustomed course, and failed to inundate its banks or render the harvests abundant. The last year of this century (1200) announced itself, says an Arabian author, like a monster whose fury threatened to devour everything. When the famine began to be felt, the people were compelled to support themselves upon the grass of the fields and the ordure of animals, [164] the poor routed up cemeteries, and disputed with the worms the spoils of coffins. When this awful scourge became more general, the population of the cities and country, as if pursued by a pitiless enemy, fled away from their homes in despair, and wandered about at hazard from city to city, from village to village, meeting everywhere with the evil they wished to avoid;s in no inhabited place could they step a foot without being struck by the appearance of a putrifying carcass, or some unhappy wretch on the point of expiring.

The most frightful effect of this universal calamity was, that the want of food gave birth to the greatest crimes, and rendered every man the enemy of his fellows. At the commencement of the famine much horror was expressed at some being reduced to feed upon human flesh, but examples of so great a scandal increased with such rapidity, that it was soon spoken of with indifference. Men contending with famine, which spared the rich no more than the poor, were no longer sensible to pity, shame, or remorse, and were restrained neither by respect for the laws, nor by the fear of punishment. They came at last to devour each other like wild beasts. At Cairo, thirty women, in one day, perished at the stake, convicted of having killed and eaten their own children. The historian Abdallatif relates a crowd of barbarous and monstrous incidents which make the blood run cold with horror, and to which we will not give a place in our history, for fear of being accused of calumniating human nature.

The plague soon added its ravages to those of famine. God alone, says contemporary history, knows the number of those that died with famine and disease. The capital of Egypt, in the space of a few months, witnessed a hundred and eleven thousand funerals. At length it was found impossible to bury the dead, and the terrified survivors were obliged to be satisfied with casting them over the ramparts. The same mortality was experienced at Damietta, Kous, and Alexandria. It was at the period of seed-time that the plague was at its height; they who sowed the seed were not the same that had ploughed the ground, and they who sowed lived not to reap the harvest. The villages were deserted, and reminded travellers of those expressions of the Koran: *"We have mown them all down and exterminated them; one cry was heard, and all have perished.*" The dead bodies that floated on the Nile were as numerous as the bulbous plants which, at certain seasons, cover the waters of that river. One fisherman counted more than four hundred that passed before his eyes in a single day; piles of human bones were met with everywhere; the roads, to borrow the expression of Arabian writers, "*Were like a field sown with dead bodies,* and the most populous provinces *were as a banqueting-hall for the birds of prey.*"

Egypt lost more than a million of its inhabitants; both famine and plague were felt as far as Syria, and the Christian cities suffered equally with those of the Mussulmans. From the shores of the Red Sea to the banks of the Euphrates and the Orontes, the whole country presented one picture of desolation and mourning. As if the anger of Heaven was not satisfied, it was not long before a third calamity, not less terrible, followed in the train of the others. A violent earthquake laid waste the cities and provinces that famine and plague had spared; [165] the shocks resembled the motion of a sieve, or that which a bird makes when he raises and lowers his wings. The rising of the sea, and the agitation of the waves presented a horrible appearance; ships were, on a sudden, carried far on to the land, and multitudes of fish covered the shore; the heights of Libanus opened and sunk in many places. The people of Syria and Egypt believed it to be the earthquake that is to precede the day of judgment. Many inhabited places totally disappeared; a vast number of men perished; the fortresses of Hamath, Barin, and Balbec were thrown down; the only part of the city of Naplouse that was left standing was the street of the Samaritans; in Damascus, all the most superb edifices were destroyed; in the city of Tyre only a few houses escaped, and the ramparts of Ptolemaïs and Tripoli were nothing but heaps of ruins. The shocks were felt with less violence in the territory of Jerusalem, and, in the general calamity, both Christians and Mussulmans returned thanks to Heaven for having spared in its anger the city of prophets and miracles.

Such awful disasters ought to have caused the treaties made between the barons and the infidels to be respected. In the fifth crusade, the sovereign pontiff urged the Christians to take advantage of these calamitous days to invade the Mussulman provinces of Syria and Egypt: but if the advice of the pope had been followed, if the Christian army on leaving Venice, had directed its march towards the countries devastated by pestilence and famine, it is most probable that the conquerors and the conquered would have perished together. At that period, death, like a formidable sentinel, guarded all the frontiers of the Christians and Mussulmans. All the scourges of nature became the terrible guardians of provinces, and defended the approaches and entrances of cities better than the greatest armies could have done.

The Christian colonies, however, began, not to repair their losses, but to forget the evils they had suffered. Amaury, king of Jerusalem, set his barons an example of wisdom and pious resignation. The three military orders, that had exhausted their treasures to support their knights and soldiers during the famine, made a strong appeal, by messengers and letters, to the charity of the faithful of the West. The Christian cities that had been destroyed by the earthquake were rebuilt, and the sums amassed by Foulque of Neuilly, the preacher of the last crusade, were employèd in restoring the walls of Ptolemaïs. As the Christians wanted labourers, they set the Mussulman prisoners to work. Among the prisoners condemned to this service, history must not pass by the celebrated Persian poet Saadi, who had fallen into the hands of the Franks, whilst on a pilgrimage to Jerusalem. [166] The author of "The Garden of Roses," and several other works, destined at a future day to obtain the admiration of the East and the West, was loaded with irons, led to Tripoli, and confounded with the crowd of captives employed in rebuilding the fortifications of that city.

The truce which had been concluded with the infidels still subsisted; but either pretensions or quarrels daily arose that were frequently followed by hostilities. The Christians were continually kept under arms, and peace was sometimes as abundant in troubles and dangers as an open war would have been. There likewise prevailed, at this time, great confusion among the Christian colonies, and even among the Mussulman powers. The sultan of Damascus was at peace with the king of Jerusalem, whilst the count of Tripoli, the prince of Antioch, with the Templars and Hospitallers, were at war with the princes of Hamath, Edessa or some emirs of Syria. [167] Every one, according to his humour, took up or laid down his arms, without any power being sufficiently strong to enforce respect for treaties.

No great battles were fought, but constant incursions upon the territories of enemies were made; cities were surprised, countries were ravaged, and great booty obtained. Amidst these disorders, which were called *Days of Truce*, the Christians of Palestine had to lament the death of their king. Amaury, according to the custom of the faithful, went to Caïfa, during holy week, to gather palm; but fell sick on his pilgrimage, and returned to Ptolemaïs to die. Thus the sceptre of the kingdom of Jerusalem again remained in the hands of Isabella, who had neither the power, nor the ability necessary to govern the Christian states. At the same time, one of the sons of Bohemond, prince of Antioch, fell under the daggers of assassins sent by the Old Man of the Mountains. Bohemond the Third, at a very advanced age, was unable to avenge this murder; and, in addition, before he died, had the mortification of seeing war break out between his second son, Raymond, count of Tripoli, and Livon, prince of Armenia. The order of the Templars, as well as that of the Hospitallers, interested themselves in this quarrel, and were opposed to each other. The sultan of Aleppo and the Turks from Asia Minor mixed themselves with the dissensions of the Christians, and took advantage of their divisions to ravage the territory of Antioch. [168] The Christian states of Syria received no more succours from the West. The remembrance of the evils that had ravaged the countries beyond the seas had damped the zeal and the ardour of pilgrims; the warriors of Europe, accustomed to face with coolness all the perils of war, had not sufficient courage to brave pestilence and famine. A great number of the barons and knights of Palestine, themselves abandoned a land too long laid desolate, some to repair to Constantinople, and others to the kingdoms of the West.

Innocent, who had up to this time made vain efforts for the deliverance of the holy places, and who could not overcome his regret at having seen great Christian armies fruitlessly dissipated in the conquest of Greece, still did not give up his vast designs; from the beginning of his reign, the sovereign pontiff had pointed out the Holy Land to the Christian nations, as the road and the way of salvation. After the example of his predecessors, he not only called piety and virtue in to the defence of the Christian colonies, but remorse and repentance. All who came to him to confess great sins, were allowed but one means of expiating their crimes,—crossing the sea to fight against the infidels.

Among the sinners condemned to this sort of punishment history quotes the names of the murderers of Conrad, bishop of Wurtzburg and chancellor of the empire. [169] The guilty having presented themselves before the pope, barefooted, in drawers, and with halters round their necks, swore in the presence of the cardinals, to pass their lives in the practice of the most austere mortifications, and to carry arms during four years against the Saracens. A knight, named Robert, scandalized the whole court of Rome by confessing in a loud voice, that, being a prisoner in Egypt during the famine, he had killed his wife and daughter, to feed upon their flesh. The pope imposed the most rigorous penances upon Robert, and ordered him, to complete the expiation of so great a crime, to pass three years in visiting the holy places.

Innocent endeavoured by such means to keep up the devotion of pilgrimages, which had given birth to the crusades, and might again revive the zeal and ardour for holy wars. According to the opinion which the sovereign pontiff sought to spread among the faithful, and by which he himself appeared penetrated, this corrupt world had no crimes for which God would not open the treasures of his mercy provided the perpetrators would take the voyage to the East. The people however were persuaded that the sins and errors of a perverse generation had irritated the God of the

Christians, and that the glory of conquering the Holy Land was reserved for another and a better age, to a generation more worthy of attracting the eyes and the blessings of Heaven.

This opinion of the nations of the West was very little in favour of the Christians of Syria, who were daily making rapid strides towards their fall. Isabella, who only reigned over depopulated cities, died soon after her husband. A son that she had had by Amaury preceded her to the tomb; and the kingdom of Jerusalem became the heritage of a young princess, a daughter of Isabella and Conrad, marquis of Tyre. The barons and knights that remained in Syria were more sensible than ever of the necessity of having at their head a prince able to govern them, and immediately set about choosing a husband for the young queen of Jerusalem.

Their choice might have fallen upon one of themselves; but they feared that jealousy would give birth to fresh discords, and that the spirit of rivalry and faction would weaken the authority of him that should be called upon to govern the kingdom. The assembly resolved to seek a king in the West, and to address themselves to the country of Godfrey and the Baldwins, — to that nation that had furnished so many heroes to the crusades, so many illustrious defenders of the Holy Land.

This resolution of the barons of Palestine had not only the advantage of preserving peace in the kingdom of Jerusalem, but also that of arousing the spirit of chivalry in Europe, and of interesting it in the cause of the Christians of the East. Aimar, lord of Cæsarea, and the bishop of Ptolemaïs, crossed the sea, and went, in the name of the Christians of the Holy Land, to solicit Philip Augustus to send them a knight or a baron who might save the little that remained of the unfortunate kingdom of Jerusalem. The hand of a young queen, a crown, and the blessings of Heaven were the rewards held out to the bravery and devotedness of him who was willing to fight for the heritage of the Son of God. The deputies were received with great honours at the court of the king of France. Although the crown they offered was nothing but a vain title, it not the less dazzled the imagination of the French knights; their valorous ambition was seduced by the hope of acquiring great renown, and restoring the throne that had been founded by the bravery of Godfrey of Bouillon.

Among the knights of his court, Philip greatly distinguished John of Brienne, [170] brother of Gauthier, [171] who died in Apulia with the reputation of a hero and the title of king. In his youth, John of Brienne had been destined for the ecclesiastical state; but, brought up in a family of warriors, and less sensible to the charms of piety than to those of glory, he refused to obey the will of his parents; and as his father was inclined to employ force to constrain him, he sought a refuge against paternal anger in the monastery of Citeaux. John of Brienne was mixed with the crowd of cenobites, and gave himself up, as they did, to fasting and mortification. The austerities of the cloister, however, did not at all assimilate with his growing passion for the noble occupation of arms; and often, amidst prayers and religious ceremonies, the images of tournaments and battles would distract his thoughts and disturb his mind. One of his uncles having found him at the door of the monastery in a state very little suited to a gentleman, had pity on his tears, took him away with him, and encouraged his natural inclinations. From that time the glory of combats entirely occupied his thoughts; and he who had been destined to the silence of cloisters and the peace of altars, was not long in creating for himself by his bravery and exploits a great and widely spread renown.

At the period of the last crusade, John of Brienne accompanied his brother in his attempt to obtain the kingdom of Naples, and saw him perish whilst fighting for a throne that was to be the reward of the victor. He had the same fortune to guide his hopes, and the same dangers to encounter, if he espoused the heir of the kingdom of Jerusalem. He accepted with joy the hand of a young queen, for the possession of whose states he must contend with the Saracens, he charged the ambassadors to return and announce his speedy arrival in Palestine, and, full of confidence in the cause he was about to defend, promised to follow them at the head of an army.

When Aymai of Cæsarea and the bishop of Ptolemaïs returned to the Holy Land, the promises of John of Brienne raised the depressed courage of the Christians, and, as it often happens in seasons of misfortune, they passed from despair to the most extravagant hopes.

It was given out in Palestine that a crusade was in preparation, commanded by the most powerful monarchs of the West; and the report of such an extraordinary armament produced a momentary terror among the infidels. Malek-Adel, who, since the death of Al-Aziz, reigned over Syria and Egypt, dreaded the enterprises of the Christians; and as the truce made with the Franks was on the point of expiring, he proposed to renew it, offering to deliver up ten castles or fortresses as a pledge of his good faith and his desire for a continuation of peace. This proposal ought to have been welcomed by the Christians of Palestine; but the hopes of assistance from the West had banished all moderation and foresight from the councils of the barons and knights. The wiser part of the Christian warriors, among whom was the grand master of the order of St. John, were of opinion that the truce should be prolonged. They reminded their companions that they had often been promised succour from the West, without this succour ever having reached the Holy Land; and that in the very last crusade, a formidable army, confidently expected in Palestine, had directed its march towards Constantinople. They added, that it was not prudent to risk the chances of war upon the faith of a vain promise; and that they ought to wait the event, before they formed a determination upon which might depend the safety or the ruin of the Christians of the East. These discourses were full of wisdom and good sense, but as the Hospitallers spoke in favour of the truce, the Templars, with great warmth, declared for war: such was, likewise, the spirit of the Christian warriors, that prudence, moderation, or, indeed, any of the virtues of peace, inspired them with a sort of disdain; for them reason was always on the side of perils, and only to speak of flying to arms was quite sufficient to win all their suffrages. The assembly of barons and knights refused to prolong the truce made with the Saracens.

This determination became so much the more fatal, from the situation of France and Europe, which could scarcely allow John of Brienne to entertain the hope of accomplishing his promise of raising an army for the Holy Land.

Germany was still agitated by the rival pretensions of Otho and Philip of Swabia: John of England laboured under the curse of an excommunication, which interdict extended to his kingdom. Philip Augustus was busily employed in taking advantage of all the troubles that were in full action around him; on one side by endeavouring to extend his influence in Germany, and on the other by constant efforts to weaken the power of the English, who were masters of several provinces of his kingdom. John of Brienne arrived at Ptolemaïs with the train of a king, but he only brought with him three hundred knights to defend his kingdom; his new subjects, however, still full of hopes, looked upon him no less as a liberator. His marriage was celebrated in the presence of the barons, the princes, and the bishops of Ptolemaïs. As the truce was about to expire, the Saracens resumed their arms, and disturbed the festivities of the coronation. Malek-Adel entered Palestine at the head of an army, and the infidels not only laid siege to Tripoli, but threatened Ptolemaïs.

The new king, at the head of a small number of faithful warriors, created great admiration for his valour in the field of battle; but he was not able to deliver the Christian provinces from the presence of a formidable enemy. When the defenders of Palestine compared their scanty ranks with the multitude of their enemies, they sank at once into a state of despondency; and even those who so lately scorned the thoughts of peace with the infidels, could not muster either strength or courage to oppose to their attacks. Most of the French knights that had accompanied the new king, quitted the kingdom they had come to succour, and returned into Europe. The dominions of John of Brienne consisted of the city of Ptolemaïs alone, and he had no army to defend even that; he then began to perceive he had undertaken a perilous and difficult task, and that he should not be able to contend for any length of time against the united forces of the Saracens. Ambassadors were sent to Rome to inform the pope of the pressing dangers of the Christian states in Asia, and once more to implore the support of the princes of Europe, and, above all, of the French knights.

These fresh cries of alarm were scarcely heard by the nations of the West. The troubles which agitated Europe at the period of the departure of John of Brienne for Palestine were far from being allayed, and prevented France especially from lending any assistance to the Christian colonies. Languedoc and most of the southern provinces of the kingdom were then desolated by religious wars, which fully employed the bravery of the French knights and nobles.

A spirit of inquiry and indocility, which had arisen among the faithful, and with which St. Bernard had reproached his age, was making alarming progress every day. The most holy doctors had already many times expressed their grief at the abasement of the holy word, of which every one constituted himself judge and arbiter, and which was treated, said Stephen of Tournay in his letters to the pope, with as little discernment as *holy things given to dogs, or pearls cast at the feet of swine*. This spirit of independence and pride, joined to the love of paradox and novelty; to the decline of sound studies, and the relaxation of ecclesiastical discipline; had given birth to heresies which rent the bosom of the Church.

The most dangerous of all the new sects was that of the Albigeois, [172] which took its name from the city of Albi, in which its first assemblies had been held. These new sectarians being unable to explain the existence of evil under a just and good God, as the Manicheans had done, adopted two principles. According to their belief, God had first created Lucifer and his angels; Lucifer having revolted from God, was banished from heaven, and produced the visible world, over which he reigned. God, to re-establish order, created his second son, Jesus Christ, to be the genius of good, as Lucifer had been the genius of evil. Several contemporary writers represent the Albigeois in the most odious colours, and describe them as given up to all kinds of error; but this opinion must not be adopted in all its rigour by impartial history. For the honour of human nature we feel bound to say, that never did a religious sect dare to endeavour to win the approbation of mankind whilst presenting an example of depravity of morals; and that in no age, among no people, has a false doctrine ever been able to lead astray any number of men, without being supported by at least an appearance of virtue.

The wisest and most earnest Christians were at that period desirous of a reform in the clergy. "But there were," says Bossuet, "vain and proud minds, [173] full of bitterness, which, struck by the disorders that reigned in the Church, and more particularly among its ministers, did not believe that the promises of its eternal duration could possibly subsist amongst these abuses. These, become proud, and thence weak, yielded to the temptation which leads to a hatred of the Church from a hatred of those who preside in it; and as if the malice of man could annihilate the work of God, the aversion they had conceived for the teachers, made them hate at the same time both the doctrine they taught and the authority they had received from God."

This disposition of men's minds gave the apostles of error a most deplorable ascendancy, and multiplied the number of their disciples. Among the new sectarians, the most remarkable were the *Vaudois*, or *Poor of Lyons*, who devoted themselves to a state of idle poverty, and despised the clergy, whom they accused of living in luxury and voluptuousness; the *Apostoliques*, who boasted of being the only mystical body of Jesus Christ; the *Popelicains*, who abhorred the eucharist, marriages, and the other sacraments; the *Aymeristes*, whose teachers announced to the world the future establishment of a purely spiritual worship, and denied the existence of a hell or a paradise, persuaded that sin finds in itself its own punishment, and virtue its own reward.

As the greater part of these heretics exhibited a sovereign contempt for the authority of the Church, which was then the first of all authorities, all those who wished to shake off the yoke of divine laws, and those even to whom their passions rendered the restraint of human laws intolerable, came at length to range themselves under the banners of these innovators, and were welcomed by a sect anxious to increase and strengthen itself, and always disposed to consider as its partisans and defenders, men whom society cast from its bosom, who dreaded justice, and could not endure established order. Thus the pretended reformers of the thirteenth century, whilst themselves affecting austerity of manners, and proclaiming the triumph of virtue and truth, admitted into their bosom both corruption and licentiousness, destroyed every regulation of authority, abandoned everything to the caprice of the passions, and left no bond to society, no power to morals, no check upon the multitude.

The new heresies had been condemned in several councils; but as violence was sometimes employed in executing the decisions of the Church, persecution only tended to sour men's minds, instead of bringing them back to truth. Missionaries and papal legates were sent into Languedoc, to convert the misled wanderers from the flock; but their preaching produced no fruit, and the voice of falsehood prevailed over the word of God. The preachers of the faith, whom the heretics reproached with their luxury, their ignorance, and the depravity of their manners, had neither sufficient resignation nor sufficient humility to support such outrages, or offer them as a sacrifice to Jesus Christ, whose apostles they were. Exposed to the scoffs of the sectarians, and gathering nothing from the labours of their missions but humiliation and contempt, they accustomed themselves to view the people they were sent to convert as personal enemies; and a spirit of vengeance and pride, which certainly came not from heaven, made them believe it was their duty to bring into the right road, by force of arms, all who had denied their power or resisted their eloquence. The sovereign pontiff, whose mind was constantly bent upon the Asiatic war, hesitated at ordering a crusade to be preached against the Albigeois; but he was led away by the opinions of the clergy, perhaps also by that of his age, and at last promised to all Christians who would take up arms against the Albigeois the same privileges as those granted to the Crusaders against the Saracens. [174] Simon de Montfort, the duke of Burgundy, and the duke of Nevers obeyed the orders of the Holy See: the hatred which this new sect inspired, but still more the facility of gaining indulgences from the sovereign pontiff without quitting Europe, drew a great number of warriors to the standards of this crusade. The Inquisition owes its birth to this war; an institution at once fatal to humanity, religion, and patriotism. Piles and stakes appeared on all sides, cities were taken by storm, and their inhabitants put to the sword. The violences and cruelties which accompanied this unfortunate war have been described by those even who took a most active part in them; [175] their recitals, which we have great difficulty in believing, frequently resemble the language of falsehood and exaggeration. In periods of vertigo and fury, when violent passions come in to mislead both opinions and consciences, it is not rare to meet with men who exaggerate the excesses to which they have given themselves up, and boast of more evil than they have committed.

For ourselves, the disastrous war against the Albigeois does not enter into the plan of this history, and if we have spoken of it here, it was only the better to describe the situation of France at this period, and the obstacles which then opposed themselves to all enterprises beyond sea. Amidst these constantly increasing obstacles, Innocent III. was deeply afflicted at not being able to send succours to the Christians of Palestine, his regret being the greater from the circumstance that at the very time the Albigeois and the count of Thoulouse were subjected to this frightful crusade, the Saracens were becoming more formidable in Spain. The king of Castile, threatened by an innumerable army, had just called upon all Frenchmen able to bear arms to come to his assistance. The pope himself had written to all the bishops of France, recommending them to exhort the faithful of their dioceses to assist in a great battle which was to be fought between the Spaniards and the Moors, about the octave of Pentecost (1212). Innocent promised the warriors who would repair to Spain, the usual indulgences of holy wars; and a solemn procession was made at Rome, to implore of God the destruction of the Moors and Saracens. The archbishops of Narbonne and Bordeaux, the bishop of Nantes, and a great number of French nobles, crossed the Pyrenees, followed by two thousand knights with their squires and serjeants-at-arms. The Christian army met the Moors in the plains of Las Navas de Tolosa, and fought a battle, in which more than two hundred thousand infidels lost either their lives or their liberty. The conquerors, loaded with spoils and surrounded by the dead, sang the *Te Deum* on the field of battle: the standard of the leader of the Almoades was sent to Rome as a trophy of the victory granted to the prayers of the Christian Church.

On learning the issue of the battle of Tolosa, the sovereign pontiff, amidst the assembled inhabitants of Rome, offered up thanks to God for having scattered the enemies of his people, and at the same time prayed that Heaven in its mercy would, in the end, deliver the Christians of Syria as it had just delivered the Christians of Spain.

The head of the Church renewed his exhortations to the faithful for the defence of the kingdom of Jesus Christ; but amidst the troubles and civil wars that he himself had excited, he could gain no attention to the complaints of Jerusalem, and shed tears of despair at the indifference of the nations of the West. About this period such a circumstance was beheld as had never occurred even in times so abounding in prodigies and extraordinary events. Fifty thousand children, in France and Germany, braving paternal authority, gathered together and pervaded both cities and countries, singing these words:—"Lord Jesus, restore to us your holy cross!" When they were asked whither they were going, or what they intended to do, they replied, "We are going to Jerusalem, to deliver the sepulchre of our Saviour." Some ecclesiastics, blinded by false zeal, had preached this crusade; most of the faithful saw nothing in it but the inspiration of Heaven, and thought that Jesus Christ, to show his divine power, and to confound the pride of the greatest captains, and of the wise and powerful of the earth, had placed his cause in the hands of simple and timid infancy.

Many women of bad character, and dishonest men insinuated themselves amongst the crowd of these new soldiers of the cross, to seduce and plunder them. A great portion of this juvenile militia crossed the Alps, to embark at the Italian ports; whilst those who came from the provinces of France, directed their course to Marseilles. On the faith of a miraculous revelation, they had been made to believe that this year (1213) the drought would be so great that the sun would dissipate all the waters of the sea, and thus an easy road for pilgrims would be opened across the bed of the Mediterranean to the coasts of Syria. Many of these young Crusaders lost themselves in forests, then so abundant and large, and wandering about at hazard, perished with heat, hunger, thirst, and fatigue; others returned to their homes, ashamed of their imprudence, saying, *they really did not know why they had gone.* Among those that embarked, some were shipwrecked, or given up to the Saracens, against whom they had set out to fight; many, say the old chronicles, gathered the palms of martyrdom, and offered the infidels the edifying spectacle of the firmness and courage the Christian religion is capable of inspiring at the most tender age as well as at the more mature.

Such of these children as reached Ptolemais must have created terror as well as astonishment, by making the Christians of the East believe that Europe had no longer any government or laws, no longer any wise or prudent men, either in the councils of princes or those of the Church. Nothing more completely demonstrates the spirit of these times than the indifference with which such disorders were witnessed. No authority interfered, either to stop or prevent the madness; and when it was announced to the pope that death had swept away the flower of the youth of France and Germany, he contented himself with saying,—"These children reproach us with having fallen asleep, whilst they were flying to the assistance of the Holy Land." [176]

The sovereign pontiff, in order to accomplish his designs, and rekindle the enthusiasm of the faithful, found it necessary to strike the imagination of the nations vividly, and to present a grand spectacle to the Christian world. Innocent resolved to assemble a general council at Rome, to deliberate upon the state of the Church and the fate of the Christians of the East. "The necessity for succouring the Holy Land," said he in his letters of convocation, "and the hope of conquering the Saracens, are greater than ever; we renew our cries and our prayers to you, to excite you to this noble enterprise. No one can imagine," added Innocent, "that God has need of your arms to deliver Jerusalem; but he offers you an opportunity of showing your penitence, and proving your love for him. Oh, my brethren, how many advantages has not the Christian Church already derived from the scourges that have desolated her, and desolate her still! How many crimes have been expiated by repentance! How many virtues revive at the fire of charity! How many conversions are made among sinners by the complaining voice of Jerusalem! Bless, then, the ingenious mercy, the generous artifice of Jesus Christ, who seeks to touch your hearts, to seduce your piety, and is willing to owe to his misled disciples a victory which he holds in his all-powerful hand." [177]

The pope afterwards compares Jesus Christ banished from his heritage, to one of the kings of the earth who might be driven from his dominions. "Where are the vassals," added he, "who will not risk their fortunes and their lives to restore their sovereign to his kingdom? Such of the subjects and servants of the monarch as shall have done nothing for his cause, ought they not to be ranked with the rebels, and be subjected to the punishment due to revolt and treason? It is thus that Jesus Christ will treat those who remain indifferent to the insults heaped upon him, and refuse to take up arms to fight against his enemies."

To raise the hopes and the courage of the Christians, the holy father terminated his exhortation to the faithful, by saying, that "the power of Mahomet drew towards its end; for that power was nothing but the beast of the Apocalypse, which was not to extend beyond the number of six hundred years, [178] and already six centuries were accomplished." These last words of the pope were sustained by the popular predictions which were spread throughout the West, and created a belief that the destruction of the Saracens was at hand. [179]

As in preceding crusades, the sovereign pontiff promised all who should take arms against the infidels, the remission of their sins and the especial protection of the Church. Upon so important an occasion, the head of the Christians laid open the treasures of divine mercy to all the faithful, in proportion to their zeal and their gifts. All prelates and ecclesiastics, as well as the inhabitants of cities and countries, were invited to raise a certain number of warriors, and support them for three years, according to their means. The pope exhorted princes and nobles who would not take the cross, to second the zeal of the Crusaders in every way in their power; the head of the Church demanded of all the faithful, prayers; of the rich, alms and tributes; of knights, an example of courage; of maritime cities, vessels; he himself engaging to make the greatest sacrifices. Processions were to be made every month in all parishes, in order to obtain the benedictions of Heaven; all the efforts, all the vows, all the thoughts of Christians were to be directed towards the object of the holy war. That nothing might divert the faithful from the expedition against the Saracens, the Holy See revoked the indulgences granted to those who abandoned their homes to go and fight against the Albigeois in Languedoc, or the Moors on the other side of the Pyrenees.

It is plain that the sovereign pontiff neglected nothing that could render the success of the holy enterprise more certain. A modern historian justly remarks, that he employed every means, even such as were not likely to succeed; for he wrote to the sultan of Damascus and Cairo, inviting him to replace the holy city in the hands of the servants of the true God. Innocent said in his letter, that God had chosen the infidels as his instruments of vengeance; that he had permitted Saladin to get possession of Jerusalem, in order to punish the sins of the Christians; but that the day of deliverance was come, and that the Lord, disarmed by the prayers of his people, was about to restore the heritage of Jesus Christ. The sovereign pontiff counselled the sultan to avoid the effusion of blood, and prevent the desolation of his empire.

This was not the first time that the head of the Church had addressed prayers and warnings to the Mussulman powers. Two years before he had written to the sultan of Aleppo, in the hope of bringing him back to the way of evangelical truth, and making him a faithful auxiliary of the Christians. All these attempts, which ended in nothing, clearly prove that the pope was perfectly unacquainted with the spirit and character of the Mussulmans. The sovereign pontiff was not more fortunate when, in his letters, he desired the patriarch of Jerusalem to use his utmost endeavours to arrest the progress of corruption and licentiousness among the Christians of Palestine. The Christians of Syria made no change in their morals, and all the passions maintained their reign amongst them; whilst the Mussulmans fortified the holy city that was demanded of them, and employed themselves in arming against the attacks of the enemies of Islamism.

Nothing could exceed the ardour and activity of the sovereign pontiff. History can scarcely follow him, whilst seeking in every direction enemies against the Mussulmans; appealing, by turns, to the patriarchs of Alexandria and Antioch, and to all the princes of Armenia and Syria. His eye took in at one view both East and West. His letters and ambassadors passed unceasingly throughout Europe. He sent the convocation for the council and the bull of the crusade into all the provinces of Christendom; and his apostolic exhortations resounded from the shores of the Danube and the Vistula to the banks of the Tigris and the Thames. [180]

Commissaries were chosen to make the decisions of the Holy See known to all Christians: their mission was to preach the holy war, and reform manners; to invoke at the same time the knowledge of the learned and the courage of warriors. In many provinces, the mission of preaching the crusade was confided to the bishops; Cardinal Peter Robert de Courçon, who was then in France, as legate of the pope, received great powers from the Holy See; and travelled through the kingdom, exhorting Christians to take up the cross and arms.

The cardinal de Courçon had been in his youth the disciple of Foulke of Neuilly, and had gained great celebrity by his eloquence. The multitude flocked from all parts to hear so distinguished a preacher of the

Word, clothed in all the splendour of Romish power. "The legate," says Fleury, "had the power of regulating everything that was connected with tournaments; and, which will appear more singular, the faculty of granting a certain indulgence to those who were present at the sermons in which he preached the crusade." Faithful to the spirit of the religion of Jesus Christ, the cardinal de Courçon gave the cross to all Christians who asked for it, without reflecting that women, children, old men, the deaf, the blind, the lame, could not make war against the Saracens; or that an army could not be formed as the Gospel composed the feast of the father of the family. Thus this liberty of entering into the holy bands, accorded without distinction or choice, only disgusted the barons and knights, and cooled the ardour of the common soldiers. [181]

Among the orators whom the pope associated with the cardinal de Courçon, one of the most remarkable was James of Vitri, whom the Church had already placed in the rank of its celebrated doctors. Whilst he preached the crusade in the different provinces of France, [182] the fame of his virtues and talents extended even to the East. The canons of Ptolemaïs demanded him of the pope as their pastor and bishop; and the wishes of the Christians of Palestine were immediately granted. James of Vitri, after having excited the warriors of the West to take arms, became afterwards a witness of their labours, and related them in a history which has come down to our times.

The preaching of the holy war awakened everywhere the charity of the faithful. Philip Augustus gave up the fortieth part of his territorial revenues towards the expenses of the crusade, and a great number of nobles and prelates followed his example. [183] As boxes had been placed in all churches to receive the alms of the charitable, these alms brought considerable sums into the hands of the cardinal de Courçon, who was accused of having appropriated to himself the gifts offered to Jesus Christ. These accusations were the more eagerly received, from the legate having taken upon him to exercise, in the name of the Holy See, an authority which was displeasing to both the monarch and his people. The cardinal, without the approbation of the king, levied taxes, enrolled warriors, forgave debts, lavished both rewards and punishments, and, in a word, usurped all the prerogatives of sovereignty. The exercise of such an unbounded power was the cause of trouble to all the provinces. [184] To prevent disorders, Philip Augustus thought it necessary to lay down regulations which should specify to the general council, the individual position of the Crusaders, and the exemptions and privileges they were to enjoy.

Whilst the cardinal de Courçon continued to preach the crusade throughout the provinces of France, the archbishop of Canterbury was earnestly engaged in inciting the people of England to take up arms against the infidels. During a length of time, the kingdom of England had been troubled by the violent contentions of the commons, the barons, and even the clergy, who had taken advantage of the excommunications [185] launched by the pope against King John, to obtain a confirmation of their liberties. The English monarch, when subscribing the conditions that had been dictated to him, had yielded much more to necessity and force, than to his own inclinations; he wished earnestly to retract what he had granted, and in order to place his crown under the protection of the Church, he took the cross, and swore to go and fight against the Saracens. The sovereign pontiff placed faith in the submission and promises of the king of England; and after having preached a crusade against this prince, whom he accused of being an enemy of the Church, he employed the whole authority of the Holy See, and all the thunders of religion in his defence.

King John had no other motive in taking the cross but to deceive the pope, and obtain the protection of the Church; the sign of the Crusaders was assumed by him only as a means of preserving his power; a false and deceitful policy, which was soon unmasked, and, without doubt, assisted much in diminishing the public enthusiasm for the holy war. The barons of England, in their turn excommunicated by the pope, employed themselves in defending their liberties, and paid no attention to the holy orators who called upon them to embark for Asia.

The empire of Germany was not less disturbed than the kingdom of England. Otho of Saxony, after having been, during ten years, the object of all the predilections of the Holy See, drew upon himself all at once the implacable hatred of Innocent, by putting forth some claims to certain domains of the Church, and to the kingdom of Naples and Sicily. Not only was he himself excommunicated, but the cities even that remained faithful to him were placed under an interdict. The sovereign pontiff opposed Frederick II., son of Henry VI., to Otho, in the same manner as he had opposed Otho to Philip of Swabia. Germany and Italy were immediately in a state of agitation and trouble. Frederick, who was crowned king of the Romans at Aix la Chapelle, took the cross, from a sentiment of gratitude, and with the hope of securing the support of the Holy See in ascending the imperial throne.

Otho meanwhile neglected no means of preserving the empire, and resisting the views and undertakings of the court of Rome. He made war against the pope, and allied himself with all the enemies of Philip Augustus, who had declared for Frederick. A formidable league, composed of the king of England and the counts of Flanders, Holland, and Boulogne, threatened France with an invasion. The capital and provinces of that kingdom were already shared among the leaders of this league, when Philip gained the celebrated battle of Bouvines. This memorable victory [186] secured the independence and honour of the French monarchy, and restored peace to Europe. Otho, conquered, lost his allies, and sunk beneath the thunders of the Church.

The period was now arrived at which the council summoned by the pope was to meet. From all parts of Europe, ecclesiastics, nobles, princes, and the ambassadors of princes, repaired to the capital of the Christian world. The deputies from Antioch and Alexandria, with the patriarchs of Constantinople and Jerusalem, came to Rome to implore the support of the nations of Christendom; the ambassadors of Frederick, Philip Augustus, and the kings of England and Hungary, in the names of their sovereigns, came to take their places in the council. This assembly, which represented the universal Church, and in which were nearly five hundred bishops and archbishops, and more than a hundred abbots and prelates from all the provinces of the East and West, took place in the church of the Lateran, [187] and was presided over by the sovereign pontiff. Innocent opened the council by a sermon, in which he deplored the errors of his age and the misfortunes of the Church. After having exhorted the clergy and the faithful, to sanctify by their morals, the measures he was about to take against heretics and the Saracens, he represented Jerusalem as clothed in mourning, exhibiting the chains of her captivity, and calling upon all the prophets to lend their voices to reach the hearts of the Christians.

"Oh! ye," said Jerusalem by the mouth of the pontiff, "who pass along the public roads, behold, and see if ye have ever witnessed grief like mine. Hasten then all, O ye that love me, to deliver me from the depth of my miseries! I, who was the queen of all nations, am now subjected to a tribute; I, who was formerly filled with people, am now left desolate and almost alone! The roads of Sion mourn, because no one comes to my solemnities. My enemies have crushed down my head; all my sacred places are profaned; the Holy Sepulchre, once so splendid, is covered with disgrace; there, where of late the Son of God was adored, worship is now offered up to the son of perdition and hell. The children of the stranger load me with outrages, and, pointing to the cross of Jesus, say to me, *Thou hast placed thy trust in vile wood; we shall see whether this wood can save thee in the hour of danger.*" [188]

Innocent after having thus made the mourning Jerusalem eloquent, conjured the faithful to take pity on her misfortunes, and arm for her deliverance. He terminated his exhortation by these words, which breathe both his grief and his ardent zeal:—"My beloved brethren, I give myself up entirely to you; if you think it best, I promise to go in person with the kings, princes, and nations; you shall see if, by my cries and my prayers, I shall be able to excite them to fight for the Lord, to avenge the insults of the crucified, whom our sins have banished from the land wetted with his blood, and sanctified with the mystery of our redemption."

The discourse of the pontiff was listened to in religious silence; but as Innocent spoke of several objects at the same time, and as his oratory was full of allegories, he did not at all succeed in awakening the enthusiasm of the assembly. The fathers of the council appeared to be not less affected by the abuses introduced into the Church, than by the reverses of the Christians of the East; in the first place the assembly employed itself in endeavouring to find means to reform ecclesiastical discipline, and check the progress of heresy.

In a declaration of faith, the council explained the doctrine of Christians, and recalled to their minds the symbol of evangelical belief. They opposed truth to error, persuasion to violence, and the virtues of the Gospel to the passions of sectarians and innovators: happy would it then have been for the Christian church, if the pope had followed this example of moderation; and if, whilst defending the rights of religion, he had not forgotten the rights of sovereigns and humanity. By an apostolic decree, proclaimed amidst the council, Innocent deposed the count of Thoulouse, who was considered the protector of heresy, and gave his states to Simon de Montfort, who had fought against, or rather slaughtered the Albigeois.

Innocent could not pardon the count of Thoulouse for having provoked a war which had agitated Christendom, and suspended the execution of his designs for the Eastern crusade. The violent policy of the sovereign pontiff aimed at striking terror into all heretics, and encouraging Christians to arm for the cause of Jesus Christ and that of his vicar upon earth.

After having condemned the new errors, and pronounced the anathemas of the Church against all who strayed from the way of the faith, the pontiff and the fathers of the council gave their attention to the Christians of the East, and the means of promptly succouring the Holy Land. All the dispositions expressed in the bull of convocation were confirmed; it was decreed that all ecclesiastics should pay the twentieth of their revenues towards the expenses of the crusade; that the pope and the cardinals should pay the tenth of theirs, and that there should be a truce of four years among all Christian princes. The council launched the thunders of excommunication against all princes that should molest the march of pilgrims, and against all that should furnish infidels with provisions or arms: the sovereign pontiff promised to direct the preparations for the war, to contribute three thousand silver marks and to supply, at his own expense, several vessels for the transport of the Crusaders.

The decisions of the council and the speeches of the pope made a profound impression upon the minds of the western Christians. All the preachers of the holy war were formally directed to recall the faithful to a sense of penitence, and to prohibit dances, tournaments, and public sports; to reform morals and to revive in all hearts the love of religion and virtue. They were commanded, after the example of the sovereign pontiff, to make the complaints of Jerusalem resound in the palaces of princes; and to earnestly solicit monarchs and nobles to assume the cross, so that the people might be induced to do so likewise.

The decrees concerning the holy wars were published in all the churches of the West; in several provinces, particularly in the north, of Europe, the prodigies and miraculous apparitions that had excited enthusiasm at the period of the first crusades, again became common; luminous crosses appeared in the heavens, and made the inhabitants of Cologne and the cities in the vicinity of the Rhine believe that God favoured the holy enterprise, and that the divine power promised the defeat and ruin of the infidels to the arms of the Crusaders.

The orators redoubled their ardour and zeal to engage the faithful to take a part in the holy war. From the pulpits imprecations were poured forth against the Saracens, always accompanied by a repetition of the words of Christ: "I am come to establish war." The eloquence of prelates, bishops, and pastors had no other aim than summoning all Christian warriors to arms. The voices of preachers were not the only trumpet-calls; poetry herself, who had but recently revived in the southern provinces of France, chose the holy expeditions as the themes of her songs; and the profane muse of the troubadours mingled their notes with the animated words of the sacred orators. The Pierres d'Auvergne, the Ponces de Capdeuil, the Folquets de Romano, ceased to sing the love of ladies and the courtesy of knights, to celebrate in their verses, the sufferings of Christ and the captivity of Jerusalem. "The times are come," said they, "in which it will be seen who are the men worthy of serving the Eternal. God now calls upon the valiant and chivalrous; they shall be his soldiers for ever, who, knowing how to suffer for their faith, and fight for God, shall prove themselves frank, generous, loyal, and brave; let the base lovers of life or seekers for gold remain behind. God now only calls upon the good and brave. It is his will that his faithful servants should secure salvation by noble feats of arms; and that glory obtained in fight should open to them the gates of heaven." [189]

One of the minstrels of the holy war celebrates in his verses the zeal, the prudence, and courage of the head of the Church; and to induce the faithful to assume the cross, sings: *"We have a sure and valorous guide, the sovereign pontiff Innocent."*

It then began to be hoped that the father of the Christians would himself lead the Crusaders, and sanctify the Asiatic expedition by his presence. The pope, in the council of the Lateran, had expressed a desire to assume the cross, and to go in person to take possession of the heritage of Christ; but the state of Europe, the progress of heresy, and, doubtless, also, the advice of the bishops and cardinals, prevented the accomplishment of his design.

As germs of dissension still subsisted between several European states, these discords might be prejudicial to the success of the holy war; and the pope sent forth emissaries to act as angels of peace; he himself repairing to Tuscany, to appease the quarrels that had broken out between the Pisans and Genoese. His words soothed down all angry passions; at his voice the most implacable enemies swore to forget their disputes, and unite to combat against the Saracens. His most ardent wishes appeared about to be fulfilled, and the whole West, obedient to his sovereign will, was ready to precipitate itself upon Asia, when he fell suddenly ill, and died, leaving to his successors the care and honour of finishing so great an enterprise.

Like all men who have exercised great power amidst political tempests, Innocent, after his death, was, by turns, praised and blamed with all the exaggeration of love and hatred. Some said he had been summoned to the heavenly Jerusalem, as God wished to reward his zeal for the deliverance of the holy places; whilst others had recourse to miraculous apparitions, and made saints speak in condemnation of his memory; sometimes he was seen pursued by a diagon, whose purpose was to inflict justice upon him; and at others he appeared surrounded by the flames of purgatory. Europe had been in a constant state of trouble during his pontificate; there was scarcely a kingdom upon which the wrath of the pontiff had not been poured out; and so many excesses, so many misfortunes had embittered men's minds, that it was natural they should take a pleasure in believing that the vicar of Christ upon earth was expiating in another life the crimes of this. Innocent, nevertheless was irreproachable in his manners; at first he had evinced some degree of moderation; he loved truth and justice; but the unhappy condition of the Church, the obstacles of all kinds which he met with in his spiritual [190] government, irritated his character, and drove him to the excesses of a violent policy; at length, preserving no propriety or self-command, he burst forth with the ever-memorable and reprehensible words: "*Sword, sword, spring from the scabbard, and sharpen thyself to kill.*" [191] As he had undertaken far too much, he left serious embarrassments to those who might assume the reins of power after him; and such was the situation in which his policy had placed the Holy See, that his successors were obliged to follow up his maxims, and complete both the good and the evil he had begun. From this period, the history of the crusades will be incessantly interrupted by the quarrels of popes and princes, and we shall follow the pilgrims to the Holy Land amidst the clashing of the thunders launched by the various heads of the Church.

Censius Savelli, cardinal of St. Lucia, was chosen by the conclave to succeed Innocent, and governed the Church under the name of Honorius III. On the day after his coronation, the new pope wrote to the king of Jerusalem, to announce his elevation, and to revive the hopes of the Christians of Syria. "Let not the death of Innocent," said he, "depress your courage; although I am far from being his equal in merit, I will show the same zeal for the deliverance of the Holy Land; and when the season shall arrive, will do everything in my power to assist you." A pontifical letter, addressed to all bishops, exhorted them to continue to preach the crusade.

In order to secure success to the Oriental expedition, Innocent had first endeavoured to re-establish peace in Europe; and certainly the necessity in which the popes found themselves at such times, to promote concord among nations, was one of the greatest benefits of the holy wars. Honorius followed the example of his predecessor, and was desirous of calming all discords, even such as owed their origin to the pretensions of the Romish see. Louis VIII., son of Philip Augustus, at the solicitation of the pontiff, had taken arms against England, and was not willing to renounce the project of invading a kingdom so long subjected to the anger of the Church. The pope even stooped to supplications to disarm the redoubtable enemy of the king of England. He hoped that England and France, after having suspended their hostilities, would unite their efforts for the deliverance of the holy places; but these hopes were never accomplished. Henry III. ascended the throne of England after the death of John, and took the cross to secure the favour of the sovereign pontiff; but he had no idea of quitting his kingdom. The king of France, constantly occupied with the war against the Albigeois, and perhaps also with the secret designs of his ambition, satisfied himself with expressing the greatest respect for the authority of the Holy See, but took no part in the crusade. [192]

Most of the bishops and prelates of the kingdom, whom the sovereign pontiff had entreated to present an example of devotedness, exhibited much greater eagerness and zeal on this occasion than the barons and knights; many of them took the cross, and prepared to set out for the East. Frederick, who owed the imperial crown to the protection of the Church, renewed, in two solemn assemblies, his oath to make war against the Saracens. The example and promises of the emperor, whatever doubt might be entertained of their sincerity, had a powerful effect over the princes and people of Germany. The inhabitants of the banks of the Rhine, those of Friesland, Bavaria, Saxony, and Norway; the dukes of Austria, Moravia,

Brabant, and Lemburg; the counts of Juliers, Holland, De Wit, and Loo; with the archbishop of Mayence and the bishops of Bamberg, Passau, Strasburg, Munster, and Utrecht, emulatively ranged themselves under the banners of the cross, and prepared to quit the West.

Among the princes who took the oath to fight against the Mussulmans, was Andrew II., king of Hungary. Bela, the father of the Hungarian monarch, had made a vow to go to the Holy Land; but not having been able to undertake the pilgrimage, he had, on his death-bed, required his son to accomplish his oath. Andrew, after having taken the cross, was for a long time detained in his states by the troubles to which his ambition had given birth, and which he had great difficulty in suppressing. Gertrude, whom he had married before the fifth crusade, made enemies of the whole court and nobility by her pride and her intrigues. This imperious princess [193] committed such extraordinary insults against the magnates of the kingdom, and inspired them with so violent a hatred, that they formed conspiracies against her life, and introduced murderers even into her palace. Disorders and misfortunes without number followed these crimes, the greatest of which, doubtless, was the impunity of the guilty.

In such circumstances policy would certainly have pointed it out to the king of Hungary, as his duty, to remain in his own states; but the spectacle of so many unpunished crimes, without doubt, alarmed his weakness, and strengthened his desire of getting at a distance from a court filled with his enemies. Like his mother, the widow of Bela, [194] he expected to find in the places consecrated by the sufferings of Christ, an asylum against the griefs which beset his life; the Hungarian monarch might likewise think that the holy pilgrimage would make him more respected by his subjects, and that the Church, ever armed in favour of royal crusaders, would defend the rights of his crown better than he himself could. He resolved at length to perform the vow he had made before his dying father, and earnestly set about preparations for his departure for Syria.

Andrew then reigned over a vast kingdom,—Hungary, Dalmatia, Croatia, Bosnia, Galicia, and the province of Lodomira obeyed his laws, and paid him tribute; and throughout all these provinces, so lately enemies to the Christians, the crusades were preached. Hordes wandering amidst forests, listened to the complaints of Sion, and swore to fight against the infidels. Among the nations of Hungary, who, a century before, had been the terror of the pilgrim companions of Peter the Hermit, a crowd of warriors eagerly took the cross, and promised to follow their monarch to the Holy Land.

Vessels and fleets for the transport of the Crusaders were equipped in all the ports of the Baltic, the ocean, and the Mediterranean; and yet, at the very same time, a crusade was being preached against the inhabitants of Prussia, who still remained in the darkness of idolatry. Poland, Saxony, Norway, and Livonia armed their warriors to overthrow the idols of paganism on the banks of the Oder and the Vistula, whilst the other nations of the West were preparing to make war against the Saracens in the plains of Judæa and Syria.

The still savage people of Prussia, separated by their religion and their customs from the other inhabitants of Europe, presented in the centre of Christendom, in the thirteenth century, a living picture of ancient paganism, and of the superstitions of the old nations of the North. Their character and their manners are worthy of fixing the attention of both the historian and his readers, fatigued, perhaps, by the constant repetition of the preaching of holy wars, and the distant expeditions of the Crusaders.

Much discussion has taken place concerning the origin of the ancient inhabitants of Prussia, and we have nothing on this head but conjectures and systems. The Prussians were, in person, like the Germans; [195] blue eyes, a spirited and lively look, ruddy cheeks, a lofty stature, a robust form, and light hair: this resemblance to the Germans was produced by climate, and not by the mixture of the nations; the inhabitants of Prussia had more affinity with the Lithuanians, whose language they spoke, and whom they imitated in their dress. They lived by the chase, fishing, and the flesh of their flocks; agriculture was not unknown to them; their mares furnished them with milk, their sheep with wool, their bees with honey; in commercial transactions they had very little to do with money: to prepare flax and leather, to split stones, to sharpen their arms, and to fashion yellow amber, constituted the whole of their industry. They marked time by knots tied in thongs, and the hours by the words *twilight, light, dawn, sunrise, evening, the first sleep,* &c. The appearance of the Pleïades directed them in their labours.

The months of the year bore the names of the productions of the earth, and of the objects presented to their eyes by each season; they knew the month of crows, the month of pigeons, that of cuckoos, of the green birch-trees, of the linden-trees, of corn, of the departure of the birds, of the fall of leaves, &c. Wars, the conflagrations of great forests, hurricanes, and inundations, formed the principal epochs of their history.

The people dwelt in huts built of earth, the rich in houses constructed of oak timber; there was not a city in Prussia. Some strong castles appeared upon the hills. This nation, though savage, recognised princes and nobles; he who had conquered enemies, and he who excelled in taming horses, attained nobility. The lords held the right of life and death over their vassals; the Prussians made no wars for the purpose of conquering an enemy's country, but solely to defend their homes and their gods. Their arms consisted of the lance and the javelin, which they handled with much skill. The warriors named their chief, who was blessed by the high priest; before going to battle, the Prussians selected one of their prisoners of war, fastened him to a tree, and transfixed him with arrows. [196] They believed in omens; the eagle, the white pigeon, the crow, the stork, the bustard, promised victory; the stag, the wolf, the lynx, the mouse, the sight of a sick person, or even of an old woman, announced defeats or reverses; when presenting their hand, they offered peace; when swearing to treaties, they placed one hand upon their breast and the other upon the sacred oak. When victorious, they tried their prisoners of war, and the most distinguished among them expired at the stake,—a sacrifice to the gods of the country.

Amidst all their barbarous customs, the Prussians had the reputation of respecting the laws of hospitality. The stranger and the shipwrecked mariner were sure to find an asylum and succour among them; intrepid in war, simple and mild in peace, grateful but vindictive, respecting misfortune, they had more virtues than vices, and were only corrupted by the excess of their superstition.

The Prussians believed in another life; they called hell, *Peckla*; chains, thick darkness, and fetid waters constituted the punishment of the wicked. In the Elysian fields, which they called *Rogus*, beautiful women, banquets, delicious drink, dances, soft couches, and fine clothes were the rewards of virtue.

In a place called *Remové*, arose a flourishing oak, which had witnessed the passage of a hundred generations, whose colossal trunk contained three images of their principal gods; the foliage daily dripped with the blood of immolated victims; there the high priest had established his abode, and there administered justice. The priests alone ventured to approach this holy place; the guilty slunk from it trembling. *Perkunas*, the god of thunder and fire, was the first among the deities of the Prussians; he had the countenance of an angry man, his beard was curled, and his head was surrounded with flames. The people called claps of thunder, the march or steps of Perkunas. Near the grove of Remové, on the banks of a sulphureous spring, an eternal fire burned in honour of the god of thunder.

Near Perkunas, *Potrimpus* appeared, in the form of a young man, wearing a crown of wheat-ears; he was adored as the god of waters and rivers; he preserved mankind from the scourge of war, and presided over the pleasures of peace. By a strange contradiction, they offered up to this pacific divinity, the blood of animals, and that of the captives slaughtered at the foot of the oak; sometimes children were sacrificed to him; the priests consecrated the serpent to him, as symbolical of fortune.

Beneath the shade of the sacred tree, was still another idol, called *Pycollos,* the god of the dead; he bore the form of an old man, with grey hair, hollow eyes, and a pale countenance, his head enfolded in a shroud; his altars were heaps of human bones; the infernal deities were obedient to his laws; he inspired both grief and terror.

A fourth divinity, *Curko,* whose image ornamented the branches of the oak of Remové, furnished mankind with the necessaries of life. Every year, at autumnal seed-time, his image was renewed; it consisted of a goat-skin, elevated upon a pole eight feet high, crowned with blades of corn; the priest sacrificed upon a stone, honey, milk, and the fruits of the earth, whilst the youth of both sexes formed a circle round the idol.

The Prussians celebrated several other festivals during spring and summer, in honour of the same god; at the spring festival, which took place on the 22nd of March, they addressed Curko in these words: "It is thou who hast chased away winter, and brought fair and fine days back to us; by thee the gardens and the fields rebloom; by thee the forests and the woods resume their verdure." The inhabitants of Prussia had a crowd of other gods, whom they invoked for their flocks, their bees, the forests, the waters, harvest, commerce, the peace of families, and conjugal happiness; a divinity with a hundred eyes watched over the threshold of houses; one god guarded the yard, another the stable; the hunter heard the spirit of the forest howl amidst the tree-tops; the mariner recommended himself to the god of the sea. *Laimelé* was invoked by women in labour, and spun the lives of mankind. Tutelary divinities arrested the progress of conflagrations, caused the sap of the birch-trees to flow, guarded roads, and awakened workmen and labourers before the dawn of day. The air, the earth, the waters were peopled by gnomes or little gods, and with ghosts and goblins, which they called *arvans.* It was believed by all that the oak was a tree dear to the gods, and that its shade offered an asylum against the violence of men or the assaults of destiny. In addition to the oak of Remové, the Prussians had several other trees of the same kind, which they considered the sanctuaries of their divinities. They consecrated also linden-trees, firs, maples, and even whole forests; they held in reverence fountains, lakes, and mountains; they adored serpents, owls, storks, and other animals: in short, in the countries inhabited by the Prussians, all nature was filled with divinities, and, up to the fourteenth century, it might be said of a European nation, as Bossuet said of ancient paganism, *"Everything there was god, except God himself."*

A long time before the crusades, St. Adalbert had left his native country, Bohemia, to penetrate into the forests of Prussia, and endeavour to convert the Prussians to Christianity; but his eloquence, his moderation, or his charity, could not disarm the fury of the priests of Perkunas. Adalbert died, pierced with arrows, and received the palm of martyrdom; other missionaries shared the same fate; their blood arose against their murderers, and the report of their death, together with an account of the cruelties of a barbarous people, everywhere cried aloud upon the Christians of the North for vengeance. The neighbouring nations were constantly entertaining the resolution to take arms against the idolaters of Prussia. An abbot of the monastery of Oliva, more able, and still further, more fortunate than his predecessors, undertook the conversion of the pagans of the Oder and the Vistula, and succeeded, with the assistance of the Holy See, in getting up a crusade against the worshippers of false gods; a great number of Christians took the cross, at the summons of the pope, who promised them eternal life if they fell in fight, and lands and treasures if they triumphed over the enemies of Christ. The knights of Christ and the knights of the sword, instituted to subdue the pagans of Livonia, with the Teutonic knights, who in Palestine rivalled in power and glory the two other orders of the Temple and the Hospital, at the first signal flocked to the standards of the army assembled to invade Prussia, and convert its inhabitants: this war lasted more than two centuries. In this sanguinary struggle, if the Christian religion sometimes inspired its combatants with its virtues, the leaders of this long crusade were much more frequently influenced by vengeance, ambition, and avarice. The knights of the Teutonic order, whose bravery almost always amounted to heroism, remained masters of the country conquered by their arms. These victorious monks never edified the people they subdued, either by their moderation or their charity; and were often accused before the tribunal of the head of the Church, of having converted the Prussians, not to make them servants of Christ, but to increase the number of their own subjects and slaves.

We have only spoken of the people of Prussia, and of the wars made against them, to exhibit to our readers a nation and customs almost unknown to modern scholars even; and to show how far ambition and a thirst of conquest was able to abuse the spirit of the crusades: we hasten to return to the expedition that was being prepared against the Saracens.

Germany considered Frederick II. as the leader of the war about to be made in Asia; but the new emperor, seated on a throne for a long time shaken by civil wars, dreading the enterprises of the Italian republics, and perhaps those of the popes their protectors, thought it prudent to defer his departure for Palestine.

The zeal of the Crusaders, however, did not abate, and in their impatience they turned their eyes towards the king of Hungary to take the command in the holy war. Andrew, accompanied by the duke of Bavaria, the duke of Austria, and the German nobles who had taken the cross, set out for the East, at the head of a numerous army, and repaired to Spalatro, where vessels from Venice, Zara, Ancona, and other cities of the Adriatic, awaited the Crusaders, to transport them into Palestine.

In all the countries through which he marched, the king of Hungary was followed by the benedictions of the people. When he approached the city of Spalatro, the inhabitants and the clergy came out in procession to meet him, and conducted him to their principal church, where all the faithful were assembled to call down the mercy of Heaven upon the Christian warriors. A few days after, the fleet of the Crusaders left the port [197] of Spalatro, and set sail for the island of Cyprus, at which place were met the deputies of the king and the patriarch of Jerusalem, of the orders of the Temple and St. John, and of the Teutonic knights.

A crowd of Crusaders, who had embarked at Brindisi, at Genoa, and at Marseilles, preceded the king of Hungary and his army. Lusignan, king of Cyprus, and the greater part of his barons, influenced by the example of so many illustrious princes, took the cross, and promised to follow them into the Holy Land. All the Crusaders embarked together at the port of Lemisso, and landed in triumph at Ptolemaïs.

An Arabian historian says, that since the time of Saladin the Christians had never had so numerous an army in Syria. [198] Thanks to Heaven were offered up in all the churches, for the powerful aid it had sent to the Holy Land; but the joy of the Christians of Palestine was quickly troubled by the serious difficulty in which they found themselves to procure provisions for such a multitude of pilgrims.

This year (1217) had been barren throughout the richest countries of Syria; [199] and the vessels from the West had only been laden with machines of war, arms, and baggage. Deficiency of food was soon felt among the Crusaders, and led the soldiers to license and robbery; the Bavarians committed the greatest disorders; pillaging houses and monasteries, and devastating the neighbouring country; the leaders had no other means of reëstablishing order and peace in the army, but by giving the signal for war against the Saracens; and, to save the lands and dwellings of the Christians, they proposed to their soldiers to ravage the cities and territories of the infidels.

The whole army, commanded by the kings of Jerusalem, Cyprus, and Hungary, encamped on the banks of the torrent of Cison. The patriarch of the holy city, in order to strike the imagination of the Crusaders, and prevent their forgetting the object of their enterprise, repaired to the camp, bringing with him a portion of the wood of the true cross, which he pretended to have been saved at the battle of Tiberias. The kings and princes came out, barefooted, to meet him, and received with respect the sign of redemption. This ceremony rekindled the zeal and enthusiasm of the Crusaders, whose ardent desire now was to fight for Christ. The army crossed the torrent, and advanced towards the valley of Jesraël, between Mount Hermon and Mount Gelboé, without meeting an enemy. The leaders and soldiers bathed in the Jordan, and passed over the plain of Jericho, and along the shores of the great lake of Genesareth. The Christian army marched singing spiritual songs; religion and its remembrances had restored discipline and peace among them. Every object and place they beheld around them filled them with a pious veneration for the Holy Land. In this campaign, which was a true pilgrimage, they made a great number of prisoners without fighting a battle, and returned to Ptolemaïs loaded with booty.

At the period of this crusade, Malek-Adel no longer reigned over either Syria or Egypt. After having mounted the throne of Saladin by injustice and violence, he had descended from it voluntarily; the conqueror of all obstacles, and having no longer a wish to form, he became sensible of the emptiness of human grandeur, and gave up the reins of an empire that nobody had the power to dispute with him. Melik Kamel, the eldest of his sons, was sultan of Cairo; and Corradin [200] was sultan of Damascus. His other sons had received, as their shares of the empire, the principalities of Bosra, Baalbec, Mesopotamia, &c. Malek-Adel, relieved from the cares of government, visited his children by turns, and preserved peace among them. All he had reserved of his past power was the ascendancy of a great renown, and of a glory acquired by numberless heroic exploits; but this ascendancy held princes, people, and army in subjection. In moments of peril, his counsels became laws: the soldiers still considered him as their leader; his sons as their sovereign arbiter; and all Mussulmans as their defender and support.

The new crusade had spread terror among the infidels, but Malek-Adel calmed their fears by assuring them that the Christians would soon be divided amongst themselves, and by telling them that this formidable expedition resembled the storms which howl over Mount Libanus, and which disperse of themselves: neither the armies of Egypt, nor the armies of Syria, made their appearance in Judæa; and the Crusaders assembled at Ptolemaïs were astonished at meeting no enemy to contend with. The leaders of the Christian army had resolved to direct their march towards the banks of the Nile; but winter, which was about to commence, would not permit them to undertake so distant an enterprise. To employ the soldiers, whom idleness always seduced into license, it was determined to make an attack upon Mount Tabor, where the Mussulmans had fortified themselves.

Mount Tabor, so celebrated in the Old and New Testament, arises like a superb dome amidst the vast plain of Galilee. The declivity of the mountain is covered with flowers and odoriferous plants; from the summit of Tabor, which forms a level of a league in extent, may be seen, travellers say, all the banks of the Jordan, the Lake of Tiberias, the Sea of Syria, and most of the places in which Christ performed his miracles.

A church, the erection of which was due to the piety of St. Helena, stood on the very spot where the transfiguration of Christ took place in presence of his disciples, and for a length of time attracted crowds of pilgrims. Two monasteries, built at the summit of Tabor, recalled for centuries the memory of Moses and Elias, whose names they bore; but, from the reign of Saladin, the standard of Mahomet had floated over this holy mountain; the church of St. Helena and the monasteries of Moses and Elias had been demolished, and upon their ruins was raised a fortress, from which the Mussulmans constantly threatened the territories of Ptolemaïs.

It was impossible to ascend Mount Tabor without encountering a thousand dangers; but nothing intimidated the Christian warriors: the patriarch of Jerusalem, who marched at their head, showed them the true cross, and animated them by his example and his eloquent words. Enormous stones rolled from the heights occupied by the infidels, who poured down an endless shower of javelins and arrows upon all the roads which led to the top of the mountain. The valour of the soldiers of the cross braved all the efforts of the Saracens; the king of Jerusalem distinguished himself by prodigies of bravery, and killed two emirs with his own hand. The summit of the mountain being attained, the Crusaders dispersed the Mussulmans, and pursued them to the gates of their fortress: nothing could resist their arms. But all at once several of the leaders began to entertain suspicions regarding the intentions of the sultan of Damascus; and the fear of a surprise acted the more strongly on their minds from no one having foreseen it. Whilst the Mussulmans retired filled with terror behind their ramparts, a sudden panic seized the conquerors: the Crusaders renounced the attack of the fortress, and the whole Christian army retreated without effecting anything; as if it had only ascended Mount Tabor to contemplate the spot rendered sacred by the transfiguration of the Saviour.

We could scarcely yield faith to the account of this precipitate flight, without the evidence of contemporary historians; [201] the ancient chronicles, according to their custom, do not fail to attribute to treachery an event they cannot comprehend; it appears to us, however, much more natural to suppose that the retreat of the Crusaders was produced by the discord and want of foresight which prevailed in all their undertakings. [202]

This retreat had most fatal results; whilst the leaders reproached each other with the disgrace of the army and the egregious error they had committed, the knights and soldiers sank into a state of discouragement. The patriarch of Jerusalem refused from that time to bear the wood of the true cross in the van of the Crusaders, as he found the sight of it could neither revive their piety nor reanimate their courage. The kings and princes who directed the crusade, wishing to retrieve so shameful a reverse before they returned to Palestine, led the army towards Phœnicia. In this new campaign no exploit signalized their arms being winter, a great number of the soldiers, overcome by cold, remained abandoned on the roads, whilst others fell into the hands of the Bedouin Arabs. On Christmas eve, the Crusaders, who were encamped between Tyre and Sarphat, were surprised by a violent tempest; wind, rain, hail, whirlwinds, incessant peals of thunder killed their horses, carried away their tents, and scattered their baggage. This disaster completed their despondency, and created a belief that Heaven refused them its support.

As they were in serious want of provisions, and the whole army could not subsist in one place, they resolved to divide themselves into four different bodies till the end of winter. This separation, which was made amidst mutual complaints, appeared to be the work of discord much more than of necessity. The king of Jerusalem, the duke of Austria, and the grand master of St. John encamped in the plains of Cœsarea; the king of Hungary, the king of Cyprus, and Raymond, son of the prince of Antioch, retired to Tripoli; [203] the grand masters of the Templars and the Teutonic knights, and Andrew d'Avesnes, with the Flemish Crusaders, went to fortify a castle built at the foot of Mount Carmel; the other Crusaders retired to Ptolemaïs with the intention of going back to Europe.

The king of Cyprus fell ill and died just as he was upon the point of embarking for his own kingdom. The king of Hungary was discouraged, and began to despair of the success of a war so unfortunately commenced. This prince, after a sojourn of three months in Palestine, thought his vow accomplished, and resolved, all at once, to return to his dominions.

The West had doubtless been surprised to see Andrew abandon his kingdom, torn by factions, to repair to Syria; and the Eastern Christians were not less astonished at seeing this prince leave Palestine without having done anything for the deliverance of the holy places. The patriarch of Jerusalem reproached him with inconstancy, and employed his utmost efforts to retain him beneath the banners of the cross; but finding Andrew would not yield to his prayers, he had recourse to threats, and displayed the formidable train of the weapons of the Church. Nothing, however, could shake the resolution of the king of Hungary, who satisfied himself with not appearing to desert the cause of Christ by leaving half his troops under the command of the king of Jerusalem.

After having quitted Palestine, Andrew remained for a long time in Armenia, appearing to forget his own enemies, as he had forgotten those of Christ. He came back into Europe through Asia Minor and beheld, whilst passing Constantinople, the wreck of the Latin empire, which ought to have roused him from his pious indolence, and have reminded him of his own dangers. The Hungarian monarch, who had left his army in Syria, took back with him a number of relics; such as the head of St. Peter, the right hand of the apostle Thomas, and one of the seven vases in which Christ changed water into wine at the marriage in Cana: his confidence in these revered objects made him negligent of the means of human prudence; and, if we may believe a contemporary chronicle, [204] when he returned into Hungary, the relics which he brought from the Holy Land suffice for the suppression of all the troubles of his states, and caused peace, the laws, and justice, to nourish throughout his provinces. The greater part of the Hungarian historians, however, hold quite another language, [205] and reproach their monarch with having dissipated his treasures and his armies in an imprudent and an unfortunate expedition; the nobility and people took advantage of his long absence to impose laws upon him, and obtain liberties and privileges which weakened the royal power, and scattered the germs of a rapid decay in the kingdom of Hungary.

After the departure of the king of Hungary, a great number of Crusaders arrived from the ports of Holland, France, and Italy. The Crusaders from Friesland, Cologne, and the banks of the Rhine had stopped on the coast of Portugal, where they had conquered the Moors in several great battles, killed two Saracen princes, and mounted the banners of the cross upon the walls of Alcazar. They described the miracles by which Heaven had seconded their valour, and the apparition of angels, clothed in resplendent armour, who had fought on the banks of the Tagus, in the ranks of the soldiers of Christ. [206] The arrival of these warriors, with the account of their victories, revived the courage of the Crusaders who had remained in Palestine under the command of Leopold, duke of Austria; with such a powerful reinforcement, nothing was talked of but renewing the war against the Mussulmans.

The project of conquering the banks of the Nile often occupied the thoughts of the Christians; since the idea of a war in Egypt had been put forth by the pope himself amidst the council of the Lateran, it had been considered as an inspiration from Heaven; they only thought of the advantages of a rich conquest, and the perils of so difficult an enterprise appeared of no importance in the eyes of the soldiers of the cross.

The Christian army, commanded by the king of Jerusalem, the duke of Austria, and William, count of Holland, embarked at the port of Ptolemaïs, and landed within sight of Damietta, on the northern bank of the second mouth of the Nile. The city of Damietta, [207] situated at the distance of a mile from the sea, had a double rampart on the river side, and a triple wall on the land side; a tower arose in the middle of the Nile, and an iron chain, which reached from the city to the tower, prevented the passage of vessels. The city contained a numerous garrison, with provisions and munitions of war for a long siege. Damietta had already several times resisted formidable attacks of the Christians. Roger, king of Sicily, had made himself master of it in the preceding century, but he was not able to retain and defend it, against the united forces of the Mussulmans.

The Crusaders arrived before Damietta early in April; having pitched their tents in a vast plain, they had behind them lakes and pools abounding in fish of all kinds; [208] before them the Nile, covered with their vessels; a thousand canals, crowned with evergreen papyrus and reeds, intersected the lands, and spread freshness and fertility around them. In the fields which had so lately been the theatre of sanguinary contests, no traces of war were to be seen; harvests of rice covered the plains in which Christian armies had perished by famine; groves of oranges and citrons loaded with flowers and fruit; woods of palms and sycamores, thickets of jasmines and odoriferous shrubs, with a crowd of plants and wonders, unknown to the pilgrims, created the image of an earthly paradise, and made them fancy that Damietta must have been the first dwelling of man in his state of innocence. The aspect of a beautiful sky and a rich climate intoxicated them with joy, kept hope alive in their hearts, and held out to them the accomplishment of all the divine promises. In their religious and warlike enthusiasm, they believed they saw Providence prodigal of its miracles for the success of their arms; scarcely had they established their camp on the bank of the Nile, when an eclipse of the moon covered the horizon with darkness; and even this phenomenon inflamed their courage, as it appeared to them a presage of the greatest victories.

The first attacks [209] were directed against the tower built in the middle of the Nile; vessels, in which were placed towers, ladders, and drawbridges, approached the walls. The soldiers who manned them, braving the arrows and murderous machines of the Mussulmans, made several assaults; but prodigies of strength, courage, and skill were useless. The most intrepid of the Crusaders, victims of their own rash bravery and devotedness, perished, swallowed up by the waves, without being able to be succoured or avenged by their companions. In all the attacks, nothing could equal the impetuous valour of the Western warriors; but this valour was not seconded by either the prudence of the commanders or the discipline of the soldiers; each nation had its leader, its machines of war, its days for fighting; no order governed either attack or retreat; the soldiers on board the vessels wished to manœuvre them, the sailors would fight.

The frequent checks they experienced, at length, however, taught them prudence: the lightest of their vessels ascended the Nile, and returning to cast anchor above the tower built in the middle of the river, attacked and broke asunder the bridge of boats which united the tower with the city. Industry likewise lent its assistance to the bravery of the Crusaders; machines of war were invented, of which no models had previously existed. An enormous wooden castle, built upon two vessels, [210] joined together by beams and joists, was admired as a miraculous invention, and considered as a certain pledge of victory. Upon this floating castle was a drawbridge, which could be lowered upon the tower of the Saracens, and galleries destined to receive the soldiers who were to attack the walls. A poor priest of the church of Cologne, [211] who had preached the crusade on the banks of the Rhine, and followed the Christian army into Egypt, was charged with the superintendence of the erection of this formidable edifice. As the popes in their letters always advised the Crusaders to take with them to the East men skilled in the mechanical arts, [212] the Christian army was in no want of workmen to perform the most difficult labours; the liberality of the leaders and soldiers supplied all the necessary expenses.

The whole army looked with impatience for the moment at which the enormous fortress should be brought near to the tower on the Nile; prayers were offered up in the camp for the protection of Heaven; the patriarch and the king of Jerusalem, the clergy and the soldiers, during several days, submitted to all the austerities of penitence,—all marched in procession barefooted to the seashore. The leaders had fixed upon the festival of the apostle St. Bartholomew as the day for the assault, and the Crusaders were filled with hope and ardour. They vied with each other in eagerness to be of the assaulting party, for which the best soldiers of each nation were selected, and Leopold, duke of Austria, the model of Christian knights, obtained the honour of commanding an expedition with which the first success of the crusade was connected.

On the appointed day, the two vessels surmounted by the wooden tower received the signal for moving. They carried three hundred warriors fully armed; and an innumerable multitude of Mussulmans assembled on the walls contemplated the spectacle with surprise mingled with dread. The two vessels pursued their silent course up the middle of the river, whilst all the Crusaders, either drawn up in battle-array on the left bank of the Nile, or dispersed over the neighbouring hills, saluted with loudest acclamations the moving fortress which bore the fortunes and the hopes of the Christian army. On drawing near to the walls the two vessels cast anchor, and the soldiers prepared for the assault. Whilst the Christians hurled their javelins and got ready their lances and swords, the Saracens poured upon them torrents of Greek fire, and employed every effort to make the wooden castle on which their enemies fought a prey to the flames. The one party was encouraged by the shouts and applauses of the Christian army, the other by the thousand times repeated acclamations of the inhabitants of Damietta. Amidst the fight, the machine of the Crusaders all at once appeared on fire; the drawbridge lowered on to the walls of the tower wavered and was unsteady; the flagstaff of the duke of Austria fell into the Nile, and the banner of the Christians remained in the hands of the Mussulmans. At this sight the Saracens uttered the most extravagant cries of joy, whilst groans and sounds of grief were heard along the shore on which the Crusaders were encamped; the patriarch of Jerusalem, the clergy, the whole army, fell on their knees, and raised their supplicating hands towards heaven.

But soon, as if God had been favourable to their prayers, the flames were extinguished, the machine was repaired, the drawbridge was replaced, and the companions of Leopold renewed the attack with more ardour than ever. From the top of their fortress they commanded the walls of the tower, and dealt mighty blows with sabre, spear, battle-axe, and iron mace. Two soldiers sprang upon the platform upon which the Saracens defended themselves; they carried terror among the besieged, who descended tumultuously to the first stage of the tower; the latter set fire to the floor, and endeavoured to oppose a rampart of flames between themselves and the enemies who rushed down in pursuit of them; but these last efforts of despair and bravery presented but a vain resistance to the Christian soldiers. The Mussulmans were attacked in all parts of the tower; and their walls, shaken by the machines, appeared to be sinking around them, and about to bury them beneath the ruins: in this hopeless condition they laid down their arms, and sued to their conquerors for life.

After this memorable victory, the Christians, masters of the tower of the Nile, broke the chain which impeded the passage of vessels, and their fleet was able to approach close to the ramparts of the city.

About the same time (September, 1217) Malek-Adel, who had rendered himself so formidable to the Christians, died in the capital of Egypt. He heard before his death of the victory which the Christians had gained at Damietta; and the Crusaders did not fail to say that he had sunk under the effects of despair, and that he carried with him to the tomb the power and glory of the Mussulmans.

The Christians, in their histories, have represented Malek-Adel as an ambitious, cruel, and stern prince; Oriental writers celebrate his piety and mildness. An Arabian historian boasts of his love of justice and truth, [213] and paints, by a single trait, the moderation of the absolute monarchs of Asia, when he says, "that the brother of Saladin listened without anger to that which displeased him."

Historians unite in praising the bravery of the Mussulman prince, and the ability he displayed in the execution of all his designs. No prince knew better how to make himself obeyed, or to give to supreme power that brilliant exterior which strikes the imagination of nations, and disposes them to submission. In his court, he always appeared surrounded with the pomp of the East: his palace was as a sanctuary which no one durst approach: he rarely appeared in public; when he did, it was in a manner to inspire fear: as he was fortunate in all his undertakings, the Mussulmans had no difficulty in believing that the favourite of fortune was the favourite of Heaven: the caliph of Bagdad sent ambassadors to salute him *king of kings*. Malek-Adel was pleased to be styled in camps Seïf Eddin [214] (the sword of religion), and this glorious name, which he had merited by his contests with the Christians, drew upon him the love and confidence of the soldiers of Islamism. He astonished the East by his abdication, as much as he had astonished it by his victories; the surprise he excited only added to his glory as well as to his power; and, that his destiny might in everything be extraordinary, fortune decreed that when he had descended from the throne, he should still remain master. His fifteen sons, of whom several were sovereigns, still trembled before him; nations prostrated themselves on his passage; up to the very hour in which he closed his eyes, his presence, his name only, maintained peace in his family and the provinces, and order and discipline in the armies.

At his death the face of everything began to change; the empire of the Ayoubites, which he had sustained by his exploits, gave tokens of decline; the ambition of the emirs, for a long time restrained, broke out into conspiracies against the supreme authority; a spirit of license began to be apparent in the Mussulman armies, and particularly among the troops that defended Egypt.

The Crusaders ought to have profited by the death of Malek-Adel, and the consequences it was sure to produce, by attacking the discouraged Mussulmans without intermission. But instead of following up their success, after they had obtained possession of the Tower of the Nile, they all at once neglected the labours of the siege, and appeared to have fallen asleep over their first victories. A great number of them, persuaded that they had done enough for the cause of Christ, only thought of embarking to return into

Europe. Every vessel that left the port recalled to the pilgrims remembrances of home; and the beautiful sky of Damietta, which had inflamed their imaginations at the commencement of the siege, was not sufficient to retain them in a country which they began to consider as a place of exile.

The clergy, however, warmly censured the retreat and desertion of the Crusaders, and implored Heaven to punish the base soldiers who thus abandoned the standards of the cross. Six thousand pilgrims from Brittany, who were returning to Europe, were shipwrecked on the coast of Italy, and almost all perished; and the ecclesiastics, with the most ardent of the Crusaders, did not fail to see, in so great a disaster, a manifestation of divine anger. When the Crusaders of Friesland, after having deserted the banners of the Holy Land, had returned into the West, the ocean all at once broke through the dykes, and overflowed its customary boundaries; the richest provinces of Holland were submerged, and a hundred thousand inhabitants, with whole cities, disappeared beneath the waters. Many Christians attributed this calamity to the culpable retreat of the Frieson and Dutch Crusaders.

The pope beheld with pain the return of the pilgrim deserters from the cause of Christ. Honorius neglected nothing to secure the success of a war he had preached; and he every day, both by prayers and threats, pressed the departure of those who, after having taken the cross, delayed the accomplishment of their vow

According to the usual custom of navigators, two periods of the year were fixed upon at which it was best to cross the sea. The pilgrims almost always embarked in the month of March and in the month of September, whether to repair to the East or to return to Europe; which caused them to be compared to those birds of passage that change their climate at the approach of a new season, and towards the end of fine weather. [215] At each passage, the Mediterranean was covered with vessels which transported Crusaders, some returning to their homes, others going to fight the infidels. At the very moment the Christians were deploring the loss of the Frieson and Dutch warriors, their spirits were restored by seeing Crusaders from Germany, Pisa, Genoa, Venice, and several provinces of France, arrive in the camp at Damietta.

Among the French warriors, history names Hervé, count of Nevers; Hugh, count de la Marche; Miles de Bar-sur-Seine; the lords John of Artois and Ponce de Crancey; Ithier de Thacy, and Savary de Mauléon; they were accompanied by the archbishop of Bordeaux, the bishops of Angers, Autun, Beauvais, Paris, Meaux, Noyon, &c. England also sent the bravest of her knights into Egypt. Henry III. had taken the cross after the council of the Lateran; but as he could not quit his dominions, at that time a prey to civil wars and torn by discord, the earls of Harcourt, Chester, and Arundel, with Prince Oliver, [216] were honoured with the charge of acquitting, in his name, the vow he had taken to fight in the East for the cause of Christ.

At the head of the pilgrims who arrived at that time in Egypt were two cardinals, whom the pope had sent to the Christian army. Robert de Courçon, one of the preachers of the crusade, was charged with the mission of inculcating the moral precepts of Christ in the camp of the Crusaders, and animating the zeal and devotion of the soldiers by his eloquence. Cardinal Pelagius, bishop of Albano, was invested with the entire confidence of the Holy See; he brought with him the treasures that were to defray the expenses of the war; the Crusaders from Rome and several other cities of Italy marched under his orders, and recognised him as their military leader.

Cardinal Pelagius, by his position, was endowed with great authority in the Christian army, and his naturally imperious character led him to assume even more power than he had received from the Holy See. In whatever affair he was employed, he acknowledged no equal, and would not endure a superior. He had been known to oppose the sovereign pontiff in the bosom of the conclave; he would have resisted the most powerful monarchs, even in their own councils. Cardinal Pelagius, persuaded that Providence meant to make use of him to accomplish great designs, believed himself fit for all works, and appointed to all kinds of glory; when he had formed a determination, he maintained it with invincible obstinacy, and was influenced by neither obstacles nor perils, nor even by the lessons of experience. If Pelagius originated any advice in council, he supported it with all the menaces of the court of Rome, and often gave cause for a belief that the thunders of the Church had only been confided to his hands, that he might secure the triumph of his own opinions.

Pelagius had scarcely arrived in Egypt, when, as legate of the pope, he disputed the command of the army with John of Brienne. To support his pretensions, he asserted that the Crusaders had taken up arms at the desire of the sovereign pontiff; that they were the soldiers of the Church, and ought to recognise no other head than the legate of the Holy See: these assumptions gave great offence to the barons and principal leaders. From that time it was easy to foresee that discord would be introduced by him whose mission it was to establish peace; and that the envoy of the pope, charged to preach humility among Christians, was about to ruin everything by his mad presumption. [217] Cardinal de Courçon died shortly after his arrival.

The continuator of William of Tyre, whilst deploring the death of this legate, who had been remarkable for his moderation, characterizes, by a single word, the conduct of Pelagius, and the consequences that might be expected from it, by saying: "Then died Cardinal Peter, and Pelagius lived, which was a great pity."

In the mean time, the approach of danger had reunited the Mussulman princes. The caliph of Bagdad, whom James of Vitri [218] styles *the pope of the infidels*, exhorted the nations to take up arms against the Christians. All the sons of Malek-Adel, who reigned over the provinces of Syria and of Yemen, prepared to march to the assistance of Egypt. The sultan of Damascus, after having made several incursions into the territories of Ptolemaïs, gathered together his whole army, and resolved to go and defend Damietta. As he had reason to fear the Christians might take advantage of his absence to seize Jerusalem and fortify themselves in it, he caused the ramparts of the holy city to be demolished. He also ordered the fortress of Tabor, and all those that the Mussulmans held along the coasts of Palestine, to be destroyed; a vigorous measure that afflicted the infidels, but was calculated to afflict the Christians still more; as it proved to them that they had to contend with enemies animated by despair, and disposed to sacrifice everything to secure their own safety.

The sultan of Cairo encamped in the vicinity of Damietta, where he awaited the princes of his family. The garrison of the city received every day provisions and reinforcements, and was in a condition to resist the Christian army for a length of time. The preparations and the approach of the Mussulmans at length roused the Crusaders from their state of inaction. Animated by their leaders, but more by the appearance of danger and the presence of a formidable enemy; still led by the king of Jerusalem, who had resisted the pretensions of Pelagius, the Christian soldiers resumed the labours of the siege and made several assaults upon the city on the river side. The winter, which had just set in, did not at all prevent their attacks; nothing could equal the heroic constancy with which they braved, during several months, cold, rain, hunger, all the fatigues of war, and all the rigours of the season. A contagious malady committed great ravages in the Christian army: a frightful storm, which lasted three days, carried away the tents and the baggage of both leaders and soldiers; but nothing diminished the fury of the contests, which were incessantly renewed.

At length the Christians, having become masters of all the western bank of the Nile, determined to cross the river, and attack the city on the land side. The passage was difficult and dangerous; the sultan of Cairo had fixed his camp on the opposite shore; the plain on which the Crusaders wished to pitch their tents was covered with Mussulman soldiers; an unexpected event removed all obstacles.

We have spoken of the seditious spirit of the emirs, who, since the death of Malek-Adel, had openly shown their ambitious designs and sought to introduce divisions into the Mussulman armies. The most remarkable among these emirs, was the leader of a troop of Curds, named Emad-eddin, [219] who had taken a part in all the revolutions of Egypt and Syria. Associated with the destinies of the sons of Ayoub, this emir had witnessed the rise and fall of several Mussulman dynasties, and held in contempt the powers of which he knew both the source and the origin. An intrepid soldier, a faithless subject, always ready to serve his sovereigns in fight or betray them in a conspiracy, Emad-eddin could not endure a prince who reigned by the laws of peace, or recognise a power which was not the fruit of his intrigues or of a revolution. As fortune had always favoured his audacity, and as all his treacheries had been well rewarded, every fresh revolt augmented his credit and his renown; an enemy to all acknowledged authority, the hope of all who aspired to empire, he was almost as redoubtable as the Old Man of the Mountain, whose menaces made the most powerful monarchs tremble. Emad-eddin resolved to change the government of Egypt, and conceived the project of dethroning the sultan of Cairo, and replacing him by another of the sons of Malek-Adel.

Several emirs were drawn into this conspiracy. On the day appointed, they were to enter the tent of Melic-Kamel, and compel him, by violence, to renounce the supreme authority. The sultan was warned of the plot prepared against him, and on the eve of the day on which it was to be carried into effect, he left his camp in the middle of the night. The next day, at dawn, the conspirators were made aware that their designs had been discovered; they endeavoured in vain to draw the soldiers into a revolt; the greatest confusion prevailed throughout the camp; among the emirs, some gathered around Emad-eddin, and swore to follow his fortunes; others, doubtful of the success of his enterprise, remained silent; many took an oath to defend Melic-Kamel. Amidst these debates, the Mussulman army, conscious that they were without a leader, feared they might be surprised by the Christians. A panic terror all at once seized upon the soldiers, who abandoned their tents and their baggage, and rushed in the greatest disorder in the traces of their fugitive sultan.

This retreat, of which the Christians could not imagine the cause, and which their historians explain by a miracle from heaven, [220] opened to them the passage of the Nile. The army hastened to cross the river, took possession of the Mussulman camp, made an immense booty, and drew near to the walls of Damietta.

The panic, however, which had put the Mussulman troops to flight, had not at all communicated itself to the garrison of the city: this intrepid garrison offered the most vigorous resistance, and gave the army of Melic-Kamel [221] time to recover from its fright. The sultan of Damascus soon joined his brother the sultan of Cairo. Emad-eddin and the other leaders of the conspiracy were arrested and loaded with chains. Order and discipline were reëstablished among the Saracens, and the Christian army had to contend with all the united forces of the infidels, impatient to repair their check, and recover the advantages they had lost.

The burning days of summer were approaching: the Nile, increased by the rains of the tropics, began to issue from its bed. The Christian army was encamped under the walls of Damietta, having the lake Menzaleh in its rear. The Saracens came and pitched their tents at a short distance from the camp of the Christians, who, oppressed by the consuming heat of the season and the climate, were subject every day to the spirited attacks of the infidels. In one of these conflicts, the Mussulmans got possession of a bridge which the Crusaders had thrown over the Nile; the banks of the river were covered with dead, and the Christian army only owed its safety to the heroic bravery of the duke of Austria, the king of Jerusalem, and the grand masters of St. John and the Temple. Soon after, another battle was fought still more bloody than the first. In this fight, as it is described by James of Vitri, an ocular witness, not a person among the Christians was idle: the clergy were at prayers or attending the wounded; whilst the women and children carried water, wine, food, stones, and javelins, to the combatants. Whirlwinds of scorching dust arose in the air, and enveloped the two armies. The cries of the wounded and the dying, the sound of the trumpets, and the clashing of arms resounded from the neighbouring hills and from both shores of the Nile. Sometimes the Saracens were put to flight, and whole battalions, says James of Vitri, disappeared submerged in the Nile, as formerly the armies of Pharaoh perished in the Red Sea. Sometimes the Christians were repulsed in their turn, and left a great number of their warriors on the field of battle: the carnage lasted during the whole day, without either side being able to claim the victory. Whilst the two armies were contending with such fury on the banks, the Genoese and the Pisans, on board their vessels, made an attack upon the ramparts of the city. Several of their ships were consumed by the Greek fire, and the bravest of their soldiers were crushed beneath the beams and stones hurled from the top of the walls. At the approach of night the Crusaders returned to their tents, despairing of ever being able to subdue the Saracens, and reproaching each other with want of courage in this unfortunate day.

On the morrow fresh disputes arose between the horse and foot soldiers, [222] each of which bodies accused the other with having been the cause of the losses the army had experienced. These debates became so warm that at length the foot and the horse both demanded, with loud cries, to be led again to battle, and rushed tumultuously out of the camp, to give convincing proofs of their bravery; the leaders could neither restrain nor direct the ardour and impetuosity of their soldiers, who fought in disorder, and were repulsed by the Saracens after a horrible carnage.

At this period a holy person, named Francis of Assise, made his appearance in the Christian army, whose reputation for piety was spread throughout the Christian world, and had preceded him into the East. From his earliest youth, Francis had left the paternal roof to lead a life of edification. One day, whilst present at mass in a church in Italy, he was struck with the passage of the Gospel in which our Saviour says, "Take with you neither gold nor silver, nor other moneys; neither scrips for the journey, nor sandals, nor staff." From that period Francis had held in contempt all the riches of this world, and had devoted himself to the poverty of the apostles; he travelled through countries and cities, exhorting all people to penitence. The disciples who followed him braved the contempt of the multitude, and glorified themselves with it before God: when asked whence they came, they were accustomed to answer, "We are poor penitents from Assise."

Francis was led into Egypt by the fame of the crusade, and by the hope of there effecting some great conversion. The day preceding the last battle, he had a miraculous presentiment of the defeat of the Christians, and imparted his prediction to the leaders of the army, who heard him with indifference. Dissatisfied with the Crusaders, and devoured by the zeal of a mission from God, he then conceived the project of securing the triumph of the faith by his eloquence and the arms of the Gospel alone. He directed his course towards the enemy's camp, put himself in the way of being taken prisoner by the Saracen soldiers, and was conducted into the presence of the sultan. Then Francis addressed Melic-Kamel, [223] and said to him, "It is God who sends me towards you, to point out to you the road to salvation." After these words, the missionary exhorted the sultan [224] to embrace the Gospel; he challenged in his presence all the doctors of the law, and to confound imposture and prove the truth of the Christian religion, offered to cast himself into the midst of a burning funeral-pile. The sultan, astonished, ordered the zealous preacher from his presence, who obtained neither of the objects of his wishes, for he did not convert the sultan, nor did he gather the palm of martyrdom.

After this adventure, St. Francis returned to Europe, where he founded the religious order of the Cordeliers, who at first, possessing neither churches, monasteries, lands, nor flocks, spread themselves throughout the West, labouring for the conversion of penitents. The disciples of St. Francis sometimes carried the word of God among savage nations; some went into Africa and Asia, seeking, as their master had done, errors to confute and evils to endure; they frequently planted the cross of Christ upon the lands of the infidels, and in their harmless pilgrimages, constantly repeated the scriptural words, *Peace be with you*; they were only armed with their prayers, and aspired to no glory but that of dying for the faith.

The Crusaders had been encamped seventeen months before the walls of Damietta, and not a single day had passed without a murderous conflict. The Mussulmans, although they had obtained some advantages, began to lose all hope of triumphing over an enemy proof against the evils of war and an unhealthy climate. Report proclaimed the approaching arrival of the emperor of Germany, who had taken the cross, and this news, whilst it sustained the courage of the Christians, made the Mussulmans tremble at the idea of having to contend with the most powerful of the monarchs of the West. The sultan of Damascus, in the name of all the princes of his family, sent ambassadors to the camp of the Crusaders to ask for peace. He offered to abandon to the Franks the city and kingdom of Jerusalem, and only to reserve to themselves the places of Krak and Montréal, for which they proposed to pay a tribute. As the ramparts and towers of the holy city had been recently destroyed, the Mussulmans engaged to pay two hundred thousand dinars to re-establish them; they further agreed to give up all Christians made prisoners since the death of Saladin.

The principal leaders of the Christian army were called together to deliberate upon the proposals of the Mussulmans. The king of Jerusalem, the French barons, the English, Dutch, and Germans, were of opinion that the terms should be acceded to, and the peace accepted: the king of Jerusalem would regain his kingdom, and the barons of the West would see the happy end of a war that had detained them so long from their homes.

"By accepting the peace they attained the object of the crusade,—the deliverance of the holy places. The Christian warriors had besieged Damietta during seventeen months, and the siege might be still prolonged. Many Crusaders daily returned to Europe; whilst crowds of Mussulman warriors as constantly joined the standards of the sultans of Cairo and Damascus. If they should take Damietta, they would be but too happy to exchange it for Jerusalem. The Mussulmans offered to give, before victory, quite as much as they could demand after having subdued them. It was not wise to refuse that which fortune offered to bestow upon them without conflicts or perils.

The effusion of blood should be avoided, and they ought to reflect, that victories purchased by the death of the soldiers of the cross, were such as were most acceptable to the God of the Christians."

The king of Jerusalem and most of the barons spoke thus, and endeavoured to bring to their opinion the Italian nobles and the body of the prelates, whom Cardinal Pelagius led in an opposite direction. The legate of the pope regarded himself as the head of this war, and he wished it to continue, in order to prolong his power and to procure for him additional renown. "He could see nothing in the proposals of the enemy but a new artifice to delay the capture of Damietta, and gain time. The Saracens offered nothing but desert countries and demolished cities, which would fall again into their power. Their only object was to disarm the Christians, and furnish them with a pretext for returning into the West. Things had gone too far to allow them to retreat without dishonour. It was disgraceful for Christians to renounce the conquest of a city they had besieged seventeen months, and which could hold out no longer. They must take possession of it first, and then they should know what was best to be done—once masters of Damietta, the Crusaders might conclude a glorious peace, and reap all the advantages of victory."

The motives alleged by Cardinal Pelagius were not unreasonable, but the spirit of party and faction reigned in the council of the leaders of the crusade. As it always happens in similar circumstances, every one formed his opinion not upon that which he believed to be useful and just, but upon that which appeared most favourable to the party he had embraced; some advised that the siege should be prosecuted, because the king of Jerusalem had offered a contrary opinion; others wished the proposed capitulation should be accepted, because this capitulation was rejected by the legate of the pope. The Christian army exhibited a strange spectacle. On one side, John of Brienne and the most renowned warriors were advocates for peace; on the other, the legate and most of the ecclesiastics demanded with great warmth the continuation of the war: they deliberated during several days without a chance of bringing the two parties to an agreement; and whilst the discussions became more intemperate, hostilities were renewed: then all the Crusaders united to prosecute the siege of Damietta.

The sultan of Cairo employed every means to throw succours into the city, and keep up the courage of the garrison and the inhabitants. Some Mussulman soldiers, taking advantage of the darkness of night, attempted to effect an entrance into the place; a few were able to gain and pass through the gates, but by far the greater number were surprised and massacred by the Crusaders, who kept constant and close watch around the walls.

The news which the sultan, Melic-Kamel, received from Damietta, became every day more alarming, the Mussulman army, not daring to succour the besieged, remained inactive, and confined themselves to the defence of their own intrenchments. Communication was soon entirely cut off between the place and the camp of the infidels; some divers crossed the Nile through the Christian fleet, attained Damietta, and returned to inform the sultan that pestilence, famine, and despair reigned throughout the city. The Mussulmans had recourse to all sorts of stratagems to convey food to the garrison; sometimes they filled leather sacks with provisions, which, being abandoned to the stream of the Nile, floated under the ramparts of the city; at others, they concealed loaves in the sheets that enveloped dead bodies, which, being borne on by the waters, were stopped in their course by the besieged. It was not long before these stratagems were discovered by the Christians, and then famine began to make horrible ravages; the soldiers, overcome by fatigue and weakened by hunger, had not the strength to fight or guard the towers and ramparts. The inhabitants, given up to despair, abandoned their houses, and fled from a city that presented nothing but images of death: many came to implore the pity of the Crusaders. The commander of Damietta, whose name history has not preserved, in vain endeavoured to keep up the courage of the people and the soldiers. To prevent desertion, he caused the gates of the city to be walled up; and from that period neither the sultan of Cairo nor the Crusaders were able to know what was passing in the besieged place, in which a dismal silence reigned, and which, according to the expression of an Arabian author, *was no longer anything but a closed sepulchre.*

The Christians had placed their machines at the foot of a tower, and as they saw no one defending it, the legate, at the head of the Italian Crusaders, took advantage of a dark and stormy night to penetrate within the first inclosure of the walls. The king of Jerusalem and the other leaders resolved at the same time to make an assault and enter the city, sword in hand. As soon as day appeared, the boldest ascended into the tower, which they found deserted, and called aloud upon their companions to join them. The Christian army applauded their success, and answered by shouts of joy; the soldiers flew to arms, and instantly put the rams in motion. The walls were scaled, the gates were beaten to pieces, and a passage opened; the eager Crusaders rushed forward with naked swords and ready lances to encounter the enemy; but when they penetrated into the streets, a pestilential odour enveloped them, and a frightful spectacle made them recoil with horror! The public places, the mosques, the houses, the whole city, were strewed with dead! [225] Old age, infancy, ripened manhood, maiden beauty, matronly grace—all had perished in the horrors of the siege! At the arrival of the

Crusaders, Damietta contained seventy thousand inhabitants; of these only three thousand of the most robust remained, who, ready to expire, glided like pale, fading shadows among tombs and ruins.

This horrible spectacle touched the hearts of the Crusaders, and mingled a feeling of sadness with the joy their victory created. The conquerors found in Damietta immense stores of spices, diamonds, and precious stuffs. When they had pillaged the city, it might have been believed, says an historian, that the warriors of the West had conquered Persia, Arabia, and the Indies. The ecclesiastics launched the thunders of excommunication against all who secreted any part of the booty; but these menaces had no effect upon the cupidity of the soldiers: all the wealth brought to the public stock only produced two hundred thousand crowns, which were distributed among the troops of the victorious army.

Damietta boasted a celebrated mosque, ornamented by six vast galleries and a hundred and fifty columns of marble, surmounted by a superb dome, which towered above all the other edifices of the city. This mosque, in which, on the preceding evening, Mussulmans had lifted their imploring, tearful eyes to their prophet, was consecrated to the virgin mother of Christ, and the whole Christian army came thither to offer up thanks to Heaven for the triumph granted to arms. On the following day the barons and prelates assembled in the same place, to deliberate upon their conquest; and, by a unanimous resolution, the city of Damietta was assigned to the king of Jerusalem. They then turned their attention to the fate of the unfortunate inhabitants who had escaped pestilence and famine. James of Vitri, when describing the miseries of Damietta, and speaking of the horrible famine which swept away so many families during the siege, sheds tears over the little children who in vain asked their dead parents for bread. [226] The fate of such of those as remained alive inspired the virtuous bishop of Ptolemaïs with pity, and he purchased many of them, in order to have them baptized and brought up in the Christian religion. The pious charity of the prelate, however, could only procure them eternal life, for they almost all died after having been baptised. All the Mussulmans who had sufficient strength to work received liberty and bread, and were employed in cleansing and purifying the city. Whilst the leaders were thus watching over a mourning city, and gave their anxious attentions to prevent new calamities, the spectacle that Damietta presented, and the empoisoned air they breathed within its walls, obliged the Christian army to return to their camp, and wait for the time at which the conquered city might be inhabited without danger.

When the news of the taking of Damietta was spread through Syria and Upper Egypt, the Mussulman nations, seized with terror, flew to their mosques to implore the intervention of their prophet against the enemies of Islamism. The sultans of Cairo and Damascus sent ambassadors to the caliph of Bagdad, conjuring him to exhort all true believers to take arms to defend the religion of Mahomet. The caliph contemplated with grief the calamities about to fall upon the princes of the family of Saladin; but other dangers threatened him more nearly. Tartar hordes had issued from their mountains, invaded several provinces of Persia, and were advancing towards the Euphrates. The caliph, far from being able to assist the Mussulmans of Syria and Egypt by his prayers and exhortations, invoked their succour to defend his capital, and turn aside the storm ready to burst over the whole East. When the Mussulman ambassadors returned to Damascus and Cairo, their accounts added new alarms to those which the conquests of the Christians had already inspired.

The Ayoubite princes, however, did not delay endeavouring to unite all their efforts against the Crusaders, postponing, to a more favourable moment, the defence of the head of Islamism. The Mussulman nations had a much greater dread of the invasion of the Christians than of the irruptions of the hordes of Tartary. The conquerors whom nations fear the most, are those that desire to change the laws and religion of the conquered country. The Tartars, whose habits and manners were not formed, easily complied with those of the people they subdued; the Christians, on the contrary, only made war to destroy all and enslave all. Already rich cities, great provinces, were in their power: everything had changed its form under their domination. Thus the Mussulman princes and people, from the Euphrates to the Red Sea, forgot or neglected the storm which growled over Persia and was advancing slowly towards Syria, and resolved to take arms against the Crusaders, who were masters of the Nile.

After the taking of Damietta, the Mussulman soldiers who defended Egypt were struck with such excessive fear, that, during several days, not one of them durst face a Christian soldier. The Egyptian warriors who guarded the fortress of Tannis, built beyond the lake Menzaleh, abandoned their ramparts at the approach of a few Crusaders, and thus one of the firmest bulwarks of the Mussulman empire fell without defence into the hands of the Franks. From that time, the Christians had reason to believe they had no more enemies on the banks of the Nile; and, during the rigours of winter, many of the pilgrims returned to Europe. Half the army took advantage of the March passage to quit Egypt; such as remained under the banners of the crusade forgot the labours and perils of war, and gave themselves up to indulgence and voluptuousness, to all the pleasure which the approach of spring, and the fine climate and beautiful sky of Damietta inspired.

During the leisure of peace, the divisions which had so often interrupted the course of the war, soon revived; the taking of Damietta had inflamed the pride of Cardinal Pelagius, who, in the Christian army, spoke as a conqueror and commanded as a master. The king of Jerusalem was so dissatisfied, that he abandoned a city that had been given to him, and quitted an army of which he was the head, to retire to Ptolemaïs.

New Crusaders, however, eager to signalize their valour against the Mussulmans, arrived daily. The duke of Bavaria, with four hundred German knights and barons, sent by Frederick II., landed on the banks of the Nile. A short time afterwards, the Christian army received into its ranks Crusaders from Milan, Pisa, and Genoa, and prelates and archbishops conducted a crowd of defenders of the cross, who came from the various provinces of Germany, and from France and Italy. The sovereign pontiff had neglected nothing to secure the success of the holy war; he sent to Cardinal Pelagius provisions for the army, and a considerable sum of money, partly from his own treasury, and partly from the charity of the faithful of the West. [227] The legate was desirous of profiting by the succours he had just received, and proposed to follow up the war, and march directly against the capital of Egypt. The clergy adopted the advice of Pelagius, but such of the Crusaders as saw with disgust a prelate at the head of warriors, refused to take up arms. The duke of Bavaria and the barons and knights would acknowledge no leader but the king of Jerusalem; the legate Pelagius was obliged to send deputies to John of Brienne, who, pressed by the pope himself, was at length prevailed upon, and consented, after an absence of several months, to come back and take the command of the army.

Whilst the Crusaders remained thus in inaction, all the Mussulmans were flying to arms: the sultans of Damascus and Aleppo, the princes of Hamah, Balbec, and of Arabia, assembled fresh armies. After the taking of Damietta, the sultan of Cairo had retired, with his troops, to the spot where the two eastern branches of the Nile separate: there he daily beheld troops of Mussulman warriors join his standard, and, awaiting a favourable opportunity, he constructed a palace in the centre of his camp, surrounded by walls.

The Mussulmans there built houses, baths, and bazaars, and the camp of the sultan became a city, called Mansourah, which was destined to be celebrated in history by the defeat and ruin of the Christian armies.

As soon as the king of Jerusalem returned to Damietta, the leaders of the Crusaders assembled in council, to deliberate upon what they had to do: the legate of the pope was the first to offer his opinion, and proposed to march against the capital of Egypt. "We must attack the evil at its source, and, in order to conquer the Saracens, destroy the foundation of their power. Egypt supplies them with soldiers, provisions, and arms. By taking possession of Egypt, we should cut off all their resources. At no period were the soldiers of the cross animated by more zeal; never were the infidels more depressed. To lose such an opportunity was to betray the common cause. When a great empire was attacked, prudence commanded the assailants not to lay down their arms till they had subdued it; by stopping after the first victory, they exhibited more weakness than moderation. The eyes of the whole Christian world were upon the army of the Crusaders; it was not only the deliverance of the holy places that was looked for from their valour, but the death of all the enemies of Christ, the destruction of every nation that had imposed a sacrilegious yoke upon the city of God."

The bishops, the prelates, and most of the ecclesiastics were loud in their applause of the speech of the legate; but John of Brienne, who did not at all partake of their opinion, arose, and protesting his devotion to the cause of Christ, began by appealing to the assembly, if any one could be more interested in the conquests of the Christians in the East, than the man who had the honour to be king of Jerusalem. He then pointed out how imprudent it would be to go up the Nile at the very moment at which that river was beginning to overflow, and would most likely inundate the roads which led to Cairo. "Mark," said he, "all the perils of the expedition proposed to you. We are to march into an unknown land, through the midst of an enemy's country: if conquered, there can be no place of asylum for us; if conquerors, our victories will only weaken our army. However easy it may be for us to conquer provinces, it will be almost impossible for us to defend them. The Crusaders, always eager to return to Europe, are incalculably more serviceable in gaining battles than in securing the possession of conquered countries. Nobody can suppose, that with the brave bands that surround us, we entertain any fear of the Mussulman armies which are gathering together from all parts; but in order to secure our safety, we must not only subdue our enemies, we must destroy them—we have not to deal with an army, but with an entire nation animated by despair. The whole Mussulman race are about to become so many intrepid soldiers, impatient to shed their blood in the field of battle. But what do I say? we shall have much less to dread from their courage than from their timid prudence. They will not fail to shun the fight, and will wait until diseases, want, fatigue, discord, the inconstancy of men's minds, the overflowing of the Nile, and the heat of the climate shall have triumphed over our efforts and secured the failure of all our enterprises."

John of Brienne strengthened his opinion by other motives, with which his knowledge of the art of war supplied him, and terminated his speech by saying, "That Damietta and Tannis were powerful enough to restrain the people of Egypt; that it was necessary to recapture the cities they had lost, before they thought of conquering countries that had never been in their possession; and that, in short, they had not assembled under the banners of the cross to besiege Thebes, Babylon, or Memphis, but to deliver Jerusalem, which opened its gates to the Christians, and which they could fortify against all the attacks of the infidels."

This moderate and pacific language would well have become the mouth of an envoy of the pope; but Pelagius listened to the king of Jerusalem with the most evident impatience: he answered, that weakness and timidity screened themselves behind the veil of moderation and prudence; that Christ did not summon to his defence such wise and far-sighted soldiers, but warriors who sought for battle rather than for reasons, and who could see the glory of an enterprise, and be blind to its dangers. The legate added several more reasons to those he had already advanced, and expressed them with great bitterness; at length, led away by the heat of the discussion, he threatened all those who did not partake of his opinions with excommunication. Most of the leaders, and the king of Jerusalem himself, fearing to be excommunicated, but dreading much more to see the least suspicion cast upon their bravery, at length yielded to the obstinate will of Pelagius: the council of the barons and the bishops decided that the Christian army should leave Damietta, and march against the capital of Egypt.

This army, composed of more than seventy thousand men, advanced up the banks of the Nile. A numerous fleet, laden with provisions, arms, and machines of war, ascended the river at the same time. The Christian army passed through Farescour and several other villages, that had been abandoned by their inhabitants; all fled away at the approach of the Crusaders, who began to believe they should meet with no obstacle to their victories, and celebrated, beforehand, the conquest of Memphis and Cairo. The legate of the pope exulted in the resolution he had dictated to the Christian army; and, full of confidence in a prediction that had been made concerning him in his youth, the presumptuous cardinal flattered himself that he was about to overthrow the worship of Mahomet; and indulged in the most insulting railleries against those who had been opposed to the war. Without fighting a single battle, the Christians gained the extremity of the Delta, at the angle formed by the arm of the river which descends towards Damietta and the canal of Almon, whose waters flow into the sea on the eastern side. The Saracens were encamped in the plain of Mansourah, on the opposite bank of the river: the Crusaders halted on the hither shore, and their fleet cast anchor as near to them as possible.

The sultan of Damascus, and the princes of Aleppo, Balbec, Hamah, and Bosra, had united their troops with those of the sultan of Cairo. The Nile, whose bank was covered with intrenchments, presented a barrier very difficult to be overcome. But Melic-Kamel did not dare to match himself with the Crusaders; dreading their rash bravery, so accustomed to sport with perils and triumph over all obstacles. Reports of the arrival of Frederick, and of the approach of the Tartars, kept the Mussulmans in a continual state of alarm, and made them anxious to terminate a war which exhausted their resources, consumed their strength, and did not promise them, even in victory, a compensation for so many efforts and so many sacrifices.

Ambassadors were sent to propose peace to the leaders of the Christian army: the Mussulmans offered their enemies, if they would consent to an entire cessation of hostilities, to give up to them Damietta and its territories, and to restore Jerusalem, with all the places of Palestine that had been conquered by Saladin.

These conditions assured to the Christians all the advantages of both war and peace. The king of Jerusalem, and most of the barons, who saw the difficulties and perils of the expedition they had entered upon, listened with as much surprise as joy to the proposals of the infidels, and did not hesitate to accept them; but they had absolutely no power in the army. The legate, who exercised an arbitrary authority, and who was constantly dreaming of conquests, persisted in thinking that these pacific proposals were only the effects of fear, and that the enemy who sued for peace was the one with whom war should be prosecuted with most spirit.

The ambassadors returned to the camp of the Mussulmans, to announce that the Christians refused the peace: their account excited indignation, and indignation roused courage. When the Ayoubite princes proposed peace, they were in possession of ample means to carry on the war with advantage; they every day received reinforcements, and their camp rapidly assumed a more formidable aspect; but soon a terrible auxiliary, against whose attacks Pelagius had no defence, came to the assistance of the Mussulmans, and procured them a complete triumph without either battles or danger.

The Christian warriors, who flattered themselves they had now only to deal with a conquered enemy, were satisfied with surrounding their camp with a ditch and a wall; the army remained for several days in this position, without making an effort either to attack the Saracens or pass the Nile. Pelagius, who was constantly promising victory to his soldiers, remained, nevertheless, in a state of inactivity in his tent. During this period, many of the Crusaders grew weary of a war in which no battles were fought; some fancied that the cause no longer stood in need of their assistance; whilst others, with more foresight, feared coming reverses: more than ten thousand Crusaders abandoned the camp and returned to Damietta.

The Christian army had been for more than a month in face of the enemy, always in expectation of the victories that had been promised to them. At length, the overflowing of the Nile, in a most alarming manner, disturbed their imagined security. The Saracens opened the sluices, and filled all the canals of Lower Egypt. The Mussulman fleet, which had not been able to ascend the Nile by Damietta, took advantage of the canals, and came up with the Christian ships. In a single engagement, the vessels of the Crusaders were almost all dispersed and consumed by the Greek fire: from that moment terror seized upon the Christians, for they were in want of provisions, and had neither means nor hopes of obtaining any. The Saracens, after having crossed the Nile on bridges, occupied all the circumjacent hills. The Christian soldiers wandered about the fields at hazard, pursued by the waves of the rising river, and by the Mussulmans, whose bravery they had so lately held in contempt. The whole army was on the point of being submerged or perishing with hunger, and had no hope but in the clemency of an enemy with whom they had recently refused to make peace.

In this extremity, the king of Jerusalem and the principal leaders of the Christians sent several of their knights to offer the Saracens battle; but the latter were neither sufficiently imprudent, nor sufficiently generous to accept a proposal dictated by despair. The Crusaders were exhausted with hunger and fatigue; the cavalry sunk into, and encumbered by mud and slime, could neither advance nor retreat; the foot-soldiers cast away their arms; the baggage of the army floated away upon the waters, and nothing was heard but groans and lamentations. "When the Christian warriors," says an Arabian historian, "saw nothing before them but death, their minds sank into a state of despondency, and their backs bent beneath the rod of God, *to whom be all praise!*"

Pelagius must then have been sensible of the full extent of his error: his project of marching to Cairo had, doubtless, something great in it, if it could have been executed; but the presumptuous legate disdained all counsels, all lessons of experience, and foresaw none of the obstacles he was certain to meet with on his route; he conducted an army filled with discontent; the soldiers had neither that confidence nor that enthusiasm that leads men to brave dangers or cheerfully encounter fatigue. The king of Jerusalem, the duke of Bavaria, and a great number of the barons were his personal enemies, and took very little interest in the success of an enterprise of which they had disapproved.

Amidst the cries and lamentations of an army to which he had promised victory, Pelagius was obliged to negotiate for peace, and his pride humbled itself so far as to implore the clemency of the Saracens. Christian ambassadors, among whom was the bishop of Ptolemaïs, went to propose a capitulation to the conquerors; they offered to give up the city of Damietta, and only asked for the Christian army liberty to return to Ptolemaïs.

The Mussulman princes assembled in council to deliberate upon the proposals of the Crusaders. Some were of opinion they should be accepted; others declared that all the Christians ought to be made prisoners of war. Among those who proposed the harshest measures, the sultan of Damascus, an implacable enemy of the Franks, was conspicuous. "No treaty can be made," said he, "with warriors without humanity and without faith. We should remember their barbarities in war and their treachery in peace. They armed themselves to ravage provinces, to destroy cities, and overthrow the worship of Mahomet. Since fortune has placed these most cruel enemies of Islamism, these devastators of the East, in the hands of *the true believers*, we ought to immolate them to the safety of the Mussulman nations, and take an advantage of our victory that will create a terror among the people of the West for ever."

Most of the princes and emirs, animated by fanaticism and vengeance, applauded this violent speech. The sultan of Cairo, more moderate, and, doubtless, more prescient than the other leaders, dreading likewise the arrival of Frederick and the invasion of the Tartars, combated the opinion of the sultan of Damascus, and advised that the capitulation of the Franks should be accepted. "All the Franks were not comprised in this army now in their power; other Crusaders guarded Damietta, and might be able to defend it; the Mussulmans had sustained a siege of eight months, the Christians might hold out as long. It was more advantageous for the princes of the family of Saladin to return to their cities than to retain a few of their enemies in chains. If they destroyed one Christian army, the West, to avenge the defeat of its warriors, was able to send numberless legions into the East. They ought not to forget that the Mussulman armies had lost a portion of that spirit of obedience and discipline that was the sole guarantee of victory; that they were worn out with fatigue, and sighed for repose. Other enemies than the now disarmed Christians, other perils than those they had just escaped, might soon hang over both Syria and Egypt. [228] It was wise to make peace at this moment, in order to prepare for fresh contests, for new wars, perhaps much more cruel than that which they had now an opportunity of terminating with so much glory to the Mussulman arms."

The speech of Melik-Kamel brought back the princes of his family to sentiments of moderation. [229] The capitulation was accepted; the sultan of Cairo sent his own son to the camp of the Christians as a pledge for his word. The king of Jerusalem, the duke of Bavaria, the legate of the pope, and the principal leaders repaired to the camp of the Saracens, and remained as hostages till the accomplishment of the treaty.

When the deputies of the imprisoned army came to Damietta and announced the disasters and captivity of the Christians, their account drew tears from the crowd of Crusaders who at that time arrived from the West. When these same deputies informed them that the city must be given up to the infidels, the most intrepid of the Franks could not restrain their indignation, and refused to recognise a treaty so disgraceful to the soldiers of the cross. The greatest tumult prevailed throughout the city. Some, filled with despair, determined to return to Europe, and prepared to desert the banners of the cross; others ran towards the ramparts, and getting possession of the towers, swore to defend them.

A few days after, fresh deputies arrived to declare that the king of Jerusalem and the other leaders of the army would be obliged to give up Ptolemaïs to the Mussulmans if they refused to surrender Damietta. In order to overcome the obstinate resistance of those who wished to defend the city, and who reproached the imprisoned army with disgracing the Christians, they added, that this army, though defeated, had obtained a prize worthy of their former exploits, for the Saracens had engaged to restore to them the true cross of the Saviour, which had fallen into the hands of Saladin at the battle of Tiberias. The fear of losing Ptolemaïs, the hope of regaining the cross of Christ, together with the speeches of the deputies, brought back the spirit of peace and resignation to the minds of the most ardent of the Crusaders, and disposed them to the performance of the conditions of the treaty.

In the mean time, the Christian army having lost their tents and their baggage, passed many days and many nights in a plain covered with the waters of the Nile. Hunger, disease, and inundation threatened their entire destruction. The king of Jerusalem, then in the camp of the Saracens, upon being informed of the horrible distress of the Christians, went to conjure Melik-Kamel to have pity on his disarmed enemies. The continuator of William of Tyre, who is our guide in this part of our history, reports, in his old, quaint language, the touching interview between John of Brienne and the sultan of Egypt. "The king sat down before the sultan, and began to weep; the sultan, on seeing the king weep, said, 'Sire, why do you weep?' 'Sire, I have good cause,' replied the king, 'for I behold the people whom God has confided to me perishing amidst the waters, and dying with hunger.' The sultan felt great pity at seeing the king weep, and he wept also; then he sent thirty thousand loaves to the poor as well as the rich; and sent the same quantity daily during four days." [230]

Melik-Kamel caused the sluices to be closed, and the waters rapidly retired from the plain; as soon as Damietta was surrendered to the Mussulmans, the Christian army began its retreat. The Crusaders, who owed their liberty and lives to the mercy of the Saracens, passed through the city which had cost them so many conflicts and so much labour; and, weeping, quitted the banks of the Nile, where so short a time before they had sworn to make the cause of Christ triumphant. They bore away in sadness the wood of the true cross, the identity of which they had reason to suspect, since it no longer performed miracles, and was not for them now the signal of victory. The sultan of Egypt caused them to be accompanied by his son, who had orders to provide for all their wants on their route. The Saracen leaders were impatient to get rid of an army that had threatened their empire; they could scarcely give credit to their own triumph, and some little apprehension was, no doubt, mingled with the pity with which their conquered enemies inspired them.

Great rejoicings had been made at Ptolemaïs for the victories obtained by the Christians on the banks of the Nile; they believed that they already saw the holy places delivered, and the empire of the Saracens destroyed. Consternation took place of their joy on seeing the army return. As in all the other reverses which their arms had met with, the Christians mutually reproached each other with their defeat; they accused the leaders of ambition, and the king of Jerusalem of weakness; the Templars and Hospitallers, who had on all occasions set an example of courage and the most generous devotedness, were obliged to make a public apology for their conduct. When it became known in the West that Damietta had fallen again into the hands of the Saracens, all the faithful were affected by the deepest grief, [231] and sought, by their prayers, to mitigate the anger of Heaven. Violent murmurs arose against the legate Pelagius, and represented him to the sovereign pontiff as the author of all the disasters of the crusade; but Honorius was not willing to condemn his minister, and reproached Frederick, who had three times renewed his vow to fight against the infidels, with having remained an idle spectator of an unfortunate war, and with having neglected to succour his brethren of the East.

Frederick, who had sent vessels, provisions, and soldiers to the holy war, thought that he had fully performed his part in the crusade, and was at first much astonished at the reproaches of the Holy See. When the pope threatened him with the anger of Heaven and the thunders of Rome, he could not restrain his indignation; in his letters the emperor complains bitterly of the tyranny of both Innocent and Honorius, and talks of opposing war to war, and vengeance to injustice. After this, Honorius, who acted less from the dictates of his own mind than after the policy of his predecessors, changed his tone, attempted to justify both Innocent and himself, and, employing prayers instead of menaces, conjured Frederick to have pity on the Church of the East.

This paternal language appeased Frederick; in an interview which he had with the pope at Veroli, the emperor of Germany repeated his vow to repair to Palestine at the head of an army. In another assembly, which was held some time afterwards at Verona, the pope endeavoured to engage Frederick, on account of his own interests; he proposed to him to espouse Yolande, daughter of John of Brienne, and heir to the kingdom of Jerusalem. The grand masters of the Templars, the Hospitallers, and the Teutonic order, with the patriarch and the king of Jerusalem, all summoned to Italy to deliberate on the affairs of the crusade, approved of a union which would secure them the assistance of a powerful monarch. Frederick accepted a kingdom which he promised to defend, and consented to undergo excommunication if he failed in his promises.

After the conference of Verona, King John of Brienne visited the principal states of Europe, for the purpose of soliciting aid for the Holy Land. At the time of John's arrival in France, the French were mourning the death of Philip Augustus. The king of Jerusalem assisted at the funeral ceremonies of his master and benefactor, who, at his death, had bequeathed three thousand silver marks to the defenders of Palestine. After having paid the last duties to Philip, John went first to England, and afterwards to Germany, in both of which countries his presence and his discourses strongly moved Christians with the misfortunes of the Holy Land.

The emperor Frederick, on his part, made all the requisite preparations for an expedition which he was to lead in person; he ordered vessels to be constructed in all the ports of Sicily for transporting the Crusaders. "Heaven and earth," wrote he to the pope, "are witnesses that I desire the success of the Christian arms with my whole soul, and that I will neglect nothing that can assist in securing the success of the holy enterprise." In all his letters Frederick exhorted the sovereign pontiff to employ every means to augment the numbers of the soldiers of Christ. Become, all at once, more zealous for the crusade than the pope himself, he reproached the court of Rome with being sparing in indulgences, and with confiding the preaching of the crusade to vulgar orators; he advised the pope to redouble his efforts to appease the quarrels of Christian princes, and to compel the kings of France and England to sign a peace, in order that the nobles and people of these two kingdoms might take part in the crusade. Frederick not being able to go into Germany, sent thither the grand master of the Teutonic order, with directions to exhort the landgrave of Thuringia, the duke of Austria, the king of Hungary, and the other princes of the empire, to take the oath to fight against the infidels. He undertook to furnish the Crusaders with vessels, provisions, arms, and everything necessary for the expedition beyond the sea; in short, he displayed so much activity, and showed so much ardour and zeal, that all the attention of the Christians was directed towards him, and he was considered as the soul, the moving principle, and the head of the holy enterprise.

The Christians of Palestine placed all their hopes in him; the patriarch of Alexandria, in a letter to the pope, said that they looked for the emperor of Germany on the banks of the Nile and the Jordan, *as formerly the saints had looked for the coming of the Messiah or Saviour of the world*. The patriarch spoke with grief of the oppression and servitude that had been inflicted upon the Christians established in Egypt since the last invasion of the Crusaders. The unfortunate disciples of Christ were not allowed to keep in their dwellings either arms or horses, nor even to bear a crucifix at the funeral processions of their relations; a hundred and fifteen of their churches had been destroyed since the conquest of Damietta. Oppressed by tributes, [232] condemned to disgraceful labours, banished from their homes, wandering around their temples and their altars, they invoked the mercy of Heaven and the valour of the warriors of the West for their deliverance.

The report of Frederick's preparations was spread even to the remote nations of Georgia; and the queen of that country wrote to the head of the Church of Rome, that the constable of her kingdom and a great number of warriors only waited for the arrival of the emperor of Germany, to fly to the assistance of Palestine. The Georgians had the reputation of being a warlike people, and were dreaded by the Mussulmans; their pilgrims enjoyed the privilege of entering Jerusalem without paying the tribute imposed upon other Christians. When the sultan of Damascus caused the ramparts of the holy city to be destroyed, the warriors of Georgia swore to avenge the outrage committed on the city of God; but an invasion of the Tartars prevented them from leaving their own territories. [233] Since that period, the hordes of Tartary having directed their ravages towards other countries, the Crusaders of Caucasus and the shores of the Caspian Sea promised to unite themselves in the plains of Syria and Egypt, with the Crusaders from the banks of the Rhine and the Danube.

Frederick, however, was not yet in a position to perform his so often repeated promises; the kingdom of Sicily and Naples contained germs of discord and rebellion; the republics of Lombardy were openly opposed to the emperor of Germany; and the Holy See, which observed with anxiety the ambitious projects of Frederick upon Italy, encouraged all the enemies of a power of which it dreaded the too close neighbourhood. Thus, the policy of the court of Rome, the revolts of Sicily, and the enterprises of the Italian republics, would not allow the emperor to lead his armies into Asia. Frederick demanded of the pope the indulgence of a delay of two years for the performance of his vow; founding his request upon the length of time required for assembling his armies, and declared that he was not willing to begin the war before the expiration of the truce made with the Mussulmans; thus showing much more respect for treaties with infidels, than had till that time been common among Christians, indeed, more respect than he had himself shown. The pope, although much dissatisfied, could not refuse the delay the emperor demanded; he, however, dissembled his anger, and contented himself with requiring fresh promises, which were made, as all the rest had been, with the greatest solemnity.

The new vows of Frederick were strengthened by his marriage with the heir of the king of Jerusalem. The marriage was celebrated at Rome, amidst the benedictions of the clergy and the acclamations of the people; all the Christians of the West heard of it with joy, and this union appeared to them to be the most certain pledge of the victories the Crusaders would gain over the infidels. John of Brienne, who assisted at the ceremony, congratulated himself upon having obtained an emperor for a son-in-law and a supporter; but his joy was not of long duration. Frederick, after his marriage, only saw in him the brother of that Gauthier de Brienne, who had borne the title of king of Naples and Sicily; he considered him as an enemy to his power, a dangerous rival, and he disputed the possession of the kingdom of Jerusalem with him. The pope was secretly pleased at this claim or pretension, as he hoped it would promote the interests of the crusade. Honorius was delighted to see the ambition of the emperor mix itself up with the great designs for the execution of which he was so anxious. Frederick was therefore acknowledged king of Jerusalem. Thus John of Brienne, who had always proved himself the most ardent apostle of the holy war, deprived of his crown, and from that time a stranger to the affairs of Palestine, was obliged to wait in retirement and silence for a favourable opportunity to avenge himself on his son-in-law, and recover his kingdom.

Frederick carried on his preparations for the holy war, and appeared more than ever disposed to set out for the East. The crusade was preached, in the name of the head of the Church, in all the kingdoms of Europe; the sovereign pontiff wrote to the princes to exhort them to suspend their divisions and occupy themselves solely with the war beyond the sea.

As hostilities had just been renewed between England and France, Honorius ordered Louis VIII. to lay down his arms, and threatened him with excommunication, if he did not immediately make peace. The king of France, before he obeyed the orders of the pope, was desirous of completing the conquest of Poitou; and whilst the thunders of Rome were growling over his head, the people and clergy were returning Heaven thanks for his victories, in every church of his kingdom.

The war against the English was not the only obstacle to the departure of the French Crusaders for the Holy Land; the exterminating crusade against the Albigeois was still going on, and Louis VIII. took a more active interest in it than his father Philip had done. When Louis VIII. had concluded a truce with England, he at length resolved to take the cross, and made a vow, not to go and fight against the Saracens in Asia, but against the heretics in Languedoc. In this crusade the king of France had the double advantage of scarcely going out of his own territories, and of making conquests that might some day enlarge his kingdom. The lords and barons followed Louis into the southern provinces, and thought no more about the deliverance of Jerusalem.

At the same time the envoys of the pope and the emperor were busy in exhorting the nations of Germany to succour the Christians of Palestine. Their orations, which at first had great success, ended by diminishing both confidence and enthusiasm. As the pope had recommended the preachers to be prodigal of the indulgences of the Church, the people beheld with astonishment the greatest criminals take the cross, and swear to expiate their sins by the holy pilgrimage. They remembered that St. Bernard had called thieves and murderers to the defence of Christ; but opinions and morals began to change, and that which had succeeded in the preceding century was now only a source of reproach. The monk of Upsberg, a contemporary author, informs us that the facility granted to the most vicious of mankind to redeem their crimes by taking up arms and the cross, only served to increase great offences, and cool the zeal of the true defenders of Christ. [234]

The orators who preached the crusade in England gathered more fruit from their labours, but owed great part of their success to celestial phenomena, which came very opportunely to second their eloquence. A luminous crucifix, with the marks of the five wounds of the Saviour, appeared suddenly in the heavens. This miraculous spectacle greatly inflamed the enthusiasm of the people; and, if we may believe Matthew Paris, more than sixty thousand English took the oath to arm themselves for the deliverance of the tomb of Christ.

Spain was constantly the seat of a sanguinary war between the Moors and the Christians; the one party supported by warriors from Africa, the other by knights and soldiers from the provinces of France, fought battles every day without destroying their means of either attack or defence: amidst such wars, in which, by turns, Mahomet and Christ were invoked, Spain was not likely to hear or attend to the complaints and appeals of Jerusalem.

Another enthusiasm than that of the crusades,—an ardent desire for liberty,—then agitated the finest countries of Italy. The greater part of the cities, acted upon by jealousy and the other passions of republics, were all at war among themselves; fighting sometimes for territory, and sometimes for independence. In all these small states, parties attacked and pursued each other with fury, and disputed the exercise of power, sword in hand. Some of the cities, principalities, and baronies invoked the authority of the pope, others that of the emperor of Germany; the factions of the Guelphs and the Ghibellines troubled every city, and created divisions in most families. These discords and civil wars naturally turned the attention of Christian nations from the crusades.

The cities of Lombardy had formed a powerful confederacy, which gave Frederick continual cause of inquietude, and detained him in the West; Honorius employed every means in his power to re-establish peace, and direct men's minds towards his darling object; and at last succeeded in getting the Lombard republics to join the emperor of Germany for the deliverance of the holy places.

Although the people had lost some portion of their enthusiasm for the holy war, it was still possible to form a redoubtable army, by gathering together all the warriors that had taken the cross in the various countries of Europe; and the new Crusaders were ordered to meet at the port of Brindisi, where vessels were being prepared to transport them to the East. On their arrival in the kingdom of Naples, the emperor of Germany supplied them with provisions and arms; everything was ready, and the pope was about, at length, to see his wishes accomplished, and receive the reward of all his labours and preachings, when inexorable death deprived Christendom of its head.

Gregory IX., who succeeded him, had all the abilities, the virtues, and the ambition of Innocent III. In the execution of his designs, he feared neither difficulties nor perils; the most violent measures had no terrors for his obstinacy or audacity, when the triumph of his will was in question. Gregory had scarcely ascended the pontifical throne, when the preparations for the holy war engrossed all his thoughts, and became the principal object of his active solicitude.

The Crusaders assembled in Apulia had much to suffer from the influences of the climate and the season; the sovereign pontiff neglected nothing to alleviate their distresses and hasten their departure. He exhorted the emperor to embark, by saying to him, "The Lord has placed you in this world as a cherubim with a flaming sword, to direct those who stray from the way of the tree of life." Frederick at length yielded to the prayers of the pope, and sailed from the port of Brindisi with his fleet and army. Prayers were being put up for the prosperity of his voyage and the success of his expedition, in all the provinces of his empire, when, at the end of three days, being attacked by the malady that had made such ravages in the Christian army, he retraced his course, and landed in the port of Otranto.

Gregory had celebrated the departure of Frederick as a triumph of the Church; he considered his return as an absolute revolt against the Holy See. The little city of Agnani, to which the pope had retired, witnessed the rage of the pontiff, and beheld the birth of that formidable storm which so long disturbed the Christian world. Accompanied by the cardinals and several bishops, Gregory repaired to the principal church, and having mounted the pulpit, before the assembled people, he pronounced a sermon which had for its text, "It is necessary that scandals should arise." After having called upon the prophets, and spoken of the triumph of St. Michael over the dragon, he launched against Frederick all the anathemas of the Church.

The emperor at first sent messengers to the pope to explain and justify his conduct; but the inexorable Gregory refused to listen to them, and complained to all the sovereigns of Europe, representing Frederick as a faithless and perjured prince. He accused him of having consigned his wife Yolande to close imprisonment, in which she died of grief; of having left the Crusaders to perish with hunger, thirst, and heat in the plains of Apulia; and of having, at last, under the frivolous pretext of sickness, violated his oath and deserted the banners of Christ, *in order to return to the customary enjoyments of his kingdom.* He made him many other reproaches; and in his anger called down upon him the maledictions of all Christians.

Frederick, exceedingly irritated, replied to the accusations of Gregory with much bitterness. In his apology, which he sent to all the princes of Christendom, he complained strongly of the usurpations of the Holy See, and exposed, in the most odious colours, the policy and ambitious designs of the court of Rome. "The Church of Rome," said he, "sends legates everywhere, *with power to punish, to suspend, and excommunicate, not with the designs of spreading the word of God, but to heap up money, and reap that which they have not sown.*" The emperor reminded the princes, in his letters, of the violences which the pope had exercised against the count of Thoulouse and the king of England; he said that the domains of the clergy did not now satisfy the ambition of the Holy See, and that the sovereign pontiffs wished to lay their hands upon every kingdom. From that moment open war was declared between the pope and the emperor; neither of them possessed a pacific character or a love of quiet; both were animated by boundless ambition, jealous to excess of their power, implacable in their revenge, and always ready to employ the arms which the Church or fortune placed in their hands. Gregory displayed an indefatigable activity, leaving his enemies no repose, but pursuing them at the same time with the thunders of religion and war. In addition to the arms of eloquence, the pontiff did not disdain to employ satire; the manifestoes which he published against his adversaries constantly recalled the spirit of the denunciations made by the prophets. These denunciations, mixed with obscure allegories, gave to his words a dark and mysterious tone, which caused him to be considered as the interpreter of angry Heaven. Frederick was neither a less able prince nor a less redoubtable enemy: the art of war contained no stratagems or secrets with which he was unacquainted; policy dictated no means that he scrupled to employ. Endowed with all the gifts of mind, and with a keen spirit of raillery, he was as competent to confound his enemies in a discussion, as to conquer them in the field of battle. Descended, on the female side, from those famous Normans who had conquered Sicily and the kingdom of Naples, he united, as they had done, courage with subtlety, and audacity with dissimulation: to please the court of Rome, he had made barbarous laws against heretics; and, now become the enemy of the popes, he did not fear to arm heretics or Saracens against the court of Rome. When the kingdom of Jerusalem was offered to him, he set no great value upon the acquisition; but he accepted it with joy, in order to increase his popularity in the Christian world, and to arm himself, one day, against the sovereign pontiff with a title, which was then held in universal veneration.

A war between such enemies must necessarily prove terrible, and spread desolation and confusion throughout Christendom. Gregory, on his return to Rome, repeated his excommunications in the church of St. Peter; Frederick, in order to revenge himself, seduced into his party most of the Roman nobles, who took up arms, insulted the sovereign pontiff at the very foot of the altar, and compelled him to abandon the capital of the Christian world. The pope, driven from his states, pursued his enemy with more fury than ever; and, availing himself of the formidable authority of the Church, he released the subjects of Frederick from their oath of fidelity, by reminding them that they could owe no obedience to those who *opposed themselves to God and his saints*. On his side, Frederick drove the Templars and Hospitallers from the kingdom of Naples, plundered the churches, and ill-treated all ecclesiastics whom he suspected of being attached to the party of the Holy See. He sent troops to ravage the patrimony of St. Peter, and enlisted the Saracens established in Sicily, under the banners of a Christian prince, to combat the head of the Christian church. The Roman states were ravaged, and given up to the horrors of war. The eyes of all Europe were fixed upon these deplorable scenes, and every one seemed to have forgotten the holy war.

The Christians of Palestine, however, never ceased to implore aid from the West. A letter to the pope from the patriarch of Jerusalem, the bishops of Cæsarea and Bethlehem, and the grand masters of the three military orders, painted in strong colours the despair into which the Christians of the East had fallen, when they learnt that Frederick had deferred his departure. The pope received their complaints with expressions of sorrow and kindness, and communicated them to the faithful with greater zeal, from their furnishing him with a fresh opportunity of accusing the emperor of Germany. But the nations of the West, occupied with their own dangers, and terrified at the sight of the violent storms that had recently burst forth, were not in the least moved by either the lamentations from Palestine or the pressing exhortations of Gregory. In this unfortunate position of European affairs, the Christian colonies, abandoned to themselves and their own feeble resources, and a prey to the greatest disorders, must have been invaded and entirely destroyed, if Providence had not stirred up fresh discords among their enemies.

During the siege of Damietta, the common danger had united the children of Malek-Adel; after victory, ambition resumed the place of fear; and the Ayoubite princes quarrelled for the provinces which their union had wrested from the power, or saved from the invasion of the Christians. Conraddin, sultan of Damascus, dreading the views of Melik-Kamel, called Gelaleddin, prince of the vast empire of Carismia, to his aid. The sultan of Cairo, in great apprehension of the consequences of this alliance, turned his eyes towards the princes of the West. During several years, the report alone of the preparations of Frederick had been a source of terror to the Mussulman powers. The emperor of Germany was considered, in the East, as the head of all the nations of Europe. The sultan of Egypt attached the greatest importance to the disarming of a formidable enemy; and as the complaints of the pope, and the report of the discords that had broken out among the Christians, had reached his ears, he conceived a hope of finding in Frederick a sincere ally and a powerful auxiliary. [235]

Melik-Kamel sent presents and ambassadors to the emperor of Germany; he invited Frederick to come into the East, and promised to deliver Jerusalem up to him. This proposition gave the emperor as much surprise as joy; and he, in reply, sent an ambassador into Egypt, to ascertain the exact intentions of the sultan of Cairo, and offer him his friendship. The envoy of Frederick was received at the court of the sultan with the greatest honours, and returned to announce to his master that Melik-Kamel was ready to favour his expedition to Palestine.

This negotiation, with which the pope and the Christians of the West were perfectly unacquainted, made Frederick determine to follow up the project of the crusade: he had, besides, several other motives for not renouncing the Eastern enterprise. He knew that John of Brienne was on the point of returning to Palestine, and resuming possession of the kingdom of Jerusalem. The pope continued to represent him as the enemy of Christ, and the scourge of Christians. To secure the failure of the plan of John of Brienne, and, at the same time, reply to the sovereign pontiff in a victorious manner, Frederick resolved to embark for the Holy Land. He was desirous of proclaiming his intention with the greatest pomp; and caused a magnificent throne to be erected in the plain of Barletta, which he ascended in the presence of an immense crowd of spectators. In all the splendour of imperial magnificence, he presented himself invested with the pilgrim's cross, and announced to the assembled people that he was about to set out for Syria. In order to give more solemnity to this pompous ceremony, and affect the hearts of the multitude, the emperor caused his will to be read with a loud voice; and the barons and nobles swore at the foot of the throne, to see that his last commands should be executed, if he should chance to lose his life, either in the perils of the sea or the wars of the East.

When the pope learnt this determination of Frederick's, he sent ecclesiastics to forbid him to embark. The sovereign pontiff reproached the emperor with presenting to the Christian world the scandal of a crusade directed by a prince reproved of God: as the fleet of Frederick consisted of only twenty galleys, and as he took with him only six hundred knights, Gregory reproached him with not having fulfilled his promises, and compared his imprudent attempts to the expedition of a captain of pirates. The emperor did not condescend to make any reply to the messengers of the pope; the more opposition the head of the Church gave to his departure, the more impatient Frederick appeared to set out and accomplish his design: in his indignation, he congratulated himself at having to brave the anger of the Church and the arms of the Saracens at the same time. He left the greater part of his army in Sicily; charging his lieutenant, the duke of Spoleto, to negotiate for peace with the pope, but at the same time to carry on the war commenced against the Roman states with unabated vigour.

When he heard of the departure of the emperor, Gregory was in the little city of Assisi, occupied in the canonization of St. Francis. During several days, he had sung nothing but hymns of hope and joy: "Francis," said he, "had appeared like the star of morning, like the orb of day, like the moon in its splendour." This language of peace, this festive pomp, were all at once interrupted by the maledictions that the pope pronounced against Frederick: the sovereign pontiff repaired to the foot of the altar, and there implored Heaven to confound the pride of impious monarchs, and frustrate all their sacrilegious enterprises.

The emperor, notwithstanding, arrived safely on the coast of Syria, and was received at Ptolemaïs by the patriarch, the clergy, and the grand masters of the military orders. For some days, the Christians of the East viewed him as the liberator and the king of Jerusalem; but a change speedily took place. Two disciples of St. Francis, sent by the pope, came to announce to the faithful that they had received a prince rebellious to the will of the Church. From that moment, contempt, hatred, and mistrust took place of respect and submission. They began by perceiving that Frederick was followed by only a small number of warriors, and that he had not troops enough to render him formidable to either the Saracens or the Christians. Nothing was talked of in Ptolemaïs but the excommunication of the pope, and the means of withdrawing themselves from obedience to a heretic prince: never had the deliverance of Jerusalem been less thought of.

At the moment in which Frederick arrived in Syria, Conraddin, sultan of Damascus, died; and the death of this prince gave birth to more discords among the Mussulman powers. The principality of Damascus was governed by a young inexperienced prince; and the spirit of license and insubordination, which had, in the last wars, been already observed among the troops of Syria and Egypt, made, every day, greater progress, and put all the Mussulman thrones in peril.

The sultan of Cairo, when informed of the arrival of Frederick, came into Palestine, at the head of an army. Some asserted that he came to defend Jerusalem, and to fight with the Christians; but his true design was to take advantage of the chances of war, and of the discords which everywhere prevailed, to get possession of Damascus, and defeat the plans of the enemies that jealousy and ambition had raised up against him among the Mussulmans and princes of his family.

The emperor of Germany marched out of Ptolemaïs, at the head of his small army, and directed his course towards the mountains of Naplouse. He had sent Count Thomas de Celano to Melik-Kamel, to remind him of his promises, and to tell him, that, being master of the most vast provinces of the West, he was not come into Asia for the purpose of making conquests; that he had no other design but that of visiting the holy places, and taking possession of the kingdom of Jerusalem, which belonged to him. [236] The sultan received the ambassador of Frederick with due respect; but whether he was ashamed to make peace before he had begun the war, or whether he feared to draw upon himself the hatred of the Mussulmans, by showing too much deference for a Christian prince, he at first made no reply to the propositions that were made to him.

Nevertheless the two princes sent fresh ambassadors, charged on both sides to express a desire for peace; both were placed in embarrassing circumstances, being surrounded by enemies who blamed their proceedings, and did not allow them to publish all their sentiments freely. The Mussulman army from Damascus, encamped in the neighbourhood of Jerusalem, watched all the movements of the sultan of Egypt, and seemed much more disposed to fight with him than to repulse the Christians. The emperor of Germany found himself in the presence of two hostile armies, and that which he himself commanded inspired him with no more confidence than he inspired in it. The Hospitallers and Templars had left him, and followed him at a distance; in the camp of the Christians no one durst pronounce the name of the prince who commanded the army. Frederick had been obliged to withdraw the standard of the empire, and his orders were only issued to the soldiers of the cross in the name of God and of the Christian republic.

In this difficult situation, Frederick and Melik-Kamel were equally sensible of the necessity for peace, and of the danger of commencing war; they therefore gave more employment to their ambassadors than to their soldiers; this crusade was nothing but a long negotiation, disapproved of by both Christians and infidels. As the two sovereigns covered their policy with a veil of profound mystery, it was easy for hatred to spread and procure countenance for sinister reports. Criminal intentions were discovered in the simplest actions. In the Christian army it was conceived that Frederick had committed a crime by sending his sword and cuirass to the sultan of Cairo, as a pledge of his wish for peace. Among the Mussulmans, Melik-Kamel was reproached with seeking an alliance with the enemies of Islamism, by sending to the leader of the Franks an elephant, some camels, and the rarest productions of Arabia, India, and Egypt. The scandal reached its height when the emperor received as a present from the sultan of Cairo, a troop of girls, brought up, according to the custom of the Orientals, to sing and dance in the banqueting-hall.

At length prejudices were carried so far on both sides, that Frederick was judged more favourably of by his enemies than by his own army; and Melik-Kamel would sooner have found grace among the Christians than among his own troops. The infidels regarded the emperor of Germany as a prince full of wisdom and moderation; Abulfeda, and all the Arabian authors, have celebrated the qualities and virtues of the monarch of the Franks, whilst the continuator of William of Tyre only speaks of this prince with bitterness, and reports in his history, that all the apostles and other Christians had great doubt and great suspicion that he was far gone in infidelity, and warm in his belief in the law of Mahomet.

Hatred soon broke out in acts of treachery and the most odious plots. As the emperor had expressed an intention of going to bathe in the waters of the Jordan, the Templars addressed a letter to Melik-Kamel, pointing out the means of surprising the head of the Christian array in his pilgrimage: the sultan of Cairo despised such treachery, and sent the letter he had received to Frederick. At the same time Melik-Kamel learnt that the sultan of Damascus had declared war against him, and would be joined by several other Mussulman princes. The sultan of Cairo and the emperor of Germany had carried on their negotiations for peace during several months, but now, pressed on all sides by enemies, and surrounded by dangers, even in their own camp, they at length resolved to end the matter, and conclude a treaty, which would permit them to dispose of their forces for their security or for their personal ambition. They agreed between themselves, that they would make a truce of ten years, and that Jerusalem, Nazareth, Bethlehem, and Thoron should be given up to Frederick or his lieutenants. [237] According to the conditions of the treaty, the Mussulmans were to retain in the holy city, the mosque of Omar and the free exercise of their worship: the principality of Antioch and the county of Tripoli were not comprised in the treaty. The emperor of Germany undertook to divert the Franks from every kind of hostility against the subjects or lands of the sultan of Egypt.

When the articles of the treaty became known in the two camps, the peace was considered by both as impious and sacrilegious. [238] The imauns and cadis, invoking the name of the caliph of Bagdad, loudly condemned a truce which conveyed away from the Mussulmans the holy city, which they called *the house of God, the city of the prophet.* The prelates and bishops, speaking in the name of the pontiff of Rome, declaimed vehemently against a treaty which left mosques standing by the side of the Holy Sepulchre, and in some sort confounded the worship of Mahomet with that of Christ. When the envoy of the emperor of Germany went to Damascus, to procure the ratification of the treaty which had been concluded, the sultan and his vizier refused to hear him. The peace made with the Christians was a subject of affliction and scandal for all true believers. One of the most celebrated orators of Islamism pronounced the panegyric of Jerusalem in the great mosque; and, when recalling in pathetic terms the loss the Mussulmans had experienced, he drew tears from all the assembled people.

The patriarch of Jerusalem placed an interdict upon the recovered holy places, and refused pilgrims permission to visit the sepulchre of Christ. Jerusalem was no longer, in the eyes of Christians, the holy city and the heritage of the Son of God; when the emperor made his public entrance, the faithful preserved a sullen and melancholy silence as he passed along. Accompanied by the German barons and the Teutonic knights, he repaired to the church of the Holy Sepulchre, which was hung with mourning, and appeared as if guarded by the angel of reprobation; all the ecclesiastics had deserted the sanctuary, and everything wore the air of abomination and desolation. Frederick himself took the crown, and placing it upon his head, he was proclaimed king of Jerusalem without any religious ceremony; the images of the apostles were veiled; nothing was seen around the altars but swords and lances; and the sacred vaults gave back no sounds but the noisy acclamations of warriors.

After his coronation, Frederick wrote to the pope and to all the princes of the West, that he had reconquered Jerusalem without the effusion of blood; in his account he endeavoured to enhance the splendour and merit of this victory, which must fulfil all the hopes of the Christian world. At the same time, the patriarch wrote to Gregory, and all the faithful of Christendom, to show them the impiety and the disgrace of the treaty Frederick had just concluded. When he heard of the success of the emperor, the sovereign pontiff deplored the conquest of Jerusalem as he would have deplored its loss, and compared the new king of Judæa to those impious monarchs whom the anger of God placed upon the throne of David.

Frederick was not able to remain long in the holy city, which resounded with imprecations against him. He returned to Ptolemaïs, where he found only revolted subjects and Christians scandalized at his successes. The patriarch and the clergy placed an interdict upon the city during the time the emperor should remain in it; all religious worship was suspended; the altars were deprived of their ornaments, and the crosses, relics, and images of the saints were cast upon the ground; no more bells, no more religious hymns were to be heard; a melancholy silence prevailed in the sanctuary, where mass was celebrated in a low voice, and with closed doors. The dead were buried in the fields, without funeral ceremonies or monumental stones; everything, in short, denoted a season of great calamities, and a dread of the vengeance of Heaven: it was thus that the liberator of Jerusalem was welcomed at Ptolemaïs.

It was Passion-week, and this religious period gave additional influence to the clergy and more solemnity to the maledictions of the Church. Frederick found himself obliged to negotiate for peace with the Christians, as he had done with the infidels, and being unable to regain their good-will he still further exasperated them by his violence. He caused the gates of the city to be closed, and prohibited the bringing in of provisions; he planted archers and arbalatiers in every place where they could insult the Templars and pilgrims; and by his orders, mendicant preaching monks were dragged from the foot of the altar, and beaten with rods in the public places of the city.

Hatred and vengeance were carried, on both sides, to the greatest excess. It was impossible for the emperor, surrounded as he was by enemies, to remain long at Ptolemaïs, in addition to which motive, he daily received letters from Europe urging his return. Two formidable armies, under the banners of the Holy See, had entered the kingdom of Naples, pillaged the cities, ravaged the country, mutilated prisoners, and committed all kinds of enormities. These armies were under the command of John of Brienne, impatient to revenge his own injuries, and two Sicilian counts, whom the emperor of Germany had driven from the kingdom of Naples.

Frederick at length quitted Palestine and returned to his own dominions. As he left Ptolemaïs, the inhabitants chanted hymns of deliverance and joy. He accused the Templars of having endeavoured to deliver him up to the Saracens; the Templars, on their part, accused him of having wished to surrender all the Christian cities to the sultan of Cairo: these accusations, and a thousand others, dictated by hatred, ought to inspire the historian with great and just suspicions. The Christians might have urged against Frederick a much more reasonable reproach; he had taken no means to secure his conquest, and they were warranted in believing that he had only made his triumphal entry into Jerusalem with the view of annoying the Holy See, and dating a reply to the inculpations of Gregory from the holy places: having attained his object, he had deceived the faithful, by inviting them to a city that he was disposed neither to defend nor fortify. In addition to this, Frederick himself felt very little pride in the advantages of which he made such a pompous display throughout Europe; and the crusade in which he had taken a part was frequently the object of his pleasantries and sarcasms.

On his return to Italy, he found a much more serious war than that he had carried on in Asia. The pope had not only levied troops to ravage his states, he had induced the Lombard republics to take up arms against him. John of Brienne, deprived of his title of king of Jerusalem, determined to endeavour to be acknowledged emperor, and his pretensions were supported by all that was then held most sacred, the authority of the Church and the right of victory. The presence of Frederick restored courage to his subjects, whose fidelity was still unshaken; he met his enemies in several engagements, in which he always gained the advantage. The army of John of Brienne was dispersed, and the pontifical troops quitted all the cities and provinces they had conquered, in the greatest disorder.

The pope, learning that fortune had deserted his banners, again had recourse to the thunders of religion, and employed the most terrible of its denunciations against Frederick. He declared that all were excommunicated who should hold any kind of commerce with the emperor, all who should sit at his table, be present at his councils, celebrate divine service before him, or offer him any mark of attachment or respect. Frederick was terrified at this sentence, which was published with great solemnity in all parts of Europe, particularly in his own dominions; and sent ambassadors to the pope, who, in spite of the thunders with which he was armed, dreaded the consequences of war, and showed himself disposed to receive the submission of an enemy he dreaded.

After a negotiation of several days, a treaty was made, in which the conquered pope dictated laws to his conqueror, and appeared, whilst receiving peace, to accord a pardon. But in spite of this treaty of peace, the effects of discord still subsisted, and were felt even in the East, where debates, raised in the name of the Church, had divided men's minds, and depressed the general courage; and where the Christian states, for which Europe had taken up arms, remained without support and without defence. As Frederick had abandoned Jerusalem without fortifying it, [239] the Christians were in constant dread of the invasion of the Mussulman peasants, whom the hopes of pillage attracted from the mountains of Naplouse. The great bell of the church of the Holy Sepulchre often gave warning of the approach of an enemy eager for carnage; and most of the inhabitants retired with their terrified families, some to the fortress of St. David, which was still standing among the ruins, and others into desert places.

The patriarch of Jerusalem, the prelates, barons, and people of Palestine, who had no longer either a leader or a king, in vain implored the assistance of the warriors and princes of the West: prayers and complaints so frequently repeated, had no power to awaken in the hearts of the faithful either the sentiments of pity or the enthusiasm which had so often caused them to take up arms and the cross. They could have no faith in perils that followed so closely upon victory; and they despaired of ever being able to assure the deliverance of a country which required to be delivered so often.

The pope, however, had not abandoned the project of the crusade, and still entertained the hope of reviving the ardour and zeal of the Christian warriors by his exhortations. He convoked an assembly at Spoleto, at which Frederick, with the patriarchs of Constantinople, Antioch, and Jerusalem assisted. It was resolved in this assembly, to renew the war in Palestine, notwithstanding the truce concluded with the sultan of Cairo.

Gregory was impatient to accomplish his designs, and proclaim the laws of the Church in the rich countries of the East; and, to employ the time till warriors could be gathered together, he sent several missionaries across the sea, armed with the sword and the word, to endeavour to convert the infidels of Syria and Egypt. The sovereign pontiff was so persuaded of the success of this pacific crusade, that he wrote to the caliph of Bagdad, the sultan of Damascus, and the principal Mussulman chiefs, to exhort them to embrace Christianity. [240] History does not say what the fate was of these mendicant preachers in the East; but the caliph of Bagdad and the Mussulman princes did not cease to be inveterate enemies to the Christians. Gregory IX. was better inspired and more fortunate when he sent sacred orators into several of the provinces of the West, to appease the troubles and civil wars that were so injurious to the cause of religion, and diverted the minds of the people from the great enterprise of the holy wars.

The disciples of St. Dominick and St. Francis of Assisi, charged with a mission worthy of the Gospel, pervaded cities and countries, preaching peace and concord. Among the preachers thus sent to pacify states, Brother John of Vicentia made himself conspicuous by the miracles effected by his eloquence. [241] In all the countries he visited, the nobles, the peasants, the citizens, and the warriors flocked to listen to him, and swore to pardon all injuries and terminate all quarrels. After having re-established peace in several cities troubled by the spirit of jealousy, and animated by the stormy passions of undefined, ill-understood liberty, he announced that he should preach in the plain of Peschiera, on the banks of the Adige. All the inhabitants of the neighbouring cities, headed by their clergy and their magistrates, repaired to the place appointed, to listen to the *Angel of Concord* [242] and the orator of public peace. In the presence of more than four hundred thousand auditors, Brother John mounted a pulpit elevated in the centre of the plain of Peschiera; a profound silence prevailed throughout the assembly; every eye was fixed upon the holy preacher; his words seemed to descend from heaven. He took for his text these words of the Scripture: "I give you my peace, I leave you my peace." After having drawn a frightful picture of the evils of war and the effects of discord, he ordered the Lombard cities to renounce their enmities, and dictated to them, in the name of the Church, a treaty of universal pacification. At no period had the middle ages presented a more sublime and touching spectacle; the historian of that time, who has nothing but troubles and wars to describe, ought to be delighted at an opportunity to tell of such an imposing and solemn scene, wherein religion recalled assembled nations to a sense of all that her maxims contain that is most consoling and salutary. The discourse of Brother John filled his auditory with a holy love of peace, and the cities then at war swore, before him, to forget for ever the subjects of their long divisions and eternal rivalries.

These evangelical discourses restored to Italy a few days of peace, and gave the Holy See an opportunity of preaching a new crusade with success. Gregory addressed pastoral instructions to all the bishops and prelates of Christendom. In his letters to the French bishops, he applied these words of Christ to the holy war: "If any one would come with me, let him renounce himself, let him take up my cross and follow me." The sovereign pontiff declared all who would not employ their utmost efforts to conquer the heritage of Christ, guilty of treason. The circulars of the pope ordered all the faithful, of both sexes, to pay a denier per week towards the expenses of the crusade. The head of the Church compared these alms to those which St. Paul solicited for the poor of Jerusalem, and did not fear to assert, beforehand, that they would suffice for the maintenance of the army of Crusaders for ten years.

The preaching of this crusade was confided to the fraternities of St. Dominick and St. Francis, which had, in Asia, missionaries for the conversion of infidels, and in the West, preachers to re-establish peace among Christians; the new apostles of the holy war received from the pope the power, not only to give the cross, but to commute the vow of pilgrimage to a pecuniary alms, a practice that had never been seen since the beginning of the crusades; they had likewise the faculty of granting indulgences for several days to all who came to listen to their sermons. According to the spirit of their institutions, the disciples of St. Francis and St. Dominick lived amidst austerities and penance; they devoted themselves to poverty, and were bound to furnish a constant example of Christian humility; but, in this instance, the pope desired they should be received into monasteries and cities with pomp and ceremony; and that the clergy should come out to meet them, with the banners and most splendid ornaments of their churches. Whether this magnificence changed the simplicity of their manners, or that the people did not like to behold men whom they had lately seen devoted to evangelical poverty, treated with ceremonial pomp, the preachers of the crusade inspired their auditors with neither esteem nor respect, and the crowd diminished every day. As they received abundant alms, of which no one could see the employment, neither the solemnity of their mission nor the sanctity of their characters could screen them from the suspicions and accusations of the multitude: the murmurs and complaints which arose on all sides, at length weakened the authority of their words, and assisted in cooling the zeal and devotion of the Christians for the holy war.

The enthusiasm of the people, which Christian eloquence could not revive, stood in need of the example of the most illustrious princes and warriors. France was then at peace; the war against the Albigeois was drawing towards its end: most of the knights and barons, reared amidst battles, could not endure rest, and sighed for an opportunity of signalizing their warlike temperament. They took the oath to go into Asia and fight against the Saracens.

Thibault V., count of Champagne, and king of Navarre, son of Thibault, who died before the fifth crusade, undertook to discharge the vow his father had made to the Church and to Christ. The king of Navarre was celebrated among knights and among troubadours; his muse, which had sung profane loves, now gave voice to the complaints of Jerusalem, and awakened, by Christian songs, the ardour of the soldiers of the cross. "Learn," said he, "that heaven is closed to all those who will not cross the seas to visit and defend the tomb of God. Yes, all the brave, all who love God and glory, will not hesitate to take up the cross and arms. Those who prefer repose to honour, those who dread perils, will remain alone in their homes. Jesus Christ, in the day of judgment, will say to the one party: 'You, who helped me to bear my cross, go to the place in which dwell the angels and my mother Mary;' he will say to the others: 'You, who have not succoured me, descend to the abode of the wicked.'" [243] The example and the exhortations of Thibault attracted princes, barons, and knights from all the provinces of France.

Pierre de Dreux, duke of Brittany, whom the clergy surnamed Mauclerc, because, in his youth, he had abandoned the ecclesiastical state, wished to expiate his numerous felonies, his unjust wars, his tyranny towards his subjects, his perfidies towards his allies, by the holy pilgrimage. Hugh IV., duke of Burgundy, the counts of Bar, Ferez, Mâcon, Joigny, Sancoure, and Nevers; Simon de Montfort, Andrew de Vitri, Amaury fils, Geoffrey d'Ancenes, and a crowd of barons and knights took the cross, and engaged to follow the duke of Brittany and the king of Navarre into Palestine.

As the preaching of the crusade had been accompanied by several abuses that might prove injurious to the success of the holy expedition, a council assembled at Tours, employed itself in remedying and stopping the evil at its source. We have seen, on preceding occasions, that preachers of the crusades, by receiving criminals under the banners of the cross, had scandalized Christian knights; and crusades, as was seen in the twelfth century, were not considered as a means of salvation for the faithful, and as the way of the Lord, in which all the world might enter. Great criminals no longer found a place in the ranks of the pious defenders of Christ. The council of Tours decided that Crusaders, arrested by justice, should be transferred to the hands of an ecclesiastical judge, who would pay no respect to their privileges, and should even take the cross from them, if he found them guilty of homicide or any other great crime committed against divine and human laws.

As in other crusades, the people were led into violent excesses against the Jews, whom they accused of having immolated the God for whom they were going to fight, and who retained immense treasures in their hands, whilst the Crusaders were obliged to pledge their property to perform the voyage to Palestine. In order to stop the course of these popular violences, the council forbade any ill-treatment of the Jews, either by plundering them of their wealth or by doing them personal injury, under pain of heavy ecclesiastical censures.

Another abuse, not less prejudicial to the Crusaders than all the others, had been likewise observed. The preachers of the holy wars and many other theologians had permitted Crusaders to buy off their vow by paying a sum of money equal to that which they would have expended in their pilgrimage: [244] this abuse caused great scandal among the faithful, but the Holy See, which derived considerable sums from it, paid no attention to the complaints made on account of it in England and many other states of Europe.

The Crusaders were preparing for their departure, when, all at once, a fresh cry of alarm resounded through the West. The empire of the Latins, at Constantinople, was reduced to the lowest extremity. After the reigns of Baldwin of Flanders and his son Henry, the family of Courtenay, called to the throne, derived nothing from their exaltation but the griefs and reverses inseparable from the government of an empire which is hastening to decay. Peter of Courtenay, count of Auxerre, when on his way to take possession of the throne of Baldwin, was surprised and massacred in Macedonia, by the orders of Theodore Comnenus, prince of Epirus. A short time afterwards, the empress, who had arrived at Constantinople by sea, died of grief, on learning the tragical end of her husband. Robert of Courtenay, second son of Peter, only ascended the throne to experience the rapid decline of the empire; conquered in a great battle by Vataces, the successor of Lascaris, he lost all the provinces situated beyond the Bosphorus and the Hellespont; whilst, on the other side, the prince of Epirus took possession of Thessaly and a great part of Thrace. Constantinople, threatened by formidable enemies, beheld from its towers the standards of the Greeks of Nice and of the barbarians of Mount Hemus, floating near its walls and insulting its majesty. Amidst these various disasters, Robert died, leaving, as his only successor, his brother Baldwin, still in his childhood. John of Brienne, whom fortune had made, for a short period, king of Jerusalem, was called to the tottering throne of Constantinople, at the moment that the Greeks and Bulgarians, animated by the ardour of pillage, were at the gates of the capital. Their fleets penetrated to the port, their numerous battalions were preparing to scale the ramparts; but the new emperor fought several battles with them, obtained possession of their ships, and dispersed their armies. The miraculous victories of John of Brienne added greatly to his renown, but only served to diminish his forces: after having defeated his enemies, he found himself without an army; and whilst the poets were comparing him to Hector, Roland, and Judas Machabæus, [245] he was obliged to wait in his capital for succours that had been promised him, and which never arrived. More than eighty years of age, he terminated his active career in contesting with the barbarians the remains of a power which had been founded by arms, and the miserable wreck of which could only be preserved by prodigies of valour.

The ruins which surrounded him in his last moments must have made him sensible of the nothingness of human grandeur, and produced sentiments of Christian humility. He had passed the early days of his life amidst the austerities of the cloister. On his death-bed he laid aside the imperial purple, and was desirous of breathing his last sigh in the habit of a Cordelier. A simple French knight, seated for some few days upon two thrones, both ready to pass away, son-in-law of two kings, [246] father-in-law of two emperors, John of Brienne only left, when dying, the remembrance of his extraordinary exploits, and the example of a wonderful destiny. Young Baldwin, who had married his daughter, and who was to have succeeded him, was unable to obtain his inheritance; and departing as a fugitive from his capital, he wandered through Europe as a suppliant, braving and enduring the contempt of princes and nations. Spectacle worthy of pity! the successor of the Cæsars, clothed in the purple, was beheld imploring the charity of the faithful, begging for the assistance granted to the lowest indigence, and frequently not obtaining that for which he sued.

Whilst the emperor of the East was thus travelling through Italy, France, and England, Constantinople was left without an army, and sacrificed for the defence of the state, even to its relics, the objects of the veneration of the people, and the last treasures of the empire. The sovereign pontiff was touched with the misery and degradation of Baldwin, and, at the same time, could not hear without pity the complaints of the Latin church of Byzantium: he published a new crusade for the defence of the empire of the East.

The Crusaders, who were about to set out for the Holy Land, were invited to lend their assistance to their brethren of Constantinople; but the prayers and exhortations of the Holy See produced but very feeble effects; opinions were divided; some wished to defend the empire of the Latins, others, the kingdom of Jerusalem.

The French princes and nobles, however, persisted in their resolution of going to fight against the Saracens in Asia. The barons and knights either pawned or sold their lands to purchase horses and arms, quitted their donjons and their castles, and tore themselves from the embraces of their wives. Thibault, their leader and interpreter, bade adieu to France in verses which are still extant, and which express, at the same time, the devotion of a Christian and the spirit of chivalry. His muse, at once pious and profane, deplores the torments of love, the griefs of absence, and celebrates the glory of the soldiers of Christ; to console himself for having left the lady of his thoughts, the king of Navarre invokes the Virgin Mary, *the lady of the heavens*, and finishes his complaints, by this verse, which so admirably paints the manners of the time:

Quand dame perds, Dame me soit aidant. [247]

Other troubadours, after the example of the king of Navarre, sang the departure of the pilgrims; they promised, in their verses, the indulgences of the crusade to the warriors that would set out for Syria, advising the dames and demoiselles not to listen to those that should be left in Europe; for, said they, there will remain none but cowards: all the brave are going to seek glory in the battles of the East. Whilst France was repeating the songs of the troubadours, and prayers were offered up to Heaven in the churches for the success of the expeditions, the Crusaders from all the provinces of the kingdom commenced their march, directing their course towards the port of Marseilles, where vessels waited, to transport them into Asia; all were animated by the most ardent zeal for the deliverance of the holy places; but the pope, at whose voice they had taken up arms, no longer applauded their enthusiasm. Gregory, who had made himself a great many formidable enemies in the West, appeared to have forgotten a war he had so warmly promoted, and was entirely engrossed by his own dangers.

Most of the leaders of the crusade were assembled at Lyons to deliberate upon the best means of carrying on their enterprise, when they received a nuncio from the sovereign pontiff, who commanded them to return to their homes. This unexpected order from Gregory IX. gave great offence to the princes and barons, who told the envoy of the court of Rome, that the pope might change his policy, and disapprove of that which he himself had set on foot; but that the defenders of the cross, they who had devoted themselves to the service of Christ, would remain steadfast in their intentions. "We have made," added they, "all our preparations; we have pledged or sold our lands, our houses, and our goods; we have quitted our friends and our families, giving out our departure for Palestine: religion and honour forbid us to retrace our steps." [248]

As the pope's nuncio wished to speak and uphold the authority of the Church, and as he accused the barons of betraying the cause they were going to defend, the Christian warriors could not restrain their indignation; the soldiers and leaders were so exasperated, that they even ill-treated the ambassador of the pontiff; and, but for the intercession and prayers of the prelates and bishops, would have immolated him to their anger.

Scarcely had the Crusaders dismissed the pope's nuncio with contempt, than deputies arrived from the emperor of Germany, equally supplicating them to suspend their march, and wait till he had collected his troops, in order to place himself at their head. The knights and barons, animated by a sincere zeal for the objects of their expedition, could not comprehend the meaning of the delays thus attempted to be thrown in the way of it, and sighed over the blindness of the powers that wished to turn them aside from the road to salvation. The king of Navarre, the dukes of Brittany and Burgundy, with most of the nobles that had taken the cross, persisted in the design of accomplishing their vow, and embarked for Syria at the port of Marseilles.

A new misunderstanding had broken out between the pope and Frederick, who were disputing the sovereignty of Sardinia; all the passions were soon engaged in this quarrel, and armed themselves, by turns, with the vengeance of Heaven and the furies of war. Gregory, after having excommunicated Frederick afresh, was determined to attack his reputation, and degrade him in the opinion of his contemporaries. Monitories and briefs from the pope were read in all the churches of Europe, in which the emperor was represented as an impious man, an accomplice of heretics and Saracens, an oppressor of religion and humanity. Frederick replied to the accusations of the sovereign pontiff by the most violent invectives; he addressed himself to the Romans, to excite them against the Holy See, and called upon all the princes of Europe to defend his cause as their own. [249] "Kings and princes of the earth," said he, "look upon the injury done to us as your own, *bring water to extinguish the fire that has been kindled in our neighbourhood*; a similar danger threatens you." The irritated pope hurled all the thunders of the Church against his adversary; and even went so far as to preach a crusade against the emperor, saying, "There was more merit in combating a prince who was rebellious to the successors of St. Peter, than in delivering Jerusalem." Throughout this scandalous contest, the Church was allowed to possess nothing that was sacred, the authority of princes nothing that was legitimate; on one side, the sovereign pontiff considered all who remained faithful subjects to the emperor as the ministers and accomplices of the demon; on the other, the emperor would not acknowledge the pope as the vicar of Christ. At last, Gregory promised the imperial crown to any

Christian prince who would take up arms against the emperor, and drag him from his throne: Louis IX., more wise than the Church itself, refused the empire which was offered to him for his brother Robert, and employed earnest but vain endeavours to restore peace to Europe, disturbed by the pretensions and menaces of the pope.

They soon came to hostilities; and Frederick, after having gained a great victory over the Milanese, and carried terror amongst all the republics of Lombardy, marched towards Rome at the head of an army. Gregory, who had no troops at all, went through the streets of his capital at the head of a procession; he exhibited to the Romans the relics of the apostles, and, melting into tears, told them he had no means of defending this sacred deposit without their assistance. The nobility and people, touched by the prayers of the pope, swore to die in defence of the Holy See. They set about preparations for war, they fortified the city with the greatest expedition; and when the emperor drew near to the gates, he saw those same Romans, who, a short time before, had embraced his cause against the pope, drawn up in battle-array on the ramparts, determined to die in the cause of the head of the Church. Frederick besieged the city, without being able to get possession of it; in his anger, he accused the Romans of perfidy, and revenged himself by exercising horrible cruelties on his prisoners. The hatred enkindled between the pope and the emperor soon passed into the minds of the people, and the furies of civil war devastated the whole of Italy.

Amidst such general disorder and agitation, the cries and prayers of the Christians of Palestine were scarcely audible. At the expiration of the truce concluded with Frederick, the sultan of Damascus re-entered Jerusalem, and destroyed the tower of David and the weak ramparts erected by the Christians: this conquest, which revived the courage of the Mussulmans, necessarily produced more than proportionate despair among the unfortunate inhabitants of the Holy Land. Instead of receiving within its walls the innumerable armies that fame had announced, Ptolemaïs only had to welcome the arrival of a few unarmed pilgrims, who had nothing to relate but the deplorable quarrels of Christian monarchs and princes. Most of the communications with the East were closed; all the maritime powers of Italy were contending for the empire of the sea; sometimes in league with the sovereign pontiff, sometimes with the emperor. Several of the Crusaders who had sworn to go to Constantinople or Ptolemaïs, took part in the crusade that had been preached against Frederick; others resolved to proceed to Syria by land, and almost all perished in the mountains and deserts of Asia Minor; the French lords and princes, who, in spite of the orders of the pope, set out for Asia from the ports of Provence, were able to bring with them into Palestine but a very small number of warriors.

At the period of the arrival of these Crusaders, the East was not less troubled than the West. Melik-Kamel, the sultan of Cairo, had recently died, and his death became the signal for many sanguinary wars among the princes of his family, who disputed by turns the kingdom of Egypt, and the principalities of Damascus, Aleppo, and Hamah. Amidst these divisions, the emirs and the Mamelukes, whose dangerous support was constantly sought for, were accustomed to dispose of power, and proved themselves more formidable to their sovereigns than to the enemies of Islamism. Supreme authority seemed to be the reward of victory or of skill in treachery; the Mussulman thrones were environed by so many perils, that a sultan of Damascus was seen abandoning his sceptre, and seeking retirement, saying, "a hawk and a hound afforded him more pleasure than empire." The princes, divided among themselves, called for the succour of the Carismians and other barbarous nations, who burnt their cities, pillaged their provinces, completed the destruction of the powers they came to defend, and perfected all the evils that were born of discord.

The Crusaders might have taken advantage of all these troubles, but they never united their forces against the enemy they had sworn to contend with; the kingdom of Jerusalem had no government capable of directing the forces of the crusade; the crowd of pilgrims had no tie, no common point of interest which could hold them together for any length of time under the same standards: scattered troops of soldiers were to be seen, but there was nowhere an army; each of the leaders and princes followed a plan of his own, declared war or proclaimed peace in his own name, and appeared to fight entirely for his own ambition or renown.

The duke of Brittany, followed by his knights, made an incursion into the lands of Damascus, and returned to Ptolemais with a rich booty; the other Crusaders, jealous of the success of this expedition, were desirous of distinguishing themselves by exploits, and formed the project of attacking the city of Gaza. As they marched without order or precaution, they were surprised and cut to pieces by the Saracens. The duke of Burgundy, who was at the head of this expedition, escaped the pursuit of the conquerors almost alone, and came back to Ptolemaïs, to deplore the loss of his knights and barons, who had all met with slavery or death on the field of battle. This reverse, instead of uniting the Christians more closely, only increased their discords; in the impossibility of effecting any triumph for their arms, they treated separately with the infidels, and made peace, as they had made war. The Templars and some leaders of the army agreed for a truce with the sultan of Damascus, and obtained the restitution of the holy places; on their side, the Hospitallers, with the count of Champagne, and the dukes of Burgundy and Brittany, concluded a treaty with the sultan of Egypt, and undertook to defend him against the Saracens who had just given up Jerusalem to the Christians.

After having disturbed Palestine by their disorders, the Crusaders abandoned it to return to Europe, and were replaced at Ptolemaïs by some English, who arrived under Richard of Cornwall, brother to Henry III. Richard, who possessed the tin and lead mines of the county of Cornwall, was one of the richest princes of the West: if old chronicles are to be believed, Gregory had forbidden him to go to the East, hoping that he would consent to remain in Europe, and would impart a portion of his treasures to the Holy See, to procure the indulgences of the crusade. When Richard arrived before Ptolemaïs, he was received by the people and the clergy, who went out to meet him, singing, "Blessed be he who comes in the name of the Lord." This prince was the grandson of Richard Cœur de Lion, [250] whose courage and exploits had rendered him so famous in the East. The name alone of Richard spread terror among the Saracens; the prince of Cornwall equalled his ancestor in bravery; he was full of zeal and ardour, and his army shared his enthusiasm for religion and glory. He prepared to open the campaign, and everything seemed to promise success; but, after a march of some days, and a few advantages obtained over the enemy, finding himself very ill-seconded by the Christians of Palestine, he was obliged to renew the truce made with the sultan of Egypt. As the whole fruit of his expedition, he could only obtain an exchange of prisoners, and permission to pay the honours of sepulture to the Christians killed at the battle of Gaza.

Without having seen either the walls of Jerusalem or the banks of the Jordan, Richard embarked for Italy, where he found the pope still engaged in the war against Frederick. All Europe was in a blaze; a council convoked for the peace of the Church had not been able to assemble; the emperor still besieged the city of Rome, and threatened the head of Christendom. Amidst this general disorder, Gregory died, cursing his implacable adversary, and was succeeded by Celestine IV., who only wore the tiara sixteen days. The war was continued with renewed fury, the Church remained without a head, and Christ without a vicar upon earth; the cardinals wandered about dispersed; Frederick holding several of them in chains. "The court of Rome," says Fleury, "was desolate, and fallen into great contempt." This deplorable anarchy lasted nearly two years; all Christendom was loud in complaints, and demanded of Heaven a pope able to repair the evils of Europe and the Church.

The conclave met at length, but the election of Innocent IV., made amidst trouble and discord, put an end to neither the public scandal nor the furies of the war, which grieved all true Christians. The new pontiff followed the example of Innocent III. and Gregory IX., and soon surpassed all their excesses. Under his pontificate, disorder continued increasing, until it had reached its height. The Christians of Greece and Palestine were quite forgotten. Missionaries in vain perambulated the kingdoms of the West, to exhort the faithful to make peace among themselves, and turn their arms against the Saracens; many of these angels of peace were proscribed by Frederick, who was, at once, at war with the sovereign pontiff, the emperor of the East, and all those who, in taking the cross, had sworn to defend Rome, or to deliver Constantinople or Jerusalem. We will not attempt to describe the violent scenes of which the West, but particularly Italy, was the theatre. Attention becomes fatigued by dwelling long upon the same pictures; the wars and revolutions which lend so much life to history finish by presenting only a wearisome, twice-told tale; and thus, likewise, may the reader perceive that the passions have their uniformity and tempests their monotony.

Each of the preceding crusades had a distinct object, a march which could be easily followed, and was only remarkable for great exploits or great reverses. That which we have just described, which embraces a period of thirty years, is mingled with so many different events, with so many clashing interests, so many passions foreign to the holy wars, that it at first appears to present only a confused picture; and the historian, constantly occupied in relating the revolutions of the East and of the West, may with reason be accused of having, as a European Christian, forgotten Jerusalem and the cause of Christ.

When we have read the twelfth book of this history, we perceive that we are already far from the age that gave birth to the crusades, and witnessed their brilliant progress. When comparing this war with those that preceded it, it is easy to see that it has a different character, not only in the manner in which it was conducted, but in the means employed to inflame the zeal of the Christians, and induce them to take up arms.

When we observe the incredible efforts of the popes to arm the nations of the West, we are at first astonished at the small quantity of success obtained by their exhortations, their menaces, and their prayers. We have but to compare the Council of Clermont, held by Urban, with the Council of the Lateran, presided over by Gregory. In the first, the complaints of Jerusalem excite the tears and sobs of the auditory; in the second, a thousand different objects intrude, to occupy the attention of the fathers of the Church, who express themselves upon the misfortunes of the Holy Land, without emotion and without pain. At the voice of Urban, knights, barons, and ecclesiastics all swore together to go and fight against the infidels; the council became, in a moment, an assembled host of intrepid warriors: it was not so at the

Council of the Lateran, in which no one took the cross, or burst forth into an expression of that high enthusiasm which the pope desired to awaken in all hearts.

We have drawn attention, in the course of our recital, to the circumstance of pilgrims being permitted by the preachers of the holy war to buy off their vow by paying a sum of money; this mode of expiating sins appeared to be a scandalous innovation: and the indulgence of the missionaries of the holy war, who thus released the faithful from the pilgrimage, made them lose a considerable portion of their ascendancy. They were not, as formerly, the messengers of Heaven; the multitude no longer endowed them with the power of working miracles; they were even sometimes obliged to employ the menaces and promises of the Church to draw hearers to their sermons; in short, at length the people ceased to consider them as the interpreters of the gospel, and saw in them only the collectors of the dues of the Holy See. This sale of the privileges of the crusade, purchased at an extravagant price, necessarily checked the effects of all generous passions, and, in the minds of Christians, confounded that which belonged to Heaven with that which belonged to earth.

Preceding ages were unacquainted with any other motive but religion and its promises. [251] The companions of Peter the Hermit and Godfrey, the warriors who followed Louis the Young, Philip Augustus, Richard Cœur de Lion, Boniface, and Baldwin of Flanders, could not have possibly believed that gold could be made a substitute for the merit and glory of the holy war.

We find another remarkable difference in the preaching of this crusade,—the refusal to admit great criminals under the banners of the cross. The astonishment which the enrolment of a crowd of obscure persons in the holy militia caused among the Christian knights, suffices to denote a great change in the manners and opinions of the Crusaders. The sentiment of honour, which is allied with a love of glory, and has a tendency to establish distinctions among men, appears to have prevailed over the purely religious feeling which inspires humility, acknowledges the equal rights of all Christians, and confounds repentance with virtue. The crusade, into which none were admitted but men of acknowledged bravery and good conduct, ceased, in some sort, to be a simply religious war, and began to resemble other wars, in which leaders have the power of selecting the soldiers they have to command.

The enthusiasm for the holy wars only revived at intervals, like a fire upon the point of going out of itself; the people required some great event, some extraordinary circumstance, some striking example of princes or warriors, to induce them to take arms against the infidels; the subtleties of theologians, who insisted upon everything being subservient to their discussions, contributed to cool the remains of that pious and warlike ardour, which, till that time, it had been found necessary to moderate and restrain within just limits. Disputes were started in the schools upon such questions as these: In what case was a Christian exempt from the accomplishment of his vow? What sum was sufficient to redeem a promise made to Christ? If certain pious exercises could be substituted for pilgrimage? If an heir was bound to fulfil the oath of a testator? Whether the pilgrim who died on his way to the Holy Land, had more merit in the eyes of God than one who died on his return? [252] Whether a wife could take the cross without the consent of her husband, or the husband without the consent of the wife? &c. From the moment in which all these questions were solemnly discussed, and, upon several points, the opinions of theologians differed, enthusiasm, which never reasons, was rendered languid by the cold arguments of the doctors; and pilgrims appeared to yield less to the transports of a generous feeling, than to the necessity of performing a duty or of following an established rule.

This sixth crusade was more abundant in intrigues and scandalous quarrels than in military exploits; the Christians never united all their efforts against the infidels; no spirit of order presided over their enterprises; the Crusaders, who only held their mission of their zeal, set out at the time their will or their fancy selected; some returned to Europe without having faced a Saracen in fight; others abandoned the colours of the cross, after a victory or a defeat; and fresh Crusaders were constantly summoned to defend the conquests or repair the faults of those that had preceded them. Although the West had counted in this crusade more than five hundred thousand of her warriors departing for Palestine or Egypt, great armies were rarely assembled on the banks of the Nile or the Jordan. As the Crusaders were never gathered together in great bodies, they were not subjected to famine, or the other scourges that had so fearfully thinned the ranks of the early defenders of the cross; but if they experienced fewer reverses, if they were better disciplined, we may say that they showed none of that ardour, or of those lively passions which men communicate to each other, and which acquire a new degree of force and activity amidst a multitude assembled for the same cause and under the same banners.

By transferring the theatre of the war to Egypt, the Christians no longer had before their eyes, as in Palestine, the revered places and monuments, which could recall to them the religion and the God they were about to fight for; they had no longer before them and around them the river Jordan, Libanus, Thabor, or Mount Sion, the aspect of which had so vividly affected the imagination of the first Crusaders.

When the people of Europe heard the head of the Church exhort the faithful to the conquest of Jerusalem, and at the same time curse Frederick, the liberator of the holy city, the object of the crusade lost its sacred character in the eyes of Christians. The emperor of Germany, after his return from his expedition, sometimes said, "If God had been acquainted with the kingdom of Naples, he never could have preferred the barren rocks of Jerusalem to it." These sacrilegious words of Frederick must have been a great subject of offence to pilgrims; but, indeed, this prince only sent to the Holy Land such of his subjects as he was dissatisfied with, or wished to punish. The popes also condemned to pilgrimage the great criminals whom society rejected from its bosom, which was very repugnant to the manners and opinions of the nobles and knights of Europe. As a crowning misfortune, the reverses or exploits of the Crusaders beyond the seas frequently created divisions among the princes of the West. From that time, Palestine was no longer, in the eyes of the faithful, a land of blessedness, flowing with milk and honey, but a place of exile. From that time Jerusalem was less considered the city of God and the heritage of Christ, than a subject of discord, or the place in which were born all the storms that disturbed Christendom.

In the other crusades, the popes had been satisfied with awakening the enthusiasm of pilgrims, and addressing prayers to Heaven for the success of the Crusaders; but in this war, the heads of the Church insisted upon directing all the expeditions, and commanding, by their legates, the operations of the Christian armies. The invasion of Egypt was decided upon in the Council of the Lateran, without a thought of asking the advice or opinions of any of the skilful captains of the age. When hostilities began, the envoys of the pope presided over all the events of the war; weakening the ardour of the soldiers of the cross, by their ambitious pretensions, as well as by their ignorance. They let all the fruits of victory slip through their hands, and gave birth to an injurious rivalry between the spiritual and the temporal powers. This rivalry, this reciprocal mistrust, were carried so far, that the sovereign pontiff and the emperor of Germany, by turns, arrested the march of the pilgrims; the first fearing that the Crusaders, on embarking for Palestine, would become the soldiers of Frederick; the second, that these same soldiers might become the defenders of the temporal power of the popes.

At the period of which we have just retraced the history, so many crusades were preached at once, that the eyes of the faithful were necessarily diverted from the first object of these holy expeditions. Called upon to defend so many causes, no one could distinguish which was the cause of God and Jesus Christ; so many interests presented themselves at the same time to the attention of Christians, and were recommended to the bravery of warriors, that they gave birth to hesitation and reflection; and these produced indifference. Europe, for a length of time in a state of fermentation, was undergoing the vague uncertainty of a change; states began to think more of their independence, people of their liberty. The passions which politics bring forth, took the place of passions of which religion is the motive.

The sanguinary quarrels of the emperor and the popes contributed greatly to the revolution which was brought about in men's minds: the motive which animated the heads of the Church was not always a religious one; the emperor of Germany and the pontiffs of Rome had pretensions to the domination of Italy, and had been, for a long time, engaged in a rivalry of ambition. Gregory could not see Frederick master of the kingdom of Naples without great pain; and when he pressed him to go into Asia, to make war upon the Saracens, he might have been compared to that personage of ancient fable, who, in order to get rid of his rival, sent him to combat the Chimera.

Four popes, although of a different character, finding themselves in the same circumstances, pursued the same policy. Frederick, by his cruelties, injustice, and extravagant ambition, often justified the violences of the Holy See, of which he was, by turns, the ward, the protector, and the enemy; like his predecessors, he made no secret of his project of restoring the empire of the Cæsars; and, had it not been for the popes, it is not improbable that Europe would have been brought under the yoke of the emperors of Germany.

The policy of the sovereign pontiffs, whilst weakening the imperial power, favoured, in Germany, the liberty of cities, and the growth and duration of small states; we do not hesitate to add, that the thunders of the Church preserved the independence of Italy, and perhaps that of France, which was less ill treated by the court of Rome than neighbouring nations. The French monarchy took advantage of the troubles that existed on the other side of the Rhine, and of the interdict set upon England, to repel the invasions of the English and Germans; and, at the same time, availed itself of the absence of the king of Navarre, the dukes of Brittany and Burgundy, with several other great vassals, whom the crusade attracted beyond the seas, to increase the prerogatives of the royal authority, and extend the limits of the kingdom.

England herself owes something to the authority of the popes, who, by overwhelming John Lackland with excommunications, rendered him powerless in his attempts to enslave the English people, or to resist the demands of the barons and the commons. This is a truth which impartial history cannot deny or doubt, and which disposes us not to approve, but to blame with less bitterness, excesses and abuses of power of which all the effects have not been deplorable. [253] The populace of London, who burn every year the effigy of the pope, would be much astonished if, amidst a fanatical delirium, they were told that the army which once fought for the independence of Great Britain was called *the army of God and of the Holy Church*; if they were reminded that the great charter of the Forest, the first monument of British liberty, was the fortunate fruit of the menaces and thunders of the Church of Rome, and that this charter would never have been granted by John, without the redoubtable influence and the imperious counsels of the sovereign pontiff. [254]

Without wishing to justify the domination of the popes, we may say that they were led to grasp at supreme power by the circumstances in which Europe was placed in the eleventh and twelfth centuries. European society, without experience or laws, and plunged in ignorance and anarchy, cast itself into the arms of the popes, and believed that it placed itself under the protection of Heaven.

As nations had no other ideas of civilization than such as they received from the Christian religion, the sovereign pontiffs naturally became the supreme arbiters between rival or neighbouring countries; amidst the darkness which the light of the Gospel had a continued and never-ending tendency to diminish, their authority must naturally have been the first established and the first recognised; temporal power stood in need of their sanction; people and kings implored their support and consulted their wisdom: they believed themselves authorized to exercise a sovereign dictatorship.

This dictatorship was often exercised to the advantage of public morality and social order; it often protected the weak against the strong; it arrested the execution of criminal plots; it re-established peace between states; and it preserved a young society from the excesses of ambition, licentiousness, and barbarism. When we cast our eyes over the annals of the middle ages, we cannot help being struck by one of the most beautiful spectacles that human society has ever presented,—it is that of Christian Europe recognising but one religion, having but one law, forming as it were but one empire, governed by a single head, who spoke in the name of God, and whose mission was to make the Gospel reign upon earth.

In the general reflections by which we shall terminate this work, we will enter into much greater developments upon this head; we will compare modern Europe with the Europe of the middle ages, and we will make it clear that, if we have acquired some wisdom in the art of civilization, we are still far from having turned it to the advantage of public liberty: nations are at the present day led away by the spirit of the French revolution, as they were in the middle ages by the spirit of the court of Rome and enthusiasm for the crusades. The French revolution began by liberal ideas, it was continued by victories. The military spirit allied itself with the fanaticism of new ideas, as it formerly allied itself with religious enthusiasm. On casting a glance over our Europe, we are astonished at seeing two contradictory things, which should naturally exclude each other; we see almost everywhere a tendency to favour the propagation of liberal ideas, and at the same time an inclination to increase the mass of armies; it is difficult to explain a policy which tends, on the one side, to multiply the apostles of liberty, on the other to multiply soldiers; which, by turns, proclaims a principle, and raises a regiment; which speaks, at the same time, of recruiting, and of a constitution; which appears never to have laws enough, and yet is insatiable of cannons and bayonets. It is easy to foresee the near and distant results of such a monstrous amalgamation. [255] Everything leads us to believe that these results, like those of the crusades and the influence of the pope in the middle ages, will not turn out *entirely* for the advantage of civilization.

But without dwelling longer on these distressing reflections, we will return to our subject, from which, perhaps, we have strayed too long. In the eleventh and twelfth centuries, the nations of Europe, subject to the authority of St. Peter, were united together by a tie more strong than that of liberty. This motive, this tie, which was that of the universal Church, for a length of time kept up and favoured the enthusiasm for and the progress of holy wars. Whatever may have been the origin of the crusades, it is certain they never would have been undertaken without that unity of religious feelings which doubled the strength of the Christian republic. The Christian nations, by the agreement of their sentiments and their passions, showed the world all that can be done by enthusiasm, which increases by communication, and that lively faith, which, spread among men, is a miraculous power, since the Gospel accords it the faculty of *moving mountains*. In proportion as people, united by one same spirit, separated, and ceased to make one common cause, it became more difficult to collect together the forces of the West, and pursue those gigantic enterprises of which our age can scarcely perceive the possibility.

It may have been observed, that the pontifical authority and the enthusiasm for the crusades experienced the same vicissitudes; the opinions and the exaltation of the religious spirit which caused men to take up arms, necessarily, at the same time, increased the influence of the sovereign pontiffs. But springs so active and so powerful could not possibly last long; they broke by the violence with which they were employed.

The popes, invested with authority without limit, exercised that authority without moderation; and as the abuse of power brings on, sooner or later, its own ruin, the empire of the sovereign pontiffs finished by declining as other empires have done. Their fall commenced with their long contests with Frederick; all Europe was called upon to judge their cause; their power, founded upon opinion, the origin of which was entirely religious, lost much of its prestige by being given over to the discussions of men of the world.

At the same time that the sovereign pontiffs abused their power, the spirit and enthusiasm that had produced the holy wars were likewise abused. Many Christian princes took the cross, sometimes to obtain the protection of the popes; sometimes as a pretext for assembling armies, and enjoying the temporal advantages accorded to the soldiers of Christ. The leaders of Christendom, without having originated the wars of the East, were eager to profit by them; in the first place, to extend their dominions, and in the next to gratify violent passions. From that moment society sought other supports than that of the Holy See, and warriors another glory than that of the crusades.

Thibault, king of Navarre, who, in his verses, had preached the war beyond the seas, was disgusted at the troubles excited in Europe by the heads of the Church, and deplored with bitterness *a time full of felony, envy, and treachery*. He accused the princes and barons of being without *courtoisie*, and reproached the popes with excommunicating those who were most in the right (*ceux qui avaient le plus raison*). If a few troubadours still raised their voices to exhort Christians to take up the cross and arms, the greater part did not partake of their enthusiasm for the holy wars; and beheld nothing in these pilgrimages beyond the seas, but the griefs of a long absence, and the rigours of a pious exile.

In a Tenson [256] which has come down to us, Folquet de Romans asks Blaccas, the model of troubadours and of knights, whether he will go to the Holy Land? After having answered that he loves and is beloved, and that he will remain at home with his ladye-love, (she was countess of Provence), Blaccas thus ends his simple song:—

> "Je ferai ma pénitence,
> Entre mer et Durance,
> Auprès de son manoir." [257]

> "I will perform my penitence
> Between the sea and swift Durance,
> Near to my lady's bower."

These sentiments belonged to the manners of troubadours and knights; but at the time of the first crusades, religious ideas were much more mixed up with ideas of gallantry; a poet, invited to take the cross, would not have dared to speak of his ladye-love, [258] without likewise speaking of the mercy of God and the captivity of Jerusalem.

During the other crusades, the religion and morality of the Gospel resumed their empire, and spread their benefits everywhere; at the voice of the holy orators, Christians became penitent and reformed their morals; all political tempests were laid by the simple name of Jerusalem, and the West remained in profound peace. [259] It was not so at the period we have just described; Europe was perhaps never more agitated, or, perhaps, more corrupted than during the thirty years which this crusade lasted.

In the relations between the Christians and Mussulmans, little respect had, to this time, certainly, been paid to treaties; but in this crusade, contempt for sworn faith and forgetfulness for the laws of nations were carried to an extreme: signing a truce was a preparation for war;—the Christian armies owed their safety to a treaty of peace; and the sovereign pontiff, far from respecting the conditions of it, preached a new crusade against the infidels. It must be allowed, also, that the most solemn treaties were often violated by the Mussulmans. The duration of peace depended solely upon the want of power in both parties to resume hostilities with advantage. The least hope of success was sufficient to induce them to fly to arms, the slightest circumstance was an excuse for rekindling all the flames of war. The continuator of William of Tyre says, with great ingenuousness, when speaking of the death of a sultan of Damascus: "When the sultan died, all the truces died with him." These words alone are sufficient to give an idea of the state of the East during the sixth crusade, and of the small degree of respect then entertained for the laws of peace and war.

If, in the preceding crusade, the expedition of the soldiers of the cross against Greece did not produce great advantages to the West, it at least illustrated the arms of the Venetians and the French. In the war we have just described, the knights and barons who took the cross, added nothing to their glory or their renown. The Crusaders who were fortunate enough to revisit their homes, brought back with them nothing but the remembrance of most shameful disorders. A great number of them had nothing to show their compatriots but the chains of their captivity; nothing to communicate but the contagious disorders of the East.

The historians we have followed are silent as to the ravages of the leprosy among the nations of the West; but the testament of Louis VIII., an historical monument of that period, attests the existence of two thousand *léproseries* (hospitals for lepers) in the kingdom of France alone. This horrible sight must have been a subject of terror to the most fervent Christians; and was sufficient to disenchant, in their eyes, those regions of the East, where, till that time, their imaginations had seen nothing but prodigies and marvels.

Among the abuses then made of the spirit of the crusades, and the misfortunes they brought in their train, we must not forget the civil and religious wars of which France and several other countries of Europe were the theatre. In their expeditions into the East, Christians had become familiarized with the idea of employing force and violence to change men's hearts and opinions. As they had long made war against infidels, they were willing to make it, in the same manner, against heretics; they first took up arms against the Albigeois, then against the pagans of Prussia; for the same reason, and in the same manner, that they had armed themselves against the Mussulmans.

Modern writers have declaimed with great vehemence and eloquence against these disastrous wars; but long before the age in which we live, the Church had condemned the excesses of blind fanaticism. [260] Saint Augustine, St. Ambrose, the fathers of councils, had long taught the Christian world that error is not destroyed by the sword, and that the truths of the Gospel ought not to be preached to mankind amidst threats and violences.

The crusade against the Prussians shows us all that ambition, avarice, and tyranny can exhibit that is most cruel and barbarous; the tribunal of history cannot judge with too much severity the leaders of this war, the ravages and furies of which were prolonged during more than a century; but, whilst condemning the excesses of the conquerors of Prussia, we must admit the advantages Europe gained by their victories and exploits. A nation that had been separated from all other nations by its manners and customs, ceased to be a foreigner in the Christian republic. Industry, laws, religion, which marched in the train of the conquerors, to moderate and remove the evils of war, spread their blessings among hordes of savages. Many flourishing cities arose from amidst the ashes of forests, and the oak of Remove, [261] beneath the shade of which human victims had been immolated, was replaced by churches, in which the virtues and charity of the Gospel were inculcated. The conquests of the Romans were sometimes more unjust, then wars more barbarous; they procured less advantages to the civilized world, and yet they have never ceased to be objects of the admiration and eulogy of posterity.

The war against the Albigeois was more cruel and more unfortunate than the crusade directed against the nations of Prussia. Missionaries and warriors outraged, by their conduct, all the laws of justice and of the religion whose triumph they pretended to aim at. The heretics, naturally, sometimes employed reprisals against their enemies; both sides armed with the steel and axe of murderers and executioners, humanity had to deplore the most guilty excesses.

When casting a retrospective glance over the annals of the middle ages, we are particularly grieved to see sanguinary wars undertaken and carried on in the name of a religion of peace, whilst we can scarcely find an example of a religious war among the ancients and under the laws of paganism. [262] We must believe that modern nations and those of antiquity have, and had the same passions; but, amongst the ancients, religion entered less deeply into the heart of man or into the spirit of social institutions. The worship of false gods had no positive dogma; it added nothing to morality; it prescribed no duties to the citizen; it was not bound up with the maxims of legislation, and existed, in some sort, only upon the surface of society. When paganism was attacked, or when a change was effected in the worship of false gods, the affections, morals, and interests of pagan society were not deeply wounded. It was not thus with Christianity, which, particularly in the middle ages, mixed itself up with all civil laws, recalled man to all the duties due to his country, and united itself with all the principles of social order. Amidst the growing civilization of Europe, the Christian religion was blended with all the interests of nations; it was, in a manner, the foundation of all society; it was society itself: we cannot wonder, then, that men were passionate in its defence. Then all who separated themselves from the Christian religion, separated themselves from society; and all who rejected the laws of the Church, ceased to acknowledge the laws of their country. We must consider the wars against the Albigeois and the Prussians in this light; they were rather social wars than religious wars.

BOOK XIII
A.D. 1242-1245

SEVENTH CRUSADE

When I began this work, I was far from being aware of the task I was imposing upon myself; animated by the interest of my subject, full of a too great confidence in my own powers, like those villagers who, when they set out for the first crusade, fancied every city they saw to be Jerusalem, I constantly believed I was approaching the end of my labours. As I advanced in my career, the horizon expanded before me, difficulties multiplied at every step, so that to sustain my courage, I have often been obliged to recall to my mind the kindness with which the early volumes of this history have been received by the public.

The difficulty did not consist in placing a narrative of the holy wars before our readers; it became necessary to present exact ideas of the manners and characters of the nations which, in any way, took part in them. We have endeavoured to make all the peoples known who have in turn passed across the scene: the Franks, with their soldier-like roughness, their love of glory, and their generous passions; the Turks and Saracens, with their military religion and their barbarous valour; the Greeks, with their corrupted manners, their character at once superstitious and frivolous, and their vanity, which with them supplied the place of patriotism: a new nation is now about to offer itself to the pencil of history, and mingle with the events of which we are attempting to give the picture. We are about to say a few words upon the manners and conquests of the Tartars in the middle ages.

The hordes of this nation, at the period of the sixth crusade, had invaded several countries of Asia, and the progress of their arms had a great influence over the policy of the Mussulman powers of Syria and Egypt, which were then at war with the Christians. At the time of which we are speaking, the fame of their victories filled the East, and spread terror even to the most remote countries of Europe.

The Tartars inhabited the vast regions which lie between ancient Emaüs, Siberia, China, and the Sea of Kamschatka; they were divided into several nations, which all boasted of having the same origin; each of these nations, governed by a khan, or supreme leader, was composed of a great number of tribes, each tribe commanded by a particular chief, called Myrza. The produce of the chase, the milk of their mares, and the flesh of their flocks, satisfied the simple wants of the Tartars; they lived under tents with their families; and moveable dwellings, drawn by oxen, transported from one place to another their wives, their children, and all they possessed. In summer, the whole tribe drew towards the northern countries, and encamped upon the banks of a river or a lake; in winter, they directed their course southward, and sought the shelter of mountains that could protect them from the icy winds of the north.

The Tartar hordes assembled every year, in either autumn or spring. In these assemblies, which they called *Couraltaï,* they deliberated on horseback, upon the march of the tribes, the distribution of the pasturages, and peace and war. It was from the bosom of this tumultuous assembly that issued the legislation of the people of Tartary; a simple and laconic legislation, like those of all barbarous nations, whose only objects are to maintain the power of the leaders, and keep up discipline and emulation among the warriors.

The nations of Tartary acknowledged one God, the sovereign of heaven, to whom they offered up neither incense nor prayers. Their worship was reserved for a crowd of genii, whom they believed to be spread through the air, upon the earth, and amidst the waters; a great number of idols, the rough work of their own hands, filled their dwellings, followed them in their courses, and watched over their flocks, their slaves, and their families. Their priests, brought up in the practices of magic, studied the course of the stars, predicted future events, and employed themselves in abusing the minds of the people by sorcery. Their religious worship, which inculcated no morality, had neither softened their rude manners nor ameliorated their character, which was as boisterous and unkindly as their climate. No monument raised under the auspices of religion, no book inspired by it, reminded them of deeds of glory, or laid before them precepts and examples of virtue. In the course of their wandering life, the dead, whom they sometimes dragged with them in their waggons, appeared to them an annoying burden, and they buried them in haste in retired places; where, covering them with the sands of the desert, they were satisfied with concealing them from the eyes or the outrages of the living.

Everything that might fix them to one spot rather than another, or lead them to change their manner of living, excited the animadversion and disdain of these races. Of all the tribes that inhabited Mogul Tartary, one alone was acquainted with writing, and cultivated letters; all the rest despised commerce, arts, and learning; which constitute the true splendour of polished societies. The Tartars disdained the idea of building; in the twelfth century their vast country contained but one city, [263] the extent of which, according to the monk Rubruquis, did not equal that of the little town of Saint Denis. Confining themselves to the care of their flocks, they regarded agriculture as a degrading occupation, only fit to employ the industry of slaves or conquered people. Their immense plains had never become yellow with harvests sown by the hand of man; no fruit had there ripened which he had planted. The spectacle most agreeable to a Tartar was the desert, upon which grass grew without cultivation or the field of battle covered with ruin and carnage.

As the limits of their pastures were under no regulation, frequent quarrels necessarily arose among the Tartars; the spirit of jealousy constantly agitated the wandering hordes; the ambitious leaders could endure neither neighbours nor rivals. Thence civil wars; and from the bosom of civil wars issued a fully-armed despotism, to support which the people flocked with cheerfulness, because it promised them conquests. The entire population was military, to whom fighting appeared to be the only true glory, and the most noble occupation of man. The encampments of the Tartars, their marches, their hunting-parties, resembled military exhibitions. Habit imparted so much ease and firmness to their seat on horseback, that they took their food, and even indulged in sleep, without dismounting. Their bow, of an enormous size, announced their strength and skill; their sharp steel-headed arrows flew to an immense distance, and struck down the bird amidst its rapid career, or pierced through and through the bear or tiger of the desert; they surpassed their enemies in the rapidity of their evolutions; they excelled them in the perfidious art of fighting whilst flying; and retreat was often, for them, the signal of victory. All the stratagems of war appeared familiar to them; and as if a fatal instinct had taught them all that could assist in the destruction of the human race, the Tartars, who built no cities, knew how to construct the most formidable machines of war, and were not unacquainted with any means that could spread terror and desolation among their enemies. In their expeditions, their march was never impeded by the inclemency of seasons, the depth of rivers, the steepness of precipices, or the height of mountains. A little hardened milk, diluted with water, sufficed for the food of a horseman during several days; the skin of a sheep or a bear, a few strips of coarse felt, formed his garments. The warriors showed the most blind obedience to their leaders, and, at the least signal, were ready to encounter death in any shape. They were divided into tens, hundreds, thousands, and tens of thousands; their armies were composed of all that could handle the bow or lance; and what must have caused their enemies as much surprise as terror, was the order and discipline that prevailed in a multitude that chance seemed to have gathered together. According to their military legislation, the Tartars were never allowed to make peace but with a conquered enemy; he who fled from battle, or abandoned his companions in danger, was punished with death; they shed the blood of men with the same indifference as that of wild animals, and their ferocity added greatly to the terror which they inspired in their enterprises.

The Tartars, in their pride, despised all other nations, and believed that the whole world ought to be subject to them. According to certain opinions, transmitted from age to age, the Mogul hordes abandoned the north to the dead they left behind them in the deserts, and kept their faces constantly directed towards the south, which was promised to their valour. The territories and the riches of other nations excited their ambition; and, possessing neither territories nor riches themselves, they had almost nothing to fear from conquerors. Not only their warlike education, but their prejudices, their customs, the inconstancy of their character, everything with them seemed to favour distant expeditions and warlike invasions. They carried with them neither regrets nor endearing remembrances from the countries they abandoned; and if it be true, when we say that country is not within the walls of a city, or the limits of a province, but in the affections and ties of family, in the laws, manners, and customs of a nation, the Tartars, when changing their climate, had always their country with them. The presence of their wives, of their children; the sight of their flocks and their idols, everywhere inflamed their patriotism, or love of their nation, and sustained their courage. Accustomed to consult their own inclinations, and take them for their sole rule of conduct, they were never restrained by the laws of morality or by feelings of humanity; as they had a profound indifference for all the religions of the earth, this indifference even, which aroused no hatred in other nations, facilitated their conquests, by leaving them the liberty of readily receiving or embracing the opinions and creeds of the people they conquered, and whom they thus completely subjected to their laws.

In very remote antiquity, the hordes of Tartary had several times invaded the vast regions of India, China, and Persia, and had extended their ravages even into the West: the ambition or the caprice of a skilful leader, excess of population, want of pasturage, the predictions of a wizard, were quite sufficient to inflame this tumultuous race, and precipitate them in a mass upon distant regions. Woe to the people whom the Tartars encountered in their passage! At their approach, empires fell with a horrible crash; nations were driven back upon one another, like the waves of the sea; the world was shaken and covered with ruins. History has preserved the remembrance of several of their invasions; the most remote posterity will never pronounce without a species of terror the names of the Avari, the Huns, the Heruli, of all those wandering nations who, some flowing from the depths of Tartary, and others dragged in the wake of the conquerors or driven before them, poured down upon the tottering empire of the Romans, and divided the spoils of the civilized world amongst them: in the middle ages, the wars of the Tartars were compared to tempests, inundations, or the bursting forth of volcanoes; and the resigned nations believed that the justice of God held these innumerable swarms of barbarians in reserve in the north, to pour out his anger upon the rest of the earth, and chastise corrupted nations by their hands.

The Tartars never proved themselves more redoubtable than under the reign of Gengiskhan. Temugin, which was the first name of the heroic barbarian, was born of a prince who reigned over some hordes of ancient Mogulistan. [264] Traditions relate that the seventh of his ancestors was engendered in the womb of his mother by the miraculous influence of the rays of the sun. At the birth of Temugin, his family remarked with joy some coagulated blood in the hands of the infant, a sinister presage for the human race, in which flattery or superstition saw the future glory of a conqueror. Some historians inform us that nothing was neglected in the education of Temugin; others, more worthy of faith, affirm that he could not read; but all agree in saying that he was born for war, and to command a warlike people. Endowed with great penetration of mind, and with a sort of eloquence, knowing how to dissemble in season, skilful in working upon the passions, uniting bravery to a boundless ambition, that was never checked by any scruple, he had all the qualities and all the vices which lead to empire among barbarians, and sometimes even among polished nations. His natural propensities developed themselves in adversity, which hardened his character, and taught him to brave everything in order to carry out his designs. From the age of fourteen, despoiled of his paternal heritage, and a fugitive with the khan of the Karaïtes, he sacrificed without pain the most holy duties of hospitality to his future grandeur. The khan of the Karaïtes was known by the name of Prester John among the Christians of the middle ages, [265] who celebrated his conversion to Christianity, and considered him as one of the most fervent apostles of the Gospel, which, doubtless, he never had known. He confided the care of his states to young Temugin, who insinuated himself into the favour of the army, and dethroned his benefactor. As he had outraged all the laws of morality to usurp empire, he violated all the laws of humanity to maintain himself in it. Seventy of his enemies plunged into seventy caldrons of boiling water, and the skull of the chief of the Karaïtes enchased in a golden box, announced very plainly what the master was whom fortune was about to place over the nations of Asia.

Victory was to achieve what treachery, violence, and ingratitude had begun; the arms of Temugin and his lieutenants subdued successively all the hordes whose camps arose between the wall of China and the Volga. Temugin was the all-powerful leader of many millions of shepherds and warriors, impatient to quit their own climate and invade the regions of the south. In order to attach the companions of his victories to his fortunes, he was desirous of reigning by their suffrages, and called together a couraltaï or general diet, in which he was proclaimed sovereign of the Moguls. The ambition of Temugin did not neglect the influence of superstition; he took the title of Gengis, *king of kings*, or *master of the world*, and fame gave out that he had received this pompous title from a prophet who descended from heaven upon a white horse.

Eastern historians have praised Gengiskhan for having given laws to nations he had conquered. These laws, the aim of which was to maintain the peace of families, and to direct the minds of the people towards war, for a length of time retained the obedience and the respect of the Moguls. As Gengiskhan, in his legislation, acknowledged one God, the sovereign of the earth and heaven, and, at the same time, permitted all kinds of creeds, some modern writers have taken occasion to boast of his religious tolerance. But what could be the tolerance of a savage conqueror, who caused himself to be styled the son of the sun, the son of God; who himself followed no worship, and to whom all religions were equally indifferent, provided they crossed neither his ambition nor his pride?

The lieutenants and warriors of Gengiskhan had recognised him with the greater joy, as universal conqueror and master of the earth, from the hopes they entertained of enriching themselves with the spoils of all the nations subdued by his arms. His first enterprises were directed against China, of which empire he had been the vassal. Neither the barrier of the great wall, nor the ascendancy of knowledge and arts, nor the use of gunpowder, said to be then known among the Chinese, was able to defend a flourishing empire against the attacks of a multitude, whom the thirst for booty and a warlike instinct, urged forward to face perils, and rendered invincible.

The wars we have seen in our days, and of which we deplore the calamities, give nothing but a feeble idea of these gigantic invasions, in which many millions of men perished by sword and famine. China experienced twice all the evils inseparable from a war which appeared to be directed by the genius of destruction; and, in the space of a few years, the most ancient and the most powerful kingdom of Asia, covered with blood and ruins, and deprived of half its population, became one of the provinces of the new empire founded by the shepherds of Mogulistan.

The conquest of Carismia soon followed that of China; Carismia was close to the frontiers of the Mogul empire, and, on one side extended to the Gulf of Persia, and on the other, to the limits of India and Turkistan. Gengis learnt that a Tartar caravan and three of his ambassadors had been massacred in one of the cities of the Carismians. It is easy to imagine the effect that this news would produce upon the emperor of the Moguls, who himself compared the anger of kings to the fire of conflagrations, which the lightest wind may light up. [266] After having fasted and prayed, during three days and three nights, upon a mountain, where a hermit announced to him, the second time, the conquest of the whole world, the terrible Gengiskhan commenced his march, at the head of seven hundred thousand Tartars. This army met that of the Carismians on the banks of the Jaxartes; Mahomet, sultan of Carismia, who had several times carried his victorious arms into Turkistan and Persia, commanded the host of the Carismians. The plain in which this battle was fought was covered by twelve hundred thousand combatants; the shock was terrific, the carnage horrible; victory was adverse to Mahomet, who, from that day, together with his family and the whole of his nation, sunk into the lowest abyss of misfortune.

The cities of Otrar, Bochara, Samarcand, Candahar, and Carismia, besieged by an innumerable multitude, fell in turn into the power of the conqueror, and witnessed the extirpation of their garrisons and inhabitants. We cannot suppress a feeling of pity when history presents to us, on one side, an entire population flying from their devastated homes, to seek an asylum in deserts and mountains; and on the other, the family of a powerful monarch dragged into slavery or groaning in exile; and this monarch himself, whose prosperity all Asia had boasted or envied, abandoned by his subjects, and dying with misery and despair in an island of the Caspian Sea.

The army of Gengiskhan returned to Tartary, loaded with the spoils of Carismia: the sovereign of the Moguls [267] appeared to form the desire of governing his conquests in peace; but the world, agitated by his victories, and always eager to throw off his yoke, together with the warlike spirit of his nation, to whom he had afforded a glimpse of the riches of other people, would not permit him again to enjoy repose; he was on the point of undertaking a third expedition against China, which seemed disposed to rebel, when death put an end to his career. Some historians assert that he was struck dead by thunder, as if Heaven had determined itself to crush the instrument of its wrath; [268] others, much more worthy of belief, inform us that the Tartar hero died in his bed, surrounded by his children, to whom he recommended to preserve union among themselves, that they might achieve the conquest of the world. Octaï, the eldest of his sons, succeeded him in the empire, and, according to the custom of the Moguls, the great men assembled and said to him, "We wish, we pray, we command you to accept of entire power over us." The new emperor answered by this formula, which contains the whole spirit of the despotic governments of the East: "If you desire that I should be your khan, are you resolved to obey me in everything; to come when I shall call you, to go where I shall send you, and to put to death all those I shall command you to kill?" After they had answered "Yes," he said to them, "Henceforth my simple word shall serve me as a sword." Such was the government of the Tartars. Octaï was about to reign over an empire composed of several great empires; his brothers and nephews commanded the innumerable armies that had conquered China and Carismia; they governed in his name in the north, in the south, and the east, kingdoms of which the extent was scarcely known; each of his lieutenants was more powerful than the greatest kings of the earth, and all obeyed him as his slaves. For the first time, perhaps, concord was preserved among conquerors; and this monstrous union effected the ruin of all the nations of Asia: Turkistan, Persia, India, the southern provinces of China, which had escaped the ravages of the first invasion, all that remained of the empire of the Abassides and of that of the Seljoucides—all fell before the arms of the redoubtable posterity of Gengiskhan. Many of the sovereigns whom, in these days of disorder and calamity the chance of war hurled from their thrones, had invoked the succour of the Moguls, and favoured the enterprises of that warlike people against neighbouring or rival powers. Fortune enveloped them all in the same ruin, and oriental history compares them to the three dervises whose indiscreet wishes and prayers reanimated, in the desert, the bones of a lion, who sprang up from the bosom of the sand and devoured them.

The conquest of the richest countries of Asia had inflamed the enthusiasm of the Tartars to such a degree, that it would have been impossible for their leaders to confine them within the limits of their own territories, or bring them back to the peaceful labours of pastoral life. Octaï, whether desirous of obeying the paternal instructions, or whether he felt the necessity of employing the restless and turbulent activity of the Moguls, resolved to turn his arms towards the West. Fifteen hundred thousand shepherds or warriors inscribed their names upon the military register; five hundred thousand of the most robust were selected for the great expedition; the others were to remain in Asia, to maintain the submission of the vanquished nations, and complete the conquests commenced by Gengiskhan. Rejoicings, which lasted forty days, preceded the departure of the Mogul army, and were as a signal of the desolation they were about to spread among the countries of Europe.

In their rapid course, the Tartars crossed the Volga, and penetrated, almost without obstacle, into Muscovy, then a prey to the fury of civil war. The devastation of their country, the conflagrations of Kiow and Moscow, and the disgraceful yoke that so long oppressed these northern regions, were the punishments due to the feeble resistance of the Muscovites. After the conquest of Russia, the multitude of Moguls, led by Batou, son of Tuli, directed their victorious course towards Poland and the frontiers of Germany, and repeated, wherever they went, the horrors of Attila and his Huns. The cities of Lublin and Warsaw disappeared on their passage, and they laid waste both shores of the Baltic. In vain the duke of Silesia, the Polish palatines, and the grand master of the Teutonic order, united their forces to arrest the progress of this new scourge of God; [269] the generous defenders of Europe succumbed upon the plains of Lignitz, and nine sacks, filled with human ears, were the trophy of the victory of the barbarians. The Carpathian mountains presented but a feeble barrier to these invincible hordes; and the Tartars soon burst like a fearful tempest over the territories of those Hungarians who, two centuries before, had, like them, quitted the deserts of Scythia, and conquered the fertile banks of the Danube. Bela, king of Hungary, had recently attracted forty thousand families of Comans into his dominions, who betrayed him; the palatines and magnates of the kingdom were divided among themselves, and not even the aspect of danger could induce them to unite or submit themselves to the laws of the monarch. Disobedience, treachery, and discord, delivered the whole kingdom up to the furies of a pitiless enemy; the flocks, the harvests, the entire wealth of the country, became the prey of the Moguls; half the population was exterminated. Of all the cities of Hungary, only three offered an earnest and true resistance, and thus preserved themselves from scenes of carnage and destruction. The shepherds of Scythia, who could not read, have left to the vanquished the task of describing their conquests, and we have great difficulty in crediting the accounts of the old Hungarian chronicles, when they describe the unheard-of cruelties by which the Moguls disgraced their victories; [270] but several provinces entirely depopulated and changed into deserts, the ruins of two thousand churches, fifty destroyed cities, the traditions of these great disasters transmitted from age to age, and the terror that pervaded Europe, are evidences so worthy of faith, that we cannot reject them.

In the general consternation, it is surprising that the Moguls did not direct their arms against the Latin empire of Constantinople, then menaced by the Greeks, and little better than a ruin; but the shepherds of the desert did not employ themselves in inquiries concerning the interior revolutions of states or of the signs of their decay; they preserved, as did all the nations of Asia, a vague and confused idea of the power of the armies of ancient Byzantium, but took little heed whether the moment were come to attack it and conquer it. The great advantages which the imperial city derived from its position between Europe and Asia, did not at all strike the Tartars, who were ignorant of both navigation and commerce, and infinitely preferred rich pastures to the sumptuous edifices of great capitals. Thus we may equally believe, either that the city of Constantine was protected on this occasion by the memories of its past greatness, or that it owed its safety to the contempt and indifference of the barbarians.

The Franks established in Syria enjoyed the same good fortune as the Greeks of Byzantium. The armies of the Moguls had not yet crossed the Euphrates.

Whilst the tumult of war and the fall of empires resounded from the Yellow River to the Danube, the Christians of Palestine, protected by the discords of the Saracens, resumed possession of Jerusalem: they were beginning to repair the walls of the holy city, and rebuild the churches; and thanked Heaven in peace, for having preserved them from the scourges that were devastating the rest of the world. The Tartars were scarcely aware of the existence or the name of a country for which so much blood had been spilt, and were not likely to be attracted to the revered but barren banks of the Jordan, by either the hopes of booty or by the remembrances which excited the warlike enthusiasm of the nations of the West. Happy would it have been for the Christian colonies, if a people, conquered by the Moguls, driven from their own territories, and seeking an asylum everywhere, had not come to disturb their transient security, and plunge the city of Christ into fresh calamities.

After the death of Mahomet, sultan of Carismia, his son Gelaleddin gathered together an army. The valour which he displayed in several battles astonished his enemies, and, for a moment, brought back to his standard the sad remains of his empire; fortune favoured his expeditions into Georgia and India; but at last he forgot the lessons of adversity amidst the intoxication of pleasures; he lost all his conquests, and perished miserably among the Curds, where he had sought refuge. The Carismian warriors, incessantly pursued by the Tartars, abandoned a country they could no longer defend, and, under the command of one of their leaders named Barbakan, spread themselves through Asia Minor and Syria.

These hordes, banished from their own country, marched, sword and torch in hand, and, in their despair, seemed to wish to avenge upon other nations the evils they had suffered from the Tartars. History describes these furious bands, wandering along the banks of the Orontes and the Euphrates, dragging in their train a multitude of men and women that had fallen into their hands; a great number of waggons conveyed the spoils of the ravaged provinces they passed through. The most brave of them ornamented their lances with the hair of those they had immolated in fight. Clothed in the produce of pillage, their army presented a spectacle at once terrific and ridiculous. The Carismian warriors had no resource but in victory, and all the harangues of their leaders consisted of these words: *You will conquer, or you will die.* They gave no quarter to their enemies on the field of battle; when conquered themselves, they submitted to death without a complaint. Their fury spared neither Christians nor Mussulmans; all they met on their passage were their enemies; their approach spread terror everywhere, put the distracted peoples to flight, and changed cities and towns into deserts.

The Mussulman powers of Syria several times united in a league against the Carismians, and drove them back to the other side of the Euphrates. But the spirit of rivalry which at all times divided the princes of the family of Saladin, soon recalled an enemy always redoubtable notwithstanding defeats. At the period of which we are speaking, the princes of Damascus, Carac, and Emessa had just formed an alliance with the Christians of Palestine; they not only restored Jerusalem, Tiberias, and the principality of Galilee to them, but they promised to join them in the conquest of Egypt, a conquest for which the whole of Syria was making preparations. The sultan of Cairo, to avenge himself upon the Christians who had broken the treaties concluded with him, to punish their new allies, and protect himself from their invasion, determined to apply for succour to the hordes of Carismia; and sent deputies to the leaders of these barbarians, promising to abandon Palestine to them, if they subdued it.

This proposition was accepted with joy, and twenty thousand horsemen, animated by a thirst for booty and slaughter, hastened from the further parts of Mesopotamia, disposed to be subservient to the vengeance or anger of the Egyptian monarch. On their march they ravaged the territory of Tripoli and the principality of Galilee, and the flames which everywhere accompanied their steps, announced their arrival to the inhabitants of Jerusalem.

Fortifications scarcely commenced, and the small number of warriors in the holy city, left not the least hope of being able to repel the unexpected attacks of such a formidable enemy. The whole population of Jerusalem resolved to fly, under the guidance of the knights of the Hospital and the Temple. There only remained in the city the sick and a few inhabitants who could not make their minds up to abandon their homes and their infirm kindred. The Carismians soon arrived, and having destroyed a few intrenchments that had been made in their route, they entered Jerusalem sword in hand, massacred all they met, and as, amidst a deserted city the conquerors found no victims to glut their vengeance with, they had recourse to a most odious stratagem to lure back the inhabitants who had taken flight. They raised the standards of the cross upon every tower, and set all the bells ringing. The crowd of Christians who were retiring towards Jaffa, marched on in silence, and advanced but slowly, constantly hoping that Heaven would be touched by their misery, and, by some miracle, lead them back to the homes they had quitted: from time to time, their eyes involuntarily turned towards the holy city. All at once they saw the banners of the Cross unfurled, and the sound of the sacred brass, which every day called them to prayers, resounded in their ears. The news soon spread that either the barbarians had marched their army in another direction, or that they had been repulsed by the Christians who were left in the city. They became soon persuaded that God had taken pity on his people, and would not permit the city of Christ to be defiled by the presence of a sacrilegious horde. Seven thousand fugitives, deceived by this hope, returned to Jerusalem and gave themselves up to the fury of the Carismians, who put them all to the sword. Torrents of blood flowed through the streets and along the roads. A troop of nuns, children, and aged people, who had sought refuge in the church of the Holy Sepulchre, were massacred at the foot of the altars. The Carismians finding nothing among the living to satisfy their fury, burst open the sepulchres, and gave the coffins and remains of the dead up to the flames; the tomb of Christ, that of Godfrey of Bouillon, the sacred relics of the martyrs and heroes of the faith, nothing was respected, and Jerusalem then witnessed within its walls such cruelties and profanations as had never taken place in the most barbarous wars, or in days marked by the anger of God. [271]

In the mean time, the grand masters of the Templars and the Hospitallers, assembled with the patriarch of Jerusalem and the nobles of the kingdom, in Ptolemaïs, endeavoured to devise means by which the Carismians might be repulsed and Palestine saved. All the inhabitants of Tyre, Sidon, Ptolemaïs, and other Christian cities, able to bear arms, repaired to their standards. The princes of Damascus, Carac, and Emessa, whose assistance the Christians implored, united their forces, and assembled an army to stop the progress of the general devastation. This Mussulman army soon arrived in Palestine. Its appearance before the walls of Ptolemaïs raised the courage of the Franks, who, in so pressing a danger, appeared to have no repugnance to fight in company with the infidels. Almansor, prince of Emessa, who commanded the Mussulman warriors, had recently signalized his valour against the hordes of Carismia. The Christians took pleasure in relating his victories in the plains of Aleppo, and on the banks of the Euphrates. He was received in Palestine as a liberator, and carpets bordered with gold and silk were spread upon his passage. "The people," says Joinville, "considered him as one of *the best barons of paganism.*"

The preparations of the Christians, the zeal and ardour of the military orders, the barons, and prelates; the union that subsisted between the Franks and their new allies, altogether seemed to form a presage of success in a war undertaken in the names of religion, humanity, and patriotism. The Christian and Mussulman armies, united under the same banners, set out from Ptolemaïs, and encamped upon the plains of Ascalon. The army of the Carismians advanced towards Gaza, where they were to receive provisions and reinforcements sent by the sultan of Egypt. The Franks became impatient to meet their enemies, and to avenge the deaths of their companions and brethren massacred at Jerusalem. A council was called, to deliberate upon the best mode of proceeding. The prince of Emessa and the more wise among the barons thought it not prudent to expose the safety of the Christians and their allies to the risk of a battle. It appeared to them most advisable to occupy an advantageous position, and wait, without giving battle, till the natural inconstancy of the Carismians, want of provisions, or discord, might assist in dispersing this vagabond multitude, or lead them into other countries.

Most of the other chiefs, among whom was the patriarch of Jerusalem, did not agree with this opinion, and could see nothing in the Carismians but an undisciplined horde that it would be very easy to conquer and put to flight: any delay in attacking them would only raise their pride and redouble their audacity. Every day the evils of war were increasing; humanity and the safety of the Christian colonies required that they should promptly put an end to so many devastations, and that they should make haste to chastise the brigands, whose presence was at once an opprobrium and a calamity for the Christians, and all the allies of the Christians.

This opinion, too congenial with the impatient valour of the Franks, prevailed in the council. It was resolved to march, and offer the enemy battle.

The two armies met in the country of the ancient Philistines. Some years before, the duke of Burgundy and the king of Navarre, surprised in the sandy plains of Gaza, had lost the best of their knights and soldiers. Neither the sight of places where the Crusaders had been defeated, nor the remembrance of their recent disaster, diminished the imprudent ardour of the Christian warriors; as soon as they perceived the enemy, they were eager for the signal for battle. The Christian army was divided into three bodies; the left wing, in which were the knights of St. John, was commanded by Gauthier de Brienne, count of Jaffa, nephew to king John, and son of that Gauthier who died at the conquest of Naples. The Mussulman troops, under the orders of the prince of Emessa, formed the right wing. The patriarch of Jerusalem, surrounded by his clergy, with the wood of the true cross borne before him, the grand master of the Templars with his knights, and the barons of Palestine with their vassals, occupied the centre of the army.

The Carismians formed their line of battle slowly, and some degree of disorder was observable in their ranks. Gauthier de Brienne was anxious to profit by this circumstance and attack them with advantage; but the patriarch restrained his valour by a severity not less contrary to the interests of the Christians than to the spirit of the Gospel. [272]

The count of Jaffa, having been excommunicated for detaining in his hands a castle to which the prelate laid claim, asked, before he commenced the encounter in which he might lose his life, to be relieved from his excommunication. The patriarch twice rejected his prayer, and refused to absolve him. The army, which had received the benedictions of the priests and bishops, arising from their knees, awaited in silence the signal for battle. The Carismians had formed their line and advanced, uttering loud cries and discharging a cloud of arrows. Then the bishop of Rama, in complete armour, impatient to signalize his bravery against the enemies of the Christians, approached the count of Jaffa, exclaiming, "Let us march,— the patriarch is wrong: I absolve you, in the name of the Father, of the Son, and of the Holy Ghost." After having pronounced these words, the intrepid bishop of Rama and Gauthier de Brienne, followed by his companions in arms, rushed amidst the ranks of the enemy, burning to obtain victory or the crown of martyrdom.

The two armies were soon generally engaged, and mingled on the field of battle. The ardour to conquer was equal on both sides; neither the Christians nor their enemies could be ignorant that a single defeat must cause their ruin, and that their only safety was in victory. On this account, the annals of war present no example of a more murderous and obstinate contest; the battle began with the dawn, and only ended at sunset. On the following morning fighting was renewed with the same fury; the prince of Emessa, after having lost two thousand of his horsemen, abandoned the field of battle, and fled towards Damascus. This retreat of the Mussulmans decided the victory in favour of the Carismians; the Christians for a long time sustained the repeated shocks of the enemy; but at length, exhausted by fatigue and overwhelmed by a multitude, almost all were either killed or taken prisoners. This sanguinary battle cost life or liberty to more than thirty thousand Christian and Mussulman warriors; the prince of Tyre, the patriarch of Jerusalem, and some of the prelates, with great difficulty escaped the slaughter, and retired to Ptolemaïs. Among the warriors who regained the Christian cities, there were only thirty-three knights of the Temple, twenty-six Hospitallers, and three Teutonic knights.

When the news of this victory reached Egypt, it created a universal joy; it was announced to the people by sound of drums and trumpets; the sultan ordered public rejoicings throughout the provinces, and all the public edifices of the capital were illumined during three nights. In a short time the prisoners arrived at Cairo, mounted on camels, and pursued by the insulting clamours of the multitude. Before their arrival, the heads of their companions and brethren killed at the battle of Gaza were exhibited on the walls. This horrible monument of their defeat foreboded all they had to fear for themselves from the barbarity of the conquerors. They were cast into dungeons, where they were abandoned to the mercies of cruel gaolers, and where they had the melancholy satisfaction of embracing the barons and knights made prisoners in the last crusade.

Whilst all Egypt was celebrating the victory of Gaza, the inhabitants of Palestine deplored the death and captivity of their bravest warriors. As long is any hope existed of conquering the Carismians with the assistance of the Mussulmans of Syria, their alliance had created neither mistrust nor scruple; but reverses quickly revived prejudices; the last disaster was attributed to divine justice, irritated by having seen the banners of Christ mingled with those of Mahomet. On the other hand, the Mussulmans believed they had betrayed the cause of Islamism by allying themselves with the Christians; the aspect of the cross on the field of battle awakened their fanaticism and diminished their zeal for a cause which appeared to be that of their enemies. At the moment of beginning the fight, the prince of Emessa was heard to pronounce these words: "I am armed for battle, and yet God tells me, in the depths of my heart, that we shall not be victorious, because we have sought the friendship of the Franks."

The victory of the Carismians delivered up the greater part of Palestine to the most redoubtable enemies of the Christian colonies. The Egyptians took possession of Jerusalem, Tiberias, and the cities ceded to the Franks by the prince of Damascus. The hordes of Carismia ravaged all the banks of the Jordan, with the territories of Ascalon and Ptolemaïs, and laid siege to Jaffa. They dragged the unfortunate Gauthier de Brienne in their train, hoping that he would cause a city that belonged to him to open its gates to them: this model of Christian heroes was fastened to a cross before the walls. Whilst thus exposed to the eyes of his faithful vassals, the Carismians loaded him with insults, and threatened him with instant death if the city of Jaffa offered the least resistance. Gauthier, braving death, exhorted the inhabitants and the garrison, with a loud voice. to defend themselves to the last extremity. "Your duty," cried he, "is to defend a Christian city; mine is to die for you and Jesus Christ." The city of Jaffa did not fall into the hands of the Carismians, and Gauthier soon received the reward of his generous devotedness. Sent to the sultan of Cairo, he perished beneath the brutal blows of a furious mob, and thus obtained the palm of martyrdom for which he had wished.

In the mean time, fortune, or rather the inconstancy of the barbarians, came to the assistance of the Franks, and delivered Palestine from the presence of an enemy nothing could resist. The sultan of Cairo sent robes of honour and magnificent presents to the leaders of the victorious hordes, proposing to them to crown their exploits by directing their arms against the city of Damascus. The Carismians immediately laid siege to the capital of Syria. Damascus, which had been hastily fortified, was able to oppose but a very slight resistance to their impetuous attacks. Having no hope of succour, they opened their gates, and acknowledged the domination of the sultan of Egypt. It was then that the Carismians, inflated by their victory, demanded, in a menacing tone, that the lands that had been promised to them in Palestine should immediately be given up to them. The sultan of Cairo, who dreaded such neighbours, attempted to defer the fulfilment of his promise. In the fury which his refusal created, the barbarians offered their services to the prince whom they had just despoiled of his states, and laid fresh siege to Damascus, in order to deprive the Egyptians of it. The garrison and the inhabitants defended themselves with obstinacy; the fear of falling into the hands of a pitiless enemy supplying the place of courage. All the evils that war brings in her train, even famine itself, appeared to them a less terrible scourge than the hordes assembled under their ramparts.

The sultan of Egypt sent an army to assist the city, which was augmented by the troops of Aleppo and of several of the principalities of Syria. The Carismians were conquered in two battles. After this double defeat, Oriental history scarcely mentions their name, or furnishes us with means of following their track. The greater part of those that escaped the sword perished with hunger and misery in the countries they had devastated; the most brave and the best disciplined went to seek an asylum in the states of the sultan of Iconium: and if faith can be given to the conjectures of some historians, [273] they were the obscure origin of the powerful dynasty of the Ottomans.

The Christians of Palestine must have been grateful to Heaven for the destruction of the Carismians; but the loss of Jerusalem and the defeat of Gaza could not permit them to indulge in many joyful sensations. They had lost their allies, and could reckon upon nothing but enemies among the Mussulmans. The sultan of Egypt, whose alliance they had rejected, was extending his dominions in Syria, and his power became every day more formidable. The cities which the Christians still retained on the coasts of the sea were almost all without defenders. The orders of St. John and the

Temple had offered the sultan of Cairo a considerable sum for the ransom of his prisoners; but the sultan refused to listen to their ambassadors, and threatened them with all the terrors of his wrath: these two bodies, formerly so much dreaded by the Mussulmans, were no longer able to serve the cause of the Christians with any advantage, and were compelled to wait, in a state of inaction, till the warlike nobility of Europe should come to replace the knights held in captivity by the infidels, or swept away on the field of battle. The emperor of Germany made not the least effort to save the wreck of his feeble kingdom; he had sent several warriors to protect his rights in Ptolemaïs; but as these rights were not recognised, the presence of the imperial troops only added to the other scourges that desolated the Holy Land, that of discord and civil war.

Palestine, threatened every day with a fresh invasion, could not entertain the smallest hope of being succoured by the other Christian states of the East. The Comans, a barbarous people from the confines of Tartary, and who surpassed the hordes of Carismia in ferocity, ravaged the banks of the Orontes, and submitted everything in the principality of Antioch to fire and sword; the king of Armenia was in dread, at the same time, of the ravages of the Tartars, and of the aggressions of the Turks in Asia Minor; the kingdom of Cyprus, a prey to factions, had recently been the theatre of a civil war, and had reason to fear the incursions of the Mussulman nations of Syria and Egypt. In this deplorable situation, it might be believed that the kingdom of Godfrey was on the eve of perishing entirely, and that all that remained of the Christians in the Holy Land would soon share the fate of the Carismians. But, on turning their eyes towards the West, the Franks of Palestine again felt their hopes and their courage revive; more than once the Christian states of Syria had owed their safety, and even a few days of prosperity and glory, to the excess of their abasement and misery. Their groans and complaints were seldom heard in vain by the warlike nations of Europe, and their extreme distress became almost always the signal for a new crusade, the very report of which was enough to make the Saracens tremble.

Valeran, bishop of Berytus, had been sent into the West to solicit the protection of the pope and the assistance of princes and warriors. The pope received the envoy of the Christians with kindness, and promised his succour to the Holy Land. But the West was at that period agitated by troubles: the quarrel that had broken out between the Holy See and the emperor of Germany was carried on with an animosity that disgraced both religion and humanity. Frederick II. exercised all sorts of violences against the court of Rome and the partisans of the sovereign pontiff; the pope, every day more irritated, invoked the arms of the Christians against his enemy, and promised the indulgences of the crusade to all who would minister to his anger.

On another side, the Latins established at Constantinople were environed by the greatest perils. The emperor Baldwin II., after having conducted a feeble reinforcement to his capital, had returned into the West, and was, the second time, soliciting the alms and the succours of the faithful to sustain the deplorable remains of his empire, exposed, almost without defence, to the attacks of the Greeks and Bulgarians. At the same time, the Tartars continued to ravage the banks of the Danube, and threaten Germany; their barbarous exploits had carried terror to the very extremities of Europe; everywhere the excited imagination of nations represented these terrible conquerors as monsters vomited up by hell, clothed in hideous forms, and endowed with strength against which no man was able to contend. The deficiency of communication, which did not allow of exact information as to their march, gave birth to the most frightful rumours. Fame declared at one time they were invading Italy, and immediately afterwards, that they were ravaging the banks of the Rhine; every nation dreaded their prompt arrival, every city believed they were at its gates.

It was amidst this general disorder and consternation, that Innocent IV., a refugee at Lyons, resolved to convoke an œcumenic council in that city, to remedy the evils that desolated Christendom in both the East and the West. [274] The sovereign pontiff, in his letters addressed to the faithful, exposed the deplorable situation of the Romish Church, and conjured the bishops to come around him, and enlighten him with their counsels. The patriarchs of Constantinople, Antioch, and Aquilæa, a great number of prelates and doctors, with several secular princes, responded to the invitation of the head of the Church. Among the crowd of bishops, one alone seemed to attract general attention; this was the bishop of Berytus; his presence, and the grief impressed upon his brow, reminded the assembly of all the misfortunes of the Holy Land. Baldwin II., emperor of Byzantium, created very little less notice; and his suppliant attitude but too plainly showed what the empire founded by the sixth crusade had become.

Most of the Western monarchs had sent their ambassadors to this assembly, in which the safety and the great interests of the Christian world were about to be discussed. Frederick in particular, who had so long been the object of the anger of the sovereign pontiff, neglected nothing to turn aside the thunders suspended over his head, and ministers invested with his confidence were commissioned to defend him before the fathers of the council. Among the deputies of the emperor of Germany, history names Pierre Desvignes, who had written, in the name of Frederick, eloquent letters to all the sovereigns of Europe, to complain of the tyranny exercised by the Holy See; and Thadæus of Suesse, who was not prevented by the profession of arms from employing the arts of eloquence, or fathoming the depths of the study of laws. The latter had often served his master with glory amidst the perils of war, but he had never had an opportunity of showing so much firmness, courage, and devotion as in this assembly, in which the court of Rome was about to put forth all its power and realize all its threats.

Before the opening of the council, the pope held a congregation in the monastery of St. Just, where he had chosen to fix his residence. The patriarch of Constantinople exposed the deplorable state of his church: heresy had resumed its empire in a great part of Greece, and the enemies of the Latin church were advancing to the very gates of Constantinople; the bishop of Berytus read a letter, in which the patriarch of Jerusalem and the barons and prelates of Palestine described the ravages of the Carismians, and showed that the heritage of Christ was upon the point of becoming the prey of the barbarians, if the West did not take arms for its defence. The dangers and misfortunes of the Christians of the East affected the fathers of the council deeply. Thadæus, taking advantage of their emotion, announced that the emperor, his master, fully partook of their profound grief, and that he was ready to employ all his powers for the defence of Christendom. Frederick promised to arrest the progress of the irruption of the Tartars, to re-establish the domination of the Latins in Greece, to go in person to the Holy Land, and to deliver the kingdom of Jerusalem; he still further promised, in order to put an end to all divisions, to restore to the Holy See all he had taken from it, and to repair all wrongs offered to the sovereign pontiff. Such lofty promises, made by the most powerful monarch of Christendom, created as much joy as surprise in the greater part of the bishops; the whole assembly appeared impatient to know what would be the reply of Innocent. The pope proved inflexible, and rejected with scorn propositions, as he said, already made several times, and which had no other guarantee but the too suspicious loyalty of Frederick. He was determined to view the new protestations of the emperor as nothing but a fresh artifice to deceive the Church, and turn aside the course of its justice. *"The axe,"* added he, *"is already lifted, and ready to cut the roots of the tree;"* words very ill assorted with the charity of the Gospel, and which plainly show that Innocent had prepared the solemn pomp of a council with less purpose to oppose the foes of Christendom than to prepare the fall, and consummate the ruin of his personal enemy.

The pope held this preparatory sitting in order to make a trial of his strength, and to become acquainted with the dispositions of the bishops. A few days afterwards, the council was opened with great solemnity in the metropolitan church of St. John; the sovereign pontiff, wearing the tiara, and clothed in pontifical robes, was placed upon an elevated seat, having on his right hand the emperor of Constantinople, and on his left the count of Provence and the count of Thoulouse. After having given out the *Veni Creator*, and invoked enlightenment from the Holy Ghost, he pronounced a discourse, for the subject of which he took the five griefs with which he was afflicted, and compared them to the five wounds of the Saviour of the world upon the cross. The first was the irruption of the Tartars; the second, the schism of the Greeks; the third, the invasion of the Holy Land by the Carismians; the fourth, the relaxation of ecclesiastical discipline and the progress of heresy; and the fifth, the persecution he endured from Frederick.

Whilst describing the misfortunes of Christendom, the pontiff could not restrain his tears. His voice, if we may believe a contemporary historian, was often stifled by sobs; he conveyed to all hearts the sentiments by which he was affected; but he soon abandoned the language of compassion and despair, and assumed that of anger and menace. The Tartars, the Carismians, and the Mussulmans, inspired him with less hatred than the emperor of Germany, and it was for this prince he reserved all the thunders of his eloquence. He reproached him, in the most vehement expressions, with all the crimes that could draw upon his head the maledictions of his age, the hatred of his contemporaries, and the contempt of posterity. When the pope had pronounced his discourse, a profound silence reigned throughout the assembly; it appeared to the greater part of the terrified bishops that the voice of Heaven had made itself heard for the purpose of condemning Frederick: all eyes were turned upon the deputies of the emperor, and no one could believe that either of them would dare to reply to the interpreter of the anger of Heaven. All at once Thadæus of Suesse arose, and addressed the council, calling upon God, who searches all hearts, to witness that the emperor was faithful to all his promises, and had never ceased to endeavour to serve the cause of the Christians. He combated all the accusations of the sovereign pontiff, and in his reply did not hesitate to allege numerous complaints against the court of Rome. [275] The angry pope replied from his lofty throne; he again accused the emperor, and evinced but too great a desire to find him guilty: the first sitting of the council, entirely occupied with these violent debates, exhibited the unedifying spectacle of a contest between the head of the faithful, who accused a Christian prince of perjury, felony, heresy, and sacrilege; and the minister of an emperor, who reproached the court of Rome with having exercised an odious despotism, and committed revolting iniquities.

This contest, the results of which were likely to prove equally injurious to the head of the Church and the head of the Empire, was prolonged during several days; it doubtless scandalized all those that the pope had not associated with him in his resentments, and most of the bishops must have been afflicted at being thus diverted from the principal object of the convocation.

At length, however, the calamities of the Eastern Christians, the captivity of Jerusalem, and the dangers of Byzantium engaged the attention of the fathers of the council. The pope and the assembly of prelates decided that a new crusade should be preached for the deliverance of the Holy Land and the Latin empire of Constantinople. They renewed all the privileges granted to Crusaders by preceding popes and councils, as well as all the penalties directed against such as should favour either pirates or Saracens: during three years all who should take the cross would be exempted from every kind of tax or public office; but if after taking the vow they did not perform it, they incurred excommunication. The council recommended to the barons and knights to reform the luxury of their tables and the splendour of their dress; they advised all the faithful, and particularly ecclesiastics, to practise works of charity, and to arm themselves with all the austerities of penitence against the enemies of God. In order to obtain the protection of Heaven by the intercession of the Holy Virgin, the pope and the fathers of the council ordered that the octave of the Nativity should be celebrated in the church. In several councils Christian knights had been forbidden to take part in the profane solemnities of tournaments; the council of Lyon renewed the prohibition, persuaded that these military festivals might turn aside the minds of the warriors from the pious thoughts of the crusades, and that the expenses they occasioned would render it impossible for the bravest of the lords and barons to make the necessary preparations for the pilgrimage beyond the seas. The council ordered that the clergy should pay the twentieth part of their revenue, and the sovereign pontiff and cardinals the tenth of theirs, to provide for the expenses of the holy war. Half of the revenues of all non-resident benefices was specially reserved for the assistance of the empire of Constantinople. The decrees of the council ordered all whose mission it was to preach the word of God, to urge princes, counts, barons, and the corporations of cities, to contribute to the extent of their power to the success of the holy war; the same statutes recommended the clergy to show to the faithful that sacrifices offered to the crusade were the surest means of redeeming their sins; but above all they recommended the clergy to excite the faithful, in the tribunal of penitence, to multiply their offerings, or at least to bequeath in their testaments something for the assistance of the Christians of the East.

It was thus the council declared war against nations opposed to the Christians, and prepared means for assuring the triumphs of the soldiers of Christ. We are nevertheless surprised that the pope said nothing about preaching a crusade against the Tartars, whose invasion he had compared to one of the wounds of the Saviour on the cross. In the state of desolation in which Hungary was then placed, none of the bishops of that unfortunate kingdom had been able to appear at the council, and no friendly voice was raised to direct attention to, or implore favour for the Hungarian nation. The Tartars, it is true, repulsed by the duke of Neustadt, had fallen back from the banks of the Danube; but there was great reason to dread their return: to prevent fresh invasions, the council contented itself with advising the Germans to dig ditches and build walls on the roads the Tartarian hordes were likely to take. These measures, which even then must have been known to be insufficient, assist us at the present day in forming an opinion of the spirit of improvidence and blindness which then presided over political councils. Who can fail to be surprised at seeing, in an assembly so grave as a council, Europe pressed to lavish its treasures and sacrifice its armies for the deliverance of Constantinople and Jerusalem, whilst the most redoubtable of the barbarians were at their doors, and threatening to invade their own territories?

We may, however, remark, that Frederick himself had solicited the powers of Europe to assist him in repelling the Tartars; and the pope took much less interest in succouring the empire than he did in endeavouring to wrest it from Frederick. Innocent seemed very little disposed to set an example of that spirit of concord and charity which the council had just recommended to Christian princes; history can but deplore the zeal and ardour he evinced in carrying out his projects of vengeance against the emperor of Germany, at the risk of arousing evil passions, of perpetuating discord, and thus giving up the West to the invasion of the barbarians. In the second sitting of the council he was preparing to crush his enemy and completely overwhelm him with the weight of ecclesiastical power, when Thadæus of Suesse demanded a delay of a few days, to allow the emperor to come in person to justify his conduct and demonstrate his loyalty. The defender of Frederick hoped that the presence of a powerful monarch, by awakening in the minds of the assembly the respect due to the majesty of kings, would bring about the triumph of justice. The pope consented, though very unwillingly, to defer the accomplishment of his menaces; but the emperor could not condescend to appear as a suppliant before an assembly convoked by the most implacable of his enemies: he did not come to the council, and when the required period of delay had expired, the sovereign pontiff took advantage of his absence to reproach him afresh with his bad faith, and his resistance to the laws of the Church.

At the moment in which the assembly of the bishops tremblingly awaited the terrible sentence, the English ambassadors arose to complain of the agents of the court of Rome, whose ambition and avarice were ruining the kingdom of England; they at the same time protested against the feudal supremacy which the pope, in consequence of a cession made by King John, pretended to exercise over the English monarchy and nation. These claims could not restrain the ever-boiling anger of the sovereign pontiff. In vain Thadæus again rose to urge that a great number of bishops were absent— that several princes had not sent their ambassadors to the council; in vain he declared that he should appeal from this to a more numerous and more solemn council; nothing could turn aside the storm or retard the hour of vengeance. Innocent at first replied with moderation to the deputies of England, and even to those of Frederick; but soon assuming the tone of a judge and a master, "I am," said he, "the vicar of Jesus Christ; all that which I shall bind on earth shall be bound in heaven, according to the promises of the Son of God made to the prince of the apostles; and therefore, after having deliberated upon it with our brethren the cardinals, and with the council, I declare Frederick attainted and convicted of sacrilege and heresy, to be excommunicated and degraded from the empire; I absolve from their oaths, for ever, all who have sworn fidelity to him; I forbid any, under pain of excommunication incurred by that single fault, to henceforth yield him obedience; to conclude, I command the electors to elect another emperor, and I reserve to myself the right of disposing of the kingdom of Sicily."

During the reading of this sentence, the pope and the prelates held lighted wax tapers in their hands, and bent towards the earth in sign of malediction and anathema. The envoys of Frederick retired filled with confusion and despair; Thadæus of Suesse was heard to pronounce these words of the Scripture: "*O terrible day! O day of anger and calamity!*" A deep and melancholy silence prevailed throughout this assembly, into the bosom of which it appeared as if the bolts of heaven had just fallen amidst awful peals. The pope alone appeared collected, and his countenance was radiant with joy; he gave out the *Te Deum*, as if he had obtained a victory over the infidels, and declared that the council had terminated its labours.

Such was the council of Lyons, too celebrated in the annals of the middle ages, which has frequently supplied the enemies of religion with a pretext for attacking the judgments of the Church. The pope in his opening discourse had deplored the progress of heresy; but always more eager to combat the enemies of his power than those of religion, he did not propose a single measure to arrest the progress of the new errors. In this council, which had no tendency to the enlightenment of the faithful, the majesty of kings was violently outraged; all the maxims of the rights of nations, and all the precepts of scriptural charity were in it trampled under foot. When Innocent announced the intention of deposing the emperor, not a single bishop raised his voice to divert the sovereign pontiff from this revolting use of his power. The real wrongs that Frederick had committed against the Church; the remembrance of the persecutions he had exercised towards several bishops; the intention which they believed he entertained of plundering the clergy; the threatening language and tone of the pope; that invincible influence under which all feel themselves in a numerous assembly—all assisted in preventing any of the bishops from pleading the cause of reason or recalling the maxims of the Gospel to the mind of the enraged pontiff. Nevertheless the fathers of the council, whatever might be their prejudices or their resentments, did not take part in all the fury of Innocent, and did not actively assist in carrying out his acts of injustice and violence.

The pope did not appeal to their wisdom, and seemed afraid to ask their opinions. Without repeating here that which has frequently been said in schools of theology, impartial history must disapprove of the silent neutrality of the council; but it must at the same time assert that the odious decree against Frederick was not an act of the Church; that the bishops and prelates did not give their formal approbation to it; and that the shame of this great iniquity fails entirely upon the memory of Innocent. [276]

It was at this deplorable period that the cardinals, by order of the pope, clothed themselves for the first time in the scarlet robe, a symbol of persecution, and a sad presage of the blood that was about to flow. Frederick was at Turin when he heard of his condemnation; at this news he called for his imperial crown, and placing it upon his head, exclaimed in a loud and angry voice, "There it is, and before it shall be wrested from me, my enemies shall well know the terror of my arms; let this pontiff tremble, who has broken every tie that bound me to him; he at length permits me henceforth to listen to nothing but the dictates of my just anger." These threatening words announced a formidable contest, and every friend of peace must have been seized with terror: the fury which animated the emperor and the pope quickly passed into the minds of the people; in the provinces of Germany and Italy all flew to arms. Amidst the agitation in which the West was then plunged, it is probable that Jerusalem and the Holy Land would have been quite forgotten, if a powerful and highly-revered monarch had not placed himself at the head of the crusade which had been proclaimed in the council of Lyons.

The preceding year, at the very moment the nations of the West heard of the last misfortunes of Palestine, Louis IX. of France fell dangerously ill. The most earnest prayers were offered up by the people of his kingdom for the preservation of the virtuous monarch. The malady, the attacks of which became every day more violent, at length created serious alarm. Louis sunk into a mortal lethargy, and the intelligence was soon circulated that he was dead. The court, the capital, the provinces were struck with the deepest grief; nevertheless, the king of France, as if Heaven had not been able to resist the prayers and tears of a whole nation, recovered, even when apparently at the portals of the tomb. The first use he made of speech, after again beholding the light, was to ask for the cross and express his determination of going to the Holy Land.

Those who surrounded him considered his return to life as a miracle effected by the crown of thorns of Christ, and by the protection of the apostles of France; they cast themselves on their knees to return thanks to Heaven, and in the joy they experienced, scarcely paid attention to the vow Louis had made of quitting his kingdom and going to fight against the infidels in the East. When the king began to recover his strength, he repeated his vow, and again asked for the cross of the Crusaders. [277] The queen Blanche, his mother, the princes of his family, and Pierre d'Auvergne, bishop of Paris, then endeavoured to divert him from his purpose, and conjured him, with tears in their eyes, to wait till he was perfectly restored to health before he directed his thoughts to so perilous an enterprise; but Louis thought he was only obeying the will of Heaven. His imagination had been forcibly affected by the calamities of the Holy Land; Jerusalem given up to pillage, the tomb of Christ profaned, were constantly present to his mind. Amidst the height of a burning fever, he had fancied he heard a voice which came from the East, and addressed these words to him: "*King of France, thou seest the outrages offered to the city of Christ; it is thou whom Heaven hath appointed to avenge them.*" This celestial voice resounded still in his ears, and would not allow him to listen to the prayers of friendship or the counsels of human wisdom. Steadfast in his resolution, he received the cross from the hands of Pierre d'Auvergne, and caused it to be announced to the Christians of Palestine—sending them at the same time succours of both men and money—that he would cross the seas as soon as he could assemble an army, and had reëstablished peace in his dominions.

This information, which conveyed such joy to the Christian colonies, spread grief and consternation through all the provinces of France. The sieur de Joinville expresses warmly the regret of the royal family, particularly the despair of the queen mother, [278] by saying, that when this princess saw her son wearing the cross, *she was struck as fearfully as if she had looked upon him dead.* The late disasters of Jerusalem had drawn tears from most Christians in the West, but without inspiring them, as in the preceding age, with any earnest desire of going to fight the infidels. It was impossible to see, in these distant expeditions, anything but great perils and inevitable reverses; and the project of recovering the city of God awakened more alarm than enthusiasm.

The sovereign pontiff, however, sent ecclesiastics into all the Christian states with a charge to preach the holy war. Cardinal Eudes, of Chateauroux, arrived in France with the express commission of publishing and causing to be executed the decrees of the council of Lyons respecting the crusade. The holy expedition was preached in all the churches of the kingdom. Contemporary history scarcely mentions the effect of these preachings, and everything leads us to believe that those who then took the oath to fight against the Saracens were induced to do so more by the example of the king than by the eloquence of the holy orators.

In order to give more solemnity to the publication of the crusade, and to excite the ardour of the warriors for the deliverance of the holy places, Louis IX. convoked a parliament in his capital, in which were assembled the prelates and magnates of the kingdom. The cardinal legate there repeated the exhortations addressed by the head of the Church to the faithful. Louis IX. spoke after the cardinal of Chateauroux, and retraced the picture of the disasters of Palestine. "According to the expression of David, an impious nation has entered into the temple of the Lord; blood has flowed like water around Jerusalem; the servants of God have been massacred in the sanctuary; and their remains, deprived of sepulture, are abandoned to the birds of heaven." After having deplored the miseries of Sion, Louis IX. reminded his barons and knights of the example of Louis the Young and of Philip Augustus; he exhorted every generous soldier who heard him to take arms, to go across the seas, fight against the infidels, and defend the glory of God and of the French name in the East. Louis, invoking by turns the charity and the warlike virtues of his auditory, endeavoured to awaken in all hearts both inspirations of piety and sentiments of chivalry. There is no necessity for repeating what was the effect of the exhortations and prayers of a king of France who addressed himself to the honour, and appealed to the bravery of his subjects. He had scarcely ceased speaking, when his three brothers, Robert, count d'Artois, Alphonse, duke of Poictiers, and Charles, duke of Anjou, took the oath to go and defend the heritage of Christ and the French colonies in Asia. Queen Marguerite, the countess d'Artois, and the duchess of Poictiers, likewise took the cross and resolved to accompany their husbands. Most of the bishops and prelates who were present at this assembly, influenced by the discourse of the king and the example of the cardinal-legate, did not hesitate to enrol themselves in a war for which, it is true, less enthusiasm was shown than had appeared in a former age, but which was still termed *the war of God*. Among the great vassals of the crown who swore to quit France for the purpose of fighting the Saracens in Asia, the friends of the French monarchy must have numbered, with much joy, Pierre de Dreux, duke of Brittany, Hugh, count de la Marche, and several other lords whose jealous ambition had so long disturbed the kingdom. Quickly after them were seen the duke of Burgundy, Hugh de Chatillon, the count de St. Pol, the counts of Dreux, Bar, Soissons, Blois, Rhotel, Montfort, and Vendôme; the seigneur de Beaujeu, constable of France, and John de Beaumont, great admiral, and great chamberlain; Philip of Courtenay, Guy of Flanders, Archambaud de Bourbon, young Raoul de Coucy, John of Barres, Gilles de Mailly, Robert de Bethune, and Oliver de Thermes. There was not an illustrious family in the kingdom that did not supply one hero for the crusade. In the crowd of these noble Crusaders, history is gratified in observing the celebrated Boilève, who was afterwards provost of the traders of Paris, and the sieur de Joinville, whose name will for ever appear in the history of France by the side of that of Louis IX.

In the assembly of prelates and barons several measures were adopted for the maintenance of public peace and the preparations for the holy war. An immense number of processes at that period disturbed the peace of families, and those processes, of which many were decided by the sword, often amounted to actual wars. The tribunals were enjoined to terminate all affairs brought before them, and in cases in which they could not oblige the parties to acquiesce in a definite judgment, the judges were directed to make them swear to a truce of five years. In agreement with the authority of the pope, and the decrees of the council of Lyons, it was ordered that ecclesiastics should pay to the king the tenth of their revenues, which created a dissatisfaction in the clergy that Louis had great trouble in dispelling. A proscript, issued by royal authority, in concert with the will of the pope, decreed that Crusaders should be protected during three years from the pursuits of their creditors, reckoning from the day of their departure for the Holy Land; this proscript, which likewise excited much murmuring, had great effect in determining many barons and knights to leave the West.

Louis IX. occupied himself constantly in carrying his design into execution, and neglected no means of winning to his purpose all the nobility of his kingdom; his piety did not disdain to employ, for what he considered a sacred cause, all the empire that kings generally possess over their courtiers; he sometimes even lowered himself to seduction and trick, persuaded that the sanctity of the crusade would excuse everything. After an ancient custom, the kings of France, at great solemnities, gave such of their subjects as were at court certain capes or furred mantles, with which the latter immediately clothed themselves before leaving the court. In the ancient *comptes* (a sort of audits) these capes were called *livrées* (whence, no doubt, our word livery), because the monarch gave them (*les livrait*) himself. Louis ordered a vast number of these to be prepared against Christmas Eve, upon which crosses were embroidered in gold and silk. The moment being come, every one covered himself with the mantle that had been given to him, and followed the monarch to the chapel. What was their astonishment when, by the light of the wax tapers, they at once perceived upon all before them, and then upon themselves, the sign of an engagement they had never contracted. Such was, however, the character of the French knights, that they believed themselves obliged to respond to this appeal to their bravery; all the courtiers, as soon as divine service was ended, joined in the laugh with *the skilful fisher of men*, [279] and took the oath to accompany him into Asia.

Notwithstanding all these efforts, the publication of the holy war created in the nation much more sorrow than warlike ardour, and the approaching departure of the monarch afflicted all France. Queen Blanche, and the most prudent of the ministers, who had at first endeavoured to divert Louis IX. from the crusade, repeated their attempts several times: resolved to make a last effort, they went to the king in a body. The bishop of Paris was at their head, and spoke for all; this virtuous prelate represented to Louis, that a vow made in the height of a disease ought not to bind him in an irrevocable manner, particularly if the interests of his kingdom imposed upon him the obligation of dispensing with it. "Everything demanded the presence of the monarch in his dominions; the Poitevins were threatening to take up arms again; the war of the Albigeois was ready to be rekindled; the animosity of England was always to be dreaded, as it paid little heed to treaties; the wars occasioned by the pretensions of the pope and the emperor inflamed all the states adjoining to France, and the conflagration was not unlikely to extend to that kingdom." Many of the nobles to whom Louis had confided the most important functions of the state, spoke after the bishop of Paris, and represented to the monarch that all the institutions founded by his wisdom would perish in his absence; that France would lose by his departure the fruits of the victories of Saintes and Taillebourg, with all the hopes that the virtues of a great prince made her entertain. Queen Blanche spoke the last. "My son," said she, "if Providence has made use of me to watch over your infancy and preserve your crown, I have perhaps the right to remind you of the duties of a monarch, and of the obligations which the safety of the kingdom over which God has placed you imposes upon you; but I prefer speaking to you with the tenderness of a mother. You know, my son, that I can have but few days to live, and your departure leaves me only the thought of an eternal separation: happy still if I die before fame may have borne into Europe the intelligence of some great disasters. Up to this day, you have disdained both my counsels and my prayers; but if you will not take pity on my sorrows, think at least of your children, whom you abandon in the cradle; they stand in need of your lessons and your assistance; what will become of them in your absence? are they not as dear to you as the Christians of the East? If you were now in Asia, and were informed that your deserted family was the sport and prey of factions, you would not fail to hasten to us. Well! all these evils that my tenderness makes me dread, your departure is most likely to give birth to. Remain then in Europe, where you will have so many opportunities of displaying the virtues of a great king, of a king the father of his subjects, the model and support of the princes of his house. If Christ requires his heritage to be delivered, send your treasures and your armies into the East; God will bless a war undertaken in his name. But this God, who hears me, believe me, never commands the accomplishment of a vow which is contrary to the great designs of his providence. No; that God of mercy who would not permit Abraham to complete his sacrifice, does not permit you to complete yours, and expose a life upon which so entirely depend both the fate of your family and the welfare of your kingdom."

On finishing these words, Queen Blanche could not restrain her tears; Louis himself was deeply moved, and threw himself into the arms of his mother; but soon resuming a calm and serene countenance, he said: "My dear friends, you know that all Christendom is acquainted with my resolution; during several months the preparations for the crusade have been carried on under my orders. I have written to all the princes of Europe that I was about to leave my dominions and to repair to Asia; I have announced to the Christians of Palestine that I would succour them in person; I have myself preached the crusade in my kingdoms; a host of barons and knights have obeyed my voice, followed my example, and sworn to accompany me into the East. What do you now propose to me? to change my projects publicly proclaimed, to do nothing that I have promised to do, or that Europe expects of me, and to deceive at once the hopes of the Church, of the Christians of Palestine, and of my faithful nobility."

"Nevertheless, as you think that I was not in possession of my reason when I took the cross; well, I give it back to you; there is that cross which gives you so much alarm, and which I only took, you say, in a fit of delirium. But now that I am in the full enjoyment of my reason I ask it of you again, and I solemnly declare that no food shall enter my mouth until you have returned it to me. Your reproaches and your complaints affect me with the deepest sorrow; but learn to be better acquainted with my duties and your own; aid me in seeking for true glory; second me in the powerful cause in which I am engaged, and do not alarm yourselves on account of my destiny or that of my family and people. The God who made me victorious at Taillebourg will watch over the designs and plots of our enemies; yes, the God who sends me into Asia to deliver his heritage, will defend that of my children, and pour his blessings upon France. Have we not still her who was the support of my childhood and the guide of my youth, her whose wisdom saved the state in so many perils, and who, in my absence, will want neither courage nor ability to crush factions? Allow me, then, to keep all the promises I have made before God and before men; and do not forget that there are obligations which are sacred for me, and ought to be sacred for you—I mean the oath of a Christian and the word of a king!"

Thus spoke Louis IX.: Queen Blanche, the bishop of Paris, and the other counsellors of the king preserved a religious silence, and from that time only thought of seconding the endeavours the monarch was making to forward the execution of an undertaking which appeared to emanate from God. [280]

The crusade was preached at this time in all the countries of Europe; but as most states were filled with agitation and discord, the voices of the sacred orators were lost amidst the din of factions and the tumult of arms. When the bishop of Berytus went into England, to entreat the English monarch to succour the Christians of the East, Henry III. was fully employed in repelling the aggressions of the king of Scotland, and in appeasing the troubles of the country of Wales. The barons menaced his authority, and did not permit him to engage in a distant war. This prince not only refused to take the cross, but forbade the preaching of a crusade in his kingdom.

All Germany was in a blaze in consequence of the quarrel between the Church and the Empire. After having deposed the emperor at the council of Lyons, Innocent IV. offered the imperial crown to any one who would take up arms against the excommunicated prince, and bring about the triumph of the Holy See. Henry, landgrave of Thuringia, allowed himself to be seduced by the promises of the sovereign pontiff, and was crowned emperor by the archbishops of Mayence and Cologne, and a few other ecclesiastical electors. From that event civil war broke out in all parts; Germany was filled with missionaries from the pope, with the power of the evangelical word against Frederick, whom they styled the most redoubtable of infidels. The treasures collected for the equipments of the holy war were employed in corrupting fidelity, laying plots, fomenting treasons, and keeping up troubles and discords; so that it may well be supposed the cause of Christ and the deliverance of Jerusalem were entirely forgotten.

Italy was not less agitated than Germany; the thunders of Rome, so often hurled at Frederick, had redoubled the fury of the Guelphs and the Ghibellines. All the republics of Lombardy were leagued in opposition to the party of the emperor; the threats and the manifestoes of the pope would not allow a single city to remain neuter, or leave peace an asylum in the countries situated between the Alps and Sicily. The missionaries of Innocent employed, by turns, the arms of religion and of policy; after having declared the emperor to be a heretic and an enemy to the Church, they represented him as a bad prince and a tyrant, and dazzled the eyes of the people with the charms of liberty, always so powerful a motive upon the minds of nations. The sovereign pontiff sent two legates into the kingdom of Sicily, with letters for the clergy, the nobility, and the people of the cities and country. "We have not been able to see without some surprise," wrote Innocent, "that, burdened as you are, living under the opprobrium of servitude, and oppressed in your persons and your property, you have hitherto neglected the means of securing yourselves the sweets of liberty. Many other nations have presented you with an example; but the Holy See, far from accusing you, is satisfied with pitying you, and finds your excuse in the fear that must hold possession of your hearts under the yoke of a new Nero." On terminating his letter to the Sicilians, the pope endeavoured to make them understand that God had not placed them in a fertile region and beneath a smiling sky to wear disgraceful chains; and that by shaking off the yoke of the emperor of Germany, they would only second the views of Providence.

Frederick, who had at first defied the thunders of Rome, was terrified at the new war declared against him by the pope. The interdict placed upon his states, the terrible array of the maledictions of the Church, strongly affected the minds of the multitude, and might at length shake the fidelity of his subjects; he himself felt his courage forsake him; his party in Italy grew weaker every day; his armies had experienced some checks in Germany; many conspiracies had been formed against his life, and amongst the conspirators, he had the grief to find some of his servants whom he had loaded with kindnesses. This haughty monarch became convinced that he had no course but to seek a reconciliation with the Church, and addressed himself to Louis IX., whose wisdom and piety rendered him the arbiter of sovereigns and nations. Frederick, in his letters, promised to abide by the decision of the king of France and his barons, and engaged, beforehand, to go in person to the conquest of the Holy Land, or to send his son, the king of the Romans. In order to interest Louis in his cause, the emperor offered to supply him with provisions, vessels, and everything he should stand in need of in the expedition to the East.

Louis eagerly embraced this opportunity for reëstablishing peace in Europe and assuring the success of the holy war. Several ambassadors were sent to the pope at Lyons, conjuring the father of the faithful to listen to the voice of mercy rather than to that of anger. The king of France had two long conferences with Innocent in the monastery of Cluni, and supplicated him afresh to appease by his clemency the troubles of the Christian world; but enmity had been carried too far to leave any hopes of peace; it was not possible for Innocent and Frederick to pardon each other sincerely the outrages they had mutually committed. The emperor had spared neither threats nor violences against the popes; he did not hate them more for the injuries he had received from them than for those he had done them. On the other side, it had for a length of time been determined, in the councils of Rome, to effect the overthrow of the house of Swabia, which was suspected, and with reason, of entertaining the project of invading Italy and establishing the seat of imperial domination in the city of St. Peter. This policy, embraced with ardour, had assumed all the character of a personal vengeance in the mind of Innocent. The triumph, even, of the pontiff, whilst flattering his pride and ambition, appeared to double his hatred, and the hope of completing the ruin of his enemy rendered him implacable.

In vain the emperor of Germany, overcome by fear rather than won by the love of peace, promised to descend from his throne, and pass the remainder of his days in Palestine, on condition that he should receive the benediction of the pope, and that his son Conrad should be raised to the empire. This entire abnegation of power, this strange abasement of royal majesty, produced no effect upon Innocent, who did not believe, or feigned not to believe, the promises of Frederick; in vain Louis IX., whose mind was incapable of suspecting Imposture, represented to the pope the advantages that Europe, Christendom, and the court of Rome itself might derive from the repentance and offers of the emperor; in vain he spoke to him of the vows and the safety of pilgrims, of the glory and peace of the Church; the discourses of the holy king were scarcely listened to, and his pious mind could not view, without being moved with disgust, this inflexible rigour in the father of the Christian world.

Whilst the report of these discords, upon gaining the East, spread joy among the infidels, the unhappy inhabitants of Palestine gave themselves up to despair on learning that so many untoward events retarded the preparations for the crusade. Several messages from the Christians beyond the seas were sent to the sovereign pontiff to intercede for a prince from whom they hoped for such powerful assistance. The patriarch of Armenia wrote to the court of Rome to demand favour for Frederick; he demanded it in the name of the threatened Christian colonies; in the name of the city of God, fallen into ruins; in the name of the sepulchre of Christ, profaned by barbarians. The pope made no reply whatever to the patriarch of the Armenians, and appeared to have forgotten Jerusalem, the holy sepulchre, and the Christians of Syria; he had, indeed, but one thought,—that of carrying on the war against Frederick. Innocent pursued his redoubtable enemy even to the East, and endeavoured to induce the sultan of Cairo to break his engagements with the emperor of Germany. The sultan of Cairo received, with as great joy as surprise, a message which informed him so authentically of the divisions that existed among the Christian princes; he answered the pope with a severity full of contempt; and the more he was pressed to be unfaithful to the treaties made with Frederick, the more he affected to display a fidelity from which he hoped to obtain an advantage over the Christian Church.

It was at this period that the emperor of Germany, urged on to despair, in some sort justified the most violent proceedings of the court of Rome by his conduct. He could not pardon Louis IX. for having remained neuter in a quarrel that interested all Christendom, and if the Arabian historian Yafey may be believed, he sent an ambassador secretly into Asia to warn the Mussulman powers of the expedition projected by the king of France. Throwing off at once the tone of submission to the pope, he resolved to repel force by force, and violence by violence. Some successes which he obtained in Germany, raised his courage, and completely dissipated all his scruples. He laid siege to the city of Parma, at the head of a formidable army. Horrible cruelties signalized his first triumphs; the bishop of Arezzo, who fell into his hands, with many other prisoners of war, were loaded with irons, and handed over to the executioner without even the ceremony of a trial.

In the intoxication of success, Frederick threatened to cross the Alps, and attack Innocent within the walls of Lyons. Heaven, however, would not permit the execution of a project formed by hatred and revenge. The Guelphs beat and dispersed the imperial army. Fortune changed, and the irresolute character of Frederick changed as suddenly with it. Victory had inflamed his pride and redoubled his fury; a single defeat cast him into despondency, and rendered him again accessible to fear. From that time he resumed the part of a suppliant to the pope; from that time protestations and prayers seemed to cost his terrified mind no effort.

As the extent of his empire gave umbrage to the court of Rome, Frederick promised to divide his dominions, and give Sicily to his son Henry, and Germany to his son Conrad. He submitted his religious belief to the examination of several bishops, and sent their decision to the pope. He went at last even so far as to promise to come in person to solicit the clemency of Innocent. The sovereign pontiff had just caused the count of Holland to be nominated emperor, in the place of the landgrave of Thuringia, who had died on the field of battle. In this state of things he dreaded less the hostilities and angry threats of Frederick, than he did his protestations of submission and repentance. The supplications of princes and nations, who demanded favour for a power he wished to destroy, annoyed Innocent; they seemed to accuse him, in the eyes of Christendom, of obstinacy in his refusal, and without inducing him to renounce his policy, only embarrassed him in the execution of his designs.

The pope remained constantly inflexible; but astonished Europe began to ask what powerful interest it was that commanded all these rigours. Frederick, pursued with so much inveteracy, found at length the number and zeal of his friends and partisans increase. Germany, Cologne, and several other cities, rejected the decrees of the Holy See, and proceeded to violent excesses. The angry pope launched all his thunders against the guilty, and by an injustice which characterizes these times of discord and vengeance, many of the penalties he pronounced extended to the fourth generation. This senseless rage completed the alienation of men's minds, and the fanaticism of heresy was added to the furies of civil war.

As the court of Rome, under the imposing pretext of the crusade, levied tributes in all the states of Europe to keep up the fire of sedition and revolt, so many violences, and so much injustice infused dissatisfaction everywhere, and gave birth to a spirit of opposition among nations even, that had been exempt from the consequences of the terrible quarrel. The commissaries of the Holy See ruined the provinces of France; they pervaded the cities and countries, compelling the curates and chaplains of the nobles to sell all their little property; they required from all, church dues; and from religious communities, now the twentieth for the crusade against Constantinople, then the tenth for that of Palestine, and at last a contribution towards carrying on the war against the emperor. The French nobility, stimulated by a feeling of patriotism, by the spirit of chivalry which led all the *preux* of that time to enter the lists against iniquity of any kind, and perhaps also by the fear of being oppressed in their turn, spoke loudly in favour of Frederick, and expressed their anger at seeing the kingdom of France a prey to the agents of the pope. Just remonstrances were at first made; but in a short time no measures were observed, and they proceeded so far as to agitate the question, whether they ought to acknowledge a pontiff, whose conduct appeared so contrary to the spirit of the Gospel, as the vicar of Jesus Christ. The principal French nobles at length formed a confederacy against the proceedings of the pope and the clergy. Throughout this new struggle, Louis IX., equally removed from that sacrilegious impiety which pretends to brave everything, and from that superstitious pusillanimity which believes itself obliged to suffer everything, managed to restrain the excesses of both parties, and maintain peace; the league which was then formed, without embittering men's minds, succeeded in enlightening them; it served, during the absence of the king, to repress the enterprises of the Holy See, and many writers trace to this period the origin of those Gallican liberties which have constituted the glory of the French clergy up to modern times.

Nevertheless, Louis IX. was constantly employed in preparations for his departure. As no other route to the East was available but that by sea, and as the kingdom of France had no port in the Mediterranean, Louis made the acquisition of the territory of Aigues-Mortes, in Provence; the port, choked with sand, was cleansed, and a city large enough to receive the crowd of pilgrims was built on the shore. Louis at the same time busied himself in provisioning his army, and preparing magazines in the isle of Cyprus, where he meant to land. Thibault, count de Bar, and the sieur de Beaujeu, sent into Italy, found everything necessary for the provisioning and transport of an army, either in the republic of Venice, or in the rich provinces of Apulia and Sicily, whither the directions of the emperor Frederick had preceded them.

The fame of these preparations soon reached Syria, and the authors of the times describe the Mussulman powers as struck with terror, and as immediately and earnestly employed in fortifying their cities and their frontiers against the approaching invasion of the Franks. Such popular rumours as were then in circulation that history has deigned to preserve, accuse the Saracens of having employed perfidious means and odious stratagems to avenge themselves upon the Christian nations, and ruin their enterprise. It was asserted that the life of Louis IX. was in danger from the emissaries of the Old Man of the Mountain; it was reported in cities, and the multitude did not fail to give credit to it, that the pepper which came from the East was empoisoned; and Matthew Paris, a grave historian, does not hesitate to affirm that a great number of persons died of it before this horrible artifice was discovered. We may well believe that the policy of the time itself invented these gross fables, to render the enemies they were about to combat more odious, and that indignation might increase and animate the courage of the warriors. It is natural also to suppose, that such rumours had their origin in popular ignorance, and that they gained credit from the opinion that was then entertained of the manners and characters of infidel nations.

Three years had passed away since the king of France assumed the cross. He convoked a new parliament at Paris, in which he at length fixed the departure of the holy expedition for the month of June of the following year (1248). The barons and prelates renewed with him the promises of fighting against the infidels, and engaged to set out at the period assigned, under the penalty of incurring ecclesiastical censures. Louis took advantage of the moment that the magnates of his kingdom were assembled in the name of religion, to require that they should take the oath of fealty and homage to his children, and to make them swear (these are the expressions of Joinville) "that they should be loyal to his family, if any misadventure should befall his person in the holy voyage beyond the seas." [281]

It was then that the pope addressed a letter to the nobility and people of France, in which he celebrated in solemn terms the bravery and other warlike virtues of the French nation and its pious monarch. The sovereign pontiff gave his benediction to the French Crusaders, and threatened with the thunders of the Church all who, having made the vow of pilgrimage, deferred their departure. Louis IX., who had no doubt requested this warning from the pope, saw with joy all the nobility of his kingdom hasten to join his standard; many nobles, whose ambition he had repressed, were the first to set the example, for fear of awakening old mistrusts or incurring fresh disgraces; others, seduced by the habitual spirit of courts, declared themselves with ardour champions of the cross, in the hope of obtaining, not the rewards of Heaven, but those of the earth. The character of Louis IX. inspired the greatest confidence in all the Christian warriors. "If, till this time," said they, "God has permitted the crusades to be nothing but a long course of reverses and calamities, it is because the imprudence of the leaders has compromised the safety of the Christian armies; it is because discord and licentiousness of manners have reigned too long among the defenders of the cross: but what evils have we to dread under a prince whom Heaven appears to have inspired with its own wisdom,—under a prince who, by his firmness, has succeeded in suppressing every division in his own country, and is about to exhibit to the East an example of all the virtues?"

Many English nobles, among whom were the earls of Salisbury and Leicester, resolved to accompany the king of France, and share with him the perils of the crusade. The earl of Salisbury, grandson of "Fair Rosamond," who had gained by his exploits the surname of "Long Sword," had just been stripped of all his possessions by Henry III. In order to place himself in a condition to make preparations for the war, he addressed himself to the pope, and said to him, "Beggar as I am, I have made a vow to perform the pilgrimage to the Holy Land. If Prince Richard, brother to the king of England, has been able to obtain, without taking the cross, the privilege of levying a tax upon those who have just laid it down, I have thought that I might obtain a similar favour;—I, who have no resource but in the charity of the faithful." This discourse, which informs us of a very curious fact, made the sovereign pontiff smile: the earl of Salisbury obtained the favour he asked, and deemed it his duty to set out for the East.

The preachings for the holy war, which had produced but little effect in Italy and Germany, had nevertheless been successful in the provinces of Friesland and Holland, and in some of the northern kingdoms. Haco, king of Norway, celebrated for his bravery and exploits, took the oath to fight against the infidels; and the Norwegians, who had several times distinguished themselves in the holy wars, followed the example of their monarch. Haco, after completing his preparations, wrote to Louis IX. to announce his approaching departure. He asked him permission to land upon the coast of France, and to furnish himself there with the supplies necessary for his army. Louis made a most cordial reply, and proposed to the Norwegian prince to share with him the command of the crusade. Matthew Paris, who was charged with the message from Louis IX., informs us in his History that the king of Norway declined the generous offer of the French king, persuaded, he said, that harmony could not long subsist between the Norwegians and the French,—the first, of an impetuous, restless, and jealous character, the others, full of pride and haughtiness.

Haco, after having made this reply, thought no more of embarking, and remained quietly in his kingdom, history being perfectly unable to discover the motives which produced this sudden change. It may be believed, that in accordance with the example of several other Christian monarchs, this prince had made use of the crusade as a cloak for his political designs. By levying a tax of a third upon the revenues of the clergy, he had amassed treasures which he might employ in strengthening his power. The army he had raised in the name of Christ might minister to his ambition much more effectually in Europe than in the plains of Asia. The pope, from whom he had received the title of king, at first exhorted him to assume the sign of the Crusaders; but everything leads us to believe that he afterwards advised him to remain in the West, where he hoped to raise in him one more enemy against the emperor of Germany. Thus the king of Norway had promised to go into the East in the hope of obtaining the favour and protection of the court of Rome; and to preserve this favour and this support, he had but one thing to do, and that was to forget his promises.

However this may be, it is certain that the pope, at that time, took but very little interest in the success of the eastern crusade. We may judge of this by the facility with which he liberated so many from their vows of fighting against the infidels: he went even so far as to forbid the Crusaders from Friesland and Holland to embark for Palestine. In vain Louis IX. made some serious remonstrances on this head; Innocent would not listen to him. Engrossed by one passion, he found it much more advantageous to grant dispensations for the voyage to Syria; for, on one part, those dispensations which were bought with solid money, contributed to fill his treasury, and on the other, they left soldiers in Europe that he might arm against his personal enemies.

Thus France was the only country in which the crusade was really an object of interest; the piety and zeal of Louis IX. brought back all those whom the indifference of the pope had cooled; and the love of the French for their king, replacing religions enthusiasm, sufficed for the removal of all obstacles. The cities whose liberties the monarch had protected, voluntarily sent him considerable sums. The farmers of the royal domains, which were then very extensive, advanced the revenues of a year. The rich taxed themselves, and poured their hoards into the coffers of the king; poverty dropped its mite into the poor-boxes of churches; and we may add, that at that period there was scarcely a will made in the kingdom which did not contain some legacy towards the expenses of the holy war. The clergy were not content with addressing prayers to Heaven for the crusade, they paid the tenth of their revenues for the support of the soldiers of the cross.

The barons, nobles, and princes, who equipped themselves at their awn expense, imposed taxes on their vassals, and found, after the example of the king of France, the money necessary for the voyage in the revenues of their domains and in the pious generosity of the towns and cities. Many, as in other crusades, pledged their lands, sold their property, and ruined themselves, to provide means to support their soldiers and knights. They forgot their families, they forgot themselves in the sad preparations for departure, and appeared never to look forward to the period of return. Many prepared themselves for the voyage as they would have prepared for exile or death; the most pious of the Crusaders, as if they only went to the East to find a tomb, were particularly anxious to appear before God in a state of grace; they expiated their sins by penitence; they pardoned offences, repaired the ill they had done, disposed of their goods, gave them to the poor, or divided them amongst their natural heirs.

This disposition of men's minds was greatly to the advantage of humanity and justice; it imparted generous sentiments to people of property; whilst, in the wicked, it awakened a remorse that was nearly allied to virtue. Amidst civil wars and feudal anarchy, a crowd of men had enriched themselves by strife, rapine, and brigandage; religion inspired them with a salutary repentance, and this time of penitence was marked by a great number of restitutions, which for a moment made the triumphs of iniquity to be forgotten. The famous count de la Marche set the example; his conspiracies, his revolts, his unjust enterprises had often troubled the peace of the kingdom, and ruined a great number of families; he became desirous of expiating his faults; and to mitigate the just anger of God, he, by his will, ordered a complete restitution to be made of all the property he had acquired by injustice and violence. [282] The sieur de Joinville tells us, with great simplicity, in his History, that his conscience did not reproach him with anything serious, but that, nevertheless, he assembled his vassals and neighbours to offer them reparation for the wrongs he might have done them without knowing it.

In those days of repentance monasteries were founded and treasures lavished on churches: "The most sure means," said Louis IX., "to avoid perishing like the impious, is to love and enrich the place in which dwells the glory of the Lord." The piety of the Crusaders was not forgetful of the poor and infirm; their numerous offerings endowed cloisters as asylums for want; hospices, or small convents, for the reception of pilgrims; and particularly leper hospitals, which were established in all the provinces, the melancholy abodes of victims of the holy wars.

Louis IX. distinguished himself by his liberality towards churches and monasteries; but that which must particularly have drawn upon him the blessings of his people, was the care he took to repair all injustice committed in the administration of government. The holy monarch knew, that if kings are the images of God upon earth, they are never so truly so as when justice is seated beside them on the throne. Restitution-offices, established by his orders in the royal domains, were charged with the repairing of all wrongs that might have been committed by the agents or farmers of the king. In most of the great cities it was the duty of two commissaries, one an ecclesiastic, the other a layman, to hear and decide upon complaints made against his ministers and officers: a noble exercise of the supreme authority, which rather employs itself in seeking out the unfortunate to assist them, than the guilty to punish them! which watches for the murmurs of the poor, encourages the weak, and submits itself to the tribunal of the laws! It was not sufficient for Louis to have established regulations for the administration of justice,— their execution excited his most anxious solicitude. Preachers announced the intentions of the king in all the churches, and as if he thought himself responsible to God for all judgments pronounced in his name, the monarch secretly sent holy ecclesiastics and good monks to make fresh observations, and learn from faithful reporters, if the judges whom he believed to be worthy men, were not themselves corrupt. The historian pauses complacently over this touching picture; so noble an example presented to the kings of the earth, appeared likely to bring down the blessings of Heaven upon Saint Louis; and when we reflect upon the deplorable results of this crusade, with the chroniclers of his own time, we feel astonished that so many calamities should have been the reward of such exalted virtue. [283]

The preparations were now carried on with redoubled zeal and activity; all the provinces of France appeared to be in arms; the people of cities and country had but one thought, and that was the crusade. The great vassals assembled their knights and troops; the nobles and barons visited each other, or exchanged messengers, in order to settle the day of their departure. Relations and friends engaged to unite their banners, and place everything in common—money, glory, and perils. Devotional practices were mingled with military preparations. Warriors were seen laying aside the cuirass and sword, and walking, barefooted and in their shirts, to visit monasteries and churches, to which the relics of saints attracted the concourse of the faithful. Processions were formed in every parish; all the Crusaders appeared at the foot of the altars, and received the symbols of pilgrimage from the hands of the clergy. Prayers were put up in all churches for the success of the expedition. In families, abundance of tears were shed at the moment of departure; and most of the pilgrims, on receiving these last endearments of their friends, seemed to feel, more than ever, the value of all they were leaving behind them. The historian of Saint Louis tells us, that after visiting Blanchicourt and Saint-Urbain, where holy relics were deposited, he would not once turn his eyes towards Joinville, for his heart was softened at the idea of the beautiful castle he was leaving, and of his two children. [284] The leaders of the crusade took with them all the warlike youth, and left in many countries nothing but a weak and unarmed population; many abandoned castles and fortresses must, naturally, fall to ruins; much flourishing land must be changed into a desert, and a vast many families must be left without support. The people, no doubt, had cause to regret the nobles whose authority was supported by kindnesses, and who, after the example of Saint Louis, loved truth and justice, and protected the weak and the innocent; but there were some whose departure was witnessed with gladness; and more than one town, more than one village, rejoiced at seeing the donjon, from which they had been accustomed to experience all the miseries of servitude, empty and abandoned.

It was an affecting spectacle to see the families of artisans and poor villagers lead their children to the barons and knights, and say to them: "You will be their fathers; you will watch over them amidst the perils of war and of the sea." The barons and knights promised to bring back their soldiers to the West, or to perish with them in fight; and the opinion of the people, the nobility, and the clergy, devoted, beforehand, all who should fail in this sacred promise, to the anger of God and the contempt of men.

Amidst these preparations, the most profound calm prevailed throughout the kingdom. In all preceding crusades, the multitude had exercised great violence against the Jews; but by the firmness and wisdom of Saint Louis, the Jews, though depositaries of immense wealth, and always skilful in taking advantage of circumstances to enrich themselves, were respected among a nation they had plundered, and which was now completing its own ruin by the holy war. Adventurers and vagabonds were not admitted beneath the banners of the cross; and, upon the demand of Saint Louis, the pope forbade all who had committed great crimes to take up arms in the cause of Christ. These precautions, which had never been observed in former crusades, were highly calculated to insure the maintenance of order and discipline in the Christian army. Among the crowd that presented themselves to go into Asia, artisans and labourers met with the best reception,—which is a remarkable circumstance, and clearly proves that views of a wise policy were mingled with sentiments of devotion, and that, though the ostensible object was the deliverance of Jerusalem, hopes were entertained of founding useful colonies in the East.

At the appointed time Louis IX., accompanied by his brothers, the duke of Anjou and the count d'Artois, repaired to the abbey of St. Denis. [285] After having implored the support of the apostles of France, he received from the hands of the legate the pilgrim's staff and scrip, and that oriflamme which his predecessors had already twice unfurled before the nations of the East. Louis then returned to Paris, where he heard mass in the church of Notre Dame. The same day he quitted his capital, not again to enter it before his return from the Holy Land. The people and clergy were softened to tears, and accompanied him to the abbey of St. Antoine, singing psalms by the way. There he mounted on horseback to go to Corbeil, at which place the Queen Blanche and Queen Marguerite were to meet him.

The king gave two more days to the affairs of his kingdom, and confided the regency to his mother, whose firmness and wisdom had defended and preserved the crown during the troubles of his minority. If anything could excuse Louis IX., and justify his pious obstinacy, it was his leaving his country in profound peace. He had renewed the truce with the king of England; and Germany and Italy were so occupied with their own internal discords, that they could not give France the least subject for alarm. Louis, after having employed every precaution against the spirit of disaffection, took with him into the Holy Land almost all the powerful nobles that had disturbed the kingdom. The county of Mâcon, sold at the end of the preceding crusade, had recently reverted to the crown; Normandy had escaped from the yoke of the English; the counties of Thoulouse and Provence, by the marriage of the counts of Anjou and Poictiers, were about to become apanages of the princes of the royal family. Louis IX., after he took the cross, never ceased in his endeavours to preserve the recent conquests of France, to appease the murmurs of the people, and remove every pretext for revolt. The spirit of justice, which was observable in all his institutions; the remembrance of his virtues, which appeared more estimable amidst the general grief caused by his departure; the religion which he had caused to flourish by his example, were quite sufficient to maintain order and peace during his absence.

As soon as Louis had placed the administration of his kingdom in other hands, he gave himself up to the exercises of piety, and appeared to be no more than the most meek of Christians. The dress and attributes of a pilgrim became the only adornments of a powerful monarch. He wore no more splendid stuffs, no more valuable furs; his arms even, and the harness of his horses, glittered with nothing but the polish of steel and iron. His example had so much influence, says Joinville, that on the voyage not a single instance of an embroidered coat was seen, either upon the king or any one else. When endeavouring to reform splendour in equipages or dress, Louis caused the money he had been accustomed to expend in these to be distributed to the poor. Thus royal magnificence was in him nothing but the luxury of charity.

Queen Blanche accompanied him as far as Cluny. This princess was persuaded she should never see her son again until they met in heaven, and took leave of him in the most affectionate manner; the tears of mother and son bearing witness to the truth of their grief at parting. On his way, he saw the pope at Lyons, and conjured him, for the last time, to be merciful to Frederick, whom reverses had humiliated, and who implored pardon. After having represented the great interests of the crusade, after having spoken in the name of the numerous pilgrims who were abandoning everything for the cause of Christ, the pious mind of the king was astonished to find the pontiff still inexorable. The king then directed all his attention to the prosecution of his journey. Innocent promised to protect the kingdom of France against the heretic Frederick and the king of England; the latter of whom he always styled his vassal: he witnessed without regret the departure of a prince venerated for his love of justice, whose presence in Europe might be an obstacle to his policy. The sovereign pontiff had not much trouble in keeping his promise of defending the independence and peace of France; for the discords he excited in other states preserved that kingdom from all foreign annoyance during the time of the crusade.

The fleet, which awaited Louis at Aigues-Mortes, was composed of twenty-eight vessels, without reckoning those that were to transport the horses and the provisions. The king embarked, followed by his two brothers, Charles duke of Anjou, and Robert count d'Artois, and the queen Marguerite, who did not dread less the idea of remaining with her mother-in-law than that of living away from her husband. [286] Alphonse, count of Poictiers, deferred his departure till the following year, and returned to Paris to assist the queen regent with his counsels and authority. When the whole army of the Crusaders was embarked, the signal was given, the priests, according to the custom in maritime expeditions, sang the *Veni Creator*, and the fleet set sail.

France had then no marine, the sailors and pilots were almost all Spaniards or Italians. Two Genoese performed the functions of commanders or admirals. A great part of the barons and knights had never before seen the sea, and everything they saw filled them with surprise and dread; they invoked all the saints of Paradise, and recommended their souls to God. The good Joinville does not at all dissemble his fright, and cannot help saying: "A great fool is he who, having any sin on his soul, places himself in such a danger; for if he goes to sleep at night, he cannot be certain he shall not find himself at the bottom of the sea in the morning." [287]

Louis IX. embarked at Aigues-Mortes, the 25th of August, and arrived at Cyprus on the 21st of September. [288] Henry, grandson of Guy of Lusignan, who obtained the kingdom of Cyprus in the third crusade, received the king of France at Limisso, and conducted him to his capital of Nicosia, amidst the acclamations of the people, nobility, and clergy.

A short time after the arrival of the Crusaders, it was decided in a council, that the arms of the Christians should, in the first place, be directed against Egypt. The reverses that had been met with on the banks of the Nile, in preceding wars, did not at all alarm the king of France and his barons; it is even more than probable that Louis, before he left his kingdom, had formed the design of carrying the war into the country from which the Mussulmans drew their wealth and their strength. The king of Cyprus, who had recently received the title of king of Jerusalem from the pope, the more strongly applauded, this determination, from its giving him reason to hope to be delivered from the most formidable of his neighbours, and the most cruel enemy of the Christian colonies in Syria. This prince also caused a crusade to be preached in his kingdom, for the sake of being placed in a condition to accompany the French Crusaders, and associate himself usefully in their conquests. He proposed to the king of France and his barons to wait till he had concluded his preparations. "The lords and prelates of Cyprus," says William of Nangis, "all took the cross, appeared before Louis, and told him they would go with him wherever it should please him to lead them, if he would stay till the winter had passed away." As Louis and the principal French nobles appeared but little disposed to delay their march, the Cypriots spared neither protestations of friendship, caresses, nor prayers to detain them. Every day was devoted to rejoicings and feastings, in which the nobility and wealthy men of the kingdom exhibited the splendour of eastern courts. The enchanting aspect of the isle, a country rich in all the delicious productions of nature, particularly that Cyprus wine which Solomon himself has not disdained to celebrate, seconded in a powerful manner the entreaties and seductions of the court of Nicosia. It was decided that the Christian army should not depart before the following spring.

It was not long before they became fully aware of the error they had committed. Amidst the excessive abundance that reigned in their camp, the Crusaders gave themselves up to intemperance; in a country in which pagan fables placed the altars of voluptuousness, the virtue of the pilgrims was every day exposed to fresh trials; a protracted idleness relaxed the discipline of the army, and, to crown these evils, a pestilential disease exercised great ravages among the defenders of the cross. The pilgrims had to lament the death of more than two hundred and fifty knights from this calamity. Contemporary chronicles mention among the lords and prelates that were victims to it, the counts of Dreux and Vendôme, Robert, bishop of Beauvais, and the brave William des Barres; the army had likewise to regret the loss of the last of the race of the Archambault de Bourbons, whose county became afterwards the heritage of the children of Saint Louis, and gave to the royal family of France a name that it has rendered for ever illustrious in the annals of that country.

A great number of barons and knights were in want of money to maintain their troops, and Louis freely opened his treasury to them. The sieur de Joinville, who had no more than one hundred and twenty livres tournois [289] left, received from the monarch eight hundred livres; a considerable sum in those days.

Many of the nobles complained of having sold their lands and ruined themselves to follow the king to the crusade. The liberality of Louis could not possibly satisfy all these complainants. A great number of knights, after being ruined by the abode in the isle of Cyprus, could not endure the idleness they were condemned to, but were anxious to set out for Syria or Egypt, hoping to make the Saracens pay the expenses of the war. Louis had a great deal of trouble to restrain them; historians agree in saying that he was *only half obeyed*; therefore, he had much more frequent occasion to exercise his patience and evangelical mildness than his authority; and if he succeeded in appeasing all discords and suppressing all murmurs, it was less by the ascendancy of his power than by that of his virtue.

Differences arose between the Greek clergy and the Latin clergy of the isle of Cyprus. Louis succeeded in putting an end to them. The Templars and Hospitallers appealed to him as judge in their constantly reviving quarrels; he made them swear to be reconciled, and to have no other enemies than those of Christ. The Genoese and Pisans resident at Ptolemaïs, had long and serious disputes, both parties having recourse to arms, and nothing appeared able to check the fury and scandal of a civil war in a Christian city. The wise mediation of Louis reëstablished peace. Aitho, king of Armenia, and Bohemond, prince of Antioch and Tripoli, implacable enemies, both sent ambassadors to the king of France: he induced them to conclude a truce: thus Louis IX. appeared among the nations of the East as an angel of peace and concord.

At this period the territory of Antioch was ravaged by vagabond bands of Turcomans; Louis sent Bohemond five hundred cross-bowmen. Aitho had just formed an alliance with the Tartars, and was preparing to invade the states of the sultan of Iconium in Asia Minor. As the Armenian prince enjoyed a great reputation in the East for skill and bravery, many French knights, impatient to display their valour, left Cyprus for the purpose of joining his standard and sharing the fruits of his victories. Joinville, after having spoken of their departure, says nothing of their exploits, and only informs us of their unhappy destiny by these words: "not one of them ever came back." [290]

Fame had announced the arrival of Louis throughout all the countries of the East, and the news produced a great sensation among both Mussulmans and Christians. A prediction, that was credited in the most distant regions, and which missionaries found spread even through Persia, announced that a king of the Franks was destined speedily to disperse all infidels and deliver Asia from the sacrilegious worship and laws of Mahomet. It was believed that the time was now come for the accomplishment of this prediction. A crowd of Christians hastened from Syria, Egypt, and all the countries of the East, to salute him whom God had sent to fulfil his divine promises.

It was at this period that Louis received an embassy that excited the curiosity and attention of the Crusaders in the highest degree; the marvellous account of it occupies a conspicuous place in the chronicles of the middle ages. [291] This embassy came from a Tartar prince, named Ecalthaï, [292] who professed himself to be converted to the Christian faith, and displayed the most ardent zeal for the triumph of the Gospel. The head of this deputation, named David, remitted to the king a letter filled with sentiments expressed with so much exaggeration as ought to have rendered it doubtful; he said that the great khan had received baptism three years before, and that he was prepared to assist the expedition of the French Crusaders with all his power. The news of this embassy soon spread through the army, and from that time nothing was talked of but the promised succour of the great khan or emperor of the Tartars; the leaders and soldiers flocked to the residence of Louis to see the ambassador of the prince Ecalthaï, whom they considered *as one of the first barons of Tartary.*

The king of France interrogated the deputies several times respecting their journey, their country, and the character and disposition of their sovereign; and as all he heard flattered his most cherished thoughts, he conceived no mistrust, and discovered no signs of imposture in their replies. The Tartar ambassadors were received at his court, and admitted to his table; he himself conducted them to the celebration of divine service in the metropolitan church of Nicosia, where all the people were edified by their devotion.

At their departure, the king of France and the legate of the pope charged them with several letters [293] for the prince Ecalthaï and the great khan of the Tartars. To these letters were added magnificent presents; among which was a scarlet tent, upon which Louis had caused to be worked "The Annunciation of the Virgin Mary, the Mother of God, and all the other points of faith." The king wrote to Queen Blanche, as did the legate to the sovereign pontiff, to announce the extraordinary embassy that had arrived from the most distant regions of the East. The propitious news of an alliance with the Tartars, who were then looked upon as the most formidable of all nations, spread joy among the people of the West, and increased their hopes of the success of the crusade.

Missionaries that were sent into Tartary by Louis were very soon satisfied that the conversion of the great khan was nothing but a fable. The Mogul ambassadors had advanced many other impostures in their accounts, which has induced some learned moderns to think that this great embassy [294] was nothing but a trick, the contrivance of which may be attributed to some Armenian monks. However it may be, there can be no doubt that the Moguls, who were at war with the Mussulmans, might have some interest in conciliating the Christians, and might be led, from that time, to consider the Franks as useful auxiliaries.

Winter, in the mean time, was drawing towards an end, and the period fixed upon for the departure of the French Crusaders was approaching. The king of France ordered a great number of flat-bottomed boats to be constructed, to facilitate the descent of the Christian army upon the coast of Egypt. As the Genoese fleet, in which the French had embarked at Aigues-Mortes, had left the port of Lemisso, it required considerable trouble to get together, from all parts, vessels sufficient to transport the army and the numerous magazines formed in the isle of Cyprus. Louis IX. applied to the Genoese and Venetians established on the coast of Syria, who, to the great scandal of the knights and barons, showed, in this instance, more cupidity than devotion, and placed an exorbitant price upon services demanded of them in the name of Christ.

At this time Louis received a communication from the emperor of Germany, still pursued by the thunders of Rome. This prince sent provisions to the Crusaders, and expressed great grief, in his letters, at being unable to share the perils of the holy war. The king of France thanked Frederick, and sighed at the obstinacy of the pope, which deprived the defenders of the cross of such a powerful auxiliary.

Preparations were continued with the greatest activity; every day fresh Crusaders arrived, who came from the ports of the West, or had passed the winter in the isles of the Archipelago, or on the coasts of Greece. All the nobility of Cyprus had taken the cross, and were preparing for their conflict with the infidels. The greatest harmony prevailed between the two nations; in the Greek as well as the Latin churches, prayers were offered up to Heaven for the success of the Christian arms; and throughout the host nothing was talked of but the wonders of the East, and the riches of Egypt, which they were about to conquer.

Whilst enthusiasm and joy were thus exuberant among the Christian warriors, the grand masters of St. John and the Temple wrote to Louis IX., to consult him upon the possibility of opening a negotiation with the sultan of Cairo. The leaders of these two orders anxiously desired to break the chains of their knights who were detained in captivity since the defeat of Gaza; they did not otherwise partake with the Crusaders their blind confidence in victory; experience of other crusades had taught them that the warriors of the West, at first very redoubtable, almost always began their wars with splendour, but that afterwards, weakened by discord, exhausted by the fatigues of a distant expedition, and sometimes led away by their natural inconstancy, they only thought of returning into Europe, abandoning the Christian colonies to all the furies of an enemy irritated by former defeats. According to these considerations, the two grand masters would have wished to take advantage of the powerful succours from the West, to conclude a useful and durable peace. The mode of negotiation presented them much greater future advantages than a war, whose chances were doubtful, and whose perils might, in the end, all recoil upon them.

Their pacific message arrived at the moment when nothing way spoken of in the Christian army but the conquests they were about to make; when all minds were heated by the enthusiasm of glory, and the hope of a rich booty. The proposition alone of peace with the infidels was a true subject of scandal for these warriors, who believed themselves called upon to destroy, throughout the East, the domination and the power of all the enemies of Christ. The general surprise and indignation gave credence to the blackest calumnies against the grand master of the Temple, who was loudly accused of keeping up a secret intelligence with the sultan of Cairo, and of having joined in barbarous ceremonies to bind this impious union. Louis IX., who did not come into the East to sign a treaty of peace and to deliver only a few prisoners, shared the indignation of his companions in arms, and forbade the grand masters of the Temple and St. John to reiterate propositions insulting to the Christian warriors, insulting to him.

The Crusaders, intoxicated with their future success, were not aware of half the obstacles they were about to encounter; they thought more about the wealth than the strength of their enemies; acquainted with neither the climate nor the country to which their wishes were directed, their ignorance redoubled their security, and fed hopes that were doomed soon to fade away.

The leaders of the crusade were particularly sanguine with respect to the divisions of the Mussulman princes, who were quarrelling for the provinces of Syria and Egypt: in fact, since the death of Saladin, discord had rarely ceased to trouble the family of the Ayoubites. But as their dissensions broke out in civil wars, and as civil wars rendered the population more warlike, their empire, which grew weaker every day inwardly, often, consequently, became the stronger outwardly; when common danger united the Mussulman powers, or that one of those powers mastered the rest, everything was to be dreaded from an empire always tottering in peace, but which seemed to derive fresh strength from the animosities and perils of a war against the Christians.

Malek Saleh Negmeddin, who then reigned in Egypt, was the son of the sultan Camel, celebrated by the victory gained at Mansourah over the army of John of Brienne and the legate Pelagius. Driven from the throne by a conspiracy, he endeavoured to recover it by arms; conquered, he fell into the chains of his rival, and profited by the lessons of adversity. Very soon, the esteem in which his abilities were held; the hatred which the prince who reigned in his place inspired; the want of change, and perhaps a certain partiality for revolt and treason, recalled him to empire. The new sovereign showed himself much more skilful and more fortunate than his predecessors; he knew how to preserve obedience in the provinces; to maintain discipline in his army; and to keep fear alive among his enemies. He had taken advantage of the arms of the Carismians to get possession of Damascus, and to crush both the Christians and their allies. From this period Negmeddin extended his conquests upon the banks of the Euphrates, and at length gathered under his laws the greater part of the empire of Saladin.

At the moment Louis IX. landed in the isle of Cyprus, the sultan of Cairo was in Syria, where he was making war against the prince of Aleppo, and held the city of Emessa in siege. He was acquainted with all the projects of the Christians, and gave orders for the defence of all the avenues of Egypt. When he learnt that the Christian army was about to embark, he immediately abandoned the siege of Emessa, and concluded a truce with enemies of whom he entertained very little dread, to return to his states that were threatened with invasion.

The Orientals considered the French as the bravest people of the race of the Franks, and the king of France as the most redoubtable monarch of the West. The preparations of Negmeddin were commensurate with the dread these new enemies naturally inspired. He neglected nothing in fortifying the coasts or in provisioning Damietta, which was most likely to be the object of the first hostilities. A numerous fleet was equipped, descended the Nile, and was placed at the mouth of the river; an army, commanded by Fakreddin, the most skilful of the emirs, encamped on the coast, to the west of the mouth of the river, at the very same point where, thirty-three years before, the army of John of Brienne had landed.

All these preparations would, no doubt, have been sufficient to meet the first attacks of the Crusaders, if the sultan of Cairo had been able to direct them himself, and command his troops in person; but he was attacked by a disease which his physicians pronounced to be mortal. In a state of things in which everything depended upon the presence and life of the prince, the certainty of his approaching end necessarily weakened confidence and zeal, cooled the general courage, and was injurious to the execution of all the measures taken for the defence of the country.

Such was the military and political situation of Egypt at the time Louis embarked from the ports of the isle of Cyprus. Many historians say, that before his departure, according to the custom of chivalry, he sent a herald-at-arms to the sultan Negmeddin, to declare war against him. In the early crusades, many Christian princes had in this manner addressed chivalric messages to the Mussulman powers they were about to attack: it is quite possible that Louis might imitate this example; but the letter attributed to him bears no character of truth about it. The same historians add, that the sultan of Cairo could not refrain from tears on reading the letter of St. Louis. His reply, quoted in Makrisy, is at least conformable to his known character, and to the spirit of the Mussulman princes. He affected to brave the unexpected threats and attacks of the disciples of Christ; he referred with pride to the victories of the Mussulmans over the Christians; and whilst reproaching the king of France with the injustice of his aggressions, he quoted in his letter this passage from the Koran:—"They who fight unjustly shall perish."

This message contained predictions that were but too fully realized in the end. There is nothing, however, to lead us to believe that any correspondence was then established between Louis and the sultan of Cairo. Prudence, at least, required the king of France to send messengers and emissaries into Egypt, to reconnoitre the state, strength, and resources of the country. It is more than probable, that in preceding crusades it was not only in obedience to the spirit of chivalry, but to ascertain the position of their enemies that ambassadors were sent; we must confess, however, that we cannot find in any chronicle of the times evidence of their having taken any precaution of this kind. A foresight which might bear the slightest association with timidity, stratagem, or even policy, was not the least in accordance with the character of Louis and his knights. History has no hesitation in affirming that the Crusaders, ready at this period to embark for Egypt, knew nothing of the countries into which they were about to carry their arms, but that which they had learnt from the uncertain accounts of common report.

The signal of departure was given on the Friday before Pentecost; and a numerous fleet, in which embarked the French army and the warriors of the isle of Cyprus, [295] sailed gallantly out from the port of Limisso. "This was a thing most beautiful to behold," says Joinville; "for it appeared as if the sea, as far as the eye could reach, was covered with the sails of vessels, which were to the number of eight hundred, as well large as small." All at once a wind blowing full from the coast of Egypt gave rise to a violent storm, which dispersed all the fleet; and Louis IX., who was forced to put back to port, found, with great grief, that at least the half of his vessels had been carried by the wind on to the coasts of Syria. At this moment of disappointment, however, unexpected reinforcements arrived, which restored the hopes of Louis and his captains. These consisted of the duke of Burgundy, who had passed the winter in the Morea; William of Salisbury, at the head of two hundred English knights; and William of Villehardouin, prince of Achaia, who forgot the dangers of the Latin empire of Constantinople to go and fight the infidels on the banks of the Nile and the Jordan. Without waiting for the vessels which the tempest had dispersed, they again set sail, and the fleet, with a favourable wind, directed its course towards Egypt. On the fourth day, at sunrise, the watch on deck cried, "Land! land!" A sailor, who served as pilot, ascended to the round top of the leading vessel, and such was the sentiment which the sight of the land inhabited by the infidels inspired in the Christians, that this man cried out, "We have nothing to do but to recommend ourselves to God; for here we are, before Damietta." These words flew from rank to rank, and the whole fleet drew as near as they could to the vessel of Louis IX. The principal leaders endeavoured to get on board of it; the king awaited them in a warlike attitude and exhorted them to offer thanks to God for having brought them face to face with the enemies of Jesus Christ. As the greater part of the leaders seemed to fear his life would be too much exposed in the course of a war which must be terrible: "Follow my example," said he to them; "leave me to brave all perils, and in the midst of the hottest fight never once think that the safety of the state and the Church resides in my person; you yourselves are the state and the Church, and you ought to see in me nothing but a man whose life, like that of any other, may be dissipated like a shadow, when it shall please the God for whom we combat." Thus Louis forgot himself and his state, and before the infidels, the king of France was but a simple soldier of Jesus Christ.

This discourse animated the courage of the barons and knights; orders were given for the whole fleet to prepare for action. In every vessel the warriors embraced each other with joy at the approach of peril; such as quarrels had alienated, swore to forget all divisions and injuries, and to conquer or to die together. Joinville says he forced two knights, who had been irreconcilable enemies, to make peace, by persuading them that their discord might draw down the maledictions of Heaven, and that union among the Christian soldiers could alone open to them the road to Egypt.

Whilst the Crusaders were thus preparing, the Mussulmans neglected nothing for their defence; their sentinels had perceived the Christian fleet, from the walls of Damietta, and the news was soon spread through the city; a bell, which had remained in the great mosque since the conquest of John of Brienne, gave the signal of danger, and was heard on both sides of the river. Four Mussulman galleys advanced to reconnoitre the strength of the Crusaders; three of them were sunk, and the fourth, getting back with great difficulty to the Nile, announced to the infidels what enemies they had to contend with.

In the mean time the Christian fleet advanced in order of battle, and cast anchor within a quarter of a league of the coast, at the moment at which the sun had performed half his daily course. The shore and sea presented the most imposing spectacle; the coast of Egypt was *lined with all the powers of the soldan, who were people goodly to look upon.* The sea appeared to be covered with ships, over which floated the banners of the cross. The Mussulman fleet, laden with soldiers and machines of war, defended the entrance of the Nile. Fakreddin, the leader of the infidel army, appeared amidst their ranks in a panoply so splendid, that Joinville, in his surprise, compares him to the sun. The heavens and the earth resounded with the noise of the bended horns and the naccaires, [296] a kind of enormous kettledrum, a thing very frightful to hear, and very strange to the French. [297]

All the leaders assembled in council in the king's vessel; some proposed to defer the descent till the vessels which had been dispersed by the tempest should rejoin them: "To attack the infidels without having all their forces, would be to give them an advantage that might greatly elevate their pride; and even if success were certain, it appeared but just to wait, that all the Crusaders might have their share of the glory they came so far to seek." Some went still further, and spoke of the embarrassments and perils of a descent in an unknown country; of the disorders which must accompany a first attack; and of the difficulty of rallying the army and fleet, if the obstacles they met with should prove invincible. Louis IX. did not at all agree with this opinion: "We have not come thus far," he said, "to listen coolly to the menaces and insults of our enemies, or to remain, during several days motionless spectators of their preparations. To temporize is to raise their courage, and weaken the ardour of the French warriors. We have neither road nor port, in which we can shelter ourselves from the winds, or from the unexpected attacks of the Saracens; a second tempest may again disperse what remains of our fleet, and deprive us of all means of beginning the war with a chance of success. To-day God offers us victory; later he will punish us for having neglected the opportunity to conquer."

The majority of the leaders were of the opinion of Louis IX., and it was resolved that the descent should be made on the morrow. A strict watch was preserved during the night; a vast number of flambeaux were kept burning, and vessels were placed near the mouth of the Nile, to observe the motions of the Saracens.

At daybreak the whole fleet weighed anchor, and the Mussulmans at the same time got under arms. Their infantry and cavalry occupied the entire shore of the point at which they expected the Crusaders to land.

When the vessels drew near the shore, the Christian warriors got into the barks that accompanied the fleet, and ranged themselves in two lines. Louis IX., accompanied by the two princes his brothers, and his chosen knights, placed himself at the right point. The cardinal legate, bearing the cross of the Saviour, was on his right hand, and in a bark in front of him floated the oriflamme of France.

The count of Jaffa, of the illustrious family of Brienne, was at the left point towards the mouth of the Nile; he appeared at the head of the knights from the isle of Cyprus and the barons of Palestine. He was on board the lightest bark of the fleet. This boat bore the arms of the counts of Jaffa, painted on its poop and prow. Around his standard floated banderoles of a thousand colours, and three hundred rowers impelled the vessel through the waves like the flight of the swallow over the stream. Erard of Brienne, surrounded by a chosen troop, occupied the centre of the line, with Baldwin of Rheims, who commanded a thousand warriors. The knights and barons stood erect in their boats, looking earnestly at the shore, lance in hand, with their horses beside them. In the front and on the wings of the army, a crowd of crossbow-men were placed to keep off the enemy. [298]

As soon as they were within bow-shot, a shower of stones, arrows, and javelins was poured at the same instant from the shore and from the line of the Crusaders. The ranks of the Christians appeared for a moment shaken. The king commanded the rowers to redouble their efforts to gain the shore. He himself set the first example; in spite of the legate, who endeavoured to restrain him, he plunged into the waves, in full armour, his buckler over his breast, and his sword in hand; the water being up to his shoulders:

the whole Christian army, after the example of the king, cast themselves into the sea, crying, "*Montjoie! St. Denis!*" This multitude of men and horses, endeavouring to gain the shore, elevated the waves which broke at the feet of the Saracens; the warriors pressed on, clashing against each other in their progress—nothing was heard but the noise of the waves and the oars, the cries of the soldiers and the sailors, and the tumultuous shock of the barks and vessels, which advanced in disorder.

The Mussulman battalions assembled on the shore could not stop the French warriors. Joinville and Baldwin of Rheims landed the first; after them came the count of Jaffa. They were drawing up in order of battle, when the cavalry of the Saracens came pouring down upon them; the Crusaders closed in their ranks, covered themselves with their bucklers, and presenting the points of their lances, checked the impetuosity of the enemy. All their companions who had reached the shore, immediately formed in rear of this battalion.

Already the oriflamme was planted on the shore; Louis had landed. Without giving the least reflection to the danger, he immediately fell on his knees to offer up his thanks to Heaven; and springing up again, filled with fresh ardour, called his bravest knights around him. An Arab historian relates that the king of the Franks then caused his tent to be pitched, which was of a bright scarlet, and attracted all eyes. At length, all the army being landed, a sanguinary contest began on every part of the coast; the Saracens and Franks, seeking and attacking each other, formed one conflicting mass. Nobody remained inactive; the two fleets quickly became engaged at the mouth of the Nile. Whilst the shore and the sea resounded thus with the shock of arms, Queen Marguerite and the duchess of Anjou, who remained on board a vessel at a distance, awaited in terrible anxiety the issue of the double battle; they offered up fervent prayers, and pious ecclesiastics assembled around them, joined in holy psalms to obtain the protection of the God of armies.

The fleet of the Saracens was soon dispersed; many of the vessels were sunk, the remainder escaped up the river. In the mean time, the troops of Fakreddin, broken in all directions, retired in the greatest confusion; the French pursuing them up to their intrenchments. After a last desperate struggle, the Mussulmans abandoned their camp and the western bank of the Nile, leaving several of their emirs on the field of battle: nothing could resist the French, animated by the presence and the example of their king.

In the course of the battle several messenger pigeons had been sent to the sultan of Cairo, whose malady confined him in a small town situated between Damietta and Mansourah: as no answer was received, a report of his death began to prevail, and completed the discouragement of the Egyptian troops. Many of the emirs were impatient to know, and at the same time were doubtful of the fate that awaited them under a new reign. Several deserted their standards, and by that means augmented the disorder: towards evening the whole army dispersed, and the soldiers, abandoned by their leaders, thought of nothing but seeking safety in flight. [299] The Crusaders remained masters of the coast and of both banks of the Nile; and this glorious victory had cost but little Christian blood, for only two or three knights were killed: of the French nobles the army had only to deplore the count de la Marche, who appeared to seek death, and, dying thus by the side of his king, expiated, say our historians, his numerous treasons and crimes.

Towards the end of the day, the tents were pitched on the field of battle; the clergy chanted the *Te Deum*, and the night was passed in rejoicings. Whilst the victorious army was thus giving itself up to exultation, the greatest confusion reigned in Damietta; the fugitives had passed through the city, spreading, as they went, the contagion of the fear that pursued them. Fakreddin himself gave no orders for the security of the place: the inhabitants expected every instant to see the French enter; some dreaded a surprise, others feared a siege; there was no one to reassure them, and the darkness of night came on to complete their terror and confusion. Fear rendered them barbarous; they pitilessly massacred all the Christians that were in the city; the troops, on retiring, pillaged the houses and set fire to the public edifices; whole families abandoned their homes, carrying with them their furniture and movable wealth. The garrison was composed of the bravest of the Arab tribe of the Benou-Kenaneh; [300] but fear gained dominion over them as well as the rest; they abandoned the towers and the ramparts intrusted to their guardianship, and fled away with the army of Fakreddin. Before the dawn of day, the city was without defenders, and almost without inhabitants.

The columns of flame that arose from the bosom of the city were soon observed in the Christian camp; the whole horizon was on fire. On the morrow, at daybreak, the soldiers advanced towards the city, all the gates of which they found open. They met with nothing in the streets but the carcasses of the victims immolated by the despair and fanaticism of the infidels, and a few living Christians, who, having contrived to conceal themselves from the murderers and executioners, had, in their turn, massacred all the Mussulmans whom age and infirmities prevented from flying with their compatriots. The soldiers returned to announce what they had seen, and could scarcely gain credit from their companions. The army advanced cautiously in order of battle. When they were assured that the city was deserted, the Crusaders took possession of it. They employed themselves, in the first place, to stop the progress of the flames; then the soldiers spread themselves throughout the city, for the purpose of pillaging it, and all that escaped the conflagration became the reward of victory.

In the mean time, the king of France, the pope's legate, and the patriarch of Jerusalem, followed by a crowd of prelates and ecclesiastics, entered Damietta in procession, and repaired to the great mosque, which was once more converted into a church, and consecrated to the Holy Virgin, the mother of Jesus Christ. The French monarch, the clergy, and all the leaders of the army, marched with heads uncovered and barefooted, singing psalms of thanksgiving, and attributing to God all the glory of this miraculous conquest.

The news of this victory was soon spread through all the Egyptian provinces. The continuator of Tabary, who was then at Cairo, informs us in his History, that this event was considered as one of the greatest calamities. All Mussulmans were sunk in despondency and fear; the most brave even despaired of being able to save Egypt.

Negmeddin was still ill, and unable to mount on horseback; the defeat of his army, and the victory of the Christians, were announced to him by the soldiers and inhabitants that had fled from Damietta. He broke into a violent rage against the garrison, and pronounced a sentence of instant death upon fifty-four of the most guilty: in vain they alleged the retreat of the emir Fakreddin as an excuse; the sultan said they merited death for having feared the arms of their enemies more than the anger of their master. One of these, condemned to suffer with his son, a young man of singular beauty, implored the sultan to allow him to die first; the sultan refused even this grace, and the unhappy father underwent the agony of seeing his son killed before his eyes, ere he himself was handed over to the executioner. When we reflect upon the barbarity of these executions, we are astonished that a prince without an army should find instruments to execute his wrath, or even that he should dare to display it in this frightful manner upon deserters and cowards; but this public and awful exhibition of punishment, which kept up the belief in the power of the master, acted strongly upon the minds of the multitude, and assisted in bringing back the vulgar crowd of the Mussulman soldiery to discipline and order. But it was not thus with the principal emirs; already but little disposed to tremble before a sovereign whom they regarded as their own work, and who stood in such need of their support. The sultan would willingly have punished Fakreddin, but the circumstances, says an Arabian historian, dictated patience. He contented himself with addressing a few reproaches to him. "The presence of these Franks," said he to him, "must have something very terrible in it, since men like you cannot support it during one whole day." These words created more indignation than fear among the emirs that were present, and some of them looked at Fakreddin, as if to tell him they were ready to sacrifice the sultan; but the print of the cold hand of death was on the brow of the sultan, and the sight of a dying man took away the wish to commit a useless crime:—deplorable situation of a prince who had within a few leagues of him a formidable enemy, that he was not able to contend with; near him traitors, that he did not dare to punish; and who, whilst seeing his authority every day diminish, and feeling himself hourly dying, appeared to have no salvation to expect for either himself or his empire!

During this time the Crusaders established themselves in Damietta without obstacle; Queen Marguerite and the other princesses, with the legate and the clergy, occupied the palaces and principal houses; the rest of the city was abandoned to the pilgrims who did not bear arms: the towers and ramparts were guarded by five hundred knights, and the Christian army was encamped upon the plain on the banks of the Nile. In this situation the Crusaders only thought of enjoying the fruits of their victory in peace, and appeared to have forgotten that they had still enemies to contend with.

The sultan of Cairo had caused himself to be transported to Mansourah, where he endeavoured to rally his army, and re-establish discipline among the troops. Whether he had recovered from his terror, or that he was willing to conceal his alarm and the progress of his malady, he sent several messages to Louis IX. In one of these letters, Negmeddin, joining menaces to irony, congratulated the king of France upon his arrival in Egypt, and asked him at what period it would please him to depart again. The Mussulman prince added, among other things, that the quantity of provisions and agricultural instruments with which the Crusaders had burdened their vessels, appeared to him to be a useless precaution; and to perform the duties of hospitality towards the Franks, in a manner worthy of himself and them, he engaged to supply them with corn during their sojourn in his states. Negmeddin, in another message, offered the king of France a general battle on the 25th day of June, in a place that should be determined upon. Louis IX. answered the first letter of the sultan by saying that he had landed in Egypt on the day he had appointed, and as to the day of his departure, he should think about it at leisure. With regard to the proposed battle, the king contented himself with replying, that he would neither accept the day nor choose the place, because all days and all places were equally fit for fighting with infidels. The French monarch added, that he would attack the sultan wherever he should meet with him; that he would pursue him at all times and without intermission; and would treat him as an enemy till God had touched his heart, and Christians might consider him as a brother.

Fortune presented King Louis with an opportunity and the means of accomplishing his threats. The Crusaders, whom the tempest had separated from the fleet, continued to arrive every day, and the knights of the Temple and of St. John, who had been accused of being anxious for peace, joined the banners of the army, and breathed nothing but war. They were acquainted with the country, and with the best manner of combating the infidels; and with this useful reinforcement, the king was able to undertake an expedition against Alexandria, or, by obtaining possession of Mansourah, render himself master of the route to Cairo. After the taking of Damietta, several of the leaders had proposed to pursue the Mussulmans, and take advantage of the terror that the first victory of the Christians had inspired. But the period was approaching at which the waters of the Nile began to rise, and the remembrance of the overthrow of Pelagius and John of Brienne, dispelled the idea of marching against the capital of Egypt. Before he pursued his conquests, Louis wished to wait the arrival of his brother, the count of Poictiers, who was to embark with the *arrière* ban of the kingdom of France. Most historians view in this delay the cause of all the evils that afterwards befell the Crusaders. We have nothing like sufficient positive documents to test the truth of their opinion; but we may say with certainty, that the inaction of the Christian army became, from that time, a source of most fatal disorders.

These disorders began to break out when the division took place of the booty made at the taking of Damietta. To animate the courage of the Crusaders, the treasures of this city, the entrepôt of the merchandises of the East, had often been boasted of; but as the richest quarters had been destroyed by the conflagration, and as the inhabitants had, when they fled, taken their most valuable effects with them, the spoils were very far from answering the hopes of the victorious army. In spite of the threats of the legate, several of the Crusaders had not brought all that fell into their hands to the common stock. The whole of the booty obtained in the city only produced the sum of six thousand *livres tournois*, [301] to be divided among the Crusaders, whose surprise and indignation found vent in violent murmurs.

As it had been determined that no division should be made of the provisions, but that they should be preserved in the royal magazines, for the support of the army, this resolution, so contrary to ancient usages, gave birth to loud complaints. Joinville informs us that the *prud'homme* John of Valery, whose stern probity and bravery were the admiration of the whole army, addressed some warm representations to the king on this subject. John of Valery alleged the laws of the Holy Land, and the custom pursued till that time in the crusades; he mentioned the example of John of Brienne, who, at the first conquest of Damietta, had only retained one-third of the riches and provisions found in the city, abandoning the rest to the general army. This custom was even less consecrated by the holy wars than by the feudal laws, according to which every lord carried on the war at his own expense, and by right had a share in all the plunder obtained from the enemy. But it might be objected, that Louis IX. furnished most of the leaders of the army with money, and by that the counts and barons had renounced the conditions of the feudal compact. This law of the division of provisions, which had, in fact, been observed in preceding crusades, sufficiently accounts for the scarcity that had so often desolated the Christian armies. The pious monarch was anxious to avoid evils that were the fruit of want of prudence and foresight, and refused to listen to the complaints of most of the French nobles. Thus, says Joinville, scarcity continued, and made the people very much dissatisfied. [302]

This spirit of dissatisfaction was quickly joined by other disorders, the consequences of which were still more deplorable. The knights forgot, in their fatal inactivity, both their warlike virtues and the object of the holy war. The riches of Egypt and the East being promised to them, the lords and barons made haste to consume, in festivities and pleasures, the money which they had obtained from the liberality of the king, or by the sale of their lands and castles. The passion for gaming had got entire possession of both leaders and soldiers; after losing their fortune, they risked even their horses and arms. Even beneath the shadow of the standards of Christ, the Crusaders gave themselves up to all the excesses of debauchery; the contagion of the most odious vices pervaded all ranks, and places of prostitution were found even in the close vicinity of the pavilion inhabited by the pious monarch of the French.

To satisfy the boundless taste for luxury and pleasure, recourse was had to all sorts of violent means. The leaders of the army pillaged the traders that provisioned the camp and the city; they imposed enormous tributes upon them, and this assisted greatly in bringing on scarcity. The most ardent made distant excursions, surprised caravans, devastated towns and plains, and bore away Mussulman women, whom they brought in triumph to Damietta. The sharing even of this sort of booty often gave rise to angry quarrels, and the whole camp resounded with complaints, threats, and confusion.

One of the most afflicting phases of this picture was, that the authority of the king became less respected daily; as corruption increased, the habits of obedience declined; the laws were without power, and virtue had no longer any empire. Louis IX. met with opposition to his wishes, even from the princes of his own family. The count d'Artois, a young, ardent, and presumptuous prince, unable to endure either rivalry or contradiction, proud of his military renown, and jealous to excess of that of others, was in the habit of constantly provoking the other leaders, and of heaping upon them, without motive, the most outrageous affronts. The earl of Salisbury, to whom he had behaved very ill, complained of him to Louis, and being unable to obtain the satisfaction he demanded, in his anger pronounced those memorable words: *"You are then not a king, if you are unable to administer justice."* This indocility of the princes, and the licentiousness of the great, completed the disorder; every day relaxation of discipline was observed to increase; the guarding of the camp, which extended far over the plains and along the banks of the Nile, was scarcely attended to; the advanced posts of the Christian army were constantly exposed to the attacks of the enemy, without being able to oppose any other means of resistance than imprudent and rash bravery, which only increased the danger.

Among the Mussulman soldiers sent to harass the Crusaders, the most successful in their mission were the Bedouin Arabs; intrepid warriors, indefatigable horsemen, having no other country but the desert, no other property but their horses and arms, the hopes of plunder supported them through all toils, and taught them to brave all dangers. With the Arabs of the desert were joined some Carismian horsemen, who had escaped from the ruin of their warlike nation. Accustomed to live by brigandage, both these watched night and day, to dog the Christian soldiers, and appeared to possess the instinct and activity of those wild animals that prowl constantly around the dwellings of man in search of their prey. The sultan of Cairo promised a golden byzant for every Christian head that should be brought into his camp; sometimes the Arabs and Carismians surprised the Crusaders who wandered from the army, and often took advantage of the darkness of night to get access to the camp; sentinels asleep on their posts, knights in bed in their tents, were struck by invisible hands, and when day appeared to lighten the scene of carnage, the barbarians fled along the banks of the Nile, to demand their wages of the sultan of Egypt.

These surprises and nocturnal attacks had a considerable effect in reanimating the courage of the Mussulmans. To raise the confidence of the multitude and the army, great care was taken to exhibit the heads of the Christians; all captives were paraded about in triumph, and the least advantage obtained over the Franks was celebrated throughout Egypt. Contemporary historians, led away by common exaggeration, talk of the most trifling combats as memorable victories; and we are astonished, at the present day, to read in the history of a period so abounding in great military events, that in the month of Ramadan thirty-seven Christians were brought in chains to Cairo, that they were followed, some days afterwards, by thirty-eight other captives, among whom were distinguished five knights. The activity of Negmeddin appeared to increase as his end approached. He employed the greatest exertions to get together all his troops; was indefatigably attentive in watching the movements of the Crusaders, and seldom failed to take advantage of their errors. Men were employed night and day in repairing the towers and fortifications of Mansourah; the Mussulman fleet, which had ascended the Nile, cast anchor immediately in front of the city. Whilst these preparations were going on, news arrived that the garrison of Damascus had taken possession of the city of Sidon, belonging to the Franks, and that the important place of Carac had just declared in favour of Negmeddin. This unexpected intelligence, the sight of the prisoners, but above all, the inactivity of the Christian army, which was attributed to fear, completed the dissipation of the terror of the Mussulmans. Whilst new reinforcements were every day arriving in the camp of the sultan, the people flocked in crowds to the mosques of Cairo and the other cities of Egypt, to invoke the protection of Heaven, and return thanks to the God of Mahomet, for having prevented the Christians from taking advantage of their victories.

BOOK XIV
A.D. 1248-1255

Whilst the Christian army was forgetting in its sojourn at Damietta both the laws of discipline and the object of the holy war, Alphonse, count of Poictiers, prepared to set out for the East. All the churches of France still resounded with pathetic exhortations addressed to the Christian warriors; the bishops, in the name of the sovereign pontiff, conjured the faithful to second, by means of charity, the enterprise against the Saracens; an apostolic brief, granted to the brother of the king not only the tribute imposed upon the Crusaders who repurchased their vow, but all the sums destined by testament to acts of piety, the object of which was not distinctly signified. These sums must have been considerable, but could scarcely suffice for the expenses of an expedition which bore the appearance of another crusade. The knights and barons who had not been affected by the example of Louis IX. showed but very little enthusiasm, or else wanted money for so long a voyage. Piety and the love of glory were not powerful enough to seduce them to join the banners of the holy war. History has preserved an agreement, by which Hugh Lebrun, count of Angoulême, consented to set out for the crusade with twelve knights, but on the express condition that the count of Poictiers should feed them at his own table during the expedition; that he would advance the seigneur Hugh Lebrun the sum of four thousand livres; and should pay him, in perpetuity, a pension of six hundred livres tournois. This agreement and several other similar ones were innovations in the military usages of feudalism, and even in the usages consecrated by the holy wars.

The English nobles, however, were impatient to follow the example set them by Louis IX. We read in Matthew Paris, that the English lords and knights had already sold or empawned their lands, and placed themselves entirely at the mercy of the Jews; which appeared to be the preliminary of a departure for the Holy Land. It is not out of place to add here, that this impatience to set out for the East, arose less from a religious motive than from the spirit of opposition that animated the barons against their monarch, Henry III., who was accused of being desirous of taking advantage of the absence of Louis IX., and did all in his power to retain the barons and lords of his kingdom; and as the latter resisted his solicitations with contempt, he resolved to employ the influence of the Church; "so that," says Matthew Paris, "like a young child who, having been ill-used, goes to its mother to complain, the king of England carried his complaints to the sovereign pontiff, adding that he proposed to go himself, and lead his barons shortly to the Holy Land." The pope, in his replies, forbade Henry III. to undertake anything against the kingdom of France; but, at the same time, he threatened with the thunders of the Church, all the knights and barons that should leave the kingdom against the will of the king. Henry, supported by the authority of the pope, ordered the commanders at Dover and the other ports to take measures that no Crusader should embark. Thus the court of Rome on one side preached the crusade, and on the other prevented the departure of the soldiers of the cross; which must have tended to dissipate all the illusions and annihilate the spirit of the holy war.

Baymoud, count of Thoulouse, had likewise taken the oath to combat the infidels; but the inconstancy of his character, and the policy of the pope, soon led him into other enterprises. His age had seen him, by turns, full of zeal for the Church, ardent to persecute it; the apostle of heresy, and the terror of heretics: sometimes abandoned to the furies of revolt, sometimes submissive to servitude; braving the thunders of the court of Rome, afterwards seeking the favour of the pontiffs; pursued by unjust wars, and himself declaring war without a motive. At the epoch of which we are speaking, the count of Thoulouse had given up all idea of fighting against the infidels, and was preparing to minister to the personal vengeance of Innocent IV., by turning his arms against Thomas of Savoy, who had recently married a daughter of the emperor Frederick, in opposition to the commands of the pope. He had already received the money necessary for his preparations from the pope, and had taken leave of his daughter, the countess of Poictiers, about to depart for the East, when he fell sick at Milan. From that time all the projects of his ambition faded away, and, to borrow the expression of a modern historian, *he went into another world to learn the result of the incomprehensible varieties of his life.*

With him the illustrious house of Thoulouse became extinct, a house of which several of the princes had been heroes of the holy wars, others deplorable victims of crusades. The county of Thoulouse thus became a property of the family of the king of France, and whilst Louis IX. was dissipating his armies and his treasures in vain endeavours to make conquests in the East, conquests less brilliant, but also less expensive, more useful and more durable, were increasing the power of the monarchy and extending the limits of the kingdom.

Germany, Holland, and Italy, filled with troubles, at that time occupied all the attention of Frederick II., and did not allow him to turn his thoughts towards the East. He sent the count of Poictiers fifty horses and a quantity of provisions, delighted, as he said, to seize an opportunity of acquitting some of the obligations he had received from France; he put up prayers for the success of the crusade, and deeply regretted his inability to take a part in it. Frederick had lived as the count of Thoulouse had done, and like him, he was soon, in another world, to behold the end of his ambition, of the inconstancy of his designs, and of the vicissitudes of fortune.

Although the count of Poictiers was little favoured by circumstances, he finished his preparations and got together an army. The new Crusaders embarked at Aigues-Mortes, at the moment the news of the taking of Damietta arrived in the West. The Christian army expected them in Egypt with greater anxiety, from the circumstance of the Sea of Damietta having been, for more than a month, agitated, unceasingly, by a furious tempest. Three weeks before their arrival, all the pilgrims had put up prayers on their account; on the Saturday of each week they went in procession to the seashore, to implore the protection of Heaven in favour of the warriors about to join the Christian army. At length, after a passage of two months, the count of Poictiers disembarked before Damietta, His arrival not only diffused joy and hope among the Crusaders, but permitted them to leave their long and fatal state of inactivity.

Louis IX. assembled the council of the princes and barons, to consult them on the line of march most advisable to be taken, and upon measures for perfecting the conquest of Egypt. Several of the leaders proposed to lay siege to Alexandria: they represented that that city had a commodious port; that the Christian fleet would there find certain shelter; and that they could there procure munitions and provisions with great facility: this was the opinion of all that had experience in war. The headstrong youth of the army, persuaded that they had sacrificed sufficiently to prudence, by remaining several months in idleness, maintained that they ought to proceed immediately against Cairo; they thought nothing of the dangers the Christian army must encounter in an unknown country, where they must expect to meet with enemies irritated by fanaticism and despair. The count d'Artois put himself particularly forward among those who wished them to attack the capital of Egypt. "When you wish to kill the serpent," cried he, "you ought always first to endeavour to crush his head." This opinion, expressed with warmth, prevailed in the council; Louis himself partook of the ardour and hopes of short-sighted youth, and the order was given for marching towards Cairo. [303]

The army of the Crusaders consisted of sixty thousand fighting men, more than twenty thousand of whom were horse. A numerous fleet ascended the Nile, laden with provisions, baggage, and machines of war. Queen Marguerite, with the countesses of Artois, Anjou, and Poictiers, remained at Damietta, where the king had left a garrison under the command of Olivier de Thermes.

The Crusaders encamped at Pharescour the 7th of December; terror had preceded their triumphant march, and every thing seemed to favour their enterprise. One circumstance, of which they were ignorant, would have increased the security and joy of the Christian knights if they had known of it; Negmeddin, after having struggled for a long time against a cruel malady, was at length dead. This death might have produced serious trouble in both the Egyptian nation and army, if it had not been carefully concealed for several days. After the sultan had breathed his last, the Mamelukes guarded the gates of his palace as if he had been still living; prayers were put up, and orders were issued in his name: with the Mussulmans, nothing interrupted the preparations for defence or attention to the war against the Christians. All these precautions were the work of a woman—a woman who had been purchased as a slave, and had become the favourite wife of Negmeddin. The Arabian historians are eloquent in the praise of the courage and talents of Chegger-Eddour, and agree in saying, that no woman surpassed her in beauty, and no man excelled her in genius.

After the death of Negmeddin, the sultana assembled the principal emirs; in this council the command of Egypt was given to Fakreddin, and they acknowledged as sultan Almoadam Touranschah, whom his father had banished to Mesopotamia: some authors assert that in this council it was resolved to send ambassadors to the king of the Franks, to propose peace in the name of the prince of whose death he was still ignorant. The ambassadors, in order to obtain a truce, were to offer the Christians Damietta with its territories, and Jerusalem with several other cities of Palestine. It was not probable that this negotiation should succeed; the Christians had advanced too far, and had too much confidence in their arms, to listen to any proposition.

The Christian army pursued its march along the banks of the Nile, and entered the town of Scharmesah, without meeting any other enemy than five hundred Mussulman horsemen. These horsemen at first evinced nothing but pacific intentions, and, from the smallness of their numbers, they inspired no dread. [304] Louis IX., whose protection they seemed to implore, forbade the Crusaders to attack them; but the Mamelukes, abusing the confidence that was placed in them, and taking advantage of a favourable opportunity, fell all at once upon the Templars, and killed a knight of that order. A cry to arms immediately rung through the French army, and the Mussulman battalion was assailed on all sides: such as did not fall beneath the swords of the Crusaders, were drowned in the Nile. In proportion with the approach of the Christians to Mansourah, the anxiety and terror of the Egyptians increased: the emir Fakreddin exposed the dangers of the country in a letter that was read at the hour of prayer in the great mosque of the capital. After the formula, *"In the name of God and of Mahomet his prophet,"* the letter of Fakreddin began by these words of the Koran: *"Hasten, great and small, the cause of God has need of your arms and of your wealth."* "The Franks," added the emir, "the Franks (Heaven curse them) are arrived in our country with their standards and their swords; they wish to obtain possession of our cities and ravage our provinces: what Mussulman can refuse to march against them, and avenge the glory of Islamism?"

Upon hearing this letter read, all the people were melted to tears; the greatest agitation prevailed throughout the city of Cairo; the death of the sultan, which began to be known, added greatly to the general consternation; orders were sent to raise troops in all the Egyptian provinces; war was preached in all the mosques, and the imauns endeavoured by every means to awaken fanaticism, in order to combat the depression of despair.

The Christian army arrived before the canal Aschmoum Theriah on the 19th of December. The Mussulman army was encamped on the opposite shore, having the Nile on its left, and behind it the city of Mansourah; close to them, in the direction of Cairo, the Saracens had a numerous fleet upon the river. That of the Christians had advanced to the head of the canal. Everything seemed to announce that the fate of the war would be decided on this spot. The Crusaders marked out their camp in the place in which the army of John of Brienne had encamped thirty years before. The remembrance of a great disaster ought to have served them as a lesson, and, at least, have tempered the excessive confidence that the too easy conquest of Damietta had given them.

The canal of Aschmoum was of the width of the Seine, its bed was deep, and its banks steep. In order to cross it, it was necessary that a dike should be constructed: the work was begun, but as fast as they heaped up the sand and stones, the Saracens dug away the earth in front of the dike, and thus removed further back the opposite bank of the canal; in vain the causeway advanced, the Crusaders had always the same distance to fill up, and each of the trenches dug by the enemy tended to make their labours useless. In addition to which, they were night and day interrupted in their works, and were constantly exposed to the arrows and javelins of the Saracens.

Although the Mussulman general had fled without fighting at the first appearance of the Franks, the chronicles of the times speak very highly of his bravery and military talents. They add that he had been made a knight by Frederick II., and that he bore the arms of the emperor of Germany with those of the sultans of Cairo and Damascus upon his escutcheon. These distinctions might draw the attention of the multitude; but that which was for Fakreddin a true title of glory is, that he was able, by his speeches and his example, to reanimate the courage and confidence of a conquered army.

Scarcely had the Crusaders seated themselves down in their camp, and begun the works necessary for the passage of the Aschmoum, than Fakreddin sent a party of troops to Scharmesah, to attack the rear of the Christian army. The Saracens, by this unexpected assault, spread disorder and terror through the camp of their enemies. The first advantage redoubled their audacity, and soon after an assault was made upon the Christians, along the whole line of their camp, extending from the canal to the Nile. The Mussulmans several times passed the intrenchments of the Crusaders; the duke of Anjou, Guy count of Forest, the sieur de Joinville, and several other knights, were compelled to exert all their bravery to repulse from their camp an enemy whom every fresh combat taught that the French were not invincible, and that it was at least possible to stop them on their march.

Conflicts took place every day in the plain and upon the river. Several vessels belonging to the Christians fell into the hands of the Mussulmans; the Arabs, constantly prowling round the camp, bore away into captivity every man that ventured to stray from his colours. As the emir Fakreddin could only learn from the reports of prisoners the state and disposition of the Christian army, he promised a recompense for every captive that should be brought into his tents: all the means that audacity and cunning could suggest were employed to surprise the Crusaders. It is related that a Mussulman soldier having buried his head in a melon that had been hollowed out, threw himself into the Nile, and swam down the stream. The melon, which appeared to float upon the water, attracted the eyes of a Christian warrior, who sprang into the river, and as he stretched out his hand to seize the floating melon, he himself was seized and dragged away to the camp of the Mussulmans. This anecdote, more whimsical than instructive, is related by several Arabian historians, who scarcely say anything of the preceding combats. Such are the spirit and character of the greater part of oriental histories, in which the most frivolous details often take the place of useful truths and important events.

Whilst the armies were thus in face of each other, the Crusaders pursued the work they had begun upon the Aschmoum. Towers of wood and machines were constructed, to protect the workmen employed in making the dike upon which the Christians were to cross the canal. On their side, the Mussulmans redoubled their efforts to prevent their enemies from completing their work. The dike advanced but very slowly, and the wooden towers that had been constructed in front of the causeway, could not defend either the workmen or the soldiers against the arrows, stones, and fiery darts that were being constantly launched from the camp of the Egyptians. Nothing could equal the surprise and terror that the sight alone of the Greek fire caused the Christian army. According to the relation of ocular witnesses, this redoubtable fire, cast sometimes through a brass tube, and sometimes by an instrument that was called the *perrière*, was of the size of a tun or large cask; the flaming tail, which it drew after it, was many feet in length; the Crusaders imagined they beheld a fiery dragon flying through the air; the noise of its explosion resembled that of thunder, which rolls in repeated peals. When it was launched during the night, it cast a lurid splendour over the whole camp. At the first sight of this terrible fire, the knights set to guard the towers, ran here and there, like men bewildered; some called their companions to their aid, whilst others threw themselves on the ground, or fell on their knees, invoking the celestial powers. Joinville could not conceal his fright, and thanked Heaven with all his heart when the Greek fire fell at a distance from him. Louis IX. was not less terrified than his barons and knights, and when he heard the detonation of the fire, he burst into tears, exclaiming: "Great God! Jesus Christ, protect me and all my people!" [305]

"The good prayers and orisons of the king," says his historian, "were of great service to us;" nevertheless, they were not able to save the towers and wooden works constructed by the Crusaders: all were consumed by the flames in sight of the Christian army, without their having any power to arrest their devastation. This misfortune was a lesson by which they ought to have profited; the Christians ought to have perceived that they had undertaken an impossible enterprise, and that they ought to seek for some means, more easy and more certain, of crossing the canal. But, unhappily, the leaders persisted in causing other erections to be made, which shared the fate of the first. They thus lost much time, and the futility of their attempts assisted in raising the pride and confidence of the Saracens.

The Mamelukes at this time learned that their new sovereign had arrived in Damascus, and that he was hourly expected in his capital. This arrival gave them fresh hopes, and rendered them more confident of victory. To redouble the ardour of his soldiers, Fakreddin often repeated, with a tone of assurance, that he should soon go and sleep in the tent of the king of the Franks.

The Christians had been a month before Aschmoum, exhausting themselves in useless efforts. Their leaders never took the trouble to examine if it were possible to ford the canal, or cross it by swimming, as the Egyptian cavalry had done. They were beginning to despair, when chance revealed to them a means of extricating themselves from their embarrassment, a means they might have known much sooner, if they had had less obstinacy and more foresight. A Bedouin Arab came to propose to Imbert de Beaujeu, constable of France, to show him, at a distance of half a league from the camp, a ford, by which the Crusaders might cross without danger or obstacles, to the opposite bank of the Aschmoum. After having ascertained that the Arab told the truth, they paid him the sum of five hundred golden byzants, which he had demanded, and the Christian army prepared to profit by this happy but late discovery.

The king and the princes his brothers, with all the cavalry, began their march in the middle of the night; the duke of Burgundy remained in the camp with the infantry, to observe the enemy, and guard the machines and the baggage. At daybreak, all the squadrons that were to cross the canal, awaited the signal on the bank. The count d'Artois was ambitious of crossing first; the king, who knew the impetuous character of his brother, at first wished to restrain him; but Robert insisted warmly, and swore upon the Gospel, that when he arrived on the opposite shore, he would wait till the Christian army had passed. Louis imprudently placed faith in the promise of a young, fiery, and haughty knight, to master his warlike transports, and resist all the temptations of glory on the field of battle. The count d'Artois placed himself at the head of the van, in which were the Hospitallers, the Templars, and the English. This van crossed the Aschmoum, and put to flight three hundred Saracen horsemen. At the sight of the flying Mussulmans, young Robert was on fire to pursue them. In vain the two grand masters represented to him that the flight of the enemy was perhaps nothing but a stratagem, and that he ought to wait for the army, and follow the orders of the king. Robert feared to lose an opportunity of triumphing over the infidels, and would listen to nothing but his ardour for conquest. He rushed on to the plain, sword in hand, drawing the whole van after him, and pursuing the Saracens to their camp, into which he entered with them.

Fakreddin, the leader of the Mussulman army, was at the moment in the bath, and, after the custom of the Orientals, was having his beard coloured. He sprang on horseback, almost naked, rallied his troops, and resisted for some time; but soon, left almost alone on the field of battle, he was surrounded, and died, covered with a thousand wounds.

The whole Mussulman army fled away towards Mansourah. How was it possible to resist the inclination to pursue them? What was to be feared from enemies that abandoned their camp? Might it not be believed that the Saracens fled as they had done at Damietta, and that terror would prevent their rallying? All these thoughts arose in the mind of the count d'Artois, and would not permit him to wait for the rest of the army to complete his victory. The grand-master of the Temple in vain renewed his representations; the young prince replied with great heat to the counsels of experience. In his passion he accused the Templars and Hospitallers of maintaining an intelligence with the infidels, and with wishing to perpetuate a war that was advantageous to their ambition. "Thus, then," replied the two grand masters, "it would appear that we and our knights have abandoned our families and our country, and would desire to pass our days in a foreign land, amidst the fatigues and perils of war, in order to betray the cause of the Christian church!" On finishing these words, the master of the Templars sternly bade the standard-bearer of his order to unfurl the banner of battle. The earl of Salisbury, who commanded the English, ventured to speak of the danger to which the army would be exposed, thus separated from its van; but the count d'Artois interrupted him by saying, sharply, "Timid counsels do not suit us!" Then the quarrels that had so often disturbed the discipline of the army were renewed, and the heat of debate completely stifled the voice of prudence. Whilst they were thus inflaming each other, the ancient governor of the count d'Artois, who was deaf, and who believed they were preparing for battle, never ceased crying, "Ores à eux, ores à eux!" [306] (Hurrah! on them! hurrah! on them!) These words became a fatal signal for warriors, urged on at once by anger and impatience for victory. The Templars, the English, the French, all set forward together, all flew towards Mansourah, and penetrated into the city abandoned by the enemy; some stopped to pillage, whilst the others pursued the Saracens along the road to Cairo.

If all the Christian troops had crossed the canal at the moment that the count d'Artois entered Mansourah, the defeat of the enemy could have been complete. But the passage was made with much difficulty and confusion; and when the French army had crossed the Aschmoum, a space of two leagues separated it from its van.

The Mussulmans, who had been driven from their camp, at first believed they had fought with all the forces of the Crusaders, commanded by the king of France; but they soon became aware of the small number of their enemies, and were astonished at having been put to flight. From the very bosom of peril and disorder, a skilful leader arose among them, whose presence of mind all at once revived their courage. [307] Bibars Bondocdar, whom the Mamelukes had recently placed at their head, having perceived the imprudence of the Christians, rallied the Mussulmans, led a part of his army between the canal and Mansourah, got possession of the gates of the city, and, with a chosen part of his troops, poured down upon the Crusaders, who were pillaging the palace of the sultan. *"The Mamelukes, lions of fights,"* says an Arabian historian, *"rushed upon the Franks, like a furious tempest; their terrible maces dealing deaths and wounds in all directions."* The Christians, dispersed about in the city, had scarcely time to rally; pressed together in narrow streets, they could neither fight on horseback nor make use of their swords. From the roofs of the houses and from the windows, the Mussulmans hurled stones and other missiles, or poured down upon them heated sand and boiling water. The gates of the city were closed, a multitude of Mussulmans occupied all the roads, and there remained not a single hope of salvation for warriors who had so recently put to flight a whole army.

This first disaster brought on several others; and soon the Christian army, which had just crossed the canal, found itself in the greatest danger. As fast as the Crusaders arrived on the other bank of the Aschmoum, some learned that the count d'Artois was pursuing the enemy, others that he was shut up in Mansourah, and most of the barons and knights, who burned, according to what they heard, to share his glory or aid him in his danger, without waiting for those who followed them, flew first towards the camp of the Saracens, and then towards the city.

The count of Brittany was one of the first who moved forward, and he was quickly followed by Guy of Malvoisin, the sieur de Joinville, and the bravest knights of the Christian army. They advanced in great haste, and without the least precaution, through a country covered with enemies; they were not long in being separated from each other, when some retraced their steps, but the greater part were surrounded by the Mussulmans. A thousand combats were fought at once upon the plain; here the Christians were conquerors, further on they were conquered; in every direction they, by turns, attacked their enemies or defended themselves, at one moment putting the Saracens to flight, and the next flying before them.

All at once a cloud of dust arose from the bank of the Aschmoum, and the sound of trumpets and clarions arose, mingled with the neighing of horses and the shouts of warriors; it was the main body of the Christian army advancing. Saint Louis, marching at the head of the cavalry, halted on the summit of an acclivity, where all eyes were turned towards him. The knights scattered about at the foot of the hill, no longer able to resist the Saracens, believed they saw the angel of battles come to their assistance; Joinville, in particular, who, though pressed hard by the enemy, was, nevertheless, struck by the majestic aspect of the monarch. Louis wore a golden helmet, and held in his hand a German sword; his armour was resplendent, and his noble bearing animated all his warriors; "in short," says the ingenuous seneschal, in whom, perhaps, the feeling of danger increased that of admiration, "I declare that a more noble armed man was never seen." [308]

Many of the knights who accompanied the French king, seeing the Christian warriors engaged with the Saracens in all directions, broke from their ranks, and rushed down to the *mêlée*. Then the confusion proceeded fast to its climax; every one hastened forward without knowing where the enemy's army was, and they very soon became equally ignorant where that of the Christians was, or the king that commanded it; there was no one to issue an order, and no signal was given, except that of peril. In this horrible tumult, prudence and caution were useless, strength and skill in arms alone were triumphant; the mace and the battle-axe dash polished casques and proudly-deviced shields to fragments; some knights sink covered with wounds, others are trampled to death beneath the feet of the horses; the cry of the French, "Montjoie, St. Denis!" and that of the Mussulmans, "Islam! Islam!" are confounded together, and mingle with the plaintive voices of the dying, and the menacing clamours of the triumphant, with the clash of cuirasses, lances, and swords. From the canal to Mansourah, and from the Nile to the shore whereon the Crusaders had just landed, the country presented but one vast field of battle, where fury and despair by turns animated the combatants, where torrents of blood were shed on both sides, without allowing either Christians or Mussulmans to claim the victory.

The Crusaders had the advantage in almost all the combats, or more properly duels, as the fights were generally man to man; but their army was in a great measure dispersed. At this moment, Bibars, having left in Mansourah a sufficient number of troops to triumph over the resistance of the count d'Artois and his knights, set forward with all his forces, directing his course towards the canal, for the purpose of sustaining the Mussulmans, who were beginning to fly, or to bring on a decisive battle. Louis and the leaders that surrounded him at once perceived the movement and the plans of the enemy. It was immediately decided that the Christian army should draw near to the canal, in order to prevent its being surrounded, and, at the same time, to preserve some communication with the duke of Burgundy, who remained on the opposite bank. The oriflamme, at the head of the battalions, already pointed out the direction the army was to take, when the counts of Poictiers and Flanders, who had advanced into the plain, sent word to the king that they must succumb unless speedily succoured: at the same moment, Imbert de Beaujeu came to announce that Robert of Artois was perishing in Mansourah. Struck by the conflicting demands, Louis hesitated for a moment, and in that moment a crowd of impetuous warriors, unable to wait for his orders, galloped off, some to the succour of the Poitevins and the Flemings, others to the aid of the count d'Artois; the Saracens completely covered the country, and the French warriors, who had thus separated themselves from the king, were totally unable to contend with such a multitude of enemies, and, falling back upon the Christian army, produced disorder and created terror.

Amidst the general confusion, a report was spread that the Mussulmans were everywhere victorious, and that the king had given orders for retreat. Several squadrons disbanded, and rushed towards the canal. In an instant the waters appeared covered with drowning men and horses. In this extreme peril, Louis in vain endeavoured to rally his troops. His voice was scarcely heard, no one executed the orders he endeavoured to give. He then precipitated himself into the thickest of the fight, and so impetuously was he carried forward by his ardour, that his squires had great difficulty in keeping up with him; at last he remained alone, surrounded on all sides by Saracens. Thus situated, he had to defend himself against six Mussulman horsemen, who were determined to take him prisoner. Louis defeated all their endeavours, and succeeded in disengaging himself, and putting them to flight. This brilliant act of bravery reanimated the flying Crusaders that witnessed it; they crowded after their gallant king, recommenced the fight, and once more dispersed the Mussulman battalions.

Whilst the whole Christian army was thus fighting to repair the faults and save the life of the count d'Artois, this unfortunate prince was defending himself with heroic bravery; but all his efforts, without the walls and within the walls of Mansourah, could not free him from the host of Saracens his imprudence had drawn upon him. Robert, with his knights, the Templars, and the English, forgetting all their fatal quarrels, resolved to die together as knights and Christian soldiers. The combat had lasted from ten o'clock in the morning till three in the afternoon; the Crusaders, covered with wounds and stained with blood and dust, fought on bravely, though only sustained by the flickering strength of exhausted life. They fell almost all at the same time; Salisbury was killed at the head of the warriors he commanded; Robert de Vair, who bore the English banner, folded it round him before he died; Raoul de Coucy expired on a heap of dead; the count d'Artois, intrenched within a house, defended himself for a long time, but at length sank amidst carnage and ruins. The Christian warriors had entered Mansourah to the number of fifteen hundred, and almost all met with death there. The grand master of the Hospitallers, left alone upon the field of battle, was taken prisoner. The master of the Templars escaped by a miracle, and came back in the evening to the Christian camp, wounded in the face, his vestments torn to rags, and his cuirass pierced in several places. He had beheld two hundred and eighty of his knights fall around him.

Most of those who advanced towards Mansourah to succour the count d'Artois, fell victims to their intrepid zeal. The brave Guy de Malvoisin succeeded in reaching the walls, but not in gaining entrance to the city. The duke of Brittany made incredible efforts to gain the place of combat; he heard the threats, cries, and tumult with which the city resounded, without being able to force the gates or scale the ramparts. He returned towards night-fall; he vomited blood in streams; his horse, stuck all over with arrows, had lost its bridle and part of its furniture; and every warrior that followed him was wounded. Even in this state he proved himself terrible to the enemy, killing or driving away, with powerful thrusts of his lance, all who dared to pursue or oppose him, and jeering at their abortive attempts. [309]

When night separated the combatants, the prior of the hospital of Rosnay came towards the king, and kissing his hand, asked him if he had received any tidings of the count d'Artois. "All that I know," replied the pious monarch, "is that he is now in Paradise." The good knight, to remove such sad thoughts, was about to expatiate upon the advantages they had gained; but then Louis, raising his eyes towards heaven, burst into tears. The prior of Rosnay became silent; the barons and lords assembled round the king were unable to offer a word of consolation, but were all oppressed with pain, compassion, and pity at seeing him weep. [310]

The Christian army, although it had to reproach the count d'Artois for all the misfortunes of this day's conflict, sympathized with the sorrows of Louis. Such was the ascendancy of bravery among the French warriors, that the greatest faults appeared to them to be expiated by a glorious death. It was likewise acknowledged in all the crusades, that they who died with arms in their hands were placed in the rank of martyrs. The Christian warriors only considered the count d'Artois as a soldier of Christ, whom God had recalled to his bosom: it was thus that piety accorded with glory, and that men honoured as saints the same persons they admired as heroes. Matthew Paris asserts in his History that the mother of Salisbury saw her son ascending into heaven on the day of the battle of Mansourah. The same opinion was established among the Saracens; all who fell in the field of battle, in the wars against the Christians, passed for martyrs of Islamism. "The Franks," says the continuator of Tabary, "sent Fakreddin to the banks of the celestial river, and his end was a glorious end."

History has not preserved the names of all the warriors who signalized their valour at the battle of Mansourah. The seneschal of Champagne was not one of those who were backward in seeking danger, or in evincing want of courage; one of six, he defended a bridge against a host of Saracens. He was twice unhorsed. In such great distress, the pious knight did not forget his patron saint, and exclaimed to him: "My lord, great sire, St. James, I supplicate thee, aid me and succour me in this my need." Joinville continued fighting during the whole day; his horse received fifteen wounds, and he himself was pierced by five arrows.

The seneschal informs us that during the battle of this memorable day, he saw several men of high distinction running disgracefully away, in the general confusion: he does not name them, because at the time he wrote they were dead, and it does not appear becoming to him to speak ill of the departed. The reserve with which the historian here expresses himself, shows plainly enough what was the general spirit of the French army, in which it was considered as an ineffaceable shame, and as the greatest of misfortunes, to have ever experienced a single moment of fear.

The greater part of the French warriors, when in the presence of danger, were never abandoned by that sentiment of honour that constituted the spirit and character of chivalry. Erard de Severy, whilst fighting bravely with a small number of knights, received a sabre-cut in the face; his blood flowed fast, and it appeared not at all likely that he would survive the wound; when, addressing the knights that fought near him, he said, "If you will assure me that I and my children shall be free from all blame, I will go and demand help for you, of the duke of Anjou, whom I see yonder on the plain." All praised this determination highly, and he immediately mounted on horseback, pierced through the enemy's squadrons, reached the duke of Anjou, and returned with him to rescue his companions, who were near perishing. Erard de Severy expired shortly after this heroic achievement: he died, bearing away with him, not the sentiments of a vain glory, but the consoling certainty that no blame, as he had desired, should stain his name, or that of his children.

That which at the same time astonishes and charms us in the relations of the old chroniclers who have spoken of this battle of Mansourah is, to find, amidst scenes of carnage, traces of French gaiety, of that gaiety which despises death and laughs at peril. We have spoken of six knights who defended the passage of a bridge against a great number of Saracens; whilst these *preux chevaliers*, surrounded by enemies, maintained such a perilous post, the count de Soissons, addressing Joinville, exclaimed: "Seneschal, let us leave this rascally *canaille* to cry and bray as they please, you and I will yet talk of this day, and in ladies' bowers too."

The Mussulmans having retired, the Christian army occupied their camp, which the van had taken possession of in the morning, and which the Arabs had plundered during the battle. The camp of the enemy, and the machines of war they had left in it, were the only fruit of the exploits of this day. The Crusaders had shown what valour could effect, and their triumph would have been complete if they had been able to rally and fight together. Their leaders had not sufficient ability or ascendancy to repair the error of the count d'Artois; the Mussulman leaders, who proved themselves to be more skilful, were also better seconded by the discipline and obedience of the Mamelukes.

When they became fully aware of the losses they had experienced, the Christians gave up all idea of celebrating their victory. To appreciate the result of so many bloody conflicts, it was quite sufficient to contemplate the contrast between the sentiments that animated the two armies. A melancholy sadness prevailed among the conquerors; whilst the Saracens, on the contrary, although driven from their camp, and obliged to fall back upon Mansourah, considered it a triumph to have stopped the march of their enemies; and, reassured as to the issue of the war, they abandoned themselves to the greater joy, from having, before the battle, entertained the most depressing fears.

In fact, nothing can paint the consternation which the first attack of the count d'Artois had created among the infidels. At the beginning of the day, a pigeon that was sent to Cairo, conveyed a message expressed in these words: "At the moment this bird is dispatched, the enemy is attacking Mansourah; a terrible battle has been fought between the Christians and the Mussulmans." At this news the people of Cairo were seized with the greatest terror; and sinister reports soon added to the alarm. The gates of the city were left open all night, to receive such as might have fled; and all of these exaggerated the danger to excuse their desertion. It was believed that the days of Islamism were numbered, and many were already abandoning the capital, to seek an asylum in Upper Egypt, when, on the morrow, another pigeon arrived, bearing news calculated to raise the spirits of the Mussulmans. The fresh message announced that the God of Mahomet had declared himself to be against the Christians; then all fears were dispersed, and the issue of the battle of Mansourah, says an Arabian author, *was the note of joy for all true believers*.

During the very night that followed the battle, the Mussulmans made several attempts to recover their camp and the machines of war that remained in the hands of the Franks. The Christian warriors, oppressed by fatigue, were repeatedly aroused by cries to arms; the continual attacks of the enemy would not allow them to repair their strength by sleep; many among them were so weakened by their wounds, they could scarcely put on their cuirasses; nevertheless, they defended themselves with their accustomed bravery.

The day after the battle was Ash-Wednesday, and the priests performed the ceremonies ordered by religion for the opening of Lent. The Christian army passed a part of the day in prayer, the rest of it in preparations for defence. Whilst the soldiers of the cross prostrated themselves at the foot of their altars, or prepared to repulse the infidels, images of mourning were mingled in their hearts with sentiments of piety and bravery. Whilst remembering their past victories, they could not forbear dreading the future; and the symbol of human fragilities, that the Church offers to each of her children on that solemn day, must have kept up their sad presentiments.

On the same day they employed themselves in throwing a bridge over the Aschmoum, in order to form a junction with the camp of the duke of Burgundy. The leaders and soldiers all lent a hand to the work, which was finished in the space of a few hours. The infantry, which had been left on the other side of the canal, came to reinforce the army, which was fated to be soon engaged in fresh contests.

Bibars, who had the command of the Mamelukes, hastened to take advantage of his first successes. When the body of the count d'Artois was found, the Mamelukes exhibited his cuirass, sown over with *fleurs des lis*, and declared it was the spoil of the king of France. They carried about the heads of several knights in triumph, and heralds-at-arms repeated in a loud voice: "The Christian army is nothing but a trunk without life, like the heads you behold on the points of these lances."

This spectacle completely inflamed the ardour of the Mussulmans. The leaders and soldiers, with great cries, demanded to be led against the Christians. The Mussulman army had orders to hold themselves in readiness for battle on the morrow, the first Friday in Lent.

Louis IX. was warned of the intention of the Saracens; he gave orders to the leaders to fortify the camp, and prepare their troops for the conflict. On the Friday, by daybreak, the Christians were all under arms; and at the same time the leader of the Mussulmans appeared in the plain, ranging his men in battle-array. He placed his cavalry in the front, behind them the infantry, and still further back, the reserve. He extended or strengthened his lines according to the positions he saw his enemies take. His army covered the plain from the canal to the river. At midday he unfurled the banners and sounded the charge.

The duke of Anjou was at the head of the camp on the side towards the Nile; he was the first attacked. The infantry of the Saracens commenced by launching the Greek fire. This fire seized the clothes of the soldiers and the caparisons of the horses. The soldiers, enveloped in flames they could not extinguish, ran about uttering the most frightful cries; the horses broke away, and created confusion in the ranks. By means of this disorder, the enemy's cavalry opened themselves a passage, dispersed such as were still fighting, and penetrated within the intrenchments. The duke of Anjou was unable to resist the multiplied attacks of the Saracens; his horse having been killed under him, he fought on foot, and, nearly overwhelmed by the number of his enemies, he at length sent to Louis IX. for aid.

The king, himself engaged with the Mussulmans, redoubles his ardour and his efforts, drives the enemy back on to the plain, and then flies where other dangers call him. The knights who follow him precipitate themselves upon the Mussulman battalions which were attacking the quarter of the duke of Anjou. Louis is not stopped, either by the numberless arrows shot at him, or by the Greek fire, which covers his arms and the caparison of his horse. In the account of this battle, Joinville is astonished that the king of France escaped being killed, and can in no other way explain this species of miracle than by attributing it to the power of God: "Then it may well be believed" (we let the seneschal of Champagne speak) "that the holy king had his God in remembrance and wish: for, in truth, our Lord was then a great friend to him in his need, and aided him so effectually, that he delivered his brother, the duke of Anjou, and drove away the Turks."

On the left of the duke of Anjou, the Crusaders from the isle of Cyprus and Palestine were encamped, under the command of Guy d'Ibelin and his brother Baldwin. These Crusaders had not been engaged in the last battle, and had lost neither their horses nor their arms. Near them fought the brave Gauthier de Chatilion, at the head of a chosen troop. These intrepid warriors were proof against all attacks, and remaining firm at the post confided to them, contributed greatly to the saving of both the camp and the army.

The Templars, having lost the greater part of their knights in Mansourah, formed an intrenchment or barricade in front of them, of the wood of the machines taken from the Saracens; but this feeble defence was of little avail against the Greek fire. The enemy rushed into the camp through the flames; the Templars formed an impenetrable rampart of their bodies, and resisted the violent attacks of the assailants during several hours. The conflict was so severe at this point, that the earth could scarcely be seen behind the spot occupied by the Templars, so completely was it covered with arrows and javelins. The grand master of the Templars lost his life in the *mêlée*, and a great number of knights died in defending or avenging him. The prodigies of their bravery at last succeeded in arresting the progress of the enemy, and the last who fell in this hardly-contested battle had the consolation, when dying, to see the Saracens fly.

Guy de Malvoisin was placed near to the post which the knights of the Temple defended so bravely; the battalion he commanded was composed almost entirely of his relations, and in battle presented the spectacle of a family of warriors, ever united and ever invincible. Guy incurred the greatest peril; he was wounded several times, but never dreamt of retiring from the contest. His example and the sight of his wounds redoubled the courage of his companions, who, at length, repulsed the Mussulmans. Not far from Guy de Malvoisin, descending towards the canal, the Flemish Crusaders were posted. William, their count, was at their head; they sustained the furious shock of the Mussulmans without giving way in the least: Joinville, with some other knights, fought on their left, and on this occasion owed his safety to the warriors of Flanders, to whom he accords the warmest praises. The Flemings, united with the Champenois, put the Mussulman cavalry and infantry to flight, pursued them out of the camp, and returned loaded with the bucklers and cuirasses they had taken from their enemies.

The count of Poictiers occupied the left wing of the army; but as this prince had only infantry under his command, he was unable to resist the cavalry of the Saracens. Such were the warriors of these remote times, that when they were not on horseback, they seemed to be disarmed, and could not fight even for the defence of intrenchments. The quarter confided to the Poitevins was attacked by the Mussulmans at an early period of the fight; the Mamelukes plundered the tents of the Christians, the brother of the king was dragged out of the camp by some Saracen horsemen, and was being carried away a prisoner. In this extreme peril the count of Poictiers could not look to Louis IX. for any assistance, as he had gone to the succour of the count of Anjou; nor to the other leaders of the Christian army, all so closely pressed by the enemy themselves. This prince was adored by the people for his goodness; and on this occasion received the reward of his virtues, by owing his deliverance to the love with which he inspired all the Crusaders. When the workmen, sutlers, and women that followed the army saw him made a prisoner, they assembled in the greatest fury, and arming themselves with axes, clubs, sticks, or anything that fell in their way, flew after the Mussulmans, delivered the count of Poictiers, and brought him back in triumph.

At the extremity of the camp, close to the quarters of the Poitevins, fought Josserant de Brançon, with his son and his knights. The companions in arms of Josserant had all left Europe well mounted and magnificently equipped: now they all fought on foot, and had nothing left but lance and sword. Their leader alone was on horseback, and rode from rank to rank, exciting the soldiers, and flying to every point where the danger seemed most pressing. This weak troop would entirely have perished, if Henry of Brienne, who remained in the camp of the duke of Burgundy, had not caused his cross-bowmen to shoot across the arm of the river, every time the Saracens renewed their attacks. Of twenty knights that accompanied Josserant, twelve were left upon the field of battle. This old warrior had been present in thirty-six battles, in all of which he had borne away the prize of valour. Joinville, when relating the exploits of this day, remembers that he had formerly seen Josserant de Brançon come out victorious from a combat against some Germans who were pillaging the church of Mâcon; he had seen him prostrate himself at the foot of the altar, and pray with ardour for the favour of dying in fight against the enemies of Christ. And Josserant obtained the blessing he had asked of God; for a few days after the battle he died of his wounds.

Such was the contest of which Louis IX., in the account which he sent to France, speaks with such admirable simplicity. "On the first Friday in Lent, the camp being attacked, God favoured the French, and the infidels were repulsed with much loss."

In this battle, as in the last, the Christians had had all the glory, the Saracens all the advantage. The Christian army lost a great number of its warriors, and almost all its horses: the enemy was reinforced every day; the Crusaders could not attempt to march upon Cairo, and prudence seemed to suggest that they should retrace their steps to Damietta. Retreat, still easy, offered a means of preserving the army for a more favourable season: but this plan could only be counselled by despair, and despair has great difficulty in mastering the hearts of the brave. Nothing could appear more disgraceful to the French than flying, or appearing to fly, before a conquered enemy: they resolved to remain.

Towards the end of February, Almoadam, whom Chigger-Eddour and the principal leaders of the Mamelukes had called to the throne of his father, arrived in Egypt, and was received with loud acclamations by the people, always desirous of change, and always delighted with a new reign. The emirs and magnates likewise displayed great joy, but their demonstrations were less sincere; they looked for the coming of the successor of Negmeddin with more anxiety than impatience; placing a very high value upon that which they had done for him, they, beforehand, expected his ingratitude. On the other side, the young prince was jealous of his authority; and the power of the emirs, the nature even of their services, gave him alarms that he had not the prudence to dissemble. It was not long before a mutual mistrust and a reciprocal estrangement arose between Almoadam and the leaders of the Mussulman army; the latter repented of having raised to empire a prince who showed a disposition to rule alone, and the former was determined to defend his power, even against those who had bestowed it upon him. This state of things and the disposition of men's minds, appeared ominous of new revolutions in Egypt; unhappily these revolutions broke out too late to allow the Christians to derive any advantage from them.

The Crusaders likewise had soon to contend with calamities more destructive to them than even the power or the arms of the Mussulmans; a contagious disease made its appearance in the Christian army. They had neglected to bury the dead after the last two battles; the bodies cast confusedly and heedlessly into the Aschmoum, and floating on its waters, stopped before the bridge of boats constructed by the Crusaders, and covered the surface of the canal from one shore to the other. Pestilential exhalations quickly arose from this heap of carcasses. Louis IX. ordered the bodies of the Christians to be buried in the ditches dug by the Saracens on the bank; but these spoils of death, moved and transported without precaution, only assisted the progress of the epidemic. The spectacle which was then presented to the eyes of the Crusaders spread the deepest grief throughout the camp, and awakened a more perfect consciousness of their losses. Christian soldiers were seen searching among bodies which wounds, the hues of death, and the action of the sun and air had disfigured, for the deplorable remains of their friends or companions. Many of those upon whom friendship imposed this pious task, fell sick and died almost instantly. The devotedness and grief of one of the knights of Robert count d'Artois, were conspicuous among these affecting instances. This inconsolable knight passed whole nights and days on the banks of the canal, with his eyes intensely fixed upon the waters, braving contagion and death, in the hope of recovering and burying the young prince, whose loss was so deeply deplored by the French army.

The fatigues of war did not at all prevent the pious warriors from observing the abstinence of Lent; and the privations and austerities of penitence completed the exhaustion of their strength. The contagion attacked the most robust as well as the most weak; [311] their flesh withered away, their skin became livid, and was covered with black spots; their gums were inflamed and swollen so as to prevent the passage of food; the flowing of the blood from the nose was the sign of approaching death. Most of the diseased viewed the grim monarch without fear, and considered his dominions as the wished-for end of all their sufferings.

Dysentery and dangerous fevers were soon added to the above malady; nothing was heard in the Christian camp but prayers for the dying or the dead; nothing was seen but the pale and haggard countenances of unhappy beings who accompanied their companions to the tomb, and whom death must soon sweep away in their turn. The soldiers capable of bearing arms did not suffice for the guarding of the avenues of the camp. A thing unheard of in Christian armies, the grooms of knights were seen clothed in the armour of their masters, and taking their places in the post of danger. The clergy, who attended the sick and buried the dead, suffered greatly from the epidemic; very quickly there were not ecclesiastics enough to minister at the altars and perform the Christian ceremonies. One day, the sieur de Joinville, himself sick, and listening to the mass in his bed, was obliged to rise and support his almoner, ready to faint upon the steps of the altar. *"Thus supported,"* adds the kindly historian, *"he finished his sacrament, chanted the mass quite through—but never chanted more."* [312]

We have seen in former holy wars, multitudes of Crusaders a prey to the most cruel scourges; the bravest of the warriors often despaired of the cause of the pilgrims, and deserted the banners of the cross; and many times the excess of their misery drew from them imprecations and blasphemies. We must here remark that the soldiers and companions of Louis IX. supported their evils with more patience and resignation. Not one knight thought of deserting the banners of the crusade, and not a seditious or sacrilegious complaint was heard in the army; the example of the pious monarch doubtless strengthened the courage of the Crusaders, and preserved them from the excesses of despair. Louis IX., deeply affected by the evils that desolated his army, employed every effort to mitigate and end them. If anything could have consoled the Crusaders in the miserable condition in which they were placed, it must have been seeing a king of France himself attending the sick, lavishing upon them every kind of assistance, and preparing them for death. In vain he was conjured not to expose himself to dangers still greater than those of the field of battle; nothing could shake his courage or check the ardour of his charity; he considered it his duty (it is thus he expressed himself) to expose his life for those who every day exposed theirs for him. One of his servants, a worthy man, being at the point of death, and exhorted by a priest to meet his fate like a Christian, replied, *"I will not die till I have seen the king."* The king complied with his desire, and the man died in peace, consoled by the presence and words of his kind master. But at length he who consoled all others fell sick himself. The king was not able to leave his tent; the desolation became more profound and more general; they who suffered began now to lose all hope; it seemed as if Providence had abandoned them, and that heaven no longer protected the soldiers of the cross.

The Saracens remained motionless in their camp, leaving their awful auxiliaries, diseases, to perform their mission undisturbed; only Almoadam, in order to add famine to the other evils his enemies experienced, resolved to interrupt all communication between the Christians and Damietta, whence they received provisions by way of the Nile. Having got together a great number of boats, the sultan caused them to be taken to pieces, and afterwards transported over-land to the mouth of the canal of Mehallah. A French flotilla came up the river without suspicion, bearing provisions for the camp, and fell directly into an ambuscade of galleys, placed behind a small island. All at once the enemies appear, surprise the Christians, attack them with fury, kill a thousand soldiers, and obtain possession of fifty vessels laden with provisions. A few days afterwards, other vessels coming up the river towards Mansourah experienced the same fate. No one arrived at the camp; no news came from Damietta, and the Christians were abandoning themselves to the most melancholy presentiments, when a vessel belonging to the count of Flanders, which had escaped the enemy by a miracle, came to announce to them that all the vessels of the Crusaders had been taken, and that the Mussulman flag dominated along the whole course of the river.

Famine soon made frightful ravages in the army; and such as had been spared by disease, were threatened with death from misery and hunger. Both leaders and soldiers were seized with the deepest despondency; and the king at length judged it best to attempt to enter into a truce with the Mussulmans. Philip de Montfort was employed in the embassy to the sultan of Egypt; commissioners were named on both sides to conclude a treaty. Those of the king of France proposed to surrender Damietta to the sultan, on condition that Jerusalem and all the other places in Palestine, that had fallen into the hands of the Mussulmans in the late wars, should be given up to the Christians. The sultan, who dreaded the bravery and the despair of the Crusaders, who, besides, had reason to fear that his enemies might receive reinforcements, and that Damietta might hold out for a considerable time, accepted the proposed conditions. When the question of hostages came to be discussed, the king offered his two brothers; but whether the sultan placed no faith in the loyalty of his enemies, or whether he was wanting in it himself, he required that the king of France should remain in his hands, as a guarantee of the treaty. Sergines, one of the commissioners, could not listen to this proposal without anger. "You ought to know Frenchmen better," cried he, "than to suppose they would ever allow their king to remain a prisoner with Mussulmans." A council was held on this subject in the Christian army. The king consented to everything, but the lords and barons exclaimed with vehemence against the giving up of their sovereign. On one side, the monarch was willing to purchase the safety of his people by his own personal danger; on the other, a crowd of warriors all warmly declared they could not suffer such a disgrace, and that *they would rather die than place their king in pledge*. The more Louis was beloved by his warriors, the less he was master in this circumstance; and every one thinking it to his honour, and almost consistent with his duty, to disobey him, the negotiation was abandoned.

To paint the frightful scarcity that desolated the Christian camp, contemporary chronicles relate, as an extraordinary thing, that a sheep was sold for as much as ten crowns, an ox for eighty livres, and an egg for twelve deniers. Such high prices exceeded the means of most of the pilgrims; some were obliged to live upon the fish caught in the Nile, others upon herbs and roots.

Louis IX. preserving his courage and tranquillity of mind amidst the general mourning and depression, as a means of endeavouring to save the miserable remains of his army, resolved to repass to the other side of the Aschmoum. Whilst the Christians were crossing the wooden bridge thrown over the canal, they were warmly attacked by the Mussulmans. Gaucher de Chatillon, who commanded the rear, at first repulsed them; but as the Saracens returned several times to the charge, and as they had greatly the advantage in numbers, victory was upon the point of being adverse to the Crusaders. The brilliant valour of the count of Anjou checked the impetuosity of the Mussulmans. Erard and John de Valeri performed prodigies of bravery. Jeffroi de Hassemburgh likewise distinguished himself by heroic actions, and merited the palm of valour in that day's fight. Thus glory was always mingled with the misfortunes of the French Crusaders: but victory procured them no advantages, and always left them still exposed to the same perils, still a prey to the same calamities. They were not more fortunate on one side of the Aschmoum than on the other; and after remaining some days in their old camp, they were obliged at length to form the disheartening resolution of returning to Damietta.

As soon as Almoadam was informed of these last dispositions of the Christians, he himself harangued his troops, distributed provisions and money to them, and reinforced them with a great number of Arabs, attracted to his standards by the hopes of booty. By his orders, boats loaded with soldiers descended the Nile, and joined the Mussulman fleet that had intercepted the convoys of the Crusaders. Bodies of light cavalry were distributed along the whole course of the roads which the French army would take in its retreat.

On the fifth day of April, [313] the Tuesday after the octave of Easter, Louis IX. ordered everything to be prepared for the departure of his army: the women, the children, and the sick were embarked upon the Nile; they waited till night-fall, to conceal these sad preparations from the enemy. The bank of the Nile presented the most heart-breaking spectacle; nothing was to be seen but Crusaders overcome by their sufferings, parting, with tears in their eyes, from friends they were doomed never to see again. Amidst these painful scenes, the Arabs, taking advantage of the darkness of the night, penetrated into the camp, plundered the baggage, and slaughtered every living creature they met with. A terrified crowd fled on all sides, and cries of alarm resounded along the whole bank of the river. The mariners perceiving, by the light of the fires in the boats, this frightful disorder, and that the Christians were being massacred, became terrified on their own account, and prepared to depart. The king, who, in spite of his weakness, was present everywhere, and watched over everything, drove the infidels from the camp, reassured the Christian multitude, and commanded the vessels which had left the shore, to put back and take the rest of the sick on board.

The pope's legate and several French nobles got on board a large vessel. The king was pressed to follow this example, but he could not make up his mind to abandon his army. In vain his anxious and loving friends represented to him that his state of weakness would not permit him to fight, and exposed him to the risk of falling into the hands of the Saracens; in vain they added, that by thus hazarding his life he compromised the safety of the army. These and many other remonstrances, dictated by sincere attachment for his person, were not able to make him change his resolution. He replied, that no danger should separate him from his faithful warriors; that he had brought them with him; that he would return with them; or, if it proved necessary, die in the midst of them. This heroic determination, the inevitable consequences of which were foreseen, plunged all his knights into consternation and grief. The soldiers, partaking the feelings of the knights, ran along the bank of the Nile, crying with all their strength to those that were going down the river, "Wait for the king! wait for the king!" [314] Arrows and javelins were falling thick upon the vessels which continued to go down the river. Many stopped; but Louis insisted upon their pursuing their course.

Most of the French warriors were borne down by disease and weakened by hunger. The fatigues and new perils they were about to undergo did not at all diminish their courage; but they could not endure the thoughts of abandoning places rendered dear to them by the remembrance of their victories. The duke of Burgundy set out on his march at night-fall; and, a short time after, the rest of the troops quitted the camp, taking away their tents and baggage. Louis, who was determined to go with the rear-guard, only kept with him the brave Sergines and a few other knights and barons who were still fortunate enough to have horses. The king, scarcely able to support himself in his saddle, appeared in the midst of them mounted on an Arabian horse; he wore neither helmet nor cuirass, and had no other weapon but his sword. The warriors who had surrounded his person, followed him in silence; and in the deplorable state to which they were reduced, evinced still some joy at having been chosen to defend their king and die by his side.

The retreat of the Christian army was already known to the Saracens. The king had ordered the bridge of Aschmoum to be broken; but this order had not been executed, and it furnished the Mussulmans with an easy means of crossing the canal. In a moment the whole plain which extended on the Damietta side was covered with enemies. The rear-guard of the Christians was stopped at every step of its route, sometimes by the crossing of a rivulet, but more frequently by a charge of Mussulman cavalry. Amidst the darkness of the night, the Crusaders could not see which way to direct their blows, and when they did obtain some trifling advantage, they did not dare to pursue their enemy; they advanced fighting, and in disorder; fearing to lose themselves, such as were at any distance from their companions, called upon them by name; such as adhered closely to the standard, ran against and impeded each other in their march: over the whole plain nothing was heard but the neighing of horses, the clash of arms, and cries of rage and despair; but the most deplorable spectacle in this defeat was that of the wounded lying stretched along the roads, holding up their hands to their comrades, and conjuring them, with tears, not to leave them exposed to the fury of the Saracens. They looked for day with the most anxious impatience; but the daylight, by discovering the small number of the Christians, redoubled the confidence of the Mussulmans: it filled the former with proportionate dread, as it showed them the multitude of their enemies.

Menaced and pursued on all sides, the knights who had taken the route by land, envied those who had embarked upon the Nile; but these latter were in no less danger than their unfortunate companions. A short time after their departure, a high wind arose, and drove back the vessels towards Mansourah: some of them were run aground, others were dashed violently against accompanying boats, and were near being sunk. Towards dawn their flotilla arrived near Mehallah, a place fatal to the Christians. The Mussulman fleet awaited them there. The archers charged to proceed along the shore and protect them, had fled, and in their place appeared a multitude of Mussulman horsemen, launching such a number of arrows armed with the Greek fire, that it might have been believed, says Joinville, *"that all the stars of heaven were falling."*

The wind disconcerted all the manœuvres of the mariners. The Crusaders, crowded closely in their vessels, could scarcely stand upright, and were most of them without arms. Turning their eyes, sometimes towards the shore, where they perceived clouds of dust at a distance, and sometimes towards heaven, whose mercy they implored, they still hoped that some unexpected event might deliver them, or else that the army advancing towards Damietta would come to their succour; thus placing their last hopes in the miracles of Providence and in those of bravery. Deceitful illusions!

one division of the Christian troops had been dispersed; the rear-guard, encouraged by the presence of the king, made incredible but useless efforts to repulse the crowd of Saracens, which increased from moment to moment. The despair of the French warriors gave birth to a thousand glorious actions; but so much heroism was only able to procure them the palm of martyrdom. Guy du Châtel, bishop of Soissons, giving up all hopes of gaining Damietta or revisiting France, resolved to seek death, and rushed, followed by several knights, into the thickest of the ranks of the Saracens, who, according to the expression of Joinville, *killed them, and sent them into the company of God.* Gaucher de Chatillon and Sergines still fought on, in the hope of saving the life of the king of France. Sergines, adhering close to the side of the king, drove away the enemies with mighty blows of the sword; danger seemed to have doubled his strength. Contemporary history, which describes him to us driving away the Saracens that surrounded Louis, compares him to the vigilant servant who carefully drives away the flies from his master's cup.

In the mean time the hope of victory inflamed the enthusiasm and the fanaticism of the Mussulmans; they were persuaded they were fighting for the cause of their prophet: their dervises and imauns, who had preached the war against the Christians, followed them on the field of battle, pervaded the ranks of the army, and excited the soldiers to carnage. [315] An Arabian historian, mixing the marvellous with his account, relates that the scheikh Ezzedin, seeing that victory for a moment inclined towards the Christians, because a whirlwind of dust covered the Mussulmans and prevented them from fighting, addresses these words to the wind: *"Oh wind, direct thy breath against our enemies!"* The tempest, adds the same historian, obeyed the voice of this holy person, and victory was the reward of the soldiers of Islamism. We only report this circumstance here, to show the spirit that animated the Mussulmans in their wars against the Christians. The Saracens did not require a miracle to triumph over a dispersed army reduced to so small a number of combatants. The rear-guard of the Christians, always pursued and unceasingly attacked, arrived with much difficulty before the little town of Minieh. [316] The king, escorted by a few knights, preceded the troops into the city, where he alighted as weak "as a child in its mother's lap," says Joinville. Fatigue, sickness, and the grief which such disasters caused him, had so overcome him, that all believed (we still quote the same author) he was about to die.

The intrepid Gaucher de Chatillon watched over his safety; alone, he for a length of time defended the entrance of a narrow street, which led to the house in which his faithful servants were endeavouring to recall the exhausted monarch to life. At one moment he rushed like lightning upon the infidels, dispersed them, cut them down; then, after turning to pull from his cuirass, and even his body, the arrows and darts with which he was stuck all over, he flew again upon the enemy, rising from time to time in his stirrups, and shouting with all his force, "Chatillon, knights! Chatillon, to the rescue! Where are ye, my gallant men?" The remainder of the rear-guard were still at some distance; nobody appeared, but the Saracens, on the contrary, came up in crowds; at length, overwhelmed by numbers, bristling with arrows, and covered with wounds, he fell; none of the Crusaders could succour him, not one could witness his heroic end! His horse, one sheet of blood and foam, became the prey of the infidels, and his last exploits were narrated by a Mussulman warrior, who exhibited his sword, and boasted of having killed the bravest of the Christians.

The rear-guard drew up upon a neighbouring hill, and still defended themselves with some advantage. Philip de Montfort, who commanded them, came to inform the king that he had just seen the emir with whom they had treated for a suspension of hostilities at the camp of Mansourah; and if it were his good pleasure, he would go and speak to him about it again. The monarch consented, promising to submit to the conditions the sultan had first required. However miserable the situation of the Crusaders, they still inspired considerable dread in their enemies. Five hundred knights remained under arms, and many of those who had gone past Minieh, retraced their steps to dispute the victory with the Saracens. The emir accepted the proposition for a truce. Montfort, as a pledge of his word, gave him a ring which he wore on his finger. Their hands already touched, when a *traitor, a rascal doorkeeper,* named Marcel, cried aloud: "Seigneurs, noble French knights, surrender yourselves all, the king commands you by me; do not cause him to be killed!" At these last words, the consternation became general; they believed that the life of the monarch was in great danger, and the leaders, officers, and soldiers, all laid down their arms.

The emir, who had begun to treat for peace, perceived this sudden change, and he broke off the negotiation by saying: "It is not customary to treat with conquered enemies." Soon after, one of the principal emirs, Djemal-eddin, entered Minieh. Finding the king surrounded by his weeping servants, he took possession of his person, and without any regard for royal majesty, without any respect for the greatest misfortunes, ordered chains to be placed upon his hands and feet; from that moment there was no safety for the Crusaders. Both the brothers of the king fell into the hands of the infidels; all those that had reached Pharescour, were seized, and lost either their lives or their liberty. Many of them might have gained Damietta; but when they learnt the captivity of the king, they lost all strength or spirit to continue their route or to defend themselves. These knights, but lately so intrepid, remained motionless on the high roads, and allowed themselves to be slaughtered or manacled, without offering the least complaint or making the slightest resistance. The oriflamme, the other standards, and the baggage, all became the prey of the Saracens. Amidst scenes of carnage, the Mussulman warriors uttered the most horrible imprecations against Jesus Christ and his defenders: they trampled under-foot, they profaned by insults, crosses and sacred images—a crowning cause for scandal and despair for Christians, who, having seen their king loaded with chains, beheld their God given up to the outrages of the conqueror!

The Crusaders who had embarked upon the Nile had no better destiny; all the vessels of the Christians, except that of the legate, were sunk by the tempest, consumed by the Greek fire, or taken by the Mussulmans. The crowd of Saracens, assembled on the shore or on board the barks, immolated all that came within reach of their arms. They spared neither the women nor the sick. Avarice, rather than humanity, saved such as could expect to be ransomed. The sieur de Joinville, still suffering from his wounds and the disease that had prevailed in the camp of Mansourah, had embarked with the only two knights he had left and some of his serving-men. Four Mussulman galleys came up to his vessel, which had just cast anchor in the middle of the river, and the soldiers threatened them with instant death if they did not at once surrender. The seneschal deliberated with the persons of his suite upon what was best to be done in such an imminent danger: all agreed that it would be most prudent to surrender, except one of his ecclesiastics, who said it would be best to be killed, that they might go at once to Paradise; but this the others were not willing to comply with. Joinville then took a little coffer, and emptying it of the jewels and relics it contained, he threw them into the water, and surrendered at discretion. In spite of the laws of war, the seneschal would have been killed, if a renegade, who knew him, had not covered him with his body, crying: "It is the king's cousin!" Joinville, scarcely able to support himself, was dragged into a Mussulman galley, and from that transported to a house close to the shore. As they had deprived him of his coat of mail, and he remained almost without covering, the Saracens, whose prisoner he was, gave him a little cap, which he placed upon his head, and threw over his shoulders a scarlet cloak of his own, furred with minever, which his mother had given him: he was trembling all over, as well from his disease as the great fear that possessed him. Being unable to swallow a glass of water that was given to him, he believed himself to be dying, and called his servants around him, who all began to weep. Among those who wept the most bitterly, was a young boy, a natural son of the seigneur Montfaucon. This child, upon seeing the persons perish who had charge of him, had thrown himself into the arms and under the protection of Joinville. The sight of abandoned infancy and the despair of the worthy seneschal, excited the compassion of some of the emirs that were present, and one of them, whom Joinville at one time calls the *good Saracen*, and at another the *poor Saracen*, took pity on the boy, and when he left the seneschal, he said to him, "Be sure to hold this little child constantly by the hand, or I am certain the Saracens will kill him."

The carnage was prolonged for a considerable time after the battle; it lasted during many days. All the captives that had escaped the first fury of the Mussulman soldiers, were landed; and woe to such as sickness had weakened or as exhibited marks of poverty! the more worthy the victims were of pity, the more they roused the barbarity of the conquerors. Soldiers armed with swords and maces, charged to execute the terrible sentence of victory, awaited the prisoners on the shore. John of Vaissy, the priest, and some other servants belonging to Joinville, crawled from the ships in a dying state: the Saracens completed the work before the eyes of their master, saying that these poor wretches were good for nothing, and could pay for neither their liberty nor their lives.

In these days of disasters and calamities, more than thirty thousand Christians lost their lives, killed on the field of battle, drowned in the Nile, or massacred after the fight. The news of this victory obtained by the Mussulmans was soon spread throughout Egypt. The sultan of Cairo wrote to the governor of Damascus, to inform him of the last triumphs of Islamism. "Let thanks be rendered," said he in his letter, "to the All Powerful, who has changed our sadness into joy; it is to him alone we owe the glory of our arms; the blessings with which he has deigned to favour us are numberless, and the last is the most precious of all. You will announce to the people of Damascus, or rather to all Mussulmans, that God has enabled us to gain a complete victory over the Christians, at the moment they were conspiring to effect our ruin." [317]

The day after that on which the Christian army had laid down their arms, the king of France was taken to Mansourah on board a war-boat, escorted by a great number of Egyptian vessels. The trumpets and kettle-drums carried the notes of triumph to a vast distance. The Egyptian army, in order of battle, marched along the eastern bank of the Nile as the fleet advanced. All the prisoners whom the fury of the enemy had spared, followed the Mussulman troops, with their hands tied behind them. The Arabs were in arms on the western bank, and the multitude flocked from all parts to witness this strange spectacle. On his arrival at Mansourah, Louis IX. was confined in the house of Fakreddin ben Lokman, secretary of the sultan, and placed under the guard of the eunuch Sabyh. A vast inclosure, surrounded by walls of earth, and guarded by the fiercest of the Mussulman warriors, received the other prisoners of war.

The news of these disasters carried consternation and despair to the city of Damietta, over the walls of which the standard of the French still floated. Confused reports at first were circulated; but soon a few Crusaders, who had escaped from the carnage, announced that the whole Christian army had perished. Queen Marguerite was on the point of being confined: her terrified imagination, at one moment, represented to her her husband falling beneath the swords of the enemy, and at the next, the Saracens at the gates of the city. Her emotions became so violent, that her servants believed her to be expiring. A knight of more than eighty years of age served her as esquire, and never left her either night or day. This unhappy princess, after having, for a moment, sobbed herself to sleep, started up in the greatest terror, imagining that her chamber was filled with Saracens about to kill her. The old knight, who had held her hand while she slept, pressed it, and said: "Be not afraid, madam, I am with you." An instant after she had reclosed her eyes, she awoke again, and uttered loud and fearful cries, and the grave esquire reassured her again. At length, to free herself from these cruel alarms, the queen ordered every one to leave her chamber except her knight, and then, throwing herself upon her knees before him, with tearful eyes, she exclaimed: "Sir knight, promise that you will grant the favour I am about to ask of you." He promised upon his oath. Marguerite then continued: "I require you, on the faith you have pledged to me, that if the Saracens should take this city, you will cut off my head rather than allow me to become their captive." "Certainly, I will do it," replied the old knight; "I meant to do so, if the thing should so happen!" [318]

On the morrow the queen was brought to bed of a son, who was named Jean Tristan, on account of the melancholy circumstances amidst which he was born. The same day her attendants informed her that the Pisans, and many Crusaders from the maritime cities of Europe, were desirous of abandoning Damietta and returning to their homes. Marguerite caused the leaders of them to be brought before her bed, and said to them: "Seigneurs, for the love of God, do not quit this city; its loss would bring on that of the king and of the whole Christian army. Be moved by my tears, have pity on the poor child that you behold lying beside me!" The merchants of Genoa and Pisa were at first but very little affected by these words. Joinville reproaches them with bitterness for their want of feeling for the cause of Christ, or for that of humanity. As they answered the queen that they had no provisions left, this princess gave orders that all the provisions in Damietta should be immediately bought up, and caused it to be announced to the Genoese and Pisans, that from that time they should be supported at the expense of the king. By this means, the city of Damietta preserved a garrison and defenders, whose presence, more than their valour, produced an effect upon the Saracens. It is even asserted that the Mussulmans, after the victory of Minieh, being desirous of surprising Damietta, presented themselves before the walls, clothed in the arms and bearing the standards of the conquered Christians; but they were betrayed by their language, their long beards, and their bronzed countenances. As the Christians showed themselves in great numbers upon the ramparts, the enemy drew off in haste from a city which they believed was disposed to defend itself, but in which, really, nothing but despondency and fear prevailed.

During this time, Louis IX. was more calm at Mansourah than they were at Damietta. That which misery and misfortune have of the most bitter for the exalted of this world, only served to develop in him the virtue of a Christian hero and the character of a great king. He had no covering at night but a coarse cassock, which he owed to the charity of another prisoner. In this state, he never addressed one petition to his enemies, nor did the tone of his language announce either fear or submission. One of his almoners afterwards attested upon oath, that Louis never suffered a word of despair or a movement of impatience to escape from him. The Mussulmans were astonished at this resignation, and said among themselves, that if ever their prophet should leave them a prey to such great adversities, they would abandon his faith and his worship. Of all his riches, Louis had only saved his book of psalms, too sterile a spoil to be worth the attention of the Saracens; and when all the world seemed to have abandoned him, this book alone consoled him in his misfortunes. He every day recited those hymns of the prophets in which God himself speaks of his justice and his mercy, reassures virtue which suffers in his name, and threatens with his anger those whom prosperity intoxicates, and who abuse their triumph.

Thus religious sentiments and remembrances sustained the courage of Louis even in fetters; and the pious monarch, surrounded every day by fresh perils, amidst a Mussulman army that he had irritated by his victories, might still cry out with the prophet-king: "Supported by the living God, who is my buckler and my glory, I will not fear the crowd of enemies encamped around me."

The sultan of Cairo, appearing inclined to soften his rigorous policy, sent Louis fifty magnificent dresses for himself and the lords of his train. Louis refused to clothe himself in them, saying that he was the sovereign of a greater kingdom than Egypt, and that he would never wear the livery of a foreign prince. Almoadam ordered a great feast to be prepared, to which he invited the king. But Louis would not accept of this invitation, as he was persuaded it was only meant to exhibit him as a spectacle to the Mussulman army. At length the sultan sent his most skilful physicians to him, and did all he could to preserve a prince whom he destined to adorn his triumph, and by whose means he hoped to obtain the advantages attached to his last victory. Before long he proposed to the king to break his chains upon condition of his giving up Damietta and the cities of Palestine that were still under the power of the Franks. Louis replied, that the Christian cities of Palestine did not belong to him; that God had recently replaced Damietta in the hands of the Christians, and that no human power had the right to dispose of it. The sultan, irritated by this refusal, resolved to employ violence. At one time he threatened Louis to send him to the caliph of Bagdad, who would closely imprison him till death; at another, he announced the project of leading his illustrious captive throughout the East, and of exhibiting to all Asia a king of the Christians reduced to slavery. At length he went so far as to threaten to have him placed in the *bernicles*, [319] a frightful punishment reserved for the greatest criminals. Louis still showed himself firm, and, as the only reply to all these menaces, said, "I am the sultan's prisoner, he can do with me what he pleases."

The king of France suffered, though he did not complain; he feared nothing on his own account, but when he thought of his faithful army, and of the fate of the other captives, his heart was a prey to the deepest sorrow. The Christian prisoners were crowded into one open court, some sick, others wounded, the greater part naked, and all exposed to hunger, the injuries of the elements, and the ill-treatment of their pitiless guards. A Mussulman was commanded to write the names of all these wretched captives, whose number amounted to more than ten thousand. They led all such as could purchase their liberty into a vast tent; the others remained in the place into which they had been driven like a flock of animals, destined to perish miserably. Every day an emir, by the sultan's orders, entered this abode of despair, and caused two or three hundred prisoners be be dragged out of the inclosure. They were asked if they would abjure the religion of Christ, and those whom the fear of death induced to desert their faith, received their liberty; the others were put to the sword, and their bodies were cast into the Nile. They were slaughtered during the night; silence and darkness adding to the horrors of the execution. During several days the steel of the executioner thus decimated the unhappy prisoners. None were ever seen to return who went out of the inclosure. Their sad companions, on bidding them farewell, wept beforehand over their tragical end, and lived in certain expectation of a similar fate. At length the lassitude of slaughter caused those that remained to be spared. They were led away to Cairo; and the capital of Egypt, into which they had flattered themselves they should enter in triumph, beheld them arrive covered with rags and loaded with chains. They were thrown into dungeons, where many died of hunger and grief; the others, condemned to slavery in a foreign land, deprived of all assistance and of all communication with their leaders, without knowing what was become of their king, were hopeless of ever recovering their liberty, or of revisiting the West.

The Oriental historians relate the scenes we have just described with indifference; many even seem to consider the massacre of prisoners of war as a second victory; and, as if the misfortune and murder of a disarmed enemy could heighten the glory of a conqueror, they exaggerate in their accounts the misery of the vanquished, and particularly the number of the victims immolated to Islamism.

The barons and knights that were shut up in the pavilion, were not ignorant of the fate of their companions in arms; they passed their days and nights in continual terrors. The sultan wished to obtain from them that which he had not been able to obtain from Louis IX. He sent an emir to inform them that he would set them at liberty if Damietta and the Christian cities of Palestine were restored to the Mussulmans. The count of Brittany replied in the name of all the prisoners, that that which was asked of them was not in their power, and that French warriors had no other will than that of their king. "It is plainly to be perceived," said the messenger of Almoadam, "that you care very little for liberty or life. *You shall see some men accustomed to sword-playing.*" The emir retired, leaving the prisoners in the expectation of an early death. The apparatus of punishment was exhibited before them. The sword remained several days suspended over their heads; but Almoadam could make no impression upon their firmness. Thus, neither the captivity of an entire army, nor the death of so many warriors, had been able to deprive the Christians of a single one of their conquests, and one of the bulwarks of Egypt was still in their hands. The conquerors prayed and threatened by turns; the conquered resisted all their endeavours, and always appeared masters.

In the mean time several French nobles offered to pay their own ransom. Louis was informed of this; and as he feared that many, not having the means to redeem themselves, would remain in chains, he forbade any particular treaty. The barons and knights, but lately so intractable, did not persist in opposing the will of an unfortunate king, and instantly gave up all idea of a separate negotiation. The king said he would pay for everybody, and that he would never think about his own liberty till after he had assured that of all others.

Whilst the sultan of Cairo was thus making useless attempts to overcome the pride and lower the courage of Louis and his knights, the favourites he had brought with him from Mesopotamia pressed their master to conclude the peace quickly. "You have," said they to him, "enemies much more dangerous than the Christians; they are the emirs, who wish to reign in your place, and who never cease to boast of their victories, as if you had not yourself conquered the Franks, as if the God of Mahomet had not sent pestilence and famine to aid you in triumphing over the defenders of Christ: hasten, then, to terminate the war, in order that you may strengthen your power within, and begin to reign." These speeches, which flattered the pride of Almoadam, induced him to make rather more reasonable proposals to his enemies. The sultan limited his demand to a ransom of a million of golden byzants, and the restitution of Damietta. Louis, aware that the city of Damietta could not resist, consented to the proposals that were made to him, *if the queen approved of them.* As the Mussulmans expressed some surprise at this, the king added, "*The queen is my lady, I can do nothing without her consent.*" The ministers of the sultan returned a second time, and told the French monarch, that if the queen would pay the sum agreed upon, he should be free. "A king of France," answered he, "is not to be redeemed by money; the city of Damietta shall be given up for my deliverance, [320] and a million of golden byzants paid for that of my army." The sultan agreed to all; and, whether he was pleased at having terminated the negotiations, or whether he was touched by the noble character the captive monarch had displayed, he reduced the sum fixed upon as the ransom of the Christian army a fifth.

The knights and barons were still ignorant of the conclusion of the treaty, and were revolving in their minds their customary melancholy reflections, when they saw an old Saracen enter their pavilion. His venerable figure and the gravity of his carriage inspired respect. His train, composed of men-at-arms, inspired fear. The old man, without any preliminary discourse, asked the prisoners, by means of an interpreter, if it was true that they believed in a God, born of a woman, crucified for the salvation of the human race, and resuscitated the third day? All having answered at once that that was their belief: "In that case," added he, "congratulate yourselves at suffering for your God; you are yet far from having suffered as much for him as he suffered for you. Place your hopes in him, and if he has been able to recall himself to life, he will not want power to put an end to the evils that afflict you now."

On finishing these words, the old Mussulman retired, leaving the Crusaders divided between surprise, fear, and hope. On the next day it was announced to them that the king had concluded a truce, and wished to take counsel of his barons. John of Vallery, Philip de Montfort, and Guy and Baldwin d'Ibelin were deputed to wait upon the king. It was not long before the Crusaders learnt that their captivity was about to end, and that the king had paid the ransom of the poor as well as the rich. When these brave knights turned their thoughts towards their victories, they never could conceive how it was possible for them to have fallen into the hands of the infidels; and when they reflected on their late misfortunes, their deliverance appeared equally miraculous to them. All raised their voices in praises to God and benedictions to the king of France.

All the cities of Palestine that had belonged to the Christians at the arrival of the Crusaders in the East, were comprised in the treaty. On both sides, the prisoners of war made since the truce concluded between the emperor Frederick and Melik-Kamel, were to be given up. It was agreed, also, that the munitions and machines of war belonging to the Christian army should remain provisionally at Damietta, under the safeguard of the sultan of Egypt.

It next became the object to perform the conditions of the treaty of peace. Four large galleys were prepared to transport the principal prisoners to the mouth of the Nile. The sultan left Mansourah, and repaired to Pharescour by land.

After the battle of Minieh, a vast palace, built of fir timber, of which the chronicles of the times have left pompous descriptions, had been erected in that city. It was in this palace Almoadam received the felicitations of the Mussulmans, upon the happy issue of a war against the enemies of Islamism. All the cities, all the principalities of Syria, sent ambassadors to salute the conqueror of the Christians. The governor of Damascus, to whom he had sent a helmet, found on the field of battle, that had belonged to the king of France, replied to him thus: "There is no doubt that God destines for you the conquest of the universe, or that you will proceed from victory to victory; who can doubt of this when we already see your slaves clothed in the spoils of conquered kings?" Thus the young sultan imbibed intoxicating draughts of praise, and passed his time in the festivities and pleasures of peace, forgetting the cares of his empire, and foreseeing none of the dangers which threatened him amidst his triumphs.

Almoadam had disgraced, and deprived of their places, many of the ministers of his father; most of the emirs were in fear of a similar fall, and this fear even led them to brave everything for the preservation of their fortunes and their lives. Among these malcontents, the Mamelukes and their leader were most conspicuous. This military body owed their origin to Saladin, and they had enjoyed the greatest privileges under the preceding reign. They reproached the sultan with preferring young favourites to old warriors, the support of the throne and the saviours of Egypt. They reproached him with having concluded a peace, without consulting those who had supported the burden of the war; and with having bestowed the spoils of the vanquished upon courtiers, who had only deserved them by coming from the banks of the Euphrates to the shores of the Nile. In order to justify beforehand all they might attempt against the prince, they attributed to him projects of the most sinister nature; and nascent rebellion inflamed itself by the recital of future persecutions. The emirs who were to die were designated; the instruments of death were named, the day was fixed, everything was appointed, everything was ready. It was asserted that the sultan, in the course of one of his nocturnal orgies, had cut off the tops of the flambeaux in his apartment, crying, "Thus shall fly the heads of all the Mamelukes." A woman animated the minds of the warriors by her discourse: this was Chegger-Eddour, who, having disposed of the empire, could not endure the neglect of the new sultan. From complaints they soon passed to open revolt; for it was less perilous to attack the prince sword in hand, than to declaim for any length of time against him. A conspiracy was formed, in which the Mamelukes and all the emirs who had outrages to avenge or to fear were concerned. The conspirators were impatient to execute their project, and fearing that the sultan, if once arrived at Damietta, might escape them, they resolved to proceed to the consummation at Pharescour.

The galleys which transported the Christian prisoners arrived before that city. The king landed, with the princes, his brothers, and was received in a pavilion, where he had an interview with the sultan. History says nothing of this conference between two princes, who equally commanded attention, and whose position was so different; the one, intoxicated by his victories, blinded by his prosperities; the other, the conqueror of ill-fortune, coming out much greater from the ordeal of adversity.

The two sovereigns had appointed Saturday, the eve of the Ascension, for the giving up of Damietta. According to this convention, the Crusaders, who had been detained more than a month in chains, had only to endure the pains of captivity three days longer; but new misfortunes awaited them, and their courage and resignation were doomed to further trials. The day after their arrival before Pharescour, the sultan of Cairo, in celebration of the peace, determined to give a banquet to the principal officers of the Mussulman army. The conspirators took advantage of this opportunity, and, towards the end of the repast, all rushed upon him, sword in hand. Bendocdar struck the first blow. Almoadam, being only wounded in the hand, arises in a state of terrified amazement, escapes through his motionless guards, takes refuge in a tower, shuts the door of it, and appears at a window, sometimes imploring succour, and sometimes demanding of the conspirators what they required of him. The envoy of the caliph of Bagdad was at Pharescour. He mounted on horseback, but the Mamelukes threatened him with instant death if he did not return to his tent. At the same moment some drums were heard, giving the signal for assembling the troops; but the leaders of the conspiracy told the soldiers that Damietta was taken, and immediately the whole army precipitated themselves upon the road to that city, leaving the sultan at the mercy of men who thirsted for his blood. The Mamelukes accuse and threaten him. He endeavours to justify himself; but his words are drowned in the tumult. A thousand voices cry out to him to descend; he hesitates; he groans; he weeps; arrows fly against the tower in showers; the Greek fire, hurled from every direction, gives birth to a conflagration. Almoadam, nearly surrounded by the flames, precipitates himself from the window; a nail catches his mantle, and he remains for a moment suspended. At length he falls to the earth; sabres and naked swords wave over him on all sides; he casts himself on his knees, at the feet of Octai, one of the principal officers of his guard, who repulses him with contempt. The unhappy prince arises, holding forth his imploring hands to all the assembly, saying, that he was willing to abandon the throne of Egypt, and would return into Mesopotamia. These supplications, unworthy of a prince, inspire more contempt than pity; nevertheless, the crowd of conspirators hesitate; but the leaders know too well there can be no safety for them but in completing the crime they have begun. Bendocdar, who had inflicted the first blow, strikes him a second time with his sabre; Almoadam, streaming with blood, throws himself into the Nile, and endeavours to gain some vessels that appear to be drawing near to the shore to receive him; nine Mamelukes follow him into the water, and pour upon him a thousand blows, within sight of the galley which Joinville was on board of! [321]

Such was the end of Almoadam, who neither knew how to reign nor how to die. Arabian authors point it out as a remarkable circumstance, that he perished at once by the sword, fire, and water. The same authors agree in saying, that he himself provoked his ruin by his imprudence and his injustice. But oriental history, accustomed to laud success and blame all who succumb, repeats the complaints of the Mamelukes without examining them; and, passing lightly over this revolution, contents itself with saying, "When God wills an event, he prepares the causes beforehand."

The Nile and its shore presented, at that moment, two very different spectacles: on one side was a prince, whilst revelling in all the pomps of grandeur, in all the triumphs of victory, massacred by his own guards; on the other, an unfortunate king, surrounded by his knights, as unfortunate as himself, inspiring them with more respect in his adversity than when he was encompassed with all the splendour of prosperity and power. The French knights and barons, although they had been victims of the barbarity of the sultan, felt more astonishment than joy at the sight of his tragical death; they could not comprehend the murderous attack of the Mamelukes; and these revolutions of military despotism, at war with itself, filled them with dread.

After this sanguinary scene, thirty Saracen officers, sword in hand and battle-axes on their shoulders, entered the galley in which were the counts of Brittany and de Montfort, Baldwin and Guy d'Ibelin, and the sieur de Joinville. These furious men vomited imprecations, and threatening the prisoners with both voice and gesture, made them believe that their last hour was come. The Christian warriors prepared themselves for death, and throwing themselves on their knees before a monk of the Trinity, asked him for absolution of their sins; but as the priest could not hear them all at once, they confessed to each other. Guy d'Ibelin, constable of Cyprus, confessed to Joinville, who gave him "such absolution as God had given him the power to give." It was thus, in after-times, history represents the Chevalier Bayard, wounded to death, and ready to expire, confessing himself at the foot of an oak to one of his faithful companions in arms. [322]

But these menaces and violences of the emirs might have a politic aim. At the conclusion of a conspiracy that had divided men's minds, in order to awaken fresh passions, it was necessary for the leaders to excite the fanaticism of the multitude, and direct the general fury against the Christians. It was important for them to make others believe, and they might have believed it themselves, that Almoadam had endeavoured to find an asylum amongst the enemies of Islamism.

The lords and barons did not meet with the fate they expected; but as if their understanding with Almoadam had been really dreaded, they were thrust into the hold of the vessel, where they passed the night with the terrible images of death constantly before their eyes.

Louis, shut up in his tent with his brothers, had heard the tumult. In ignorance of what was passing, he concluded that either they were massacring the French prisoners, or else that Damietta was taken. He was a prey to a thousand terrors, when he saw Octaï, the chief of the Mamelukes, enter his tent. This emir ordered the guards to retire, and pointing to his bloody sword, exclaimed: "Almoadam is no more; what will you give me for having delivered you from an enemy who meditated your destruction as well as ours?" Louis made no reply. Then the furious emir, presenting the point of his sword, cried, "Dost thou not know that I am master of thy person? Make me a knight, or thou art a dead man." "Make thyself a Christian," replied the monarch, "and I will make thee a knight." [323] Without insisting further, Octaï retired, and in a very short time the tent of the king was filled with Saracen warriors, armed with sabres and swords. Their demeanour, their cries, the fury painted on their countenances, announced sufficiently that they had just committed a great crime, and that they were ready to commit others; but by a species of miracle, changing, all at once, both countenance and language at the sight of the king, they approached him with respect; then, as if they felt in the presence of Louis the necessity for justifying themselves, they told him that they had been forced to kill a tyrant, who aimed at their destruction as well as that of the Christians; now, they added, they had only to forget the past; all they required for the future was the faithful execution of the treaty concluded with Almoadam. Then lifting their hands to their turbans, and bending their brows to the ground, they retired in silence, and left the monarch in a state of astonishment at seeing them thus pass, all at once, from transports of rage to sentiments apparently the most respectful.

This singular scene has made some historians say that the Mamelukes offered the throne of Egypt to St. Louis. This opinion has rather gained ground in our days, so easy is it for us to give faith to everything that appears favourable to the glory of the French name. The sieur de Joinville, who is quoted in support of this assertion, only relates a conversation he had held with Louis. The king asked him what he thought he ought to have done, in case the emirs had offered him the supreme authority. The good seneschal conceived it was not possible to accept a crown from the hands of those seditious emirs, who had killed their sovereign. Louis was not of this opinion, and said that, truly, if they had proposed to him to become the successor of the sultan, he would not in the least have refused to be so (*il ne l'eût mie refusé*). [324] These words alone prove sufficiently that they had proposed nothing to the captive monarch. Joinville, it is true, adds to this recital, that according to reports that were circulated in the Christian army, the emirs had caused the trumpets to be sounded and the drums to be beaten before the tent of the king of France, and that at the same time they deliberated among themselves, whether it would not be best to break the chains of their prisoner, and make him their sovereign. The sieur de Joinville relates this fact, without affirming it; and as oriental history preserves the most profound silence upon it, an historian of the present day cannot adopt it without compromising his veracity. It is, without doubt, possible that the emirs might have expressed the desire of having a prince amongst them possessed of the firmness, bravery, and virtues of Louis IX.; but how can it be believed that Mussulmans, animated by the double fanaticism of religion and war, could have, for a moment, entertained a thought of choosing an absolute master among the Christians, whom they had just treated with unexampled barbarity; and thus place their property, their liberty, their lives in the hands of the most implacable enemies of their country, their laws, and their faith?

The supreme power, of which the emirs had shown themselves to be so jealous, and which they had wrested with so much violence from the hands of Almoadam, appeared at first to terrify their ambition, when they had it in their power to dispose of it. In a council called to nominate a sultan, the wisest declined to rule over a country filled with troubles, or command an army given up to the spirit of sedition. Upon their refusal, the crown was given to Chegger-Eddour, who had had so great a share, first in the elevation, and then in the fall of Almoadam. As governor with her, in the quality of Atabec, they chose Ezz-Eddin Aybek, who had been brought a slave into Egypt, and whose barbarous origin procured him the surname of the *Turcoman*.

The new sultana soon arrived at Pharescour, and was proclaimed under the name of Mostassemieh Salehieh, queen of the Mussulmans, mother of Malek-Almansor Khalil. Almansor Khalil, a young prince, the son of Negmeddin, had preceded his father to the tomb. Thus finished the powerful dynasty of the Ayoubites, a dynasty founded by victory, and overturned by an army which the pride of victory had rendered seditious. Whilst they were thus forming a new government, the body of Almoadam was abandoned on the banks of the Nile, where it remained two days without sepulture. The ambassador from the caliph of Bagdad at length obtained permission to bury it, and deposited in an obscure place the sad remains of the last successor of Saladin.

The elevation of Chegger-Eddour astonished the Mussulmans; the name of a woman or of a slave had never till that time been seen engraved upon the coins, or pronounced in public prayers. The caliph of Bagdad protested against the scandal of this innovation; and when he afterwards wrote to the emirs, he asked them if they had not been able to find a single man in all Egypt to govern them. The supreme authority, placed in the hands of a woman, could neither restrain the passions which troubled the empire, nor cause treaties to be respected; which became very fatal to the Christians, condemned to suffer by turns from the revolt and the submission, from the union and the discord of their enemies.

Among the emirs, some wished that the treaty concluded with the sultan should be executed; whilst others were desirous that a fresh one should be made: many were indignant that the Christians should be treated with at all. After long debates, they returned to that which had been done at first, adding to it the condition that the king of France should give up Damietta before he was set at liberty, and that he should pay half of the sum agreed upon for the ransom of himself and his army, before he left the banks of the Nile. These last conditions announced the mistrust of the emirs, and might give the Christian prisoners reason to fear that the day of their deliverance was not yet arrived.

When the observance of the treaty was to be sworn to, the forms of the oaths caused some discussion. The emirs swore that if they failed in their promises, "they consented to be jeered at like the pilgrim who makes the journey to Mecca bareheaded; or else to be as much despised as he who takes back his women after having left them." The Mussulmans, according to their manners and customs, had no more solemn expression with which to guarantee their sworn faith. They proposed to Louis IX. the following formula: "If I keep not my oath, I shall be like to him who denies his God, who spits upon the cross, and tramples it under-foot." This formula of the oath which they wished the king to take, appeared to him to be an insult to God and himself. He refused to pronounce it. In vain the emirs showed their anger and their passion; he braved all their menaces. This resistance of St. Louis, celebrated by his contemporaries, will not perhaps obtain the same eulogies in the age we now live in; nevertheless it must be considered that the king was not only restrained on this occasion by the scruples of an exaggerated devotion, but by a feeling of royal dignity. It may be remembered, that in the third crusade, Richard and Saladin had judged it unworthy of the majesty of kings to degrade their word to the formula of an oath; and had been satisfied with a touch of the hand, to cement the peace. Seditious emirs, still stained with the blood of their master, might undervalue the dignity of the supreme rank; but, on important occasions, Louis never forgot he was a great king; and the supposition of a perjury, the thought even of a blasphemy, could not ally itself in his mind with the character of a Christian prince and of a king of France.

The Mussulmans, irritated at seeing a king in fetters dictate laws to them, and resist all their demands, began to talk of putting him to death accompanied by tortures. "You are masters of my body," he replied, "but you have no power over my will." The princes, his brothers, implored him to pronounce the required formula; but he was as firm against the entreaties of friendship and affection, as he had been against the threats of his enemies. Even the exhortations of the prelates had no more effect. At length the Mamelukes, attributing such an obstinate resistance to the patriarch of Jerusalem, seized this prelate, who was more than eighty years of age, fastened him to a post, and tied his hands behind him so tightly, that the blood sprang from beneath the nails. The patriarch, overcome by the pain, cried, "Sire! Sire! swear; I will take the sin upon myself." But Louis, who was throughout persuaded that they insulted his good faith, and that they demanded of him a thing unjust and dishonourable, remained immovable. The emirs, at length subdued by so much firmness, consented to accept the simple word of the king, and retired, saying that "this Frank prince was the most haughty Christian that had ever been seen in the East."

All now gave their attention to the execution of the treaty. The galleys, on board of which were the prisoners, heaved their anchors, and descended towards the mouth of the Nile; the Mussulman army accompanying them by land. The Christians were to deliver up Damietta the next morning at daybreak. It is impossible to describe the trouble, consternation, and despair that reigned in the city throughout the night. The unfortunate inhabitants ran about the streets, asking each other questions, and communicating their fears with breathless anxiety. The most sinister reports prevailed; it was said that the whole of the Christian army had been massacred by the Mussulmans, and that the king of France was poisoned. When they received orders to evacuate the place, most of the warriors declared aloud that they would not obey, and that they preferred dying on the ramparts to being slaughtered as prisoners of war.

At the same time excitement began to prevail in the Mussulman army. It was whispered that the king of France refused to execute the treaty, and that he had ordered the garrison of Damietta to defend themselves. The soldiers and their leaders repented of having made a truce with the Franks, and appeared determined to take advantage of the least pretext for breaking it.

The commissioners of Louis IX., however, at length persuaded the Christians of Damietta to evacuate the city. Queen Marguerite, scarcely recovered from her confinement, went on board a Genoese vessel. She was accompanied by the duchess of Anjou, the countess of Poictiers, and the unhappy widow of the count d'Artois, who, amidst present calamities, still wept over the first misfortune of the war. Towards the end of the night, Olivier de Thermes, who commanded the garrison, the duke of Burgundy, the pope's legate, and all the Franks, except the sick that remained in the city, embarked on the Nile.

Geoffrey de Sergines having entered Damietta, brought the keys to the emirs; and when day broke, the Mussulman standards were seen floating over the towers and ramparts. At sight of this, the whole Egyptian army rushed tumultuously into the city. The reports that had been circulated during the night, had excited the fury of the soldiers, and they entered Damietta as if the opening of the gates had been the result of a sanguinary contest; they massacred the sick wherever they found them, they pillaged the houses, and gave to the flames the machines of war, the arms, and all the munitions that belonged to the Christians.

This early violation of the treaty, the intoxication of carnage, and the impunity of license, only served to inflame still further the minds of the Mussulmans, and to lead them to greater excesses. The emirs, partaking of the fury of the soldiers, formed the idea of putting all the Christian prisoners to death. The galleys in which the French barons and knights were crowded, immediately received orders to reascend the river towards Pharescour, "which caused great grief amongst us," says Joinville, "and many tears issued from our eyes; for we all believed they were about to kill us."

Whilst the galleys re-ascended the Nile, the Mussulman leaders deliberated in council upon the fate of the king of France and the French warriors. "Now we are masters of Damietta," said one of the emirs, "and a powerful monarch of the Franks, with the bravest of his warriors, may receive from our hands death or liberty. Fortune offers us an opportunity of securing peace to Egypt for ever, and with it the triumph of Islamism. We have shed the blood of Mussulman princes without scruple; why should we then respect that of Christian princes, who have come into the East to set fire to our cities and reduce our provinces to slavery?" This opinion was that of the people and the army; and most of the emirs, actuated by the general spirit, held similar language. An emir of Mauritania, whose name Joinville has not preserved, opposed, almost alone, this violation of the laws of war and peace. "You have," said he, "put to death your prince, whom the Koran commands you *to cherish as the apple of your eye*. This death might, doubtless, be necessary for your own safety; but what can you expect from the action that is proposed to you, except the anger of God and the maledictions of men?" This speech was interrupted by murmurs; the language of reason only added heat to hatred and fanaticism. As violent passions are never at a loss for motives of self-justification, or for excuses for their excesses, the Crusaders were accused of perfidy, treachery, and all the crimes that they themselves contemplated against them. There was no imputation that did not appear probable, consequently no violence that did not appear just. "If the Koran ordered Mussulmans to watch over the lives of their princes, it likewise commanded them to watch over the preservation of the Mussulman faith: death ought to be the reward of those who came to bring death, and their bones ought to whiten upon the same plains that they had laid waste. The safety of Egypt and the laws of the prophet required that it should be so."

After a very stormy deliberation, the terrible sentence of the captives was about to be pronounced; but cupidity came to the aid of justice and humanity; [325] the emir who had spoken in favour of the Christian prisoners, had, in his speech, more than once repeated the words, *Dead men pay no ransom*; and they at length acknowledged that the sword, by immolating the Crusaders, would only rob victory of its dues, and deprive the conquerors of the fruit of their labours. This observation at length calmed the minds of the assembly, and brought about a change of opinions. The fear of losing eight hundred thousand golden byzants caused the treaty to be respected, and saved the lives of the king of France and his companions in misfortune.

The emirs issued orders for the galleys to be brought back towards Damietta. The Mamelukes appeared, all at once, to be governed by the most pacific sentiments; and, as it is natural for the multitude to pass from one extreme to another, they treated with all the attentions of hospitality the very men whom, a few hours before, they had wished to put to death. On their arrival before the city, the prisoners were treated with fritters cooked in the sun, and with hard eggs, "which," says Joinville, "in honour of our persons, were painted of various colours."

The knights and barons at length had permission to leave the ships that had been their prisons, to go and join the king, whom many of them had not seen since the disaster of Minieh. As they left their vessels, Louis was marching towards the mouth of the Nile, escorted by Mussulman warriors; an innumerable multitude followed him, and contemplated, in silence, the features, the bearing, and the arms of the Christian monarch. A Genoese galley awaited him; as soon as he was on board, eighty archers, with their crossbows strung, appeared suddenly upon the deck of the vessel; the crowd of Egyptians immediately dispersed, and the ship glided away from the shore. Louis had with him the count of Anjou, the count de Soissons, Geoffrey de Sergines, Philip de Nemours, and the seneschal de Joinville. The count of Poictiers remained as a hostage in Damietta, until the payment of the four hundred thousand golden byzants, which the king ought to have paid to the emirs before he put to sea, should be completed. Louis had not enough by thirty thousand livres; this sum was requested of the Templars, who, to the great scandal of the lords and barons, at first refused it. They were threatened with being forced to furnish it; and then complied. The amount stipulated in the treaty was paid to the Saracens. The count of Poictiers had left Damietta, and everything was ready for the departure of the Crusaders, when Philip de Montfort, who had been directed to make the payment, returned to give an account of his mission, and told the king that he had contrived to cheat the emirs out of ten thousand livres. Louis expressed himself much dissatisfied with such a proceeding, and sent Philip de Montfort back to Damietta, to make restitution of the money he had kept back—a lesson of justice which he wished to give to both his enemies and his servants. This last mission is spoken of by an Arabian author, who attributes it to a very whimsical and singular motive. He says that Philip de Montfort was sent to the emirs to tell them that they were deficient in religion and good sense; in religion, because they had murdered their sovereign; in good sense, because, for a moderate sum, they had released a powerful prince, who would have given half of his kingdom to recover his liberty. This explanation, however improbable it may be, at least serves to inform us of the opinion then common in the East, that the Egyptian emirs were reproached with having destroyed their sultan, and allowed their enemy to escape.

Louis IX., with the miserable wreck of his army, soon passed out at the mouth of the Nile, and in a few days arrived at Ptolemaïs, where the people and the clergy were still putting up prayers for his deliverance.

The Egyptians celebrated the restitution of Damietta with public rejoicings; the Mussulman army broke up their camp, and returned towards the capital. The sultana, Chegger-Eddour, caused vests of gold and silver to be distributed to the leaders, and her liberality even extended to the soldiers. An Arabian poet composed some verses upon this occasion, which history has preserved, and which contain the remarkable passage that follows:—

> "When thou shalt see this Frenchman (the king of France), tell him these words from the mouth of a sincere friend:
>
> Thou camest into Egypt, thou covetedest its riches; thou believedst that its powers would fade away as smoke.
>
> Behold now thine army! see how thy imprudent conduct has precipitated it into the bosom of the tomb!
>
> Fifty thousand men! and not one that is not either killed, a prisoner, or covered with wounds!
>
> And if he should be ever tempted to come to avenge his defeat; if any motive should bring him back to these places;
>
> Tell him, that the house of the son of Lokman is reserved for him; that he will still find there both his chains and the eunuch Sabyh." [326]

Whilst Louis IX. was landing at Ptolemaïs, general consternation prevailed in the West; as it always happens in distant wars, fame had spread the most extraordinary reports relative to the expedition of the Crusaders. At first it was believed that the Christian standards were floating from the walls of Cairo and Alexandria; but to these news other rumours soon succeeded, announcing great disasters. The most marvellous accounts had found plenty of credulous minds in France to receive them; they refused to believe in reverses, and the first who spoke of them were given up to the hands of justice, as enemies of religion and of the kingdom. The sinister reports, however, were not long in being confirmed; the people passed from the excess of joy to the excess of grief; there was not a family in the kingdom that had not to deplore a loss in the disasters of which they acquired the painful certainty. But for the French, that which rendered so many misfortunes irreparable, and for which no one could find consolation, was the captivity of the king! Dances, festivals, spectacles, [327] everything that bore the air of joy or pleasure, was forbidden: the kingdom, plunged in sorrow and abasement, appeared, all at once, to be like one of those cities of which the Scripture speaks,—threatened with the wrath of God, they gave themselves up to grief, and covered themselves with the mourning garb of penitence.

The whole Church deplored so great a misfortune with torrents of tears; the father of the faithful was nearly in despair for the safety of Christendom. He addressed letters filled with affliction to all the prelates of the West. He ordered the clergy to put up public prayers; he exhorted the faithful to take up arms. Innocent wrote to Blanche to console her, and to Louis to sustain him in his adversity. When addressing the king of France, he is astonished at finding one man oppressed by so many calamities, and endowed with so many virtues; and demands of God what justice had been able to find in the most Christian of kings, which deserved to be expiated by misfortunes so great.

England was likewise much afflicted by the captivity of the French monarch; the barons and knights were indignant towards their king for having prevented them from going into the East to share the perils of the Crusaders. The King of Castile, then at war with the Moors, was sensible only of the evils of the Christians beyond the seas, and swore to go and fight with the victorious infidels on the banks of the Nile or the Jordan. No monarch of the West expressed more grief than Frederick II., emperor of Germany; in his letters he spoke of the king of France as his best friend, and deplored the disasters of the crusade with bitterness. Frederick, still at variance with the pope, did not neglect this opportunity of accusing Innocent, whom he reproached with the ruin of the Christians. Frederick repaired to Sicily, for the purpose of arming a fleet that might convey prompt assistance to the Crusaders; and whilst the vessels were getting ready, he sent an embassy into the East, to solicit of the sultan of Egypt the deliverance of the king of France and his army.

Amidst the universal desolation, a single Christian city gave demonstrations of joy: Florence, according to Villani, celebrated the reverses of the French Crusaders with festivities. Some pirates from Genoa, Pisa, and Venice took advantage of the disasters of Louis IX. to put to sea, and pillage the Crusaders that were returning into Europe. The joy of the Florentines, and the brigandages of the Italian pirates, were subjects of great scandal for all Christendom.

Louis IX., on his arrival at Ptolemaïs, had only been able to retain a small number of faithful knights; many of the French nobles, the companions of his captivity, instead of following him to Palestine, returned into the West. Among those who had quitted the banner of the crusade, were the duke of Burgundy and the brave count of Brittany: the latter, worn out with sickness and covered with wounds, died on his passage: his mortal remains, preserved by his knights, were transported to the abbey of Villeneuve, near Nantes, where, many ages afterwards, his tomb was still to be seen.

The appearance of the sad remains of the Christian army must have excited the compassion of the inhabitants of Ptolemaïs. Both knights and soldiers were almost naked; the seneschal of Champagne, in order to appear at the king's table, was forced to make himself a vestment of the shreds of a bed-quilt. An epidemic disease, the fruit of lengthened misery and all sorts of privations, broke out among the Crusaders, and soon extended its ravages to the city. Joinville, who was lodged in the house of the curé of Ptolemaïs, informs us that he saw daily twenty convoys pass beneath his windows; and that every time he heard the funeral words, "*Libera me, Domine*" he burst into tears, and addressed himself to God crying, *Mercy!*

In the mean time the king of France was engaged in endeavouring to deliver the captives that still remained in Egypt. These captives amounted to twelve thousand, and most of them might be able to resume their arms and serve under the banner of the crusade. Louis sent his ambassadors to pay the four hundred thousand francs that he still owed to the Saracens, and to press the execution of the last treaties. These ambassadors found Egypt filled with troubles; the emirs were divided into several factions, all disputing for power: fanaticism animated these divisions; they reciprocally accused each other of having favoured or spared the Christians. Amidst these debates, many captives had been massacred, and some forced to abjure the faith of Christ. The messengers of Louis IX. could scarcely obtain a hearing; in answer to their demands, they were told that the king of France might esteem himself fortunate in having regained his liberty, and that the Mamelukes would soon go and besiege him in Ptolemaïs. At length the Christian ambassadors were obliged to quit Egypt without having obtained anything; and only brought back to Palestine four hundred prisoners, the greater part of whom had paid their own ransom.

On their return, Louis IX. was plunged in the deepest distress; he had just received a letter from Queen Blanche, who exhorted him to leave the East. He, thereupon, was desirous of returning to France; but how could he make up his mind to abandon twelve thousand Christians in slavery, or to quit the Holy Land when it was threatened with invasion? The three military orders, the barons, and the nobles of Palestine, conjured Louis not to abandon them; repeating with accents of despair, that if they were deprived of his support, the Christians of Syria would have no other resource than to follow him into the West.

Louis was touched by their prayers, but before he would form a resolution, he was desirous of consulting his two brothers and the principal nobles that had remained with him. He exhibited to them the reasons he had for returning to France, and those that would lead him to remain in Palestine: on the one side, his kingdom threatened by the king of England, and the impossibility of his undertaking anything against the infidels, ought to induce him to quit the East; on the other side, the want of good faith in the emirs, who had failed in executing the first conditions of the treaty; the perils to which the Holy Land would be exposed by his departure; the hope, in short, of receiving succours, and profiting by them, to break the chains of the Christian prisoners and deliver Jerusalem, in some sort, imposed upon him the obligation to defer his return.

After having thus described the state of things, without saying a word that might reveal his own opinion, he requested his knights and barons to reflect seriously upon the line of action it would be best for them to pursue. On the following Sunday he again convoked them, and demanded their opinion. The first that spoke was Guy de Malvoisin, whose bravery in fight and wisdom in council were admired and respected by all the Crusaders. "Sire," said he, addressing Louis, "when I consider the honour of your person and the glory of your reign, I do not think you ought to remain in this country. Remember that flourishing army with which you left the ports of Cyprus, and then turn your eyes upon the warriors you have with you; on that day we reckoned two thousand eight hundred knights with banners in the Christian army; now, one hundred knights constitute your whole force; most of them are sick; they have neither arms nor horses, nor the means of procuring any; they have not the power of serving you with either honour or advantage. You do not possess a single city of war in the East; that in which you now are belongs to several different nations; by remaining here, you inspire no fear in the infidels, and you allow the audacity of your enemies in Europe to increase; you expose yourself to the risk of losing both the kingdom of France, where your absence may embolden ambitious neighbours, and the kingdom of Jesus Christ, upon which your presence will draw the attacks of the Mussulmans. We are all persuaded that the pride of the Saracens should be punished; but it is not in a country far distant from home that the preparations for a decisive and glorious war can be carried on. Thus, then, we advise you to return into the West, where you will watch in safety over the welfare of your states; where you will obtain, amidst a peace which is your own work, the necessary means for avenging our defeats, and, some day, repairing the reverses we have undergone."

The duke of Anjou, the duke of Poictiers, and most of the French nobles, who spoke after Guy de Malvoisin, expressed the same opinion. When they came to the count of Jaffa, he refused to speak, saying, "that he possessed several castles in Palestine, and might be accused of defending his own personal interests." Upon being pressed by the king to give his opinion as the others had done, he contented himself with saying, "that the glory of the Christian arms, that the safety of the land of Jesus Christ, required that the Crusaders should not at that time return to Europe." When it came to Joinville's turn, the good seneschal remembered the advice that his cousin, the seigneur de Bollaincourt, had given him on the eve of his departure for the crusade. "You are going beyond the seas,"—it was thus the good seigneur Bollaincourt expressed himself,—"but take care how you return; no knight, either poor or rich, can come back without shame, if he leaves any of the common people in whose company he quits France in the hands of the Saracens." Joinville, full of the remembrance of these words, declared that they could not abandon the great numbers of Christian prisoners without shame. "These unhappy captives," added he, "were in the service of the king as well as in the service of God; and never will they escape from their captivity if the king should go away." There was not one of the lords and knights who had not either relations or friends among the prisoners; therefore, many of them could not restrain their tears whilst listening to Joinville; but this kindly feeling was not sufficiently strong to stifle in their hearts their desire to revisit their own country. In vain the seneschal added that the king had still a portion of his treasure left; that he could raise troops in the Morea and other countries; and that with the succours which would come from Europe, they should soon be in a condition to renew the war. These reasons, with many others, made no impression upon the greater part of the assembly: they could only view the crusade as a long and painful exile. The sieur de Chastenai, and Beaumont marshal of France, were all that agreed with the opinion of Joinville. "What shall we reply," said they, "to those who shall ask us on our return what we have done with the heritage and the soldiers of Jesus Christ? Listen to the unfortunate inhabitants of Palestine: they accuse us of having brought war to them, and reproach us with preparing their entire ruin by our departure. If we do not receive succours, it will be then time enough to go; but why anticipate days of despair? The Crusaders, it is true, are not in great numbers; but can we forget that their leader, even when in chains, made himself respected by the Saracens? Report, likewise, tells us, that discord prevails among our enemies, and that the sultan of Damascus has declared war against the Mamelukes of Egypt." These two knights spoke amidst the murmurs of their companions; and the more reasonable the opinions they advanced appeared, the greater was the impatience with which they were listened to. The seigneur de Beaumont was about to continue; but he was interrupted with great warmth by his uncle, John de Beaumont, who loaded him with the most bitter reproaches. In vain the king urged the right that every one had to express his opinion; authority of blood prevailed over the authority of the king; the stern old man continued to raise his voice, and reduced his nephew to silence. When he had received the opinions of the assembly, the king dismissed them, and convoked them again for the following Sunday. Upon leaving the council, Joinville found himself exposed to the railleries and insults of the knights, for having expressed an opinion contrary to that of the general meeting. To complete his chagrin, he thought he had incurred the displeasure of the king; and in his despair, he formed the resolution of joining the prince of Antioch, his relation. As he was revolving these gloomy thoughts in his mind, the king took him aside, and opening his heart to him, declared that it was his intention to remain some time longer in Palestine. Then Joinville forgot all the scoffs of the barons and knights; he was so joyous with what the king had told him, that all his griefs were at an end. On the following Sunday the barons assembled for the third time. The king of France invoked the inspiration of the Holy Ghost by a sign of the cross, and pronounced the following words:—"Seigneurs, I thank equally those who have advised me to remain in Asia, and those who have advised me to return to the West. Both, I am convinced, had no other view but the interest of my kingdom and the glory of Jesus Christ. After the most serious and lengthened reflection, I think I may, without injury or peril to my states, prolong my sojourn in this country. The queen, my mother, has defended the honour of my crown in troublesome times; she will now exhibit the same firmness, and will meet with fewer obstacles. No, my kingdom will not suffer by my absence; but if I quit this land, for which Europe has made so many sacrifices, who will protect it against its enemies? Is it to be wished, that, having come here to defend the kingdom of Jerusalem, I shall be hereafter reproached with its ruin? I remain then to save that which is left, to deliver our prisoners, and if possible, to take advantage of the discords of the Saracens. I am not willing, however, to impose restraint upon anybody; such as are desirous of quitting the East are free to depart; as to those who shall determine to remain beneath the banners of the cross, I promise that they shall want for nothing, and that I will ever share with them both good and ill fortune."

After these words, says Joinville, most were astonished, and many began to shed hot tears. From that time, the dukes of Anjou and Poictiers, with a great number of the leaders, made preparations for their departure. Louis charged them with a letter addressed to the clergy, the nobility, and people of his kingdom. In this letter, Louis described, with a noble simplicity, the victories, defeats, and captivity of the Christian knights, and conjured his subjects of all classes to take up arms for the assistance of the Holy Land.

As soon as the two brothers of the king were gone, a levy of soldiers was commenced, and Palestine was placed in a state of defence. But that which most materially favoured the Crusaders, and gave a chance of security to the Christian colonies, was the discord that then prevailed among the Saracens. After the murder of Almoadam, the Mussulmans of Syria refused to recognise the authority of the Mamelukes. The principality and city of Damascus had recently been given up to Nasser, who was preparing to march against Cairo, at the head of a formidable army; the greatest agitation reigned amongst the Mamelukes of Egypt, in whom remorse seemed to be accompanied by fear. The sultana, Chegger-Eddour, was forced to descend from the throne, and to yield the supreme authority to the Turcoman Ezz-Eddin, whose wife she had become. This change allayed agitation for a time; but in such a state of things, one revolution seemed immediately to bring on another. The turbulent, restless soldiery, that had overthrown the empire of the Ayoubites, could neither endure that which was ancient, nor that which was new. To suppress sedition, the leaders at one time exhibited to the multitude a child of that family which they had proscribed, and decorated him with the vain title of sultan. They afterwards declared that Egypt belonged to the caliph of Bagdad, and that they governed it in his name.

It was at this period that the sultan of Aleppo and Damascus sent ambassadors to Louis IX. to invite the French monarch to unite with him to chastise the pride and the revolt of the soldiery of Cairo. He promised the Christians to share with them the spoils of the conquered, and to restore to them the kingdom of Jerusalem. These brilliant promises were likely to produce an effect upon the king of France, and at least merited all his attention. The emirs of Egypt equally solicited the alliance of the Christians, and proposed very advantageous conditions. In the choice before him, there were powerful motives to incline the king to the party of the sultan of Damascus. He had, on one side, to treat with emirs whose good-will was very uncertain, whose fortune might be transitory, and whose authority was menaced and tottering. On the other, he had to deal with a powerful prince, whose authority being much better established, offered a more sure guarantee to his allies. Another motive, which could not be indifferent in the eyes of the virtuous monarch, was, that the only aim of the policy of the Mamelukes was to secure impunity for a great crime, and that the sovereign of Damascus was aiming to avenge the cause of princes. All these considerations were, no doubt, presented in the council of Louis, and must have left the monarch great difficulty in deciding which side it would be best for him to take. But he could not forget that he had signed a treaty with the emirs, and that nothing could liberate him from his oath; but above all, he could not forget that the Mamelukes still held in their hands the destiny of twelve thousand Christian prisoners, and that by breaking with them, he should renounce the hope of delivering the unhappy companions of his captivity. Louis answered the Syrian ambassadors, that he would willingly join his arms to those of the sultan of Damascus, if the Mamelukes did not perform their treaties. At the same time, he sent John de Valence to Cairo, with directions to offer the emirs peace or war. The latter promised at length to fulfil all the conditions of the treaty, if Louis should consent to become their ally and auxiliary: more than two hundred knights were immediately set at liberty.

These unfortunate victims of the crusade arrived at Ptolemaïs about the month of October (1251): the people flocked in crowds to see them land; they exhibited too evident signs of their late captivity, and the remembrance of what they had undergone, together with their present wretchedness, drew tears of compassion from all the spectators. These prisoners, whose chains Louis had succeeded in breaking, brought with them, in a kind of triumph, a coffin, containing the bones of Gauthier de Brienne, who fell into the hands of the infidels at the battle of Gaza, and had been massacred by a furious mob at Cairo. The clergy accompanied the remains of the Christian hero to the church of the Hospitallers; and the companions in arms of Gauthier described his exploits and the glorious death he had undergone for the cause of Christ. Religion displayed all its pomps, and in its holy songs celebrated the glory of a martyr, and the devotion that it alone had inspired. The charity of the faithful relieved and consoled the misery of the captives, and Louis took into his service all whom age or infirmities rendered incapable of bearing arms.

The king learnt with much pain that many Christian prisoners still remained in Egypt. As the Egyptian ambassadors arrived at that time at Ptolemaïs, Louis IX. declared that they must not at all depend upon the alliance they came to solicit, if the emirs did not hasten to liberate all the captives and all the children of Christians brought up in the Mussulman faith, and even send to him the heads of the Crusaders that had been exposed upon the walls of Cairo.

Thus the position of the Christians was ameliorated daily by the divisions among their enemies. The king of France dictated the conditions to the emirs, and if he had had troops, he might have repaired some of the reverses he had experienced in Egypt; but the East furnished him with but a very small number of soldiers, and the West did not seem at all disposed to send him any supplies.

The king of Castile, who had taken the cross, died at the moment he was preparing to set out. In England, Henry III., who had likewise assumed the cross, obtained from the pope and the parliament the power to levy a tenth upon his people and clergy; he at the same time imposed enormous taxes upon the Jews of his kingdom. The preachers of the crusade were directed to announce his approaching departure for the East, and he himself swore upon the Gospel, in the presence of the assembled barons and people, that he would go to the Holy Land, at the head of his army; but after having obtained what he wanted, he forgot all his promises.

Frederick II., at the moment he was about to assist Louis IX., died at Naples; and his death proved to be a fresh source of trouble and agitation for Christendom. Although he had, when dying, bequeathed a hundred thousand ounces of gold for the succour of the Holy Land, and by his testament had restored to the Church all that had belonged to it, Innocent received the news of his death with a joy that he did not seek to conceal. "Let the Heavens rejoice!" wrote he to the clergy and people of Sicily; "let the earth be in gladness!" and he pursued with anathemas the memory of a prince who had borne the title of king of Jerusalem during thirty-eight years. He excommunicated Conrad, whom Frederick had named as his successor to the empire; he sent emissaries into the kingdom of Naples, to corrupt the fidelity of the people; and ecclesiastics in Germany received the mission to preach a crusade against the princes of the house of Swabia.

France was not less agitated than other countries on the return of the dukes of Anjou and Poictiers, the letter of Louis addressed to his subjects was read in all the churches. This letter revived all the sorrow that had been felt when the account was received of the captivity of the king and his army. The exhortations which Louis addressed to the French to obtain assistance, together with the news that arrived daily from the East, affected all hearts; and as the people have no idea of moderation in either grief or joy, a spirit of sedition, mixed with enthusiasm for the crusade, agitated the cities, pervaded the provinces, and, for a time, placed the kingdom in peril.

Princes and magnates having failed in their enterprise, the multitude was led to believe that Christ rejected the great ones of the earth from his service, and was only willing to have for defenders humble men, shepherds, and labourers. A man appeared, who undertook, with the help of this popular opinion, to inflame the public mind, and to create a general movement. This man, named Jacob, born in Hungary, and far advanced in age, was said to have preached the crusade of children, of which we have spoken in the twelfth book of this work. A long beard, which descended to his girdle, with a pale face and mysterious language, gave him the air of a prophet. He passed from hamlet to hamlet, saying that he was sent by Heaven to deliver the city of God, and avenge the king of France. Shepherds left their flocks, labourers laid down the plough to follow his footsteps.

Jacob, who was called the master of Hungary, caused a standard to be borne before him, upon which was painted a lamb, the symbol of the Saviour of the world; provisions were brought to him from all parts, and his disciples asserted that, like Christ, he had the gift of multiplying loaves.

The name of *Pastors* was given to these village Crusaders. Their first meetings, to which little attention was paid, were held in the provinces of Flanders and Picardy; they then directed their course towards Amiens, and afterwards towards the capital; increasing as they went, with a crowd of vagabonds, thieves, and prostitutes. Although they had committed some disorders, Queen Blanche tolerated them, in the hope they might be the means of procuring some assistance for the king. The implied protection of the queen regent inflamed their pride, and impunity increased their license and redoubled their audacity. The impostor Jacob and the other heads of his gang, with whom chance or corruption had associated him, declaimed with vehemence against the wealth and the supremacy of the clergy, which pleased the multitude they drew at their heels; to the great scandal of all pious men, they themselves performed sacerdotal functions, and took the place, in the pulpits, of the sacred orators, employing violence against the ministers of the altars, and seeking to awaken the passions of the people. At length, assembled to the number of more than a hundred thousand, these redoubtable pilgrims left Paris, and divided themselves into several troops, to repair to the coast, whence they were to embark for the East. The city of Orleans, which happened to be in their passage, became the theatre of frightful disorders. The progress of their enormities at length created serious alarm in the government and the magistracy; orders were sent to the provinces to pursue and disperse these turbulent and seditious bands. The most numerous assemblage of the pastors was fixed to take place at Bourges, where the master of Hungary was to perform miracles and communicate the will of Heaven. Their arrival in that city was the signal for murder, fire, and pillage. The irritated people took up arms and marched against these disturbers of the public peace; they overtook them between Mortemer and Villeneuve-sur-le-Cher, where, in spite of their numbers, they were routed, and received the punishment due to their brigandages. Jacob had his head cut off by the blow of an axe; many of his companions and disciples met with death on the field of battle, or were consigned to punishment; the remainder took to flight. [328]

Thus this storm, formed so suddenly, was dispersed in the same manner; another band, which had directed its course towards Bordeaux, was likewise subdued; some of the pastors who succeeded in getting to England, were served in the same way. A report was spread that correspondences with the Saracens had been found upon the persons of their leaders, and they were accused of having formed the project of delivering up Christian people to the swords of the infidels; which accusation, however improbable, completed the hatred the people began to entertain for them. The government, which had not at first strength enough to oppose them, armed the passions of the multitude against them, and tranquillity was soon reëstablished in the kingdom.

In the mean time the crusade to the East was preached in most of the countries of Europe; new indulgences were added to those which had been accorded to the soldiers of Christ; the bishop of Avignon received power to absolve those who had struck clerks, or burnt churches; the same bishop had the faculty of converting all vows, except that of religion, into a vow for the crusade: similar powers were given to the prior of the Jacobins at Paris. These new encouragements might have aroused a momentary ardour in the faithful, if the court of Rome had not been constantly diverted from the cares of a crusade in the East, by the war it had declared against the house of Swabia. The Holy See willingly granted dispensations to Crusaders who took a part in its cause, or who paid it a tribute; which made the good bishop of Lincoln accuse Innocent of exchanging the treasures of heaven for those of earth, and of selling the Crusaders as the heifers and rains of sacrifice were formerly sold in the Temple. At length, no longer concealing either his hatred or his ambition, the sovereign pontiff ordered the Cordeliers to preach a crusade against the heir and successor of Frederick; the indulgence for those who took the cross extended to the father and mother of the Crusaders, a thing that had never taken place in any other crusade. At the moment when Louis IX. was so earnestly requesting succour, the preaching of this impious crusade excited great scandal among the French nobility; the new Crusaders were treated as rebels; Queen Blanche caused their lands to be seized; and the princes and lords followed the example of the queen in their domains. The Cordeliers were severely reprimanded, and their preaching proved ineffectual.

Whilst the crusade against Conrad was being suppressed, no increased zeal was exhibited for the war in the East. Those who entertained the warmest attachment for Louis IX. might with justice believe, that by sending him assistance they should prolong his absence. Thus, in spite of the reiterated prayers of the king, France, which had shed so many tears over his captivity, could not resolve to take up arms to succour him, and was satisfied with putting up vows for his return.

All that Blanche was able to do for her son was to send him a vessel laden with money, which was lost on the coast of Syria. A small number of those who had taken the cross in the West, determined to cross the sea; the young count of Eu, and Raymond count of Turenne, whom the queen commanded to set out for Palestine, were almost the only nobles of this party. Most of the knights and barons that had remained in Palestine with the king, having spent everything, and being entirely ruined, fixed so high a price upon their services, and, according to the expression of the commissaries of Louis, *made themselves so dear*, that the treasury of the monarch would not suffice to support them. [329] Levies were made in Greece, in Cyprus, and in the Christian cities of Syria; but these levies only brought to the banners of the crusade a few adventurers, very ill calculated to share the labours and dangers of a great enterprise.

Among the warriors whom the love of danger and distant adventures led at this time to the Holy Land, history speaks of Alemar of Selingan. This knight had come from a country of the West, [330] in which the summer, he said, had almost no nights. Selingan and his companions sought every opportunity for signalizing their skill in arms and their romantic bravery. Whilst waiting for the happy moment, at which they might fight with the Saracens, they made war upon the lions, which they pursued on horseback into the deserts, and killed with their arrows; which was a subject of great surprise and admiration for the French warriors.

Another very noble knight also arrived, says Joinville, who was called De Toucy. The chevalier de Toucy had been regent of the Latin empire of Constantinople, in the absence of Baldwin, and prided himself upon belonging to the family of the kings of France. In company with nine other knights, he abandoned an empire which was falling rapidly to ruin, in order to endeavor to support the miserable remains of the kingdom of Jerusalem. Toucy related the misfortunes of Baldwin, and the deplorable circumstances that had forced a Christian emperor to ally himself with a chief of the Comans. According to the custom of the barbarians, the prince of the Comans and the emperor of Constantinople had punctured themselves, and mixing the blood in a cup, had both drunk of it, as a sign of alliance and brotherhood. The knights who accompanied the seigneur de Toucy had borrowed this practice of the barbarians: the French warriors at first were disgusted with it; but soon, led away by the strange novelty of the thing, they themselves mingled their blood with that of their companions, and diluting it with floods of wine, they got intoxicated together over the mystical draught, which, as they said, made them brothers.

The manners and customs of the Eastern nations strongly raised the curiosity and fixed the attention of the Crusaders. When the missionaries whom Louis IX. had sent into Tartary returned to Ptolemaïs, the French warriors were never tired of interrogating and listening to them. Andrew de Lonjumeau, who was at the head of the mission, had set out from Antioch, and travelling ten leagues every day, had prosecuted his journey for a year before he arrived at the place at which the great khan of the Tartars resided. The missionaries traversed deserts where they met with enormous heaps of human bones—sad monuments of the victories of a barbarous people: they related marvellous things of the court of the monarch of the Moguls, of the manners and customs of the countries they had travelled through, of the conquests and legislation of Gengiskhan, and of the prodigies which had prepared the power and greatness of the conqueror of Asia. Among the extraordinary and somewhat fabulous circumstances they related, the Christians learned with much joy that the religion of Christ was extending its empire among the most distant nations; the missionaries declared they had seen, in a single horde of Tartars, more than eight hundred chapels, in which the praises of the true God were celebrated. Louis IX. hoped that the Moguls might some day become auxiliaries of the Christians in the great struggle against the infidels; and this hope made him resolve to send fresh missionaries into Tartary.

But if the Crusaders were thus astonished at all they heard concerning the most distant regions of Asia, they had close to them a barbarous colony which must have excited their surprise to a still greater degree. Some months after his arrival, Louis received an embassy from the Old Man of the Mountains, who, as we have already said, reigned over about thirty villages or towns, built on the southern declivity of Mount Libanus. The envoys of the prince of the Assassins, when admitted into the presence of the king of France, asked him if he was acquainted with their master. "I have heard of him," replied the monarch. "Why, then," added one of the ambassadors, "have you not sought after his friendship by sending him presents, as the emperor of Germany, the king of Hungary, the sultan of Cairo, and so many other great princes have done?" The king listened to this strange language without anger, and appointed the ambassadors another audience, at which the grand masters of the Templars and the Hospitallers were present. The name alone of the two military orders, which the poniard of the Assassins did not venture to attack, inspired some degree of terror in the Old Man of the Mountain, who had been constrained to pay them a tribute. In the second audience, the two grand masters sternly reproved the ambassadors, and told them that if the lord of the Mountain did not send presents to the king of France, his insolence would draw upon him a prompt and just chastisement. The envoys repeated these threatening words to their master, who himself experienced some of the fear he wished to inspire, and sent them back to Louis to express much more pacific sentiments. Among the presents which they were charged to offer to the king of the Franks, there were several vases, a chess-board, and an elephant in rock crystal; to these the lord of the Mountain added a shirt and a ring, as symbols of alliance, according to which, said the envoys to the French monarch, "you and our master will remain united as the fingers of the hand are, and as the shirt is to the body." [331]

Louis IX. received this new embassy with distinction, and by their hands sent to the prince of the Assassins vases of gold and silver, and stuffs of scarlet and silk; he commanded brother Yves, a man learned in Arabic, to accompany them. Yves, who remained for some time at the court of the Old Man of the Mountain, on his return related many curious particulars, which history has not despised. The prince of the Assassins belonged to the sect of Ali, and professed some admiration for the Gospel. He had, in particular, a veneration for *Monseigneur St. Peter*, who, according to his belief, was still living, and whose soul, he said, had been successively that of Abel, Noah, and Abraham. Brother Yves spoke strongly of the terror with which the Old Man of the Mountain inspired his subjects. A fearful silence reigned around his palace, and when he appeared in public, he was preceded by a herald-at-arms, who cried with a loud voice, "Whoever you may be, dread to appear before him who holds the life and death of kings in his hands."

Whilst these marvellous recitals were amusing the leisure of the Crusaders, war was declared between the sultans of Damascus and Cairo. The Christian warriors, impatient for fight, sighed at being thus condemned to waste their time in listless idleness. But they mustered scarcely seven hundred knights beneath the banners of the cross; and their small number would not permit Louis to think of attempting any important enterprise.

Whilst anxiously looking forward to the perils and hazards of war, the holy monarch never relaxed in his endeavours to ameliorate the destiny and break the chains of the captives who still remained in the hands of the Mussulmans. But the captivity of the Christian warriors was not the only grief with which his heart was afflicted: it added greatly to his sorrow to learn that many of his companions in arms had embraced Islamism. It is a singular circumstance to remark, [332] that the Crusaders, whose aim always was to bring about the triumph of Christianity, present us with frequent examples of apostasy, and history does not hesitate to affirm, that during the course of the holy wars more Christians became Mussulmans than Mussulmans became Christians. Joinville informs us in his Memoirs, that most of the mariners who manned the Christian fleet in the retreat from Mansourah, renounced their faith to save their lives: in these disastrous days, many warriors were unable to resist the menaces of the Saracens, and the fear of death made them forget a religion for which they had taken up arms. We have seen what evils the Crusaders had endured in the expeditions to the East; among the crowd of pilgrims there were always some who had not sufficient virtue to pass through the ordeal of great misfortunes: on the arrival of Louis IX. in Egypt, that country already contained many of these perjured and unfaithful Christians, who, in the perils and calamities of preceding wars, had forsaken the God of their fathers. All these renegadoes were despised by the Saracens. Oriental authors quote a saying of Saladin's on this subject, which expresses an opinion generally established, and which was maintained to the very last days of the crusades; he said that *a good Christian was never made of a bad Mussulman, nor a good Mussulman of a bad Christian.* History affords a few details upon the lives of these degenerate Franks, who had renounced their religion and their country; many employed themselves in agriculture and the mechanical arts; a great number were enrolled in the Mussulman armies; some obtained employments, and succeeded in amassing great wealth. We may well, however, believe, that remorse empoisoned every moment of their lives, and would not permit them to enjoy the advantages they had acquired among the infidels: [333] the religion they had quitted still inspired them with respect, and the presence and language of the Franks, who had been their brothers, recalled to them the most saddening remembrances; but, withheld by I know not what false shame, and as if God had struck them with an eternal reprobation, they remained chained to their error by an invincible link, and although sensible of the misery of living in a foreign land, they did not dare to entertain the idea of returning to their own country.

One of these renegadoes, born at Provins, who had fought under the banners of John of Brienne, came to salute Louis IX., and bring him presents, at the moment the monarch was embarking on the Nile, to repair to Palestine. As Joinville told him, that if he persisted in practising the religion of Mahomet, *he would go straight to hell after his death*; he replied, that he believed the religion of Christ to be better than that of the prophet of Mecca; but, he added, that if he returned to the faith of the Christians, he should sink into poverty, and that during the rest of his life he should be loaded with infamous reproaches, and be everywhere hooted as a renegado! a renegado! Thus, the fear of poverty, together with a dread of the judgments of the world, held fast the deserters from the Christian faith, and prevented their return to the belief they had abandoned. Louis IX. neglected no means to bring them back to the right path; his liberality always met half-way such as were disposed to revert to Christianity; and to shield them, from the contempt of men, he issued an ordinance that none should reproach them with their apostasy.

The king of France expended considerable sums in placing several of the Christian cities in a state of defence; the towers and walls of Cæsarea, as well as those of Ptolemaïs, were heightened and enlarged; the walls and fortifications of Jaffa and Caïpha, which were almost in ruins, were repaired.

Amidst these useful labours, carried on in peace, the warriors remained idle, and not a few of them began to be forgetful of both military discipline and Gospel morality. The precaution that the sieur de Joinville took to place his bed in such a manner as to remove all evil thoughts respecting his familiarity with women, proves that the morals of the Christian knights were not entirely free from suspicion at least. Louis was much more severe against licentiousness of manners than he had been during his abode at Damietta. History mentions several instances of his severity; and such was the strangeness of the penal laws charged with the protection of public decency and morality, that excess of libertinism would at the present day appear less scandalous than the punishments then inflicted on the guilty.

The clergy, however, never relaxed in their endeavours to recall the Crusaders to the principles of the Christian religion; and their efforts were not fruitless. There was no city, no place in Palestine, that did not remind the warriors of the holy traditions of the Scriptures, or of the mercy and justice of God. Many of the French nobles, who had been models of courage, showed an equally bright example of devotion and piety; it was common to see the bravest knights lay down their arms, and assuming the scrip and staff of the pilgrim, repair to the spots consecrated by the miracles and the presence of Christ and the holy personages whose memory is preserved by religion. Louis himself visited Mount Thabor and the village of Cana several times, and went on a pilgrimage to Nazareth. The sultan of Damascus, who sought every opportunity of forming an alliance with him, invited him to come as far as Jerusalem; and this pilgrimage would have crowned the wishes of the pious monarch; but his barons, and more particularly the bishops, represented to him that it was not befitting for him to enter Jerusalem as a simple pilgrim, and that he had come into the East not only to visit, but to deliver the holy tomb. They added, that the Western princes who should take the cross after him, would believe, from his example, that they had fulfilled their duty, and performed their vow, by merely visiting the holy city; and thus the devotion of the Crusaders would no longer have the deliverance of the sepulchre of Christ for its object. Louis IX. yielded to the representations of the prelates, and consented not to visit Jerusalem at that time, as he still cherished the hope of one day entering it sword in hand. But this hope was doomed soon to fade away—God never afterwards permitted the holy city to be wrested from the yoke of the infidels.

The sultans of Cairo and Damascus continued to negotiate with the monarch of the Franks. Each of these two Mussulman princes hoped to have the Christians for allies, and was particularly anxious not to have them for enemies. Every time they entertained a fear of being vanquished, the emirs of Egypt renewed their proposals, and they at length accepted all the conditions that the Christians required. A treaty was concluded, by which the Mamelukes engaged to liberate all the captives that remained in Egypt, the children of Christians brought up in the Mussulman faith, and, which had often been demanded by Louis, the heads of the martyrs of the cross that had been exposed upon the walls of Cairo. Jerusalem and all the cities of Palestine, with the exception of Gaza, Daroum, and two other fortresses, were to be placed in the hands of the Franks. The treaty likewise stipulated that, during fifteen years, the kingdom of Jerusalem should have no war with Egypt; that the two states should combine their forces; and that all conquests should be shared between the Christians and the Mamelukes. Some ecclesiastics expressed their doubts and scruples upon an alliance with the enemies of Christ; but the pious monarch disdained to notice their representations; no treaty had ever offered so many advantages for the Christian cause, if good faith had presided over its execution: but the generous loyalty of Louis rendered him incapable of suspecting fraud or perfidy in his allies, or even in his enemies.

The leaders of the Mussulmans were to repair to Gaza, and from thence to Jaffa, to confirm the alliance they had just contracted, and to arrange with the French king the plan for carrying on the war. When the sultan of Damascus heard of the treaty thus entered into, he sent an army of twenty thousand men to take a position between Gaza and Daroum, so as to prevent the junction of the Egyptians and Franks. Whether the Mamelukes were prevented by their internal divisions, or whether they did not dare to face the troops of Damascus, they did *not* appear at Jaffa at the time agreed upon. They, however, fulfilled all the other conditions of the treaty, and added to the convoy of captives and funereal relics, the present of an elephant, which Louis sent to Henry III. of England. As they often repeated their promise of coming to Jaffa, Louis was constantly in expectation of them, and waited for them an entire year. The French monarch being thus deceived in his hopes, might, without injustice, have renounced a treaty that the other contracting party did not execute; he might again have opened a communication with the sultan of Damascus, who offered the same advantages, with much more probability of his promises being fulfilled. The emirs of Egypt had sought the alliance of the Christians when their own situation appeared desperate, and when they had reason to believe that the king of France would receive succours from the West; seeing, however, that Louis had no army, and that all the forces he could muster did not amount to more than seven hundred knights, they were fearful of entering too deeply into engagements that would expose them to the hatred of the Mussulmans, without offering them any substantial support against their enemies. All these emirs besides, only fought to secure for themselves impunity for their crime, and to be left in quiet possession of the fruits of their revolt. They were at all times ready to lay down their arms, if they procured pardon for the past, and had Egypt abandoned to them. The caliph of Bagdad was always anxious to establish peace among the Mussulman powers; he prevailed upon the sultan of Damascus and Aleppo to forget his causes of resentment, and upon the emirs of Egypt to express repentance, with a desire for peace. Several battles were fought without any decisive results; in one of these battles a party of Syrian troops were defeated by the Mamelukes, and fled away towards Damascus; whilst other bodies of Mamelukes were beaten by the Syrians, and pursued up to the gates of Cairo. A war in which victory was always uncertain, necessarily weakened the courage and exhausted the patience of both parties; and they appealed to the spiritual father of the Mussulmans to arbitrate between them. The sultans of Syria and Egypt at length concluded a peace, and agreed to unite their arms against the Christians. From that time the hopes of the Crusaders all vanished; the king of France, from having procrastinated so long, and at the same time neglected a favourable opportunity, had, all at once, two united enemies to dread. It is necessary to be perfectly acquainted with the situation and policy of the Mussulman powers, to ascertain how far history has reason to blame the indecision and tardiness of Louis IX. Le père Maimbourg does not scruple to blame him with much severity, and declares plainly, *that to be a saint, it appears not necessary to be infallible, particularly in political affairs, and even still less in those of war.*

The treaty concluded between the Mamelukes and Syrians was the signal for war; the sultan of Damascus, at the head of an army, came under the very walls of Ptolemaïs, and threatened to ravage the gardens and fields which supplied the city with provisions, if the inhabitants did not pay him a tribute of fifty thousand golden byzants. The Christians were not in a condition to resist their enemies, if the latter had then had any intention of attacking them in earnest; but the Syrians, exhausted by fatigue, were in want of provisions, and returned to Damascus, whilst the Mamelukes, at the same time, retook the route to Cairo; both of them departing with an intention of returning on the first favourable occasion to invade and desolate Palestine.

The threats of the Mussulmans redoubled the zeal and the efforts of Louis to place the Christian cities in a state of defence; he determined to restore the fortifications of Sidon, which had been demolished by the Saracens of Damascus, at the time that the Crusaders landed in Egypt. He sent a great number of workmen into this city, and the works were rapidly advancing, when they were all at once interrupted by the most deplorable occurrence. The place having a weak garrison, was surprised, and every

Christian it contained put to the sword by the Turcomans, a wandering, ferocious race, accustomed to live by murder and plunder. Louis was at Tyre when he learned this disastrous news, and was about to go to Sidon. Some of the few Syrian inhabitants that had escaped the carnage, described to him the unheard-of cruelties of the barbarians; the fury of the Turcomans had spared neither age nor sex, and in their retreat they had slaughtered two thousand prisoners. Louis, deeply afflicted by what he heard, formed at once the determination to go and attack the Turcomans in Belinas, to which place they had retired. At the first signal all the warriors that accompanied him eagerly assumed their armour. The king wished to place himself at their head, but the barons strongly opposed his intention, saying, "that he must not expose a life of so much consequence to the Holy Land, in such an expedition." The Christian warriors set forward on their march. Belinas, or Cæsarea Philippi, was built upon a declivity of Mount Libanus, near the sources of the Jordan: the place was only to be approached by narrow roads and steep ascents; but nothing could stop the Crusaders, impatient to avenge their murdered brethren. Upon their arrival at Belinas, the enemy fled in all directions; the city was taken, and this victory would have been complete, if the Christian warriors had observed the laws of discipline, and followed the orders of their leaders. Whilst the French were taking possession of Belinas, the Teutonic knights went to attack a Mussulman castle, built upon the neighbouring heights, whose towers appeared mingled with the peaks of Libanus. The Saracens, who had rallied at this place, and began to recover their courage, repulsed the assailants, and pursued them across the rocks and precipices. The precipitate retreat of the Teutonic knights threw the other Christian warriors into confusion; these latter being huddled together upon a mountainous piece of ground, where they could neither fight on horseback nor form a line of battle. The sieur de Joinville, who led the king's guards, was more than once upon the point of losing his life, or of falling into the hands of the Turcomans. At length the French, by hard fighting, repaired the error of the Germans; Olivier de Thermes, and the warriors he commanded, succeeded in repulsing the Mussulmans. The Crusaders, after having pillaged Belinas, abandoned it, and returned to Sidon.

Louis IX. arrived there before them: on his approach to the city, what was his sorrow at seeing on his route the ground covered with plundered and bloody carcases! These were the miserable remains of the Christians that had been slain by the Turcomans. [334] They were putrefying fast, and there had been no one to undertake the charge of burying them. Louis stopped at beholding the melancholy spectacle, and turning to the legate, requested him to consecrate a cemetery, and then gave orders for the burial of the dead that covered the roads; but instead of obeying him, every one turned away his eyes and recoiled with disgust. Louis then sprang from his horse, and taking in his hands one of the bodies from which exhaled an infectious odour, exclaimed, "*Come, my friends, come, let us bestow a little earth upon the martyrs of Jesus Christ.*" The example of the king reanimated the courage and the charity of the persons of his suite; all were eager to imitate him, and the Christians, whom the barbarians had slaughtered, thus received the honours of sepulture. This act of pious devotedness of Louis IX. to the memory of his companions in arms, has been celebrated by all historians; it presents a strange contrast to the insensibility of a hero of modern times, who, in a circumstance almost similar, and in the same country, caused all the wounded who were left upon a field of battle to be poisoned.

The king remained several months at Sidon, employed in fortifying the city. In the mean time Queen Blanche was constantly writing to him and entreating him to return to France, as she greatly feared she should never see her son again.

Her presentiments were but too quickly realized. Louis was still at Sidon, when a message arrived in Palestine, announcing that the queen regent was no more. It was the legate of the pope who first received this melancholy news. He went to seek the king, accompanied by the archbishop of Tyre and Geoffrey de Beaulieu, Louis's confessor. As the prelate announced that he had something important to communicate, and at the same time exhibited marks of great grief upon his countenance, the monarch led him into his chapel, which, according to an old author, "*was his arsenal against all the crosses of the world.*" The prelate began by reminding the king that all that man loves upon the earth was perishable; "be thankful to God," added he, "for having given you a mother who has watched over your family and your kingdom with such anxious care, and so much ability." The legate paused for a moment, and then, breathing a profound sigh, continued, "This tender mother, this virtuous princess, is now in heaven." At these words, Louis uttered a piercing cry, and then burst into a torrent of tears. As soon as he had a little recovered himself, he fell on his knees before the altar, and joining and raising his hands, exclaimed, "I thank you O my God! for having given me so good a mother; it was a gift of your mercy; you take her back to-day as your own; you know that I loved her above all creatures; but since, before all things, your decrees must be accomplished, O Lord! be your name blessed for ever, and for ever!" Louis sent away the two prelates, and, remaining alone with his confessor, he recited the service for the dead. Two days passed away before he would see anybody. He then desired Joinville to be called, and upon seeing him, said, "Ah! seneschal, I have lost my mother." "Sire," replied Joinville, "I am not surprised at that; you knew that she must die at some time; but I marvel at the great and extravagant grief that you feel for it, you who have always been so wise a prince." When Joinville left the king, *Madame Marie de bonnes Vertus* came to beg that he would come to the queen and endeavour to console her. The good seneschal found Marguerite bathed in tears, and could not refrain from expressing his surprise by saying to her, "It is a difficult matter to believe you are a woman by your weeping, for the grief you show is for the loss of a woman that you hated more than any other in the world." Marguerite replied that it was not, in fact, for the death of Blanche she was weeping, "but for the great uneasiness in which I see the king, and also for our daughter, left under the guardianship of men."

Louis IX. was present every day at a funeral service celebrated in memory of his mother. He sent into the West a great number of jewels and precious stones to be distributed among the principal churches of France; at the same time exhorting the clergy to put up prayers for him and for the repose of the queen Blanche. In proportion with his endeavours to procure prayers for his mother, his grief yielded to the hope of seeing her again in heaven; and his mind, when calmed by resignation, found its most effectual consolations in that mysterious tie which still unites us with those we have lost, in that religious sentiment which mixes itself with our affections to purify them, and with our regrets to mitigate them.

The death of Queen Blanche seemed to impose an obligation upon Louis IX. to return to his dominions; and the news he received from the West convinced him that his presence was becoming more necessary every day. A war for the succession of Flanders had broken out again; the truce with England had just expired; the people were murmuring: on the other hand, Louis had now nothing he could undertake in Palestine. He therefore gave his serious attention to the subject of his return; but as if, on this occasion, he mistrusted his own understanding, he determined, before he formed a definitive resolution, to consult the will of God. Processions were made, and prayers were put up in all the Christian cities of Palestine, that Heaven might deign to enlighten those who had been charged with the directing of a war undertaken in its name. The clergy and barons of the kingdom of Jerusalem, persuaded that the presence of Louis was no longer necessary, and that his return to the West might rouse the enthusiasm of the French warriors for a new crusade, advised him to embark for Europe; at the same time expressing their fervent gratitude for all the services he had rendered to the cause of Jesus Christ during five years. On preparing for his departure, Louis left a hundred knights in the Holy Land, under the command of Geoffrey de Sergines, who fought against the Saracens for thirty years, and became, in his old age, viceroy of Jerusalem. Louis quitted Sidon, and, with the queen and three children that he had had in the East, repaired to Ptolemaïs, in the spring of 1254. A fleet of fourteen vessels was ready to receive him and all that remained of the warriors of the crusade. The day being arrived (April 24th), the king, walking on foot, followed by the legate, the patriarch of Jerusalem, and all the nobles and knights of Palestine, took the road to the port, amidst an immense crowd collected on his passage. All classes, as they saw him depart, recollected the virtues of which he had given so bright an example, particularly his kindness to the inhabitants of Palestine, whom he had treated as his own subjects. Some expressed their gratitude by warm acclamations, others by a melancholy silence; but all proclaimed him *the father of the Christians*, and implored Heaven to shower its blessings upon the virtuous monarch, and upon the kingdom of France. The countenance of Louis plainly indicated that he fully partook of the regrets of the Christians of the Holy Land; he addressed a few consoling words to them, gave them useful counsels, reproached himself with not having done enough for their cause, and expressed an earnest desire that God would some day judge him worthy of finishing the work of their deliverance.

At length the fleet set sail. Louis had obtained permission from the legate to take with him, in his vessel, the Holy Sacrament, for the assistance of the dying and the sick; so, when beholding altars raised on board a ship, priests clothed in their sacerdotal habits, celebrating divine service, and invoking the protection of Heaven at every hour in the day, it was easy to recognise the pious wreck of a crusade, and the last trophies of the war of Jesus Christ. [335] As the fleet approached the isle of Cyprus, the vessel in which the king was struck violently against a sand-bank; all the crew were seized with terror; the queen and her children uttered piercing cries; but Louis prostrated himself at the foot of the altar, and addressed himself to Him who commands the sea. When the vessel was examined, it was found that it had received considerable damage, and the pilots pressed the king to leave it; but seeing that they themselves did not purpose to abandon the ship, he determined to remain in it. "There is no one here," said he, "who does not love his body as dearly as I do mine; if I leave, they will leave also, and, perhaps, will not see their country for a length of time; I prefer placing myself, my queen, and my children in the hands of God, to doing such an injury to so great a number of people as there are here." These words, inspired by an heroic charity, revived the courage of the sailors and the pilgrims, and they resumed their course. When leaving the coasts of Sicily, the fleet very carefully kept clear of the coast of Tunis, as if a secret presentiment warned the French Crusaders of the misfortunes that awaited them upon that shore in a still more disastrous expedition. A tempest placed the fleet in great peril; it was upon this occasion Queen Marguerite made a vow to offer a ship of silver to St. Nicholas of Lorraine, and requested Joinville to become her security with the patron saint of such as are shipwrecked. Whilst everybody else was in despair, Louis found calmness in a philosophy derived from religion; and when the danger was past, he said to his companions: "See if God has not proved to us how vast is his power, when by means of a single one of the four winds, the king of France, the queen, their children, and so many other persons have escaped drowning." The navigation lasted more than two months, during which many marvellous adventures and accidents were encountered by the pilgrims, which history has preserved an account of, and which would not figure unworthily in a Christian Odyssey.

The fleet at length cast anchor at the isles of Hières. Louis crossed Provence, and passing by Auvergne, arrived at Vincennes on the 5th of September, 1254. The people flocked from all parts to greet him on his passage; the more they appeared to forget his reverses, the more strongly was Louis affected by the remembrance of his lost companions; and the melancholy that clouded his countenance formed a painful contrast with the public joy. His first care was to go to St. Denis, to prostrate himself at the feet of the apostle of France; on the following day he made his public entrance into his capital, preceded by the clergy, the nobility, and the people. He continued to wear the cross upon his shoulder, the sight of which, whilst recalling the cause of his long absence, gave his subjects reason to fear that he had not yet abandoned his enterprise of the crusade. The greater number of the barons and knights that had gone with Louis, had found a grave in either Syria or Egypt. Such as had survived so many disasters, reëntered their castles, which they found deserted and falling to ruins. The good seneschal, after having revisited his home, repaired, barefooted, to the church of St. Nicholas of Lorraine, to discharge the vow of Queen Marguerite. He then set earnestly about repairing the evils his absence had caused, and swore never again to quit the castle of Joinville to seek adventures in Asia.

Thus terminated this holy war, the commencement of which had filled the Christian nations with so much delight, and which had, in the end, plunged the whole West into mourning. Throughout the events I have just described, the seneschal de Joinville has been my guide, and I cannot terminate my recital without paying him the just tribute of my gratitude. The unpretending tone of his narration, the simplicity of his style, the gaiety of his character, have afforded me a happy relief amidst a labour always dry and sometimes revolting. I take delight in beholding him intrepid in the field of battle, preserving his cheerfulness amidst the misfortunes of war, resigned in his captivity, and in all his actions recalling to our minds the true spirit of chivalry. Like his compatriot Villehardouin, he often makes his heroes weep, and as often weeps himself. He braves danger, when danger is present; but he thanks God with all his heart when he has no longer anything to fear.

When I read his memoirs, I am transported back to the thirteenth century, and I think I am listening to a knight who is returned from the crusade, and who tells to me all he has seen and all he has done. He has neither method nor rule; he drops the line of his discourse, and takes it up again; and he extends or abridges his narration, as his imagination is more or less struck by that which he relates. When we read the narratives of Joinville, we are not surprised that Louis should have taken so much delight in his conversation; there is not one of his readers who does not feel the same confidence and friendship for him that the virtuous monarch accorded him, and history adopts without hesitation all that he affirms *upon his honour*, persuaded that he who was bold enough to speak the truth in the courts of kings will not deceive posterity.

The crusade of St. Louis was like that which immediately preceded it. The enthusiasm for these distant expeditions was daily losing its vivacity and its energy: the crusade no longer appeared anything to the knights beyond a common war, in which the spirit of chivalry was a more powerful principle than religion. It was only a religious affair to Louis IX.

The manner in which this crusade was preached in Europe, the troubles amidst which the voices of the preachers were raised, and particularly the means that were employed to levy the tributes in the West, were calculated to turn away all minds from the object that would be supposed to be the governing one in a holy expedition.

And yet Louis took precautions that had been neglected in preceding wars. Three years were employed in preparing this great enterprise; the knights who arrived in the isle of Cyprus could not express their astonishment at seeing the casks of wine piled one upon another, so high that *they appeared like houses*; and heaps of wheat, barley, and other grains, so immense, *that they might be believed to be mountains*. There is no doubt that the princes and nobles who accompanied Louis imitated his example: happy had it been for the Crusaders, if their leaders had shown in war the same prudence and sagacity they displayed in preparing for their expedition!

The French warriors upon all occasions evinced their accustomed bravery; but throughout the crusade there was never exhibited one instance of the genius of a great captain; Louis himself, when in danger, afforded no example to his troops beyond courage and firmness. We have related the prodigies of French valour, and we have described the prodigies of pious resignation in reverses; the Crusaders and their leaders merited, even in their disasters and in the depth of their misery, the esteem and admiration of their enemies; and it is here that history presents the most beautiful spectacle she can offer to man: *"Glory, the faithful companion of misfortune."*

We have had occasion, in the course of our narrative, to remark that French gaiety never abandoned the cross-knights in their distant expeditions. This gaiety often mixed itself with the saddest images, and sometimes even did not respect severe propriety. We beg to be permitted to repeat on this head a singular anecdote related by Joinville. On the eve of the battle of Mansourah, one of the knights of the seneschal of Champagne, named Landricourt, died; and whilst the funeral honours were being paid to him, six of his companions in arms talked so loud that they interrupted the priest who was chanting mass. Joinville reproved them warmly, and they then laughed aloud, saying they were talking about remarrying the wife of Messire Hugh de Landricourt, *who was on the bier there*. The good Joinville was very much scandalized at such discourse, and ordered them to keep silent. When speaking of this indiscreet gaiety of his knights, the seneschal takes care to add that God punished them on the day of battle; for of all the six, he says, there was not one that was not killed and buried, and whose wife did not afterwards find it convenient to marry again.

The manners of the European knights formed a very striking contrast with those of the Mussulmans, who were always grave and serious, even amidst the festivities in which they celebrated the deliverance of their country and the defeat of the Christians.

We have spoken many times of the want of discipline of the Crusaders; the Saracens were very little better in this respect; but in addition to having the advantage of fighting in their own country, with every foot of which they were acquainted, fortune gave them, in their greatest dangers, skilful and experienced leaders, who knew how to take advantage of all the errors of the Christians, and bring back to their banners that victory that appeared to have been driven away by the valour of their enemies.

History describes the whole Egyptian nation as struck with terror at the first appearance of the Crusaders; but the Mussulmans, reassured by their leaders, soon felt as much security and confidence as they had experienced alarm; and as if there was nothing that men forgot so easily as danger, a year after the taking of Damietta, they could not conceive what species of madness had led a king of France to the banks of the Nile. The continuator of Tabary relates a circumstance on this subject, which paints at once the opinion and the character of the Mussulmans. The emir Hossam-Eddin, in the course of a conference with the captive monarch, said to him: "How did it come into the mind of the king, whom I perceive endowed with wisdom and good qualities,—how did it ever enter his thoughts to trust himself to a fragile wooden bark, to brave the rocks of the sea, to venture into a country filled with warriors impatient to fight for the Mussulman faith; how could he possibly believe that he should take possession of Egypt, or that he should land upon these coasts, without exposing both himself and his people to the greatest dangers?" The king of France smiled, but made no reply; and the emir thus continued: "Some of the doctors of our law have decided that he who embarks upon the sea twice consecutively, by thus exposing his life and his fortune, renders himself unfit to have his evidence taken in a court of justice, because such gross imprudence sufficiently proves the weakness of his reason and the unsoundness of his judgment." Louis IX. again smiled, and answered the emir: "He who said so was not deceived; that is a wise decision." [336]

We have transcribed the account of the Arabian historian, without according him more credit than he merits. Christian authors have not been less severe towards St. Louis, and can find no excuse for his expedition beyond the seas. Without seeking to justify this crusade, we will content ourselves with saying here, that the aim of Louis IX. was not only to defend the Christian states of Syria and to fight with the enemies of the faith, but to found a colony which might unite the East and the West by the happy interchange of productions and knowledge. We have produced, in the thirteenth book of this history, a letter from the sultan of Cairo, by which it may be plainly perceived, that the king of France had other views than those of a mere conqueror. The historian Mezerai formally says that the project of the king of France was to establish a colony in Egypt, a project of which the execution has been attempted in modern times. "For this purpose," says Mezerai, "he took with him a great number of labourers and artisans, capable, nevertheless, of bearing arms and fighting in case of need." To support our opinion, we might add to the authority of Mezerai that of Leibnitz, who, in a memoir addressed to Louis XIV., does not hesitate to affirm that the motives which determined Louis IX. to undertake the conquest of Egypt, were inspired by profound wisdom, and merited the attention of the most skilful statesmen, and of the most enlightened political writers.

We must however believe that Louis IX. did not contemplate in their full extent the advantages that might be derived from his expedition, or that have been discovered in our age. All the policy of those distant ages consisted in religious ideas, which insinuated themselves into human affairs, and often directed them towards an end that human intelligence was incapable of perceiving. What we do now for the interests of commerce or civilization, was then done for the interests of Christianity; and the results were often the same. Religion, in those times of barbarism and ignorance, was like a mysterious reason, like a sublime instinct, given to man to assist him in his search for all that was doomed to become good and useful to him. We must not forget that the Christian religion always directed the conduct of Louis IX., and that it was to the religious inspirations of this monarch, that France owed those treaties, at which frankness and good faith presided; those institutions that consecrated the principles of justice; and all those monuments of a wise policy, to which modern philosophers have not been able to refuse their admiration.

The expedition of Louis IX. produced two results for Egypt that were not at all expected. Two years after the deliverance of the king, and whilst he was still in Palestine, the Mamelukes, fearing a fresh invasion of the Franks, in order to prevent their enemies from taking Damietta and fortifying themselves in that city, entirely destroyed it. Some years after, as their fears were not yet removed, and the second crusade of Louis IX. spread fresh alarms throughout the East, the Egyptians caused immense heaps of stones to be cast into the mouth of the Nile, in order that the Christian fleets might not be able to sail up the river. Since that period a new Damietta has been built at a small distance from the site of the former city; but the entrance to the Nile is still, in our days, closed against all vessels, a sad and deplorable testimony of the terror which the arms of the Franks formerly inspired.

History has a deeper lament to make over the second consequence of this crusade. It is certain that it contributed greatly to change the form of the Egyptian government, and to fill that unhappy country with all the scourges that military despotism brings in its train. It was a spectacle worthy of our attention and our pity, to see, after a bloody revolution, a rich and vast country abandoned all at once to slaves purchased in the most barbarous regions of Asia. Despotism, which always suspects everything that approaches it, dreaded the natural defenders of Egypt, and was willing to confide its safety to men without country and without family; to those men who, according to the expression of Tacitus, when speaking of the guards of Artabanus, have not the least idea of virtue, are incapable of remorse, are instruments always ready for crime, and only know the hand that pays them. Most of the dynasties of Syria had already perished victims of their imprudent confidence in foreign soldiers. That of Saladin shared the same fate, and was, like all the others, overthrown by the barbarians whom it had intrusted with its defence. The dynasty of the Baharite Mamelukes, which succeeded that of Ayoub, was not destined to have a long duration; and a body of slaves, purchased in Circassia, in their turn got possession of the power that had armed them. Two centuries after, the Ottoman empire overcame the second dynasty of the Mamelukes; but their military government, amidst the crimes of tyranny and excesses of disorder, for a long time braved the power of the conqueror, and subsisted to the end of the eighteenth century, when the presence of a French army completed its annihilation. Thus, two French expeditions into Egypt were marked, one by the revolt and elevation of the Mamelukes, the other by their destruction.

Philosophy and humanity, however, derived some advantages from the expedition of St. Louis, which history does not dispute. The French monarch heard in Syria that a powerful emir was collecting a great number of books, and forming a library which was to be open to all the learned, and to all desirous of gaining knowledge. He became anxious to imitate this noble example, and gave orders for having all the manuscripts preserved in the monasteries transcribed. This literary treasure, confided to the care of Vincent de Beauvais, was placed in an apartment near the holy chapel, and became the first model of those bibliographical establishments, of those precious depositories of letters and sciences, of which the capital of France is now so justly proud.

It has often been said, that the hospital of the Quinze-Vingts was established by Louis IX. as an asylum for three hundred gentlemen who had returned blind from the holy war. The ordinance by which Louis founded this hospital says nothing to confirm the opinion at first spread by several writers, and which has since become sanctioned as a popular tradition. [337] Joinville speaks of the institution of the Quinze-Vingts; but he says nothing of the motives that induced the pious monarch to found this establishment. Besides, we should add that the origin of the Quinze-Vingts is posterior by several years to his return from the crusade. Mezerai relates in his history, that an hospital for the blind was established at Rouen in the middle of the twelfth century; and this ancient monument of charity might give Louis the idea of founding a similar institution in his capital.

Before this crusade, Tartary was only known by the formidable emigrations of the Moguls. This vast region was in some sort revealed to the West by the missionaries sent thither by the king of France. William de Longjumeau, who set out from the isle of Cyprus, collected a great number of fabulous traditions in the course of his voyage; but he likewise brought back some curious notices and some exact observations. Rubruquis, who started during the king's abode in Palestine, and returned after the departure of the Crusaders, did not succeed in his embassy to the powerful emperor of the Moguls; but, as a traveller, he observed with sagacity the country, the manners, and the laws of the Tartars; and his relation is still a valuable monument, that more recent voyages have not thrown into oblivion.

The chroniclers of the time, even Joinville himself, who never turned their attention to anything but the events of the war, and gave no heed to the progress of civilization, have said nothing of the knowledge Louis might have acquired concerning the legislation of the East. What interest would not the old chronicles possess in our eyes, if they had reported the conversations of the royal legislator with the Oriental Christians versed in the study of the laws and customs that prevailed in the colonies of the Franks! It was during the sojourn of the king in Syria, that the chancellor of the kingdom of Cyprus collected all the laws that formed *the Assizes of Jerusalem*. Should we not be warranted, then, in saying that we owe this precious collection to the counsels, and still more to the encouragement, of Louis IX.? It is certain that the pious monarch neglected nothing that would enable him to acquire a knowledge of the usages and customs of the countries he visited; and that the Assizes of Jerusalem served as a model for the monument of legislation which afterwards constituted the greatest glory of his reign.

One advantage of this crusade, and that, doubtless, the greatest of all, was, that Louis returned much better than he was when he went, and that adversity developed and perfected in him all the qualities to which his subjects looked for their future prosperity. A Protestant historian, when speaking of this subject, makes use of these remarkable words: "The fruit of his voyage and of his affliction was, that he returned a much better man, having increased in zeal, modesty, prudence, and diligence; and that he was more honoured and beloved by his people than he had ever been before his departure; and by the universal earth was held in singular admiration for his good life and constancy amidst dangers, as a miracle among kings." [338]

Far from seeking to forget his misfortunes, Louis was constantly referring to them, as a great example that God had been willing to present to the world. He attributed them principally to his own faults; and the austerities to which he condemned himself during the remainder of his life, were, says Father Daniel, a kind of mourning, which he always wore for the brave men who had perished in the crusade. On his return, he reformed the coinage, and by his order, silver Parisis and Gros Tournois were struck, upon which chains were figured, in order to preserve the memory of his captivity. These remembrances rendered him more dear to his people, and greater in the eyes of all Christians. Happy are princes upon whom the lessons of misfortune are not lost! happy also is the age in which men are not judged according to the favours of fortune, and in which the adversity of the great ones of the earth has in it something respectable and sacred!

The misfortunes of the time, as we have already said, had ruined a great number of the most illustrious families of the kingdom. We know that many nobles had sold their lands to provide means for undertaking the crusade; and history has preserved acts passed in the camp, even of Mansourah, by which several gentlemen sold their domains to the crown. Louis was not at all willing that his companions in arms should be condemned to poverty for having followed him into the East, and for having shared with him the labours and perils of the holy war; he therefore ordered a list to be made of the indigent nobility, and found means to assist them out of his own revenue; he relieved, with affecting kindness, the widows and orphans of the brave knights he had seen fall by his side; and his solicitude extended even to the poor labourers who had suffered, either in the war of the Pastors, by his absence, or by the inefficiency of the laws. "Serfs," said he, "belong to Jesus Christ as well as to us, and in a Christian kingdom we ought never to forget that they are our brethren." Since his war with the Mussulmans, he could not endure the idea of the blood of Christians being shed in battle. His ordinances forbade war between individuals in all the domains of the crown; and the authority of his example contributed to maintain order and peace throughout the provinces.

Before his departure, Louis had sent commissaries to repair the iniquities committed in the government of his kingdom. On his return, he was determined to see everything himself, and pervaded his provinces; being convinced that God will not pardon kings who have neglected any opportunity or means of becoming acquainted with the truth. What a touching spectacle it must have been to see a king as anxious to discover all the ills that had been effected in his name, as other men are to trace out any injustice done to themselves! In short, his paternal vigilance succeeded in destroying all abuses, and repairing all faults; "and finally," says the noble confidant of his thoughts, "in lapse of time, the kingdom of France multiplied so greatly by the justice and rectitude that reigned in it that the domains, feudal fines, rents, and revenues, increased in one year by a half, and vastly improved the kingdom of France."

We cannot finish the account of this crusade without speaking of the emperor Frederick II. and Innocent IV., who had so much influence over the events we have described. It may be said of Frederick, that his glory underwent as many vicissitudes as his fortune. Contemporary chronicles sometimes praise him with exaggeration, and at others blame him without measure. Such is ever the fate of princes who have lived amidst the conflict of parties. The spirit of party, which has judged them in their lifetime, leaves to history nothing but uncertainties, and appears still to exist for them in posterity. No historian has denied the talent or the genius of Frederick; he was one of the most illustrious captains of his times; he is placed among the princes who, by their example and their munificence, encouraged the revival of letters in the middle ages. He displayed great qualities upon the throne, but he did not know how to put himself in harmony with the spirit of his contemporaries; [339] he had neither the defects nor the virtues of his age, and that is the reason that he succumbed in the obstinate struggle with the popes. If this struggle had not troubled and divided Europe, and if Frederick had been animated by the same sentiments as St. Louis, there is no doubt that Christianity would have triumphed over Islamism, and that the Crusaders would have subdued a great portion of the East.

The memory of Innocent IV. has been judged as variously as that of his redoubtable adversary. When looking at his manifestoes, his warlike enterprises, his spiritual and temporal triumphs, we might believe that the most able and ambitious of conquerors was seated in the chair of St. Peter. The events to which he has attached his name, and which he directed by his policy, leave us nothing to say regarding his genius or his character. After the death of Frederick, this pontiff returned to Italy, which country he traversed in triumph; but by a singular contrast, he who had shaken the power of emperors, only entered Rome tremblingly. The Romans had sent envoys to him to express their surprise at seeing him lead a wandering life far from his capital, and from the flock of which he would have to render an account to the sovereign judge.

Although obedient in this respect to the will of the people of Rome, Innocent pursued his projects against the remains of the imperial family, and death surprised him in the kingdom of Naples, of which he was taking possession in the name of the Church; having lost all care for the fate of the Christian colonies of the East. The pontiff who succeeded him, although he had neither his ambition, nor his authority, nor his genius, followed not the less the career that had been marked out for him. He endeavoured to accomplish all the threats of the Holy See, and the thunders of Rome reposed no more in the hands of Alexander VI. than they had done in those of his predecessors.

That which might justify the persevering, obstinate ardour with which the popes pursued the posterity of Frederick, is that by it they liberated Italy from the yoke of the emperors of Germany; and that this rich country remained sixty years without seeing the armies of the Germanic empire. But, on the other side, this advantage was purchased by so much violence, and by so many calamities, that the nations were never able to enjoy or know the value of it. The popes, who were not always sufficiently strong to maintain the work of their policy, were sometimes obliged to call in foreign princes to their aid, who introduced fresh subjects of discord into Italy. War constantly brought on war; conquerors were expelled by other conquerors. This revolution lasted during several centuries, and became fatal, not only to Italy, but to Germany, France, and Spain, to all who wished to partake of the spoils of the house of Swabia.

It is not our task to describe these afflicting scenes: to return to that which more particularly belongs to our subject, we will glance, whilst terminating these general considerations, at the crusade which was then being preached in all the Italian cities against Eccelino de Romano, whom the voice of the people, as well as the voice of the Church, had declared to be the enemy of God and men.

This Italian noble had taken advantage of the disorder of the civil wars, to usurp a tyrannical domination over several cities of Lombardy and Trevisano. All that we are told of the tyrants of fabulous antiquity falls short of the cruelties of Eccelino. Contemporary history compares his barbarous reign to pestilence, inundations, conflagrations, and the most terrible convulsions of nature. The pope at first excommunicated Eccelino, *in whom he could see nothing but a wild beast in a human form*; a short time afterwards he published a crusade against this scourge of God and humanity. John of Vicenza, who had preached public peace twenty years before, was the first preacher of this holy war. The faithful who took up arms against Eccelino, were to receive the same indulgences as those who went to Palestine. This crusade, which was undertaken in the cause of humanity and liberty, was preached in all the republics of Italy: the eloquence of the holy orators easily prevailed over the multitude; but that which most inflamed the zeal and ardour of the people, was the sight of the wretches whom Eccelino had caused to be mutilated amidst tortures, and the groans and lamentations of the families from which the tyrant had chosen his victims. In most of the provinces of Italy, the inhabitants of the cities and country took up arms to defend the cause of religion and their native land; eager to obtain the civic crown, if they triumphed over tyranny, and the crown of martyrdom, if they chanced to fall.

The standard of the cross was displayed at the head of the army; the crowd of Crusaders marched against Eccelino, singing this hymn of the Church,—

"Vexilla regis prodeunt,
Fulget crucis mysterium."

The army of the faithful at first obtained rapid successes; but as the archbishop of Ravenna, who commanded it, wanted skill, and as the Crusaders of each town had no leaders but monks and ecclesiastics, they did not profit by their early advantages. The intrigues of policy and the spirit of rivalry relaxed the ardour of the combatants; victory was sometimes balanced by reverses: four years of labours and perils scarcely sufficed for the suppression of an impious domination, or to avenge humanity by the defeat and death of Eccelino.

I regret that the plan of this work does not permit me to speak in greater detail of this war, in which religion so happily assisted the cause of liberty, and which forms so great a contrast with most contemporary events. At this period such a number of crusades were preached, that history can scarcely follow them, and we feel astonished that the population of the West was not exhausted by so many unfortunate wars. Whilst Louis IX. was returning from the East, where he had left his army, and a holy league was being formed in Italy against the tyrant Eccelino, sixty thousand Crusaders, commanded by a king of Bohemia, marched against the people of Lithuania, still addicted to the worship of idols; and another army of Crusaders was leaving the banks of the Oder and the Vistula to combat the pagans of Prussia, so many times attacked and conquered by the Teutonic knights. History is gratified at being able to remark that in this last expedition the cities of Brunsbad and Konigsberg were founded; but the founding of two flourishing cities cannot obliterate the remembrance of the desolation of many provinces. If any advantages could arise from these sanguinary expeditions, they were certainly the progressive steps of Christianity, which brought together people till that time separated by difference in manners and religious belief; they were the lessons of misfortune and the fruits of experience, which in the end enlightened Europe, and gave to the human mind a new direction more conformable with the laws of justice and reason, more favourable to the interests of humanity. It is thus that Providence, always mixing good with evil, renews human societies, and sows the prolific seeds of civilization in the very heart of disorder and barbarism.

FOOTNOTES:

[1]The author wrote the history of the fourth, fifth, and sixth crusades during the last usurpation of Buonaparte. [How easily an observant reader may tell when a book was published—the above note was, doubtless, written after Buonaparte's failure.—Trans.]

[2]Almélik-Alazoz, Emad-eddin Otsman. We have given the names of the Mussulman princes as the greater part of our historians write them; we shall take care to point out in notes how they are pronounced by Arabian authors.

[3]Alemélek Almansour, Nassir-eddin Mohammed.

[4]Almélek Aladel Seïf-eddin Aben-beer Mohammed.

[5]Aboulfeda and some other Arabian historians point out sufficiently succinctly the division that the Ayoubite princes made of the vast provinces that formed the empire of Saladin. This empire included Syria, Egypt, almost all Mesopotamia, and even a great portion of Arabia.

Aziz, as we have said, established himself in Egypt; Afdhal and Thaher shared Syria between them, one reigning at Damascus, and the other at Aleppo. Adel retained, as his part, the cities situated beyond the Euphrates, which composed the *eastern provinces*, that is, Mesopotamia proper. To these three great divisions were attached several feudatory princes, who governed as fiefs various cities of the empire. Hamah, Salamiak, Moanah, and Mambedj belonged to Mansour; it was from this branch that issued the celebrated Aboulfeda: the family of Chirkoùh was established at Emessa; Thaher, son of Saladin, enjoyed Bosra; Amdjed, great-grandson of Ayoub, was prince of Balbek; Chëizer, Abou Cobaïs, Sahyoun, Tell-Bacher, Kaubeb, Adjloun, Barin, Kafar-Tab, and Famieh were possessed by various emirs who had served in the armies of Saladin.

As to Yémen, a province of Arabia, in which Touran-chah established himself, the family of the Ayoubites reigned there till 1239.

[6]Almélek Alafdhal, Noureddin Ali.

[7]At the death of Saladin Jerusalem came into the possession of Afdhal, his son, who gave it in fief to the emir Azz-eddin Djerdik. Aziz becoming

master of Damascus, the holy city fell into the hands of another emir, Ilm-eddin Caísser; to him succeeded Aboulhedj, the favourite of Adel; for in the division that this prince and his nephew Aziz made of Egypt and Syria, Palestine remained in the power of Adel. Aboul-Hédj was in his turn replaced by the famous emir Aksankar-el-Kébir, and he by Meïmoun, 1197. When the empire became reunited under the dominion of Adel, his son Moaddhem had Damascus, of which Palestine and Jerusalem were dependencies.

[8]This is the text of the oath, as it has been preserved by an historian:—
"I, such a one, devote myself entirely from this moment to the service of the sultan Elmélek Alnaser Salak-eddin, as long as he shall live. I swear to consecrate my life, my property, my sword, and my powers to the defence of his empire, and to be always obedient to his orders. I swear to observe the same engagements after him to his son and heir Almélek Alafdhal. I swear to submit myself to him, to fight for his empire and states with my life, my wealth, my sword, and my troops. I swear to obey him in everything; I devote myself to him inwardly and outwardly, and I take God for a witness of this engagement."

[9]This vizier was named Nasr-allah, and bore the surname of Dhiaeddin, 'the splendour of religion;' he was brother of the celebrated historian Ibn-Elatzir, author of the *Tarikh Kamel*, and himself cultivated letters with success. The study of most of the sciences occupied his youth, and his memory was adorned with the most beautiful passages of the ancient and modern poetry of his nation. Saladin had given him as vizier to his son, and Nasr-allah proved by his conduct that he was worthy of the honour. If he committed faults as a minister, he at least honoured his character by remaining faithful to his master, sharing his misfortunes, and following him into exile. After remaining some time at Samosata, whither Afdhal was banished, he came to Aleppo, and entered into the service of Thaher, who reigned there; and becoming dissatisfied with his conduct, he quitted the court, and retired to Mossoul, where he took up his residence. He died at Bagdad in 1239, whilst fulfilling a diplomatic mission with which the prince of Mossoul had charged him. Nasr-allah left several literary works, the nomenclature of which is contained in the biography of Ibn-Khilcan.

[10]M. Am. Jourdain has published a curious account of Aboulfeda and his family, the materials for which were supplied by the works themselves of this historian: it is printed in the fourteenth volume of *Les Annales des Voyages*, &c. of M. Malte Brun.

[11]The Hospitallers then possessed within the limits of Christendom *nineteen thousand manors*; the Templars had only *nine thousand*. Matthew Paris expresses himself thus:—Habent insuper Templarii in

Christianitate novem millia maneriorum; Hospitalii vero novem decem, præter emolumenta et varios proventus ex fraternitatibus et prædicationibus provenientes, et per privilegia sua accrescentes.—*Matth. Paris.*, ad annum 1244, in Henry III., lib. xi. p. 615. A manor in the middle ages *was the labour of one plough.*

[12]We possess two letters written by Celestine to Hubert, archbishop of Canterbury, to engage him to preach the crusade. The pope commands the archbishop to employ ecclesiastical censures against those who, after taking the cross, delayed their departure for the Holy Land; and to require such as could not possibly set out, to send, at their own expense, one or two men to fight against the infidels.

[13]This reminds us of the plans of conquest laid down by Pyrrhus, king of Epirus,—and of the traveller, who intended to perambulate the globe,— that he might, at the end of his wanderings, *plant cabbages in Hanover.*— Trans.

[14]All the facts relative to the preaching of this crusade are to be found in Roger de Hoveden, Matthew Paris, Godfrey Moine, William of Newbridge, Otho of St. Blaise, and Arnold of Lubeck. The latter gives the most details; he does not fail to tell us that forty burgesses of Lubeck took the cross on this occasion.

[15]The long lists of the names and titles of the Crusaders may at first appear tiresome to the reader; but as each name represents a territory or an estate, the lists are, in fact, the best means of becoming thoroughly acquainted with the extent of this astonishing mania.—Trans.

[16]Roger de Hoveden gives this account of the death of Henry of Champagne. Arnold of Lubeck says that this prince had placed himself at a window to take the air. The same Arnold adds that many thought that God had punished Henry for the regret he had evinced on the arrival of the Germans, whom he envied the glory of delivering the kingdom of Christ.

[17]We possess a very precious monument upon the battle of Sidon; it is a letter from the duke of Saxony, written to the archbishop of Cologne. The duke was present at the battle.

[18]Arnold, who gives an account of this message of the dove, appears to fear that it will not be believed. This is the manner in which he expresses himself in the third chapter:—Hic quiddam dicturus sum non ridiculum, sed ridiculè à gentibus tractum, qui quoniam sapientiores filiis iucis in generatione suâ sunt, multa excogitant, quæ nostrates non noverunt, nisi fortè ab eis didicerint. Solent enim ex untes ad quælibet negotia secum exportare columbas, quæ domi aut ova aut pullos noviter habent creates,

et si in viâ fortè accelerare volunt nuncium, scriptas literas sub umbilico columbæ subtiliter ponunt, et eam avolare permittunt. Quæ cum ad suos fœtus properat, celeriter amicis desideratum nuncium apportat.

[19]The picture of Falcandus is perfectly prophetic, and describes events exactly like those which came after him. We will quote the most curious passages:—Intueri mihi jam videor turbulentas barbarorum acies, eo qua feruntur impetu irruentes, civitates opulentas et loca diuturnâ pace florentia metu concutere, cæde vastare, rapinis atterere, et fœdare luxuriâ. Ingerit se mihi, et lachrymas a nolente futuræ species calamitatis extorquet. Occurrunt hinc cives aut resistendo gladiis intercepti, aut se dedendo miserâ servitute depressi. Illine virgines in ipsis parentum conspectibus constupratæ; matronæ post varia et preciosa capitis, colli, et pectoris ornamenta direpta, ludibrio habitæ defixis in terrâ oculis inconsolabiliter deplorantes, venerabile fœdus conjugii fœdissimæ gentis libidine violari. Nec enim aut rationis ordine regi, aut miseratione deflecti, aut religione terreri Theutonica novit insania, quam et innatus furor exagitat, et rapacitas stimulat, et libido præcipitat. Hæc autem in Apuliâ vicinisque provinciis geri, licet horrendum ac triste sit facinus, et multo cum mœrore deflendum, utcunque tamen tolerabile putaretur, si in cispharinis tantum partibus barbarorum immanitas desæviret. Servire barbaris jam cogetur antiqua illa Corinthiorum nobilitas qui patriis olim relictis sedibus, in Siciliam transuentes, et urbi construendæ locum idoneum perquirentes, tandem in optimâ et pulcherrimâ parte Siciliæ inter inæquales portus mœnia sua loco tutissimo construxerunt. Quid tibi nunc prodest philosophorum quondam floruisse doctrinis, et poëtarum ora vatifici fontis nectare proluisse? satiùs tibi quidem esset ac tutiùs, Siculorum adhuc tyrannorum sævitiam pati, quam barbaræ fœdæque gentis tyrannidem experiri. Væ tibi fons celebris et præclari nominis Arethusa, quæ ad hanc devoluta est miseriam, ut quæ poëtarum solebas carmina modulari, nunc Theutonicorum ebrietatem mitiges, et eoram servias fœditati.—See *Historia Sicula*, ap. Muratori, vol. vii.

[20]Roger de Hoveden says that the Mussulman prince of Jerusalem had offered to deliver the city up to the Franks, and even to become a Christian. If the Mussulman prince had really made such a proposition, we cannot easily guess why the Christians should not have accepted it. But Roger is the only historian that mentions this perfectly incredible circumstance: Oriental historians are silent.

[21]Otho of St. Blaise says, that after the first crusade the Saracens had fortified Jerusalem:—Pagani summâ industriâ civitates et castella quæ obtinuerunt, muniverunt, et præcipuè Hyerusalem, duplici muro antemurali opposito, et fossatis profundissimus cingentes, inexpugnabilem

reddiderunt, dato Christianis securissimo conductu visendi sepulcrum Dominicum, quæstûs gratiâ.—See *Oth. de St. Blaise* ap. Urtii collect.

[22]Arnold of Lubec enters most fully into the details of this siege: this historian is almost our only guide in this part of our narrative. We have found some useful documents in the continuator of Tabary.

[23]After describing the corruption of the Crusaders, Arnold adds:— Veniam non peto, non enim ut quempiam confundam, hæc scribo, sed dilectos in Christo moneo.

[24]Oriental historians say little of the siege of Thoron; the continuator of Tabary expresses himself thus:—"The Franks attacked Tebnyn (Thoron), and made breaches on various sides. When Malek-Adel learnt this, he wrote to Melic-Alaziz, sultan of Egypt, to desire him to come in person; 'for if you do not come,' said he, 'we shall not be able to protect the frontier country.' Alaziz then came with his troops. As to the Mussulmans who were in the castle, when they saw the breaches made in their walls, and they had no hope but defending themselves at the point of the sword, many among them surrendered to the Franks, and demanded a safeguard for themselves and their property, offering to deliver up the castle. The command was given to the priest Kandelard (Conrad), a German; but a Frank of the Sahel (coast of Syria) said to the Mussulmans, 'If you give up the fortress, these men will make you prisoners, and will kill you: preserve your own days then.' The Mussulmans left them as if to give up the fortress; but when they had re-ascended, they persisted in defending themselves, and fought in despair, so that they kept the castle till the arrival of Melic-Alaziz at Ascalon."

[25]Nec inter ista defuit spiritus procellæ, tonitruis et coruscationibus, et pluviarum inundationibus et grandine de cœlo fugientes infestandâ.— *Arnold Lub.* cap. 5.

[26]Otho de St. Blaise appears convinced that the Templars had received money to betray the cause of the Christians. He expresses himself as follows:—Nam sicut fertur, quidam de militibus Templi, à paganis corrupti pecuniâ, animam Conradi cancellarii, qui in hâc ipsâ obsidione præcipuè clarebat, cum quibusdam aliis inflexerunt, eisque auri maximo pondere collocato, obsidionem solvere persuaserunt; sicque vendito Christo tradito paganis per castellum, sicut olim Judæis, recesserunt. Nec tamen de pretio taliter acquisito aliquod emolumentum, sicut nec Judas de triginta argenteis, consecuti sunt. Si quidem pretio corrupti, corruptum à paganis aurum metallo sophistico, auro in superficie colorato receperunt; sicque in opprobrium sempiternum cum notâ infamiæ meritò consecuti sunt.— See *Oth. de St. Blaise*, in the collection of Urtius.

[27]We are astonished to find so little concerning this crusade in the continuator of William of Tyre. He speaks of this battle and of the division among the Christians, but without any circumstance worthy of being communicated to our readers.

[28]Arnold of Lubec says that the news of the death of the emperor of Germany arrived before the siege of Thoron; but it is not probable that the Crusaders, who were suddenly so anxious to return to the West on account of the troubles that threatened Germany, should have undertaken the siege of Thoron after hearing of a death which must give rise to great events in Europe. Henry died in the month of September, 1196; the siege of Thoron was begun nearly at the same time; thus the Crusaders could not be informed at that period of a circumstance which made them so suddenly renounce the holy war.

[29]Le Père Maimbourg bestows the greatest praise upon the widow of Bela. "This example," says he, "makes apparent that which has often been seen in other princesses, that heroic virtue is not at all dependent on sex, and that it is possible to make up for weakness of temperament and body by greatness of soul and strength of mind."

[30]Fuller, an English historian, speaks of this disaster at great length. As his work is scarce, I will translate the passage from it relative to this crusade, in which the impartial reader will find the gross misrepresentations of a violent enemy of the Crusaders. "In this war," says he, "we may contemplate an episcopal army which might have served for a synod; or, more truly, it offers us a picture of the *Church militant*. Many captains returned home secretly, and when the soldiers wanted to fight, the officers went away: what remained of this army fortified themselves in Jaffa. The feast of St. Martin, that great saint of Germany, fell at this time. This holy man, a German by birth, and bishop of Tours in France, distinguished himself eminently by his charity. The Germans changed his charity for the poor into excess for themselves, observing the 11th of November in such a manner that it ought no longer to be called a saint's day, but a day of festivity. Drunkenness reduced them to such a state, that the Turks, falling upon them, killed more than twenty thousand of them. This day, which the Germans write in red letters in their calendars, takes its colour from their own blood, and as their camp was a slaughter-house, the Turks were their butchers. We may compare them to the oxen of St. Martin, which differ little from droves of drunkards." — *Nicol. Fuller*, b. ii. chap. xvi. p. 133. [I really cannot see that old Fuller is so very widely wrong. — Trans.]

[31]This is the picture of the Germans in the chronicle of Usperg:—
Bellicosi, crudeles, expensarum prodigi, rationis expertes, voluntatem

pro jure habentes, ensibus invicti; in nullis, nisi hominibus suæ gentis confidentes; ducibus suis fidelissimi, et quibus vitam citiùs quam fidem posses auferre.

[32]The Latin and Greek chronicles both describe the cruelties of Henry VI. in Sicily. Nicetas, in his history, makes a long enumeration of the punishments invented by the emperor of Germany, and says that Greece was on the eve of seeing all the evils that afflicted Sicily fall upon her territory, when Henry VI. was removed, as if by an extraordinary interposition of Providence.

[33]We shall see in the end that Sicily cost Frederick II., but particularly young Conrad, the last prince of the family of Swabia, much embarrassment and many misfortunes.

[34]Our excellent author has conceived a kind of parental affection for the crusades, which makes him blind to their defects. If we speak of the *spirit* of Christianity, certainly the philosopher of Geneva has the advantage of him, as his own pages show. Divested of their mundane motives, the crusades were little else than "a savage fanaticism." There was, at least, as much religious merit in the Mussulmans, who fought to defend their faith. A philosopher may deduce beneficial results from the crusades, particularly to Europe; but he will be much puzzled to prove that that which we now consider a truly Christian spirit, influenced many of the warriors that carried them out, or the churchmen that promoted them. The Inquisition and the crusade against the Albigeois were of the same age, and the principal agents in them equally prostituted the name of religion in their horrors.—Trans.

[35]We have a life of Innocent III. which extends to the thirteenth year of his pontificate. This life, *Gesta Innocentii*, is the more valuable from being written by a contemporary.

[36]We may consult, for the preachings of this crusade, the letters of Innocent III. Some details will be found in Roger de Hoveden, Matthew Paris, &c. &c.

[37]Villehardouin expresses himself thus when speaking of the indulgences of the pope:—Por ce cil pardon fut issi grand, si s'en emeurent mult li cuers des genz, et mult s'en croisièrent, porce que li pardon ne si grand. (The pardon was so great that the hearts of people were moved, and many took the cross because the pardon was so great, or complete.)

[38]Gretser has spoken at great length of the indulgences granted to the Crusaders.—*De Cruce*, vol. iii. b. ii. c. 3.

[39]The *Chronicle* of St. Victor speaks thus of Foulques de Neuilly:—Et verba ejus quasi sagittæ potentis acutæ, hominum pravâ corda consuetudine obdurata penetrarent et ad lacrymas et pœnitentiam amolirent.

[40]If we may believe contemporary chronicles, Foulques addressed Richard Cœur de Lion, and said to him,—"You have three daughters to dispose of in marriage, Avarice, Pride, and Luxury." "Well," replied Richard, "I give my pride to the Templars, my avarice to the monks of Citeaux, and my luxury to the bishops." This anecdote is quoted by Rigord.

[41]The Latin history of the diocese of Paris thus designates the prostitutes—Multæ mulierculæ quæ corpore quæstum faciebant.

[42]Alberic, Rigord, Otho of St. Blaise, James of Vitri, the manuscript chronicle *Autore Radulfo Coggehalensi*, the *Chronicle* of Brompton, and Marin Sanul, have left particulars of the life of Foulques. The *Ecclesiastical History* of Fleury, vol. xvi., has collected all the materials scattered about in the old chronicles. The Abbé Lebeuf, in his *History of Paris*, quotes a *Life of Foulques*, 1 vol. in 12mo. Paris, 1620, which we have in vain endeavoured to procure.

[43]The monk Gunther gives some account of this sermon in the history he has left us of the conquest of Constantinople. The monk Gunther bestows the warmest praise upon Martin Litz, who was his abbot, and gives curious details of the sermons of the latter. He puts into the mouth of the preacher of the crusade a discourse in which we find the same reasons, and almost the same words, as in all the discourses of those who had previously preached holy wars; it is probable that the people were more affected by the spirit that reigned in Europe than by the eloquence of the orators.—See Gunther, in the *Collection* of Canisius.

[44]The castle of Ecry was situated on the river Aisne, not far from *Château Porcien*.

[45]The author of a *History of Jerusalem*, who wrote in the twelfth century, says, when speaking of the Champenois:—Et quædam pars Franciæ, quæ Campania dicitur, et cùm regio tota studiis armorum floreat, hæc quodam militiæ privilegio singulariùs excellit et præcellit; hinc martia pubes potenter egressa, vires quæ in tyrociniis exercitaverat, in hostem ardentiùs exerit, et imaginaria bellorum prolusione proposita, pugnans animos ad verum martem intendit.

[46]The name of Villehardouin took its origin from a village or castle of the diocese of Troye, between Bar and Arcy; the elder branch, to which the historian belonged, only subsisted to 1400; the younger, which acquired the principality of Achaia, merged in the family of Savoy. Ducange has left a very long historical notice of the genealogy of this family.

[47]Complures tantâ pontificii indulgentissimi gratiâ illecti, et Fulconis persuasionibus excitati, rubram crucem amiculo, quo dexter humerus tegitur, certatim consuere.—*Rhamnusius de Bell. Constant.* lib. i.

[48]Rhamnusius gives a very minute list of the knights and barons that took the cross. Le Père d'Outreman likewise gives a very extensive list. In the notes that accompany the history of Villehardouin, Ducange has left us many curious particulars upon the knights and barons of Flanders and Champagne who took part in this crusade.

[49]Villehardouin has preserved the names of the six deputies. The Count Thibault named two: Geoffrey of Villehardouin, Miles of Brabant. Baldwin of Flanders, two others: Canon de Bethune, and Alard de Maqueriaux; and the count of Blois, two: Jean de Friaise and Gauthier de Goudonville.

[50]Innocent III. said of the republic of Venice: Quæ non agriculturis inservit, sed navigiis potiùs et mercimoniis est intenta.—See the first book of the *Collection of the Letters of Innocent.*

[51]Nicetas says in his history, that Dandolo was styled "The Prudent of the Prudent."

[52]Several historians say that Dandolo was blind, and that the emperor Manuel Comnenus had deprived him of sight during an abode he made at Constantinople. One of his descendants, André Dandolo, says merely in his history that his ancestor was short-sighted (*visu debilis*). The part of the story connected with Manuel Comnenus appears to be a fable. Historians differ as to the age of Dandolo: Ducange, at the period of the crusade, gives him ninety-four years. Gibbon does not doubt of his blindness, though he has no faith in its having been caused by Manuel; but he certainly assigns to him actions that could scarcely be performed by a blind man. He does not believe the accounts of his very advanced age, saying,—"It is scarcely possible that the powers of mind and body should support themselves at such an age."—Trans.

[53]Weight of Cologne or Geneva. See the terms of the treaty.

[54]The Venetians undertook, in the treaty, to distribute to each individual of the army of the Crusaders, six setiers of bread, corn, wheat, or vegetables, and half a pitcher (*demi-cruche*) of wine; for each horse three bushels, Venetian measure, and water in sufficient quantities. We are not able to value the six setiers of corn, or the half-pitcher of wine, having no means of ascertaining the Venetian measures.

[55]The original treaty may be seen in the *Chronicle* of Andrew Dandolo, pages 325, 328 of vol. xii. of Muratori.

[56]From the thirteenth century the aristocracy began at Venice to get the better of the democracy.—See *History of Venice*, by Laugier.

[57]Several authors have thought that Villehardouin could not write; and they found their opinion upon what he himself says,—"*I, who dictated this work.*" However that may be, the history of Villehardouin has been pronounced by learned men to be a model of the language that has ceased to be French. In the sixteenth century the language of the marshal of Champagne was already not understood; his history was turned into modern French by Blaise de Vigenère towards the end of the sixteenth century; this translation has itself become so old as to be now scarcely intelligible. The new version that Ducange made of it in the seventeenth century still bears an impression of antiquity, which preserves something of the *naïveté* of the original. We shall often have occasion to quote Villehardouin; but we shall only quote the ancient versions, and sometimes from a translation we have ourselves made, always endeavouring to preserve as far as possible the simplicity of the old language.

[58]Gibbon says, "A reader of Villehardouin must observe the frequent tears of the marshal and his brother knights; they weep on every occasion of grief, joy, or devotion."—Trans.

[59]Maintenant li six messagers s'ageneuillent à la pies mull plorant.—*Villehardouin*, lib. i.

[60]Persuasum omnes habent, solos Venetos mari, Gallos terrâ præpotentes esse.—*Rhamn.* lib. i.

[61]Vigenère, the translator of Villehardouin, informs us that in his time the treaty between the Venetians and the French, concluded in the month of April, 1201, was still preserved in the Chancery of Venice.

[62]The author of the *History of the Republics of Italy* recapitulates thus the sum that was due to the Venetians by the Crusaders:—

For four thousand five hundred horses, at four marks per horse	18,000
For the knights, at two marks per knight	9,000
For twenty thousand foot-soldiers, at two marks per soldier	40,000
For two squires per horse, nine thousand squires	18,000
	— — —
Total marks	85,000
	— — —

Eighty-five thousand marks of silver are equal to four
millions two hundred and fifty thousand francs.

[63]Thibault was buried in the church of St. Stephen of Troyes; his
epitaph finishes with these verses:—

> Terrenam quærens, cœlestem repperit urbem;
> Dum procul hæc potitur, obviat ille domi.

[64]The *History of Burgundy* by Courtépée and Béguillet has here
committed a great error in making Eudes III. set out on the crusade, and
take a part in the capture of Constantinople.

[65]Villehardouin makes thus the eulogy of Boniface, marquis of
Montferrat:—"The marquis Boniface is, as every one knows, a very valorous
prince, and most esteemed for knowledge of war and feats of arms of any
one at the present day living."

[66]At the same time that Egypt experienced all the horrors of famine,
Richard of St. Germain and the Chronicle of Fossa-Nova (see *Muratori*) say
that a great dearth was felt in Italy and Spain; one of them adds that this
year, 1202, was known under the name of "annus famis." Mézerai speaks
of this famine, which was felt in France, and attributes it to the war then
carried on between Philip and Richard. "The two kings," says he, "pillaged
the lands, pulled up their vines, cut down the trees, cut the harvest whilst
unripe, and destroyed more cities and towns in one day than had been built
in ages. Famine followed these horrible ravages, says an author; so that
many of the richest were reduced to beg their bread, and finding none to
give it to them, ate grass and burrowed in the earth for roots."

[67]The pope was satisfied with liberating the Crusaders from the
usurious debts which they owed to the Jews. At that period all interest upon
money lent was considered usury.

[68]Jacques of Vitri, when speaking of the suspicions and murmurs that
arose against Foulques of Neuilly, expresses himself thus:—Et crescente
pecuniâ, timor et reverentia decrescebant.

[69]The Abbé Lebeuf, in his *History of the Diocese of Paris*, vol. vi. p. 20,
gives us a description of the tomb of Foulques of Neuilly, which was still
standing in the last century. "The tomb of Foulques, the famous curé of this
place about the year 1200, is in the nave, before the entrance to the choir,
built of stone a foot and a half high. It is the work of the age in which this
pious personage died. Foulques is represented in relief upon the monument,
clothed as a priest, his head bare, having the tonsure on the top, and the hair
so short that the whole of his ears is visible. A book is laid upon his breast,

which he does not hold, as his hands are crossed above, the right placed upon the left. His chasuble and his manipule represent the vestments of his times. He has under him a kind of footstool, cut in the stone, and two angels in relief incense his head, which is placed towards the west; for, after the ancient manner, his feet are pointed to the east, or the altar. It is not true, as has been said, that this tomb is incensed, nor has it any arms. He is called in the country Sir Foulques, and sometimes Saint Sire Foulques. There is a tradition that the canons of St. Maur formerly endeavoured to carry it away; but the immobility of the car with which this story is adorned, tells us what degree of faith may be attached to it." M. l'Abbé Chastelain names his death, in his *Universal Martyrology*, as having taken place on the 2nd of March, 1201, and qualifies him as *venerable*.

[70]Villehardouin says, when speaking of the arrival of the Crusaders at Venice, "No nobler people were ever seen, nor better appointed, nor more disposed to do something good for the honour of God and the service of Christendom."

[71]Upon the sojourn of the Crusaders at Venice, *Gesta Innocentii*, Villehardouin and Ducange, Sanuti, Hérold, D'Outreman, Fleury, *Histoire Ecclésiastique*, vol. xviii., l'Abbé Langier, &c. &c., may be consulted.

[72]Then might be seen so many beautiful and rich vessels of gold and silver heaped up here and there, and carried to the hotel of the duke as part of their payment.—*Villehardouin*.

[73]The Venetians might have said, and no doubt did say on this occasion, that the king of Hungary had taken the cross many years before, and had done nothing yet towards the fulfilment of his vow. Andrew did not set out for Palestine till many years after the taking of Constantinople.

[74]The monk Gunther does not at all spare the Venetians, and reproaches them bitterly with having diverted the Crusaders from their holy enterprise. The pious resolution of the leaders of the crusade, says he, was subverted by the perfidy and wicked artifices of these masters of the Adriatic,—fraude et nequitiâ Venetorum.

[75]With the true spirit of an antiquary, M. Michaud delights in throwing a character of the "olden time" into the language of Villehardouin, which is in a degree effective in the French, but is with much difficulty conveyed into English.—Trans.

[76]Irene, the daughter of Isaac, had been affianced to William, son of Tancred, king of Sicily; being taken into Germany, with the rest of the family of Tancred, she had married Philip of Swabia.

[77]Villehardouin and Gunther give very circumstantial details of the siege of Zara, and of the debates that followed it. (See also, on the subject of these debates, the letters of Innocent.) The Abbé Fleury, in the sixteenth volume of his *Ecclesiastical History*, displays sufficiently the spirit that then actuated the Crusaders. M. Lebeau, in the twentieth volume of the *History of the Lower Empire*, and the Abbé Laugier, in the second volume of his *History of Venice*, say a great deal concerning the siege of Zara.

[78]Katona, in his *Histoire Critique des Rois de Hongrie*, expresses himself with bitterness against the Crusaders, and relates facts very little favourable to the Venetians and French who laid siege to Zara. Archdeacon Thomas, one of the historians of Hungary, does not spare the Venetians, whom he accuses of tyranny, and who made, he says, their maritime power detested by all the excesses of violence and injustice.

[79]We feel bound to present the text of this oath:—B. Fland. et Hain., L. Blesen et Clar. et H. S. P. comites, Oddo de Chanliet, et W. frater ejus, omnibus ad quos litteræ istæ pervenerint, salutem in Domino. Notum fieri volumus, quod super eo quod apud Jaderam incurrimus excommunicationem apostolicam, vel incurrisse nos timemus, tam nos quam successores nostros sedi apostolicæ obligamus, quod ad mandatum ejus satisfactionem curabimus exhibere. Dat. apud Jaderam, anno Domini 1203, mense Aprilis.

[80]The pope adds, whilst speaking of the Venetians: "Excommunicated as they are, they still remained tied by their promises; and you are not the less authorized to require the performance of them; it is further a maxim of right, that in passing over the land of a heretic or an excommunicated person, you may buy or receive necessary things from him. Moreover, excommunication denounced against the father of a family, does not prevent his household from communicating with him."

[81]This permission to live by pillage, even in a friendly country, is remarkable, particularly as the pope pretends to authorize it by examples from Scripture.—*Fleury, Hist. Eccl.* book lxxv.

Innocent, in giving the Crusaders permission to take provisions wherever they may find them, adds, "Provided it be with the fear of God, without doing injury to any person, and with a resolution to make restitution."

[82]We find in the continuator of William of Tyre the following circumstance:—Malek-Adel being informed that the Crusaders were assembling at Venice, conceived great uneasiness regarding their ulterior designs. He called together the heads of the Christian clergy at Cairo, and announced to them that a new expedition was preparing in Europe, and that they must provide themselves with horses, arms, and provisions. The

bishops, to whom he addressed himself to obtain the succour of which he stood in need, replied that their sacred ministry did not allow them to fight. "Well," answered Malek-Adel, "since you cannot fight yourselves, you must provide me with men to fight in your place." He then demanded of them an account of the lands they possessed, and ordered that these lands should be sold; and the money produced by this confiscation was sent to Venice, to corrupt the leaders of that republic, and to engage them to divert the Crusaders from an expedition into Egypt or Syria. Malek-Adel at the same time promised the Venetians all sorts of privileges for their trade in the port of Alexandria. This singular circumstance, related at first, as we have said, by the continuator of William of Tyre, is to be found also in Bernard *Thesaurarius,* and in the *Chronicle* of St. Victor. Marin. Sanut, it is true, passes it by in silence, and contents himself with saying that Malek-Adel went into Egypt and there collected a treasure. But it may be observed that Marin. Sanut was a Venetian, and had a good reason not to report all the details of a fact which was not to the glory of his country. Bernard when relating it, adds:—Qualiter autem hujus rei effectus fuerit in opinione patenti multorum est, si legantur quæ Veneti cum baronibus ipsis peregerunt, detrahendo eos ad obsidionem Jadræ, et deinde Constantinopolim.

[83]The marshal of Champagne lets no opportunity escape for blaming with bitterness those who abandoned the army of the Crusaders.

[84]A double alliance and the dignity of Cæsar had connected the two elder brothers of Boniface with the imperial family. Reinier of Montferrat had married Mary, daughter of the emperor Manuel Comnenus; Conrad, who had defended Tyre before the third crusade, was married to Theodora Angela, sister of the emperors Isaac and Alexius.

[85]The army was no longer to be dreaded by the emperors as it had been in the early days of the empire; but it was no more an object of fear to its enemies than to its master. A modern historian, M. Sismondi, finds in the government of the Greek empire a complete and incontestable evidence of the natural and necessary effects of the worst of governments. The ancients were acquainted with scarcely any medium between liberty and despotism. The government of Constantinople had retained, up to the middle of the middle ages, all which characterized the despotism of the ancients, although we must allow that this despotism was sometimes tempered by religion and the influence of the patriarchs of Byzantium.

[86]Lebeau, in his *History,* describes at length the decline of the Greek empire and the vices of the emperors. Gibbon, a much more enlightened observer, sometimes neglects important details connected with this period,

and in his latter volumes, too often forgets the Greeks to speak of the barbarous nations of the East and West that had shared the wrecks of the Roman empire.

[87]We may consult, for an account of this expedition, the marshal of Champagne, Gunther, and some passages of Nicetas. Rhamnusius has only made a pompous paraphrase of Villehardouin. Lebeau and the Abbé Laugier say a great deal of the events we are relating. This expedition of the Crusaders has been splendidly described by the historian Gibbon.

[88]Villehardouin.

[89]It would be difficult to give a very exact idea of the city of Constantinople as it was at the period of this crusade. Among the travellers who have described this capital at a time nearer than our own to the middle ages, we ought to remark Peter Gilles and Grelot, who saw Constantinople, the one in the reign of Francis I., and the other in the reign of Louis XIV. Their description has furnished those who came after them with many documents. Revolutions, wars, the Turks, and fires change every day the aspect of this city, which was already much altered in the times of the travellers we have named. Ducange, in his *Christiana Constantinopolis*, and Banduri, in his *Imperium Orientale*, have collected all the information of the old travellers and the Greek historians. Among modern travellers *Constantinople, Ancient and Modern*, by the Englishman Dallaway, and *Le Voyage de la Propontide*, by M. Lechavalier, may be consulted with advantage.

[90]Having cast anchor, such as had never been there before began to contemplate this beautiful and magnificent city, the equal to which they thought could not be found in the whole world. When they perceived those high walls and large towers so near to each other, with which it was furnished all round, and those rich and superb palaces and churches rising above all, and in such great number, that they could not easily believe they saw them with their eyes; together with the fine situation of the city, in its length and breadth, which of all other cities was the sovereign, &c.— *Villehardouin*.

[91]Ducange, in his observations upon Villehardouin, gives a very learned note upon the arms and escutcheons which the warriors of the middle ages caused to be ranged on board their vessels, and which served them as battlements to shelter them from all the arrows of the enemy.

[92]The Greek historian Nicetas says, that the navigation of the Crusaders had been so favourable and so rapid, "that they arrived in the port of St. Stephen without being perceived by anybody."

[93]Nicetas, speaking of the Crusaders, says they were almost all as tall as their spears.

[94]Nicetas says, among the Venetian vessels there was one so large that it was called *the World*.

[95]The Varangians, who were in the service of the Greek emperors, have given rise to many discussions among the learned. Villehardouin says that the Varangians were English and Danes. The count de St. Pol, in a letter written from Constantinople, calls them English, Livonians, Dacians. Other historians call them Celts, Germans. The word Varangians appears to be taken from an English word *waring*,(a) which means warrior; this word is met with in the Danish, and several other tongues of the north of Europe. Ducange thinks the Varangians came from Danish England, a small province of Denmark, between Jutland and Holstein. M. Malte Brun, in the notes that accompany the *History of Russia*, by Lévesque, thinks the Varangians drew their recruits from Scandinavia; that some came from Sweden by Norvogorod and Kiow, others from Norway and Denmark by the Atlantic and the Mediterranean. We still possess a dissertation upon the Varangians by M. de Villoison, in which we find more learning than criticism. The most probable opinion is that of Ducange and M. Malte Brun. We have but one observation to make, which is, that it is probable the Varangians were not members of the Roman church; if they followed the Greek religion, may we not believe that they belonged to the nations of the North, among whom it had been introduced?

(a) An Englishman is rather at a loss to tell where our author finds this word. Johnson derives *war* from *werre*—old Dutch.—Trans.

[96]Le Père d'Outreman speaks thus of Conon de Béthune: Vir domi militæque nobilis et fœcundus in paucis.—*Constantin. Belg.* lib. iii. Villehardouin says that Conon de Béthune "was a wise knight and well-spoken."

[97]Thus went they sailing along by the side of the walls, where they showed Alexius to the Greeks, who from all parts flocked to the mole: Sieurs Greeks, behold your natural lord, of that there is no doubt, &c. &c.— *Villehardouin*, book iii.

[98]It was nearly at this period that the city of Chrisopolis began to be called Scutari. The name of Scutari is employed by Villehardouin.

[99]The breaking of the chain of the port, according to the account of Nicetas, spread the greatest consternation among the Greeks; and misfortune, says the historian of Byzantium, assumed so many different forms, and produced so surprising a number of afflicting images, that no mind is able to conceive them.

[100]For the first siege we may profitably consult the *Letter of the Crusaders to the Pope*; the *History* of Villehardouin; Nicetas, *Reign of Alexius*; the *Chronicle* of Dandolo; the *War of Constantinople*, by D'Outreman, Rhamnusius *de Bell. Constantinop.* &c. &c.

[101]The name of Barbysses is at present unknown to the Turks, who call this river Kiathana; the Greeks call it Karturicos, names which, in both languages remind us of the paper-mills that are at its mouth.

[102]Nevertheless the superb palaces were ruined by the stones of an extraordinary size that the besiegers launched with their machines, and they were themselves terrified by the heavy masses that the Romans rolled upon them from the walls.—*Nicetas, Hist. of Alexius Comnenus*, book iii.

[103]The historian of Byzantium says, with regard to this fire, that so lamentable a spectacle was capable of producing floods of tears sufficiently abundant to have extinguished the conflagration.

[104]The marshal of Champagne describes to us the order of battle of the Latins, as it was drawn up according to the tactics of the middle ages. The Crusaders issued from their camp divided into six bodies; they ranged themselves before their palisades. The knights were on horseback, their sergeants and esquires were behind them close to the quarters of their horses; the crossbow-men and archers were in front.

[105]Certes, voila une capitulation bien étrange, répondit l'empereur, et ne voy pas comme elle se puisse accomplir, tant elle est grande et excessive. Nompourtant vous avez tout fait pour lui et pour moy, que si l'on vous donnerait tout cet empire entièrement, si l'avez vous bien desuivi.— *Villehardouin*, book iv.

[106]The Crusaders addressed Otho, and not Philip of Swabia, which is very strange, as Philip was the brother-in-law of Alexius; but it is to be observed that at this period the pope had declared in favour of Otho, and threatened Philip with the thunders of the Church.

[107]This speech is given in its entirety by Villehardouin.

[108]The Greeks and Latins were divided on three principal points; first, the addition made by the Latin Church to the creed of Constantinople, to declare that the Holy Ghost proceeds from the Father; 2nd the refusal on the part of the Greeks to acknowledge the primacy of the pope; 3rdly the pretension of the Greeks that it is not possible to consecrate in the Eucharist with unleavened bread. Photius began the schism; the patriarch Cerularius established it; this latter wished to be acknowledged as the head

of the universal Church instead of the pope. L'Abbé Fleury, in his *Histoire Ecclesiastique*, thinks that the schism of the Greeks only really began at the period the Latins were masters of Constantinople.

[109]The Bulgarians had shaken off the yoke under the first reign of Isaac. They had for leaders two brothers, Peter and Asan, who had for successor a third brother, Joannices.

[110]Nicetas devotes an entire chapter to the description of this fire. Villehardouin, in the fourth volume of his *History*, speaks thus of it: De quoi les pélerins Français farent mult dolent, et mult en eurent grand pitié.

[111]Nicetas gives a sufficiently long description of this statue of Pallas.—See the *History of Isaac Angelus*, chap. iii. This statue was thirty feet high; its eyes, says the Greek historian, were turned towards the south, so that those who were ignorant of the science of angles considered she was looking towards the West, and that she invited the nations from the north of Europe to come to the shores of the Bosphorus.

[112]Nicetas.

[113]The continuator of William gives the Greek prince the name of Marofle.

[114]Lebeau, *Histoire du Bas-Empire*, says that Mourzoufle had been employed to put out the eyes of Isaac.—See *Hist. du Bas-Emp.* liv. xciv.

[115]Jacques de Vitri, Alberic, and the continuator of William of Tyre speak of this battle fought between Antioch and Tripoli; Villehardouin likewise makes mention of it, and names many knights that were killed or made prisoners.

[116]Vigenère, when translating Villehardouin, renders thus the passage in which the marshal of Champagne expresses the dissatisfaction of the Crusaders, and the ill-conduct of Alexius towards them:—Alexis les menait de délai en délai, de respit en respit, le bec dans l'eau, quant au principal, et pour le regard de certaines menues parties, qu'il leur fournissait comme à lesche doigt, formait tant de petites difficultés et chicaneries, que les barons commencèrent à s'ennuyer.

[117]Villehardouin, after having described the court of Alexius, in this ceremony naïvely adds: Tout cela se sentait bien sa cour d'un si puissant et riche prince. The title of *puissant* scarcely suited a prince who was hearing war declared against him in his own palace; and the epithet *rich* was hardly more applicable to him, since he could not pay what he had promised, and thereby redeem his empire from the greatest danger.

[118]Là-desseus bruit se leva fort grand au palais; et les messagers s'en retournuèrent aux portes, où ils montèrent habilement à cheval; n'y ayant celui, quand ils furent hors, qui ne se sentit très heureux et content en son esprit, voire estonné, d'être reschappé à si bon marché d'un si manifeste danger; car il ne tint presque à rien qu'ils n'y demeurassent tous morts ou pris.—*Villehardouin, liv. vi.*

[119]Mourzoufle deprived Nicetas of the place of Logothete, to give it to his brother-in-law Philocales. Nicetas treats Mourzoufle with much severity, and among the reproaches he addresses to him, we may remark one which suffices to paint the court of Byzantium. The greatest crime of the usurper was not that of having obtained sovereignty by parricide, but postponing the distribution of his favours.

[120]The two attempts to burn the Venetian fleet are described in a letter of Baldwin to the pope.—See *Gesta Innocent.* The marshal of Champagne only mentions the first attempt of the Greeks.

[121]Dandolo demanded of Mourzoufle fifty centenaries of gold, which have been valued at 50,000 pounds' weight of gold, or 48,000,000 of francs (about £2,000,000 sterling.—Trans.). Nicetas alone speaks of this interview, of which Villehardouin and other historians make no mention.

[122]The whole of this interview militates very strongly, as indeed do all the scenes in which the doge is an actor, against the story of his blindness.—Trans.

[123]The monuments we have consulted for the second siege of Constantinople are the *History* of Villehardouin, the reign of Mourzoufle in Nicetas, the account of Gunther, and the second letter of Baldwin to the sovereign pontiff, which is found in the Life of Innocent (*Gesta Innocent.*).

[124]Eidem civitati de quâ fugere non audebant, obsidionem ponebant.—*Gunther.* The same Gunther describes the Crusaders as trembling and distracted: De victoriâ tantæ multitudinis obtinen lâ, sive expugnatione urbis nulla eis spes poterat arridere.

[125]This treaty, made under the walls of Constantinople, is still preserved, and is to be found in *Muratori,* vol. xii.

[126]Et là, il eut maintes choses alléguées se trouvant en grand emoy ceux de l'ost, pour leur être ainsi pris ce jour là.—*Villehardouin, liv. v.*

[127]Et sachez qu'il y en avait qui eussent volontiers desiré, que la vague et le vent les eussent ravis jusqu'au delà de l'archipel; car à tels ne chaillait sinon que de parter de là, et aller leur voie droite en leurs maisons.—*Idem.*

[128]According to Gunther, the taking of Constantinople was more wonderful than all that has been related by Homer and the poets of antiquity.

[129]Gunther says it was a German count that set fire to the city,—*comes Teutonicus;* he did it to prevent the Greeks from rallying:—Comes Teutonicus jussit urbem in quâdam parte succendi, ut Græci duplici laborantes incommodo, belli scilicet atque incendii, faciliùs vincerentur; quod et factum est, et hoc illi consilio victi penitùs in fugam conversi sunt.

[130]The crowd of Greeks fled principally by the Golden Gate. M. le Chevalier, in his *Voyage de la Propontide,* informs us that vestiges of the Golden Gate are still to be seen within the inclosure of the seven towers. This gate was a triumphal arch erected by Theodosius, after his victory over Maximus; it was surmounted by a statue of Victory in bronze, and ornamented profusely with gold. On the remains of this gate may still be read these Latin verses:—

> Theodosi jussis, gemino nec mense peracto,
> Constantinus ovans hæc mœnia firma locavit;
> Tam citò tam stabilem Pallas vix conderet arcem.

Raoul de Dicetto, quoted by Ducange, says that these words were upon the Golden Gate:—Quando veniet rex flavus occidentalis, ego per meipsam aperiar. Raoul de Dicetto wrote thirteen years before the taking of Constantinople.

[131]Agnes, daughter of Louis VII., had been at the age of eight years, given in marriage to Alexius Comnenus, the son of Manuel, in 1179. After the death of Alexius, his murderer Andronicus usurped the empire and married Agnes, but had no children by her. Agnes remained a widow at Constantinople to the time of its being taken, when she married Branas, who was attached to the party of the Latins.

[132]Nicetas speaks of the carnage which followed the taking of Constantinople. We have quoted the words even of Villehardouin, who does not materially contradict Nicetas. The pope in his letters warmly reproached the Crusaders on this subject. Gunther only carries the number of slain, on the entrance of the Crusaders into Jerusalem, to two thousand persons, and attributes this slaughter to the Latins established at Constantinople, who had great cause of complaint against the Greeks. The same historian informs us that the ecclesiastics that followed the army contributed, by their discourses, to put an end to the massacre. He does not omit this occasion to praise the piety and humanity of Martin Litz, who went through the ranks of the victorious army, preaching moderation to the conquerors.

[133]There was nothing so difficult, says Nicetas, as to soften the fierce temper, appease the anger, or gain the affections of these barbarians. Their bile was so heated, that it only required a word to set it in a blaze; it was a ridiculous undertaking to attempt to render them tractable, a folly to speak reason to them.

[134]This is a very remarkable passage; it describes the hero of the crusades with the pencil of the painter as well as with the pen of the historian.—Trans.

[135]The lamentations of Nicetas are not always natural; whilst deploring the fate of Byzantium he says, "I complained to the walls, that they alone should be insensible to calamities, and should remain standing, instead of melting away in tears."

[136]The eleventh and twelfth volumes of the *Memoirs of the Royal Society of Gottingen* contain a beautiful work of the illustrious Heyne, upon the monuments of art that have existed at Constantinople. In the first memoir he gives the nomenclature of the ancient monuments,—*Priscæ Artis Opera*. In the second those that were erected under the emperors of Byzantium. In two other memoirs, the same learned author describes the loss of these same monuments: *De Interitu Operum cum antiquæ tam verioris ætatis*.

[137]The Bellerophon. This statue is that of Theodosius, showing a trophy placed upon a neighbouring column; it was thus the Pacificator was represented: *fuit a Deo pacificatoris habitus*. Nicetas says that in his left hand he held a globe. The statues of the other emperors of Constantinople present a similar sign, to which a cross is attached. The people believed that under the hoof of the left fore foot, was the figure of a Venetian or a Bulgarian, or of a man of some other country which had no intercourse with the Romans. The statue being destroyed by the Latins, it was said that the figure of a Bulgarian was found concealed in the hoof, crossed by a nail and incrusted in lead. This statue came from Antioch in Syria. At the quadrilateral base was a basso-relievo, in which the populace, ever superstitious, fancied they beheld the prediction of the fall of the empire. They even said that the Russians there represented would accomplish the prediction.

[138]One of the French translators of Gibbon, of a single statue has made two; he speaks of a statue of Joshua and of another of Bellerophon. It is true that this gross error is only met with in one French translation; the English original says that in the opinion of the vulgar, this statue passed for that of Joshua, but that a more classical tradition recognised in it that of Bellerophon and Pegasus; the free and spirited attitude of the courser indicating that he trod on air rather than on the earth.

[139]Heyne attributes it to Lysippus; he thinks it is the same as the colossal Hercules of Tarentum, which was brought to Rome and placed in the Capitol. From this city it went to Constantinople, with ten other statues, under the consulate of Julian and the reign of Constantine, that is to say, about 322; but it was not till after being exhibited in the Basilic that it was placed in the Hippodrome.

[140]Gibbon calls this *an osier basket*; Michaud says, *un lit d'osier*, which I have preferred. I can imagine Hercules sitting upon a bed or mattress of osier, but not upon a basket.—Trans.

[141]The learned Harris, in his historical Essay upon the literature and arts of the middle ages, thinks that the monument which represented the wolf suckling Romulus, was the same as that to which Virgil makes allusion when describing the buckler of Æneas:—

Illam tereti cervice reflexam

Mulcere alternos, et corpora fingere linguâ.

Æneid, b. viii.

[142]Cum ergo victores victam, quam jure belli suam fecerant, alacriter spoliarent, cœpit Martinus abbas de suâ etiam prædâ cogitare, et ne ipse vacuus remaneret, proposuit et ipse sacratas manus suas ad rapinam extendere.—*Gunther.*

The same Gunther relates how Martin committed violence upon a Greek priest to obtain relics from him. When speaking of Martin Litz Gunther employs these singular expressions—*prædo sanctus.*

[143]We have spoken in the early part of the work of the true cross which the kings of Jerusalem caused to be borne before them in battle, and which was taken by Saladin at the battle of Tiberias; Saladin refused to deliver it up to Richard, as many of the Crusaders must have known. How then could the true cross be found at Constantinople? The Greeks, however, were not very nice with respect to the authenticity of their relics, and the Christians of the West on this point yielded very easy faith to them. [I cannot but think our author a little out in his criticism here: they were but fragments or portions of the cross, at Constantinople the Saracens still held the main body of the true cross—*if true it was.*—Trans.]

[144]Villehardouin, when speaking of the rigorous justice exercised upon all who endeavoured to conceal any part of the plunder, says: Et en y eut tout plein de pendus.

[145]One edition of Villehardouin makes the plunder of Constantinople amount to five hundred thousand silver marks, equivalent to twenty-

four millions; if we add to this sum the fifty thousand marks due to the Venetians, and deducted before the division, and the part which they had in the division itself, we shall find the total amount of booty fifty millions four hundred thousand francs (about £2,100,000.—Trans.). As much, says the modern historian who supplies us with this note, perhaps, was appropriated secretly by individuals. The three fires which had consumed more than half the city had destroyed at least as much of its riches, and in the profusion that followed the pillage, the most precious effects had lost so much of their value, that the advantage of the Latins probably was not equivalent to a quarter of what they had cost the Greeks. Thus we may suppose that Constantinople, before the attack, contained 600,000,000 of wealth (£25,000,000). (What would the plunder of London amount to in 1852?—Trans.)

[146]The ceremony of the lighted flax still takes place at the exaltation of the popes; these words are addressed to them: *Sic transit gloria mundi.*

[147]Nicetas relates all the circumstances of the sharing of the lands of the empire. We find in *Muratori* the treaty for the division which was made before the siege; we do not offer it to our readers, because it is unintelligible in several places, and cannot shed any light over geography. The names of the cities and provinces of the empire are given in a very unfaithful and imperfect manner. The Venetians without doubt furnished the necessary information for the drawing up of the treaty, but this information was very incomplete.

[148]The pope would not at first recognise this election, which appeared to him a usurpation of the rights of the Holy See; but as Morosini was an ecclesiastic of great merit, Innocent was not willing to choose another. Morosini was sent to Constantinople not as if elected by the Crusaders, but as if appointed by the pope.

[149]Innocent, when speaking of the sack of Constantinople, expresses himself thus in his letter:—Quidam nec religioni, nec ætati, nec sexui pepercerunt; sed fornicationes, adulteria, et incestus in oculis omnium exercentes, non solum meretriculas et viduas, sed et matronas et virgines Deoque dicatas exposuerunt spurcitiis garcionum. The pope is more severe towards the Crusaders than Nicetas himself; the indignation that the disobedience of the Crusaders had created, led him to exaggerate their faults. The word *incestus*, applied to warriors who had no family relations with the Greeks, alone serves to prove that there is more bitterness than truth in the letter of Innocent.

[150]Some modern writers have asserted that the column from which Mourzoufle was precipitated is still to be seen at Constantinople: but

there existed two columns in that city; one of Theodosius and the other of Arcadius. The first was destroyed by Bajazet, and nothing remains of the other but the pedestal, which is in the Avret Baras (the women-market). See the *Voyage to the Propontis*, by M. le Chevalier, who has cleared up this fact on the spot.

[151]Claudian has made in his panegyrics of Stilicho, a picture of the invasion of the Goths in the provinces of Greece. These beautiful countries had not been invaded since the third century. The Franks scarcely knew how to guard their conquests better than the barbarians that had preceded them.

[152]There is in the king's library a manuscript in modern Greek, bearing the number 2,898; the first part of this manuscript is a romance in verse, entitled "Les Amours de Thésée et des Amazones." The second part of the manuscript is a poem on the crusades; all the tenth canto describes in detail the conquests of the Franks in Greece. M. Khazis, professor of modern Greek, had made a short analysis of this poem.

[153]The letters of Innocent speak of the city of Athens, which was no longer dedicated to Minerva, but to the holy virgin.—See b. xx. epis. vi. *Idem.*

[154]It is here that for the last time we quote the *History* of Villehardouin; we shall perhaps be reproached with having quoted it too often, and by that means given too much monotony to our account. We will answer, that the natural relation and expressions of such an historian, who relates what he has seen and that which he has experienced, have appeared to us above all that talent or the art of writing could substitute in their place. We are pleased at believing, that if our recital has been able to interest our readers, we owe a great part of this interest to the multiplied quotations from Villehardouin and other contemporary historians.

[155]Among the romantic accounts that were circulated concerning Baldwin, we must not omit the following:—The emperor was kept close prisoner at Terenova, where the wife of Joannice became desperately in love with him, and proposed to him to escape with her. Baldwin rejected this proposal, and the wife of Joannice, irritated by his disdain and refusal, accused him to her husband of having entertained an adulterous passion. The barbarous Joannice caused his unfortunate captive to be massacred at a banquet, and his body was cast on to the rocks, a prey to vultures and wild beasts.

But people could not be convinced that he was dead. A hermit had retired to the forest of Glançon, on the Hainault side, and the people of the neighbourhood became persuaded that this hermit was Count Baldwin. The solitary at first answered with frankness, and refused the homage they wished to render him. They persisted, and at length he was induced to play a part, and gave himself out for Baldwin. At first he had a great many partisans; but the king of France, Louis VIII., having invited him to his court, he was confounded by the questions that were put to him: he took to flight, and was arrested in Burgundy by Erard de Chastenai, a Burgundian gentleman, whose family still exists. Jane countess of Flanders caused the impostor to be hung in the great square of Lisle.—See *Ducange, Hist. de Constant.* book iii.

[156]Dandolo was magnificently buried in the church of St. Sophia, and his mausoleum existed till the destruction of the Greek empire. Mahomet II. caused it to be demolished, when he changed the church of St. Sophia into a mosque. A Venetian painter, who worked during several years in the court of Mahomet, on returning to his own country obtained from the sultan the cuirass, the helmet, the spurs, and the toga of Dandolo, which he presented to the family of this great man.

[157]Nicetas did not know whether he ought to give a place in his *History* to the Latins, who were for him nothing but barbarians, but he makes up his mind to continue—"when God, who confounds the wisdom of human policy, and lowers the pride of the lofty, has struck with confusion those who had outraged the Greeks, and delivered them up to people still more wicked than themselves."—See the history of that which happened after the taking of Constantinople, chap. i.

[158]How is it that our author, who is evidently partial to Villehardouin, has neglected to speak of his skilful retreat from Adrianople, upon which Gibbon bestows such high praise "His masterly retreat of three days would have deserved the praise of Xenophon and the ten thousand." Gibbon has fine passages on Villehardouin.—Trans.

[159]Innocent, to get rid of the neighbourhood of the emperor, demanded of Philip Augustus a knight who might marry a daughter of Tancred, and possibly reconquer Sicily. The adventures and the wars of Gauthier de Brienne are related by Conrad, abbot of Usberg, Robert the Monk, Alberic, and, as we have already said, by the author of the *Acts of Innocent.*

[160]We cannot refrain from offering our readers a curious passage from an excellent manuscript memoir which M. Jourdain has communicated to us, entitled *Recherches sur les Anciennes Versions Latines d'Aristote employées par les Ecclésiastiques du 13me Siècle.* "Two circumstances contributed in the thirteenth century to materially spread the knowledge of the Greek language in the West. Baldwin, who was placed upon the imperial throne, wrote to Pope Innocent III. to beg of him to send to him men distinguished by their

piety and knowledge, chosen from the religious orders and the University of Paris, to instruct his new people in the Catholic religion and Latin letters. The pope wrote to several monastic orders and to the University of Paris. About the same time Philip Augustus founded at Paris, near the mountain St. Geneviève, a Constantinopolitan college, destined to receive the young Greeks of the most distinguished families of Constantinople. The intention of this prince was to extinguish in the hearts of these young men the hatred they had imbibed against the Latins, by offering to them all sorts of kind treatment, and perhaps also to secure hostages against the fickleness and bad faith of the Greeks." We can conceive that this circumstance contributed powerfully in diffusing the knowledge of Greek, not only in France but in all the West, for Paris was then the most celebrated school, and almost all the men to whom Latin translations from the Greek are attributed, had studied in that city: we must also assign to the same cause the Latin versions of Aristotle made from the Greek and published before St. Thomas. Nevertheless, if the Arabs had not previously spread throughout the West a taste for the Peripatetic philosophy, it is very doubtful whether the relations established between the East and the West by the inauguration of Baldwin, would have produced any desire to obtain it from purer sources.

[161]Since their restoration to Venice, the history of these three celebrated horses has given birth to three dissertations. In one (*Narrazione Storica dei Quatro Cavalli di Bronzo*, &c.), Count Cicognara, president of the Royal Academy of Fine Arts at Venice, pretends that this monument was cast at Rome in the reign of Nero, in commemoration of the victory over Tiridates. M. Schlegel (*Lettera ai Signori Compilatori della Biblioteca Italiana*) rejects this opinion of the count, and thinks that the four bronze horses are from the hands of a Greek statuary of the time of Alexander.—*Dei Quatro Cavalli della Basilica di S. Marco*. Andre Mustoxidi, a very learned young Greek, makes this superb group come from Chios, which was rich in skilful sculptors, and believes they were transmitted to Rome in the time of Verres, and to Constantinople under Theodosius the Great.

[162]We find in the first volume of an Italian work entitled *Storia d'Incisa e del già celebre suo Marchesato*, published at Asti, in 1810, a precious monument; this is a charter which proves the sending of the seeds of maize to a city of Montferrat. This is a very interesting document.

[163]It is well worthy of remark that it is very little more than a quarter of a century since this sentence was written; and, in that short period, what has not science effected!—the East, of which we were then said to be so ignorant, is better known to Europeans than it was at any time during the crusades.—Trans.

[164]The account of this famine, and the disasters by which it was followed, is to be found in its details, in *Les Relations de l'Egypte*, translated from Abdallatif by M. Letvestre de Lacy. This Arabian author was a skilful physician and an enlightened man; and his recital, which contains many extraordinary facts, bears all the characters of truth.

[165]The circumstances of this earthquake are related by Abdallatif, the Latin historians scarcely name this great calamity.

[166]M. Langlès has furnished us with this valuable incident, which he has taken from the Persian biographer Daulet Chah. The biographer adds, that a merchant of Aleppo redeemed Saadi, by paying the Christians the sum of ten golden crowns, and he likewise gave the poet another hundred as the dowry of his daughter, whom he gave him in marriage.

[167]History has great trouble in following the events of this period through the cloud of anarchy which reigned everywhere; and that which increases the difficulty is, that the authors of our old chronicles were only acquainted with the kingdom of Jerusalem, and knew nothing of what was going on in the interior of the states. The Arab historians, on the contrary, take much more note of the expeditions of the interior than of the events that happened at Ptolemaïs, situated on the sea-coast, and in some sort isolated from the rest of Syria.

[168]We find few details upon this epoch in the continuator of William of Tyre, or the other historians of the middle ages who mention the Christian colonies.

[169]This penitence and that which follows are mentioned by Fleury, in the sixteenth volume of his History; the guilty were condemned, in addition to the pilgrimage, to wear neither vair, grey squirrel fur, ermine, nor coloured stuffs; they were never to be present at public games; after becoming widowers, were never to marry again; to walk barefooted and be clothed in woollen, and to fast on bread and water on Wednesdays, Fridays, Ember-week, and Vigils; to perform three Lent fasts in the course of the year, to recite the Pater Noster a hundred times, and make a hundred genuflexions every day. When they came to a city, they were to go to the principal church barefooted, in drawers, with halters round their necks and rods in their hands, and there receive from the canons discipline, &c. &c.

[170]Son of Erard II., count of Brienne in Champagne, and Agnes Monthéliard.

[171]The continuator of William of Tyre relates that the barons of Palestine themselves demanded John of Brienne of the king of France.

[172]As Gibbon has done, I have preferred the real name of this sect to the Latinized *Albigenses.*—Trans.

[173]Bossuet, *Histoire des Variat.* vol. ii. L'Abbé Paquet, in his *Dictionnaire des Hérésies,* and Fleury, in his *Histoire Ecclésiastique,* express the same opinion.

[174]Notwithstanding the partiality I naturally feel for an author whose work I am translating, and to which task I was led by my admiration of it, I cannot allow such opinions of the war against the Albigeois to pass unnoticed. A very sensible French historian says:—"The inhabitants of these provinces were industrious, intellectual, and addicted to commerce, the arts, and poetry; their numerous cities flourished, governed by consuls with forms approaching to republican; all at once this beautiful region was abandoned to the furies of fanaticism, its cities were ruined, its arts and its commerce destroyed, and its language cast back into barbarism. The preaching of the first religious reform gave birth to the devastation of these rich countries. The clergy were not distinguished there, as in France or the northern provinces, by their ardour to improve themselves and diffuse knowledge; they signalized themselves by gross disorders, and sank daily into greater contempt. The need of reform had been long felt among the people of Provence and many reformers had already appeared. For a length of time associations had existed whose aim it was to purify the morals and the doctrines of the Church; such were the Paterins, the Catharins, and the Poor of Lyons; and the greater part of these had obtained the sanction of the popes, who considered them as so many orders of monks, highly calculated to awaken public devotion. But the reforms that were operated extended gradually; dogmas even were attacked, priests were subjected to the insults of the people, and the domains of the Church were invaded. Such was the state of things when the famous Innocent III., at the age of thirty-nine, ascended the pontifical throne in 1198. To his great task he brought the talents of an ambitious, and the energy of a violent and an inflexible character. This pontiff, who dominated over Europe by indulgences and excommunications, watched for and punished with severity every free exercise of thought in religious matters; he was the first to feel how serious and threatening for the Church of Rome that liberty of mind must be that had already degenerated into revolt. He saw with great inquietude and anger the new tendency of men's minds in Provence and Languedoc, and proscribed the reformers, the most numerous of whom, and who gave their name to all the others, were known under the names of Albigeois and Vaudois. Some among them were Manicheans, that is to say, admitted the two principles; *but the greatest number of them professed doctrines differing but very little from those which, three centuries later, were preached by Luther.*

They denied transubstantiation in the sacrament of the Eucharist, rejected confession, and the sacraments of confirmation and marriage, and taxed the worship of images with idolatry." In this war papacy put forth all its most dreaded powers; indulgences to its brutal, mercenary soldiers; heaven for wholesale slaughterers of their fellow-creatures; hell for all who dared to think when they worshipped, or to breathe a word against the veriest nonsense of Romish rites: many instances occurred in which the odious doctrine of *no faith to be observed with heretics*, was unblushingly advanced and cruelly acted upon. I will close my notice of this war against men who ventured to entertain a shade of difference in opinion from their fellow-Christians and the head of the Church, by a quotation that vividly stamps its character. "The Crusaders precipitated themselves in a mass upon the lands of the young viscount de Béziers, took his castles and burnt all the men, violated the women and massacred the children they found in them; then, turning towards Béziers, they carried it by assault. A prodigious number of the inhabitants of the circumjacent country had taken refuge in this city; the abbot of Citeaux, legate of the pope, upon being consulted by the knights as to the fate of these unhappy beings, a part of whom only were heretics, replied by these execrable and ever-memorable words: '*Kill away! kill away! God will take care of his own!*'" The crusade against the Albigeois is one of the blackest pages in the history of mankind, and ought to be described as such by every historian whose disagreeable duty it is to name it.—Trans.

[175]The abbot of Vaux-de-Cernai, who signalized himself in the crusade against the Albigeois, has left us a history of this period, in which he relates with an air of triumph, facts which passed before his eyes, at which religion as well as humanity ought to blush. When we have read his account, we are persuaded of two things: the first, that he was sincere in the excess of his fanatical zeal; the second, that his age thought as he did, and did not disapprove of the violences and persecutions of which he so candidly exposes the history. Le Père Langlois, a Jesuit, has written, in French, a history of the crusades against the Albigeois. The *Histoire Ecclésiastique* of Fleury, and *L'Histoire de la Province de Languedoc* may be consulted with advantage.

[176]This crusade of the children is related by so great a number of contemporary authors, that we cannot entertain any doubt of it. We will refer to our Appendix the different versions of the ancient chronicles of this singular event.

[177]Vetus est hoc artificium Jesus Christi, quod ad suorum salutem fidelium diebus istis dignatus est innovare.—*Epist. Innocent.*

[178]The year 1263 answered to the year 602 of the Hegyra.

[179]Montesquieu foretells the fate of Mahometanism; not as Innocent did, but philosophically. He likewise predicts "that France will fall by the sword;" but whether the sword will be drawn by foreigners or her own sons, he does not say.—Trans.

[180]Gibbon says: "Some deep reasoners have suspected that the whole enterprise, from the first synod at Placentia, was contrived and executed by the policy of Rome. The suspicion is not founded either in matter or fact. The successors of St. Peter appear to have *followed*, rather than *guided* the impulse of manners and prejudice." With great respect for our illustrious historian, I cannot quite agree with him; the popes were in many instances the first to kindle the flame, and were always anxious to keep it burning. In the part of our history now before us, it is plain it would have gone out but for the great exertions of Innocent. The crusades were a powerful engine in the hands of the popes; they could not afford to let them go to decay.— Trans.

[181]The cardinal de Courçon was an Englishman by family. He had studied at the University of Paris, and from that was connected with Lothaire, who became pope under the name of Innocent III. It is to this friendship that Peter Robert de Courçon owed his elevation. There is a very long notice of this person by the late M. du Theil, in *Les Notices des Manuscrits*, tom. vi.

[182]The continuator of William of Tyre expresses himself thus:—Il ot en France un clerc qui prescha de la croix, qui avait nom mâitre Jacques de Vitri; cil en croisa mult, là où il étoit en la predication, l'eslurent les chanoines d'Acre, et mandèrent à l'apostolle (le pape) qu'il lor envoyast pour estre évesque d'Acre; et sachiez s'il n'en eust le commandement l'apostolle, il ne l'eust mie reçu, mais toutes voies passa-t-il outremer, et fust évesque grand pièce, et fist mult de biens en la terre; mais puis resigna-t-il, et retourna en France, et puis fut il cardinal de Rome. [As M. Michaud has placed this note all in the text, and has only given it to show the curious mode of expression, I have followed his example.—Trans.]

[183]Philip granted this fortieth, without reference to the future—*absque consuetudine*, and upon condition that this voluntary gift should be employed wherever the king of England and the barons of the two kingdoms should think best.—See *Le Rec. des Ord.* tom. i. p. 31.

[184]In the royal regulations of Philip Augustus, there is an order relative to the debts contracted by the Crusaders as members of a commune. We think our readers will not be displeased by the particulars of this order. "As to the Crusaders, members of certain communes, we order," says the king, "that if the commune itself be charged with any levy, whether for foot or horse soldiers (l'ost et la chevauchée), the inclosure of the city,

the defence of the city in the event of a siege, or for any debt that is due, and contracted before they took the cross, they shall be held subject to the payment of their proportion, equally with the other inhabitants who have not taken the cross; but as to the debts contracted after the period at which they shall have taken the cross, the Crusaders shall remain exempt, not only until their approaching departure, but until their return."—See the *Recueil des Ordonnances, Dachery*, and the sixth vol. of the *Notices des Manuscrits, dissertation de M. du Theil sur Robert de Courçon.*

[185]In the charter granted by King John, that monarch expressly says that he grants this charter by the advice of the archbishop of Canterbury, of seven bishops, and the pope's nuncio.

[186]This victory of Bouvines, which had such happy results for the French monarchy, will be worthily celebrated in the poem of *Philip Auguste*, by M. Perceval de Grand-maison: we cannot sufficiently praise our poets who take their subjects from the greatest periods of our annals.

[187]Upon the holding of this council, the Chronicle of Opsberg, the monk Godfrey, Matthew Paris, Albert Stadensis, the Chronicle of Fassano, and particularly the collection of the councils, may be consulted. Fleury enters into very copious details.—See the sixteenth vol. of the *Histoire Ecclésiastique.*

[188]The discourse of the pope is preserved in its entirety in the collection of the councils.—See the fourth Council of the Lateran.

[189]M. Raynourd, who has made profound researches into the language and poetry of the troubadours, communicated to us this piece of Pierre of Auvergne, with several others which appear to us of great interest, and which we will insert in our Appendix.

[190]In a dissertation upon the cardinal de Courçon, M. du Theil has undertaken to make the apology of Innocent III. We have the greatest respect for this *savant*; but he evinces too strong an inclination to justify Innocent in all respects; and an application of the common proverb, *"He who proves too much proves nothing,"* is quite in place here.

[191]Innocent pronounced these words against Louis, the son of Philip Augustus, whom he had induced to make war against the king of England; and whom he afterwards wished to excommunicate, because this prince persisted in continuing a war begun by the commands and advice of the Holy See.

[192]I have observed more than once, that our author is so absorbed in the history he has undertaken, that he is somewhat loose in his remarks upon that of the nations nearest to him. It was not likely that Henry III., a

boy of nine years old, should take the cross, or that the prudent Pembroke and his other counsellors would allow the forces of an unsettled kingdom to be wasted upon such a scheme. The king of France again, who he says was constantly occupied in the war against the Albigeois, had absolutely nothing to do with that war. The southern provinces subjected to this calamity were fiefs of the crown of Aragon, and did not belong at that time to France in any way. Whilst these wars were raging, Philip was prudently extending his dominions to the north and north-east.—Trans.

[193]Bonfinius, the historian of Hungary, says that Gertrude gave up the wife of Banc, the chancellor of the kingdom, to the criminal desires of her brother. He adds that Banc killed the queen to avenge this injury; but this assertion is contradicted by all historians. The same author says that the wife of Andrew was assassinated during his voyage to the Holy Land; but this assertion is as false as the first. Gertrude was assassinated on the 18th of September, 1213.—See Palma, *Notitia Rer. Hung.* t. i.

[194]Marguerite, queen of Hungary, set out for Palestine after the death of Bela, her husband.—See the ninth book of this History.

[195]The Chronicle of Peter Durburg, a priest of the Teutonic order, may be consulted on the manners and religion of the ancient Prussians. This chronicle, whose purpose is to describe the conquests of the Teutonic knights, contains several historical dissertations, which appear to us to have great merit; the most curious are, *Dissertatio de Diis Veterum Prussorum*; *Dissertatio de Sacerdotibus Veterum Prussorum*; *Dissertatio de Cultu Deorum, de Nuptiis, de Funeribus, de Locis Divino Cultui dicatis*, &c. &c. A Latin dissertation, *De Moribus Tartarorum, Lithuanorum, et Moschorum*, may likewise be consulted. This work contains curious details upon the worship and manners of Lithuania and Samogitia, which bore a strong resemblance to the worship and manners of the Prussians. M. Kotzbue, in his history of the Teutonic knights, has thrown great light upon the origin of the legislation, and the customs and religion of the ancient inhabitants of Prussia.

[196]A letter from Pope Honorius to the archbishop of Maïence, says that there is in Prussia a nation of barbarians, of whom it is said that they kill all the girls but one born of each mother; that they prostitute their daughters and wives, immolate captives to their gods, and bathe their swords and lances in the blood of these victims, to bring them success in battle— See *Raynal*, 1218. We refer our readers to our Appendix, for some details upon the manners of the Prussians.

[197]Le Père Maimbourg and most historians make the king of Hungary embark at Venice; but they are unacquainted with the Chronicle of Thomas, deacon of Spalatro, who furnishes the fullest details of the passage

of Andrew II. into the Holy Land, and his return to his dominions. This Chronicle, it is true, contains many doubtful things concerning the crusade, and the kingdom of Hungary on the return of Andrew; but it is quite worthy of confidence in all that passed at Spalatro.

[198]"This year," 614 of the Hegyra, says the continuator of Tabary, "the Franks received succours by sea from Rome the great, and other countries of the Franks, both west and north. It was the chief of Rome, a prelate much revered among the Christians, who directed them; he sent troops from his own country under various commanders, and he ordered the other Frank kings either to march in person or send their troops."

[199]A letter from the master of the soldiers of the Temple, addressed to Honorius III., enters into several details respecting the situation of the Holy Land at this period. This letter speaks of the scarcity experienced in Syria; the master of the Templars adds, that they could procure no horses. "For this reason," said he to the pope, "exhort all who have taken the cross, or intend to take it, to furnish themselves with such things as they cannot procure here."

[200]This prince was named Cheref-Eddin Melik Moaddham.

[201]It is our duty to quote here what is met with in the continuator of Tabary, or the false Tabary, relative to this expedition of the Christians: "They undertook to besiege the castle of Thour (Tabor), and reached the top of the mountain and the foot of the walls. They were very near becoming masters of it; but one of their princes being dead, they retired, after having remained seventeen days before the fort." This account is quite contrary to that of the western historians, and otherwise bears no mark of probability. It is true that the king of Cyprus died during this campaign of the Crusaders; but he died at Tripoli, and more than a month after the expedition of Mount Tabor.

[202]According to the chronicles of the times, and the report of travellers, there is no water on Mount Tabor. It is probable that the want of water prevented the Crusaders from undertaking the siege of the fortress.

[203]The unimportant accounts of this period are to be found in the continuator of William of Tyre and in James of Vitri, who was then bishop of Ptolemaïs.

[204]The archdeacon Thomas describes with great simplicity the miracles effected by the relics of the king of Hungary.

[205]One of these historians, Palma, expresses himself thus:—Hæc eadem expeditio Hierosolymitana adeo nervos omnes monarchiæ Hungaricæ absumpsit, ut unius propemodum seculi spatio ad pristinam opulentiam

viresque redire nequiverit. Another historian adds, that the long absence of Andrew, and the imbecility of his son, so completely alienated the minds of his subjects, that his return created no joy, and that Benedict, the chancellor of Queen Yollande, had difficulty in persuading a few prelates to go out and meet him.

[206]The register of Honorius in Rinaldi, and particularly the letter written by William of Holland to the pope, may be consulted for the details of this campaign against the Moors. William asks permission of the sovereign pontiff to remain in Portugal a year; but this permission was refused him by the Holy See, at that time only interested in the crusade beyond the sea. Some details concerning the expedition of the Crusaders in Portugal may be found in James of Vitri, and in the monk Godfrey.

[207]Savary has rectified an error committed by several learned moderns, who have confounded the city of Damietta, which existed in the times of the crusades, and which is called *Thamiatis* by Stephen of Byzantium, with the city of that name which exists at present. Aboulfeda informs us that the ancient Damietta was set fire to and demolished in the year 618 of the Hegyra, after the crusade of St. Louis, and that another city, under the same name, was constructed at two leagues from the sea. The assertion of Aboulfeda agrees in this point with the description of Macuzi.

[208]James of Vitri gives a sufficiently particular description of Egypt and its productions; this portion of his history is not unworthy of the perusal of the learned, and may give a just idea of the knowledge of geography and natural history of the thirteenth century.

[209]For particulars of the siege of Damietta, James of Vitri, the continuator of William of Tyre, Marin Sanut, Matthew Paris, the correspondence of Honorius in *Raynaldi*, Godfrey, and the Monk of Alberic may be consulted. We have examined the account attributed to Olivier, priest of Cologne, which may be found in the *Gesta Dei per Francos*, but this account is repeated by James of Vitri. The Arabian authors and the Chronicle of Ibn-ferat have afforded us great assistance in our labours, and have informed us of very important facts of which the Franks and their historians were ignorant.

[210]Le Père Maimbourg gives a long account of this machine, not necessary to be repeated.

[211]This priest, who was named Olivier, afterwards became bishop of Paderborn and a cardinal of St. Sabina; it is the same that signed his name to the account we have mentioned in a preceding note.

[212]Gretser, in his treaty *de Cruce*, says formally that the popes required the commanders of the pilgrims to take with them both agriculturists and workmen.

[213]The Chronicle of Ibn-ferat collects the judgments of all the Arabian historians upon Malek-Adel. These historians all express themselves in the same manner. The continuator of William of Tyre, who appears to have lived in the East, speaks of the pomp and of the air of majesty which were remarked in the brother of Saladin: the latter otherwise treats Malek-Adel with great severity.

[214]It is under the name of Seïf-Eddin, by corruption Saphadin, that Malek-Adel is known in our Histories of the Crusades.

[215]A Latin dissertation, by Boecler, entitled *De Passagiis*, may be consulted on this subject.

[216]I cannot make out who this Prince Oliver was.—Trans.

[217]In the letter by which Honorius announced to the leaders of the crusade the powers he had given to Cardinal Pelagius, his holiness expresses himself thus: Ut exercitum Domini cum humilitate præcedens, concordes in concordiâ foveat, et ad pacem revocet impacatos.

[218] *Califas papa ipsorum*. The continuator of William of Tyre calls the caliph the *Apostle of the Miscreants*. The same historian adds:—"Après manda (le soudan du Caire) au calife de Baudac, qui apostoille était des Sarrasins, et par Mahomet qu'il le seccurût, et s'il ne le seccurait, il perdrait la terre. Car l'apostolle de Rome y envoyait tant de gent, que ce n'était mie conte ne mesure, et qu'il fait preschier par Payennisme ainsi comme faisaient par Chretienté, et envoyât au soudain grant seccurs de gent par son preschement."—"The sultan of Cairo afterwards sent to the caliph of Bagdad, who was the apostle of the Saracens, and implored him, in the name of Mahomet, to assist him, assuring him that if he did not assist him, he should lose his dominions. For the apostle of Rome sent so many people that they were beyond all count or measure, and that the caliph must order preaching throughout Paganism as was practised in Christendom, and he might send the sultan great assistance in consequence of his preachings."

[219]The Chronicle of Ibn-ferat, from which we have drawn that which we relate, says that Emad-eddin was the son of Seïf-Eddin-aboul-Hassan-Ali-ben-Ahmed Alhékari, surnamed Ibn-almachtoub (son of the Scarred), on account of a wound which had marked his face. The same chronicle adds that the emir, the son of the Scarred, despised the futile things of kings, and that most extraordinary circumstances were related of his revolts against sovereigns.

[220]All the Christian historians of the middle ages, and Maimbourg after them, appear persuaded that Providence, by a miracle of its will, put the Saracens to flight.

[221]Our historians of the crusades name this prince Meledin.

[222]The infantry must have rendered, during the siege, greater services than the cavalry, in defending the intrenchments, mounting to the assault, or fighting on board the ships. This dispute alone proves that the infantry had made great progress; for till that time they would not have dared to compare themselves with the cavalry.

[223]The continuator of William of Tyre speaks at length of the interview between St. Francis and his companion and the sultan of Cairo. St. Francis at first proposed to the sultan to renounce Mahomet, under pain of eternal damnation.

[224]Li soudan dist qu'il avait archevesques et évesques de sa loi, et sans eux ne pouvoit-il crier ce qu'ils diraient. Les clercs lui respondirent: "Mandez les guerre;" et ils vinrent à lui en sa tente. Si leur conta ce que li clercs li avaient dist; ils respondirent: "Sire, tu es épée de la loi. Nous nous te commandons, de par Mahomet, que tu lor fasse la teste couper." A tant puient congé, si s'en allèrent. Li soudan demora et li dist clercs, dont vint li soudan, si lors dist, "Seignors, ils m'ont commandé, de par Mahomet, et de par la loi, que je vous fasse les testes couper; mais j'irai en contre le commandement," &c. &c. The sultan—we translate our old historian—said he had archbishops and bishops of the law, and without them he could not listen to what they had to say. The clerks, St. Francis and his companion, answered him, "Send for them here"—and they came to him in his tent. He then related to them what the clerks had said, and they answered: "Sire, thou art the sword of the law. We command you, by Mahomet, to order their heads to be cut off." They then made their obeisance and went away. The sultan and the said clerks remained. Then the sultan came towards them, and said, "Seignors, they have commanded me, by Mahomet, to order your heads to be cut off; but I shall act contrary to the commandment," &c. &c. The historian adds, that the sultan offered them presents, which they refused—he ordered them refreshment, and sent them back to the Christian army.

[225]Ingredientibus nobis fœtor intolerabilis, spectus miserabilis; mortui vivos occiderunt; vir et uxor, dominus et servus, pater et filius, se mutuis fœtoribus interemerunt. Non solum plateæ erant mortuis plenæ, sed in domibus et cubiculis et lectis jacebant defuncti; extincto viro, mulier impotens surgere, sublevandi carens subsidio vel solatione, putritudinem non ferens expiravit. Filius juxta patrem, vel e converso; ancilla juxta

dominam, vel vice versâ, languore deficiens jacebat extincta; parvuli petierunt panem, et non erat qui frangeret eis. Infantes ad ubera matrum pendentes, inter amplexus morientium vocitabant; delicati divites, inter acervos tritici interierunt fame; deficientibus cibis, in quibus erant nutriti, pepones et allia, cepas et alitilia, pisces et volatilia, et fructus arborum, et olera frustra desiderantes. Multitudo vulgi contracta vel molestiis diutius fatigata deficiens aruit.—*J. Vitr. Hist. Or. l. iii.*

[226]M. Michaud is accused by some French critics of being too rhetorical—in this instance he has not made his story so effective as he might have done. If the reader will turn to the extract from *James of Vitri*, at the foot of the last page, he will find the old chronicler much more powerful than the modern historian.—Trans.

[227]Two letters which Honorius wrote to Pelagius, when sending him the money, are still extant; they appear to us to be very curious, and merit a place in our Appendix.

[228]The Chronicle of Ibn-ferat gives some details of this council of the Mussulman princes. The Western historians say nothing of it. It is a pity that James of Vitri, who was sent to the camp of the Saracens to propose the capitulation, should have preserved a profound silence upon so important a circumstance. We have several times remarked that the Arabian historians, when the Mussulmans experience reverses, content themselves with saying, *"God is great; may God curse the Christians!"* We find the same inconvenience in the Western historians, who are almost always silent when the Christians are conquered.

[229]We cannot refrain from observing that the deliberations of the Mussulmans generally end in resolutions of moderation and mercy; and that those of the Crusaders have, as often, a very different result.—Trans.

[230]As translation can scarcely do justice to this touching little *morceau*, I subjoin the original.—Trans. Le roi s'assit devant le soudan, et se mist à plorer; le soudan regarda le roi qui ploroit, et lui dist: "Sire, pourquoi plorez vous?" "Sire, j'ai raison," repondit le roi, "car je vois le peuple dont Dex m'a chargié, perir au milieu de l'eve et mourir de faim." Le soudan eut pitié de ce qu'il vit le roi plorer, si plora aussi; lors envoya trente mille pains as pauvres et as riches; ainsi leur envoya quatre jours de suite.

[231]Muratori has preserved a little elegiac poem in Latin, upon the taking of Damietta.—See *Script. Rer. Ital.* vol. vii. p. 992.

[232]See the letter of the patriarch of Alexandria, in the Appendix. The patriarch, at the end of his letter, gives the pope some remarkable opinions upon the manner in which the emperor and the Crusaders were to arrive in Egypt.

[233]The letter of the queen of Georgia is to be found in the continuator of Baronius, under the year 1224. Curious details of the manners of the Georgians in the thirteenth century may likewise be found in James of Vitri, *Hist. Orient.*

[234]The Chronicle of Upsberg attributes the murder of the respectable Engelbert, archbishop of Maïence, to this indulgence of the preachers of the crusade.

[235]These details, unknown to all the historians of the West, are related by Abulfeda and the greater part of the Arabian historians who treat of the events of this period. The same authors name the Mussulman envoy *Fakreddin*; they disfigure the name of Frederick's envoy, and say that this prince selected for this mission the person who had been his governor in his childhood.

[236]The perusal of Arabian authors throws great light upon this part of the history of the crusades; the continuator of William of Tyre, the letters of the patriarch of Jerusalem, or the correspondence of the pope, give but very incomplete information.

[237]The Arabian authors who speak of this treaty, say that one of the conditions was, that the fortifications of Jerusalem should not be repaired; this condition is not named in the treaty which is found in the continuator of Baronius.

[238]Quant l'apostelle oi ces nouvelles, si n'en fu mie lies, parce que l'empereur était excommunié, et qu'il li etoit avis qu'il avait fait mauvaise paix, parce que les Sarrasins tenaient le temple et per ce ne volut-il soffrir un le sçut fait par lui, ne que sainte église en fit fête, ains recommanda par toute Chrestianeté qu'on excommuniat l'empereur come renvoyé et mescréant.— *Cont. of William of Tyre.* (When the apostle heard these news, he was not at all pleased, because the emperor was excommunicated, and he thought he had made a bad peace, as the Saracens were to retain the temple. Therefore he was not willing it should be thought he consented to the peace, or that the Church should offer up thanks for it; and he ordered that the emperor should be excommunicated throughout Christendom, as a castaway and an infidel.)

[239]Un poi après que l'emperor se fust parti de la terre de Jerusalem, s'assemblèrent villains de la terre as Sarrasins, et allèrent à Jerusalem une matinée, pour occir les Chrétiens qui dedans estoient.—*Cont. de Guill. de Tyr.* The same author adds that the Christian knights then at Ptolemaïs came to the assistance of Jerusalem, and that they killed a great number of the Mussulmans.

[240]The letters addressed by the pope to the Mussulman princes may be found in the continuator of Baronius.

[241]For the preachings of John of Vicentia consult *L'Histoire Ecclésiastique*, of Fleury, vol. xvii., and *L'Histoire des Républiques d'Italie*, by Sismondi.

[242]This was then a common epithet. St. Thomas Aquinas was called *the Angel of the School.*—Trans.

[243]This poetical exhortation, addressed to all knights, may be found printed among the poetry of Thibault.

[244]Matthew Paris speaks warmly against this abuse, which created much murmuring in England.

[245]

> N'aie, Ector, Roll', ne Ogiers,
> Ne Judas Maahebeus li fiers
> Tant ne fit d'armes en estors
> Com fist li Rois Jehans cel jors
> Et il defors et il dedans
> La paru sa force et ses sens
> Et li hardement qu'il avoit.

Philip Mouskes, 1274.

[246]John of Brienne married, as his second wife, a daughter of the king of Arragon.

[247]"My lady lost, holy lady be my aid."—Trans.

[248]See Raynold, Matthew Paris, Alberic, Richard of St. Germain, and the *Ecclesiastical History* of Fleury, regarding this circumstance.

[249]Upon the quarrels of the pope and the emperor, *L'Italia Sacra*, tom. viii., Richard de St. Germain, and particularly Matthew Paris, who reports the letters of Frederick, may be consulted.

[250]This is a mistake; Richard had no legitimate children. Richard, duke of Cornwall, who was likewise king of the Romans, was the son of John, Richard's brother. In the same manner Gibbon calls Edward I. Richard's nephew;—he was his *great-nephew.*—Trans.

[251]It appears to be almost incredible that our author should be so blind himself, or expect his readers to be so, to the lessons taught by his History! If the early Crusaders could not buy off their pilgrimages, more of them were attracted by what they might obtain on earth, than by "religion and its promises."—Trans.

[252]Most of these questions may be found in the work of the Jesuit Greutzer, which bears for title *De Cruce.*

[253]Although this is very like "damning with faint praise," I cannot see how the popes or their abuses are entitled to any mitigation of contempt or disapproval: the beneficial results were the work of Providence, and were never contemplated by the pontiffs.—Trans.

[254]King John was a bad prince: he inspired mistrust in his subjects, who demanded a pledge of him, and this pledge became the English constitution. If France, before the revolution of 1789, had never asked her kings for a pledge, it was because none of them had inspired mistrust in his people: the best eulogy that can be made upon the kings of France is, that the nation had never felt under their government the want of a written or guaranteed constitution, and that they were in all times considered as the safest guardians of the public liberty.

[It is scarcely conceivable how a writer of the nineteenth century could offer his readers such opinions as these (both text and note). Some of the best portions of British liberty were obtained from better kings than any France had, with the exception of Henry IV., from Louis IX. to the end of the monarchy. Our Charles I. and James II. had their faults, but they are as "unsunned snow" by the side of nine French monarchs out of ten.]—Trans.

[255]M. Michaud is here more happy than usual in his political and philosophical reflections. We might fancy him prescient of the 2nd of December.—Trans.

[256]A dispute upon an affair of gallantry, between two or more troubadours.—Trans.

[257]These verses are quoted by M. Raynourd in his grammar of the Romance language.

[258]We have but to compare the piece of the Provençal with that of Raoul de Courcy, who died in the third crusade.

[259]M. Michaud's parental partiality for his elder born makes him very oblivious. If we look back to his own account of the morals of the early crusades, particularly those of Jerusalem, we cannot see the justice of these remarks. The Crusaders only "remembered to be pious and penitent" when they experienced reverses.—Trans.

[260]It may be questioned whether the weapons since employed for the same purpose, the cunning and the tongue of Jesuits, were not in all senses as bad as the sword and lance of the Crusaders.—Trans.

[261]The city of Thorn was built on the spot where the consecrated oak grew.

[262]We may name, among the Greeks, the sacred war undertaken for the lands which belonged to the temple of Delphos; but on reading closely the history of this war, it is easy to see that they did not fight for a dogma or a religious opinion, as in the wars which, among the moderns have had religion for a motive or a pretence.

[263]Karakoroum, the residence of the principal branch of the successors of Gengiskhan. It is only lately that the true situation of this city has been fixed by M. Abel-Remusat; it was on the left bank of the Orgon, not far from the junction of that river with the Selinga to the south of the Lake of Baïkal, by the 49° of latitude and the 102° of longitude. The same country has since been the residence of the Grand Lama.

[264]M. Petis de Lacroix has published a life of Gengiskhan, according to Eastern authors. This history, though fable is sometimes mixed with truth, is one of the best works that can be consulted. M. Deguignes, in his History of the Huns, has spoken at great length of the Tartars and of Gengiskhan; he announces that he has deviated from the account of Petis de Lacroix; but as he does not always name the sources from which he has drawn, he does not inspire perfect confidence for this part of his history. We find some details upon Gengiskhan in *La Bibliothèque Orientale* of D'Herbelot.

[265]The Chronicles of the middle ages often speak of Prester John. A letter written by a prince of this name to Louis VII. has been preserved. Seven barbarous princes have been reckoned who bore the name of Prester John. The researches made to ascertain the truth would be uninteresting nowadays.—See the *Precis de la Geographie Universelle,* by M. Malte Brun, tom. i. p. 441.

[266]According to what we know of Gengiskhan, we should with difficulty believe that among modern historians he has been able to find panegyrists; but Petis de Lacroix has not been able to avoid the example of most historians, who generally appear infatuated by the hero whose life they are writing. An Arabian historian relates, that on learning the massacre of his ambassadors, Gengiskhan was not able to refrain from tears. Here Petis de Lacroix is very angry with the Arabian, and reproaches him bitterly with having given the emperor of the Moguls *a feminine* character. All others, says he, have given a portrait of him more worthy of a hero.

[267]There have been long disputes upon the terms Mogul and Tartar. We think we can make out, amidst much uncertainty, that the Moguls originally formed a distinct tribe of the vast countries of Tartary; and that the Tartars, being in great numbers in the armies of the conquering Moguls,

obliterated in a degree the names of their conquerors in the kingdoms of Europe and Asia to which these armies penetrated.

[268]Father Gaubil has translated a Chinese history of Gengiskhan; this history yields but little information, and gives no curious details but upon the family and the successors of the conqueror.

[269]Matthew Paris speaks of the terror which the Moguls spread through Europe: his history contains an exhortation to all the nations of the West to fly to arms; each nation is in this history characterized by an honourable and flattering epithet.

[270]The reader may consult *Thurocsius*, vol. i., *Rerum Hungaricarum*, and particularly the *Carmen Miserabile* of Roger of Hungary, canon of Varadin, who has described in poetical prose the disasters of which he himself was a witness.

[271]See in the Appendix the details which many of the Chronicles give of the ravages of the Carismians in Palestine.

[272]Joinville gives many particulars of this war which he had learnt during his sojourn in Palestine. The continuator of William of Tyre may likewise be consulted. Matthew Paris has preserved two letters, one from the patriarch of Jerusalem, the other from the grand master of the Hospitallers, which describe this battle.

[273]This is the opinion of M. Deguignes, in his *Histoire des Huns*.

[274]Consult Matthew Paris, and the *Annales Ecclésiastiques*, for particulars concerning the council of Lyons.

[275]Matthew Paris affords some very curious details upon the council of Lyons; Le Père Labbe may also be consulted.

[276]We find in the great theology of Tournely (*Traité de l'Eglise*, tom. ii.) a very learned dissertation upon this deposition of the emperor Frederick II. at the first council of Lyons. This theologian asserts that the council had nothing at all to do with this great act of authority of Innocent IV., and brings several reasons to support his opinion. We will quote some of them, leaving our readers to appreciate their value.

"Whilst all the bulls of the pope, published in council, begin by these words: 'We have decreed, with the approbation of the council, according to the advice of the sacred council, &c. (sacro approbante concilio, ex communi concilii approbatione, statuimus),' we read at the head of the bull in question: 'Sentence pronounced against the emperor Frederick by the pope, Innocent IV., in presence of the council (sacro præsente concilio),' an essential difference, which is likewise observable in the body of the bull, when the sovereign pontiff only speaks in his own name, and as holding the place of Jesus Christ upon earth. All the fathers of the council, says Matthew Paris, on hearing the sentence, *were struck with surprise and horror*, sentiments they certainly would not have felt if they had had any part in the judgment.

"All the historians of the time attribute this act of authority to the pope, without even mentioning the council; and Frederick II., when accusing the incompetence of the judge, his partiality, his blindness, and his ingratitude, when writing to the kings of France and England and the barons of his kingdom on the subject, only complains of the pontiff, and does not attach the least reproach to the prelates who composed the assembly. The sentence was considered as so completely the work of the pope, that the Church, which received the decisions of the council, attached little importance to the bull, and that this bull became absolutely a party affair. It was rejected by a great number of the churches of Germany and Italy. The kings of France and England considered it as injurious to sovereign majesty, and continued to treat Frederick as legitimate emperor. It only rendered the wars between the Guelphs and Ghibellines more active and more inveterate.

"The pope said truly that he had deliberated with the fathers of the council; but he adds, that the deliberation turned upon no other object but the excommunication of the emperor; that he did not at all speak of the article of the deposition, and that thence came the surprise and horror which the prelates manifested.

"It is nevertheless objected that the pope and the fathers of the council, after the reading of the sentence, turned down the waxlights which they held and extinguished them, and that afterwards the pope gave out the *Te Deum*, in which the prelates assisted; but Matthew Paris believes that the circumstances are here not exact. He thinks that some priests only, attached to the court of Rome, lent themselves to the passion of the pope against Frederick, and performed the ceremony of the waxlights, which may still further only relate to the excommunication; otherwise how can we reconcile this passage of the historian with the surprise and horror that were manifested, according to him, in the assembly at the reading of the sentence.

"The pope did not even endeavour to persuade anybody that he was supported by the authority of the council. He declared that he should know how to maintain irrevocably *all that he had done* relative to Frederick."

After having discussed all these points, Tournely raises doubts upon the œcumenicity of the first council of Lyons.

"The council of Florence," says this theologian, "which makes an enumeration of the general councils held before that period, passes by that of Lyons in silence, and in fact several countries, as Germany, Italy, Spain,

Brittany, Sweden, and Poland, had no bishops there; there were few prelates from France or England."

"In the same way the council of Constance, enumerating in a formula, that the pope about to be elected was to sign all the œcumenic councils which had preceded, only mentions one council of Lyons. Now, this could only be the second, for that was very solemn. There were more than five hundred bishops at it, as well from the East as the West, and the Greeks in it acknowledged *the divine filiation.*"

Thadæus of Suesse, representative of the emperor Frederick II. at the council of Lyons, and zealous defender of the rights of that prince, appealed publicly from this council to a future general and *œcumenic* council. One of the causes which might, according to Tournely, lead several bishops into error, but which will appear very strange at the present day, was, that they imagined the empire really was a feudatory of the court of Rome. It is the sovereign pontiff, they say, who crowns the emperor; he has then a particular and special right over the empire; he can depose the head of it for a serious matter. Frederick, in his letters to the kings of France and England, mentions and combats strongly this ridiculous prejudice, and the foolish pretensions of the popes. Gregory IX., in a letter addressed to Stephen, archbishop of Canterbury, informs him that Frederick is engaged by oath to go to the Holy Land, abandoning, if he failed in his promise, his states and his person to the sovereign pontiff. According to this, the fathers might believe that the deposition was a consequence of the penalty the prince had incurred as a perjurer. We must refer to the ages in which these questions were agitated to appreciate the influence they had upon events.

[277]This great incident in the life of Louis IX. is differently, and indeed more strikingly, related by most French historians. "When he felt himself better, to the great astonishment of all, he ordered the red cross to be affixed to his bed and his vestments, and made a vow to go and fight for the tomb of Christ. His mother, and the priests themselves, implored him to renounce his fatal design. It was all in vain; and scarcely was he convalescent than he called his mother and the bishop of Paris to his bedside, and said to them, 'Since you believe that I was not perfectly myself when I pronounced my vows, there is my red cross, which I tear from my shoulders; I return it to you: but now, when you must perceive that I am in the full enjoyment of all my faculties, restore to me my cross; for He who is acquainted with all things, knows also that no kind of food shall enter into my mouth until I have again been marked with His holy sign. 'It is the hand of Heaven,' cried all who were present; 'its will be done.'" (*Bonnechose*).—Trans.

[278]English readers should acknowledge a familiar acquaintance in this excellent mother and good queen: she is the *Lady Blanche* of Shakespear's *King John.*—Trans.

[279]See in our Appendix this fact related by Matthew Paris.

[280]It is Matthew Paris who furnishes us with information relative to this attempt to persuade St. Louis. This is the chronicler that throws most light upon the events of that period; such as the council of Lyons, the quarrel of Frederick and the pope, and the crusade of the king of France. We also find some details in William of Nangis, in Joinville, and in the *Ecclesiastical Annals* of Raynaldi.

[281]Que loyauté ils porteraient à sa famille, si aucune malle chose avenait de sa personne au saint veage d'outremer.

[282]We do not observe that this worthy penitent opened his hand and relaxed his grasp whilst living; death-bed repentances and posthumous restitutions are very suspicious affairs.—Trans.

[283]These calamities were but a portion of God's great law of cause and effect—they were begun in error and ended in failure. What connection is there between Louis' just government of his kingdom and his mad and foolish expeditions to the East?—Trans.

[284]Il ne voulut oncques retourner ses yeux vers Joinville, pour ce que le cœur lui attendrit du biau chastel qu'il laissait, et de ses deux enfants.

[285]Concerning the departure of Saint Louis, and the facts that follow consult William of Nangis, William of Puits, Matthew Paris, Sanuti, &c.

[286]Like many good and affectionate mothers, Blanche was very jealous of the influence of a young wife over her son. Principally for territorial advantages, Louis married Marguerite of Provence, when he was nineteen and the princess thirteen. Immediately after the ceremony, Blanche separated the newly-married couple and kept them apart for six years, under pretext of the youth of the new queen.—Trans.

[287]Bien fou celui qui, ayant quelque péché sur son âme, se met en un tel danger; car si on s'endort au soir, on ne sait si on se trouvera le matin au fond de la mer.

[288]Michaud has omitted to mention the cause of Louis' unfortunate choice of a route,—the residence in Cyprus proving so injurious to the army. The most regular and advisable route would have been by Sicily; but after Louis had in vain tried every means of subduing the anger of the pope, his superstitious reverence for the head of the Church prevailed over even his good sense and his prudence, and he declined stopping in Sicily, because that island was part of the dominions of an excommunicated prince.—Trans.

[289]The French had a custom of reckoning sums by *twenties*: in the text of Joinville this stands, "six vingts livres tournois." —Trans.

[290]Oncques nul d'eux ne revint.

[291]Matthew Paris, William of Nangis, said Zanfliet are agreed concerning this embassy. We shall revert to it in our Appendix.

[292]Deguignes informs us that the prince Ecalthaï was the lieutenant of the khan of the Tartars in Asia Minor.

[293]Most of the articles which form the correspondence between Christendom and the Tartars are collected in the book of Moshemius, entitled *Historia Tartorum Ecclesiastica*: the letters of this correspondence do not all merit the same attention or the same confidence.

[294]M. Abel-Remusat, in his learned Memoir upon the Tartars, explains several doubtful circumstances of this embassy; he examines the opposite versions, and does not at all adopt the opinion of M. Deguignes, who views the Mogul ambassadors as nothing but impostors. If it may be allowed me, after these two great authorities, to offer an opinion, I should say that the arrival of Louis having created a great sensation in the East, Ecalthaï, governor of all the provinces of Asia, might send emissaries to ascertain the designs and strength of the Franks; and it may be believed that these emissaries, to perform their mission with more success, feigned several circumstances calculated to increase their credit in the minds of the Christians. It appears to us that this opinion may reconcile that which is opposite in that of the two writers quoted.

[295]No chronicle says that the king of Cyprus went with Louis, although he had taken the cross. This prince is never mentioned in any of the events of the war.

[296]This word comes to us from the Arabs, with the instrument which it designates. The Arabs pronounce it *nakarah*.

[297]——chose épouvantable à ouïr et moult étrange aux Français.— *Joinville*.

[298]An admirable subject for a large historical picture.—Trans.

[299]Upon the battles that preceded the taking of Damietta, and upon the taking of that city, Joinville may be consulted, as the historian that furnishes the greatest number of details. William of Nangis, Matthew Paris, but particularly Guy de Melun, may be read with advantage. We have quoted in our text the Arabian authors that have spoken of these events.

[300]At this period the national troops had neither the courage nor the constancy that the labours of war require. The Arabs, who had entered Egypt as conquerors with Amron-Ben-al-As, had disappeared, without

leaving successors capable of supporting their reputation. There were no means of recruiting the army but by slaves bought in the north of Asia and in Europe, or by wandering Arabs, who, accustomed to a hardy, active life, still showed some energy. This latter measure presented another advantage. By bringing these nomads under the yoke of military discipline, the nations were delivered from the depredations of men who lived by war. It was with this motive that the pacha of Egypt of the present day has enrolled the Arabs of his states under his banners.—See the *Voyage of Belzoni in Egypt and Numidia.*

[301]The livre Tournois was so called from being coined at Tours, and was one-fifth less in value than the livre coined in Paris; thus afterwards the livre Tournois was valued at twenty sous, that of Paris at twenty-five. The sum mentioned would thus only amount to little more than £200 which appears almost impossible.—Trans.

[302]Ainsi demeura la besogne, dont maintes gens se tinrent mal satisfaits.—*Joinville.*

[303]At this period Louis IX. was but thirty-three years old.—Trans.

[304]There is here an apparent contradiction between the version of Ducange and that of MM. Melot, Sallier, and Caperonier: in the latter we read that these five hundred Mussulmans were sent to harass the French army, but there is no mention of a deceit, or *ruse de guerre;* in that of Ducange, on the contrary, we find this sentence: "He [the sultan] sent to the king, as a *ruse,* five hundred of his best-mounted horsemen, they telling the king that they were come to assist him, him and all his army." We find nothing like this in the edition of MM. Melot, Sallier, and Caperonier; it is probable that this sentence may have been interpolated in the manuscript, for we cannot believe that five hundred Mussulman horsemen could have been received as friends in the Christian army, who stood in no need of auxiliaries, and who certainly did not look for them among the Saracens. We avail ourselves of this opportunity to warn our readers that the various editions of Joinville often vary in important circumstances, and that they should at all times be subjected to a very critical examination.

[305]Il s'écriait, pleurant à grant larmes: "Beau Sire, Dieu Jesus Christ, garde moi et toute ma gent."—*Joinville.*

[306]This word *ores,* which was employed to animate the courage of combatants, and which is still in use among the people in several provinces of France, may it not be the same as the word *houra,* which the Russians employ? May it not have been introduced by the Franks and the other barbarians who conquered the Gauls?

[307]This is the same person who, later, made himself so formidable to the Christians when he had united Egypt and Syria under his power; he had preserved the name of Bondocdar from that of his ancient master, so called because he was the *bondocdar*, or general of the arbalatiers, in the reign of Malek-Saleh.

[308]Je vous promets que oncques plus bel homme armé ne vis.

[309]Leur disant paroles en signe de mocquerie.—*Joinville.*

[310].... et tous furent moult oppressés d'angoisse, de compassion et de pitié de le voir ainsi plorer.—*Joinville.* [I hope my readers will excuse my repetitions of this kind; I make them from a sense of inability to convey the touching and characteristic simplicity of the original, and from a wish that others should partake with me the feeling they create.]—Trans.

[311]This disease was the scurvy; "it was such," says Joinville, "that the flesh of our legs dried away to the bone, and our skins became of a black or earth colour, like an old saddle which has been a long time laid aside: and besides this, we who were afflicted by this disease were soon subjected to another persecution, in a complaint of the mouth, which arose from our having eaten of those fish; it putrified the flesh of the gums, so that it rendered the breath horribly stinking." Joinville here speaks of the *burbotte*, a fish of the Nile, which is a voracious fish, and feeds upon dead bodies. The seneschal adds, in another passage of his memoirs, "that the malady having seized upon the army, it became necessary for the barbers to cut out the swollen flesh of the gums of all who were afflicted with this disease, so that they could not eat. Great pity was it to hear all from whom this dead flesh had been cut, going about in the army, crying and moaning. They appeared to me like poor women who are in labour with their children when they come upon earth: nobody can tell how pitiable that sight was."

[312]... ne oncques plus ne chanta. [The readers of Michaud have reason to congratulate themselves, when he is availing himself of such authorities as Villehardouin and Joinville; he seems to have a sympathy with them that procures us some very delightful traits.]—Trans.

[313]Bernard Thesaurius, the author of the Continuation of the History of William of Tyre, has fixed the precise epoch of each fact. We shall most likely have occasion to draw the reader's attention to the *Annales Ecclésiastiques* of this writer in a future volume.

[314]This generous trait of St. Louis, who refused to quit his army, is attested by both French and Oriental historians. Joinville expresses himself thus:—"Seeing the king had the same disease as the army, and great weakness, as others had, we thought he would be much safer on board one of the great galleys; but he said 'he would rather die than leave his people.'"

Geoffrey of Beaulieu, equally an eyewitness, attests this fact. To the evidence of these two historians we may add that of the Arabian historian Aboul Mahassem. "The king of France," says he, "might have escaped from the Egyptians, either on horseback, or in a boat; but this generous prince would never consent to abandon his troops."

[The conduct of Louis might be imprudent, but it was noble and heroic. The admirers of the modern French idol, Buonaparte, would be very much at a loss to find such a trait in his history; it was always *sauve qui peut* with him, when he met with reverses.] — Trans.

[315]See the extract from *Soyouti* in Appendix.

[316]This is the Minieh of Aboul-Abdallah.

[317]What a lesson is this letter to all such as designate their God "the God of armies," or are worshippers of military glory! The archbishop of Canterbury could not have written a better, or one apparently more pious, after the battles of Trafalgar or Waterloo. — Trans.

[318]Très volontiers le ferai, et si ai-je eu en pensée d'ainsi faire, si le cas y échéait. — *Joinville.*

[319]I am unable to discover the nature of this punishment, or the meaning of the word, but cannot help thinking they are connected with the French proverbial expression, *Envoyer quelqu'un au berniquets*, as meaning to ruin him. — Trans.

[320]Joinville speaks of a sum of five hundred thousand livres. Ducange has made a dissertation on this head, that gives very little information: — in the first place, we must be able to ascertain what was then the value of 500,000 livres of our money.

[321]The continuator of Tabary and the *History of St. Louis*, by Joinville, furnish information upon this event. Their accounts agree exactly.

[322]Would not the death of the accomplished Sidney assort worthily with these pictures, as not only exemplifying the good and true knight, but the Christian hero, imbued with charity, the great principle of the Gospel? — Trans.

[323]This is really one of those tales that require "seven justices' names" to vouch for their authenticity. How such a man, at such a time, could be ambitious of the honour of knighthood, it is very difficult to imagine. But when we recollect that the evidence of sixty-five miracles performed by him, was produced to procure his canonization, we must not be sceptical in what regards Louis IX. — Trans.

[324]We had at first consulted the edition of Ducange; and we have been surprised to find an account and expressions totally different in that

of Caperonier, otherwise called the edition of the Louvre; however this may be, we cannot conclude, from either one version or the other, that any proposal of the kind was made to Louis IX. [As the reader may like, without trouble, to see the opinion of our great historian upon this interesting subject, I venture to subjoin it:—"The idea of the emirs to choose Louis for their sultan is seriously attested by Joinville, and does not appear to me so absurd as to M. de Voltaire. The Mamelukes themselves were strangers, rebels, and equals; they had felt his valour, they hoped for his conversion; and such a motion, which was not seconded, might be made perhaps by a secret Christian, in their tumultuous assembly."—*Gibbon*.]—Trans.

[325]If we compare this council with that of the Christians which sat after the taking of Jerusalem, and the results of both, we shall be less inclined to blame the hesitation of the Mussulmans. The Crusaders were the invaders of the country of the Mussulmans, the assailants of their faith—can it be wondered at if they awakened vindictive passions?—Trans.

[326]These Arabian verses were translated by M. l'Abbé Renard. See *L'Extrait d'Abulfeda*, vol. xi.

[327]Matthew Paris gives curious details upon the effects produced by the news of the captivity of the king.

[328]Among the great number of historians who have spoken of this movement, William de Guy, Matthew Paris, William of Nangis, and the *Annals of Waverley* may be consulted.

(Some historians relate the catastrophe differently. One says: "The pastors were accustomed to preach, surrounded by armed men for their defence; one day, by the command of Blanche, an executioner introduced himself among these, and gliding behind Jacob, struck his head off at a blow, before the eyes of the spectators, who were chilled with horror. Some knights then appeared and dispersed the pastors.")—Trans.

[329]There can be no doubt that this was the case with those who remained with him; even the worthy seneschal and all. His determination to go to Antioch proves that he had no resource in Europe. It was a desperate game, and they were obliged to play it out.—Trans.

[330]Norway.

[331]The reader may remember a curious ceremony of alliance, in the last volume, wherein the one party passes through the shirt of the other whilst he has it on.—Trans.

[332]M. Michaud observes this is a remarkable circumstance; but it is much more remarkable, that whilst instructing his readers, he appears to gather no wisdom himself. Every page of his book tells us, that though there

were many examples of sincere piety and virtue among the Crusaders, the bulk of them were *adventurers*, to whom the most profitable religion would be the best. He is so in love with his drama, that he wishes to think the actors and their motives of action much better than they are.—Trans.

[333]M. Ancelot, in his tragedy of *Louis IX.*, has painted with much truthfulness the character of a renegado.

[334]Joinville's account is very confused here; indeed, almost unintelligible. He says at first that the king was at Sidon, and that he retired into the castle on the arrival of the Saracens. Two pages further on he says: "When the king had finished the fortifying of Jaffa, he formed the intention of doing the same for Sidon as he had done for Jaffa." We cannot fail to observe a contradiction here. We can suppose that Louis had been to Sidon, had left it, and had again returned; but one circumstance proves the contrary. History says that two thousand Christians were killed at Sidon, or in the vicinity of that city; if Louis had then been upon the spot, it is most probable he would have buried the dead before his departure, and would not have deferred the performance of this pious duty till his return. It is evident that Joinville's account has been altered at this part; unfortunately, this alteration is not the only one which this precious historical monument has undergone.

[335]It is not uninteresting or barren of instruction, to think how different would be the reflections of a Voltaire or a Gibbon on this subject! The reader may safely take a position between the two extremes: Louis was a good and pious man, but a very mistaken one; as king of a great people, he certainly had not performed his duties during the last five years.—Trans.

[336]The continuation of the conversation of King Louis with the emir has for its object the manner in which the Mussulman doctors interpret the precept for the pilgrimage to Mecca.

[337]But there is one piece of internal evidence in this tradition, that we think should obtain it credit, notwithstanding the silence of history. When we remember how the European armies in Egypt, at the end of the last century, suffered from *ophthalmia*, we think there is strong reason to believe that Louis might found such an institution on his return.—Trans.

[338] *Verit. Invent. de l'Histoire de France,* by John de Serres, p. 152.

[339]One thing worthy of remark is, that the emperor Frederick resembled closely, both in character and policy, Frederick II., king of Prussia; but the latter was in harmony with his age, and his age has named him the *great Frederick.*